D1239131

HISTORY OF
THE SECOND WORLD WAR

The author of this, as of other official histories of the Second World War, has been given free access to official documents. He alone is responsible for the statements made and the views expressed.

GRACE LIBRARY, CARLOW COLLEGE
PITTSBURGH, PA. 15213

BRITISH

FOREIGN POLICY

IN THE

SECOND WORLD WAR

BY

SIR LLEWELLYN WOODWARD

*Fellow of All Souls College
and formerly Professor of Modern History
in the University of Oxford
Professor Emeritus at the Institute for
Advanced Study, Princeton, N.J.*

D
750
W62
V.4

Volume IV

LONDON: 1975
HER MAJESTY'S STATIONERY OFFICE

CATALOGUED

© *Crown copyright* 1975

HER MAJESTY'S STATIONERY OFFICE

Government Bookshops

49 High Holborn, London WC1V 6HB
13a Castle Street Edinburgh EH2 3AR
41 The Hayes, Cardiff CF1 1JW
Brazennose Street, Manchester M60 8AS
Southey House, Wine Street, Bristol BS1 2BQ
258 Broad Street, Birmingham B1 2HE
80 Chichester Street, Belfast BT1 4JY

*Government publications are also available
through booksellers*

Printed in England for Her Majesty's Stationery Office by
The Campfield Press, St. Albans

Dd. 507346   K.40   5/74

ISBN 0 11 630055 8*

FOREWORD

THIS volume, with chapters on British policy towards Spain, Portugal, Argentina, Turkey and the countries of the Middle East, and China, illustrates the multifariousness as well as the complexity of the problems upon which the Foreign Office had to advise His Majesty's Government. Until the end of 1943 British policy could do little more in Spain than counter, largely by meeting Spanish economic needs, the efforts of the Axis Powers to bring General Franco into the war on their side. After the summer of 1942 General Franco, whose chief concern was in fact to keep the war out of Spain, was little more than a nuisance to the Allies (Chapter XLVII). Great Britain had an alliance with Portugal dating from 1373, which had more than sentimental value since Portuguese neutrality prevented German submarines and other warships from using Portuguese harbours and territorial waters. The Allies had a vital interest in the exclusion of the Axis from the Portuguese Atlantic islands; in 1943 a skilful exercise of British diplomacy was able to secure (on the basis of the old alliance) the use of bases in the Azores (Chapter XLVIII). In South America, for obvious reasons, Great Britain left the direction of Allied policy mainly to the United States. The only matter upon which there were important Anglo-American differences was the treatment of Argentina where, partly out of nationalist dislike of the dictatorship of the United States, partly out of a belief that Germany would win the war, the Argentine Government would not adopt the anti-Axis measures recommended to them from Washington. In the summer of 1943, after a revolution in Argentina, the United States refused to recognise the revolutionary Government unless they complied with these anti-Axis measures. Mr. Hull insisted that the British Government should support his attitude, and a lively controversy followed in which Mr. Churchill pointed out to President Roosevelt the serious consequences to British food supplies which would follow a breach with Argentina (Chapter XLIX). The controversy was ultimately settled when Mr. Hull resigned and his successor adopted a less rigid policy towards Argentina.

From the point of view of British policy Turkey was the most important country between Constantinople and the Persian Gulf. After the collapse of France Great Britain could hardly expect Turkey to fulfil the terms of the Anglo-Franco-Turkish Treaty of 1939 and to enter the war on the British side. In any case, at a time when British assistance could have been only minimal, Turkish neutrality, which at least set a barrier to a German advance into Syria, was of more practical value than Turkish belligerency. Here, as at the western end of the Mediterranean, a change came after 1942. A strong German move eastwards was now improbable; the Allies had regained the strategic initiative and His Majesty's Government could consider whether it was now desirable to put pressure on Turkey to enter the war. Mr. Churchill, in particular, was in favour of such pressure and more hopeful than the Foreign Office and H.M. Ambassador in Turkey that such a policy would succeed. The policy did not succeed (Chapter L–LII). Turkey, with her long experience in eluding the demands of the Great Powers, feared the results of a total victory of Russia at least as much as those of a total victory of Germany; Turkish interests would be served best if she remained neutral and conserved such strength as she had by avoiding the losses of war. In any case His Majesty's Government (and their military advisers) were for a long time uncertain whether they could supply the large (and, in the British view, unnecessarily large) amount of material assistance without which the Turkish Government refused to risk war even with a weakened Germany. The negotiations with Turkey therefore petered out, and in spite of earlier British threats that Turkey might find herself in a dangerous isolation after the war, the British representatives at the Potsdam Conference defended her—as the Turkish Government had expected—against Russian demands for territorial annexations and the right to establish a naval base in the Straits.

Chapters LIII–LV deal with British policy towards Syria and Lebanon, and the development of Arab nationalism. The affairs of Syria and Lebanon took up an inordinate amount of time and attention and caused unnecessary controversy owing to the difficulty of working with General de Gaulle. The primary British aim was the maintenance of military security and political tranquillity in an area which was inevitably disturbed by the general shipping shortage, the currency inflation and other economic problems caused by the presence of large Allied forces in the Middle East. As the most obvious means of keeping down political dissatisfaction the British authorities wanted the French in Syria and the Lebanon fully and without delay to implement the promise of independence to the two countries which Great Britain and France had jointly guaranteed at the time of the expulsion of Vichy rule in 1941. General de Gaulle, however, was extremely unwilling to give up any part of the traditional French position in the Levant and unfortunately convinced that the real British intention was to oust the French in order to take their place. General de Gaulle's behaviour nearly caused a complete breach between himself and the Fighting French Movement and His Majesty's Government. At the same time his continual delays in implementing the grant of independence alienated Syrian and Lebanese opinion with the result that the Levant States refused any recognition of French privileges.

The end of the war did not bring peace in Syria and the Lebanon. The situation in Palestine was even more serious. During the war His Majesty's Government had been able to hold in suspense the difficult questions of Jewish immigration and the political status of Palestine. Even this policy, which obviously settled nothing, was not easy to carry out in view of persistent Zionist agitation in the United States, and the influence of the large American-Jewish vote on the United States Government. Since the Zionist agitation brought into being a corresponding increase in the intensity of Arab nationalism, His Majesty's Government had repeatedly to point out to the United States Government that they were urging upon Great Britain a policy which would lead to civil war in Palestine while they were refusing any practical share in putting this policy into effect. The War Cabinet appointed a ministerial committee in June 1943 to consider what solution to put forward after the war. The committee reported in favour of the partition of Palestine, but the Foreign Office opposed their recommendations as unfair to the Arabs. No agreement on British policy had therefore been reached in the summer of 1945.

A fourth set of problems (Chapters LVII–LVIII), less intractable but not easy to solve, arose out of the Anglo-Russian treaty of 1942 with Iran. Iran was the only country outside Europe during the war in which a common political supervision was shared by the three major Allies. For reasons of political security Great Britain and Russia had sent troops into the country and compelled the Iranians to agree to an occupation, while promising to restore full Iranian independence at the end of the war. The United States had no combat troops in Iran, but had provided economic advisers and taken over the direction of the Trans-Iranian railway which was the main route of supplies to the U.S.S.R. The measure of this three-Power co-operation and of the unwilling compliance by the feeble and corrupt Iranian administration was increasingly affected on the Anglo-American side by evidence that Russia was using the opportunity to weaken the Iranian régime and to establish herself permanently in the north of the country. The Foreign Office was indeed so much concerned at the end of the war with getting British troops out of Iran at once (and thus leaving the Russians with no pretext for keeping their own troops in the country) that they came into conflict with the Chiefs of Staff who wanted to leave a force for the protection of the British-controlled oil installations.

Finally British policy towards the Arab States had to make an unexpected adjustment in relation to the emergence of a new interest of the U.S. Government in Arabia resulting from the very large oil concessions obtained by American companies. This adjustment (Chapter LVI), especially in Saudi Arabia, was not made easier by the tendency of American officials, and American public opinion, to discredit the long-established British position in the Middle East as an outmoded form of 'imperialism', while in the British view the policy of the United States seemed hardly less 'imperialistic'.

British and American views also came into some conflict over China (Chapters LIX–LX). Here also in the American view British policy was affected by an imperialism from which the United States was held to be wholly free (Russian imperialism, because it had been carried into effect on land, and not by overseas expansion, was curiously ignored by official and unofficial American opinion). The Americans, including President Roosevelt and his successor, therefore suspected the realist British disbelief that China in any calculable future would play a part as a leading Power in the arrangements for world security. For obvious reasons Great Britain in fact had to accept the American lead in decisions about China, and could look on only with dismay at the increasing weakness and corruption of General Chiang Kai-shek's Government and the practical certainty of civil war in China after the expulsion of the Japanese.

LLEWELLYN WOODWARD

January 1973

CONTENTS

Page

CHAPTER LV. British policy in Syria and the Lebanon from January 1944 to July 1945.

CHAPTER LVI. The co-ordination of Anglo-American policy in the Middle East, 1942–45: Palestine: the question of oil resources: Saudi Arabia.

CONTENTS

KEY TO REFERENCES

FOREIGN OFFICE RECORDS

The great majority of the references quoted in this book are to Foreign Office files. These references are always preceded by a letter, indicating the department responsible for the file in question. Thus, A indicates the American department, E the Eastern, N the Northern, etc.

CABINET OFFICE RECORDS

CA	Confidential Annex (or Secretary's Standard File) to Cabinet Conclusions
JSM	Joint Staff Mission, Washington
PMM . . .	Cabinet Office printed series of Prime Minister's minutes
WM	War Cabinet Conclusions
WP	War Cabinet Papers

No. 10 DOWNING STREET RECORDS

Churchill Papers   .   Sir Winston Churchill's personal files
(Public Record Office Group PREMIER 3)

PRINTED SOURCES

F.R.U.S. . . . *Foreign Relations of the United States*

NOTE

Throughout these volumes, footnotes are indicated in the text by numerals, 1, 2, 3, etc. The marginal notes in brackets, (a), (b), (c), etc., indicate references to sources which are printed at the foot of each page.

CHAPTER XLVII

British relations with Spain from July 1941 to the Potsdam Conference

(i)

British policy towards Spain from July 1941 to June 1942.

IN a speech of July 18, 1941, commemorating the fourth anniver- (a)
sary of his successful insurrection, General Franco had committed
himself to a statement that the Allies had lost the war. The War
Cabinet had decided to take no positive action as the result of the
speech but at their suggestion Mr. Eden took the opportunity of
saying in the House of Commons on July 24 that we had been compelled by General Franco's speech to review our attitude towards
Spain, and that we were not prepared to continue our efforts to
provide supplies and financial assistance while the Head of the
Spanish State adopted so unfriendly an attitude towards Great
Britain.

For the next few months, however, there was little change in
Anglo-Spanish relations. In spite of his pro-Axis talk, General
Franco did not want to commit Spain to war against Great Britain.
The unpopularity of Señor Suñer increased, mainly owing to domestic reasons—the maladministration of the Falange and its failure
to deal with the food shortage—and the subservience of the Government to Germany was generally disliked. Rumours indeed were
continually reaching the British Government of plans by the Spanish
generals for getting rid of Señor Suñer and possibly of General
Franco himself. These reports did not incline the Foreign Office to
change their policy of non-intervention in Spanish affairs. A military
coup d'état seemed unlikely since the generals would obviously be
afraid of German reactions. Even if the *coup* succeeded, a new Spanish
Government would be unable to escape from falling under German
influence.

The most important political factor in Anglo-Spanish relations
was the change in the military situation after it was clear that the
Germans were not winning an immediate and decisive success in
Russia, and would be committed to an eastern campaign in 1942.
At the end of 1941 neither Señor Suñer nor General Franco were as

---

(a) C8194/46/41.

I

rashly certain as they had been six months earlier of the ultimate victory of the Axis Powers.

(a)   In a general review of the position during the latter part of November 1941, the Foreign Office considered that, while there was no change in their declared policy (i.e. non-belligerency), the Spanish Government were in fact behaving with some good will, or at all events with less ill will. The most recent conversation on economic matters between Sir S. Hoare and the Spanish Minister of Commerce had been relatively cordial. Even Señor Suñer had gone out of his way to meet us on various points where we might have expected difficulties. He had agreed not to send back to German-occupied territory against their wish Czechoslovak and Polish prisoners of war interned at Miranda del Ebro, although the Spanish Government might have been technically justified in regarding the Czechs as German citizens since Spain had not recognised a Czecho-slovak Government. Señor Suñer seemed also to have said no more about an earlier suggestion that the Spanish Government might require the withdrawal of the Polish Embassy from Spain in the face of German pressure. The Spanish Government had protested vigorously against the sinking of a British merchant vessel in Spanish territorial waters, and Señor Suñer had told Sir S. Hoare that his (Señor Suñer's) investigations had shown that the sinking of a Spanish ship off Ceuta was not due to a British submarine. There was also a circumstantial report of a conversation in which Señor Suñer had said that he would do his best to maintain Spanish neutrality even if the United States entered the war, whereas he had previously said that American belligerency would compel Spain to join the German side.

After months of prevarication the Spanish Government appeared to have decided to adopt a policy of economic collaboration with the United States. Hitherto Señor Suñer had been the main obstacle to such a policy, but he had now declared his intention of giving it his full support, and the discussions were being pursued on the Spanish side with a good deal of energy. The Spanish Government seemed therefore to have come to the conclusion that their interests would be served by collaboration with the sterling area and the United States rather than with the Axis Powers. They were putting great difficulties in the way of German purchases in Spain owing to the fact that the Germans were unwilling to pay for their purchases in goods.

The Ministry of Economic Warfare had surprisingly few complaints against the Spanish Government, and no evidence of serious contraventions of Spanish war trade undertakings. The Spanish

---

(a) C13096/46/41.

authorities had recently been facilitating British purchases of various foodstuffs such as apricot pulp, and of minerals, especially mercury, although in the latter case we had not fulfilled our undertaking to supply in return commodities such as rubber and tin. We were likely to get a good proportion of the Spanish orange crop if we wished to buy it. We had also just received a report that the Spanish authorities had agreed to renew our contracts for iron ore which expired at the end of the year. The renewal would be at the existing prices although the prices charged to the Germans had been raised.[1]

We also had little complaint to make on military grounds with the Spanish Government. Arrangements for the passage of escaped British personnel through Spain were working satisfactorily. We had no evidence that the Spanish Government were allowing the use of Spanish territory for the refuelling of submarines. When we had complained that certain German ships at Teneriffe were being used as fuelling bases for submarines, the Spanish authorities at once moved the ships to the inner harbour. Finally, we had had no Spanish complaints about the use we were making of Algeciras Bay and the airfield at Gibraltar.

After the entry of the United States and Japan into the war the (a) Foreign Office again reviewed the position. They considered that events in Libya, the increased strain on our naval forces owing to the war in the Far East, and the possibility of a stabilisation on the eastern front, might tempt the Germans to try to establish themselves in the western Mediterranean by the occupation of the Iberian peninsula and of French North Africa. The Germans were already intensifying the 'war of nerves' in Spain and Portugal: the next stage might be the entry of German troops and the occupation of bases. There was, however, nothing to show that these military moves were imminent; the eastern front indeed was not yet stabilised.

The British Chiefs of Staff wanted on strategic grounds to maintain Spanish and Portuguese neutrality as long as possible. We did not expect to induce either Spain or Portugal to offer organised resistance to a German invasion of the Peninsula, but we hoped that we might be able to dissuade the Spanish Government from voluntarily joining the Axis and to persuade the Portuguese Government, if attacked, to continue resistance overseas.[2] Hitherto British policy —in consultation with the United States Government—had been to demonstrate to the Spanish Government, or at least to influential elements of opinion in Spain, through the provision of limited

---

[1] Thirty per cent of British iron ore supplies came from Spain. Owing to the short shipping haul, the Spanish source of supply was of additional importance at this time.
[2] See below, p. 41.

(a) C14052/108/41.

supplies and economic assistance, that Spanish interests lay in maintaining a connexion with the sterling area and the Americas rather than in joining the Axis in a war for which Spain was totally unprepared.

The point had now been reached when we could supply only a very limited quantity of Spanish economic requirements without the help of the United States. An increase in German pressure on Spain might soon bring about a deterioration in Anglo-Spanish relations, and lead to a rupture. We ought therefore to convince the United States Government of the paramount strategic importance of keeping Spain and Portugal out of the war, and, to this end, of continuing to send supplies to Spain and not laying down too severe conditions in the negotiations[1] which they (the United States Government) had already begun with Spain. This policy would not only help to prevent or delay Spanish belligerency on the Axis side but might encourage anti-German elements in Spain and increase the prospect of active opposition to a pro-Axis policy and to invading Axis forces.

A telegram to this effect was sent to Lord Halifax on December 19, 1941. He was also informed that the occupation of Timor by Allied troops[2] had involved a set-back to closer Anglo-Portuguese co-operation, and that it was most important for us to do everything possible to treat the Portuguese as Allies and to meet their needs and susceptibilities. Hence we proposed to maintain our 'generous' policy in regard to imports into Portugal and not to make difficulties over minor blockade questions. We should not allow a large accumulation of stocks in Portugal, and we should try to persuade the Portuguese Government to keep as much material as possible in their colonial possessions.

A fortnight later, on January 1, 1942, the Foreign Office again telegraphed to Lord Halifax on the urgency of the negotiations with Spain. The United States Government did not seem to realise both the importance of the matter and the need of rapid action. They appeared to be taking no steps to get to grips with the Spaniards in their economic negotiations; they failed to realise how actively our enemies were working. In view of the desirability of trying to prevent an extension of the war to the Iberian peninsula while our commitments and needs were so great, the Foreign Office suggested that the Prime Minister during his visit to the United States might raise the matter with the President.

---

[1] The negotiations had begun in Washington. The British view was that this choice of place would mean long delays, and possibly failure, since neither side had adequate knowledge of the background facts, and the Spanish negotiators would not have sufficient authority to complete an agreement.

[2] See Chapter XLVIII, pp. 42 ff.

Throughout the first half of the year 1942 there was again no change either in British policy towards Spain or in the attitude of the Spanish Government. The evidence at the end of 1941 continued to show that the Spanish generals who were hostile to the Falange were planning a *coup* to get rid of Señor Suñer and possibly of General Franco himself. On the other hand, they had been making threats of this kind for the past year, and had always drawn back—doubtless through fear of bringing the Germans into the country. As earlier, the Foreign Office considered that any Spanish Government, once in office, would fall under German influence, and that we might not gain very much from the substitution of a new Government for the unpopular régime of Señor Suñer and the Falange. There was thus no strong reason for us to change our policy of non-intervention in Spanish domestic policies. Meanwhile, the economic negotiations between the United States and Spanish Governments went on slowly. Owing largely to British mediation an agreement was finally reached. During the period of negotiation the British Government found great difficulty in persuading the Americans to supply sufficient oil to Spain to prevent an economic breakdown, and in persuading the Spaniards to agree to the conditions laid down by the Americans for the shipment of oil.[1]

Lord Halifax, at the end of January 1942, asked for the support (a) of the President in getting the immediate release of two tankers, but, in spite of a promise of support, the ships were not released. The Foreign Office therefore now thought it desirable that the Prime Minister should send a message to the President. They drafted a message repeating that the agreed policy of the two Governments was to keep Spain out of the war and to stimulate Spanish resistance to German pressure, to obtain from Spain an increasingly large quantity of raw material and to deny such material to the enemy. We could achieve these objectives only by supplying goods to Spain and for this purpose American co-operation was essential. We ought to give the Spaniards a sense of what they would lose by joining the Axis Powers. We had found the Spaniards 'though woefully subject to German pressure in many respects, not unresponsive in trade matters if carefully handled'. We had no liking for the Spanish régime, but we did not want to be deprived of one of our important sources of supply and to increase our commitments in the western Mediterranean and Atlantic.

This message was not sent because on February 7 Lord Halifax (b)

---

[1] These conditions included the sending of 'oil observers' to ensure that the American supplies were not re-exported to Germany. The British Embassy in Washington strongly criticised the handling of the question of Spanish oil supplies in the State Department.

(a) C1402/25/41. (b) C1488/25/41.

reported that the United States Government had agreed to the release of the two tankers. Nevertheless in the British view the State Department still did not take sufficient account of the military importance of economic concessions to Spain and were too much inclined to think that they could get what they wanted by 'treating the Spaniards rough'.

Meanwhile, although the Spanish Government persisted in what might be called a policy of malignant neutrality, the element of neutrality predominated, and the trend of events, from the Spanish point of view, was not favourable to a more active anti-Allied policy. In particular, the attempts of General Franco and Señor Suñer to draw the Latin American Republics towards Spain and into the Axis orbit received a set-back from the Conference of these Republics at Rio de Janeiro in January 1942. The Conference recommended that the Republics should break off relations with Germany, Japan and Italy. The declaration of war on the Axis Powers by Brazil and other South American States increased Spanish isolation. General

(a) Franco, at his own suggestion, met Dr. Salazar at Seville on February 13, 1942. During this meeting General Franco told Dr. Salazar that he intended to maintain non-belligerency unless the war spread to North Africa and threatened the Spanish position there or unless Spain was driven by economic necessity to rely on German supplies. He complained of British—and still more of American—treatment of Spanish interests.

(b)   On March 10, 1942, in reply to a complaint from Señor Suñer about the British delay in answering a Spanish note about an incident at Fernando Po, Mr. Yencken, British Chargé d'Affaires at Madrid (in Sir S. Hoare's absence) took the opportunity to point out to Señor Suñer the delay on the Spanish side in answering British representations on various matters, including the case of an Italian ship which had taken part in the sinking of a British ship in Spanish territorial waters in October 1941. Mr. Yencken said that he would give Señor Suñer a list of all our complaints, some of which had been mentioned in notes which the Spanish Government had not even answered. Sir Samuel Hoare presented this list on March 28

(c) to the Under-Secretary of State at the Ministry of Foreign Affairs. Sir S. Hoare told the Under-Secretary that it seemed hardly worth while for us to continue economic negotiations with Spain over difficult matters such as rubber when the Spanish Government were giving way to German pressure. The Under-Secretary agreed that we had reason to complain but hoped that we should not change our policy since, in spite of the many signs of surrender to the Germans, there was a steadily growing resistance to German pressure.

(a) C2450/658/41.   (b) C2954, 3236/26/41.   (c) C3025, 3735/175/41.

(ii)

British relations with Spain from July 1942 to July 1943: the North African landings: Spanish proposals for a compromise peace.

In the summer of 1942 the British defeat in Libya had a serious (a) though temporary effect on British prestige in Spain. The Foreign Office realised that, if the German attack were held, the Spanish attitude would improve, and that meanwhile we could do nothing more to influence opinion. The Spanish people were as anxious as ever to keep out of the war, and, as far as could be seen, the Government were not intending a change of policy. There would certainly be greater German pressure on Spain; the result might be more manifestations of Spanish sympathy with the Axis which, though unimportant from the point of view of action, might lead—so Mr. Makins wrote in a minute of July 4—'all the elements, both here and in the U.S.A., who think emotionally about Spain and regard relations with General Franco as a sin, to become vocal and to try to sabotage our policy'. We ought to resist attempts of this kind, and to give no encouragement to Spanish refugee groups, especially those connected with Dr. Negrín. Similarly we ought to refuse requests from the Service Departments, and especially from the Admiralty, to agree to violations of Spanish sovereign rights. At the same time we should keep in touch with the elements of opposition in Spain itself, though we could not expect them to do anything at present, and should not ourselves attempt to upset the régime until we were in a position to support our friends with supplies or by direct intervention.

The British Ambassador in Madrid had in fact continued to (b) receive approaches from Spanish leaders hostile to the Falangist régime and wishing to resist German pressure. These leaders were representatives of the monarchists, the Church and the centre parties. Their programme was based upon the return of a moderate monarchist régime. They asked for British support in the case of a German invasion of Spain or a voluntary entry of Spain into the war against us, or in the case of the overthrow of the existing régime without Spain becoming involved in the war.

The Foreign Office had instructed Sir S. Hoare to give discreet encouragement to the opposition leaders on the understanding that their movement (i) represented the principal sections of moderate opinion, including moderate republican opinion; (ii) maintained a policy of full neutrality and friendship with Portugal; and (iii) introduced a political amnesty in Spain. As before, however, we did not wish to undertake definite commitments or even to develop our

---

(a) C6827/175/41.   (b) C7033/27/41.

contacts with the opposition to a point which might endanger our relations with the existing régime. We had also come to the conclusion that the Spanish refugee groups could not provide an alternative to the present Government since these groups had no unity or settled policy, and no following in Spain capable of organising successful resistance to German influences.

From August 21 to October 5, 1942, Sir S. Hoare was in London for consultation on the measures to be taken to prevent trouble with Spain when preparations for some action in the Mediterranean became evident, and later when the Allied landings in North Africa had taken place. At first trouble had seemed likely before the begin-

(a) ning of the operations. Already on May 27, Sir S. Hoare had given General Franco a long memorandum of protest from the British Government with regard to certain installations for night observation which the Germans were known to be installing—and to be intending to operate—on both sides of the Straits of Gibraltar. Señor Suñer objected to the British protest, but General Franco promised an investigation. On June 3 the Spanish Government, while admitting that German experts were installing German apparatus 'necessary for the defence of the coasts of Spain', rejected a suggestion that they (the Spanish Government) had been granting facilities to 'foreign interests'. The Spanish note of reply gave an assurance that Spanish territory would not be used by any belligerent, and that British and Allied shipping would not be attacked by Axis ships or aircraft as a result of information obtained by the installations.

On July 1 Sir S. Hoare again raised the matter with Señor Suñer. He was assured that the work on the installations had been stopped and the German personnel sent home, but the Germans themselves boasted that information—which must have come from these installations—had assisted their attack on a convoy passing through the Straits on the night of July 11–12. For the time, however, the British Government accepted Spanish assurances. Apart from the immediate repercussions of the Libyan defeats and the German successes in Russia on Spanish opinion, there was an increasing risk, after the preparations for the North African expedition had begun, that the Spaniards, under pressure from Axis agents, would reply to further protests by asking questions, for example, about the construction at Gibraltar of a vast runway jutting out into the harbour, the accumulation of large numbers of aircraft and the use of Spanish territorial waters adjacent to Gibraltar.

Before Sir S. Hoare's return to Madrid, an internal crisis in Spain

---

(a) C8568/63/41 (1943).

had led to one fortunate development from the Allied point of view.[1] Señor Suñer was dismissed on September 3, 1942, and his place as Minister for Foreign Affairs taken by General Jordana.[2] On October (a) 8 Sir S. Hoare paid his first visit to the new Foreign Minister. He (b) said that after his talks in London he was able to repeat his previous statements that the British Government had no intention of interfering in the internal affairs of Spain or of violating the neutrality of Spanish metropolitan or overseas territory. In order to counter enemy propaganda that British policy was to impose a 'red' régime on Spain, Sir S. Hoare said that he had noticed a growing support in Spain for the restoration of the monarchy. This fact was regarded with interest in England, but we should not interfere in Spanish affairs; the choice lay entirely with the Spaniards themselves.

On October 19 Sir S. Hoare repeated to General Franco the (c) assurances which he had given to General Jordana. He said that we wanted to make it as easy as possible for the Spanish Government to maintain its attitude of neutrality and non-belligerency; for this reason we had been planning to meet Spanish economic needs— particularly with regard to oil, wheat, rubber and cotton. If, however, the policy desired by Spain and ourselves—i.e. keeping Spain out of the war—were to succeed, it was essential to avoid dangerous 'incidents'. We would do our best to prevent the recurrence of such 'incidents' as the flight of British aircraft over Ferrol (about which the Spanish Government had complained). We hoped that the Spanish Government would take similar steps to prevent a repetition of actions such as the provisioning of Axis submarines by German ships at Vigo. Our view was that the only safe policy was to prohibit —as in the First World War—the use of Spanish ports to all belligerent submarines. Sir S. Hoare also referred again to the installations in the Straits.

General Franco said that Spanish policy was unchanged, and that there was no reason why Spain should not continue to keep out of the war. He was grateful for our economic help, but asked why we and the United States found it necessary to continue the blockade of Europe from which the neutral and occupied countries alone

---

[1] This crisis arose out of a bomb thrown by Falangist gangsters on August 25 at Bilbao.

[2] General Jordana (who was a strong monarchist) had been dismissed from this office in August 1939, mainly owing to his resistance to the attempts made by Ciano and Señor Suñer to bring Spain into the war. One act of political importance which showed the fundamental intention of General Jordana's policy of neutrality was a five-day visit to Lisbon in the latter part of December 1942. During this visit the Spanish and Portuguese Governments reaffirmed their non-aggression treaty of March 17, 1939. On July 29, 1940, a protocol to this treaty bound each party to consult with the other in the event of a threat to the integrity of their territory. (See below, p. 40.) At the meeting in December 1942 General Jordana spoke of the two nations as an 'Iberian bloc' which would keep the Peninsula out of the war.

(a) C8568, 8623/220/41. (b) C9702/175/41. (c) C10035/175/41.

suffered. Germany herself had more food than she needed; only a week earlier she had sent 8,000 tons of wheat to Spain in compensation for wheat in a Spanish ship which the Germans had sunk. He promised to do his best to avoid 'incidents', but we should remember the difficulties of his own position.

The Foreign Office thought the interview satisfactory, in view of the facts that General Franco was obviously not yet sure that Germany would not win the war, and could not overlook the possibility of a German invasion of Spain. On the Spanish side the assurances given by Sir S. Hoare had some effect, and prepared the way for the announcement of the Allied invasion of North Africa three weeks later. Meanwhile on October 12 the Duke of Alba had (a) given to Sir A. Cadogan a note on Spanish policy. Although the Ambassador did not say so, the Foreign Office were fairly sure that he had received the note almost verbatim from General Jordana. After stating that Spain would never be the instrument of Axis Powers or of any other nation, the note explained that Spain agreed with Germany on the need to fight Communism, but this agreement did not mean that she shared 'ideas, doctrines, or aspirations which were quite alien to her'. Spanish hatred of communism was not confined to a desire to see the defeat of the Soviet armies; Spain wanted the defeat of the doctrines of revolutionary communism everywhere. Hence the Spanish anxiety at the prolongation of the war which created an atmosphere favourable to revolutionary tendencies.

The Spanish view was that there were no fundamental differences which could not be 'arranged' between 'the two adversaries' and that some way might be found of ending the war. Spain did not intend to intervene at the moment, but wished the belligerent nations to know that there were countries outside the conflict which in due course might be able to find a formula acceptable to both sides. In the economic sphere Spain would regard the complete defeat of any one of the Great Powers as a world-wide disaster.

The Foreign Office did not regard this note as a peace approach suggested by the Germans. On the other hand they thought it important to point out plainly to the Spanish Government that we could not accept their view that there were no fundamental differences between the belligerents. A reply was therefore given to the Spanish Ambassador on October 27 that there was 'no prospect whatever' that the United Nations in general, or the British Government in particular, would encourage any effort by the Spanish Government to bring about a 'compromise' peace. The United Nations were determined upon the complete defeat of the Axis

---

(a) C9815/14/41. C10410/175/41.

Powers, the complete liberation of the territories overrun by them, and the final removal of the menace of invasion and oppression by the aggressor States.

The major concentration of forces at Gibraltar before the invasion (a) of North Africa could not escape Spanish notice. On November 5 the Minister of War told the British Military Attaché—without asking any questions—that he hoped we were not planning a landing in French Morocco, since this action might lead to a rising of the tribes throughout North Africa. On the same day General Jordana spoke in similar terms to Sir S. Hoare. He asked whether the Ambassador could give him assurances that we would avoid dangers of trouble in Algiers and French Morocco. Sir S. Hoare said that he could not be expected to say anything about future military operations, but that he could not imagine His Majesty's Government taking action which would injure Spanish interests or start subversive movements against the Spanish Government.

The plans for informing the Spanish Government of the North African landings were that the United States Ambassador should give to General Franco at, or as soon as possible after, 'zero hour', a message from President Roosevelt, and that Sir S. Hoare should communicate a message from the British Government to General Jordana. The United States Ambassador therefore saw General Jordana at 'zero hour', and told him that he had a personal message for General Franco from the President. General Jordana arranged that the Ambassador should see General Franco at 9 a.m. Sir S. Hoare delivered his message at 11 a.m. The fact that these two messages were to be delivered was of help to General Jordana in restraining a move by the Minister of War and others to send Spanish troops at once to stake out claims in French Morocco.

The texts of the messages had been agreed between the British (b) and United States Governments. Mr. Roosevelt did not mention British participation. The British message—which was the longer of the two—spoke of operations of the United Nations which were being carried out primarily by the Americans, with the participation, under American command, of substantial British forces. Both messages stated that these operations were not being directed against Spanish territory, metropolitan or overseas. Spanish territory would be fully respected and Spanish interests would not be compromised.

The British message added that the operations would not affect the existing *modus vivendi* in Tangier, or the Anglo-Spanish trade agreement and exchanges of goods between Spain and British territories or—as far as the British Government were concerned—the exchanges between Spain and other countries for which navicerts

---

(a) C10813/10738/41.　(b) C10806, 10807/10738/41.

had been granted. Finally, the two messages referred to the Spanish desire to remain out of the war. Here again the British message was more explicit in stating that the British Government were in full sympathy with the Spanish intention, and wished Spain to have 'every opportunity to recover from the devastation of the civil war and to take her place in the reconstruction of the Europe of the future'.[1]

(a)   General Franco received the President's message in a satisfactory way. He said, however, that he was surprised at the British action, since the British Government had given an undertaking at the time of the attempt to take Dakar that they would keep out of French Morocco. Sir S. Hoare, in his interview with General Jordana, corrected this statement by General Franco. He said that our assurance had been limited to the Dakar operation.[2]

The change in the course of the war in the last two months of 1942 inevitably had an effect on Spanish opinion. General Franco became more anxious to bring about a compromise peace which would not mean an outstanding victory for Russia and the complete collapse of the totalitarian régimes. In spite of the plain statement in October 1942 to the Duke of Alba,[3] General Franco persisted in putting his views before the British Government. On January 7,

(b) 1943, Count Mamblas, before leaving Madrid, apparently to take up the post of Chargé d'Affaires in London during the Duke of Alba's absence, told Sir S. Hoare that he had a message from General Franco to the Prime Minister. General Franco thought that, the longer the war lasted, the greater would be the predominance of Russia and the United States over their British ally. This change would be a calamity for the world, and particularly for Europe. General Franco therefore urged the British Government to come to terms with 'influential sections' in Germany who would save central Europe from communism and Russian control. General Franco said that he had some detailed reports of the Prime Minister's conversations with Stalin in which he had promised Russia a predominant influence over all Europe east of the Rhine.

Sir S. Hoare told Count Mamblas that General Franco's message showed a complete misunderstanding of the British attitude towards the war and that he was entirely misinformed about the conversations in Moscow. The Foreign Office fully agreed with Sir S. Hoare's reply, and thought that there was no need for the Prime

---

[1] Mr. Churchill used similar language in a reference to Spain in his speech at the Mansion House on November 10, 1942.

(c)   [2] The actual words used on September 24, 1940, were that 'this important self-contained operation is not intended to be followed by a similar *coup* in Morocco'.

[3] See above, p. 10.

(a) C10866, 10867/10738/41.   (b) C280, 589/155/18.   (c) C10864/10738/41.

Minister to see Count Mamblas. The Prime Minister, on January 9, 1943, asked Mr. Eden whether it would be useful for him to send a civil reply to the message and, in congratulating General Franco on having kept Spain out of the war so far, to add that we were thinking not so much about our place in the world as our duty to civilisation and freedom. Mr. Eden thought that a reply was unnecessary; the Prime Minister agreed with this view. In the middle of April the (a) Prime Minister, in conversation with the Duke of Alba about the possibility of an early peace, said that we should insist upon an unconditional surrender, and that 'anyone who thought otherwise was wasting his time'.

General Franco, however, continued to make public references to the possibility of an early peace, and the Spanish press, which had made no protests about the bombing of civilians by Germany, now began to suggest limitations on air attack. The Duke of Alba told (b) Mr. Eden in June 1943 that the General's talk about peace was not German-inspired, and had caused almost as much resentment in Germany as in Great Britain.[1]

(iii)

American military demands for a more drastic policy towards Spain: Sir S. Hoare's interview of August 21 with General Franco: Foreign Office decision to put stronger pressure on General Franco (August–December 1943).

In the late summer of 1943 the more cautious policy towards Spain advocated by the Foreign Office came under criticism from the American military authorities. Lord Halifax reported on August (c) 6, 1943, the views of the State Department on the Spanish situation. General Franco had now admitted to the United States Ambassador in Madrid, Dr. Carlton Hayes, that the Allies would win the war; he was still unwilling to say so in public. Mr. George of the State Department thought that only lack of agreement among General Franco's opponents enabled him to stay in power. The position of the régime was critical, but the State Department did not see what they could do except wait on events. The Allies could get rid of General Franco by cutting off economic assistance to Spain; the State Department thought, however, that the time had not come for such drastic action, and that for the present we had nothing to gain by a major change of policy.

The Foreign Office agreed with this view. They realised that the

---

[1] See also below, p. 29, note 1.

(a) C4404/75/41. (b) C7121/24/41. (c) C9026/63/41.

change in the military situation might well affect Allied economic policy towards Spain. Earlier in the war the Foreign Office had urged that supplies should be sent to Spain in order to strengthen the Spanish groups in favour of keeping out of the war. Spain was now unlikely to come into the war against us even if we reversed our economic policy towards her. On the other hand she had become a valuable source of supply of important raw materials, such as iron ore, pyrites, wolfram and mercury; we were also trying by pre-emption to deprive the Germans of these supplies—especially of wolfram. Hence on purely economic grounds the Ministry of Economic Warfare and the Supply departments had even more reason than the Foreign Office for maintaining our present policy. On political grounds the Foreign Office took the view of the State Department that we had no interest in provoking a change of régime since we could not be sure that the change would be in our favour.

Lord Halifax was instructed on August 19, 1943, to put the British view to the State Department, and to point out that our methods had been more successful than those of the Germans. The latter had bullied the Spanish Government, charged exorbitant prices and taken little trouble to give them the goods which they required. Hence their whole purchasing programme in Spain had (a) broken down owing to Spanish obstinacy. Meanwhile Sir S. Hoare had already been instructed on August 13 to warn General Franco of our dissatisfaction at his failure to meet our complaints and to tell him that our policy towards Spain after the war would be seriously influenced by the policy followed by the Spanish Government from the present time until the end of the war.

(b)   The United States Chiefs of Staff, however, were inclined on military grounds to a more drastic policy. They pointed out at the Quebec Conference that Spain was assisting the Axis Powers not only with her economic resources but with her armed forces. Spanish troops were disposed defensively against the Allies, with little or no dispositions against the Axis. We therefore had to maintain large forces for the protection of our communications through the Straits of Gibraltar, and to make plans to meet a German offensive against Gibraltar if Spain should allow passage to the Germans across Spanish territory. General Franco seemed, however, to be realising that the Allies would win the war, and to be moving towards a position of real neutrality. The United States Chiefs of Staff considered that we should take full advantage of the changed circumstances and require Spain to move the bulk of her defensive forces from Morocco and southern Spain to northern Spain, and to cease military and economic aid to Germany.

(a) C8919/63/41. (b) C9664/26/41, C10232/24/41, COS(43)513(o).

The British Chiefs of Staff agreed generally with the desirability of taking a sterner line towards Spain. They pointed out, however, that the Spanish Government would be unwilling to risk military action which might bring German retaliation. An attempt on our part to coerce them would merely unite them against us. We also should not press them to a point which would involve us in military commitments in support of our threats. Hence the British Chiefs of Staff thought it inexpedient to ask for the transfer of any Spanish forces. On the other hand they were in favour of making certain demands, including (i) the discontinuance of supplies of raw materials (especially wolfram) to Germany, (ii) the withdrawal of the Blue Division, (iii) a redistribution of the Spanish forces in Morocco in order to remove any suspicion of distrust of the United Nations, (iv) the cessation of the use of Spanish shipping for the benefit of our enemies.

Mr. Eden, on reading in Quebec the memorandum from the British Chiefs of Staff, minuted to the Prime Minister that the time had very likely come for a firmer policy with the Spaniards, but that 'how and when' were matters for political decision.[1] The Prime Minister agreed that the decision on a 'harder policy' should not be included in the final report of the Combined Chiefs of Staff. Mr. Eden consulted the Foreign Office on the recommendations. Sir O. Sargent telegraphed in reply on August 23 that the report of Sir S. Hoare's interview with General Franco showed that we had already taken a firmer line on several of the matters mentioned by the Chiefs of Staff, and that the Spanish Government seemed anxious to satisfy us. One of the main reasons for the German loss of influence in Spain was their policy of bullying. With the tide in our favour, we should gain nothing by adopting the German methods. Sir S. Hoare would be in London on August 27, and the American proposals could then be discussed with him.

Sir S. Hoare telegraphed on the night of August 21–22, 1943, an (a) account of his interview with General Franco. The interview took place at Corunna; General Jordana was also present at it. Sir S. Hoare pointed out very plainly the new facts of British military strength, and the significance of the collapse of Fascism in Italy. He said that the three main obstacles to good Anglo-Spanish relations were the Falange, the Blue Division and the Spanish policy of 'non-belligerency'. He pointed out that there was ample evidence to support the British view that the Spanish Government had always

---

[1] Sir A. Cadogan, who was with Mr. Eden in Quebec, agreed that the Chiefs of Staff were asking too much, and that their demands involved important political considerations.

(a) C9602, 9908/24/41.

desired, and still desired, an Axis victory; that, whatever assurance were given by successive Ministers of Foreign Affairs, Falangist officials refused fair and equal treatment to British interests. The Falange was the central machine of government in Spain; General Franco was its chief director, and the British Government were justified in complaining to him of the actions of his Government.

Sir S. Hoare said that the term 'non-belligerency'[1] was associated in British minds with the 'pre-belligerency' of Mussolini, and that it had in fact meant differentiation in favour of the Axis. Now that the last phase of the war had been reached, General Franco might consider whether a status so closely associated with Axis influence was to the advantage of Spain. General Franco replied by referring to his failure to get British help in the early days of the Civil War. He had then been driven against his will to accept help from Germany and Italy. He argued that the bias of Spanish civilians against us was due to these facts. Spain had now repaid its debt to the Axis, and the civil authorities and party officials had been given the strictest orders that there was to be no discrimination against us. General Franco admitted that many adventurers and criminals had got into the Falange; he was now doing his best to expel them.

General Franco said that he would not have moved from neutrality if France had not collapsed and Italy had not entered the war. In his view neutrality meant 'disinterest'. When the war reached Africa and the Mediterranean, and still more when Russia entered it, the Spanish move from neutrality to non-belligerency marked a direct interest, but did not mean 'pre-belligerency' or hostility to the Allies. In any case General Franco now distinguished between the Spanish attitude to Russia—which was not one of disinterest or indifference— and that of genuine neutrality towards the Western Allies.

General Franco insisted that the sending of the Blue Division to fight against Russia was merely a symbolic gesture, and that he would withdraw the division at once if there were a risk of it coming into conflict with British or American forces. Sir S. Hoare left a memorandum recounting the detailed complaints of the British Government against unneutral Spanish acts. He mentioned in particular Spanish connivance at Axis acts of sabotage. General Franco appeared to be genuinely anxious to stop such acts. Sir S. Hoare thought that the interview would have some results, even though General Franco's self-complacency remained unshaken. General Franco had shown clearly that he wanted to be on good terms with

---

[1] The American Ambassador at Madrid reported to his Government on October 4, 1943, that General Franco had used the term 'neutrality' to describe the international position of Spain. The Ambassador did not expect to hear again the term 'non-belligerency'. *F.R.U.S.* 1943, II, 621.

the Allies; his interpretation of neutrality was likely to be more favourable.

Mr. Eden did not regard General Franco's reply as very satisfactory: 'there are some vague promises; it remains to be seen whether any one of them is fulfilled . . . Franco is a poor fish, and almost a stranded one'. Our own position was now very strong, and we should take advantage of it. Mr. Eden's doubts were justified by General Franco's attitude during the next three months. For a time the Spanish attitude had seemed more favourable. The Spanish reaction to the Allied agreement over the Azores[1] was satisfactory. General Franco gave way to our demands for the withdrawal of the Blue Division, and took measures to secure the effective internment of U-boats and their crews which had taken refuge in Spanish harbours and had continued to provide facilities for the escaped Axis prisoners of war and refugees. The tone of the Spanish press was better; there was also an improvement in the attitude of the (a) Spanish authorities in Tangier and Morocco. On the economic side the Spanish Government agreed to modify the sterling-peseta rate in our favour, and to keep exports of wolfram to Germany at a low level. Nevertheless we still had serious grievances. There was no effective action against German sabotage[2] and espionage organisations. A Spanish air squadron was on the eastern front and was receiving reinforcements. The Spanish Government, although recognising the Badoglio Government in Italy, were delaying the departure of Italian ships from Spanish ports. We had also a long and imposing list of minor complaints, including the pro-Axis activities of certain Spanish officials.

General Franco appeared to have gained confidence since his opponents in Spain had failed to take advantage of the shock to the régime from the fall of Fascism. The improvement in the economic situation of Spain worked in his favour. He was naturally self-complacent and believed that the Allies were not seriously dissatisfied with him; his own dependence on the Falange made him think that he could avoid taking drastic measures to remove pro-Axis influences. To a certain extent this calculation was shrewdly justified. We did not want to intervene in the internal affairs of Spain or to make trouble for the Spanish Government if they maintained true neutrality. The Foreign Office realised—the facts indeed were obvious—that the United Nations could force General Franco out of power; they expected him to be removed after the war, but there

---

[1] See Chapter XLVIII, section (ii).
[2] These acts of sabotage included putting bombs in the cargoes of ships carrying Spanish oranges to Great Britain.

(a) C14887/24/41.

were no reasons for diverting our military resources to get rid of him at once or to deal with the anarchy in Spain which might follow his collapse.

(a)   Mr. Eden, however, and Sir S. Hoare came independently to the conclusion in the middle of December that we could well put more pressure on General Franco, and that we should again make our views clear to him. The Foreign Office therefore decided to instruct Sir S. Hoare to present another memorandum of complaints, and to say that since the Spanish Government seemed now to have adopted a policy of giving the minimum satisfaction to our requirements, we must infer that they wanted to give as much support as they dared to the Germans. Sir S. Hoare would then ask General Franco whether he had considered the consequences of this policy, and tell him that he would be well advised to stop all acts of unneutral assistance to Germany and change his policy in favour of the United Nations with whom after the war Spanish political and economic relations would be mainly conducted.

(b)   The United States Government at this time also decided that a stronger line was necessary towards General Franco. Sir S. Hoare reported on December 15, 1943, that, since General Franco was claiming the regular arrival of American oil supplies as evidence of American support of his régime, the United States Ambassador in Madrid was proposing to warn General Jordana early in the New Year that the intensification of Allied military operations would probably cause difficulties in the supply of oil to Spain. Delays in loading tankers would follow this statement, and would show General Franco that he could not take Allied supplies for granted. Sir S. Hoare told the Ambassador that he agreed with this policy if it were not pushed to the point where it would cause a break in economic relations with Spain and the disruption of Spanish economic life. Mr. Eden instructed Lord Halifax on December 23 to tell the State Department that we also wanted to shake General Franco's complacency. We agreed with the suggestion about the supply of oil, and thought that the United States Government should take the initiative in mentioning it to the Spanish Government, while Sir S. Hoare would carry out the instructions sent to him with regard to our own requirements.

(c)   Oil shipments to Spain were in fact suspended at the end of January 1944.[1] Meanwhile, on December 29, 1943, Sir S. Hoare

---

[1] The State Department, in a fuller announcement of this suspension on January 29, said that the Spanish Government had shown 'a certain reluctance to satisfy requests both reasonable and important by the State Department and concerning which representations have continuously been addressed to the Spanish Government for some time

(*continued on page 19*)

(a) C14756, 14887, 15295/24/41.   (b) C14872/24/41.   (c) C393/23/41.

left with General Jordana a note on the outstanding questions about which the British Government had reason to complain. General Franco, however, was unwilling to give an interview to Sir S. Hoare. Sir S. Hoare made it clear to General Jordana on January 21 that (a) he was not asking for the interview as a favour, but solely in order to point out to General Franco that the British Government took a grave view of the situation. The Spanish Government, if they wished, could refuse to hear what Sir S. Hoare intended to say, but matters would then become worse from their point of view.

General Franco accepted this advice, or rather, warning, and saw (b) Sir S. Hoare on January 28, 1944. Sir S. Hoare put to him the British complaints, including the Spanish exports of wolfram to Germany.[1] General Franco seemed anxious to avoid a breach with Great Britain; he repeated his usual attempts at justifying Spanish policy and his usual assurances that he was trying to suppress sabotage activities. He said that the question of the expulsion of the German Consulate at Tangier was under consideration; that the Blue Division was being completely withdrawn from the eastern front and that the Blue Air Squadron was no longer a working unit.[2] Sir S. Hoare understood from General Jordana that, in fact, all the British demands would have been accepted, if there had not been a leakage in Washington, followed by our special announcement about the stoppage of oil shipments.

(iv)

American demand for a complete cessation of Spanish exports of wolfram to Germany: Anglo-American differences of view: American acceptance of a compromise (February–May 1944).

The question of joint Anglo-American representations now (c) became complicated by the insistence of the State Department in going beyond the warnings suggested by the British Government and in demanding from the Spanish Government a total prohibition

---

(*continued*)
past'. The requests concerned the internment of Italian warships and merchant ships in Spanish ports, the export to Germany of materials such as wolfram, the activities of Axis agents, the continued activities of a part of the Blue Division, and a new financial arrangement with Germany. *F.R.U.S.* 1944, IV, 307.

[1] See note 1 on p. 20.

[2] Among General Franco's remarks were (i) that no one in Spain knew who was going to win the war and (ii) that, owing to confusion in Germany, there were long delays in getting any answers from the German Government. Mr. Eden had also spoken to the (d) Duke of Alba on January 24 in strong terms about the British complaints, and had received the usual bland assurances and excuses.

(a) C1010/23/41.   (b) C1288, 1309, 1320, 1321/23/41.   (c) C1791, 2237/23/41.
(d) C1083/23/41.

of the export of wolfram to Germany.[1] The British Embassy in Madrid had already asked for an embargo on exports of wolfram to Germany, and had warned the Spanish Ministry of Foreign Affairs in September 1943 that by a continuation of these exports Spain would be prolonging the war. No representations were made by the Americans until November. Ten days later—without waiting for a full statement of British views—the United States Ambassador presented a memorandum to the Ministry of Foreign Affairs in which one of the demands was for an embargo on wolfram. The United States Ambassador in Madrid agreed with Sir S. Hoare that the Spaniards would be under very heavy pressure from the Germans not to agree to a demand of this kind; if we persisted in it, and especially if we accompanied it by a threat to withhold oil supplies to Spain, we should get a stubborn refusal on the Spanish side to meet any of our grievances. The United States would then have to carry out a blockade of Spain, and in the meantime we should have lost the chance—at a critical period in the war—of getting rid of enemy agents in Spain and Tangier. Lord Halifax was instructed to put the British point of view to the State Department, but the latter were convinced that General Franco would give way. Mr. Stettinius made matters even more difficult by telling the Spanish Ambassador in Washington that the United States did not intend to interfere in the internal affairs of the country or to destroy its economic life. The Foreign Office considered that the Spanish Government would feel justified in interpreting Mr. Stettinius's mildness as evidence that they need not take the American demands too seriously.

(a)   On February 11, 1944, Sir S. Hoare reported that the United

---

[1] The most important use of wolfram for military purposes was in connection with machine tools and armour-piercing shells, including anti-tank projectiles. The chief sources of supply were in the Far East and the Iberian peninsula. The normal Spanish output was about 5,000 tons, slightly lower than that of Portugal. Except for small quantities reaching Germany through blockade-runners, the Germans lost their Far Eastern supplies after the entry of Russia into the war. Hence the importance of the supplies from Spain and Portugal.

(b)   In 1942 the British Government came to the conclusion that these supplies of wolfram from the Iberian peninsula were essential to the German armaments industry; the German requirements were estimated at about 5,000 tons a year. The War Cabinet therefore authorised the Ministry of Economic Warfare to try to buy up the whole of the Spanish supply. (For the negotiations with Portugal over the export of wolfram, see Chapter XLVIII, section (iv).) The result was a sudden rise in prices, and a consequent increase in production. In 1941 the Germans had bought 300 tons, and the Allies none. In 1942 the German purchase was 900 tons against an Allied figure of 760 tons. In 1943 the Allies bought 3,035 tons, and the Germans 1,309 tons. The Germans were at this time short of Spanish currency. At the end of 1943, however, the Spanish Government repaid its Civil War debt to Germany, while the Germans sold large quantities of arms and machinery to Spain. The Germans now had ample supplies of pesetas. They had also made an agreement on August 28, 1943, with the Spanish Government for the unrestricted purchase of wolfram. They did not begin, however, until the early part of 1944 to ask for a substantial increase in their export licences.

(a) C2237/23/41.   (b) C6242/2/41 (1944).

States Ambassador had received instructions to tell General Jordana that the United States Government insisted upon a total and permanent embargo on the supply of wolfram to Germany, and that, if this demand were not met, they would continue the suspension of oil supplies to Spain. Sir S. Hoare persuaded Dr. Hayes not to act at once on his instructions in view of the fact that Anglo-American discussions were taking place on a common policy towards Spain.

Mr. Churchill was inclined to accept the American proposal. He wrote a minute to Mr. Eden on February 12 that on the whole he was inclining to the view that the United States had come so far out into the open against Spain that it would be a mistake to try to upset their rough treatment. The Americans were not unreasonable in saying that if the Spaniards wanted American oil they must stop sending wolfram to Germany. The Prime Minister was not at all sure that the Spaniards would not give in. Anyhow there were great disadvantages in a 'blow hot, blow cold' policy. Later, however, Mr. Churchill asked Mr. Eden if he wanted him to say anything to the President about the dangers of American policy towards Spain.

The Prime Minister in fact told the President on February 13 (a) that we would support the 'decided action' taken by the United States, though he added that it would be 'tiresome if Germany gives the gasoline and Spain becomes even more definitely associated with the Nazis'. Mr. Churchill, however, also thought that the United States Government should be told of a warning from Sir S. Hoare that by concentrating wholly on the wolfram question, and (b) neglecting the question of German agents in Spain, we should be ignoring the greatest obstacles to Spanish neutrality and to the fulfilment of the promise to refrain from unneutral acts. The Foreign Office—with much reluctance—felt it necessary to support the (c) American action, since otherwise the Spanish Government would realise that the Allies were divided.

The President replied to the Prime Minister on February 15 that (d) as a result of the suspension of tanker loadings, the Spanish situation was developing satisfactorily, and that, if the British and United States Governments held firm, we should be able to secure a complete and permanent Spanish embargo on the export of wolfram to any country. The President's information showed that the Germans were very short of wolfram, and that supplies obtained at this time could be 'directly translated into terms of British and American casualties'. The President did not agree with the 'disposition on the part of your Ambassador and ours at Madrid to accept some compromise short of a complete embargo'. He saw no danger that

(a) T299/4, No. 577 (Churchill Papers/405; C2115/23/41).   (b) C2166/23/41.
(c) C2154/23/41.   (d) T316/4, No. 467 (Churchill Papers/405; C2614/23/41).

insistence upon such an embargo before the loading of tankers was resumed would produce a serious reaction in Spain.

(a)   The Foreign Office suggested an answer that, while we had agreed to support the demand for a total embargo on wolfram, we regarded as equally important our demands for the suppression of the German Consulate at Tangier, and the expulsion of German spies and saboteurs from Spanish territory, since their activities could also be directly translated into terms of British and American lives. The risk was that, if the Spanish Government turned obstinate, they might hand over to the Germans in return for gasoline some 500–700 tons of wolfram which were now stocked near the Pyrenees. The removal of these stocks was being prevented for the time by a temporary embargo during our discussions. We had also to consider the effect of a deadlock upon our own important war requirements from Spain, i.e. iron ore and potash. We had a good hand to play with the Spaniards but the Germans might be able to offer certain short-term economic advantages.

The Prime Minister thought that this draft message again pointed both ways, and that the President might be puzzled about our real wishes. The Prime Minister thought it better to send a message saying 'We will back you up but extend your line of attack', or to give a warning 'Be careful in what you do lest they deny us our iron

(b) ore and potash'. At this time a telegram from Lord Halifax on the night of February 19–20, and telegrams from Sir S. Hoare showed a new situation. Sir S. Hoare had seen General Jordana on February 17 and had secured from him certain definite undertakings: (i) to close the German Consulate at Tangier and remove all German agents from Tangier and from Spain, (ii) to dissolve and repatriate all Spanish units on the Russian front, (iii) to release all Italian merchant ships, (iv) to give every facility for ensuring a drastic limit of wolfram exports. Sir S. Hoare had proposed to General Jordana that, while the Spanish Government would maintain its sovereign right to export any commodity, it would in fact cut down wolfram exports to a point which would prevent Germany from getting any during the next six months. General Jordana agreed to consider this proposal, but implored the Allied Governments meanwhile to remove the threat of oil sanctions.

The Foreign Office thought it most desirable to agree to a settlement on these lines. We should have won a major political victory in the closing of the German Consulate at Tangier, and should also be depriving the Germans of Spanish wolfram for six months. According to Lord Halifax's telegram, however, the State Department remained unwilling to consider a resumption of oil loadings

---

(a) C2614/23/41.   (b) C2296, 2350, 2500/23/41, C2266/23/41.

until the Spanish Government had agreed to a complete embargo on wolfram, and instructions had been sent accordingly to the United States Ambassador at Madrid. The officials of the British Embassy to whom this information was given protested strongly that the instructions to Dr. Hayes had been sent without consultation with the British Government. The State Department nonetheless refused to cancel the telegram. Lord Halifax therefore complained to Mr. Stettinius that the American move was yet another example of unilateral action in a matter which was supposed to be one of joint policy.

In view of the new situation the Prime Minister telegraphed to (a) the President on February 21 that the reports from Madrid showed that a satisfactory settlement could be reached on all points if we acted at once. The settlement would include the cessation of Spanish wolfram exports to Germany for six months. The Prime Minister commented: 'If all goes as we hope, I do not think we need anticipate much difficulty in maintaining this position when the six months have elapsed.' The Prime Minister said that Mr. Eden was tele- (b) graphing at greater length to the State Department, and that he (Mr. Churchill) hoped that we should 'immediately clinch matters'.

The President replied in somewhat obscure terms on February 23 (c) that 'it was very pleasing to know that a settlement of our current controversy with Spain promises to be accomplished quickly.' The Foreign Office interpreted this to mean that the President agreed to an immediate settlement on the lines reached in the discussions with General Jordana, but the Americans continued to ask for the complete embargo on wolfram.

On February 28 Dr. Hayes told General Jordana that the United (d) States Government were prepared to accept the proposal which the Spanish Government had previously made, i.e. a reduction of exports of wolfram to Germany of 10 per cent of the 1943 figure, but that there must be no exports for the coming six months. General Jordana said that a few days earlier he could have agreed to this arrangement, but there had been an almost complete disclosure of the negotiations in the *New York Times*, with the result that he had received a formidable protest from the German Government, and now had to consult the Spanish Council of Ministers.

On March 7, after a week of meetings of the Council, General (e) Jordana told Dr. Hayes that, owing to their previous agreement with Germany, the Spanish Government were unable to accept the 10 per cent proposal or any total embargo. Hence the negotiations

---

(a) T355/4, No. 586 (Churchill Papers/405; C2481/23/41).　(b) C2266/23/41.
(c) T380/4, No. 478 (Churchill Papers/405; C2738/23/41).　(d) C2754/2/41.
(e) C3138/2/41.

dragged on through March.[1] The Spanish Government were in fact willing to cut down the exports of wolfram to Germany to a small figure. They were also prepared to agree to the other British
(a) demands; Sir S. Hoare reported on March 18 that they had begun
(b) to expel German agents. The Foreign Office therefore continued to argue that it was wholly unwise to abandon the opportunity of getting satisfaction on the other demands made on Spain merely for the sake of a small quantity of wolfram. The United States Government refused to resume oil shipments to Spain unless the Spanish Government accepted a total embargo. The Foreign Office pointed out that the State Department had agreed with the British Government in January that the increase of pressure on General Franco should not be taken to the point of a fundamental change in Allied policy, or be allowed to cause a deadlock in Allied relations with
(c) Spain. On March 27 Mr. Eden told the War Cabinet that the figure in dispute had been narrowed by discussions in Madrid to the export of some 150 tons of wolfram before June 30. Mr. Eden hoped to persuade the United States Government that this figure was not worth a serious economic conflict with Spain.

(d)   The Prime Minister sent a message to the President on March 30 putting in detail the case for accepting the compromise solution. He asked the President most earnestly to take into consideration the British view, especially since British strategic and economic interests were more concerned than those of the United States. He said that he could not support in public the policy which the United States
(e) was enforcing on us. Mr. Eden also instructed Lord Halifax to point out to Mr. Hull that proposals made by the State Department for a long-term economic agreement with Spain were 'unrealistic'. The negotiation of such an agreement would take months during which we should get none of our other *desiderata*. From the Spanish point of view the Americans were unable to offer with any certainty to provide the chief imports—arms and machinery—which Spain obtained from German-controlled Europe, while from our standpoint they also had not made any proposals for replacing our essential imports of iron ore and potash which we were likely to lose if the negotiations broke down.

(f)   The President telegraphed on April 5 that he was most reluctant to accept a compromise on the wolfram question, but that, in the absence of full Anglo-American agreement in the matter, he was asking the State Department to work out with the British Embassy

---

[1] Dr. Hayes wrote to the State Department on March 9, 1944, a somewhat critical review of American policy towards Spain. *F.R.U.S.* 1944, IV, 359–62.

(a) C3754/23/41.   (b) WP(44)170; C4044/2/41.   (c) WM(44)41; C4130/2/41.
(d) T687/4, No. 631 (Churchill Papers/405; C4131/2/41).   (e) C4131/2/41.   (f) T718/4, No. 512 (Churchill Papers/505; C4794/2/41).

a 'mutually agreeable line to take with the Spanish'. The Prime
Minister and the Foreign Office again took this message to mean
that the President was actually willing to accept a compromise.[1]
Meanwhile General Jordana told the United States Ambassador on (a)
the night of April 11–12 that although the Spanish Government
would not agree to a total embargo on exports of wolfram to Germany during the next three months, they would accept a limitation
of 60 tons from the actual moment up to June 30.[2] He said that if
this offer were to hold it must be accepted quickly. Dr. Hayes and
Sir S. Hoare recommended strongly an immediate acceptance.

The Foreign Office view was that we ought to accept this proposal.
The Germans would get very little wolfram, much less than the
amount actually in store on the Franco-Spanish frontier. The
arrangement would be regarded generally as a victory for the
Allies, and the Spanish Government would have made the other
concessions, which, in the British view, were of more value than
60 tons of wolfram.

It became clear, however, that the real objections on the American
side to a compromise proposal arose out of the domestic position in
the United States. Mr. Acheson told Lord Halifax on April 11 that (b)
the foreign policy of the Administration had been under heavy
attack in view of the Presidential election in November 1944, but
that Mr. Hull's speech of April 9, 1944, had greatly improved the
position. One of the most important passages in this speech had been
Mr. Hull's statement that the time for giving way to neutrals had
passed, and that the United States Government were now determined not to send supplies to neutrals who were assisting the enemy.
Mr. Acheson said that the Administration could not risk public
criticism by allowing oil shipments to Spain while condoning
Spanish export of wolfram to Germany. In any case we could not
make an exception in the case of Spain when we were trying to get
Sweden to stop the export of ball-bearings and Turkey the export
of chrome.

Lord Halifax pointed out that the proposed terms of settlement
with Spain could be presented as a success for Mr. Hull's policy,
since instead of getting 2–3,000 tons of wolfram during the rest of
the year the Germans would obtain practically nothing. The State
Department would be in a much more difficult position if they had
to admit that the negotiations had broken down, and that as a result
of the policy of the State Department, the Germans were securing

---

[1] On April 4 the State Department telegraphed to Dr. Hayes that, in response to
Mr. Churchill's appeal, the United States Government was prepared to recede from their
demand for a complete embargo on wolfram exports. *F.R.U.S.* 1944, IV, 377.
[2] The proposed restriction was 600 tons for the year; 300 tons had been delivered.

(a) C4804, 4805/2/41. (b) C4760/3/41.

large quantities of wolfram of which they would otherwise have been deprived. Mr. Acheson held to his opinon that the negotiations would not break down, and that the Spaniards would not dare to hand over the wolfram now in store on the frontier. He proposed to stand firm on the basis of an export of 300 tons after July 1, and nothing until then.

(a)   On April 17 Mr. Hull[1] told Lord Halifax that the wolfram question was 'terrific dynamite' at a time when all 'polecat' elements were doing their best to destroy the President and the Administration. Mr. Hull suggested as a way out of the difficulty that the British Government should sponsor the oil shipments to Spain, and that, if we did so on the basis of the proposed compromise about wolfram, the United States Administration would go as far as they could in supporting us. Lord Halifax said that Mr. Hull's proposal meant shifting the burden of an unpopular decision from the United States Government to the British Government; the American public reaction would be to contrast once more British 'opportunism' with the devotion of the United States to moral principles.

(b)   The Prime Minister replied to Lord Halifax that he was 'perfectly ready to take full responsibility for doing a sensible thing whether it is popular or unpopular, whether it is supported by the United States or merely agreed with. We have not got an election here, and anyhow we can take whatever is coming to us. You should, however, tell Mr. Hull that I must hold myself free if attacked to defend myself by a pretty considerable disclosure of the facts. There is not much agitation in this country about this point because people are thinking of the solemn events impending. But anyhow I could in half-an-hour's speech to the House of Commons convince them that our action was right and wise'.

(c)   The Foreign Office were more doubtful about the proposal. They did not in fact expect much support from Mr. Hull, and thought that once again we might be accused of 'appeasing' General Franco while the Americans appeared to be holding to their principles. On the other hand a breakdown in the negotiations would not only lose us the chance of getting satisfaction from the Spanish Government on our other demands—especially the closing of the German Consulate at Tangier and the expulsion of German agents from Spain—during the coming critical months; we should also be unable, through lack of currency, to continue our purchases of pyrites, iron ore and potash, with serious consequences to our own war production and agriculture. On balance, therefore, the Foreign Office agreed with the Prime Minister that we should accept the American suggestion.

---

[1] The President was at this time on holiday in South Carolina.

(a) C5051/2/41. (b) T880/4 (Churchill Papers/505; C5051/2/41). (c) C5838/2/41.

The War Cabinet took a similar view. Sir S. Hoare was therefore (a)
instructed—as soon as we had received confirmation that the United (b)
States Government would accept Mr. Hull's proposal—to inform
General Jordana that we were prepared to accept his wolfram offer
together with satisfactory assurances regarding our other demands.
On these terms oil shipments to Spain would be resumed at once,
and, as a matter of convenience, these shipments would now come
from British-controlled sources.

There were, however, further difficulties. The President tele- (c)
graphed a message on April 22 which did not mention Mr. Hull's
proposal but suggested that the two Governments should make yet
another attempt to persuade the Spanish Government to agree to a
complete embargo until June 30. General Jordana, however, said
that it was impossible for the Spanish Government to go beyond (d)
their offer, and that they could not continue the negotiations
indefinitely. Sir S. Hoare was afraid that General Jordana might
find it necessary to resign. The Prime Minister now proposed to
send a somewhat angry message to the President that since he (the (e)
President) had refused any compromise, including Mr. Hull's
suggestion, he proposed to 'retire from the business', and to 'leave
the direction and the responsibility' entirely in the President's hands.
This message was not sent because on April 25 the President tele- (f)
graphed that he had authorised Mr. Hull to accept what he called
Lord Halifax's proposal. It appeared from a telegram sent by Lord (g)
Halifax during the night of April 25–26 that the United States
Government had in fact decided to accept the previous British
proposals without any important change. Dr. Hayes had been
instructed to agree to a settlement in which the exports of wolfram
did not exceed 20 tons for each of the months of May and June.
On the following night, however, Lord Halifax reported that Mr.
Hull had changed his mind again. Dr. Hayes had been told to ask
for an immediate meeting with General Franco and to put the
request for a total embargo up to June 30. If this demand were
refused, Dr. Hayes could then agree to the compromise plan.

The Foreign Office considered it unnecessary to protest against (h)
the delay, and also to the form of a proposed American statement
putting the responsibility on Great Britain for the acceptance of
anything less than a total embargo. Dr. Hayes saw General Jordana (i)
on April 28. He found, as he had expected, that there was no chance
that General Franco would agree to a total embargo. He then proposed the compromise on the basis of an export of not more than

---

(a) WM(44)52. (b) C5051/2/41. (c) T903/4, No. 529 (Churchill Papers/505;
C5302/2/41). (d) C5311/2/41. (e) C5710/2/41. (f) T960/4, No. 531 (Churchill
Papers/505; C5529/2/41). (g) C5413/2/41. (h) C5565/2/41. (i) C5654/2/41.

40 tons up to June 30 and 40 tons monthly thereafter. On April 29 General Jordana told Dr. Hayes that General Franco had agreed to this proposal. Mr. Eden made an announcement of the general settlement, of which the wolfram proposals formed part, in the House of Commons on May 2. The terms of the announcement,

(a) which were agreed with the United States Government, were that for some time past the two Governments had been in negotiation with the Spanish Government over matters in which the latter's attitude had seemed contrary to the declared policy of Spanish neutrality. These matters were the presence and activities of the German Consul-General at Tangier and of German agents throughout Spain and Spanish-controlled territory, the continued presence of Spanish units on the eastern front and the level of exports of Spanish wolfram to Germany. The Spanish Government had now accepted a settlement of the demands which the British Government regarded as satisfactory 'on account of the military and economic benefits accruing therefrom to the United Nations, and because it marks a notable step towards the fulfilment of that strict neutrality which the Spanish Government have declared to be their policy'.

(v)

The Prime Minister's speech of May 24, 1944: General Franco's letter of October 18, 1944, to the Prime Minister: the Prime Minister's letter of warning to General Franco.

(b)   On May 24, 1944, the Prime Minister referred in the House of Commons to Spain. He spoke with approval of the Spanish policy of keeping out of the war, and said that the Spanish Government had 'made amends', in the period before the Allied landings in North Africa, for any assistance they had previously given to Germany.[1] The Prime Minister considered that 'a service was rendered at this time by Spain not only to the United Kingdom, and to the British Empire and Commonwealth, but to the cause of the United Nations'.[2] He had no sympathy with those who took every occasion to insult and abuse the Spanish Government. He

---

[1] The Prime Minister pointed out later to Mr. Eden that he and the Foreign Office had seen the draft of his speech, and had not commented on it. See below, p. 33, note 1.

(c)   [2] On April 21 Sir A. Clark Kerr reported a Tass message from London in the Moscow press quoting a Spanish newsletter to the effect that Spain had been a German supply base since 1939. The Prime Minister sent a personal message to Sir A. Clark Kerr: 'All the same it was a very good thing that Franco did not let the Germans through to attack Gibraltar and get across into North Africa. This has to be considered too, and you might remind our friends, as opportunity serves, that at that time we were absolutely alone in the world. So do not let us all be too spiteful about the past.'

(a) C5816/2/41. (b) *H. of C. Deb.*, Vol. 400, cols. 768–72. (c) C5708/129/41.

hoped Spain would be a strong influence for peace in the Mediterranean after the war. He regarded Spanish internal political problems as matters for the Spaniards themselves.

The United States press commented unfavourably on this speech. The Prime Minister, however, defended himself in a characteristic message of June 4 to the President: 'I see some of your newspapers (a) are upset at my references in the House of Commons to Spain. This is very unfair, as all I have done is to repeat my declaration of October 1940. I only mentioned Franco's name to show how silly it was to identify Spain with him or him with Spain by means of caricatures. I do not care about Franco, but I do not wish to have the Iberian peninsula hostile to the British after the war. I do not know how I can depend on a de Gaullist France. Germany would have to be held down by main force, and we have a 20-years alliance with Russia. . . . We should not be able to agree with her in attacking countries which have not molested us because we dislike their totalitarian form of government. I do not know whether there is more freedom in Stalin's Russia than in Franco's Spain. I have no intention to seek a quarrel with either.'

The Allied victories and the German withdrawal from France removed all danger of Spanish participation in the war on the German side. The problem now was to decide upon the attitude which the western democracies would take towards the Spanish régime after the war. For General Franco himself this problem, oddly enough, did not appear to exist.[1] His own position in Spain was stronger than ever, and his complacency greater. He was unlikely to be overthrown from within owing to the disunity of his opponents and the general fear in Spain of a renewal of the horrors of the civil war. He had to reckon on the implacable hatred of the Russians, but he gained more from his public hatred of them and from his pose as the defender of Spain against a Communist invasion. He did not expect the Western Powers, however much they disliked his régime, to take active steps to turn him out by armed intervention. He could reckon on a division of opinion in France, on the importance to Great Britain of economic relations with Spain, and on the unwillingness of the United States to be committed to armed action in the internal affairs of a European country.

---

[1] General Franco, however, had not given up his hopes of an early peace. On March 24, (b) 1944, General Jordana gave Sir S. Hoare a message from General Franco to the Prime Minister and Mr. Eden assuring them of the desire of the Spanish Government to maintain friendly relations with Great Britain. General Jordana said how greatly alarmed he and General Franco were at the danger to European civilisation from a prolonged war. They looked particularly to Great Britain as the guardian of European civilisation and prayed that the war might soon end. Sir S. Hoare made the usual answer that peace could come only after a decisive Allied victory.

(a) T1192/4, No. 692 (Churchill Paper/472; C7647/23/41). (b) C3811/23/41.

(a)   Lord Templewood,[1] who was leaving the British Embassy at his own wish in the late autumn, suggested in a memorandum of October 16, 1944 to the Foreign Office, that the Allied Governments should give a warning to General Franco—with the possibility of supporting it by economic sanctions—that their relations with him after the war would be seriously affected if he did not change for the better the character of his Government. Sir A. Cadogan, after discussing with Lord Templewood the possibility of such a warning, had doubts whether there was anything we could do without abandoning our general policy of non-interference in the internal affairs of other countries unless they threatened aggression. Sir A. Cadogan thought that the only form of remonstrance likely to be of use would be to warn General Franco that unless he reformed his régime, Spain would not be elected to membership of a World Organisation. Even so, there was nothing General Franco could do to meet the Russian opposition to Spanish membership. The Foreign Office generally took this view, and, in particular, regarded it as impolitic to indulge, in Sir A. Cadogan's words, 'in the luxury of economic sanctions for ideological ends'. On the other hand we wanted to encourage the opposition in Spain to the Falangist régime, especially after the discouraging effect produced on them by the Prime Minister's speech in May 1944.

(b)   Mr. Attlee, in a memorandum of November 4, also raised the question of policy. He said that all our Allies wanted to see the régime destroyed and that we were in danger of being regarded as its sole external supporters. Mr. Attlee admitted that it was unlikely, owing to the divisions among the Spaniards, that a democratic government could be established at once in Spain. He also thought that, in view of Spanish xenophobia, we could not take overt action to change the situation. Somewhat inconsistently, however, he suggested that we might 'in the economic field work with the United States and France to deny [it] facilities'.

(c)   This memorandum brought a rejoinder on November 14 from Lord Selborne, Minister of Economic Warfare, pointing out that the régime of General Franco was at all events better than the Spanish régime which it displaced; that its atrocities were 'fewer and less horrible' and that General Franco was not more authoritarian or more severe to his political opponents than our Allies, Stalin and Dr. Salazar. Lord Selborne considered that a policy of 'economic pinpricks and strangleholds against Spain' would do us no good and bring us no credit. We had no moral justification for such attacks

---

[1] Sir S. Hoare was elevated to the peerage as Viscount Templewood on July 3, 1944.

(a) C14492/23/41.   (b) WP(44)622; C15487, 15948/23/41.   (c) WP(44)651; C15974/23/41.

on a country which had not seriously attacked us, and for whose non-belligerency in 1940 we were much indebted. The main sufferers would be British traders and the Spanish people.

Meanwhile, before Mr. Eden had put Lord Templewood's pro- (a) posal to the War Cabinet, the Spanish Ambassador had told the Foreign Office, on November 9, that he would like to deliver, if possible early in the following week,[1] a letter from General Franco to Mr. Eden. Sir A. Cadogan said that he hoped the letter did not contain any 'injudicious remarks', since it seemed to him that some of General Franco's public statements in the last few days showed that he was suffering from certain illusions. Thus he seemed to claim that Spain should be represented at the Peace Conference. Sir A. Cadogan pointed out that it was unthinkable that, with the memory of the activities of the Blue Division against Russia, Spain under the present régime should be invited to participate in a European settlement.

After discussion in the Foreign Office and with Lord Templewood (b) Mr. Eden submitted to the Prime Minister a draft memorandum which he proposed to circulate to the War Cabinet, and also a draft telegram of instructions to Lord Halifax. In these instructions Lord Halifax was asked to enquire whether the State Department would join in a warning to General Franco that, while the British and United States Governments did not wish to interfere in Spanish internal affairs, a development of really friendly relations was impossible as long as internal conditions in Spain remained in complete contradiction with the principles of the United Nations. There could be no question of allowing Falangist Spain a seat at the Peace Conference; her admission to a future World Organisation was unlikely. If this warning did not break down General Franco's complacency, it might be desirable to take more positive action to show that the United Nations were unwilling to condone General Franco's support of the Falangist régime. This action might include the suspension of oil shipments, but we should have to take care to avoid harming our own vital economic interests or rallying the Spanish people round General Franco or producing chaotic and revolutionary conditions in Spain.

The Prime Minister, in an unusually long minute to Mr. Eden, considered that the whole matter, including the instructions to Lord Halifax, should be brought before the War Cabinet. He did not think that any neutrals

'should be allowed to come to the Armistice (*sic*) Conference except at a much lower level than the United Nations and at a long interval

---

[1] Mr. Eden's comment was: 'We need not hurry unduly.'

(a) C15489/23/41. (b) C15949, 16068/23/41.

after it has begun. On the other hand, definitely to interfere in the internal government of a country with whom one has not been at war and who has done us much more good than harm in the war is a serious step. I am no more in agreement with the internal government of Russia than I am with that of Spain, but I certainly would rather live in Spain than Russia.'

The Prime Minister did not believe that our warnings would weaken General Franco's position:

'He and all those associated with him will never consent to be butchered by the Republicans, which is what would happen. It is a life and death matter in Spain and I do not think we should, without more careful consideration, make ourselves responsible for starting another blood-bath. What you are proposing to do is little less than stirring up a revolution in Spain. You begin with oil; you will quickly end in blood.'

The Prime Minister agreed that Lord Templewood might put many of the points to General Franco in conversation; on the other hand we ought not to 'try to work up the United States'. We were already accused of handing over the Balkans and Central Europe to Russia, and would be making needless trouble for ourselves 'if we now lay hands on Spain'. If the Communists gained control of Spain, the 'infection' would spread very fast through Italy and France. 'It would be far better to allow these Spanish tendencies to work themselves out instead of precipitating a renewal of the civil war, which is what you will do if you press this matter'. Every country liberated or converted by our victories was now seething with Communism. 'All are linked together and only our influence with Russia prevents their actively stimulating this movement, deadly as I conceive it to peace and also to the freedom of mankind.'

The Prime Minister could 'well believe' that the Left Wing in Great Britain would support a doctrinal war, but he doubted whether the Conservative Party would agree to it. He personally would be unable to seek a fleeting popularity by such paths. He would be glad to see a monarchical and democratic restoration in Spain, but once we had identified ourselves with the Communist side we should lose all our influence. The Prime Minister asked Mr. Eden to

'consider the three principal tenets to which I hold: opposition to Communism, non-intervention in the domestic affairs of countries which have not molested us, and no special engagements in Europe requiring the maintenance of a large British Army, but rather the effective development of a World Peace Organisation thoroughly armed.'

Mr. Eden replied on November 17 that he had no wish to provoke or precipitate revolution in Spain, and regarded it as at present unlikely, but information, based on the views of moderate and conservative Spaniards, not Left Wing *émigrés*, suggested that an explosion was bound to come if General Franco were not persuaded to look for support to the moderate monarchist and republican forces rather than to the discredited Falange which he was still 'bolstering up more than ever'. If we did not give General Franco a warning now, the moderates would lose all influence and another civil war be inevitable 'sooner or later and probably sooner'. Mr. Eden gave examples of an expression of this view by conservative Spaniards. He asked the Prime Minister to agree to the circulation of his paper to the War Cabinet. He pointed out that there was no question of economic sanctions or threats. He had now put the warning in the form of a letter from the Prime Minister to General Franco since it would be necessary to reply to the letter which the Spanish Ambassador was bringing from the General, and the Prime Minister's position in Spain was such that our warning had most chance of being effective if it were made personally by him.[1]

The Prime Minister replied on November 18 that he agreed to the circulation of Mr. Eden's memorandum, but that the discussion of the matter should await the Spanish Ambassador's communication. The Prime Minister repeated his disagreement with the proposal to consult the United States Government 'at this stage'. He reminded Mr. Eden that he (Mr. Eden) had in fact tried to moderate the American views in recent negotiations. He was willing in principle to write to General Franco that we did not seek special association with the present régime in Spain or propose to support the inclusion of any neutrals in the conference of the United Nations after the victory over Germany, but that we wished to live in friendly relations with Spain and the Spanish people as a whole. The Prime Minister added: 'I should wish to write my own letter myself after having seen the exact nature of the Spanish communication, and having had the advantage of hearing the Cabinet discussions on the subject. Mr. Eden circulated his memorandum to the War Cabinet (a) but did not include a draft telegram to Lord Halifax.

General Franco's letter (dated October 18, 1944) was mainly a (b) complaint about British policy and the activities of British propaganda services and agents in Spain. The Duke of Alba, to whom the letter was formally addressed, presented a copy of it on November 21. (c) The Foreign Office drew up a letter of reply but the Prime Minister, while regarding this letter 'as very well drafted' and saying 'the most freezing things with suitable diplomatic restraint', minuted on (d)

---

[1] The Foreign Office also thought that a letter from the Prime Minister was desirable (e) in order to correct the Spanish misinterpretation of his speech of May 24.

(a) WP(44)665; C16069/23/41. (b) C16185/23/41. (c) C16786/23/41. (d) C17372/23/41. (e) C15950/23/41.

December 11 that the 'balance of help and hindrance given us by Spain in the war' was not fairly stated. 'The supreme services of not intervening in 1940 or interfering with the use of the airfield and Algeciras Bay' in the months before the North African landings in 1942 outweighed the minor complaints which we had against General Franco. The Prime Minister thought the draft 'too sharp a break' with what he had said in the House in May 1944: 'Remember it is Franco we want to snub and would like to see disappear, and not Spain.' The Prime Minister added that he wanted to send a copy of his reply to Stalin.

> 'I believe it would give him great satisfaction and also help to clear away any doubts which may have been engendered by de Gaulle during his visit that we have desired to build up a Western *bloc* against Russia. I have no doubt de Gaulle endeavoured to acquire as much merit as possible by stating his opposition to such an organism. I am increasingly impressed (up to date) with the loyalty with which, under much temptation and very likely pressure, Stalin has kept off Greece in accordance with our agreement, and I believe we shall gain in influence with him and strengthen a moderate policy for the Soviets by showing them how our mind works.'

(a)   The Foreign Office now revised the draft letter to General Franco in order to meet more definitely the points in General Franco's own letter. The new draft was circulated to the War Cabinet on December 12. In a covering note Mr. Eden again suggested that the two letters should be communicated to the United States Government in order to get their support before the delivery of the Prime Minister's letter.

(b) The War Cabinet approved the drafts on December 18. The Foreign Office then prepared the draft of a message from the Prime Minister
(c) to Stalin. This draft was submitted to the Prime Minister on
(d) December 25. The Prime Minister, in a minute of December 31, repeated his unwillingness to ask the United States Government to make simultaneous representations to General Franco. He wrote that he did not consider that we should 'make suggestions to the State Department to beat up the Spaniards'. We need not do more than tell them our answer to General Franco's approaches. Mr. Eden replied on January 8, 1945, that the reason for asking the State
(e) Department to make simultaneous representations in Madrid was that, owing largely to the behaviour of the American Embassy, General Franco had the impression that the United States Government approved of him and of his régime. General Franco on this account was complacently discounting our dissatisfaction with him. The British Chargé d'Affaires in Madrid (who had reported on the unsatisfactory attitude of the American Embassy) had advised the

(a) C17372/23/41. (b) WM(44)171; C18082/23/41. (c) C18083/23/41. (d) M1254/4, Z537/537/41 (1945). (e) PM/45/8, Z537/537/41.

Foreign Office to get simultaneous American action, and the State Department, according to Lord Halifax, were likely to be ready to support us.

The Prime Minister replied on January 11 complaining that his (a) letters to General Franco and Stalin had not been despatched. He repeated his view that it would be enough to tell the United States Government what we had said without 'urging them to join in an anti-Spanish coalition'. The Americans were 'very anti-Franco and also anti-Spanish', and would keep in step with us in their own way and in their own time. The Prime Minister himself had 'not the slightest intention of starting an anti-Franco crusade any more than [he wished] to walk down the street with him arm in arm'. The War Cabinet decided to send the Prime Minister's letter through the Spanish Ambassador to General Franco, and to send copies 'with the minimum comment' to President Roosevelt and Stalin. In view of the Prime Minister's minute, the letter and copies were sent within the next few days, but no request was made for simultaneous representations at Madrid by the United States Government.

The text of the letter in its final form referred to the facts that, while Spain had not taken action against Great Britain at two critical moments of the war—the collapse of France and the North African invasion—throughout the war German influence had been allowed to predominate in Spain and a Spanish division had been sent to assist our enemies against our Russian ally. We had had to make many complaints against unneutral activities in Spain; General Franco himself had delivered speeches disparaging Great Britain and other countries associated in the United Nations and describing their defeat as desirable and inevitable.

We could not overlook these past actions, or the consistently hostile attitude of the Falangist party. We were concerned more with the future than with the past. We had noted an improvement in Spanish policy towards Great Britain, but the change had not gone far enough to allow really close relations. We could not support Spanish claims to take part in the Peace Conference, and thought it unlikely that Spain would be invited to membership of the World Organisation.

The letter concluded by a plain statement that General Franco was wrong in thinking that the British Government would consider 'any grouping of Powers in Western Europe or elsewhere on a basis of hostility towards or of the alleged necessity of defence against our Russian allies'. Our policy was firmly based on the Anglo-Russian treaty of 1942, and we regarded Anglo-Russian collaboration within the framework of the United Nations as essential to the interests of Great Britain and of Europe as a whole.

(a) M52/5, Z971/537/41.

In the last week of January it became clear that there had been some leakage with regard to the exchange of letters between the (a) Prime Minister and General Franco. On February 4, Lord Halifax reported that there was fairly widespread knowledge in Washington of the substance of the correspondence, although the exact content was not known. A report was current that General Franco's letter and the Prime Minister's reply had been telegraphed to all Spanish Missions abroad. Lord Halifax thought that, if this report were true, there was a risk that, unless the real tenor of the correspondence were known, some deal between the British Government and General Franco would be assumed. This assumption would add to the number of complaints already being made against us. From the American point of view, therefore, it would be most desirable to publish the Prime Minister's letter. Suspicion of our Greek policy was linked with earlier suspicions of our attitude towards General Franco.

In transmitting this telegram to Sir A. Cadogan at Yalta on February 4 the Foreign Office agreed that publication of the correspondence would have a good effect on public opinion not only in the United States but in Great Britain. It would be, however, a breach of confidence and of established usage to publish the correspondence without General Franco's consent, and we were unlikely to get this consent. General Franco's objection to publication would not matter much in itself, but he might use the occasion of hostile criticism abroad to improve his position with his own public opinion. The Spanish people would certainly resent publication without General Franco's consent. However much we might dislike the Franco régime and wish to see it disappear, we wanted to establish and maintain friendly relations with Spain, and therefore to avoid doing anything which might be interpreted as directed against the Spanish people and not merely against General Franco himself. The Foreign Office therefore thought that publication was undesirable.

(b)   Mr. Eden replied on February 7 that he agreed that we should not publish the correspondence without General Franco's consent, but that we might have to reconsider our decision if there were any publicity about the letters on distorted or tendentious lines. The

(c) Prime Minister wrote a minute to Mr. Eden on February 14 that he saw no reason why his own letter should not be published even if we had no right to publish General Franco's. On their return to London Mr. Eden replied (March 4) to the Prime Minister's minute that, while we could publish his letter, unilateral publication would be contrary to normal diplomatic rule, and might create a precedent which foreign governments would use against us. On the whole,

---

(a) Z1507, 1588, 1678/537/41. (b) Z1836/537/41. (c) Z2004/537/41.

therefore, Mr. Eden remained against publication. *The Times* of February 10 had given a fairly accurate summary of the letter; this summary had received favourable comment in Great Britain and in the United States. The Spanish Government, on the other hand, had protested against *The Times* article and would certainly object strongly to the publication of the actual text of the letter. General Franco's annoyance would not of itself matter, but the Spanish people might take publication as an insult to their honour, and give General Franco a chance to rally them behind him. In any case public interest in the affair had now died down. We did not want to 'turn the limelight' on General Franco again, and give him the impression that we attached importance to him or that his fate was a matter of great concern to us.

Meanwhile there were no signs that General Franco was at all shaken by the Prime Minister's letter. The Duke of Alba told Mr. (a) Bowker, the British Chargé d'Affaires at Madrid, on February 12 that General Franco still took the line that Great Britain and Spain would be the only 'virile nations' left in Western Europe after the war. Great Britain would then need Spanish help against Russia. Any change in the Spanish régime would weaken the country against Russia. General Franco intended at a suitable time to restore the monarchy, but he defended the Falange as based on the best Spanish tradition. He also said that we were always making difficulties and that the United States were more understanding.

General Franco sent an acknowledgement of the Prime Minister's (b) letter towards the end of February. The reply showed that he had not understood—or anyhow that he was pretending not to understand—the implications of the letter, and that he still thought that only some further 'clarification' was necessary to enable the British and Spanish Governments to reach agreement. Earlier in the month a conversation between Lord Halifax and Mr. Culbertson, Chief of (c) the Western Division of the State Department, gave the Foreign Office an opportunity to state once again to the United States Government the main features of British policy towards Spain. Mr. Culbertson said that the State Department were considering whether the time had now come for a more openly critical attitude towards the Franco régime. They were, however, aware of the danger that the removal of General Franco and the Falange might lead to a renewal of the civil war, with serious consequences for the rest of Europe. Mr. Culbertson did not favour putting economic pressure on Spain. He thought that the best policy would be to make public statements, when opportunity offered, in condemnation of the

---

(a) Z2099/537/41. (b) Z2712/537/41. (c) Z1907/537/41.

Falange. He hoped that the British Government would give general support to this policy.

Owing to the absence of the Prime Minister and Mr. Eden, instructions to Lord Halifax were not sent until March 10. The (a) Foreign Office then told Lord Halifax that they also thought that occasional public statements condemning the Falange would be more effective than a policy of economic pressure. Our own position had been made clear by the publicity given to the Prime Minister's recent reply to General Franco. In view of the importance of co-ordinating Anglo-American policy, especially when a new American Ambassador was going to Madrid,[1] and in order to prevent General Franco from playing off one Government against another, the Foreign Office had thought it desirable to tell the United States Government of the general lines of British policy towards Spain.

We regarded a friendly Spain as desirable in our long-term strategic interests. We also wanted to expand our trade with Spain. For both these reasons we had not wished to do anything likely to encourage a recurrence of civil war in the country. On the other hand, we did not think it possible to be on cordial terms with a Spanish Government as long as General Franco and the Falange remained in power. We should welcome their disappearance partly for the sake of Anglo-Spanish relations and partly because the continuance of the régime was offensive to democratic sentiment and a temptation to trouble-makers. The Spanish people themselves, however, must settle what kind of régime should replace that of General Franco. We had no direct interest in the matter, though we hoped that any new régime would be based on democratic principles, moderate, stable and independent of outside influence. We did not propose to make suggestions to the Spanish people; the opposition was very much divided, and we wanted to avoid playing into General Franco's hands by giving the impression that we were trying to interfere in Spanish domestic affairs.

For the time, therefore, we should continue to treat the Spanish régime as one with which we could not expect to have a cordial relationship, and we should make it clear that in our view the interests of Spain and of the Spanish people, with whom we had no quarrel, would suffer as long as General Franco and the Falange remained in power. Our attitude would therefore be one of cold reserve, though we would take advantage of General Franco's apparent desire to ingratiate himself with the Allies, i.e. we would try to obtain satisfaction on minor matters such as the expulsion of

---

[1] Mr. Norman Armour was about to succeed Dr. Hayes as Ambassador.

(a) Z1907/537/41.

German agents. We should also avoid giving the impression that General Franco, or his future, mattered much to us. Above all we should work closely with the United States Government, and ensure that the Spanish Government did not play the United States off against the United Kingdom. If, as we hoped, the State Department agreed with our policy, we should like instructions to be given to the new United States Ambassador accordingly, since the Spanish Government had been alleging that the United States Government was less hostile than the British Government towards them.

The State Department replied on April 7 that they were in general (a) agreement with the British view, and that they did not understand why we should take seriously the Spanish allegation that there was a difference of view between the two Governments.

At the time of General Franco's reply to the Prime Minister's letter, the attitude of Spain had already ceased to be of immediate importance to the Allies. Neither the British nor the United States Governments had reason to change the policy of 'cold reserve' to General Franco. There were, however, indications in the Moscow press before the Potsdam Conference that the Soviet Government intended to raise at the Conference the question of the continuation of the Franco régime. The Foreign Office therefore drew up a brief (b) on the matter for the British delegation. This brief repeated in general the views already expressed in the telegram of March 10 to Lord Halifax. The Foreign Office pointed out that, in spite of the unsatisfactory political situation, the Spanish Government, since the defeat of Germany, had been co-operative on questions such as the handing over of German official premises, the expulsion of undesirable Germans, the blocking of German assets and the surrender of German ships in Spanish ports. It was also 'at least doubtful' whether British interests would gain by the substitution of a Communist régime for the Franco régime—probably the Russian objective—and certain that our interests would not benefit if such a substitution were the result of another civil war.

(a) Z4450/537/41. (b) Z8401/537/41.

CHAPTER XLVIII

British relations with Portugal, 1939–1945

(i)

Portuguese neutrality: Anglo-Portuguese staff conversations: Portuguese protests against the landing of Australian and Dutch troops in Portuguese Timor (September 1939–February 1942).

AT the beginning of the war the Portuguese Government, in agreement with the British Government, declared the neutrality of Portugal. Portuguese opinion generally, however, was most favourable to Great Britain. The Russo-German pact, and the German attack upon Poland—a Catholic State—nullified the effect of assiduous propaganda that Portugal should look not to her ancient ally[1] but to Germany for protection against communist interference and infiltration. The Portuguese Government took measures to prevent the use of their coast by German submarines; they were also willing to agree to British requests concerning, for example, the sale of Portuguese trawlers to the Admiralty and the suppression of meteorological bulletins which might be useful to the enemy.

The collapse of France and the entry of Italy into the war put the Portuguese into a very difficult position. They were especially concerned with the pro-Axis attitude of Spain. In July 1940, the Spanish Ambassador in Lisbon told Dr. Salazar that, if the Germans asked for a passage through Spain to attack Gibraltar, the Spanish Government would not oppose them. According to the Portuguese Ambassador in London the Spanish Government might well agree to join in an invasion of Portugal.

Dr. Salazar, however, signed on July 29, 1940, a protocol with General Franco providing for consultation between the two Governments in the case of a threat to their territories. This protocol was annexed to the Spanish-Portuguese treaty of friendship and non-aggression signed in March 1939, and was described as having a similar validity, 'whatever the treaty connexions or engagements of either of the contracting Powers with third parties'. The protocol thus recognised indirectly the obligations of Portugal under her alliance with Great Britain.

---

[1] The Anglo-Portuguese alliance dated back to 1373.

In December 1940 Dr. Salazar asked the British Government (a) whether they would agree to a secret discussion on the possibilities of Anglo-Portuguese collaboration in the event of a German invasion of Portugal. A Portuguese military mission came to London in February 1941 to hold staff conversations on the question. The British Government could not make a definite commitment, but offered to provide material and to make arrangements for sending military aid on the hypothesis that there was some resistance on the part of Spain, and that a Portuguese appeal was received as soon as the Germans crossed the Pyrenees. The Portuguese Government would not accept these conditions; they wished to be left free to make their appeal only in the event of an actual attack on Portugal.

The British Government therefore advised the Portuguese that their best policy, in the event of an attack, would be to move their Government to the Azores, and offer only a token resistance on the mainland. The Portuguese accepted this plan, and began at once to reinforce the islands. Further staff conversations were held in November 1941; the Portuguese continued to take the view that they would not ask for assistance until they had been attacked, but they were willing to consider detailed plans for British co-operation in the defence of the islands.[1]

The British Government let the United States Government know confidentially, as early as May 1941, of the arrangements with Portugal, and the United States authorities agreed that the discussions with Portugal should be left to Great Britain in view of the Anglo-Portuguese alliance. Meanwhile German propaganda, especially after the entry of the United States into the war, took every chance of disturbing Portuguese opinion by suggesting that the Allies intended to seize the Atlantic islands. The British Government were most careful to prevent references to the islands in the press which might cause suspicion in Portugal, but it was impossible to secure a similar reticence in the United States. Early in May 1941, Senator Pepper referred to the strategic importance of the islands in a speech in the United States Senate. The Portuguese Government thereupon issued a statement that they had received an explicit declaration from the United States Government that Senator Pepper's view had no relation to United States policy, and that this policy was one of strict respect for Portuguese sovereignty. The statement went on to explain that no one of the belligerents had made any request or proposal concerning any Portuguese possessions, and that the Portuguese Government had themselves provided for the reinforcement of the defence of their Atlantic possessions.

---

[1] See also p. 48, note (1).

(a) C2170/44/36 (1943).

Dr. Salazar's determination to maintain the strict neutrality of his country and his extreme sensitiveness to any infringement of Portuguese sovereignty resulted soon after the extension of the war to the Far East in a serious crisis over the defence of—or rather, over an attempt to defend—Portuguese Timor. The Australian

(a) Government in September 1941 suggested a discussion with the Netherlands Government on possible action—with or without Portuguese consent—in the event of a Japanese invasion of Timor. The Australian Government was willing to provide the necessary forces. The question was somewhat urgent, not only in view of the general situation in the Far East, but also because the Portuguese had allowed the Japanese commercial facilities at an aerodrome in their part of Timor.

(b)   At the beginning of November 1941, the Portuguese Ambassador in London told Mr. Eden that Portugal would resist a Japanese attack on Timor and might ask for British assistance under the terms of the Anglo-Portuguese alliance. On November 13 the Ambassador said that the Portuguese Government, which had a very small force in Timor, would welcome and indeed expect assistance from their ally. There were in fact very few Portuguese troops in Timor, and the Portuguese Government was unable to reinforce them. The two Governments then considered the means of arranging a plan for joint action. The Netherlands Government was also consulted, and promised its co-operation. The arrangements had not been

(c) concluded before the outbreak of war with Japan. On December 11, 1941, with the consent of the Australian and Netherlands Governments, the Portuguese Government was given an immediate offer of assistance (which would be provided by Australian and Dutch forces) in the event of attack, and was told that the British Government hoped that the Governor of Portuguese Timor would be instructed to 'invite such assistance if the occasion arose or to acquiesce in its being furnished in the event of there being no time for an invitation to be addressed to His Majesty's Government or to the local authorities'. The Portuguese Government accepted this offer on December 12 and agreed to send instructions at once to the Governor of Portuguese Timor to make contact with his Dutch colleague. The plan envisaged was that, if necessary, Australian and Dutch forces would go to the help of the Portuguese.

(d)   On December 16 Sir R. Campbell was instructed to inform the Portuguese Government that the Dutch authorities in London had received reports that Japanese submarines had been seen near Timor. The Dutch thought the presence of these submarines meant

---

(a) F9812 .10890/222/61.   (b) F11814, 12289/222/61.   (c) F13576, 13577, 13579, 13607, 13785, 13807/222/61. (d) F13808, 13839/222/61.

that the Japanese were about to attack Timor. The Dutch authorities therefore considered it essential to send reinforcements forthwith to Portuguese Timor. They arranged with the Australian Government that Dutch and Australian officers should see the Governor, and that, in anticipation of an invitation from him to land, some 350 Dutch and Australian troops should arrive two hours after the interview. The Foreign Office, on hearing of this plan, thought that the time-table did not allow sufficient interval for consultation. It was, however, too late to make any change.

The reactions of the Portuguese Government were sharp and violent. They refused to give the Governor power to accept assistance except in the event of an attack. They argued that the admission of Allied troops before a Japanese attack had taken place would mean the abandonment of Portuguese neutrality and would be followed by a Japanese seizure of Macao. Meanwhile the troops had begun to land. The Portuguese Government then protested most strongly against the landing and described it as an unworthy violation of their sovereignty.

The situation now showed the difficulties which inevitably follow (a) the loss of the military initiative in war. On the one hand Timor was of the greatest importance to Australia at a time when she was threatened with isolation and invasion. The Australian and Dutch forces in Timor might not be sufficient to ensure its defence, but they could at least fight a delaying action, and might be reinforced. On the other hand, a break with Portugal—which was not unlikely, in view of Dr. Salazar's temperament—might lose us the chance of getting the use of the Azores and Cape Verde islands in the event of a German occupation of the Portuguese mainland. We might even find that facilities in the islands were being given to the Axis, and we had not at present the forces required for an expedition to seize and hold the islands for ourselves. We should lose and Germany would obtain the whole of the Portuguese supply of wolfram. Furthermore a break with Portugal might well have as its consequence a total break with Spain, from whom we obtained 30 per cent of our iron ore as well as other vital commodities and, most serious of all, we might lose the use of Gibraltar as a naval base.

In these circumstances the Foreign Office thought it unwise to (b) argue in reply to the Portuguese Government that the latter had suddenly changed their minds. From Sir R. Campbell's telegrams the Portuguese appeared to have interpreted our offer as applying only after an attack had taken place. In any case the Portuguese Government evidently considered it safer to maintain that the landing had taken place against their wishes. The Foreign Office

---

(a) F472/2/61 (1942). (b) F14197, 14305/222/61.

therefore recommended that we should announce our regret for the action which we had been compelled to take in view of the inability of the Portuguese in Timor to defend their territory; we should also say that the Allied forces would be withdrawn on the arrival of Portuguese reinforcements.

The Portuguese Government let Sir R. Campbell know informally that they would accept this solution. Sir R. Campbell, who was summoned home for consultation, was instructed early in January (a) to return to Lisbon with the proposals for a settlement on the basis: (i) that the Australian and Dutch troops in Timor would be withdrawn on the arrival of some 700–800 Portuguese reinforcements whom the Portuguese Government intended to send to Timor; (ii) that a formal and unqualified announcement to this effect should be made at once; but that (iii) the Portuguese Government should give a private and secret assurance that Allied forces would be recalled in the event of a Japanese attack, and that the staff conversations which had been planned before the despatch of the present Allied contingents in Timor should be renewed. This proposal for a secret understanding was made in order to meet the request of the Australian Government for some such arrangement before the Allied troops were withdrawn. Sir R. Campbell, however, had said that the Portuguese Government were unlikely to accept any conditions qualifying the promise to withdraw. The British Government hoped that, during the staff conversations, the Portuguese might be persuaded not to wait until an attack had taken place before calling upon their allies for help.

(b)   Dr. Salazar accepted this arrangement. Mr. Churchill, however, thought that the Portuguese obviously could not protect their neutrality, and that we should say to them that we were guarding Timor until their reinforcements arrived. 'Nevertheless when they do arrive we should not go. We should leave our troops, the Dutch troops and their troops all on the spot.' We need not yet raise the question, since the Portuguese reinforcements would not arrive for (c) several weeks.[1] Mr. Eden, however, replied in a note of January 18 to the Prime Minister that the Chiefs of Staff did not think that the importance of keeping the troops was sufficient to justify the risk of a breach with Portugal. Mr. Eden thought it would be dangerous to change our policy, and that, in any case, the 380 Australian and

(d)   [1] The Prime Minister was influenced by a telegram from General Wavell to the Chiefs of Staff on January 15 that he was deeply concerned at the prospect of the withdrawal of Allied troops, since the Portuguese could not be relied upon to resist a Japanese attack, and Japanese intrigue and pressure would be renewed as soon as the Allies had left.

(a) F474/3/61.   (b) F544, 745/2/61.   (c) F745/2/61.   (d) F1589/2/61.

Dutch troops in the Portuguese end of Timor—a mountainous area nearly as large as Wales—would be insufficient to keep the Japanese out of it if they attacked in force. The War Cabinet also considered (a) that, for the present, we should not change our plan.

The Portuguese representatives agreed during conversations with (b) General Wavell that the Governor of Portuguese Timor would ask for Allied assistance as soon as it was clear that the Japanese were intending to attack. Before the arrival of the Portuguese reinforcements the situation changed owing to Japanese landings, on (c) February 19–20, in Dutch and Portuguese Timor. As the Foreign Office had anticipated, the small Allied force could not prevent the landings, and had to withdraw inland. The Japanese Minister in Lisbon informed the Portuguese Government that, as a measure of self-defence, the Japanese General Staff had decided that it was (d) necessary to expel the foreign troops in occupation of Portuguese Timor but that Portuguese 'territorial integrity' would be respected and the Japanese troops would be withdrawn when their presence was no longer necessary. The Japanese also warned the Portuguese Government, in view of the fighting around Java, that their convoy bringing Portuguese troops should not go beyond longitude 90°E.

The Portuguese Government protested against the Japanese (e) action, but obviously without success. From this time until early in June the Allied force managed to hold on in the hills in Portuguese territory. Early in June the Portuguese transmitted a suggestion (f) that, if the force surrendered, the Japanese might agree to withdraw from the island. The Australian Government, however, thought that this proposal was merely a Japanese move to secure the surrender, and that the Allied troops were well organised and supplied and could hold out.

Here the situation remained. The Allied troops continued a (g) guerrilla warfare against the Japanese, though they would have been withdrawn if there had been signs of Japanese intentions to attack them in force. On the other hand the Allies were not yet able to land an expedition for the recovery of Timor. At the beginning of September 1942, Dr. Salazar told Sir R. Campbell that since May the Japanese had prevented the Governor of Portuguese Timor from sending radio messages. It was also impossible for the Portuguese to send supplies to Timor. From the Portuguese point of view, the favourable turn in the Allied military position at the end of the year gave hope of regaining Timor as well as of keeping the rest of the Portuguese colonial empire.

(a) WM(42)9.   (b) F1589/2/61.   (c) F1909/2/61.   (d) F1703, 1705/2/61.   (e) F1744, 1756/2/61.   (f) F4295/2/61; F4298, 4459, 4519, 4651, 4991/2/61.   (g) F6422/2/61.

Note to section (i). The Portuguese Government and the recovery of Timor.

(a)   In June 1943, when the Allies asked for facilities in the Azores,[1] Dr. Salazar said that Portugal intended to maintain her neutrality except, possibly, in the Far East where he hoped that Portuguese troops would take part in the recapture of Timor. The Australian Government were informed of this statement when we asked them to associate themselves with our guarantee of Portuguese colonial territories; they welcomed the Portuguese wish to be associated with operations against Timor. Dr. Salazar was told of the Australian statement, and assumed that we agreed in principle with his proposal.

(b)   On October 4, 1943, the Portuguese Government asked the Foreign Office with whom they should discuss detailed arrangements for the association of Portuguese forces in the operations. The Chiefs of Staff, who were consulted, did not answer for more than two months; they then said that we should suggest to the United States
(c)   Government that our reply should be that we should welcome staff conversations in London with Portugal to draw up a plan of Portuguese co-operation in the war against Japan. The Foreign Office made a suggestion in this sense to the United States Government on December 22, 1943, but the United States Chiefs of Staff had not decided upon an answer by the end of January. They appeared to think that there would be no military advantage in a Portuguese declaration of war against Japan, but that an answer satisfactory to the Portuguese would facilitate the negotiations which were taking place between the United States Government and Portugal over the Azores.[2]

(d)   The Foreign Office considered it desirable to give Dr. Salazar— who was not unreasonably dissatisfied at the long delays—at least an interim reply that we would welcome Portuguese participation in the war against Japan and would make proposals for holding staff talks as soon as was practicable. As further delay seemed likely on the American side Lord Halifax was asked on February 12, 1944, to enquire whether the State Department would agree to this interim
(e)   reply. The United States military authorities, however, continued to take the view that there would be no military advantages in a declaration of war by Portugal against Japan, and that staff conversations with the Portuguese would lead to a discussion of Allied strategy in the Far East with serious risks of leakage of information. Operations against Timor were not yet included in any plan, and could be considered only when the strategical situation made them possible. The Americans therefore suggested that there was nothing to be gained by acceding to Dr. Salazar's request unless the Portuguese accepted the American demands with regard to the Azores.

---

[1] See below, section (ii).
[2] See below, section (iii).

(a) 7523; 7732/82/36. C7241/46/36.   (b) C11559/82/36.   (c)   C14734/66/36.
(d) C1788/89/36. (e) C2764, 2794/89/36.

The British military representatives in Washington did not disagree with this view.

The Foreign Office regarded the American view as extraordinary.   (a)
The entry of Portugal into the war would enable us to establish bases in Portuguese East Africa and possibly in the Cape Verde Islands. The Combined Chiefs of Staff changed their view in May 1944 but, in view of the pressure which the British and American Governments were then putting on Dr. Salazar with regard to the export of wolfram,[1] the Foreign Office thought a certain delay to be desirable. At the beginning of July, after the wolfram question had been settled,   (b)
the two Governments offered Dr. Salazar staff conversations in Lisbon. These conversations were held in September 1944. It was then   (c)
agreed that Portuguese forces would participate directly in operations in Timor, but no details could be settled since there were still no plans for an expedition to Timor. At the beginning of February 1945,   (d)
the Portuguese Chargé d'Affaires in London brought a memorandum to the Foreign Office expressing concern at the long delays in implementing the general proposals agreed in the previous September. The Portuguese Government were afraid that if a sudden decision were taken to attack the island, they might be left out of the Allied contingents. The military authorities were inclined to say that no arrangements could be made until after the end of the war with Germany, but the Foreign Office thought that we ought to honour our promise and to give a less disappointing answer. No details, however, were settled; the Combined Chiefs of Staff did not communicate their final views until the end of July 1945, and even then   (e)
merely pointed out that military operations against Timor would have to await the end of operations against 'higher priority Japanese held objectives'. The Combined Chiefs of Staff would, however, give the Portuguese military authorities notice in time for them to arrange the despatch and preparation of their force.

The Portuguese Ambassador in London was informed of the Combined Chiefs of Staff conclusions on August 7, 1945. He was satisfied with the promise to notify the Portuguese military authorities in good time. He was told that there would doubtless be plenty of time, in the event of a military collapse on the Japanese mainland, before any action was taken at Timor.

---

[1] See below, section (iv).

(a) C3204, 5785, 6137/89/36. (b) C8634/89/36. (c) C9038, 14734/89/36. (d) Z1674, 2821/50/36. (e) Z8863/50/36.

(ii)

British approach to the Portuguese Government—in virtue of the Anglo-Portuguese alliance—for the use of facilities in the Azores: Anglo-Portuguese agreement of August 18, 1943, with regard to facilities in the Azores (February–August 1943).

Although it was obvious that the acquisition of bases in the Spanish or Portuguese islands—and especially in the Azores[1]—would have been of great value in the war against enemy submarines, there was clearly no chance of obtaining such facilities in the Spanish islands from General Franco. There was also no chance of persuading Dr. Salazar to provide them in the Portuguese islands as long as the Germans were likely to retaliate by an invasion of Portugal. In the early part of 1943 a German move of this kind was less likely. Meanwhile, in view of the growing transport of American troops as well as supplies, the naval authorities in the United States as well as in Great Britain became increasingly anxious to secure bases as well as facilities for transit aircraft in the islands.

(a)   On February 12, 1943, Sir N. Charles reported from Rio de Janeiro that the Brazilian Minister for Foreign Affairs had told him of a suggestion made by President Roosevelt to the President of Brazil that Brazil should take over the defence of the Cape Verde and other Portuguese islands of strategic importance in the Atlantic. The Foreign Office view of this proposal—of which they had previously heard nothing[2]—was that Dr. Salazar would certainly refuse it. Sir R. Campbell, in telegrams from Lisbon, agreed with the Foreign Office view, and recommended that if it were necessary for the Allies to use the islands, it would be more expedient as well as more honest for us to invoke the Anglo-Portuguese alliance and ask for Dr. Salazar's help in shortening the war.

(b)   On February 12 the Foreign Office were also informed that the Admiralty were raising with the Chiefs of Staff the question of

---

[1] For the earlier question of a possible occupation of the Azores in order to forestall a German seizure of the islands, see Vol. I, Chapter XIV, section (iii). After the entry of the United Sates into the war, and the full development of anti-submarine warfare by means of air attack, the establishment of Allied bases in the Azores would have brought enemy submarines within range of Allied aircraft everywhere in the North Atlantic. These submarines would thus have been less able to attack or even to come to the surface to recharge their batteries. The bases would also have been of use against enemy raiders or blockade runners, and as a point of transit for flying Allied aircraft to the Mediterranean.

(c)   [2] The Foreign Office considered at first that, since Mr. Roosevelt had previously agreed to leave all questions of Allied relations with Portugal primarily in British hands, he must have discussed the question of the islands with the Prime Minister at Casablanca before making his suggestion to the President of Brazil. The Prime Minister, however, in a minute of February 16 to Mr. Eden, said that there had been no discussion of the matter at Casablanca.

(a) C1675, 1696, 1790/237/36.   (b) C1856/237/36.   (c) C1709/237/36.

securing early use of the islands. The Foreign Office recommended that the matter should be considered in relation to the general strategic situation in the Iberian peninsula and the western Mediterranean. We had hitherto encouraged Portugal to remain neutral, and had told Dr. Salazar at the time of the North African invasion that we had no designs against Portuguese territory and wanted to keep Spain and Portugal out of the war.

The Brazilian Government did not make an approach—at all (a) events formally—to the Portuguese Government, and the United States Government agreed not to take any action until we had given (b) further consideration to the question and discussed it with them. For some time—while the North African campaign was still unfinished—the proposal was put aside, though a study of it continued in a somewhat desultory way. On April 1, 1943, in a long despatch, (c) Sir R. Campbell took the view that, although Dr. Salazar would dislike a request for the grant of facilities, he would probably agree to honour the Anglo-Portuguese alliance. He would want definite assurances that the islands would be fully restored to Portugal at the end of the war, and was also likely to ask for a guarantee of the Portuguese African possessions, as well as guarantees of the military and air defence of Portugal and of the maintenance of Portuguese sea-borne imports.

On May 19, 1943, the Prime Minister, who had gone to Washing- (d) ton for strategic discussions, telegraphed that during the voyage across the Atlantic the Chiefs of Staff had asked for his approval to discuss with the Americans a combined approach to the Portuguese Government with regard to the Azores. The Prime Minister was disposed to agree, and to go as far as telling the Portuguese that, if they refused our proposal, we would take over the islands by force. The Prime Minister agreed with the Chiefs of Staff that the Germans were not likely to retaliate by an invasion of the Iberian peninsula, and that with our victory in Tunisia the opportunity for an approach to Portugal was specially favourable.

The Defence Committee considered the Prime Minister's telegram (e) and replied on May 12 that they agreed with the proposal for an approach to the Portuguese Government, but that they were opposed to an attempt to seize the islands. In any case an operation to seize them could not be undertaken before the end of August owing to a shortage of landing craft and trained assault troops. The Foreign Office held most strongly that a forcible seizure of the islands would be unjustified morally, and that it was undesirable from the general political and economic point of view.

(a) C1940, 2237, 3395. (b) C2366. (c) C3921/46/55. (d) Pencil 18 (Churchill Papers/ 362; C5438/237/36); COS(43)256(O) Part I. (e) Alcove 181 (Churchill Papers/362; C5438/237/36).

(a)   These views were put in a telegram to the Prime Minister. He replied on May 21 that he saw no chance of getting Portuguese agreement unless we confronted the Portuguese Government with our intentions on the night before we proposed to land, and warned them of the danger of bloodshed if they tried to oppose us. The Prime Minister said that Admiral Pound and Admiral King were greatly in favour of an occupation. The Prime Minister's own view was that it might save us a million tons of shipping and several thousand lives. The Combined Chiefs of Staff regarded this figure as an underestimate. The Prime Minister wanted to be able to tell the President that we were willing to act if the United States Government were also committed.

The Prime Minister said that he could not see:

'any moral substance in the legalistic point involved in overriding the neutrality of Portugal in respect of these islands which are of no peace-time consequence, but have now acquired vital war significance. The fate of all these small nations depends entirely upon our victory. Both the German and the Japanese aggressors have openly violated all neutralities. Timor is the latest example. Are we not putting the good cause to an undue disadvantage if in these circumstances we are not to take the steps which are necessary for the future law and freedom of the world? It is a painful responsibility to condemn so many great ships of the British and American flag to destruction and so many of our merchant seamen to drowning because our inhibitions prevent us from taking the action which would save them. I do not fear, nor does the President, any adverse reaction in our own countries, though, of course, Hitler, Mussolini and Tojo will be inexpressibly shocked. I beg you to look up what we did in Greece in 1916. We went to war in 1914 because of the violated neutrality of little Belgium and a vast volume of rhetoric and argument was presented on that theme. However, by 1916 the struggle had become so severe that the Allies had no hesitation in violating the neutrality of Greece and landing at the Piraeus by force of arms and installing a Government favourable to their interests. I have not the records with me, but I cannot recall the slightest protest that was made by any of those who wished to see us win. In this case the issue is far more precisely pointed because the rate of new buildings over sinkings is the measure of our power to wage war and so to bring this pouring out of blood and money to a timely end.'

The Prime Minister added that we should offer the Portuguese several million pounds for the lease of the islands, and promise their return with all the improvements we should have made to their air transport facilities. It might also be desirable to associate Brazil with the occupation.

(a) Pencil 159 (Churchill Papers/362; C5975/46/36); COS(43)286(O), Parts II and III.

Mr. Attlee and Mr. Eden replied on May 21 on behalf of the (a)
War Cabinet that the latter felt very strong objections of principle
to the course proposed; action within the next few weeks was hardly
practicable on military grounds without impairing other vital
operations (e.g. Sicily). Hence the only disadvantage of attempting
a diplomatic approach was that it would give some warning. The
War Cabinet asked that a decision should be postponed until after
the Prime Minister's return.

The Prime Minister replied on May 23 that postponement of the (b)
decision would 'paralyse action'. He thought that he could have
persuaded the President, but saw no hope of a satisfactory solution
unless he could settle the matter before leaving Washington. He
added, somewhat angrily: 'Of course it is very easy to avoid taking
this kind of hard decision. It merely means more ships sunk, more
sailors drowned and the war prolonged. Apart from this there is
every advantage in letting things slide.' The Prime Minister then
suggested that an expedition should be prepared, and should sail
as soon as possible, and that the Portuguese should be told twelve,
fourteen or thirty-six hours before its arrival 'that we must have the
islands, and that the descent in overwhelming force is imminent'.
They should be asked to submit under protest, and with all guarantees for the return of the islands. The negotiations should be conducted by a Minister who would go to Portugal for the purpose. If
the Portuguese refused, and our bluff failed, we would call off the
expedition. The Prime Minister thought that this plan had a three-
to-one chance of success whereas a mere request 'with nothing behind
it' would certainly fail.

Mr. Attlee and Mr. Eden replied on May 24 that the War Cabinet (c)
had considered this new plan. They understood that the operation
could not be carried out for two months at the earliest; hence there
was time for further consideration of plans. They remained convinced that it would be better to try first a diplomatic approach
and to base our approach on the obligations of Portugal under her
alliance with us. Sir R. Campbell, who had been called to London
for consultation in April, had thought that Dr. Salazar was more
likely to accept an approach of this kind than to give way to an
ultimatum. The War Cabinet agreed, however, that preparations
should be begun at once for an expedition. They added that an
expedition which had a generally British appearance would meet
with less resistance and resentment than would an American
expedition. The Prime Minister replied on May 24 that the President (d)

(a) WM(43)74.1, C.A.; Alcove 334 (Churchill Papers/362; C5975/46/36). (b) Pencil
216 (Churchill Papers/362; C6030/46/36). (c) WM(43)76, C.A.; Alcove 387 (Churchill
Papers/362; C5976/46/36). (d) Pencil 231 (Churchill Papers/362; C6031/46/36).

was in favour of 'going through with' the proposed expedition, and not 'bluffing'. The Prime Minister, however, had reserved the British decisions on the grounds of principle.

(a)   The Foreign Office continued to argue in favour of a diplomatic approach and on June 7 the Defence Committee agreed to this method. On June 8 Dr. Salazar asked Sir R. Campbell for a
(b) renewal of the Anglo-Portuguese staff conversations in view of the changed military position.[1] Sir R. Campbell thought that Dr. Salazar's conversation might mean that he hoped we should appeal
(c) to the alliance. The War Cabinet, at a meeting on June 10, took a similar view, though the Prime Minister still doubted whether we should be able to avoid a threat of force. The War Cabinet agreed that we should make it clear to Dr. Salazar that we would return the islands after the war, together with the improved facilities which we had introduced. We should also offer assurances regarding the future of the Portuguese colonial empire and facilities for the protection of Portuguese shipping, e.g. in convoy. If our diplomatic approach failed we should have to use force, but we should warn Dr. Salazar shortly before our action that it would be in his power, by accepting our demands, to avoid bloodshed and the termination of our alliance.

The Prime Minister agreed to telegraph to President Roosevelt for his approval of our plan. The Prime Minister telegraphed to the
(d) President on June 11 that, if Dr. Salazar agreed, we would be saved the trouble of mounting a considerable expedition and any stigma that might attach to the use of threats or force against our oldest ally. If he refused, no great harm would be done. We should continue our military preparations and, having invoked the alliance in vain, use force to get what we wanted. We thought it best not to use the influence of Brazil but to rely in the first instance on the force and validity of our 600-year-old alliance. We should like to associate the United States Government with our requests and assurances,
(e) especially with regard to the Portuguese colonies. The President agreed at once with the proposals, though he did not mention an American guarantee.
(f)   Sir R. Campbell put the British proposals to Dr. Salazar on

---

[1] Dr. Salazar considered that there was no longer reason to assume (see above, p. 41) that the Germans could and might invade the Iberian Peninsula, that Great Britain would be unable to provide effective assistance and that the Portuguese Government would have to move to the islands. The staff conversations were renewed in October
(g) 1943. The British representatives at this time thought an attack on Portugal by Germany or Spain most unlikely. For the question of Portuguese entry into the war against Japan, and participation in the recovery of Timor, see above, note to section (i).

(a) C6788/46/36. (b) C6584, 6585/82/36. (c) WM(43)84.1, C.A. (d) T777/3, No. 305 (Churchill Papers/362; C6663/282/36). (e) T784/3, No. 282 (Churchill Papers/362; C6663/1282/36.) (f) C6976, 7020, 7042, 7099/46/36; C6708/46/36. (g) C13058/82/36.

June 18. Dr. Salazar evidently had not expected them at this time, but did not refuse them. He was more afraid of a land attack from Spain than from Germany. The British requests were for facilities on Sâo Miguel and Terceira for operating reconnaissance aircraft, and unrestricted fuelling facilities for naval boats at Sâo Miguel or Fayal.

Dr. Salazar's formal reply was given to Sir R. Campbell in a note (a) of June 24. He accepted the requests in principle, and under the terms of the alliance, but subordinated the actual use of facilities in the Azores to an examination of the relevant political, military and economic considerations. Mr. Eden had already offered to go to Lisbon, but Dr. Salazar thought it better that the discussions should take place between himself and the British Ambassador with the necessary expert assistance. He wanted, if possible, to provide the facilities without bringing Portugal into the war. He was also unwilling to allow any troops other than British into the islands.

The Foreign Office thought it better to say little about this latter point, since we should not find it too difficult, once we had secured the facilities, to extend them in any way which seemed necessary, e.g. to cover the operation of American aircraft from the islands. Dr. Salazar had accepted our argument that the 'mixed' arrangements of convoys would make it inconvenient to restrict all facilities to British ships; he had therefore agreed to allow American warships and merchant ships refuelling facilities. The Foreign Office also regarded it as satisfactory that Dr. Salazar did not want to come into the war, since we should not be able to promise much help on land. They agreed to the holding of discussions in Lisbon. The Prime Minister thought it desirable to fix a time-limit of July 15 for the discussions, but the Foreign Office explained that Dr. Salazar (b) knew that we expected an early conclusion, and that the mention of a time-limit might have the appearance of an ultimatum.

The discussions were opened at Lisbon on July 6. The head of (c) the British Service Delegation was Air Vice-Marshal Medhurst; Mr. F. K. Roberts went with him as representing the Foreign Office. The Portuguese made it clear that they wanted to give us the necessary facilities, but in a manner which would attract the least notice. They were afraid, in particular, of provoking the hostility of General Franco, thus bringing about a Spanish attack on Portugal; they also feared, more vaguely, a sudden descent of German airborne troops on Portugal. They therefore wanted us to begin by keeping as low as possible the numbers sent to the islands, and by leaving all but the most essential services to be prepared by

---

themselves. There was no doubt that they would allow us to expand
our forces once we were in the islands.

(a)   Meanwhile the Prime Minister had sent a message to President
Roosevelt on June 29 saying that he hoped for the President's
authorisation to tell the Portuguese Government that the United
States associated themsleves with the assurances which we were
giving to Portugal. The Prime Minister also explained the position
in regard to the restriction to British forces of the facilities to be
granted. No answer had been received from the President or the
State Department at the end of July, though on July 19 Mr. Winant
had said to Mr. Eden that there would be no doubt about the
American willingness to 'underwrite' our assurances. Mr. Eden
wrote to Mr. Winant again on August 4, but did not get a reply
until August 13. The reply then seemed to link the assurances of the
(b) United States Government with the satisfaction of their demands
for facilities in the islands.

(c)   The Prime Minister, in a minute of July 11 to Mr. Eden, agreed
that we should begin in a quiet way and on a small scale.

> 'The great thing is to worm our way in and then without raising any
> question of principle, swell ourselves out. We shall use cash locally
> to make ourselves popular and smooth the way. The only thing that
> matters is getting a couple of squadrons at work in a month from
> now.'

It was therefore essential that the United States Government
(d) should not ask for facilities for themselves. The State Department,
however, had informed the British Embassy in Washington on July 7
that the United States Army Air Corps had already asked Pan-
American Airways to explore the possibility of obtaining Portuguese
permission to establish landing facilities for land planes in the
Azores under cover of supposedly commercial developments. Pan-
American Airways had approached the Portuguese Air Council, but
the United States Government had made no official representations.
They now proposed to do so, and asked for British support. The
Foreign Office replied by telling the State Department of the satisfactory development of the discussions with the Portuguese and of
our view that we did not expect any difficulty in securing landing
facilities for United States aircraft on their way to Africa, but that
it was inadvisable for the United States Government to press their
request while our negotiations were in progress.

(e)   The State Department agreed with this view. On July 20, however,
Sir R. Campbell reported from Lisbon that the United States
Legation had been asked urgently by the State Department to obtain

---

(a) C7521/82/36. (b) C9258/82/36. C10394/82/36. (c) C7936/82/36. (d) C7844, 7858,
8184/82/36. (e) C8315/46/36.

permission for the Weather Bureau of the United States Department of Commerce to establish a weather observation bureau in the islands. The British delegation in Lisbon thought it most undesirable that this proposal should be put while their own negotiations were in progress. Lord Halifax was instructed to make representations to the State Department who replied that the United States Legation (a) had been told to suspend action. They did not wish to give up their request (or that of Pan-American Airways) but they agreed that for the time being neither matter should be raised.[1]

After a fortnight of negotiations in Lisbon the British delegation (b) realised that the Portuguese intended to delay the grant of facilities for at least two and a half months after the arrival of the anti-aircraft and the defence material for which they had asked in view of possible German retaliation. The Prime Minister wrote to Mr. Eden on (c) July 24 that we could not accept a policy of procrastination. We had fixed August 20 as 'the date when ultimate sanction could be applied. But then came the hope of parley, invoking the alliance and so forth. . . . Now, after all this vast verbiage and haggling', Sir R. Campbell was suggesting that September 1 was too early a date 'to be insisted upon', but the Prime Minister considered that the Portuguese had 'ample argumentative munitions to spread the matter out into the winter weather. The time has come to let them know that this nonsense must cease'. Mr. Churchill thought that the Portuguese should be told that unless they agreed to offer the facilities 'freely and without fail by August 15',[2] we should 'take our own measures and in our own time'.

Mr. Eden replied on July 27 that he agreed about forcing a decision, but was not sure whether the Prime Minister's date was possible, since our own expedition could not arrive before September 1. The Chiefs of Staff proposed that we should tell Dr. Salazar that our first convoy must arrive in the islands not later than September 15, and that we were making the necessary arrangements on the assumption that we had Portuguese consent. If Dr. Salazar refused we should discontinue negotiations and withdraw our delegation. We should leave no doubt about the effect of a refusal on our relations with Portugal and the Portuguese Empire and on the Anglo-Portuguese Alliance, but we should give no hint of our intention to take the facilities for ourselves. The Prime Minister agreed, with the comment, 'But don't let's miss September 15'. Sir R. Campbell was

---

[1] The State Department explained that, for security reasons, not all the members of the Department had been informed of our negotiations, and it had therefore not been possible to prevent the instructions from being sent to Lisbon.

[2] The original minute has the figure '12' pencilled above '15'.

(a) C8498/82/36. (b) C8432, 8433/82/36. (c) C8639/82/36.

therefore instructed to tell Dr. Salazar that this was our latest date.

(a)   The American Chiefs of Staff now complicated the issue by saying that they could not accept an agreement limiting the use of facilities in the islands to British Empire aircraft and that they also must have the facilities for which we were asking.[1] The Foreign Office continued to hold that we could not introduce these new American demands with the Portuguese while our own negotiations were in progress;[2] we should tell the Americans that as soon as we were in the islands we should try to extend the benefits of our arrangements to them, and that meanwhile we would try to incorporate in our agreement with the Portuguese the grant of transit facilities for all aircraft of the United Nations. Air Vice-Marshal Medhurst telegraphed on the

(b) night of August 9–10 that the British delegation regarded it as most undesirable to introduce a demand for sharing the facilities with the Americans. The Portuguese had made it absolutely clear that the facilities were to be granted to us in accordance with the Anglo-Portuguese alliance; the word American 'has invariably had strong and unfavourable reactions'. Once we were installed in the islands, the matter would be on a different footing. The British Embassy in

(c) Washington was accordingly instructed to explain the position to the State Department.

(d)   By August 13 Mr. Eden was able to telegraph to the Prime Minister (who had earlier left for Quebec) that Dr. Salazar had accepted all our proposals, except (i) the form of our assurance about the protection of the Portuguese mainland in the event of attack, and (ii) the date of our entry into the islands. On (i) we had offered an assurance of military support. Dr. Salazar wanted us to make clear that our meaning was not merely general support, but assistance 'for effective defence against such an attack'. Mr. Eden thought that we should agree to this amendment. On (ii) Dr. Salazar said that his own military preparations would not be ready before October 15. On October 8 they would be sufficiently advanced for him to risk German reactions, but October 1—the date to which we had moved forward our limit—was too soon. Mr. Eden thought, on balance, that it would be wise for us to accept October 8. The Prime Minister

---

[1] It appeared during the Quebec Conference that the American Chiefs of Staff had not been told fully by the President of information given to him by the Prime Minister on June 29, and that they felt a certain grievance that they had not been adequately consulted over the agreement. The Foreign Office also considered that American commercial air interests were exercising some influence in the matter.

[2] The Chiefs of Staff agreed with the Foreign Office that there was no chance of Portuguese agreement to the extension of the facilities to the Americans. (This American demand was different from the requests mentioned above (pp. 54–5) which we had been asked to support.)

(a) C8999, 9089/82/36. (b) C9124/82/36. (c) C9258/82/36. (d) Concrete 176 (Churchill Papers/362; C9248/82/36.)

accepted this date, and the agreement with the Portuguese Government was signed on August 18.[1]   (a)

(iii)

British attitude towards requests of the United States Government for extended facilities for American forces in the Azores (August 1943–September 1944).

The Prime Minister told the President on August 19 that, as soon (b) as we were in occupation of the islands we would 'make every effort by diplomacy to obtain the permit for United States entry'. The Foreign Office expected that—since the British entry into the Azores was not to take place until October 8, or to be given public announcement until October 12—the Americans would allow time for observing German reactions before putting forward their demands.

The United States Chiefs of Staff, however, before they had even (c) seen the terms of the Anglo-Portuguese agreement, put forward at the beginning of September proposals for what amounted to an American occupation of two islands with a force of about 10,000 (d) men. They were thus asking for much more than we had been able to obtain with considerable difficulty and after invoking our special alliance with the Portuguese. Moreover, in the British view, the facilities which the Americans wanted were unnecessary since they were duplicating to a large extent those required for anti-submarine action which had already been provided in the Anglo-Portuguese agreement.

The British Chiefs of Staff, with the approval of the Foreign Office, asked the Joint Staff Mission in Washington on September 18 to explain to the United States Chiefs of Staff the difficulties in their proposals, and to put forward counter-suggestions with the purpose of bringing the Americans into the islands as soon as possible, in view of Portuguese reluctance to extend facilities to them. In particular the British proposals concentrated first upon ferry plans for American aircraft which were obviously of great importance to the United Nations war effort and could be put into effect, at least in their early stages, under British cover.

The Foreign Office and the Chiefs of Staff, however, found the Prime Minister more inclined to accept the immediate American

---

[1] The agreement was dated August 17, though signed on the following day. The main facilities were at the ports of Horta and Ponta Delgada, and the airfield on Terceira Island. The British entry took place, as arranged, on October 8. The Portuguese (e) co-operation was and continued to be satisfactory.

(a) C9480/82/36. (b) C10100/82/36. COS(43)513(O), Part A. (c) C10562/82/36. (d) C10840/82/36. (e) C9475, 10007, 10875/82/36.

(a) demands. On September 20 the Prime Minister telegraphed to Field-Marshal Sir John Dill asking him to tell Admiral King that 'he must have confidence in my resolve and undertaking to bring the United States fully into these islands for all purposes of the war. Everything is moving in our favour, but the vital thing is to get established there and get our foot in the door'. Mr. Churchill said that he was considering the possibility of a 'more violent incursion' at a somewhat later stage. He said that Admiral King should remember that 'the Portuguese are more frightened of the Americans than of the English because they think that the Americans want the Azores, whereas the English at least in this respect are innocent lambs'.

The Foreign Office thought that this message was not easy to reconcile with the instructions sent by the Chiefs of Staff. Mr. Eden therefore spoke to the Prime Minister, and on September 27, at the (b) suggestion of the Foreign Office, sent him a minute to the effect that

'owing to the history of the negotiations with the Portuguese the United States Chiefs of Staff should not open their mouths so wide or press the pace. . . . It was a notable achievement on our part to obtain facilities in [the Azores] by diplomatic negotiation from a small neutral State, which thereby ran what in its own eyes was a serious risk of being involved in the war. The satisfactory Portuguese response based entirely on loyalty to the Anglo-Portuguese alliance, contrasts more than favourably with the conduct of other neutrals, cf. examples of Turkey and Eire.'

We should therefore

'work to secure for the Americans approximately the same advantages as we have obtained from [the] Portuguese for ourselves. If [the] Americans want more, as they appear to do for whatever reason, they will have to try to get that for themselves.'

(c)   The Prime Minister, in a minute of September 30, agreed generally, but thought we should take steps immediately after our entry to secure for the Americans equal facilities with ourselves on the basis of American participation in the guarantee of Portuguese sovereignty over their colonies.

Mr. Eden replied on October 3 that he was already trying to do what the Prime Minister had suggested. The Chiefs of Staff had sent Air Vice-Marshal Medhurst to Washington. So far, however, we had been told only of 'a very ambitious American plan, drawn up in ignorance of the Lisbon negotiations and of the terms of the final agreement'. We could not approach the Portuguese Government until we knew the views of the United States Chiefs of Staff

---

(a) T1359/3, OZ2860 (Churchill Papers/362; C11253/82/36).   (b) C11253/82/36.
(c) C11672/82/36.

after they had heard Air Vice-Marshal Medhurst's views. We should not be fully established in the islands until six weeks after our entry. We should depend on Portuguese goodwill for the essential local services and did not yet know how soon the facilities in the islands could be developed sufficiently for the Americans to send in forces of their own. Hence a communication to the Portuguese Government on the day of our entry into the islands would not accelerate the actual use of the facilities by the Americans, while it would have a bad effect on Dr. Salazar, and,

> 'given the deep-seated Portuguese distrust of the Americans, might change the present Portuguese attitude of willing co-operation into one, at best, of grudging acquiescence. . . . It is important that the Americans should realise that modern Portugal, which for all practical purposes means Dr. Salazar, is not a second Guatemala, from whom anything the Americans desire can be obtained simply by threats or bribes. The present facilities have been granted to ourselves only in virtue of the Anglo-Portuguese alliance, and we shall have our work cut out to get them extended to the Americans.'

The Prime Minister had suggested that the change in the war situation was favourable to our negotiations. Mr. Eden was not sure whether this change would 'influence Dr. Salazar so much, since his object is not to "climb upon the Allied band wagon" in good time'. We knew Dr. Salazar and the Americans did not know him. The Azores were in our own and not in the American sphere of strategical responsibility; we should therefore be allowed to decide the best method of approach to Dr. Salazar.

Sir R. Campbell agreed entirely with the Foreign Office. He also (a) pointed out that the Americans were unaware of the practical difficulties in the way of the construction of the aerodromes for which they were asking, and that they were entirely wrong in thinking that negotiations through Pan-American Airways would be of any use.

The United States Government agreed to offer a colonial (b) guarantee—if the Portuguese asked for it. They also appeared— from a message sent by the President to the Prime Minister on (c) October 7—to be limiting their demands to facilities for air transport and ferrying, though they still seemed unaware of the political difficulties. Neither Admiral King nor General Arnold had attended the meeting at which Air Vice-Marshal Medhurst explained these difficulties, and the American Chiefs of Staff had shown little interest in them. On October 8 the Prime Minister suggested to the President (d) that we should approach Dr. Salazar as soon as he had had a few

---

(a) C11781/82/36.   (b) C11522, 11598, 11705/82/36.   (c) T1525/3, No. 376 (Churchill Papers/362; C12016/46/36).   (d) T1545/3, No. 444 (Churchill Papers/362; C11799/82/36).

days in which to observe the German reactions to our entry into the islands.

(a)   The President replied on October 9 agreeing with this plan, and again referring to the 'ferry service' without any mention of the

(b) larger proposals. Five days later, however, he telegraphed to the Prime Minister that he had received information that the Portuguese Government would be likely to agree to an American request; he therefore thought it best to approach the Portuguese Government himself, though he would like British support. The Prime Minister and the Foreign Office accepted this plan, and indeed welcomed it, since it relieved them of the difficulty of going to the Portuguese Government and 'asking for more', and from any responsibility if the Americans found that their request was refused. The Prime

(c) Minister told the President that, in supporting the American request, we should use a phrase 'friends to friends' which had been employed in the original treaty of 1373.

(d)   Sir R. Campbell, however, found that though the President had not mentioned the fact to the Prime Minister, the Americans were now reverting to their earlier proposals for facilities going far beyond those granted to us and amounting to an occupation of the Azores. Mr. Kennan, the United States Chargé d'Affaires at Lisbon, said to Sir R. Campbell that he expected a Portuguese refusal and that he was asking for permission to fly home in order to explain the position. The Foreign Office thought that the American action was a piece of 'very sharp practice'. The Prime Minister considered that they had definitely withdrawn these 'very heavy-footed demands' after Air Vice-Marshal Medhurst's discussions in Washington. The Prime Minister suggested on October 19 that he should telegraph to the President

> 'how unwise it would be to use such a battering-ram at the present time and how much better it is to build up gradually, and in any case that we should find great difficulty in supporting them beyond the reduced proposals'.

(e)   The Prime Minister telegraphed to the President on October 19 that he feared that there was a misunderstanding about the proposed direct approach. He did not mention directly the question of British support, but said that he thought there was very little chance of getting a favourable answer to the demand for such far-reaching facilities.

(f)   The Prime Minister asked the Foreign Office on October 25 whether they considered it advisable for him to arrange a meeting

---

(a) T1565/3, No. 384 (Churchill Papers/362; C11799/82/36). (b) T1622/3, No. 387 (Churchill Papers/362; C12306/46/36).   (c) T1633/3, No. 458 (Churchill Papers/362; C12210/46/36).   (d) C12197/46/36.   (e) T1669/3, No. 466 (Churchill Papers/362; C12307/46/36).   (f) C12848/46/36.

in November (i.e. on his way to Teheran) with Dr. Salazar at Gibraltar, but the Foreign Office replied that Dr. Salazar was most unlikely to be willing to risk arousing German suspicions still further about Portuguese policy towards the Allies. The Prime Minister (a) proposed on October 29 to suggest that Mr. Kennan should be instructed to ask Dr. Salazar to allow the United States to share the British facilities. We would support this request, 'pointing out that British and American air and convoys are so intermingled that no other solution is possible, that it adds nothing to his risks and doubles his security'. The Foreign Office, however, thought that the President would assume that we expected Dr. Salazar to agree, whereas in fact we were afraid he would refuse. Meanwhile Mr. Kennan had gone to Washington. On November 9 the President (b) informed the Prime Minister that he (Mr. Kennan) was returning with instructions to ask for 'what we consider minimum necessary facilities in the Azores for the operation of the air transport, ferrying, anti-submarine and convoy operations by United States forces in that area'. The President asked again for British support; he did not make it clear whether the Americans were putting forward all their larger proposals, though they were clearly asking for more than we considered wise in the first instance.

Once again the Prime Minister was inclined to offer full support, but the Foreign Office pointed out that we ought to know more definitely what demands we would be supporting. Mr. Eden suggested therefore to the Prime Minister on November 11 that he should remind the President that we had thought it wise in the first instance to concentrate upon the ferry service, and that we should like details of the new proposals in order to enable us to send appropriate instructions to Sir R. Campbell.

The Prime Minister had left England before he could reply to this suggestion. He let the Foreign Office know that he would discuss the matter with the President. Meanwhile Sir R. Campbell was instructed on November 16 to give full support to Mr. Kennan unless the latter's instructions were so framed as seriously to prejudice the chances of a favourable Portuguese reply.

On his return to Lisbon (in advance of the newly-appointed (c) United States Minister to Portugal) Mr. Kennan told Sir R. Campbell that he had a personal letter from the President to Dr. Salazar asking that the United States should be allowed to share the facilities granted to the British at Horta and Terceira. Mr. Kennan himself was not sure what the United States Government

---

(a) C12913/46/36. (b) T1912/3, unnumbered (Churchill Papers/362; C13262/46/36). (c) C13756/46/36.

really wanted,[1] but he made it clear that they preferred to handle the matter themselves without too much British assistance.

The Foreign Office therefore considered that we must leave the Americans to make their approach. Dr. Salazar, however, would certainly assume that we knew of this approach, and we were likely to have to find a way out of the difficulties which the Americans had created for themselves by too great haste. The Foreign Office did not expect the United States Government to use force since Dr. Salazar would then be able to invoke the Anglo-Portuguese alliance and ask us to defend Portuguese territory against American invasion. In any case it would be impossible for the Americans to justify under the Atlantic Charter the use of force. Moreover they had now associated themselves with our colonial guarantee to the Portuguese.[2]

(a)   Mr. Kennan saw Dr. Salazar on November 23. Dr. Salazar did not object to the American use of facilities at Horta as already provided for in the Anglo-Portuguese agreement. He was also willing to allow the Americans to use the airfield on Terceira provided that during their stay the aircraft could be described technically as 'aircraft of the British Commonwealth'. Dr. Salazar, however, made it clear that he had allowed facilities to Great Britain in view of the Anglo-Portuguese alliance, and that he could not grant them to the United States without giving up the neutrality which he had
(b) hitherto maintained. On December 1 Dr. Salazar again repeated to Mr. Kennan that any facilities granted to the Americans should
(c) be within the framework of the British agreement. The Americans, in fact, finally agreed with this proposal and at the end of the year
(d) the matter was settled in this sense.[3]

The acceptance by Dr. Salazar of a formula for the 'cover' operation of American units in the Azores was not the end of the matter. In accordance with the formula all American operational units would be 'on loan to His Majesty's Government, operating under the command of a British officer from a base under British

---

(e)   [1] Lord Halifax telegraphed on the night of November 20–1 that the State Department had informed the British Embassy that Mr. Kennan's talks in Washington were 'mostly at a very high level', and that they themselves were 'not quite certain what his final instructions were. They are telegraphing to him to let them know exactly what he is instructed to ask for'.

(f)   [2] A Foreign Office summary of the position on November 20 concluded: 'It should perhaps be added that American suspicions of our motives are being kept alive by American aviation interests. Although they are groundless so far as the Foreign Office and Chiefs of Staff are concerned, there may be more substance in them so far as Lord Beaverbrook and British aviation interests come into the picture.'

[3] For an official American account of these negotiations see *F.R.U.S.* 1943. Europe, Vol. II, pp. 527–581. For Mr. Kennan's account see G. F. Kennan, *Memoirs*, 1925–50 (New York, 1967), Chapter VI.

(a) C13925/46/36. (b) C14255/46/36. (c) C14492/46/36. (d) COS(43)791(O), Parts II and III. (e) C13775/46/36. (f) C14303/46/36.

control'. Mr. Norweb, the United States Minister, told Dr. Salazar that American personnel in considerable numbers would now be (a) sent to the islands, the number of ferry aircraft would be very large and American naval squadrons of anti-submarine aircraft would soon be operating from Lagens airfield on Terceira on loan to the British Government.

Dr. Salazar made no objection. There was, however, a misunderstanding between him and the United States Minister. Dr. Salazar (b) did not realise that the Americans proposed to send an operational squadron to the islands and that the construction personnel for this squadron had already sailed.[1] Dr. Salazar refused to agree to the (c) despatch of the squadron but, when the American construction units actually arrived, consented (after the intervention of Sir R. Campbell) to their landing. He argued that the operation of an American combatant unit was contrary to the Anglo-Portuguese agreement of August 17, and that he had not agreed to the establishment of American aircraft or forces—other than construction forces—on Terceira. Dr. Salazar gave orders that the landing of American combatant troops would be resisted, if necessary, by force. The (d) President, on January 17, telegraphed to the Prime Minister that he proposed sending the squadron in spite of Dr. Salazar's refusal.

The Prime Minister, in a message of January 12 to Mr. Eden, (e) had already said that Sir R. Campbell should be told to back up the Americans vigorously and to impress on Dr. Salazar the consequences which would follow from resisting American troops. Dr. Salazar was no longer in any danger of a German invasion and the alliance was one of 'friends to friends'. The Prime Minister concluded: 'There is no need for us to be apologetic in dealing with any of these neutrals who hope to get out of Armageddon with no trouble and a good profit.'

The Foreign Office explained to the Prime Minister that there (f) had been a misunderstanding, but that the only question now unsettled was that of the operation of an American squadron. The Chief of Air Staff considered that there was no reason why this particular squadron in the Azores should be American rather than British, and that it would be unwise to prejudice really vital needs such as the ferry requirements and the extension of our own facilities, e.g. an enlargement of the aerodrome, by insisting on the presence of an American operational squadron. The Foreign Office agreed

---

[1] The State Department omitted to send the United States Minister actual instructions (g) with regard to the formula until mid-December; he was therefore unable to see Dr. Salazar until after Christmas.

(a) C128/11/36 (1944). (b) C329, 347, 352/11/36. (c) C357, 369, 476/11/36. (d) T68/4, No. 443 (Churchill Papers/362; C1016/11/36). (e) Frozen 1254 (Churchill Papers/362; C606/11/36). (f) C1016/11/36. (g) C15231/46/36.

with the Chief of the Air Staff, and regarded the American approach as 'somewhat clumsy and inept', whereas Dr. Salazar had loyally carried out his original agreement with the United States Minister. President Roosevelt did not know Dr. Salazar, who was 'quite capable of repeating his threat to oppose American landing by force . . . if the Americans continued to proceed by *faits accomplis* rather than by negotiation'.

(a)   The Prime Minister agreed to put the Foreign Office recommendations to Mr. Roosevelt. He telegraphed to him on January 19 explaining that there must have been a misunderstanding. The Prime Minister pointed out that the Germans, 'making a virtue of necessity', had apparently told Dr. Salazar that they would respect Portuguese engagements under the treaty with Great Britain, but that they would not recognise any right on his part to admit the entry of American forces. Dr. Salazar, however, was prepared 'to lend himself to any fiction or camouflage' in the matter. The Prime Minister pointed out that Dr. Salazar had been willing to meet our needs

> 'to a very great extent in spite of the fact that we gave no guarantee to send an army to defend Portugal at a time when things looked more dangerous for him than they do now. . . . Although we possess overwhelming strength, it would be . . . inconsistent with our general attitude towards such Powers to override them roughly in matters of neutrality.'

The Prime Minister said that the difficulty would be avoided if the American squadron would operate as a British unit with British markings,[1] but with American crews wearing some badge to indicate that they were temporarily incorporated in the Royal Air Force. The Prime Minister reminded the President that we had been willing to put large numbers of British troops into American uniform at the time of the North African landings.

(b)   The President agreed on January 22 to delay sending the squadron, but asked for further British support in trying to persuade Dr.

(c)   Salazar. For the next few months the question was argued at length. Sir R. Campbell could not get Dr. Salazar to agree to the introduction of the American squadron as an American combatant unit, while the Americans were unwilling to give up the demand or to allow the squadron to wear British insignia. At the end of April Sir R. Campbell had been able to get Dr. Salazar to ask him to find out whether the Americans would agree on the question of wearing British insignia, with (if desired) American insignia along-

---

[1] General Marshall had made this suggestion at the Cairo Conference.

(a) T81/4, No. 549 (Churchill Papers/362; C1017/11/36).   (b) T110/4, No. 448 (Churchill Papers/362; C1001/11/36).   (c) C10199/11/36.

side in rather less conspicuous form. Early in June the Americans accepted this proposal, but Dr. Salazar still held out until July 18, 1944.

(iv)

The export of Portuguese wolfram to Germany.[1]

Apart from the question of the islands, and the short but very sharp reaction of Dr. Salazar to the Allied action with regard to Timor, the main difficulties in Anglo-Portuguese relations occurred over the enforcement of the blockade, and, in particular, over the (a) sale of Portuguese wolfram to Germany. There was a certain paradox in the fact that economic negotiations generally were more difficult with Portugal than with Spain. One reason was that in Spain General Franco himself took little direct part in these negotiations; the arrangements were left almost entirely to the Minister of Commerce and Industry, and were settled (in spite of the trouble deliberately caused by Señor Suñer during his tenure of the Ministry of Foreign Affairs) in accordance with Spanish material interests, whereas in Portugal Dr. Salazar himself undertook the negotiations and brought into them his own sensitiveness about Portuguese sovereignty.

Furthermore Portugal, with her overseas Empire, depended less than Spain on supplies from the United Nations; Spain was also in greater need of help owing to poverty and scarcity following the long civil war. In other respects also Portugal was better off than Spain —she was, for example, more able to distribute her domestic supplies by sea, and therefore less dependent on imports of rubber for tyres. The Portuguese financial position was stronger. Spain, at the outbreak of war, was in debt to the United Kingdom to the extent of some £5 million. Until the end of 1941 she was increasing her debt, and had been given British loans of £4 million. Portugal, on the other hand, began earlier to accumulate large sterling balances, while the British Government was unable to supply Portuguese requirements of iron and steel. Finally, Dr. Salazar was in a position to use, at least until 1943, the argument that the Germans were likely to respect Portuguese neutrality only as long as they gained advantages from it; hence it was inexpedient as well

---

[1] This section deals only in short outline with the complicated history of Anglo-Portuguese economic negotiations, including those on wolfram. The subject is treated fully in W. N. Medlicott, *The Economic Blockade*, Vol. I (H.M.S.O., 1952) and Vol. II (H.M.S.O., 1959). For an account of the negotiations over wolfram with Spain, see Chapter XLVII, section (iv).

(a) C4089/444/36 (1943).

as unneutral for Portugal to refuse to supply the Germans with the commodities for which they asked.

The negotiations with the Portuguese Government for a formal War Trade Agreement were therefore long and difficult, and the British authorities had to work on the basis of an exchange of memoranda (with partly divergent texts). There was a deadlock for several months over the question of the export from Portugal to the Axis Powers of indigenous products similar to those imported through the blockade. In the spring of 1942 negotiations were begun for a formal Supply-Purchase Agreement covering a period of twelve months. Before the settlement of the main agreement, a special discussion took place about wolfram.

In Portugal, as in Spain, competition between British and German buyers had raised prices to an extent which had disorganised the national economy. In Spain the problem, from the British point of view, was mainly one of pre-emption; as long as British trade with Spain was maintained to an extent sufficient to secure an adequate supply of currency, there was little difficulty in securing the wolfram, since the Spanish Government, on their side, could not do without the Allied supplies. In the case of Portugal the matter was more complicated because early in 1942, in order to check the inflated prices which were having disturbing effects on the economy of the country, the Portuguese Government set up a Commission to buy and market all supplies of wolfram.[1] Dr. Salazar also made an agreement in January 1942 (without consulting the British Government, and at the time of his indignation over the Allied action in Timor) with the Germans to provide them with export licences for up to 2,800 tons of wolfram for twelve months from March 1, 1942. The Germans in return agreed to provide steel products and fertilisers which the Allies were unable to supply. After exasperatingly troublesome negotiations with Dr. Salazar the Allies secured in November 1942 a general War Trade Agreement, and a Supply-Purchase Agreement including a special wolfram agreement. The latter ran from March 1, 1942, to February 28, 1943, and enabled the Allies to secure 3,400 tons of the total supply of wolfram.

Early in 1943, while the British and American Governments were negotiating a new wolfram agreement, in which they were asking for a larger share of the total available supply, Dr. Salazar—again without previously informing the British and American negotiators—made another agreement for twelve months with the Germans. Mr.

---

[1] A further complication was caused by the fact that just over half the total quantity of wolfram was produced from British owned mines, $8\frac{1}{2}$ per cent from German owned mines.

Eden, in a strong protest to the Portuguese Ambassador on May 13, (a) described this action as 'incomprehensible' on the part of an ally. We could not, however, compel Dr. Salazar to repudiate the agreement without taking retaliatory measures which would have been more harmful to the Allies than to the Portuguese. Moreover Dr. Salazar did in fact concede the greater part of the Anglo-American demands and had at this time the special argument that, if he refused the Germans all supplies of wolfram, they might be less willing to tolerate the Portuguese grant of facilities to the Allies in the Azores.[1] Hence the British Government limited themselves for the time to suggestions for administrative action which might diminish the supply of wolfram without a technical violation of the Portuguese-German agreement.

After the Anglo-Portuguese agreement over the Azores had (b) brought (as the British Government expected) only a formal protest to Portugal from Germany, and as the Wolfram Agreement of 1943–44 was approaching its term, the British Government considered whether they would try to secure a complete embargo on wolfram supplies to Germany. The fact that they were negotiating with Spain for a drastic reduction in the export of Spanish wolfram to Germany made it even more important to secure a similar denial of Portuguese wolfram.[2]

The Portuguese Government continued to be unwilling to go as far as an embargo. The Foreign Office were inclined to think that, since in any case we were hoping within a few months to cut off the Germans from access to the Spanish and Portuguese supplies, the matter was not worth pushing to an extreme by a threat of a general embargo on Allied imports into Portugal. On the other hand the United States Government were strongly urging a total stoppage of Spanish and Portuguese supplies of wolfram to Germany. In view of this American insistence, the Foreign Office decided that an approach to this end should be made to Dr. Salazar. If, as was (c) most probable, Dr. Salazar refused a joint Anglo-American request —which would be put in terms of shortening the war—we should

---

[1] According to a Foreign Office minute the Prime Minister appears to have told the (d) Portuguese Ambassador in October 1943 that he saw no reason why the Portuguese should not continue to send wolfram to Germany, and indeed increase their exports if such action were necessary to keep the Germans quiet.

[2] The capacity of the German steel industry was already being affected by the Russian recovery of the manganese mines at Nikopol and the prospective total loss of Turkish chrome. There was, nevertheless, some doubt whether the Germans were really short of wolfram, and whether their heavy purchases had not been intended—like those of the Allies—mainly as measures of pre-emption. In any case the Germans would probably have been able to secure a considerable supply by smuggling across the Portuguese and Spanish frontiers.

(a) C5366/444/36.   (b) C7419/33/36 (1944).   (c) C580, 631, 704/33/36. (d) C14289/444/36.

ask him to limit exports to Germany to 250 tons a quarter, and to limit the duration of the Portuguese agreement with Germany to six months (with a right to cancellation at the end of three months). We should not object to similar limitations on the export of wolfram to the United Nations, and in return we would do everything possible by increasing other purchases to mitigate the economic loss to Portugal and to supply commodities which she might otherwise have received from Germany.

(a)   Sir R. Campbell made an approach to Dr. Salazar on January 23, 1944, about an embargo, but was given no definite reply. Dr. Salazar was obviously waiting to see the result of the Anglo-American discussions with the Spanish Government over the export of wolfram from Spain. At the beginning of March the Foreign

(b) Office thought that further action should be taken, and that Dr. Salazar should not be left to see what the Spaniards decided to do, but should be told that we expected him as an ally to set an example to Spain. The Foreign Office therefore suggested that the Prime Minister should send a personal letter to Dr. Salazar[1] in which, without formally invoking the alliance, he would point out the bad effect upon Anglo-Portuguese relations of the refusal to meet our demands about wolfram.

(c)   In this letter of March 15 the Prime Minister wrote that public opinion in Great Britain would ask with increasing concern why our ally 'who responded so generously in the Azores Agreement to our request for the facilities required to increase the safety of our shipping routes and so to shorten the war, nevertheless provides Germany with the essential means to pierce British armour, kill British troops and so prolong the war, with all its attendant suffering and danger to the great values of Christian civilisation'. The Prime Minister said there was no longer any German threat to Portugal which might justify Portuguese hesitancy to cut off German supplies.

(d)   Dr. Salazar replied on March 28, 1944, with a long letter explaining why he could not go as far as an embargo. He also showed his own attitude towards the moral issues involved in the war.

'If England, our friend and ally, were the only enemy against whom Germany was fighting, the considerations arising from what should represent for us the lives of British citizens would certainly find in our soul a stronger and more decisive echo than they can when it is

(e)   [1] Dr. Salazar had refused—in friendly terms—an invitation from the British Government to come to London for general political and economic discussions. On March 31, however, the Portuguese Ambassador told Mr. Eden that Dr. Salazar, while unable for the time to accept the invitation, would like to do so later.

(a) C1015, 2903, 3318/33/36.   (b) C3636, 3637/33/36.   (c) Churchill Papers/505; C4341/33/36.   (d) Churchill Papers/505; C4341/33/36.   (e) C657, 866, 989, 1556/262/36; C4261/33/36.

known that the German war effort is likewise directed against other enemies whose activity against Christian civilisation, which Great Britain defends, has unfortunately been well-marked and is well known.'

In view of Dr. Salazar's obstinacy the Prime Minister was inclined for the time at least to take no special action in the matter. He wrote a minute to Mr. Eden on April 9 that 'we must never forget that (a) they [the Portuguese] have let us into the Azores and that we should then have been very glad to shut our eyes to wolfram misdemeanours for the sake of what we got. The pressure should be kept up, but in a tone more in sorrow than in anger'. The Prime Minister said that he was ready to send a message to the President in this sense.

The Prime Minister, however, suggested a somewhat sharper attitude after Mr. Hull's speech of April 9 on the behaviour of those neutrals who were supplying Germany with material of military value. He wrote a minute to Mr. Eden on April 13 that: (b)

'we should become cool with Salazar and let him feel it. We should keep up the pressure, both negative and positive, on Portugal. We should let the Americans go ahead without discouragement in this field. We are entitled gradually to change our position as the danger of Portugal being involved recedes. This may well happen in the next two or three months. New situations are developing, and the relations of Salazar with his old allies as well as his general position in the war come sharply on to the table. We must see how "Over-lord" goes[1] before taking a more decided line. He should receive no answer, no compliments and no comfort. I am not asking for more than that.'

Sir R. Campbell thought that Dr. Salazar would probably offer (c) a reduction from 1,550 tons (the 1943 figure) to 1,050 tons in the annual export to Germany. The Minister of Economic Warfare suggested an appeal to Dr. Salazar fully to implement the Anglo-Portuguese alliance and to join the United Nations. The Foreign Office, however, regarded such an appeal as useless. Dr. Salazar was not attracted 'by the prospect of climbing on to the Allied band-wagon merely because we are winning the war'. He also realised that we should not find it in our interest to have a serious quarrel over so 'short-term' an issue as wolfram. We could not denounce the alliance while we were benefiting from it in the Azores. Our means of exerting economic pressure on Portugal were small. We were already in arrears in our economic commitments under the Azores agreement, and depended on Dr. Salazar for financing all our purchases in Portugal, including those of wolfram.

---

[1] i.e. the cross-Channel invasion.

(a) C4654/33/36. (b) C4929/33/36. (c) C4968/33/36.

(a)   On April 30 the Prime Minister—after getting figures of the Portuguese exports from Lord Cherwell—wrote to Mr. Eden that 'we should now put the screw hard on Salazar, who thinks that he is entitled to mince and frill before the world'. Mr. Churchill was ready to support 'a pretty rough policy towards him. A little time ago I was still contented with his concessions about the Azores, but I think we should now shift from one leg to the other'. The Foreign Office also thought that more pressure should be put on Dr. Salazar, especially since he had not yet suggested any steps for reducing exports to Germany. The negotiations with Spain were now practically complete,[1] and the Turkish Government had agreed to cut off German supplies of chrome.[2] Public opinion would therefore regard it as more than absurd if Portugal allowed Germany greater benefits than she could get from Spain and Turkey.

(b)   The Prime Minister, on May 5, was still ready to accept a compromise whereby the Portuguese would export to Germany no more wolfram than the Spaniards. The Foreign Office suggested an

(c)   arrangement roughly on this basis. Dr. Salazar, in spite of a direct appeal from General Smuts, was unwilling even to go as far as this suggestion, while the United States Government refused to be satisfied with anything short of a complete embargo. As in the case of Spanish wolfram, the State Department seemed to the Foreign Office to take no account of the fact that while the negotiations were continuing—with little prospect of success—the Germans were getting much larger quantities than they would receive under a compromise plan. Moreover there was even less chance of moving Dr. Salazar, since he had received the impression from the United States Ambassador that the United States Government would not in any circumstances impose economic sanctions on Portugal.

(d)   After another appeal—which was supported by the Brazilian Government—on May 24 Dr. Salazar was willing to impose a general embargo on the export of wolfram, but he still insisted on sending to Germany 98 tons due under the previous year's agreement, although the Germans had already received about 400 tons since the expiry of this agreement.

(e)   The Foreign Office telegraphed to Sir R. Campbell on June 2 that Dr. Salazar's insistence upon these 98 tons would have unfortunate results for Portugal. With the approaching liberation of Europe the demands upon the strictly limited supply of commodities available would increase. The claims of neutrals—unless they

---

[1] The agreement with Spain was announced on May 2.
[2] See Chapter LII, section (i).

(a) C6002/33/36. (b) C6468/33/36. (c) C6003, 6310, 6375, 6716/33/36. (d) C6469 7003, 7019, 7441, 7742/33/36. C7419/33/36; Churchill Papers/505. (e) C7581/33/36.

qualified for special consideration by taking a helpful line now—would come below those of our Allies who were fighting and suffering. Unless, therefore, Dr. Salazar gave way over the 98 tons, we saw little or no hope of persuading the United States Government to meet him over the essential requirements of Portugal and we should feel unable to make a special effort to move them. We should also have to announce the facts in Parliament, and to say that the Portuguese response to our appeal had been so very grudging that we could conclude only that they attached little value to the Anglo-Portuguese alliance or to their relations with 'the United Nations in general and the British Commonwealth in particular'. Dr. Salazar (a) finally gave way on June 5, and accepted the British demand.[1]

---

[1] The Prime Minister would have been willing to allow Dr. Salazar the small additional (b) tonnage. He wrote to Mr. Eden on June 7 before hearing that a settlement had been reached: 'This 100 tons will save his [Dr. Salazar's] face, and I am quite prepared, if you wish, to press the President on this point. I think it very likely he will not worry about it now so much else is going on.'

After the successful conclusion of the negotiations the United States Minister at Lisbon reported that it seemed 'undeniable that it was the invocation of the Anglo-Portuguese Alliance which finally carried the day'. The Minister also thought that the support of Brazil, which had taken Dr. Salazar completely by surprise, had also been very helpful. *F.R.U.S.*, 1944, IV, 131–2.

(a) C7552, 7553/33/36. C7419/33/36. (b) C7819/33/36.

CHAPTER XLIX

Great Britain's relationship towards Argentina: British and United States policy during the period 1942 to 1944

(i)

British acceptance of American leadership in policy towards the Latin American States: the attitude of the Argentine Government in 1942–43.

THE area of Anglo-American differences on policy—though small in relation to the wide extent of friendly agreement and co-operation—was increased in 1943–44 owing to the unwillingness of the Foreign Office to follow Mr. Hull in what seemed, in the British view, an unwise interference in the domestic affairs of Argentina. Before and after the entry of the United States into the war British policy towards the Latin American States followed the lead set by the State Department. Any attempt at separate British action would have caused resentment both in Washington and throughout Latin America, and was in fact unnecessary because the decisions taken at Pan-American meetings were favourable to British interests. The Latin American States generally were disinclined to support Germany, and resented (not without a certain anxiety) the strident efforts made by the Germans to organise as a distinct body the large populations of German descent in parts of South America. On the other hand, after the collapse of France, when Latin American opinion expected a British defeat, the countries outside the area of immediate protection by the United States did not want to risk the enmity of Germany by undertaking any positive action against the Axis Powers. They agreed, however, at the Havana Conference of July 1940, to a declaration of common interest that 'any attempt on the part of a non-American State against the integrity or inviolability of the territory, the sovereignty, or the political independence of an American State' should be considered as an act of aggression against all the States signing the declaration.

(a)   The United States Government called a meeting of the Latin American States at Rio de Janeiro on January 15, 1942, for the implementation of this declaration of July 1940. Before the meeting took place the Latin American countries near to the United States had declared war on the Axis Powers or at least broken off diplo-

---

(a) A1612/1/51.

72

matic relations with them. The United States Government did not regard the belligerency of all Latin America as necessary or even desirable, but they wanted every State to break off diplomatic and commercial relations with the common enemy if only to put a stop to espionage and the organisation of 'fifth column' activity.

The opposition to this policy came mainly from Argentina, and was due partly to nationalist dislike of dictation by the United States, and partly to the belief that Germany would win the war. On December 31, 1942, at the request of the United States Government, (a) the British Government issued through the Foreign Office a public statement regretting that Argentina had not broken off relations with the Axis, and pointing out that trade with her would no longer be possible unless steps were taken to prevent German agents from giving information to submarines about the movement of British shipping. The Argentine Government took some measures— (b) including the deportation of the German naval attaché—to stop these activities, but in February 1943 reaffirmed their neutrality.

In June 1943 the dictatorship of President Castillo was overthrown by a military *coup*. The British and United States Governments hoped that there would now be a change of foreign policy, but the new Government made it clear that they intended to delay a break with the Axis as long as possible, and meanwhile to bargain for American economic and military aid. At the end of the year there (c) was evidence of the complicity of the Argentine Government and German agents in a military revolution overthrowing the Bolivian Government.

At this point Mr. Hull proposed to take strong action to discredit the Argentine military dictatorship and to secure the establishment of a more democratic and co-operative régime. He asked for British support, and for the next twelve months this question caused much controversy between the Foreign Office and the State Department. The Foreign Office agreed with Mr. Hull about the character of the dictatorship; British economic interests in Argentina were greater than those of the United States, and the threat to such long-term interests from adventurers like Colonel Perón—who soon became the dominant figure in the régime—were serious. The Foreign Office, however, thought that Mr. Hull was greatly exaggerating the damage done by the Argentine Government to the Allies, and that anyhow his attempt to bring about the overthrow of the régime would fail. Opinion generally in the Argentine regarded the public indictment of the Government by foreigners as an insult; the effect of these attacks was merely to strengthen Perón's position. The Foreign

---

(a) A461/4/2, A11847, 12089, 12116, 12121/3188/2. (b) A3079/4/2; A477, 646/283/2.
(c) Tel. No. 53, Churchill Papers/50.

Office argued again and again that official gestures of disapproval, such as the withdrawal of Ambassadors, were ineffective and that an attempt to apply economic sanctions would do more harm to the Allies than to the Argentine Government. Mr. Hull suspected that the British attitude was due to the pressure of financial interests, but the Foreign Office pointed out the inescapable facts that the stoppage of supplies of meat, corn and hides from Argentina would greatly hamper military operations in 1944, and was of general concern to the United Nations. The Combined Chiefs of Staff agreed with this view; Mr. Hull refused to accept it or to regard Argentina as likely to hold out against Allied action.

(a)   On January 6, 1944, the State Department gave Lord Halifax a copy of a memorandum[1] recounting at length the complaints against

(b) Argentina. Two days later Sir D. Kelly, British Ambassador to Argentina, reported that the U.S. Ambassador had spoken to him of Mr. Hull's views. Sir D. Kelly had doubts about the value of 'talking tough' to the Argentine Government. Mr. Eden agreed

(c) with him. On January 10 Lord Halifax reported that the U.S. Ambassador was to be recalled and an embargo imposed on exports from Argentina to the U.S.A. Mr. Churchill (who was at Marrakesh) at first thought that we should support Mr. Hull's action,[2] but Mr.

(d) Eden telegraphed to him that we could not afford a break with Argentina, which was sending us 31 per cent of our meat in addition

(e) to other essential supplies. Mr. Churchill then noted (January 21) that he now saw the 'grave reasons' against a break: Mr. Eden therefore telegraphed to Lord Halifax his 'hope that he (Lord Halifax) would be able to keep Mr. Hull in play a little longer'. Lord Halifax saw Mr. Hull and reported their conversation of

(f) January 23.[3] On January 25 Mr. Roosevelt, to whom Mr. Churchill had telegraphed giving the British view, replied with the 'good news' that Argentina was about to break off her relations with Germany. Mr. Hull then agreed to postpone further action and to give the Government a chance of carrying out measures against German activities. The break of relations took place on January 26, 1944, but the Government did nothing to suppress Axis activities.

---

[1] For Mr. Hull's complaints, see his *Memoirs* (Hodder & Stoughton, 1948), p. 1390.

(g)   [2] Mr. Churchill telegraphed that he did not 'see why we should not join in with Mr. Hull in bashing Argentina'.

[3] The Argentine Government at this time realised that a German victory was less likely, and that they might find themselves in an isolated position in comparison with that of Brazil.

(a) Tel. No. 80. Churchill Papers/50.   (b) Tel. No. 14. Churchill Papers/50.   (c) Tel. GRAND 139. Churchill Papers/50.   (d) PM/44/2, 17 Jan. 44. Churchill Papers/50. (e) Note on a minute of H. L. Ismay. Churchill Papers/50.   (f) Tel. 357. Churchill Papers/ 50.   (g) Tel. FROZEN 1264. Churchill Papers/50.

(ii)

*Coup d'état of February 1944 in Argentina: Mr. Hull's refusal to recognise
the new Government: differences between Mr. Hull and the Foreign Office
over the treatment of the Argentine Government: the question of British meat
contracts: change in American policy and recognition of the Argentine Government, April 1945.*

Mr. Hull's impatience with the behaviour of the Argentine Government was not lessened by another turn in the domestic politics of the
country. In February 1944 a group of officers headed by Colonel
Perón deposed the President of Argentina, and installed a new
President (General Farrell) while keeping real power in their own
hands. The United States Government refused to recognise the
legality of this latest Government unless they met the American
requirements.

Perón and Farrell would not give way to American pressure. Mr.
Hull became even more indignant, and more convinced about the
need to get rid of the régime, while the Foreign Office held to their
view that denunciation merely strengthened the position of the
dictators, and that we should be wiser to limit ourselves to saying
that we counted upon the new Government loyally to carry out the
policy of co-operation with the United Nations begun by their
predecessors. We should thereby be putting on Farrell and Perón
the responsibility for action contrary to our interests. In view of
Mr. Hull's insistence, however, Mr. Eden instructed the British
Ambassador, Sir D. Kelly, to limit his communications with the (a)
Argentine Government to matters of routine.[1]

The deadlock was unbroken at the end of May. Meanwhile, under
Perón's impulsion, the Argentine Government continued to reorganise the country on totalitarian lines. With the full agreement
of the United States Ambassador (who had consulted the State
Department) Sir D. Kelly had a private discussion on April 28 with (b)
President Farrell on the question of recognition. The President
complained that the attitude of the United States was greatly resented
by the Argentine people, and that the 'public orders' given to him
by the State Department made it impossible for him to carry out
conciliatory measures.

The Secretary of State instructed Lord Halifax on June 3 to tell
Mr. Hull that in our view it would be wiser to give up the idea of a

---

[1] The Prime Minister was especially anxious to go as far as possible in supporting
Mr. Hull. In a minute of February 7 to Mr. Eden he wrote: 'When you consider the
formidable questions on which we may have difficulty with the United States, oil, dollar
balances, shipping, policy to France, Italy, Spain, the Balkans, etc., I feel that we ought
to try to make them feel we are their friends and helpers in the American sphere.'

(a) AS1327/4/2. (b) AS2353/81/2.

'diplomatic victory' over the Argentine Government and to concentrate on finding a practical solution by laying down clear and definite terms of recognition. At the suggestion of a senior official of the State Department, who was intending to submit a memorandum to Mr. Hull, Lord Halifax waited before carrying out his instructions. On

(a) June 16, however, he telegraphed that he had heard in confidence from the State Department that the United States Ambassador might be withdrawn from Buenos Aires, and that the United States Government might ask us to withdraw Sir D. Kelly.

Mr. Eden therefore instructed Lord Halifax not to delay any longer his representations to Mr. Hull. If Mr. Hull raised the question of the withdrawal of the British Ambassador, Lord Halifax should say 'forcibly' that we would not agree to withdrawal unless the Argentine Government committed an unfriendly act of a kind which in normal circumstances would justify a rupture of diplomatic

(b) relations.[1] On the night of June 23–24 Lord Halifax reported that Mr. Hull had told him that he was withdrawing the United States Ambassador, and hoped that we would recall Sir D. Kelly. Lord Halifax asked whether it would not be a good thing to tell the Argentine Government what we wanted of them, with the implication that we would recognise them if they met our wishes. Mr. Hull did not agree. He said that the Argentine Government already knew what we wanted, and that they were trying to break South American solidarity and to hold on to their German connexions.

(c) The Prime Minister was inclined to give way to Mr. Hull. He wrote on June 25 to Mr. Eden again that we had 'so many differences open with the State Department at this moment that this might be an opportunity to do them a service'. Mr. Eden replied on June 26

(d) that Mr. Hull's motives were not 'founded on good policy', but on irritation over his previous failure and over attacks on his policy by Mr. Sumner Welles. He also seemed to think that 'being tough with neutrals' would help towards winning the Presidential Election. Our constant support of Mr. Hull and his policy had not earned us much thanks, but was 'landing us into ever deeper trouble'. Mr. Hull had not consulted us before recalling the United States Ambassador, and in those circumstances we had to consider our interests. 'First and foremost' was the question of meat supply. Our contract with the

---

[1] Mr. Hull described Argentina as a 'deserter'. The Foreign Office pointed out there was an analogy between the position of Argentina in regard to the Pan-American Union, and that of Eire in regard to the Commonwealth from which she obtained protection and many other advantages. The British Government, however, had decided to leave moral judgments in the matter to be applied by others, and not to upbraid Mr. De Valera or put pressure on him, but, far from 'appeasing' him, to ensure that Eire, and, if possible, its government, made the maximum contribution to the war effort.

(a) AS3131/78/2.   (b) Tel. No. 3377, Churchill Papers/50.   (c) M755/4. Churchill Papers/50.   (d) AS3438/78/2. PM/44/470: Churchill Papers/50.

Argentine Government was due for renewal at the end of August. It was most important that the matter should be handled by our Ambassador, and that the political atmosphere should be as little unfavourable as possible. We also had very large capital interests in Argentina which were already threatened and we were handicapped in protecting them because we were not officially in relations with the Government. In any case the withdrawal of an Ambassador was 'about the most futile diplomatic move' which could be taken.

On June 27 Lord Halifax telegraphed that a senior official in the (a) State Department said to him privately that he was greatly disturbed at Mr. Hull's policy towards Argentina, and that we should do the United States a valuable service by refusing to be rushed into a critical decision. President Roosevelt, however, telegraphed to Mr. Churchill on June 30 asking that we should recall Sir D. Kelly for (b) consultation. After a discussion with Mr. Eden, the Prime Minister replied on July 1 that he would agree to the recall, but that he was (c) acting only in response to the President's request. He did not see what we expected to get from this policy. He added: 'I hope you will not mind my saying, as is my duty, that we ourselves were placed in an invidious position by the American decision, to which we are now asked to conform, being taken without consultation with us.'

The President sent on July 6 a telegram of thanks in which he said (d) that, if we continued to stand firm, there was a good chance that the entire matter would soon be cleared up. Mr. Eden, in a minute of July 13 to Mr. Churchill, said that this view was 'absurdly optimistic', (e) since an Argentine Government which gave way to pressure from the United States would at once be overthrown. Sir D. Kelly did not consider that the Axis war effort was getting any real assistance from Argentina. He also believed that this was the view of the United States naval and military authorities. We ought therefore to decide upon what we regarded as reasonable terms of recognition, and put these terms to the State Department.

The Ministry of Food, with Mr. Eden's approval, drew up a note (f) on the serious consequences which would follow a failure to get a renewal of the meat contract. The Prime Minister sent this note to the President on July 14 with a covering message that we wanted to (g) do all we could to help him and Mr. Hull with the South American countries, but that he ought to see the 'formidable arguments' put forward by the Minister of Food. We were importing over 40 per cent of our meat ration from Argentina, and could not risk losing this

---

(a) Tel. No. 3479, AS3381/78/2. (b) Tel. No. 575, T1386/4, PM/412/6. (c) T1394/4, PM/412/6. (d) Tel. 579, T1415/4: PM/412/6. (e) Tel. No. 523, PM(44): Churchill Papers/50. (f) T1448/4: PM/412/6. (g) No. 730, T1447: PM/412/6.

source of supply. Mr. Churchill wrote: 'The stamina of the workman cannot be maintained on a lesser diet in meat. You would not send your soldiers into battle on the British Service meat ration, which is far above what is given to workmen. Your people are eating per head more meat and more poultry than before the war while ours are most sharply cut.'

(a)   The President replied on July 23 that he would do nothing to cut down the British meat supply or to prevent a new contract. He thought, however, that we could state firmly our disapproval of the pro-Axis sentiments and practises of the Argentine Government, and at the same time get our meat contract. He also asked the Prime Minister to consider a statement by Mr. Hull which was being sent through Mr. Winant to Mr. Eden.

(b)   On July 27 Mr. Hull issued to the press a public indictment of Argentina. The Foreign Office considered that the charges were put more strongly than the facts warranted, and that Mr. Hull had again shown great lack of consideration in issuing this statement without allowing us time to discuss it with him or with Sir D. Kelly. We could not now send Sir D. Kelly back or recognise the Argentine Government at least for some time, though we might try in some private way to make them behave better and also 'to lower the temperature all round'. We could not back Mr. Hull very strongly because his facts and methods were wrong.

At Mr. Eden's suggestion, the Prime Minister in Parliament on August 2, in a review of the war situation referred to the attitude of the Argentine Government.[1] The Foreign Office thought that

(c)   Argentina had done much of what we required of her, though so slowly and grudgingly that she deserved no credit. They suggested that the Combined Chiefs of Staff should be asked to state what injury Argentina had caused to the United Nations and what assistance she could now provide. We should not send our Ambassador back, or recognise the Argentine Government until we had

(d)   discussed the situation with the United States. Mr. Churchill, in a message of August 23 to Mr. Roosevelt, hoped that the United States, having said in public what they thought of the Argentine Government, would now 'ignore them for a good many weeks, thus giving both of us an opportunity to examine a common policy, and the Argentines a chance to mend their ways, which they can never do under the glare of public indictment'.

---

[1] The Prime Minister's words were: 'We must all feel deep regret that in this testing-time for nations, she [Argentina] has not seen fit to declare herself wholeheartedly, unmistakably, and with no reserve or qualification whatsoever, on the side of freedom, godliness and decent humanity.'

(a) Tel. No. 588, T1481/4: PM/412/6; AS3941/78/2. (b) AS3263/325/45. (c) AS3851/78/2. (d) Tel. No. 766, T1655/4: PM/412/6.

Here, on the British side, the matter rested, as far as the political issue was concerned, until Mr. Hull's resignation. Mr. Stettinius then met the wishes of the other Latin American States by taking a more conciliatory line. Before the end of the year a private agreement was made with the Argentine leaders on the question of recognition. On April 9, 1945, the Argentine Government, which had declared war on Germany on March 27, was officially recognised by the United States Government.[1]

Meanwhile, in the last few months of 1944, there were further differences with the State Department over the question of a British meat contract. The British Government had taken the President's telegram of July 23 to mean that there were no American objections to the negotiation of a new meat contract. The Prime Minister had (a) in fact telegraphed on August 23 to the President that we were (b) going ahead with the negotiations and hoped that nothing would happen to hazard them.[2] Mr. Roosevelt had replied on (c) August 26 that he had no doubt that a satisfactory contract would be arranged. The Ministry of Food therefore asked the Argentine negotiators in London to find out whether their Government would be interested in a four-year contract.

At the Quebec Conference, however, the Americans asked us not to conclude a contract even for two years. Mr. Hull spoke contemptuously of the 'petty commercial advantages of a long-term (d) bargain with a fascist government', but the reasons on the British side for wanting the contract were unchanged. If we lost the Argentine supplies altogether, our small meat ration would be reduced by some two-thirds. If we refused a contract, the Argentine Government would not be embarrassed, as Mr. Hull argued, because other purchasers would come in. The Belgian, Dutch and French Governments (who had gold at their disposal) were anxious to buy, and prices would therefore be raised. We could not hold off these Governments indefinitely; we had told them of our intention to purchase the whole supply on a long-term basis, and to allocate shares to the liberated European countries.

---

[1] The Americans were in a weak position on this question because Mr. Roosevelt had told Stalin at Yalta that Argentina would not be eligible for membership of the United Nations unless she changed her policy. Mr. Stettinius, however, had agreed at an Inter-American Conference at Mexico City later in February to support the admission of Argentina. Mr. Molotov tried at San Francisco to 'trade' the admission of Argentina against that of the Warsaw Government.

[2] The United States Government had frozen £2,000,000 of Argentine gold assets in the United States on August 16, 1944, but the State Department's proposals for a general freezing of Argentine assets in the U.S.A. met with strong resistance from other United States Departments.

(a) AS3941/78/2. (b) Tel. No. 766, T1655/4: PM/412/6. (c) Tel. No. 607, T1679/4: PM/412/6. (d) AS4901, 4902/78/2.

The Foreign Office considered that Mr. Hull, since he knew these facts, had no right to put pressure on us. On the other hand we could not forget the great debt which we owed him for his support.[1] The Prime Minister, as before, thought that we ought to do our utmost to fall in with American wishes. He suggested to the War Cabinet on October 4 that we should state the whole case again to Mr. Hull, and say that we would delay signing the contract until

(a) after the American elections, but Mr. Roosevelt telegraphed on October 11 that he hoped we should continue only on a month-to-month basis and not conclude a long-term contract. The Prime Minister replied on October 13 that he had given instructions that

(b) no long-term contract should be negotiated during the next two months.[2] The Ministry of Food, however, before they knew of these instructions, had already discussed with the Argentine representatives the reply of their Government to the proposal made to them in August. The Ministry now held up further discussion; since there was a serious risk that a refusal to do so would endanger the success of the large economic and financial negotiations with the United States, they finally agreed to continue to another half-year, i.e. till June 1, 1945, on a month-to-month basis.

(c) [1] One Foreign Office comment at this time was that dealing with Mr. Hull was like attempting to deal with Mr. Gladstone in his old age.

[2] The Prime Minister was in Moscow at this time.

(a) Tel. DRASTIC 38, T1917/4: PM/412/6. (b) Tel. HEARTY No. 64, T1923/4: Churchill Papers/50. (c) AS4369/78/2.

CHAPTER L

British relations with Turkey from January 1942 to June 1943

(i)

British attempts to remove Turkish suspicions of Russian policy: reassurances to Turkey with regard to the Anglo-Soviet treaty of May 26, 1942: British and Russian declarations to Turkey (January–June 1942).

SINCE the collapse of France, British diplomacy had been concerned with the grave dangers of a German attack on Turkey or a demand for the passage of German troops and war material through Turkish territory. The most critical time, after the crisis of 1940, had been in the spring of 1941.[1] At the beginning of 1942 the threat to Turkey remained but was for the time less immediate. On the Turkish side, however, the possibility of a vast German defeat in Russia was as disquieting—from the point of view of Turkey's future—as the menace of a German invasion. Thus, while the Turkish Government began to be more confident of their ability to resist German pressure, they were more inclined to listen to German propaganda about the 'bolshevisation of Europe' and to suspect that Great Britain might give way to demands from Russia at Turkish expense.

The Foreign Office therefore regarded the improvement of Russo- (a) Turkish relations as of great importance. They tried to reassure the Turkish Government, and considered that they had satisfactory statements from the Russian side. On his return from Moscow in January 1942,[2] Mr. Eden told the War Cabinet that Stalin's (b) attitude to Turkey was most reasonable. He had agreed that we should treat Turkey well and offer her inducements to remain neutral, since as a neutral she provided an effective 'pad'. He had not suggested a change in the régime of the Straits.

The Turkish Government, however, were nervous about the (c) discussions in Moscow. Before leaving Moscow, Mr. Eden had given Sir H. Knatchbull-Hugessen a personal message for the

---

[1] See Vol. I, Chapter XVI.
[2] For Mr. Eden's visit to Moscow in December 1941, see Vol. II, Chapter XXVI, sections (i)–(ii).

(a) R480/480/44. (b) WM(42)1.4, C.A. (c) N7478/7462/38 (1941); R314/72/44.

President of the Republic that the Soviet Government had not themselves raised any question about Turkey during the conversations, and had shown a most friendly attitude when Mr. Eden had mentioned the subject. In the House of Commons on January 8, 1942, Mr. Eden said that the references to Turkey had been in all respects friendly and such as the Turkish Government themselves would have been glad to hear. Turkey had nothing to fear from an Allied victory. Her territorial integrity was not menaced by the Allies, and the Anglo-Soviet pledges given to Turkey would be honoured. Both Russia and Great Britain wished to see Turkey strong and prosperous.

(a)   Sir H. Knatchbull-Hugessen called on the Turkish Minister for Foreign Affairs on January 10 to tell him of the Moscow conversations in so far as Turkey was concerned. He mentioned a broadcast statement by Mr. Eden as well as his speech in the House of Commons and said that there was every reason to believe in Russia's determination to adhere to the guarantees already given to Turkey. Nonetheless the Turkish Government remained suspicious. On

(b) January 15 Mr. Eden gave Dr. Aras, the Turkish Ambassador, a note repeating what he had said in the House of Commons about the Moscow discussions and the attitude of Stalin. Mr. Eden offered an additional assurance that he would never discuss a question regarding the Straits or any Turkish frontier or interest[1] with a third party without first informing the Turks. These assurances seemed to satisfy M. Aras. On the other hand, Sir H. Knatchbull-Hugessen continued to report the 'morbid state of suspicion' of the Turkish Government; they were not satisfied with the information given

(c) them about the Moscow talks.[2] The Foreign Office authorised him if necessary to repeat to the President or Minister for Foreign Affairs the assurance in Mr. Eden's note of January 15.

(d)   On January 19 the Soviet Ambassador gave the Turkish Minister for Foreign Affairs an account of the Moscow conversations which corresponded closely with the British version. He said that the Straits were not mentioned, and that Stalin desired a strong and inviolate Turkey. He told M. Saracoglu of Stalin's suggestions that Turkey should have the Dodecanese and also a portion of Bulgaria south of

---

[1]At the Ambassador's suggestion, Mr. Eden inserted 'or any Turkish interest' after 'Turkish frontier' in the last sentence but one of the note.

(e)   [2] On February 18 *Pravda* published a report that Herr von Papen, German Ambassador at Ankara, had made a special report to the Turkish President about Mr. Eden's negotiations in Moscow, alleging that Mr. Eden promised the Bosphorus and the Persian Gulf to the Soviet Union. *Pravda* denied the report.

(a) N200/200/38; N114/5/38; R316, 317, 318/72/44.   (b) R403/403/44; R293, 448/72/44. (c) R293, 318/72/44. (d) R451, 501/72/44. (e) R1227/481/44.

Burgas where the population was Turkish. Stalin had also said that Turkey had interests regarding the Syrian frontier.[1]

On January 20 Sir H. Knatchbull-Hugessen spoke to the President (a) of the Republic about the Moscow conversations. The President said that he was entirely satisfied and had full confidence in us. As long as Turkey was convinced of our faith in her she would withstand any propaganda or menace. He spoke of Russia in a most friendly way. On January 23 Mr. Eden informed Sir H. Knatchbull- (b) Hugessen that in Moscow he had asked Stalin about his ideas for improving the situation in Turkey. Stalin had suggested an offer of the Dodecanese. Mr. Eden had said that Greece wanted these Greek-inhabited islands. Stalin then suggested an exchange of islands between Greece and Turkey. He said that Turkey's main interest was to secure control of the islands blocking the outlet from the Dardanelles and that she would also like Dedeagatch. He did not, however, suggest an offer of this port, since he agreed that the Greeks would raise objections.

Mr. Eden made no comment in his telegram to Sir H. Knatchbull-Hugessen on the frontier adjustment proposed by Stalin between Turkey and Bulgaria. He said that a change in the Syrian frontier was impossible in view of the British recognition of Syrian independence and integrity, and that, owing to Greek claims and our obligations to Greece, we should not be prepared to agree to the surrender of the Dodecanese to Turkey.[2]

On March 25 M. Orbay,[3] who was succeeding Dr. Aras as Turkish (c) Ambassador to Great Britain, brought warm personal messages of friendship from the President of the Republic. The President had asked him to assure Mr. Eden of his most sincere goodwill for the success of the British Government and people, and to repeat that the policy of Turkey was unchanged, and that she was unshakeably loyal to her friendship. Mr. Orbay added that Turkey's interests and those of the British Empire were indissolubly linked. If we were defeated there was no future for Turkey.

Mr. Eden asked M. Orbay to reciprocate cordially the President's message. We had understood the difficulties of the Turkish position,

---

[1] The Turkish and Soviet accounts of this interview differed. The Turkish account said that Stalin spoke of 'some rectification on the Syrian frontier.'

[2] On February 27 the Minister for Foreign Affairs told Sir H. Knatchbull-Hugessen that Turco-Soviet relations were better. The Soviet Government had moved nearly all (d) their troops from the Turkish frontier and were using the area only as a training ground. The Soviet Ambassador was maintaining closer and more frequent contact with him.

[3] M. Husseyin Rauf Orbay had been Prime Minister of Turkey in 1922. The Foreign Office regarded him as a strong character who had spoken his mind fearlessly under the (e) Ataturk dictatorship and has consistently upheld Anglo-Turkish friendship.

(a) R482/72/44; R698/70/44. (b) R451/72/44. (c) R2216/72/44; R2075/403/44. (d) R1469/72/44. (e) R634/480/44.

but had always felt sure that, if faced with German demands incompatible with her interests, Turkey would resist and fight. M. Orbay said that this was undoubtedly so. The mind of the President, Government and people was made up on this issue and we could count on their loyalty. Finally, M. Orbay asked for help in obtaining American equipment to assist them in the resistance which they were determined to make.

(a)   The Secretary-General, M. Numan Menemencioglu, reaffirmed M. Orbay's assurances of Turkish loyalty. On May 10 he repeated to the British Air Attaché that Turkey was unflinchingly with Great Britain. If Great Britain won, Turkey had hopes. If she sank, Turkey sank with her. The Secretary-General stated that even if Germany pushed back the Russians, advanced into Iran and Iraq and at the same time moved through the islands to Syria, Turkey would still fight. The Air Attaché understood him to mean that in such circumstances Turkey would go to war rather than allow herself to be encircled. The Secretary-General said that Turkey would follow Britain's lead in all circumstances and that, whatever plans we might have for the future, Turkey would be with us. Meanwhile

(b)   on March 27 Sir H. Knatchbull-Hugessen had reported that the primary object of Turkey was to avoid war unless she were directly attacked. She would be careful not to take provocative action which might lead into war, but would actively resist any foreign aggression.

(c)   The proposals for an Anglo-Soviet treaty revived Turkish suspicions that we were abandoning Turkey and committing ourselves

(d)   to concessions at Turkish expense, e.g. over the Straits. On the night of April 3–4, Sir H. Knatchbull-Hugessen telegraphed that he realised the political necessity for the treaty, but that he must state his view of its effect in Turkey. Our experiences since June 1941 showed that, the closer our relations with Russia the more difficult our position in Turkey, whose distrust of Russia was ineradicable.[1] Sir H. Knatchbull-Hugessen thought that the conclusion of an Anglo-Soviet treaty might give the impression that we were ready to yield to any Russian demands. The effect of informing the Turkish Government only after the treaty had been signed would be most unfortunate. The Turks had always asked that as our allies they should be taken into our confidence; they had insisted on keeping the Soviet Government informed of negotiations for the Anglo-Turkish treaty. Sir H. Knatchbull-Hugessen urged that the Turkish Government should be told confidentially of the negotiations and

---

[1] In March an attempt was made to assassinate Herr von Papen with a bomb. Two employees of the Soviet Consulate-General at Istanbul were tried for alleged participation. The Soviet Government strongly objected to this trial.

(a) R3078/24/44. (b) R2075/403/44. (c) R2643/480/44. (d) R2219/72/44.

that the treaty should contain or be accompanied by some undertaking that both parties would respect Turkish territorial integrity
and sovereignty. This undertaking should be so worded as to refute
any allegation that we had handed over south-eastern Europe to
the Russians.

The Foreign Office were already preparing to reassure Turkey. (a)
On April 5 Mr. Eden submitted a memorandum to the War Cabinet
pointing out that the signature of the proposed treaty was bound to
cause anxiety which the British and Soviet Governments should
dispel, before the treaty was signed, by addressing joint or simultaneous declarations to the Turkish Government. These declarations
should explain that the motive of the two Governments in concluding
the treaty was to facilitate the defeat of Germany; they should also
reaffirm the assurances of August 10, 1941:[1] (i) that the British and
Soviet Governments had no aggressive intentions or claims regarding
the Straits; (ii) that they remained faithful to the Montreux Convention which regulated the régime of the Straits; (iii) that both
Governments were prepared to observe scrupulously the territorial
integrity of the Turkish Republic; (iv) that both Governments were
prepared to send Turkey every help and assistance in the event of
her being attacked by a European Power.

The War Cabinet approved Mr. Eden's proposals on April 8. (b)
On that day the Foreign Office informed Sir H. Knatchbull- (c)
Hugessen that they agreed about the need to tell the Turks of our
intentions well before the signature of the treaty, and the need for
the British and Soviet Governments to make reassuring declarations
to the Turkish Government before it was published. The Foreign
Office would suggest to the Soviet Government at the outset of the
negotiations a declaration to the following effect: (i) that the motive
of the two Governments in deciding to conclude the treaty was the
better to pursue their common object of defeating Germany;
(ii) the British Government would recognise the right of the Soviet
Government to their 1941 frontiers in Finland, the Baltic States and
Roumania as they existed before the German invasion (the frontier
between Poland and the Soviet Union being reserved for future
negotiation). We considered that it was as much in our own interests
as in those of the Soviet Government that the Soviet Union should
thus recover her strategic position in order to ensure that Germany
was not again in a position to violate the peace of Europe.

The object of these two clauses was to emphasise to Turkey that
Stalin's demands concerned Germany, and that the frontiers in
question were vital to Russian existence and the peace of the world

---

[1] See Vol. II, p. 21.

(a) WP(42)144.   (b) WM(42)44.4, C.A.   (c) R2219/72/44.

against Germany. The fact that both the British and Soviet Governments regarded the Polish-Soviet frontier as a matter for future discussion between the Polish and Soviet Governments should convince the Turks that we had not 'sold' the Poles, and encourage them in the belief that we would not sell Turkey to Russia.

A third clause would reaffirm the Anglo-Soviet assurances of August 10, 1941, to Turkey. We would suggest that a passage should precede the Soviet declaration stating that they were informing the Turkish Government of their intention to conclude a treaty with His Majesty's Government in pursuance of their obligation under the protocol of December 17, 1929, renewing the Turco-Soviet Treaty of Friendship and Neutrality of December 17, 1925.

The proposed British declaration would state that it was intended to be merely a repetition of our undertaking towards Turkey as set out in Article 1 of the Treaty of Mutual Assistance, and did not in any way modify, extend or detract from that treaty. The Foreign Office also informed Sir H. Knatchbull-Hugessen that they appreciated the importance of reassuring Turkey about the alleged Russian designs on Bulgaria and the mouths of the Danube. They were considering the inclusion in the treaty of a clause committing the Soviet Government to approval of the principle of confederation in certain areas including the Balkans. They proposed thereby to make clear that Roumania and Bulgaria should participate as independent units in any Balkan confederation.

Owing to the refusal of the British Government to accept the Russian demands,[1] the Anglo-Soviet treaty was in form no more than a military alliance with a reference in general to post-war (a) collaboration. On May 26—the morning of the signature of the treaty—Mr. Eden gave to the Turkish Ambassador a declaration that the United Kingdom Government as the ally of Turkey desired to let the Turkish Government know of their intention to conclude a treaty with the Government of the U.S.S.R. This treaty would confirm and replace the Anglo-Soviet Agreement of July 12, 1941. The declaration stated that:

> 'His Majesty's Government in the United Kingdom confirm their fidelity to the Montreux Convention and assure the Turkish Government that they have no aggressive intentions or claims with regard to the Straits; His Majesty's Government in the United Kingdom, as also the Soviet Government, are prepared scrupulously to observe the territorial integrity of the Turkish Republic; while fully appreciating the desire of the Turkish Government not to be involved in war, His Majesty's Government in the United Kingdom, as also the

---

[1] See Vol. II, Chapter XXVI, section (iv).

(a) R3383/72/44; R1423/55/44.

Soviet Government, would nevertheless be prepared to send to Turkey every help and assistance in the event of her being attacked by any European Power.'

Before the publication of the treaty, M. Vyshinsky read to the (a) Turkish Chargé d'Affaires at Kuibyshev a statement that the Soviet Government considered the Soviet assurance to Turkey of August 10, 1941, to be in full force; that they had accepted the Atlantic Charter and that they called the attention of the Turkish Government to the provisions of the new treaty regarding an agreement not to conclude a separate peace.

On May 27 Sir H. Knatchbull-Hugessen spoke to M. Saracoglu (b) about the negotiations. The Minister took particular note of the passage in the treaty that the two Powers would not seek territorial aggrandisement and would not interfere in the internal affairs of European peoples. He said that he personally was 'very satisfied'. Three days later he informed the Ambassador that President Inönü and the Turkish Government were also satisfied with the British and Russian declarations. The Minister for Foreign Affairs remarked that in some respects the Russian declaration was fuller than ours. Meanwhile M. Numan had informed Sir H. Knatchbull-Hugessen (c) that the Russian declaration was generally on the same lines as ours, but that the Soviet Government had not quoted the assurances of August 10, 1941.

M. Numan mentioned that, in the text of these assurances, as stated in our declaration, the reference to the Montreux Convention and the Straits was made only in the name of His Majesty's Government, whereas the assurances in the rest of the document included both the British and Soviet Governments. Sir H. Knatchbull-Hugessen said that, if he remembered rightly, the Soviet Government had given a corresponding assurance at the time.[1]

(ii)

The question of British military aid to Turkey: German offer of arms to Turkey: British policy of outbidding the Germans: British promise to supply arms by the end of 1942 (January–November 1942).

Under the Anglo-Turkish Treaty of Mutual Assistance of October 1939, the British Government had given a promise to provide Turkey

---

[1] The text of the Anglo-Soviet Treaty was made public on June 11 after a statement (d) in the House of Commons. Mr. Eden did not mention Turkey explicitly in this statement. The Turkish Government subsequently gave the Soviet Government an assurance of their good intentions.

(a) R3956/24/44. (b) R3494, 3537/72/44. (c) R3542/72/44. (d) R3830, 4394/72/44.

with war material. They had done their best to supply this material although deliveries had not been up to schedule. In July 1940 the Foreign Office had recommended that we should do what we could to provide Turkey with means of perfecting her own defences, developing her own industries, improving her means of transport and enabling her to depend less on Germany who still represented a vital source of supply.

The German invasion of Russia made it necessary to strengthen (a) in every way our position in Turkey. In April 1941 Mr. Eden had predicted to the War Cabinet the likelihood of an Anglo-German 'tug-of-war' over Turkey. He thought that, if the Foreign Office considered that there was a good chance of holding the Turks, we should do all we could to ensure that they did not capitulate to German demands and that they stood up to a German attack. The occupation of Bulgaria and the mainland of Greece made it possible for Germany largely to isolate Turkey and restrict her intercourse with Great Britain and Egypt. Mr. Eden believed that some of the Turkish leaders were ultra-cautious and determined that Turkey should not be launched into an adventure which might end ill for her. Nevertheless he had confidence in Turkey's underlying loyalty to the British cause.

The difficulty was to induce the Turks to take an active line. Germany's position was increasingly strong as the result of her successes, and Turkey was unlikely to abandon a negative attitude for some time to come. Our fundamental requirement of Turkey was, however, negative rather than positive. In view of her lack of offensive power, we asked for political not military action. A secondary aim of the British policy of 'a Turkish buttress' was to build up Turkish economic and war potential, improve the training and operational experience of the Turkish fighting forces and see that the Turks adopted the best strategical plan of defence. Mr. Eden thought that we should accept the Turkish view that Turkey's role must be passive, and should accelerate the programme of (b) military and civil supplies.[1] The Prime Minister and War Cabinet agreed that we should continue to send supplies but not at a greater rate.

(c)   Sir H. Knatchbull-Hugessen reported in June 1941 that if we cut off a large proportion of their military supplies, the Turks would at once turn to the Germans for them. The Germans would then be encouraged to make further demands such as the dismissal of British personnel, the rejection of British pre-emptive purchases, the passage of war material or the suppression of British news. The situation was

---

(d)   [1] Up to August 1942 Great Britain sent Turkey over 100,000 tons of cereals.

(a) WP(41)77.   (b) WM(41)44.   (c) WP(41)141.   (d) R5428/1574/44.

changed, however, to some extent by the Turkish undertaking[1] to deliver up to 90,000 tons of chrome a year to Germany in 1943–44 against delivery to Turkey by the Germans[2] of war material. The (a) Foreign Office thought that, in fact, the Turks had held off the Germans fairly well. At the end of September 1941, the War Cabinet (b) considered the question of military assistance to Turkey in order to counteract further German pressure. Mr. Eden thought it important to work with the Minister of State in Cairo and Chiefs of Staff the best offer of assistance we could make to the Turks, and to send this offer to them as soon as possible. He raised the matter again with the (c) War Cabinet on November 10, 1941. He was anxious lest the urgency of Russian needs should cause us to overlook the importance of continuing our supplies to Turkey.

Mr. Eden thought Turkish resistance to Germany of crucial importance to our position in the Middle East and to the Soviet Union. In view of Russian requirements, we should decide what we considered essential minimum war material for Turkey in addition to supplies promised under the treaty. Mr. Eden referred to secret discussions about our aid to Turkey in the event of a German attack. The Turkish General Staff had asked for considerable military assistance; we had offered four infantry and two armoured divisions, two army tank brigades and twenty-four squadrons of aircraft in the event of a German attack in the spring, on condition that Turkish communications and administrative facilities were sufficient to enable this force to be maintained,[3] and that the situation elsewhere allowed us to provide and maintain it.

On November 17 the War Cabinet approved Mr. Eden's proposal (d) for a special effort to supply a minimum programme of Turkish requirements for infantry equipment, engineering stores and mechanical transport by a given date of which the Turks should be informed.

The spring of 1942 was likely to bring a renewal of the danger of (e) a German attack on Turkey. The German objectives would be the oilfields of the Caucasus and possibly also of Mosul, and a general undermining of the British position in the Middle East. Meanwhile the Libyan campaign and the outbreak of war in the Far East had weakened British resources. The Foreign Office informed Sir. H. (f) Knatchbull-Hugessen that, while a greater limiting factor was the

---

[1] In the agreement concluded by Dr. Clodius in October 1941. See note at end of section (iii).
[2] See Vol II, Chapter XIX, section (iv).
[3] Four squadrons of fighters would, however, be sent at once irrespective of these conditions.

(a) WM(41)101. (b) WM(41)96.1, C.A. (c) WP(41)265. (d) WM(41)115; R1104/70/44 (1942). (e) R1104/70/44. (f) R28/28/44; R235/70/44; JP(42)28; COS(42)9.

state of Turkish communications, we should probably be unable to carry out in full the promises of assistance which we had made in the previous autumn.

(a)   On January 20 Sir H. Knatchbull-Hugessen reopened with the Turkish Government the question of our military aid. He said that our forces could arrive in time to be of value only if the Turks made

(b) advance preparations and improved their transport facilities. The reaction to this advice showed that, for the first time for many months, the Turks were prepared to concert plans to resist a German attack. The War Office instructed the Commander-in-Chief, Middle

(c) East, to take advantage of this more helpful attitude.

(d)   On March 2 Mr. Eden told the Prime Minister that our Turkish policy seemed to be uncertain. He asked for a comprehensive study of possible developments in view of the danger of a German offensive to gain the Persian Gulf.[1] The Prime Minister consulted the Chiefs of Staff. They had already asked the Joint Planning Staff to consider ways of stiffening Turkish resistance. The latter reported that there was no possibility of sending equipment, mainly owing to the shortage of shipping. They considered political measures such as an offer of the Dodecanese or the Duck's Bill,[2] and concluded that this would not produce any good results. They suggested an energetic propaganda policy stressing the growing strength of Allied production and war effort.

(e)   As early as May 1942, and increasingly during the next two months the Foreign Office had evidence of a German campaign in Turkey aimed at displacing Great Britain as the principal supplier of industrial and military requirements, and thereby undermining the Anglo-Turkish connexion. Germany had offered Turkey large quantities of war material, including nearly 200 tanks, several hundred anti-tank and anti-aircraft guns and fighter and bomber aircraft. The price for these arms was 400 million marks. The Foreign Office considered counter-measures, but took the line with the

---

[1] At a meeting of the Chiefs of Staff on February 24, the Chief of Air Staff had suggested —contrary to previous policy—that we might consider sending to the Turks anti-aircraft and anti-tank guns and tanks. Since, in any case, the Turks were not trained in the use of this equipment, Mr. Eden did not agree with this proposed change of policy. Meanwhile the Turks, who were known to be afraid of an attack in the spring, were keeping to the plan (which the British military authorities regarded as unsound) of concentrating their forces in Thrace. Mr. Eden therefore regarded it as necessary to consider how we could best use our available resources in assisting Turkey.

(f)   [2] The name given to the extreme north-east corner of the Jezireh in Syria. This territory extended to the Tigris and was crossed by the Baghdad railway. A Foreign Office memorandum of January 3, initialled by Mr. Eden, pointed out that we had recognised the independence and integrity of Syria. They noted also that the effect on the Arabs of the cession of the Duck's Bill to Turkey would be deplorable, and further that we had implicitly pledged ourselves to the United States Government not to enter during the war into any commitments regarding post-war territorial changes.

(a) R485/70/44. (b) R697, 706/70/44. (c) R968, 1055/70/44. (d) R1287, 1671, 2232/70/44; JP(42)226. (e) WP(42)304; R4864/486/44; R3514/810/44. (f) R28/28/44.

Turkish Government that the latter, as our allies, and in view of our efforts to send equipment, should resist these German manoeuvres, restrict relations with Germany to the minimum and adopt an attitude not of neutrality but of non-belligerency in our favour.

On May 15 the Turkish Secretary-General informed Sir H. (a) Knatchbull-Hugessen that his Government had made it clear to Germany that if she agreed to supply arms, they could accept no political conditions with regard to their use but would employ them against any aggressor. Six days later Herr von Papen[1] proposed (b) that the Turkish Government should send a delegation to Berlin for negotiations. A delegation left for Berlin on May 23. M. Numan later showed the British Ambassador the text of the correspondence with Herr von Papen about the proposed armaments credit. On June 22 Mr. Eden informed M. Maisky of these developments. He said that the Turkish Government had kept us informed of the negotiations with Germany and had given us a day's prior notice of the departure of the delegation.

According to the Turkish Government, Hitler received the (c) delegation personally and with considerable ceremony, although it contained no officers of the highest rank and only a junior official of the Turkish Ministry of Foreign Affairs. Hitler said that everything would be done to satisfy Turkish demands for war material without great delay. He wanted to supply Turkey with the most modern and efficient weapons, and his only ambition was to see her capable of self-defence. He assured the delegation of Germany's friendship for Turkey and full confidence in her.

Hitler mentioned chrome as one of the commodities which Turkey could supply in return for arms. The Turkish Government, however, told Sir H. Knatchbull-Hugessen that the delegation had been instructed to keep the arms agreement separate from the question of chrome supplies.[2] On June 16 the Secretary-General informed (d) him that an agreement had been reached about tanks and anti-aircraft guns. One hundred and seventy tanks were to be supplied; deliveries would begin in July and end in October. This arrangement had been made without waiting for the settlement of financial arrangements.

---

[1] On December 8, 1942, Sir H. Knatchbull-Hugessen gave his opinion that Herr von (e) Papen had very little influence in Turkey. He said that the Turkish Government had done their best to avoid receiving him as Ambassador, and that they neither liked nor trusted him. He had made various attempts to flatter the Turkish Foreign Minister by suggestions that the war might be brought to an end by Turkish mediation. Sir H. Knatchbull-Hugessen said it was clear that von Papen hoped for a compromise peace with Great Britain.

[2] The Foreign Office knew from other sources that there had been continual mention (f) of chrome in the conversations between the Germans and the Turkish delegation in Berlin.

(a) R3181/50/44. (b) R4084/486/44; R3908/50/44. (c) R3894, 4084/486/44. (d) R4004/50/44. (e) R8543/24/44. (f) R4004/50/44.

(a) These German overtures had given greater urgency to the question of Allied military assistance to Turkey. On April 7 M. Orbay had asked Mr. Eden for anti-tank and anti-aircraft guns. In view of shipping and supply difficulties and demands elsewhere it was still impossible without an Anglo-American decision on the highest level to do more than send Turkey a small quantity of specialised equip-

(b) ment. On May 13, however, the Prime Minister made a proposal to Mr. Eden which he later defined as giving 'for the first time . . . a practical and hopeful policy towards Turkey'. As soon as the Russian front shut down for the winter, Turkey should receive 'a substantial packet of tanks, A.T. guns and flak'. He specified 1,000 tanks[1] and 1,000 anti-tank and anti-aircraft guns. If deliveries could begin in November, the promise of them would keep Turkey neutral during the summer. Mr. Churchill hoped that the arrival of these weapons would make Turkey a belligerent ally in the spring of 1943.

(c) The Foreign Office thought that the Prime Minister's proposal assumed either that there would be no German attack on Turkey until the spring of 1943, or no attack at all, in which case she might be used as a base for attacking the Axis. Meanwhile, all that we asked was that she should remain faithful to her alliance with us and keep out intruders. On this assumption the Foreign Office supported the proposal. On May 14 Mr. Eden wrote to the Prime

(d) Minister accordingly. He said, however, that our offer must be additional to existing promises, and that we must stand by our policy if Turkey were attacked before the spring of 1943. Mr. Eden pointed out the shipping and supply difficulties in the way of an unconditional promise and concluded: 'Until we see our way clearer I feel it would be very risky to say anything to the Turks.'

(e) The Prime Minister replied the next day that as far as possible we should keep promises already made, but that if Turkey were attacked during the summer or autumn of 1942, there were practically no forces to send. Even if we had large forces, communications from Syria would make their movement difficult. Mr. Churchill said that his idea was a joint Anglo-American offer, operative after November, to encourage Turkey through 'these anxious months' and enable her to participate in a campaign in 1943 'should our affairs in these regions prosper'.

(f) Mr. Eden answered on May 18 that he supported the new programme if there were reasonable hope of fulfilling it despite shipping and other difficulties. A Foreign Office minute of the third

---

[1] The Prime Minister had in mind the expected large increase in American production from which this allocation might be made.

(a) R2343/403/44. (b) M178/2, R3225/70/44; M201/2, R3742/70/44. (c) R2732/70/44 (d) PM/42/93, R3225/70/44. (e) M187/2, R3741, 3742/70/44. (f) PM/42/118, R3742/70/44.

week of May noted that the Germans had just offered the Turks a division of tanks. Mr. Eden later pointed out to the Prime Minister that the despatch of equipment to Turkey on the scale proposed might mean that other areas, e.g. the United Kingdom and theatres of war dependent on American supplies, might have to go short. He concluded: 'It goes without saying that if the proposal is now put to the Turks we must at all costs carry it out when the moment comes.'

At the request of the Prime Minister the Foreign Office drafted (a) a message from him to Mr. Roosevelt. The draft described the role which we wanted Turkey to play as that of a 'protective pad' in the Middle East, and outlined Mr. Churchill's plan for a promise of a substantial quantity of munitions in the hope of turning Turkey into an active ally in the spring of 1943 and giving her confidence meanwhile. The Prime Minister asked Mr. Roosevelt to co-operate in making a promise to the Turks, though this promise must avoid the impression that we were trying to drag the Turks into the war, since they remembered the successful German efforts to commit them to the last war. The Prime Minister accepted the (b) draft and wrote to Mr. Eden on June 13 that he would hand it to the President himself[1] after he had received the comments of the Chiefs of Staff Committee.

Meanwhile the Foreign Office considered other counter-measures (c) to the German pressure on Turkey. Turkish generals and journalists were being invited to visit Germany. The re-opening of the railway between Turkey and Bulgaria would make possible the resumption of Turco-German trade. Turkish merchants would then exert pressure on the Turkish Government to permit an extension of trade with Germany which would increase the volume of goods and so lower prices. The Foreign Office thought that the Turkish Government might acquiesce in order to alleviate a disturbing internal situation. They had already instructed Sir H. Knatchbull-Hugessen to inform the Turks that we disliked their acceptance of the German arms credit and offer a division of tanks.

On June 5 Mr. Eden informed Sir H. Knatchbull-Hugessen that he had considerable misgivings about the German offer of war material and the alacrity with which the Turks had accepted it. The only certain counter was successful competition, and the Foreign Office were considering urgently the possibility of increasing supplies. Mr. Eden asked how we could hold our position. We wanted to be sure that the Turkish Government were resisting German attempts to establish a position for themselves, and thereby to undermine the

---

[1] The Prime Minister arrived in Washington on June 18.

(a) R3743/70/44; Churchill Papers/446. (b) M247/2, R3743/70/44. (c) R3729/486/44.

Anglo-Turkish connexion and to repeat in Turkey the technique of demoralisation successfully applied to Yugoslavia.

(a)   On the previous day Mr. Eden had told the Turkish Ambassador that he was increasingly anxious about German pressure. As an ally we felt justified in warning the Turkish Government against German manoeuvres, and we expected the latter to resist them. We were doing our best to supply arms and hoped to be able to provide more. M. Orbay reassured Mr. Eden. He said that Turkey was suspicious of Germany after her experience in the last war, and would not accept the fate of a mere German dependency. Mr. Eden warned M. Orbay that Germany wished to see Turkey embroiled with Russia, and asked him to warn his Government of the risk which we thought they were running.

(b)   On June 13 M. Orbay told Sir O. Sargent that he was instructed to assure His Majesty's Government that they could continue to have confidence in the Turkish Government. They could consider Turkey as the 'rampart' against any penetration by Germany through Turkey. It was out of the question that Turkey would enter a combination against Russia or foster designs to the detriment of that Power. His Majesty's Government could so inform the Soviet Government. Sir O. Sargent warned M. Orbay in strong terms of

(c)   Germany's plans and intentions. Meanwhile on June 11 Sir H. Knatchbull-Hugessen had telegraphed to the Foreign Office that we were faced with a determined German drive in Turkey, but that it was a potential rather than an actual danger and should not be exaggerated. The real danger lay in Germany's 'industrial drive'. The general course of the war would be the most important factor determining the Turkish attitude, but at the moment there was no leaning towards Germany.

(d)   On June 20 Sir H. Knatchbull-Hugessen had an audience with President Inönü, who repeated the usual formula about his loyalty to the Anglo-Turkish connexion and confidence in our policy and sympathy with it. Sir H. Knatchbull-Hugessen said that our policy was a long-term rather than a wartime one, and that it was based on the strengthening of political and economic relations and closer collaboration in the post-war period. He warned the President against German manoeuvres, and pointed out that, if Germany were allowed to regain her economic foothold, Turkey might find herself in the position from which she had tried three years ago to extricate herself, i.e. political allegiance to Great Britain but economic bondage to Germany. The President and M. Saracoglu said that they realised this danger and would avoid it. They had

---

(a) R3717/486/44.   (b) R3908/50/44.   (c) R3854/810/44.   (d) R4092/72/44; R4106/403/44.

always made clear to von Papen that they could do nothing contrary to the Anglo-Turkish alliance, and must inform us of their dealings with Germany. The President said that he supported our Russian policy.

A month later Mr. Eden mentioned to the War Cabinet the (a) progress of the Turkish negotiations in Berlin. He said that the original agreement for the supply of German arms provided only for an expenditure of 100 million marks to be covered by a credit. M. Numan had assured Sir H. Knatchbull-Hugessen that the Turkish Government would not accept anything costing more than a total of 100–110 million marks, but it was uncertain whether the Turks would refuse the balance of such valuable equipment, none of which we or the United States could supply. If the Turkish Government accepted these arms, Germany would go far to renew her hold on the Turkish economy. Dr. Clodius was now discussing semi-official proposals with the Turkish delegation in Berlin to discover ways whereby the extra cost of the arms over the agreed 100 million mark credit could be covered. These proposals included some form of barter agreement which would cover a wide range of Turkish products then being purchased by Great Britain for supply or pre-emptive reasons.

Mr. Eden believed that the Germans were in earnest in their promise to deliver the equipment within the next six months. If they did so, the comparison of German with British supplies would be extremely unfavourable to us. In 1939 we and the French had granted the Turks an armaments credit of £25,000,000 but three years later only half of it had been used. If, therefore, the Germans fulfilled their promises, they would be supplying Turkey in one-sixth of the time with three times as much equipment as we had done.[1] Mr. Eden pointed out that circumstances made it impossible for us to outbid the German offer, and that there was little we could do.

On August 4 the Prime Minister arrived in Cairo to discuss the military situation with the Commanders-in-Chief, Middle East. The Chiefs of Staff Committee also came to the conclusion that a (b) German move through Turkey was unlikely while the Germans were engaged against Russia. The Turks were also unlikely to accept German demands unless our position in the Middle East had gravely deteriorated or they had lost faith in an ultimate Allied victory and the Germans had built up an adequate force to coerce them. The

---

[1] There seems to be an error in these calculations. Taking the 1939 rate of RM.20 = £1, RM.100,000,000 would equal £5,000,000 or approximately two-fifths of £12,500,000, not 'three times as much'.

(a) WP(42)304; R4864/486/44. (b) WP(42)335; COS(42)357.

(a) Chiefs of Staff thought that an attack through Anatolia on the northern front of the Middle East theatre was improbable before the spring of 1943.

(b)   On August 6 the Turkish Prime Minister made a declaration in the Chamber outlining the policy of the new Government.[1] He reaffirmed Turkey's intention to resist aggression and described her attitude as one of active neutrality. He said that the Anglo-Turkish alliance constituted the fundamental factor in Turkish policy, and that a 'further clear and loyal manifestation of [the] same policy reveals itself in [the] Turco-German part [*sic*? Pact] which sealed once again reciprocal comprehension and friendship of two countries'. M. Saracoglu did not mention Russia. Mr. Eden noted: 'All that we ask of Turkey now is that she should protect her territories against all comers, and stay at home.'

(c)   On August 25 Mr. Eden told the War Cabinet of an interview with the Turkish Ambassador earlier in the day. The Ambassador's attitude had changed and showed much anxiety about the position. He had said that if Turkey were attacked she would fight, but that it would be of great assistance to know what help in arms she could count on receiving from us by a given date. At Mr. Eden's request, the Prime Minister agreed to see M. Orbay. In making this enquiry M. Orbay had acted without instructions. Sir H. Knatchbull-Hugessen, however, in a series of telegrams recommended to the

(d) Foreign Office that we should make an immediate gift of specialized equipment. He thought that Turkey would resist attack in any circumstances; he was not so sure about the possible effect of an outstanding German success in Russia and the Middle East on the Turkish attitude to German demands for the passage of troops or war material. On September 2 he said that the provision of some

(e) tanks, aircraft and anti-tank guns at a moment when the Germans had only given promises and were apparently bargaining about them might have a decisive effect on the Turkish will to resist, but such equipment must be supplied at once if the Turks were to withstand the temptation to bargain for it with Germany.

(f)   The War Cabinet referred the Ambassador's suggestion to the
(g) Chiefs of Staff, but the Foreign Office noted that nothing could be released from the Middle East for the moment; even if we could spare something from other sources, it would not reach Turkey before

---

(h)   [1] Sir H. Knatchbull-Hugessen reported on July 9 the formation of a new government (owing to the death of the former Prime Minister, Dr. Refik Saydam) by M. Saracoglu. M. Numan Menemencioglu later succeeded M. Saracoglu as Minister for Foreign Affairs.

(a) WM(42)104.2, C.A.   (b) R5215, 5200/810/44.   (c) WM(42)118.2, C.A.
(d) R5690/486/44; R5730, 6044/486/44.   (e) R5828/2/44.   (f) WM(42)119.
(g) R6436/2/44. (h) R4534, 4624/810/44.

the end of November. They suggested, however, to the Chiefs of Staff that the psychological effect on the Turks of giving them some specialised weapons of their own would yield political results out of all proportion to the purely military effect on the Turkish army. On the Prime Minister's personal initiative the Chiefs of Staff (a) worked out a scheme for supplying Turkey with arms. Mr. Churchill asked that a promise should be contingent upon a favourable turn of events in the Western Desert. He later spoke of the gift as 'a token (b) of comradeship and comprehension'.

The Prime Minister saw M. Orbay on September 24. He read (c) him the list of equipment to be sent to Turkey before the end of the year. He said that the only thing that would prevent the despatch of this material would be a very unfavourable turn of events on the Egyptian front, of which there was no danger. Mr. Eden later instructed Sir. H. Knatchbull-Hugessen to give the list of equipment to the President of the Republic and to make the most of 'this considerable contribution on our part to Turkey's security and ability to play her part when necessary in joining against our common enemies'.

Sir H. Knatchbull-Hugessen carried out his instructions on (d) October 1. The President expressed 'gratification' and M. Saracoglu the 'greatest pleasure' on seeing the list. Otherwise the Turkish Government showed no enthusiasm about the offer, and the Foreign Office were disappointed at its off-hand acceptance. On October 17 Sir H. Knatchbull-Hugessen met M. Berter, the Secretary-General, and contrasted the Turkish behaviour to the Germans and ourselves. They had not even thanked us for this gift, but to the Germans they showed anxiety even to stretch their existing obligations to agree about further supplies of chrome. M. Berter said that we had made our promise subject to military needs in Egypt, and that the moment to thank us would be when the material arrived. The Foreign Office recognised the importance of the Prime Minister's offer as a political (e) gesture, but thought that even as such it had apparently failed.

(iii)

The question of Turkish chrome: British and American attempts to prevent the supply of chrome to Germany (June–December 1942).

The Prime Minister had intended that the British gift of arms (f) should be kept separate from the chrome negotiations which Sir H. Knatchbull-Hugessen had been instructed to start in June. In Mr.

(a) R6135, 6190/2/44. (b) M432/2, R6946/2/44. (c) R6459/2/44. (d) R6492, 6578, 6946, 6947/2/44; R6547/1429/44. (e) R6947/2/44. (f) M432/2, R6946/2/44.

Churchill's own words, 'I am after the Turk; I am not after your
(a) chrome'. The Foreign Office in fact attached more importance than
the Prime Minister to success in the negotiations for chrome. We
wanted to prevent the Germans, who were short of chrome, from
getting any of it from Turkey. We (and the Americans) also wanted
the chrome.[1] Furthermore, if, after challenging Germany on this
issue, we failed to get our way, our prestige would suffer. Sir A.
Cadogan also thought that we should regard the question as the
(b) touchstone of Turkish friendship. Mr. Eden endorsed this view that
the matter was a test of German ability to coerce Turkey and of the
Turkish will to resist German coercion. Nevertheless Mr. Eden
(c) agreed with the Prime Minister that the offer of arms, which was
spontaneous and unconditional, should not be used to bargain about
chrome.

(d)   On October 5 Sir H. Knatchbull-Hugessen had set out the British
proposals about chrome in a letter to the Turkish Prime Minister.
He asked that we should receive the whole of the 1942 output to
which we were entitled, that we should be given at least equality
of treatment with the Germans in 1943 and 1944, and that we should
have an option over Turkish chrome from 1945 onwards.

(e)   The Turkish Government had agreed to the first and third
demands but maintained that for 1943 and 1944 their obligations
to Germany must take priority over our demands. On this basis,
assuming the total Turkish annual production to be 100,000 tons,
Germany would receive 72,500 tons in 1943.[2] There was a further
possibility that the Turks might argue when the time came that
they must satisfy the total German requirements before they could
turn to ours. This would mean that the Germans would receive
over the two years 180,000 tons, and that only 20,000 tons would be
left for us. The Ministry of Economic Warfare and the Treasury
agreed on an attempt to gain at least equality of treatment with
Germany in 1943 and 1944.

(f)   At the request of Sir H. Knatchbull-Hugessen, Sir A. Cadogan
saw M. Orbay on October 16 on Mr. Eden's behalf. He handed
him a *communication orale* setting out the state of our negotiations
with Turkey and giving an *exposé* of our claims. Sir A. Cadogan
emphasised the repeated assurances of the Turkish Prime Minister
and Minister for Foreign Affairs that the Berlin negotiations were not

---

[1] See note at end of this section.

[2] See note at end of this section. The promise to Germany was for 45,000 tons plus a
second instalment also of 45,000 tons in 1943. After providing the Germans with the
first 45,000 tons the Turks would have 55,000 tons for disposal. If they divided this
quantity between Great Britain and Germany each would receive 27,500 tons. The total
German amount would thus be 72,500 tons.

(a) R6306/111/44. (b) R6837/134/44. (c) PM/42/211, R6946/2/44. (d) R6673/134/44.
(e) R6753/134/44; R283/49/44 (1943). (f) R6837, 6935, 6936/134/44.

connected with chrome; he also referred to the earlier assurance of October 1941 that, notwithstanding the provisions of the Clodius Agreement, we should be accorded equal treatment with the Germans and that our needs would be met.

Sir A. Cadogan said that we based our claims to chrome on the Anglo-Turkish alliance as well as on Turkish assurances. M. Orbay at once replied that we could rely on him to do his 'duty'. As allies we were of course entitled to equal treatment and more. He was sure that there was a misunderstanding, and would telegraph immediately to his Government. He had come to London on the assumption that Turkey and Great Britain would co-operate as allies; if that were not to be so, he would not stay.

The Foreign Office, with the full support of the United States (a) Government,[1] employed 'maximum' diplomatic pressure on the Turkish Government during October. Sir H. Knatchbull-Hugessen reported that in their anxiety to get war materials, the Turks had been drawn into the trap against which we had warned them, and had gone further with the Germans than the strict letter of the (b) Clodius Agreement necessitated. They had broken many assurances to us and were now in a tangle, but we should not hold them to all their promises to the point of forcing on them a choice between embroilment with Germany or a major quarrel with ourselves. If we and the United States presented an uncompromisingly united front they might give way. On the other hand a rigid insistence on the assurances given to us might defeat our immediate object and damage permanently our relations with the Turks. Sir H. Knatchbull-Hugessen thought that we should get the question on to the broader basis that no chrome should be available to Germany except that genuinely mined after January 8, 1943, and that deliveries to Germany in 1943 and 1944 should be kept to the minimum.

On the night of November 3–4, Sir H. Knatchbull-Hugessen (c) telegraphed that we were not entirely justified in regarding the supply of chrome as the test of our relations with Turkey. Turkey was cautiously trying to stand well with both sides; there were no signs of any wish to join Germany or a weakening of determination to resist German pressure if it came. If it were a straight issue between friendship with ourselves and friendship with Germany, he would not be so reluctant to force a choice on Turkey, and in such case he thought that her ultimate decision would not be in doubt; the doubt arose, however, from the Russian factor. Turkey's

---

[1] Mr. Laurence Steinhardt had presented his letters of credence as American Ambas- (d) sador to Turkey on March 10, 1942. Sir H. Knatchbull-Hugessen spoke of him as a 'most willing collaborator'.

(a) R7058, 7059, 6886/134/44.   (b) R7264, 7296/134/44.   (c) R7391/134/44.
(d) R4841/788/44.

'historical distrust of Russia' was as strong as ever, and her sympathies with the United Nations were 'tempered by the fact that Russia is one of them'. Sir H. Knatchbull-Hugessen was sure that 'one of the motives which prompted [Turkey] to seek arms at all costs from Germany' was 'the desire to be strong against Russia'.

(a)   The Foreign Office had noted on November 2 that we had not intended a serious change in our policy if we failed to get our way over the chrome issue. For major strategical reasons we had to continue investing money and material in Turkey. Moreover, our firm attitude had produced some results. Turkey had not signed the arms agreement in Berlin, and had refused the German request for unconditional delivery of the first 45,000 tons of chrome provided for under the Clodius Agreement. Further, the Turkish delegation in Berlin had received instructions not to sign the supplementary chrome agreement for which the Clodius Agreement provided until the £T18,000,000 worth of war material stipulated for in the Clodius Agreement had been delivered.

The alternative to continuing to hold out for our demands would be to strike an immediate bargain regarding the 1942 production, and to remind the Turks that we were prepared to pay a higher price for it.[1] As matters were, our offer of a higher price for 1942 chrome was conditional on a satisfactory solution of our chrome demands for 1943 and 1944. Under the alternative we should rely on Turkish generosity to give us the best treatment possible in 1943 and 1944, having regard to their 'prior obligations' to Germany.

(b)   On November 4 the Foreign Office accordingly instructed Sir H. Knatchbull-Hugessen that they had considered whether we should hold out for equal treatment with the Germans or relax our pressure and trust to Turkish goodwill to restrict deliveries to Germany to a minimum. We had never contemplated a serious change of policy towards Turkey in the event of failure over this issue. We thought, however, that for the moment we should hold out for our demands. We might eventually be forced to close the deal regarding 1942 chrome by paying the higher price without insisting on the conditions then attached regarding 1943 and 1944 production, but it would be a mistake to throw in our hand while the battle for Egypt was undecided. We should maintain our pressure, but there was no reason for increasing it. Our object should be to prevent the Turkish Government from concluding with Germany agreements to our

---

(c)   [1] This offer was first made on October 5, and repeated on October 20. In an *aide-mémoire* of that date, Sir H. Knatchbull-Hugessen informed the Turkish Government that, in return for equality of treatment with the Germans in 1943 and 1944, we were prepared to pay for 1942 chrome at the price which the Germans were offering for 1943 chrome. This price was considerably above the price laid down in our agreement for 1942.

(a) R7330/134/44.   (b) R7330/134/44.   (c) R7330/134/44.

disadvantage and to hold out for our own requirements. Sir H. Knatchbull-Hugessen was instructed to make it clear to the Minister for Foreign Affairs that he would gladly co-operate with him in finding ways of satisfying British requirements in the manner least likely to involve Turkey in difficulties with Germany.

On November 4 M. Orbay asked to see Mr. Eden on the chrome (a) question. Mr. Eden impressed on him that German acquisition of Turkish chrome in 1943 would be of the utmost importance to Germany's war effort; we felt entitled as an ally to ask that Turkey should limit her export of chrome to Germany to an amount compatible with the strictest possible interpretation of her obligations. M. Orbay agreed that under the alliance we ought to receive at least as much Turkish chrome as Germany; he felt sure that this was his Government's intention in so far as they could carry it out honourably without breaking their engagement with Germany.

By the third week in November the position was more hopeful. (b) The Berlin negotiations were at a standstill and the arms agreement was not signed. The Turks were insisting on the Germans fulfilling the conditions of the Clodius Agreement. The Foreign Office thought that the British negotiations might drag on into January without a conclusive result, and a point might be reached when it would be in our interest to close the deal regarding 1942 production by paying the higher price without insisting on conditions regarding 1943 and 1944 production. The Foreign Office asked Treasury consent to this step.

Late in November Sir H. Knatchbull-Hugessen came to London (c) for consultation. On December 7 the position was discussed with him at a meeting in the Foreign Office. After further discussions with representatives of the Treasury, Ministry of Economic Warfare and Chrome Control, the Foreign Office accepted on December 10 the view that we ought not to delay if we were to obtain possession of all chrome mined and above ground on January 7, 1943. We should withdraw our original conditions, and offer to pay unconditionally the increased price for 1942 chrome. A delay in the negotiations in order to get satisfactory terms in 1943 and 1944 would risk our position regarding 1942 production.

On December 11 the British Minister at Ankara, Mr. Sterndale- (d) Bennett, was instructed to inform the Turkish Government that, in view of the substantial progress in reaching agreement, His Majesty's Government made a formal offer to pay the German price for all chrome mined between September 25, 1942, and January 8, 1943,

---

(a) R7404/134/44. (b) R7506, 7698/134/44. (c) R8325, 8467/134/44. (d) R8467/134/44.

(a) not yet declared.[1] The Foreign Office reported to Lord Halifax that by announcing our readiness to pay the increased (i.e. German) price for 1942 chrome, we hoped to absorb all existing supplies from Turkey and so make it impossible for the Germans to obtain their 45,000 tons for a considerable period in 1943. Lord Halifax was instructed to ask whether the United States Government would share the extra cost. The United States Government agreed to do so.

(b)   On December 12 Mr. Sterndale-Bennett reported that he had now received the Turkish reply to Sir H. Knatchbull-Hugessen's letter of October 5 to the Prime Minister. It took the form of a letter, enclosing a *communication orale*, from the Turkish Minister for Foreign Affairs to the British Minister dated December 11. The Assistant Secretary-General hoped that the proposals would not be the subject of further argument or be accepted grudgingly. The Turkish Government had made an effort to give us the greatest possible satisfaction to clear away the chrome dispute. In practice obligations to Germany would be interpreted with the utmost rigidity. Mr. Sterndale-Bennett thought that we should accept the reply since we were ultimately dependent on Turkish goodwill in the matter. He proposed that we should answer that we appreciated the effort made to meet us and that we accepted the Turkish communication as constituting an agreement between the two Governments about

(c) chrome. On December 21 Mr. Sterndale-Bennett informed M. Numan that His Majesty's Government were happy to accept his letter of December 11 and the enclosed communication together with Sir H. Knatchbull-Hugessen's letter of October 5 as the basis of Anglo-Turkish arrangements for disposal of the Turkish chrome production.

(d)   The position in December thus was that we were to obtain physical possession of all chrome above ground on January 1, 1943. As for 1943 and 1944 production, the Turkish Government would give us all the chrome which they were not obliged to give to the Germans under the Clodius Agreement and the supplementary agreement contemplated therein.

Note to section (iii)

Turkish chrome[2]

In the early years of the war Turkey was producing about

---

[1] i.e. not yet declared by the mines. There was evidence that the mines were holding back the chrome in the expectation of getting higher prices from the Germans if not from the British Government. They knew of the British conditional offer of October 5 and were waiting for it to be made official and unconditional.

[2] For the negotiations with Turkey over chrome, see Medlicott, *The Economic Blockade* Vol. I (London, 1952), Chs. VII and VIII, also Vol. II (London, 1959), Ch. VIII.

(a) R8567/2/44.   (b) R8548, 8553/134/44.   (c) R6673/134/44; R283/49/44 (1943). (d) R8569/134/44.

100,000 tons of chrome ore per annum. The importance of the chrome to Great Britain and the United States at the end of 1942 was mainly pre-emptive, since at this time the American deficiency of chrome due to the loss of the Philippines had been largely offset. The availability of Turkish chrome to Great Britain was limited by the shipping problem. On the other hand Germany's need for Turkish chrome was vital since her stocks were expected to be exhausted at the end of 1942 and her minimum needs at the tempo of operations at that time were estimated at 215,000 tons per annum, of which she could obtain only about 140,000 tons from territories under her control.

Turkish obligations to Great Britain were laid down in an Anglo-Franco-Turkish Agreement dated January 8, 1940, by which Turkey agreed to supply Great Britain and France (in a proportion of 11 : 4) with the whole of her existing stocks of chrome plus the amount produced during the period covered by the agreement, which was concluded for two years and renewable for a third. French rights under this agreement were assumed by Great Britain after the collapse of France; the last of a series of subsidiary purchase agreements laid down arrangements for our purchase of the total stock at the end of 1941 (amounting to some 50,000 or 60,000 tons) plus the whole of Turkish production between January 1, 1942, and January 8, 1943. The price agreed on was 140s. per ton for 48 per cent ore, but a higher price was subsequently offered.

Turkish obligations to Germany arose from the Clodius Agreement of October 9, 1941, which provided *inter alia* for the exchange on a value basis of goods figuring on lists appended to the agreement and including Turkish chrome and German war material. The total amount expended by either side at any given moment was to be kept approximately equal; no single item in the Turkish list was to figure excessively in the total. The total value of goods to be exported from the German list in question was £T55 million, including £T18 million worth of war material. The maximum amount of chrome which the Turks undertook to export was 45,000 tons of specified grade, deliverable after January 15, 1943. A subsequent agreement fixed the price of Turkish chrome to be supplied to Germany at 270s. for 48 per cent ore. (Both the British and German prices followed a sliding scale, i.e. the price per ton rose or fell if the grade was more or less than 48 per cent.)

In addition the Clodius Agreement provided that after the Germans had supplied the £T18,000,000 worth of war material, and before March 31, 1943, the Turks would conclude a further agreement for the export of chrome against war material and would then allow the export of 90,000 tons of chrome for each of the years 1943 and 1944—a total of 180,000 tons, including the 45,000 tons referred to above. It was arguable that the supply of the first 45,000 tons was subject to the same condition as the conclusion of the new agreement,

(a) R8026/134/44.

viz. the preliminary supply by Germany of £T18,000,000 worth of war material; but the Turkish Government did not maintain this interpretation.

(a)   The importance of chrome was due to the fact that it was an indispensable ingredient in the manufacture of certain types of high-grade steel required for tanks, aircraft engines and many other munitions. His Majesty's Government did not hope at the end of 1942 to deprive Germany of more than one-half of the annual Turkish production. If Germany, however, succeeded only in getting 50,000 tons from Turkey, she would be left with a deficit of 25,000 tons below her estimated minimum annual requirements. Even so relatively small a deficit would have an appreciably adverse effect on the German output of high-grade steels. If Germany obtained the full amount which she was demanding from Turkey, i.e. 90,000 tons annually, she would amply cover her requirements.

(iv)

The Prime Minister's proposals for persuading Turkey to enter the war: Sir H. Knatchbull-Hugessen's discussions with the Foreign Office and the Chiefs of Staff: Mr. Eden's message to the Turkish Ministers: Turkish views in favour of maintaining neutrality (November 18, 1942–January 22, 1943).

After the battle of El Alamein and the landings in North Africa the Prime Minister was more hopeful of persuading Turkey to enter the war, and more insistent that a very strong effort should be made to persuade her to do so in the spring of 1943. At this time— immediately after the success of the landings—President Roosevelt was inclined to continue and enlarge the scope of Allied action in
(b) the Mediterranean. In a telegram of November 12 to the Prime Minister he hoped that the latter, with the Chiefs of Staff in London, and the President himself with the Combined Staff in Washington, might 'make a survey of the possibilities', including a 'forward movement directed against Sardinia, Sicily, Italy, Greece and other Balkan areas', with the 'possibility of obtaining Turkey's support for an attack through the Black Sea against Germany's flank'.
(c)   Mr. Churchill replied on the following day:

'Nothing pleases me more than to read what you say about bringing Turkey in. Our minds have indeed moved together on this as in so much else. It seems to me that there are four stages: (a) the clearance of the North African coast and the opening of the Mediterranean for military traffic; (b) a guarantee to Turkey by Great Britain, Russia

---

(a) R7206/134/44. (b) T1483/2, No. 210, Churchill Papers/446. (c) T1491/2, No. 189. Churchill Papers/446.

and the United States of her territorial integrity and *status quo*;
(c) the rapid stocking up of Turkey with British and American arms,
particularly tanks, flak and anti-tank guns; (d) the movement of the
air forces to the Russian southern flank, which must in any case be
pressed forward at once, and the gathering during the winter of a
considerable army in Syria. I hope next week to make you specific
proposals and suggestions.'

Mr. Eden was less confident of the chances of this plan. He minuted
on the draft of the telegram: 'I doubt the value of (b). Russia has (a)
already given assurances jointly with us to Turkey. We must remember that the one fixed point in Turkish policy so far has been to keep
out of the war.' Mr. Eden suggested the omission of (b), and the
addition of a warning about 'Turkish policy hitherto'. He doubted
whether 'any promises or cajolery will bring Turkey into the war.
If we mean to do this, we must try to embroil her with Germany
whilst at the same time giving her arms and assurances of assistance.'
Mr. Eden did not insist on his proposed changes. The Prime Minister
therefore sent the telegram as drafted to Mr. Roosevelt.

On November 18 the Prime Minister wrote a note to the Chiefs (b)
of Staff in which he said definitely: 'I wish to record my opinion
that Turkey may be won if the proper measures are taken.' He
thought that the Turks would want a place at the Peace Conference. They also wished to be well armed. Their army had been
mobilised for nearly three years and was 'warlike'. Hitherto 'Turkey
had been restrained by fear from fulfilling her obligations, and we
have taken an indulgent view of her policy on account of our own
inability to help. The situation has now changed.' We could now
build up a 'powerful British land and air force to assist the Turks'.

The Prime Minister suggested the following 'order of procedure,
political and military': Turkey should be offered a Russian-
American-British guarantee of territorial integrity and *status quo*.
We should follow this offer by the despatch of a strong Anglo-
American Military Mission. During the winter we should equip
Turkey from Egypt and the United States on the largest possible
scale. We should urge the Russians to clear the Caucasus and to
resume their intention of striking south-west from the region north
of Stalingrad towards Rostov-on-Don. The ultimate result of these
operations would be the opening of the Dardanelles.

The Prime Minister sent a copy of this minute to the President. (c)
The President replied on November 19 in more guarded terms than (d)
those of his earlier telegram. He said that the Combined Chiefs of

---

(a) PM/42/272, Churchill Papers/446.   (b) Churchill Papers/446.   (c) T1524–5/2,
Nos. 194–5, Churchill Papers/446.   (d) T1540/2, No. 217, Churchill Papers/446.

Staff were now studying the possibilities of future action in the Mediterranean. He did not mention Turkey.

(a)   On November 24 the Prime Minister telegraphed to Stalin that President Roosevelt agreed with him generally in thinking that we should make a new effort to bring Turkey into the war.[1] For this purpose the Prime Minister proposed that the United States should join in an Anglo-Soviet guarantee of the territorial integrity and status of Turkey. We were already sending Turkey a considerable quantity of munitions, including 200 tanks. We hoped by the spring to have an army in Syria ready to go to assist the Turks. It was evident that Russian operations in or north of the Caucasus would have a great influence on the Turkish decision. The Prime Minister pointed out that if Turkey entered the war, we should be able not

(b) only to open the Dardanelles, but also to bomb the Roumanian oilfields. Stalin replied[2] on November 27 that he agreed with the Prime Minister and the President about the desirability of bringing Turkey into the war in the spring. He implied, however, that he did not regard Turkish belligerency (and a consequent change in Allied strategical plans) as an alternative to a second front in Europe in the spring of 1943. He said that he had 'paid close attention to your communication that you and the Americans do not relax preparations along your south-eastern and southern coasts in order to keep the Germans pinned in the Pas de Calais, etc., and that you are ready to take advantage of any favourable opportunity'. Stalin hoped that this did not mean a change of mind 'with regard to your promise given in Moscow to establish a second front in Western Europe in the spring of 1943'.

(c)   The Prime Minister sent to the President a copy of his message to Stalin, and of the latter's reply. Northing further, however, seems to have been said at this time about the proposed guarantee to Turkey. Meanwhile the Foreign Office—in view of the reports of Sir H. Knatchbull-Hugessen—were much less confident about the possibility of convincing the Turks that it was to their interest to enter the war. During Sir H. Knatchbull-Hugessen's visit to London they and the Chiefs of Staff went into the whole question raised by

(d) the Prime Minister. On December 4 the Chiefs of Staff discussed with the Ambassador the Turkish attitude. He pointed out that the main preoccupation of the Turks was not to come into the war but to keep out of it, and to remain strong against the possibility of pressure from Russia later on. He thought that the Turks fully

---

[1] Mr. Churchill also mentioned planning for 1943 in other theatres of war.
[2] This reply dealt with a number of other subjects, including the question of Admiral Darlan.

(a) T1584/2, Churchill Papers/446. (b) T1608/2, Churchill Papers/446. (c) T1633/2, No. 216, Churchill Papers/446. (d) COS(42)335; R8534/24/44.

realised that their interests lay in an Allied victory; that they were now convinced that the Allies would win the war, and that recently there had been a definite improvement in their relations with Russia.

Sir H. Knatchbull-Hugessen said that the Germans were making little progress in Turkey. The German Embassy took every opportunity of encouraging trouble or discontent; they doubtless had a small number of people in their pay and would use bribery and subversive methods to encourage any feeling against the Turkish Government. Sir H. Knatchbull-Hugessen reported gradual economic deterioration in Turkey, increasing inefficiency, widespread corruption and probable food shortages. The main problem was in regard to communications; railways and roads were inadequate and there was a great shortage of rolling stock. Nonetheless the maintenance of close ties with Great Britain remained a fundamental factor in Turkish foreign policy; American influence was not of great account.

Sir H. Knatchbull-Hugessen pointed out to the Chiefs of Staff the difficulty of persuading Turkey to enter the war on our side or to allow us to cross Turkish territory for an attack on Europe, since the Turks had never forgotten that they had been tricked into war in 1914. A second factor was the course of events at the time Italy entered the war. The British and French Governments had pressed the Turks to declare war in accordance with the terms of their treaty but had not informed them of the position in France.[1] The Turks thought that we had been trying to jockey them into war to help us at the sacrifice of their own interests. These two considerations had probably affected the Turkish attitude in 1941, when, although we had asked for no military action, we had urged them to put up a stiff political front. The Turks had not distinguished between military and political action, and had suspected that we were trying to involve them in war indirectly. Mr. Eden noted that this summary of the Turkish attitude was probably correct.

Sir H. Knatchbull-Hugessen thought that it would be extremely hard to draw the Turks into action unless they considered that it was in their interests to come into the war. They would not take this view as long as there was a serious threat of German retaliation.[2] It would thus be useless to make a definite request or proposal to the Turkish Government. The only practicable policy was to let the Turkish Government realise in general discussions of the situation that the problem of belligerency would present itself. The Turkish General Staff had already suggested that a British proposal for

---

[1] Sir H. Knatchbull-Hugessen agreed that the Turkish Ambassador in France had kept the Turkish Government informed. The Turks, however, may have resented the fact that the British Government did not frankly explain the position.

[2] There was a non-aggression clause in the Turkish Treaty with Germany.

further staff conversations would be well received. If such conversations could be begun, the problem of Turkey's future action was certain to arise. A second possible opening might be through the discussions which Sir H. Knatchbull-Hugessen was being instructed to hold with the Turks about schemes for a future Balkan settlement.[1]

(a)   Sir H. Knatchbull-Hugessen attended a meeting at the Foreign Office on December 4 when the internal position in Turkey was discussed. He said that Turkey was determined to stay out of the war and that only three things would bring her into it: direct attack or a situation where attack seemed likely; an internal situation where economic crisis and political agitation became so aggravated that participation in the war would seem to the Government the only way of pulling the country together; desire to participate in the peace settlement by becoming a member of the United Nations, i.e. by abandoning their attitude of neutrality. Their fear was now not of a separate Russo-German peace, but of an Anglo-Russian arrangement for collaboration after the war to Turkey's detriment.

As the result of these discussions the Foreign Office agreed upon the action which Sir H. Knatchbull-Hugessen should take on his return to Turkey. We had not reached a point where we could make definite proposals to the Turkish Government which would not either frighten or antagonise them, but the occasion would be a good one for sending a message in general terms as a starting-off point for further talks between Sir H. Knatchbull-Hugessen and the Turkish Minister for Foreign Affairs on Turkey's future policy in view of the new war situation in the Mediterranean. Sir H. Knatchbull-Hugessen should therefore make the Turkish Government realise that the time was coming when it would be in their own interests to take a more active part in the war. We could raise with them the question of the post-war settlement of the Balkan problem. The Turks would probably be in favour of the idea of a Balkan Confederation, particularly as a means of excluding Russian influence. Turkey was, however, not likely to have any say in the matter at the peace settlement unless she qualified as one of the United Nations.

(b)   On December 18 Mr. Eden approved the instructions to Sir H. Knatchbull-Hugessen. He was first to deliver messages of good wishes from Mr. Eden to the Turkish Prime Minister and the Minister for Foreign Affairs. Mr. Eden repeated that close co-operation and friendship based on the Anglo-Turkish Treaty of 1939 formed one of the main points of British policy.

Mr. Eden gave Sir H. Knatchbull-Hugessen a note outlining a plan

---

[1] See below, pp. 109–10.

(a) R8381/810/44. (b) R8381/810/44.

for a possible organisation of the Balkans after the war. The note mentioned three *desiderata*—common defence and a common economic system and foreign policy—and also a federative system and some form of centralised or collective organisation to which each Government would delegate some of its sovereign powers. Mr. Eden stated that the British Government had therefore viewed with interest and sympathy the conclusions reached in the Greco-Yugoslav Agreement of January 15, 1942.[1] The British Government thought that a Balkan confederation should consist of all the Balkan countries, including Albania and Bulgaria; neither the external nor internal frontiers of the confederation were specifically discussed. Mr. Eden also authorised Sir H. Knatchbull-Hugessen to invite the Turkish Government to hold further staff conversations. He told Sir H. Knatchbull-Hugessen for his own information that the British Government would be prepared to arrange for a high military authority from the Middle East to go to Turkey and carry the conversations further.

Sir H. Knatchbull-Hugessen had explained to the Foreign Office (a) that the Turkish Air Force was practically non-existent for the purposes of modern warfare. The Foreign Office understood that we were giving the Turks as much military equipment as they could absorb, but thought that much more could be done in the way of air supplies. They therefore raised the matter with the Air Ministry; Mr. Eden suggested that the offer of more aircraft might be a considerable inducement to the Turks to take risks which they could not otherwise consider. He thought that the Turks had some grounds for complaint to us about aircraft supplies.[2]

At the beginning of January 1943, before the Prime Minister left (b) for the Casablanca Conference, the Foreign Office considered once again what inducements we had to offer Turkey. The Prime Minister's proposal for an Anglo-American-Soviet guarantee of Turkish frontiers did not seem practicable. Sir H. Knatchbull-Hugessen thought that the Turkish Government would resent it, and that American association with the guarantee might offend the Soviet Government.[3] Moreover, a guarantee of this kind would

---

[1] This agreement laid down detailed plans for a Balkan Union after the war, with common foreign, defence and economic policies, and various co-ordinating arrangements.

[2] In October 1942 a telegram from Ankara had drawn attention to the rapidly waning (c) strength of the Turkish Air Force as a result of our inability to supply it with modern operational aircraft. The Prime Minister had asked the Chief of Air Staff to consider the matter and, as a result, the Air Officer Commanding-in-Chief, Middle East, had offered the Turks 20 modern Hurricane cannon fighters to be delivered in November and December 1942.

[3] Sir H. Knatchbull-Hugessen does not seem to have known that the Prime Minister had already proposed such a guarantee to Stalin. See above, p. 106, Sir H. Knatchbull-Hugessen later changed his views about a guarantee. See below, pp. 121–2.

(a) R337/337/44 (1943).   (b) R8961, 9083/24/44.   (c) R8028/2/44; R6548/1206/44; R289/337/44 (1943).

merely convince the Turks that their policy of strict neutrality was right, since they would have little to lose by not participating in the war. The Turkish Government had territorial aspirations in Syria, the Dodecanese and Bulgaria, but a promise of territory in any of these three regions would not have a decisive influence on Turkey and would cause us difficulties in other directions. We had no right to give away Syrian territory. An offer of the Dodecanese to Turkey would lead at once to trouble with the Greek Government. Concessions of territory in Bulgaria would be only of minor importance. We could also do no more in the way of economic and financial assistance. We had offered Turkey ample credit to pay for military and civilian goods which were available; Turkish difficulties were those of internal finance, in which we could give no real help. We were already sending as much civil and military material as Turkish communications could carry; it was indeed doubtful whether the Turkish Army could absorb more military material.

The Foreign Office therefore continued to think that we could do little more than exploit the favourable turn in the war situation, and invite the Turkish Government to engage in further staff conversations. We could discuss the future of the Balkans with the Turkish Government in the hope of inducing them to co-operate in our plans. Lastly, we could supply Turkey's cereal requirements. Before next harvest Turkey would have a deficiency of 150,000–200,000 tons of grain; a supply of this quantity would end the agitation for demobilisation of the Turkish Army on the grounds that the men were required for agricultural work. Such demobilisation was undesirable from our point of view since it would be another argument in favour of Turkish political neutrality. Proposals were therefore being worked out in London and Cairo to supply 150,000 tons of grain as soon as possible.[1]

(a)   On January 3 Sir H. Knatchbull-Hugessen gave to the Minister for Foreign Affairs Mr. Eden's personal message and a translation of the Foreign Office note on the general war position. The Minister said that he greatly appreciated the message. He accepted at once a suggestion for staff talks. Sir. H. Knatchbull-Hugessen told the United States Ambassador of his conversation in very general terms, without mentioning the proposal for staff talks. Mr. Steinhardt thought that Turkey wanted to get all she could and also to keep out of the war.

(b)   The following day Sir H. Knatchbull-Hugessen gave Mr. Eden's message to the Turkish Prime Minister and showed him the note on

---

[1] See above, p. 88, note (1).

(a) R138, 140, 438/55/44. (b) R169/55/44.

the war position and the statement of Mr. Eden's views on Balkan federation. He reported that the conversation was most friendly. On January 9 Sir H. Knatchbull-Hugessen again saw M. Saracoglu, (a) and two days later the Minister for Foreign Affairs. Both spoke in favour of keeping out of the war and gave the impression that they intended to do so. The Prime Minister said that Turkey had certain small *desiderata*, but could do without them.

The two Ministers mentioned Turkey's internal difficulties and lack of air defence, and said that to fight would weaken her and increase the chance of her becoming a Russian satellite; Turkey could help us better by reserving her strength and influence in the Balkans and Middle East for the post-war period, since she was the only Power of any weight in these areas. Neither Minister seemed alarmed at the idea of isolation or absence from the peace conference. Sir H. Knatchbull-Hugessen believed that they thought Turkey essential to our future policy and that we could not drop her or exclude her from the peace conference. Sir H. Knatchbull-Hugessen (b) asked the Prime Minister whether his policy of acquiring as much war material as possible from all sources was to make Turkey strong against a possible Russian threat. The substance of what he said in reply made it clear that this assumption was correct. M. Saracoglu agreed that Turco-Russian relations were better than usual, but showed his distrust and anxieties.

Sir H. Knatchbull-Hugessen pointed out to M. Saracoglu that (c) the 'protective pad' policy had been merely the consequence of Turkey's desire to keep out of the war; that it had benefited us only indirectly and that Turkey could not have followed it successfully in isolation. He spoke of the effect on British public opinion if Turkey remained neutral until the end of the war. He reported to the Foreign Office on January 13 that since his return he had seen no sign of modification of the Turkish attitude; Turkey would resist attack but would not take offensive action or make operational plans now or for the summer. He thought that the only course was to continue to talk over the whole question frankly and dispassionately. An expression of disapproval or criticism would only increase the difficulties; a change in the policy of supplying Turkey on the ground that she would never fight would almost certainly defeat its object. The Foreign Office instructed Sir H. Knatchbull-Hugessen on (d) January 22 to continue the conversations along the lines which he had suggested.[1]

---

[1] The Foreign Office informed the State Department of the conversations.

(a) R399/55/44. (b) R954/55/44. (c) R466/55/44. (d) R467/55/44.

EBFP

(v)

Discussions on Turkey at the Casablanca Conference: the Prime Minister's proposal to meet the Turkish Ministers: reluctance of the War Cabinet to agree to the proposal: the Prime Minister's discussions with the Turkish Ministers at Adana, January 30–31, 1943.

Although Sir H. Knatchbull-Hugessen's reports had confirmed the Foreign Office view that the Turkish Government was still a long way from belligerency, the Prime Minister still hoped that they might be persuaded to enter the war if they were sure of adequate

(a) military and air support. One of the arguments used by the British Chiefs of Staff at the Casablanca Conference to convince the Americans of the desirability of undertaking the invasion of Sicily, was that by driving Italy out of the war we might induce the Turks to come into it. The Prime Minister discussed the question with the President and arranged with him that Great Britain should take immediate responsibility in negotiations with the Turkish Government.[1]

(b)   The Prime Minister reported this decision (in his own words: 'It was agreed that we play the hand in Turkey whether in munitions or diplomacy') by telegram to the War Cabinet on January 20. He said that, with the President's approval, he now proposed to get into direct touch with the Turks. He asked that, if Mr. Attlee and Mr. Eden approved of this plan, the latter should propose at once a meeting between him (the Prime Minister) and members of the Turkish Government.

In view of the reports from Sir H. Knatchbull-Hugessen of the

(c) Turkish reaction to the approach already made to them, Mr. Attlee and Mr. Eden thought it unwise of the Prime Minister to suggest this personal meeting. They were afraid that he would meet with

---

(d)   [1] See below, p. 119. As a counterpart to the arrangement about Turkey, the Prime Minister agreed that the Americans should take the lead in China, and continue to take it in French North Africa. Sir H. Knatchbull-Hugessen was not told officially of the decision about Turkey until March 11. In the first week in March the United States Ambassador said to him that he understood that Turkey and the Middle East were to be a British sphere and that he was to play a secondary role *vis-à-vis* the British Embassy.

(e)   He promised to support Sir H. Knatchbull-Hugessen in every way. See also below, p. 128, note 1. On July 10, however, Mr. Hull wrote to Lord Halifax: 'Notwithstanding any military understanding reached, I am not aware of any commitment made by the President at Casablanca which relates in any way to the surrender by the United States of its full independence of action with regard to relations between the United States and Turkey in either the political or the economic sphere, either during the war or after.' The British Embassy at Washington informed the Foreign Office of the State Department's verbal explanation that the letter had the approval of the President, but that they did not believe that there was any practical difference of views between the two Governments.

(a) COS(43)33(o).   (b) Stratagem 102, Churchill Papers/446.   (c) Telescope 182, Churchill Papers/446.   (d) R1962/55/44.   (e) R13353/55/44.

'a rebuff or a refusal'. They suggested also on general grounds that it would be better from the point of view of Parliament and public opinion that the Prime Minister should come home after the Conference to give a report on it to the House of Commons.[1]

The Prime Minister replied on January 21 that if he did not carry (a) out his plan 'a golden opportunity' might be lost. He had not intended 'to extort any pledge, but only to explain [to the Turks] the ways in which we are now able to help them place themselves in a position of security', i.e. '(i) by the guarantees; (ii) by substantial munition aid; (iii) by reinforcing them in the event of attack. . . . I should not feel at all rebuffed if they were afraid to come.' Mr. Eden then (b) sent a personal message to the Prime Minister supporting the arguments of the War Cabinet. The Prime Minister discussed the matter again with the President, and held to his proposal. He tele- (c) graphed on January 24 asking that the War Cabinet should reconsider the plan as quickly as possible and that a telegram should be sent to the Turkish President proposing a meeting in Cyprus. He sent the texts of this proposed message and also of a message which Mr. Roosevelt had agreed to send. He argued that 'even if the Turks should say "no" it will do no harm. I have no false pride in these matters. The capture of Tripoli, the increasing Russian victories and the fact that I speak for the two great allies creates a most favourable occasion.'

The War Cabinet on January 24 considered both the political (d) and military aspects of the question. Their objection to the Prime Minister's proposal was that if the offer was refused or if a meeting were held without achieving the desired result, the position would be worse. They thought it unlikely that President Inönü would accept the invitation to a meeting; if he did so he would put forward a long series of demands to be fulfilled before Turkey could enter the war on our side. It was better that such demands should be analysed in Staff conversations rather than that they should be dealt with in high-level discussions. The view of the War Cabinet was that high-level discussions were unlikely to succeed until the ground had been further prepared. A draft telegram from Mr. Eden to Mr.

---

[1] They added an argument which was, in fact, more likely to influence the Prime (e) Minister in the opposite direction. They said that he was taking unnecessary personal risks. The Prime Minister in reply pointed out that there was no difficulty about flying from Marrakesh to Cairo; he hoped that the War Cabinet would 'give me strict latitude in my personal movements which I deem necessary to the public interest'. After the War Cabinet had agreed that the meeting with the Turkish Ministers should take place, the Foreign Office strongly opposed Ankara as a meeting place. In view of the attempted assassination of Herr von Papen, the security arrangements at Ankara would not be adequate.

(a) Stratagem 144, Churchill Papers/446. (b) Telescope 230, Churchill Papers/446. (c) Stratagem 198, Churchill Papers/446. (d) WM(43)13 and 14, C.A. (e) Stratagem 198, Churchill Papers/446.

(a) Churchill was considered in detail, and finally approved and despatched.

(b)   The Prime Minister replied on January 25 that there was no question of persuading Turkey to come into the war 'without regard to circumstances and conditions. . . . However, it seems to me a subject of surprise if right conditions were created that anyone should have doubt about the advantages of Turkey entering the war on our side.' The Prime Minister said that the Chief of the Imperial General Staff as well as the President and his advisers agreed with his view. If the Turks refused, the rebuff would not have noticeable consequences, while if they accepted, it would not be in their interest to let this important contact with the winning side lapse into a failure. The War Cabinet met at once on January 25

(c) to consider this further telegram from the Prime Minister. After some discussion they agreed to the despatch of the telegram from

(d) Mr. Churchill to President Inönü. They also agreed to ask the Prime Minister—in view of Stalin's message of November 27, 1942[1]—to consider sending a suitable telegram informing Stalin of

(e) his plan to meet the Turks. On January 31 Stalin replied that the importance of the meeting was clear to him.

(f)   President Inönü replied that he would be glad to meet Mr. Churchill anywhere in Turkey, but that he could not leave Turkey without appointing a *remplaçant*, and therefore would be unable to keep the meeting secret. If a meeting could not take place in Turkey, the President of the Council, M. Saracoglu, would meet Mr. Churchill in Cyprus. Adana was finally accepted as the meeting-place.

     The Prime Minister flew to Adana from Egypt on January 30,

(g) 1943.[2] He met there the President of the Turkish Republic, General Inönü, and M. Saracoglu, M. Numan Menemencioglu and Marshal Cakmak. The Prime Minister first read, and then handed to the Turkish President, a note which he had prepared as a background

(h) for the discussion.[3] This note pointed out that the Russian victories over the Germans had removed the danger to Turkey from the north

---

[1] See above, p. 106.

[2] At the Prime Minister's request Sir A. Cadogan flew to Egypt in order to go with him to Turkey.

(i)   [3] Mr. Churchill later reported to the War Cabinet: 'I pursued a method of perfect trust and confidence, asking for no engagement but giving to the utmost in our power. In this atmosphere the President said that the note was wholly favourable to his views, that if Turkey was allowed to be judge we should get all we wanted. . . . He and his Ministers reiterated again and again that they longed for the victory of England.'

     (a) Telescope 274 (Churchill Papers/446; R709/55/44). (b) Stratagem 222 (Churchill Papers/446; R709/55/44). (c) WM(43)15.1, C.A. (d) Telescope 278-9 (Churchill Papers/446; R709/55/44). (e) Telescope 373 (Churchill Papers/446; R709/55/44). (f) Telescope 303, Churchill Papers/446. (g) WP(43)64. (h) WP(43)64; Stratagem C/4 (Churchill Papers/446; R709/55/44). (i) Stratagem C/3 (Churchill Papers/446; R709/55/44).

for the time being; the danger from the south had been removed by the British victories in North Africa. Germany's need for oil and her eastern ambitions remained; she might try to force her way through the centre in the summer, and Turkey must be in the best possible condition to resist such aggression. Mr. Churchill said that he had come, with President Roosevelt's agreement, to find out how best to help Turkey at 'this serious but at the same time hopeful juncture', and that he and President Roosevelt were prepared to speed up and increase the supply of modern munitions to Turkey, and wished Turkey to be 'closely associated with the two great Western democracies not only during the concluding stages of the war, but in the general work of world rehabilitation which will follow.'

Mr. Churchill said that the assembled military experts must examine the first stage in his proposals for assisting Turkey to prepare her own defence. We considered that Turkey might be drawn into the war either by German aggression or by a state of anarchy in Bulgaria and the Balkans needing the intervention of the Turkish Government in protection of its own interests. The note outlined plans for Allied aid in an immediate emergency including a hostile initial air attack. We expected the crisis to come in the early summer of 1943, when we should be conducting large-scale operations in the Mediterranean and the Russians might be sending troops across the Black Sea. The British and Americans together would certainly provide at least twenty-five squadrons of aircraft immediately if Turkey were drawn into the war. Mr. Churchill mentioned further detailed plans for military assistance, and said that at the Casablanca Conference the two Allies had decided upon plans to drive Italy out of the war. The defeat of Italy would lead to contact with the western Balkans and with the 'highly hopeful resistance maintained both by General Michailovitch in Croatia and the Partisans in Slovenia'.[1] Mr. Churchill spoke of extensive operations in the Mediterranean in the summer months; these operations, and above all the Italian attitude, would cause the 'very greatest agitation' throughout the Balkans. A further advance of the Russian armies could not be excluded. He went on to say that Stalin was most anxious to see Turkey well-armed and ready to defend herself against aggression. Both Mr. Roosevelt and the British Government wanted Turkey to be a full partner in the Peace Conference. Mr. Churchill reaffirmed in plain terms the Allies' conviction that they would win the war.

---

[1] On February 9, on the Prime Minister's instructions, the Foreign Office had their (a) copies of this text corrected. It should have read: 'General Mihailovic in Serbia and the Partisans in Croatia and Slovenia.'

(a) R709/55/44.

(a)   At the second meeting the President referred to the possibility of a German attack, and said that for this reason Turkey must be strengthened. If Germany did not attack, the only other factor which might affect Turkey would be a state of chaos in the Balkans. The President asked how Turkey could collaborate during and after the war. Mr. Churchill said that Turkey should be strong and ready. There might be anarchy in the Balkans; there might be some change in Germany or a collapse. Turkey must be ready to throw in her weight when that moment arrived and when her interests were obviously involved. He thought that it was very important for her to have a seat at the peace conference. He did not ask her to act until it was in her interest to do so and in that of the grand coalition, but a moment would come when she would be in a position to let us use her territory either for refuelling or as air bases.

Mr. Churchill then spoke of post-war conditions. He said that the United States were aiming at a solid international structure, involving the disarmament of aggressors and international justice. Russia, who had accepted the Atlantic Charter, would be part of this organisation, and the United States would certainly join. Mr. Churchill said that post-war Russia might be even more imperialistic than the Russia of former years, and that the best protection for Turkey was an international arrangement perhaps accompanied by special guarantees applying to her. Russia (and also possibly the United States) was ready to give these guarantees.

M. Saracoglu noted that Mr. Churchill thought that Russia might become imperialistic. This danger made it necessary for Turkey to be very prudent, especially since 'all the defeated countries would become Bolshevist and Slav if Germany was beaten'. Mr. Churchill replied that 'things did not always turn out as badly as was expected. But if they did so it was better that Turkey should be strong and closely associated with the United Kingdom and the United States'. The Turkish Ministers agreed. Mr. Churchill said that he would never propose that Turkey should come into the war if she were not ready, or suggest that she should do so in any way which would involve exhaustion of her resources. She might even render assistance without entering the war, e.g. in allowing us to attack Ploesti from Turkish bases. M. Saracoglu agreed and said, 'Very good.' Mr. Churchill said later to M. Numan that there might be a moment when Turkey could strike in the war without risk of exhaustion or invasion. He would not advise her to enter the war at the present time or to do so until ready, but a moment might come when we should have the right to make a firm proposal. M. Numan agreed that this was extremely reasonable.

(a) WP(43)64.

The Turkish Ministers asked the object of the supply of British and American munitions to Turkey without payment. Mr. Churchill said that it was threefold: (i) to secure the defence of Turkey against the passage of German forces; (ii) to secure the association of the greatest number of Powers; (iii) if the opportunity came and did not prove too costly or dangerous, we wished Turkey to be able to enter Bulgaria and the Balkans and assist in the general advance on the retreating German army.

Mr. Churchill met the Turkish Ministers again on January 31. In the meantime he had prepared a paper setting out his views on post-war security. He said these views were only his personal ideas since he had not been able to consult his Government. The object of the paper was to reassure the Turks. Mr. Churchill referred to (a) the Anglo-Soviet Treaty and the Atlantic Charter, and said that it was the intention of the 'Chiefs of the United Nations to create a world organisation for the preservation of peace, based upon conceptions of freedom and justice and the revival of prosperity. As a part of this organisation an instrument of European Government will be established.' The units forming this body would be not only 'the great nations . . . but a number of Confederations formed among the smaller States', including a Danubian *bloc* and a Balkan *bloc*. Mr. Churchill said that the greatest post-war security for Turkey would be found by her taking her place as a victorious belligerent ally at the side of Great Britain, the United States and Russia. He thought that Turkey's interests might require her to intervene to help prevent total anarchy in the Balkans. He also referred to the possible value of air bases in Turkey for British and American aircraft operating against the Roumanian oilfields, or in the event of a British attack on the Dodecanese and Crete. There was also the question of opening the Straits to Allied traffic and closing them to Axis traffic. Mr. Churchill said that in listing these things he was contemplating a case in which Turkey would have departed from strict neutrality and have sided with the United Nations without engaging her armies offensively against the Germans and the Bulgars.

Mr. Churchill's note also considered the possibility of Turkey becoming a full belligerent and of her armies advancing into the Balkans side by side with the Russians and British. In such an event Mr. Churchill promised the utmost aid from all her allies and offered a guarantee—with which Mr. Roosevelt would probably associate himself—of Turkish territory and post-war rights in a treaty either alone or with Russia.

The President read Mr. Churchill's note and said that in general

---

(a) WP(43)64, Annex II; Stratagem C/6, Churchill Papers/446.

he agreed with all of it, and that a European organisation on the lines indicated would be ideal. Mr. Churchill again suggested that Turkey should voluntarily enter the war and later come to the Peace Conference relatively unweakened, since this course of action would give the best prospects for her security. The President said that he was in entire agreement.

Military discussions were also held with the Turks at Adana by Generals Sir A. Brooke, Sir H. Maitland Wilson and Sir H. Alexander. It was agreed on January 31 that the Turkish military representatives would furnish lists of the naval, military and air equipment which they required. The British representatives would examine these lists with a view to supplying available equipment as quickly as possible. The British and Turkish Staffs would prepare a plan for the movement into Turkey and subsequent maintenance in Turkey of British forces in the event of Turkey being drawn into the war.

At Adana the general assumption was that Turkey would not be required to take positive action before her armed strength had increased, unless in the meantime there were a withdrawal of German forces to a greater distance from the Turkish frontiers, dissension in the Balkans or increasing resistance to German and Italian tyranny in the occupied countries of central and south-east Europe. The Turks were clearly much relieved that they had not
(a) been asked to come into the war at once. Mr. Churchill sent Stalin an account of the meeting with a short summary of his two notes.[1]

(b)   On February 7 Mr. Churchill gave the War Cabinet a summary of his tour in the Mediterranean, and said that it had been highly satisfactory that the Americans had agreed at Casablanca to our dealing with Turkey. The Turkish attitude at Adana had been realistic and encouraging, and the Turks were obviously impressed by the news reaching them about conditions inside Germany. On
(c) February 2 Sir A. Cadogan reported to Mr. Eden that the Turks 'could not have been more cordial or friendly, and they made no difficulty about any point'. He added: 'Their real pre-occupation is of course Russia.'

(d)   President Roosevelt raised the question of Turkey with Mr. Eden towards the end of the latter's visit to Washington between March 12 and 30, 1943. The President thought that in May the moment might come when we should put pressure on Turkey to give us certain facilities, such as the use of aerodromes, in order to assist Allied operations in the Eastern Mediterranean. Mr. Eden said that Mr.

---

[1] Sir A. Clark Kerr later gave Stalin the text of the notes.

(a) T92/3, Churchill Papers/446. (b) WM(43)25.2, C.A. (c) Stratagem 330, R709/55/44. (d) T412/3, Washington tel. 1484, Prisec.

Churchill held similar views. He agreed that the moment for such an approach would not come at least until Tunis was cleared of the enemy. President Roosevelt said that he had agreed with Mr. Churchill that Turkey was a British sphere and that he had no desire to alter the decision. He would be glad to join us later, if we so wished, in a joint *démarche*.

(vi)

Turkish insistence upon a policy of neutrality: the question of a new Anglo-Turkish treaty of alliance: British reaction to the Turkish policy (March–June 1943).

In the first week in March 1943, the Foreign Office prepared a (a) memorandum repeating their view that Turkish policy was governed by a determination to keep out of the war unless directly attacked, or unless they could participate without serious effect on their internal or external position, and by a deep-rooted distrust of Russian intentions after the war. In order to guard against the latter, Turkey wanted to strengthen herself by every means, including the drawing of supplies of arms from both belligerent camps. The Foreign Office agreed that the Turks wanted a British victory, provided that it did not involve a Soviet victory which would make Russia the predominant Power in Central Europe and the Balkans.

The memorandum also restated British policy towards Turkey since the Adana Conference. We no longer needed Turkey as a 'protective pad' against German economic or military penetration into the Middle East. We now wanted to use her as an 'aircraft carrier' for an attack on the occupied countries of south-eastern Europe and the Roumanian oil-wells. After Allied forces had gained a foothold in Greece or Yugoslavia, we should wish Turkey to enter the war; at the moment we wished her only to stretch her neutrality in British favour.

The Foreign Office thought that the gulf between the objects of Turkish and British policy could be bridged by supplying Turkey with enough munitions to enable her to feel secure in taking minor risks with the Germans. We must show her that, if she were involved in war, we were ready and able to come to her aid with sufficient forces for the successful defence of her frontiers. We should persuade her that the only means of protection against Russia was active co-operation with the United Nations in war in anticipation of the post-war settlement.

On April 1 Sir H. Knatchbull-Hugessen reported that Turkish (b)

(a) R2299/55/44. (b) R2958/55/44.

E*BFP

policy remained one of neutrality, and that—contrary to some assumptions in London—there was no sign of a willing advance

(a) even towards non-belligerency. On April 9 he telegraphed that the general attitude of the Minister for Foreign Affairs was that Turkey was still in a period of preparation; that we had left her a free choice and would not ask her to take undue risks or come into the war against her judgment. The Minister would maintain this attitude as long as possible in the hope that Germany might collapse before the moment came for Turkish action. Sir H. Knatchbull-Hugessen recommended that we should be frank but not too pressing in keeping our point of view before the Turkish Government. The Foreign Office agreed with this view. Sir A. Cadogan wrote on April 16 that the objective of our Turkish policy was clear enough; the Turks knew what it was, and Sir H. Knatchbull-Hugessen must be left to decide upon the tactics to be employed in attaining it.

The Commander-in-Chief, Middle East, paid a visit to Ankara in

(b) April.[1] General Wilson went with the Ambassador to see the Minister for Foreign Affairs on April 16. He said that his object was to carry the Adana conversations a step further. We had no intention of trying to force Turkey into the war. Our objective was a strong Turkey; we wanted to complete our preparations so that in the event of a German attack we could give Turkey all necessary support and ultimately turn to the offensive in Europe. M. Numan hoped that we should 'attain an equality' in the area concerned before taking action. He made it clear that he referred to equality with Russia during and after the war.

(c) On April 17 Sir H. Knatchbull-Hugessen and General Wilson saw the Turkish Prime Minister. The Ambassador said that we were not thinking as yet of asking Turkey to enter the war. The eventual decision rested with the Turkish Government, but a day would come—probably not until September and possibly later—when we would have to tell the Prime Minister that by joining in or letting us use Turkish territory, Turkey could greatly assist in shortening the war. Our request might be for the use of airfields during operations against the Dodecanese and the opening up of the Aegean. The Prime Minister gave no sign of dissent. General Wilson pointed out that from the military angle the Turks would lose a great deal if they did not come into the war and obtain experience of modern warfare. At each of his two interviews with M. Saracoglu, General Wilson made it clear that we would be putting requests to the Turkish Government at a later date.

---

[1] Air Chief Marshal Sir Sholto Douglas, Air Officer Commanding-in-Chief, Middle East, had visited Turkey in March.

(a) R3258/55/44. (b) R3573, 3666/55/44. (c) R3667, 3668, 3913/55/44.

The Foreign Office thought that the conversations during General Wilson's visit represented a definite advance. The Turks had been warned of an approximate date when we would ask them to help in future operations, and discussions were taking place about military command and the date when British troops would enter Turkey after the first signs of a German threat. This latter point had not been discussed in staff contacts with the Turks since the collapse of France. Sir H. Knatchbull-Hugessen thought that there had been solid material but not political progress since Adana. At best the only points on which we and the Turks agreed were that: Turkey would fight if attacked; Turkey must be made as strong as possible as quickly as possible; if Turkey fought, she would receive direct British and American help.

Sir H. Knatchbull-Hugessen, however, doubted whether the (a) Turks would ever change their attitude. One obstacle to their coming in—lack of preparation—could be remedied. The second obstacle was fear of Russia and Germany. We had tried to bring Russia and Turkey together by promoting conversations,[1] with the result that a friendly spirit existed on the surface, although underneath the old distrust remained as strong as ever. We had held out hopes of Anglo-Russian-American guarantees and even of an independent British guarantee. We had pointed out the danger which Turkey incurred by not joining the Allies at the right moment. As for Germany, Sir H. Knatchbull-Hugessen thought that the Turks might be hoping for a German revival in time for the latter to act as a makeweight to Russia. He had recently seen a disquieting secret report indicating that the Turks intended to maintain commercial relations with Germany in order to be sure of an alternative market after the war, when their failure to come in on the Allied side might have lost them the sympathies of the Western Powers.

Sir H. Knatchbull-Hugessen considered that the provision of arms and munitions, whatever the quantities, was not likely to turn the political scale with the Turks. He suggested an approach to the Turkish Government with a direct request. If they refused, we could either repeat our request with Russian and American support, or let Russia make an independent and direct request. We should accompany these *démarchés* by a promise of a guarantee in return for

---

[1]After Adana at the Prime Minister's suggestion the Foreign Office arranged for (b) Turco-Soviet conversations in Moscow. Both sides were willing to hold such talks but neither could produce a definite agenda. The talks were a failure and no communiqué was issued at their close. The Turks claimed that their only result was a strong impression that Russia wished to isolate Turkey from Great Britain and at an appropriate moment discuss alone with her such questions as the future of the Balkans and the Straits.

(a) R4389/55/44.   (b) R2300, 9968/650/44.

Turkish belligerency. The implication would be clear that the Turks would not get the guarantee if they did not come into the war.

(a)   On May 5 the Turkish Ambassador came to see Mr. Eden before he returned to Turkey for a visit. Mr. Eden said that he hoped that Turkey would soon cease to be 'non-belligerent'. From Turkey's own point of view, as well as from that of Europe, she should attend the Peace Conference as a belligerent ally. M. Orbay asked what active military part Turkey could take. Mr. Eden said that before long the time might come when, without being an active belligerent, Turkey could provide facilities to her ally which might help to shorten the war. M. Orbay said that if this were the fact, he hoped

(b)   that we should tell the Turks so. A week later he asked to see Mr. Eden again. Mr. Eden said that the programme for delivery of supplies as agreed at Adana was now complete and that the flow had begun. The Allied war effort was gathering momentum, and before long we might be asking Turkey for facilities to help shorten the war.

(c)   On May 7 Sir H. Knatchbull-Hugessen gave the Turkish Prime

(d)   Minister lists of the war material to be delivered in 1943.[1] He also brought a message from Mr. Churchill. M. Saracoglu was most grateful. He said that he realised from the message that Mr. Churchill wanted Turkey to be strong and independent so that she could face any danger. He made it clear that he was thinking both of Germany and of Russia. Sir H. Knatchbull-Hugessen said that our only idea was to beat Germany as quickly as possible.

(e)   In a later conversation Sir H. Knatchbull-Hugessen spoke plainly to the Turkish Prime Minister about the choice between participation and isolation. He said that the danger of a German attack was negligible; that time was passing and that a request to Turkey to join the Allies would certainly come. A favourable answer would range her with the United Nations and give her the collective security which was the best answer to her fear of Russia. A negative answer would have a bad effect on British public opinion, and amount to first step by Turkey towards voluntary isolation. The Prime Minister admitted that he no longer feared a German attack, but that he was very anxious about an air raid on Istanbul or a military *coup* in Thrace if Turkey came in. Sir H. Knatchbull-Hugessen said that the best safeguard was to allow British forces into Turkey in good time before such an attack could develop; he spoke of the importance of Turkish air bases. The Prime Minister

---

[1] This list included our 7,000 guns, 700 tanks and 470 aircraft. See also p. 131, note 2, and p. 178, note 1.

(a) R4054/55/44. (b) R4242/55/44. (c) R4131/55/44. (d) T603A/3, Churchill Papers/446; Tel. 621 to Ankara, Prisec. (e) R4188/55/44.

asked what could Turkey do? She would only be crippled. Sir H. Knatchbull-Hugessen suggested that Turkey should act on the defensive while allowing us to conduct operations from her territory.

On May 13 the Foreign Office telegraphed to Sir H. Knatchbull- (a) Hugessen that we were supplying Turkey with arms not only to strengthen her against attack but to make it safe for her to grant us facilities. We expected this return before the end of the war. The Turks must understand that we were not giving them arms to enable them to withstand post-war Russian designs; such a suggestion would imply disloyalty on our part to our Russian allies. Sir H. (b) Knatchbull-Hugessen gave the substance of this telegram to M. Saracoglu on May 16 and at his request repeated it three times. M. Saracoglu deprecated the suggestion that we were supplying him with war material for use against Russia. He said that Turkey had lived for over twenty years on friendly terms with the Russians and asked only to continue to do so. He did not refer to the proposal that Turkey should grant us facilities for war operations.

On May 25 Sir H. Knatchbull-Hugessen reported that the Soviet (c) Ambassador confirmed his own impression that the Turks were drawing back and intended to remain neutral and refuse any request for facilities to attack Germany. The Soviet Ambassador did not rule out the possibility of ultimate acceptance of the British proposals for suitable compensation; he agreed that it was in the Turkish interest to come into the war.

Meanwhile Sir H. Knatchbull-Hugessen had an unofficial con- (d) versation with the Minister for Foreign Affairs. The Minister had argued that it would be contrary both to Turkish and British interests for Turkey to come into the war in view of the freedom of choice left to her. M. Numan later told the Yugoslav Ambassador (e) at Ankara that he did not see why Turkey should 'immolate herself' and sacrifice her big towns for what would merely be an 'episode' in the war. Turkey would go to war only in her own major interests; if Great Britain pressed him to come in, he would refuse. M. Numan said that Turkey had conferred great benefits on the Allies by acting as a rampart against Germany and leaving the Allies free to manoeuvre in the Middle East. Sir H. Knatchbull-Hugessen reported that M. Orbay and other Turkish officials were using this argument.

The Foreign Office concluded from these and other reports that the Turks certainly were drawing back. The Turkish press was taking the same line as the Government. The Foreign Office thought that with the end of the Tunisian campaign the Turks expected a new and possibly decisive phase in the war to open, and would

---

(a) R4131/55/44. (b) R4410/55/44. (c) R4667/55/44. (d) R4669/55/44. (e) R4752, 4744, 4875/55/44.

wait until they saw how matters developed both on the German-Russian and Mediterranean fronts. One military phase had ended with the successful Russian defence at Stalingrad and the ejection of the Axis from North Africa; a diplomatic phase had also ended, or rather, in the Foreign Office view, had been brought to an end deliberately by the Turks. This diplomatic phase had included the Adana conversations and the first phase of mild British pressure. The Turks were now anxious to avert the second diplomatic phase —British pressure on them to take a more active part in the war— until they saw more clearly the outcome of the second military phase. The Foreign Office recommended that we should not make a major change in policy towards the Turks for the present, but that we should adopt an attitude (as distinct from a policy) to meet the attitude of the Turks. Thus we should reply to the Minister for Foreign Affairs on two points: his fear of German strength and his claim that we should need Turkey because we should not be able to rely on the United States.[1] We might also introduce a more critical tone into our propaganda to Turkey.

(a)   Sir O. Sargent noted on May 24 that when the Prime Minister decided to send quantities of war material unconditionally into Turkey, we were taking a gamble which was necessary in the circumstances. Since then the chances of the gamble succeeding had not improved. Our victories, so far from encouraging the Turks to move towards belligerency, had if anything increased their fears, because they could not foresee how future developments were going to affect the Turkish political and military position. It was difficult to decide how to check this trend. Threats to withhold further war material and to leave Turkey in the lurch at the peace settlement would only increase their fears of Russia without being forcible enough to induce them to abandon neutrality. Blandishments such as the offer of a seat at the peace settlement had proved equally ineffective. Sir O. Sargent noted that the Foreign Office did not want to force the issue at the moment because Allied operational plans in the Middle East were still uncertain. On the other hand, we ought to consider again our course of action if the Chiefs of Staff were to announce suddenly that they wanted to use Turkish territory on a given date.

Sir O. Sargent thought that we needed new methods if we were to get a return during the war for the material we had given the

---

[1] M. Numan had suggested to Sir H. Knatchbull-Hugessen that the prospects of Anglo-American co-operation after the war were not improving, and that Mr. Churchill's visit to Washington (in May) was a sign of disagreement between the British and United States Governments. M. Numan told the Yugoslav Ambassador at this time that the Americans wanted to avoid large-scale participation in the European theatre of war.

(a) R4390/55/44.

Turks. We would have to give definite and far-reaching promises, such as a guarantee that Russia would not attack or threaten Turkish territory or interests (this guarantee would come into force only when Turkey entered the war on our side); or a new Anglo-Turkish treaty of alliance to replace the existing treaty which was now out of date. There was a strong case for a new treaty on the understanding that it came into force only when Turkey entered the war. A new treaty might embody the proposed guarantee and might also provide for post-war economic assistance, to which the Turks attached considerable importance. The Foreign Office would have to consider whether the United States and Soviet Governments should be invited to be parties to the treaty and guarantee, or whether these should be purely British obligations.

Sir A. Cadogan on May 24 ruled out the offer of a guarantee. He (a) questioned the desirability of a new Anglo-Turkish treaty of alliance. He thought that we should wait until the moment when we wanted to use Turkish bases and then ask for them. Mr. Eden saw no harm in working out a treaty, but agreed with Sir A. Cadogan that we could not give a guarantee: 'Let us be most prudent never to promise in the future what we cannot perform.'

In the last week of May Sir H. Knatchbull-Hugessen reported (b) that we had now reached a stage where it was clear to the Turkish Government that we wanted them soon to allow us to use their territory for offensive warfare, and that we genuinely considered it to be in their interests to agree when we made the request. Sir H. Knatchbull-Hugessen's view was that we had to reckon with some understanding between Turkey and Germany that neither would attack the other. He thought that von Papen had threatened that, if Turkey attacked Germany or allowed the Allies to use her territory, the large Turkish towns would be bombed. Further, M. Numan had suggested that Sir H. Knatchbull-Hugessen's recent attitude was not in keeping with the understanding reached at Adana, and that he was trying to force the Turks into the war against Turkish interests. Sir H. Knatchbull-Hugessen thought it important not to exert any more pressure for the time being.

On May 30 Sir H. Knatchbull-Hugessen again referred to a (c) Turkish 'decision' not to attack Germany. He thought that it amounted to a decision and was not sure that it was not a mutual understanding. The Turkish Government had already reacted against the suggestion that they should grant us the use of bases. M. Saracoglu had replied instantly: 'Istanbul would be in ashes in twenty-four hours.' Sir H. Knatchbull-Hugessen thought that there was little possibility of ever getting the Turks to take offensive

---

(a) R4390/55/44.   (b) R4874/55/44.   (c) R5035/55/44.

action, and doubted whether British policy towards Turkey was practicable. There had been a great change in the last few weeks; the Turks now had neither the wish nor the intention to become a belligerent ally. Hence it was a mistake to go on pouring arms into Turkey and making plans based on Turkey's readiness to act up to the treaty and then at the last moment get a negative answer.

(a)   On May 31 Sir H. Knatchbull-Hugessen again spoke of the 'present overwhelming symptoms of Turkish reluctance'. The answer to the question 'Will Turkey ever come in willingly?' was almost certainly 'No'. He suggested that as a form of pressure we should make it clear that supplies of war material over those already promised, and the supply of spare parts for upkeep of the existing material, would depend on some firm undertaking by the Turks to give us facilities when required. We could become less communicative on post-war problems, a Balkan confederation and political matters generally, in order to let the Turks feel the sting of isolation. The press could modify its tone, and we could show a certain lack of interest in Turkey and less care for Turkish susceptibilities. We could be less ready to supply civilian goods and could buy less from Turkey. Turkey would then be faced with the choice between active co-operation and isolation, collective security or no guarantees, a seat inside the Peace Conference or in the 'waiting-room' with Spain, Portugal and Sweden. In the last resort it would be a question of the continued validity of the Anglo-Turkish treaty. Hitherto on the grounds of expediency we had acquiesced in non-fulfilment of Turkey's obligations under that treaty. If when we invoked them Turkey attempted to evade them, she could not expect us to regard our own obligations as continuing in full force.

(b)   Sir H. Knatchbull-Hugessen thought that the Foreign Office should take into account the fact that the Turks were incapable of using or maintaining the equipment sent to them. There was wastage and muddle in every branch of their services; our co-operation was not sought. Communications were in a bad condition, the coal supply was precarious and rolling stock deficient. These facts had an immediate effect on the part which the Turkish army could play. Sir H. Knatchbull-Hugessen doubted whether Turkish administration, organisation and finance would stand the strain of war. He considered that the Turkish Army was not an effective force for offensive action against Germany. The most that we could expect from it was a simple defensive role dependent on us for anti-aircraft and anti-tank protection. Only very limited British forces could be maintained in Turkey, and we would have to be ready for a contingent liability for maintenance of the civilian life of the country.

(a) R5038/55/44.   (b) R5038, 5297/55/44.

On the other hand, if an atmosphere of co-operation existed, we could make use of Turkish influence in the Middle East and Arab world, and her prestige in Moslem countries including India. The use of such influence against us would cause us difficulty. Turkey might emerge at the end of the war intact and equipped with modern war material sufficient to give her a commanding position in relation to some of the Balkan countries which were likely to be exhausted after the war. She would then be in a position to take advantage of our wide preoccupations.

The Foreign Office noted on June 13 that Sir H. Knatchbull- (a) Hugessen's letters were written on the assumption that the accumulating signs of Turkish reluctance to enter the war probably represented a political decision. The Foreign Office at first held the view that they were a Turkish 'barrage' put down for tactical reasons; later they were compelled to conclude that this explanation was optimistic. The question was, when and how were we going to put Turkey a direct request to abandon neutrality. The Prime Minister had proposed on June 12 that we should do so at once by means of (b)] a message from him to the Turkish President complaining of Turkish neutrality and hinting that, unless there were more liberal interpretations of neutrality, Turkey would not receive a tripartite guarantee from Great Britain, the United States and Russia.[1] Mr. Eden, however, thought that the moment for such a message would be shortly before we asked the Turks for the use of bases. Mr. Churchill accepted his advice.

On June 5 the Foreign Office instructed Sir H. Knatchbull- (c) Hugessen to show the Turkish Government that their arguments did not impress us. We contended that a policy of belligerency was the best way of safeguarding Turkish interests both *vis-a-vis* Russia and in the general peace settlement. M. Numan should be told that it was not safe to assume that Turkey would be too important to us after the war for us to dare to leave her isolated. On the suggestion of Sir A. Cadogan, the Foreign Office proposed that, instead of

---

[1] During the military conference at Washington (at which no Foreign Office repre- (d) sentative was present) between May 12 and 25 the Prime Minister had repeated his view that, if Italy were driven out of the war, and the three major Allies then asked Turkey for permission to use Turkish bases for bombing Ploesti and clearing the Aegean, such a request could 'hardly fail to be successful', if 'the moment were chosen when Germany could take no powerful action against Turkey'. President Roosevelt was also optimistic about Turkish entry into the war. The final report of the Combined Chiefs of Staff also included in its objectives the preparation of 'the ground for the active or passive participation of Turkey in the war'. During the discussions with General Eisenhower in North Africa after the Washington Conference the Prime Minister and Mr. Eden took a hopeful view of the Turkish attitude after the collapse of Italy.

(a) R5038, 5624/55/44. (b) R5427/191/44. (c) R4669/55/44. (d) COS(43)281(O); COS(43)286(O); COS(43)290(O).

counter-argument, an ominous silence and obvious disinclination to discuss these matters further might make the Turks think that demands on them were impending. This line of diplomacy might not be very convincing while we continued to send warlike stores, conduct military discussions and give the Turks all kinds of technical assistance. Sir H. Knatchbull-Hugessen was therefore asked for his

(a) opinion. On June 12 he replied that he agreed with Sir A. Cadogan, but suggested a 'calculated' rather than an 'ominous' silence to make the Turks apprehensive of their dependence on us and so get them into a more realistic mood against the moment when we should ask for their co-operation. He did not want to force the issue until the next major military development. Until then he recommended general uncommunicativeness on wider issues, unresponsiveness to further requests and an attitude of mild criticism and lack of interest. He thought that the policy of military preparations should be continued. Delays in the military sphere would strengthen the Turkish case for refusal of co-operation; we ought also to avoid giving the Turks any ground for claiming that we were defaulting in our promises.

(b)   At this point the Commander-in-Chief, Levant, Admiral Sir John Cunningham, visited Ankara. In conversations with the Prime Minister and Minister for Foreign Affairs Admiral Cunningham spoke of the optimism in London about the prospects of the war, the increasing success of the battle of the Atlantic, increasing German weakness, especially in the air, and the closeness of Anglo-American co-operation.[1] He hoped that Italy would be out of the war by the winter. We should then be able to threaten the Axis through Greece, Yugoslavia, Albania and the Balkans generally. The position in the Aegean would thus change from one of quiet to one of extreme activity. M. Numan said that there should be complete confidence between the two Governments and that *surtout de notre côté* this confidence existed. M. Turgut Menemencioglu, who was interpreting, translated *surtout* as 'at least'.

(c)   Sir H. Knatchbull-Hugessen reported on June 19 that the tone of the press and of conversations with officials, suggested that Turkey intended to keep out of the war at all costs. They paid lip-service to the Allies but seemed, whenever possible, to be favouring the Germans. Sir H. Knatchbull-Hugessen now recommended slowing down our supplies. He thought, however, that the Turks might

---

(d)   [1]At the end of June the United States Ambassador in conversation with the Minister for Foreign Affairs spoke of the close agreement between the British and American Governments.

(a) R5164/55/44.   (b) R5283, 5721/55/44.   (c) R5366, 5378/55/44.   (d) R5678/55/44.

welcome an opportunity to claim that they were not sufficiently prepared for war. After the invasion of Sicily we might try to interfere with Turkish railway traffic to Germany (i.e. through Bulgaria), and thereby reduce the risk of Turkish retaliation for the loss of British supplies by sending more chrome to Germany. Sir H. Knatchbull-Hugessen reported that at a lunch party including von Papen, M. Numan had said that Turkey wanted to come out of the war like Switzerland; she did not wish the destruction of Germany and would not co-operate in it.

At the end of June the British Government were becoming increasingly exasperated in the face of these signs that Turkey was determined not to enter the war. Sir H. Knatchbull-Hugessen again (a) reported that in various conversations with members of the Turkish Government there was no sign of a consciousness on the Turkish side of their obligations to us under the Treaty of Alliance. The Government professed fear of Germany and showed a strong inclination to keep out of the war at all events in 1943. They represented that Turkey was left free at Adana to choose her own time for coming into the war and not merely to say 'yes' or 'no' when we asked for her active collaboration. Sir H. Knatchbull-Hugessen said that the prevalent idea in Turkey was that the war was of no concern to her. He pointed out on the other hand that we could not deny the strength of some of M. Numan's points, such as the fact that Turkey had stood by the alliance in 1940, and that the support which we could have afforded her in 1940 and 1941 would not have been very effective.

On July 12 Sir H. Knatchbull-Hugessen saw M. Orbay.[1] He went (b) through all the British grievances regarding the general attitude of the Turkish Government, which appeared to favour Germany, the continual use of the words 'neutral Powers', etc., and the obstructiveness of the Turkish General Staff. On the general political question, M. Orbay gave every assurance that Turkish policy had not changed. Sir H. Knatchbull-Hugessen said that the alliance had two aspects, war-time and long-term. We had a right to ask Turkish assistance at the proper moment; our demand would be the crucial test of the survival value of the alliance. He said that he felt certain that the Germans had threatened the destruction of Istanbul, and that Turkey seemed to want to nurse Germany as a future counterweight to Russia. M. Orbay strongly denied both these statements. He said that the only solution of Turkey's difficulties with Russia was co-operation with ourselves, Russia and the United States. On

---

[1] The Turkish Ambassador in London, who was at this time on leave in Turkey.

(a) R5840, 8032/55/44. (b) R6428/55/44.

(a) July 17 he gave the Ambassador a definite assurance from the President and Marshal Cakmak that they were entirely on our side and that the alliance remained as firm as ever. In justification of the recent Turkish attitude, he maintained that, if Germany thought that the Turkish Government were about to assist us, she would seize the Dardanelles. She was still in a position to do so; M. Orbay said that the Turkish attitude was intended to avert this danger.

(a) R6566/55/44.

CHAPTER LI

British relations with Turkey from
July 1943 to March 1944

(i)

Reconsideration of British policy to Turkey: military decision not to invite Turkey to enter the war: the slowing of supplies to Turkey: Turkish secret co-operation during the operations in the Dodecanese (July–October 1943).

The Turkish change of attitude since the Tunisian victory had led Sir H. Knatchbull-Hugessen on June 19, 1943, to recommend a slowing down of all deliveries promised by the Prime Minister at the Adana meeting.[1] The Middle East Defence Committee made a similar recommendation on June 25. General Wilson suggested (a) slowing down the delivery of offensive military equipment, but maintaining the delivery of defensive equipment, especially anti-tank mines, at the existing level in order to counter the Turkish plea that they were too weak to resist German attack.[2] The Foreign Office noted on June 27 that it seemed impossible to formulate a positive policy until the Chiefs of Staff had decided what they expected of Turkey.

At the end of June the Foreign Office prepared a memorandum (b) on policy towards Turkey for submission to the Chiefs of Staff. They thought that they must now reckon with a change in Turkish policy in the form of a determination to remain neutral. Turkey had always hoped that the war would end in a compromise which would leave Germany strong enough both militarily and politically to act as a counterpoise to Russia in the Balkans. She hoped also that all three great European Powers would emerge from the war so much weakened that Turkey would be courted by all of them and thus

---

[1] See above, p. 128.
[2] The approximate value of military equipment given to Turkey up to June 18, 1943, was £14,000,000. This figure did not include the value of 5 ships, 40 railway engines, 470 railway wagons, 4,000 tons of coal, 387 horses, 97 aircraft and miscellaneous stores (approximately value £2,000,000); 2,000 tons of petrol for the Turkish Air Force had also been delivered. After deducting the use of shipping which would in any case have been allotted for voyages to Turkey to collect chrome, etc., the average expenditure of Allied shipping effort in delivering stores to Turkey between January and May 1943 was estimated as the equivalent of three-and-a-half 3,000-ton coastal vessels and nearly five 6,000-ton ocean vessels in continuous use. See also p. 178, note 1.

(a) R5624/55/44. (b) R5624/55/44.

be able to play an important part in south-eastern Europe. These dreams were now fading as the prospect of complete Allied victory became clearer, but the Turks felt even more strongly that they must keep out of the war in order that they might be able to fend for themselves in the post-war world. Although they were breaking faith with Great Britain in so doing, they were convinced that the maintenance of an independent Turkey in control of the Dardanelles was so much bound up with British interests in the Mediterranean that Great Britain could not afford to abandon her politically.

We had to consider means of persuading the Turkish Government to abandon this policy of neutrality if operational plans required active Turkish belligerency. The Foreign Office suggested that an early capture of the Dodecanese would upset Turkish calculations about the immediate development of the war. It would strengthen our general position and by extending our blockade to the Aegean, increase Turkish dependence on us, since Turkish trade with the Axis would be confined to the material which could be carried on the Turkish overland communications and the sea route between Istanbul and the Black Sea ports.

The Foreign Office considered whether we could force Turkey into the war by slowing up or stopping the arms supply, withholding vital civilian and industrial supplies and threatening to abandon political support of Turkey during and after the war. They doubted whether a threat to cut off the supply of arms would be enough, since the Turkish Army would probably take over six months to absorb the material already accumulated, and thereafter could count on a flow from German sources.

The Foreign Office memorandum suggested that we could soon cause a crisis in the Turkish economy owing to our monopoly of certain raw materials, even though the Germans would try to increase civilian supplies from Germany and German-occupied Europe. If, however, we cut off Turkey's civilian supplies, we should reduce her rapidly to a state of economic chaos and largely neutralise her value as a belligerent. If—as was possible but unlikely —Germany attacked her she would be unable to offer effectual resistance and might not resist at all, while as long as our relations with Turkey were friendly there was every prospect that she would resist if attacked. Economic collapse might drive Turkey into the German camp. The Foreign Office advised against taking any step which would result in German-Turkish collaboration, even though only in the political and economic spheres. Furthermore, if the Turks, who had always relied upon a Great Power to support them against Russia, considered that they could rely neither on Great Britain nor on Germany, they might compound with Russia in the form of a Turco-Soviet agreement similar to that which M. Saracoglu had refused to sign in 1939, and which would give Russia practical control over the Straits.

The Foreign Office considered whether Turkey would be more of a liability than an asset as a co-belligerent. She would employ considerable British forces which were needed elsewhere. It was doubtful whether she could yet stand the strain of being an 'aircraft carrier' for offensive operations, except possibly against the Dodecanese. The Foreign Office thought that the capture of the Dodecanese and the Greek Aegean islands would alter the possibilities of using Turkey as an Allied base. It would relieve pressure on communications and thereby enable us to maintain air forces for offensive operations against Balkan targets and also to send in any support necessary for Turkish defence.

The Foreign Office asked the Chiefs of Staff whether they regarded it as necessary that Turkey should come into the war. Sir A. Cadogan noted on July 1 that the Foreign Office must know the value (a) attached to Turkey's participation in the war and to the grant of facilities in the country. He asked whether British policy should still insist on excluding Russia from the control of the Straits; 'conditions change, with the development of submarine and other forms of warfare, and I do not know whether the possession of the shores of the Dardanelles nowadays assures an exit for a fleet into the Mediterranean'.

The Chiefs of Staff considered the Foreign Office memorandum on July 23. They decided for the time to give a general priority to (b) operations affecting the elimination of Italy over plans for operations in the eastern Mediterranean. They thought that this decision did not mean a change in long-term policy towards Turkey. They had not yet taken a decision on operations after an Italian collapse, but did not wish to prejudice the issue either by abandoning Turkey or attempting to manoeuvre her into war. From the military point of view, therefore, they recommended that the existing policy should be maintained until the Combined Chiefs of Staff had settled the strategy in the Mediterranean area after the collapse of Italy.

On July 26 the Prime Minister prepared a memorandum for the (c) War Cabinet on the fall of Mussolini. This memorandum was endorsed by the War Cabinet and the Chiefs of Staff Committee. President Roosevelt accepted it with some amendments. Mr. Churchill then proposed that the revised document should become a joint directive conveying the instructions of the two Governments. In the course of a survey of the war situation, the Prime Minister's memorandum referred to the effects of Mussolini's fall and of an

---

(a) R5624/55/44.   (b) COS(43)364(O); COS(43)170th meeting; R6787/1027/44.
(c) WP(43)339 and 353; WM(43)109; R7089/242/22.

Italian capitulation upon Bulgaria, Roumania and Hungary. Mr. Churchill thought that the collapse of Italy should fix the moment for putting the strongest pressure on Turkey to act in accordance with the spirit of the alliance, and that Great Britain and the United States, acting jointly or severally,[1] should if possible be joined or at least supported by Russia in their demands. The War Cabinet on August 2 approved the revised memorandum (with two further amendments not dealing with Turkey) as constituting a joint directive to the United Kingdom and United States Governments.

(a)   Subsequently, on Mr. Churchill's instructions, the Chiefs of Staff told the Commanders-in-Chief, Middle East, in the first week in August to make all preparations to exploit the situation in the eastern Mediterranean occasioned by weakening Italian resistance. To this end all supplies intended for Turkey but needed to re-equip the 10th Indian Division, the Greek Brigade and the 9th Armoured Brigade had been stopped temporarily, and the Commanders-in-Chief were authorised to stop any further supplies for Turkey if they needed them for immediate operations in the Aegean. The Foreign Office noted that these orders meant that we could not maintain our Turkish policy on its existing basis and that the policy agreed at Adana would be given up. We would now have to tell the Turks that we could not keep our promises. We should thus be in a more difficult position later if we wanted Turkey in the war.

Sir A. Cadogan, however, noted on August 5 that he did not think, and never had thought, that Turkey intended to come into the war on our side or to give us in the foreseeable future the use of facilities such as air bases which would expose her to participation in the war. He doubted the wisdom of continuing to arm Turkey or to argue with her. He thought that she might come into the war just before the end. In such case Sir A. Cadogan hoped that we should make it plain that we had no obligations to her. If the Turks protested against the stoppage of supplies, our reply should be that until we had some indication that the arms would be used in the interests of the United Nations, we felt that they were better employed elsewhere. Mr. Eden wrote on August 6 that he had never liked the Adana meeting or the policy resulting from it, and that he had no hesitation in supporting General Wilson's urgent demands to enable him to capture the Dodecanese against the issue of further supplies to Turkey.

On August 10 the Foreign Office noted that events had developed so fast that the July decision of the Chiefs of Staff was now out of date. It seemed probable that Italy would be out of the war within

---

[1] These words were suggested by President Roosevelt.

(a) R7114/55/44.

two or three months. The Prime Minister had suggested that an Italian collapse should fix the moment for putting the strongest pressure on Turkey. The Foreign Office were therefore faced with a paradoxical situation. The imminent collapse of Italy made it necessary to maintain our previous policy towards Turkey, while at the same time the delivery of war material which was one of the main features of this policy had ceased to be possible. Further, our Ambassador at Ankara had been without guidance for two months. Mr. Eden took a less gloomy view of the situation than the Southern Department. He thought that if we could capture the Dodecanese we should have done more to encourage the Turks to come into the war than by the delivery of a certain amount of equipment which they could not use.

Meanwhile on August 3 M. Orbay had called to see Mr. Eden. (a) He said that his Government's attitude to the war was unchanged, although he was disturbed by the increasing suspicion in our attitude. Mr. Eden said that our suspicions were due to the Turkish attitude as defined by their press and statement of their national leaders, and especially by the growing insistence on 'neutrality'. M. Orbay admitted these facts, but said that Turkey was loyal to the alliance. If we had anything to ask of her, why did we not ask it? Mr. Eden replied that at some time or other we should have requests to make of her which would not in our judgment be unreasonable. He thought that it would be to Turkey's benefit to come in on the side of the Allies before the end of the war. M. Orbay did not disagree. He repeated his assurances of unbroken Turkish loyalty to her engagements with us.

A fortnight later M. Orbay saw Sir O. Sargent. The discussion was friendly throughout. Sir O. Sargent pointed out that, while we were grateful to Turkey for her resolute attitude in 1940 and 1941, Turkish neutrality was now no longer a protective barrier against German penetration into the Middle East, but a wall preventing us from getting at our enemies. M. Orbay said that, as a result of his visit to Turkey, he was reassured that Turkish policy was based wholeheartedly on the alliance, and that her neutrality was in accordance with it.

In a letter of August 16 Sir H. Knatchbull-Hugessen referred to (b) the invasion of Sicily, the fall of Mussolini and the bombing of Ploesti from non-Turkish aerodromes. The Germans had suffered new reverses in Russia, and there was accumulating evidence that they were being driven on to the defensive on all sides. The Turks must now be thinking that we could secure without them the objectives which we had said at Adana would need their co-operation.

(a) R7116/55/44. (b) R8032/55/44.

They must also realise the disappearance of the German threat
behind which they had been sheltering. Their pretexts for not
coming into the war were now much thinner. Sir H. Knatchbull-
Hugessen did not think that Turco-Russian relations were improving.
Hitherto we had considered the question of the entry of Turkey into
the war or at least her active collaboration by the grant of facilities
from the point of view of advantage to our strategy against the Axis.
Turkish help was now less important for us from this point of view,
but we might have to look at the matter rather from the standpoint
of our post-war policies towards Turkey and Russia. Sir H.Knatch-
bull-Hugessen suggested encouraging Turkish participation in the
war in the interests of improved Turco-Russian relations. Furthermore, if we decided to continue strengthening Turkey's defensive
security with a view to the post-war period, Turkish active collaboration with the United Nations might be the only basis on which we
could do so without alienating Russia from ourselves. Sir H.
Knatchbull-Hugessen said that, although the Adana objectives had
faded, there might still be reasons for seeking Turkish participation
and in asking Russia and the United States to join us in pressing
for it.

(a)   In the middle of August Sir H. Knatchbull-Hugessen was told of
the Chiefs of Staffs' decision of July 23. The collapse of Italy might
now come much sooner than was expected. We might then want to
put the strongest pressure on Turkey in order to gain the full benefit
of the effects on the Balkans of Italian capitulation. We had decided
to divert supplies from Turkey, with the result that the military
considerations which made it desirable to maintain our existing
policy to Turkey also compelled us to withhold the delivery of war
material which formed part of that policy.

Mr. Eden telegraphed on August 3 to Sir H. Knatchbull-Hugessen
to tell him of a conversation he had had with M. Orbay, which
would give him some guidance as to our policy. The Ambassador
should leave the Turks in no doubt that ultimately we should make
demands on them and that a decision affecting Turkey's future
would be required of her. Sir H. Knatchbull-Hugessen was to try
to convince the Turks that the war would determine the whole
history of the world; that Turkey in her own interests must assume
her share of sacrifices but that we should not ask her to take any
action until it was in her own interests and power to do so, and
until her contribution to a United Nations victory was proportionate
to the sacrifice which this contribution might involve.

(b)   Meanwhile the Prime Minister discussed the Turkish problem
with the Chiefs of Staff while in the *Queen Mary* on the way to the

---

(a) R7114, 7661/55/44. (b) COS(43)513(O), Part B.

Quebec Conference. As a result Mr. Eden informed the Foreign (a)
Office on August 20 that the Chiefs of Staff had told the Prime
Minister that small forces would be available to enter the Dodecanese but that there was no surplus of resources for large-scale
operations in the eastern Mediterranean. Major operations from
Turkey were out of the question. The Chiefs of Staff thought that
the time had not come to ask Turkey to enter the war. With the
agreement of the Prime Minister they suggested that we should ask
Turkey: (i) to interpret the Montreux Convention strictly so as to
exclude the passage of all German shipping of military value
through the Straits; (ii) to stop supplies of chrome to Germany;[1]
(iii) to continue to improve her internal communications, to complete airfields and storage facilities and to raise the effectiveness of
her fighting forces. The Chiefs of Staff recommended that we should
continue to supply such equipment as we could spare and the Turks
could absorb.[2]

Mr. Eden thought that these 'comparatively small' demands
should be put to the Turks at once and that we should not wait
until we had greater demands to make on them. With the concurrence of the Vice-Chiefs of Staff the Foreign Office instructed (b)
Sir H. Knatchbull-Hugessen on September 1 for his own most secret
information that there was little prospect of needing Turkish
co-operation in any eastern Mediterranean operations in the near
future, and that we were unlikely to require the early use of Turkish
air bases.[3] There would be no question of making major demands
on Turkey in 1943. Sir H. Knatchbull-Hugessen was informed of
the minor demands and told that, subject to his views, it seemed
better to let the Turks know what we wanted instead of merely
repeating our complaints about their unsatisfactory attitude and our
warnings that at some future date we should require them to abandon
their neutrality.

Mr. Eden therefore approved the idea of an interview with the
Minister for Foreign Affairs. Sir H. Knatchbull-Hugessen could not
explain that Turkish belligerency was not yet wanted, since a leakage
of this information to the Germans would enable them to guess our
strategical plans for the eastern Mediterranean. He was instead to

---

[1] To the end of July the Germans had only received 14,000 tons as against 90,000 to
which they had a theoretical claim in 1943. See Chapter L, section (iii).

[2] The Foreign Office noted on October 5 that the reduction in military supplies was (c)
so large that the Turks were getting far less than they could absorb, while we were open
to the charge of not fulfilling our promises. We were pressing the Turks to speed up their
re-armament without giving them the means to do it.

[3] The word 'early' was added at the request of the Vice-Chiefs of Staff. The Vice- (d)
Chiefs of Staff also suggested that if Turkey knew that we intended to make no major
demands on her for the time being, she might be less willing to meet our minor demands.

(a) Welfare 250, R7834/55/44. (b) R7834/55/44. (c) R9672/55/44. (d) R8134/1027/44.

discuss frankly future possibilities as between Allies, and to make it clear that Turkey was still under a treaty obligation which we had waived for the moment; meanwhile we expected help in other ways, particularly in the completion and speeding up of military work.

(a)   On September 4 Sir H. Knatchbull-Hugessen saw the Minister for Foreign Affairs. He explained that our failure to make a definite request was due to the strategical position. He said that we were not basing ourselves only on Turkish interests but on our treaty. He mentioned cases in which we felt that the Germans were unduly favoured, e.g. delay and obstruction in the arrests of Axis-owned vessels and various press matters. M. Numan undertook to examine these questions sympathetically, and said that he would continue to use every opportunity for small delays in chrome deliveries to Germany but could not default on his obligations. Sir H. Knatchbull-Hugessen said that we regarded the question of chrome as of extreme importance. He reported that M. Numan did not object or disagree with what he said about an eventual request for Turkish assistance.

(b) On September 11 the Foreign Office agreed with his recommendation that we should await the results of his approach to M. Numan.

(c)   After the unconditional surrender of Italy, the Prime Minister had been strongly in favour of a rapid move to capture the islands of the Dodecanese, and in particular Rhodes. The capture of these islands was necessary in order to clear the Aegean and open the port of Smyrna, which in turn was essential for monitoring an Allied force of any size in Anatolia. The Chiefs of Staff hoped that the Italians in Rhodes might facilitate an Allied landing by disarming the Germans, but the opposite happened; the Germans on September 12 seized control from the Italians. Allied forces, however, took Leros, Cos and Samos in the next two days. Mr. Churchill wanted to continue the plan for an attack on Rhodes, but President Roosevelt and General Eisenhower were afraid that the operation, which would have to be a more serious affair, would be a risky division of strength from the campaign in Italy and, by delaying the movement of assault craft and other shipping from the Mediterranean, might cause a postponement in the date of the cross-Channel invasion. After the American refusal Mr. Churchill still wanted to hold the smaller islands, but it soon became clear that it would be impossible to keep them and to assault Rhodes without the use of air bases (at first, only landing strips) in south-west Anatolia. Sir H. Knatchbull-Hugessen had already been asked on September 17 to make a request to the Turkish Government about supplies for the British garrisons in the islands from British dumps in Turkey, and supplies for civilians from Turkish resources. The use of food and petrol from dumps

---

(a) R8383/55/44.   (b) R8384/55/44.   (c) R8838, 8839/55/44.

would in practice need the consent of the Turkish Government, whose co-operation or acquiescence was also necessary for transport to the coast and thence to the islands. This request amounted to using Turkey as a supply base in the Dodecanese operations. The justification of the request, which had the support of the Chiefs of Staff and the Commanders-in-Chief, was that Turkey was not a neutral but our ally.

The Foreign Office pointed out that we were making our first specific request for semi-military assistance; the Ambassador was to explain that we should regard the Turkish reaction to our demand as a test of their loyalty to the alliance. At the same time Mr. Eden asked M. Orbay for the co-operation of the Turkish Government in accordance with the alliance in furnishing the needed supplies. (a) M. Orbay said that he felt sure that his Government would be glad to help us. Sir H. Knatchbull-Hugessen made the British request on September 19 to the Minister for Foreign Affairs. The Minister agreed to do all he could 'within the framework of his present position'. Two days later M. Orbay called on Sir A. Cadogan to say that his Government gladly complied with our request and agreed as to procedure.

Meanwhile the Prime Minister had written to Mr. Eden that the (b) time had nearly come for a message from him to the Turkish President 'as was arranged at Adana'. The Foreign Office commented that the Turks had taken a cautious but definite step forward towards co-operation; that we should not press them too hard or fast, and that there was no need for a message from the Prime Minister. Apart from supplies to the occupied islands, we wanted nothing more for the time. Mr. Eden spoke to Mr. Churchill, who agreed to take no action.

On October 12 the Commanders-in-Chief, Middle East, asked (c) urgently for a more systematic despatch of supplies, including ammunition, engineering, ordnance and signal stores and petrol to the islands. They asked that, if necessary, the supplies should be speeded up by special trains[1] from the Middle East. By October 16 the Turkish Government had agreed to this request subject to conditions of complete secrecy. Sir H. Knatchbull-Hugessen reported to the Foreign Office that the Turks had said nothing about the flight of military transport planes over Turkey, and that they had shown their readiness to assist in other matters, such as cutting off at our request the lights at a lighthouse. They had been so ready in

---

[1] This request was presumably for the passage of trains carrying British supplies across Turkish territory to ports in western Asia Minor. Cos had fallen on October 4 and an attack was expected on Leros. See below, p. 148, note 1.

(a) R8912, 8913, 9270, 9672/55/44.　　(b) M590/3, R9410/55/44.　　(c) R10243, 10301/55/44.

sending supplies for the occupied islands that there had been an accumulation at the port where British caiques were to fetch them. They had even given us flour and wheat free of charge.

The Foreign Office considered the Turkish co-operation[1] to be most satisfactory, though they thought that the Turks had in mind the importance of the decisions to be taken at the forthcoming Foreign Minister's Conference at Moscow.[2] Sir O. Sargent noted on October 21 that the improvement in the Turkish attitude might be due in part to the realisation that we were involved in an Italian campaign which made it impossible for us to undertake a Balkan offensive. After the Tunisian victory they had been afraid that we might decide to carry our offensive into the Balkans instead of Italy, and that we might suddenly ask them to come into the war.

(ii)

The Foreign Ministers' Conference at Moscow, October 1943: Russian proposal to put pressure on Turkey to enter the war: British and American unwillingness to accept the Russian proposal: decision to ask Turkey at once for the grant of air bases: protocol of the Conference.

(a)   During this time both the British and Turkish Governments continued to be anxious about the unsatisfactory state of Turco-Russian relations. The Foreign Office thought that some attempt to improve these relations should be taken before the Foreign Ministers' Conference in Moscow; the Turkish Foreign Minister had also asked British advice on the matter. Sir H. Knatchbull-Hugessen proposed that before the Conference the Turks should make a confidential declaration of temporary 'non-belligerent co-operation', in which they would state their intention of aligning themselves with the United Nations at an opportune moment; we should give them in return an assurance that such non-belligerency would make Turkey to all intents and purposes one of the United Nations. The Foreign Office considered, however, that the Turks should not try to placate the Russians by making their declaration a few days before the Conference.

The Foreign Office realised that there was a danger of friction

---

(b)   [1]After the fall of Leros the Turks continued to give secret assistance. The supply depôt set up at Kusada during the islands operations in the autumn continued to function in the same manner, and was of considerable value to Allied naval and military forces conducting raiding operations. These forces also made free use of Turkish waters and parts of the Turkish coast. Allied ships engaged in night operations constantly lay up during the day in Turkish waters both before and after their operations.

[2] See below, section (ii), and above, Vol. II, Chapter XXXIV, section (v).

(a) R9005, 9009/55/44. (b) R4995/7/44 (1944).

with the Soviet Government over Russian and British policy towards Turkey, and that the Turkish reaction to Russian displeasure might be to withdraw further into neutrality. The Foreign Office suggested that we should make the best possible case to the Russians at the Conference about what we wanted of the Turks, and that we should explain that we did not require their immediate entry into the war. We could then hope to find out the Russian demands. Mr. Eden and Sir A. Cadogan agreed that the only way was to discuss the matter with the Russians and then to approach the Turks. Mr. Eden was sure that the Russians would not be satisfied with Turkish non-belligerency; he thought that the more the Turks had done for us before the Conference, e.g. as in the Dodecanese, the stronger our position would be for argument with the Russians that our policy was right. On October 2 therefore the Foreign Office informed Sir (a) H. Knatchbull-Hugessen that we did not yet know what either we or the Russians wanted of the Turks, although it seemed likely that we should soon want active Turkish co-operation.

Meanwhile Mr. Eden had submitted a memorandum on Turkey (b) to the War Cabinet stating that British short-term policy was to bring Turkey into the war or persuade her to grant us facilities at a moment appropriate to our strategy in the eastern Mediterranean. From reports of conversations in Moscow between the Soviet Government and the Turkish Ambassador, and in Ankara between the Soviet Ambassador and the Turkish Government, as well as from articles in the Russian press, the Soviet Government seemed to be dissatisfied with Turkish neutrality, and regarded it as wholly to the advantage of Germany.[1] They said that their attitude to Turkey would be governed by Turkey's attitude to Germany. Mr. Eden mentioned indications that Russia viewed with disfavour reports that Turkey wished to intervene in the Balkans in the event of anarchy after a German withdrawal from that area. There were signs that the Russians did not understand the purpose of our supplies of arms to Turkey, and that they suspected that we were giving them to Turkey for ultimate use against Russia.

Mr. Eden thought that there was no conflict between British and Russian long-term interests regarding Turkish territorial integrity or the Straits, but there was some misunderstanding about immediate policy. Both Great Britain and Russia wanted Turkish participation in the war on the side of the United Nations; the only difference was that Russia wanted immediate participation and that for military reasons we wanted Turkey to come in at a later stage. We were not

---

[1] On October 14 the Soviet Ambassador called on Sir H. Knatchbull-Hugessen and (c) complained of Turkish neutrality and unhelpfulness.

(a) R9009/55/44. (b) WP(43)420; R9617/55/44. (c) R10243/55/44.

supplying war material to Turkey to strengthen her against supposed Russian aggressive intentions. If Turkey failed later to fulfil her obligations under the treaty, we should stop these military supplies. We had no interest in Turkish intervention in the Balkans after the withdrawal of the Germans, although we should welcome Turkish help in clearing the enemy out of the area. Mr. Eden asked that the War Cabinet should agree to a statement in this sense to the Soviet Government.

(a)   At a meeting of the War Cabinet on October 5 the Prime Minister said that while he could not wish to press Turkey to enter the war at this stage on conditions involving the diversion to Turkey of military resources required elsewhere, he would be glad if Turkey entered the war on her own initiative. Subject to this point, the War Cabinet approved Mr. Eden's proposed course of action.

(b)   The British agenda for the Moscow Conference proposed a discussion on the desirability or otherwise of Turkey's entry into the war as an active belligerent either at once or at a later date and on the assistance which Turkey could give to the United Nations war effort as a non-belligerent. At their first formal meeting at Moscow

(c) on October 19 the Foreign Ministers agreed to consider measures to shorten the war against Germany and her allies in Europe. M. Molotov proposed that the three Powers should suggest to the Turkish Government their immediate entry into the war. On

(d) October 20 the Conference discussed the Soviet proposal. Mr. Eden said the difference between the British and Russian views was only on the question of timing. We could not give Turkey the support which she was entitled to expect if she entered the war at once.[1] We and the Russians would like to see Turkey help us to drive the Germans out of the Balkans; neither of us would welcome Turkish aspirations in that area. M. Molotov agreed. Mr. Eden spoke of the importance of a common policy with Russia in the matter and suggested that the Conference should consider it later. M. Molotov agreed and Mr. Hull did not dissent. Mr. Eden thereupon sent a telegram to the Prime Minister asking for his views. He thought that he should ask the Russians to give their reasons for thinking that Turkey should enter the war at once. He himself preferred to work for a decision of the Conference that Turkey should come into the war at an appropriate moment to be decided by the three Governments in the light of the military situation.

(e)   [1] The British Government had promised to make available 25 air squadrons when Turkey came into the war on our side. These squadrons could not, however, have been made available to Turkey in November 1943.

(a) WM(43)135.3, C.A. (b) Tel. 35 Extra to Moscow, R9971/55/44. (c) Moscow tel. 43 Space, R10557/55/44; N6165, 6921/3666/38. (d) Moscow tel. 48 Space (Churchill Papers/446; N6221/3663/38). (e) WM(43)148.2, C.A.

The Foreign Office thought that, until we had made further (a) progress in the Dodecanese, the Turks would refuse an invitation to enter the war. If Turkey did come in, we probably could not take advantage of her belligerency owing to the insufficiency of our military resources in the Middle East. Turkey might prove more of a liability than an asset, and might even temporarily collapse. The Russians might in consequence spread over into Turkish territory.

The Foreign Office and the Chiefs of Staff submitted a draft (b) telegram to the Prime Minister on October 22. The draft said that Mr. Churchill agreed that the Russians should be pressed to give their reasons for wanting Turkey in at the moment. Our policy should be to get Turkey to enter the war as soon as, but not before, we could exploit fully the military advantages from her entry. This condition was not likely to be fulfilled until we had sufficient forces available for the eastern Mediterranean to enable us to: (i) assist Turkey to maintain her position in Thrace; (ii) occupy the necessary island bases in the Aegean, e.g. Rhodes, Cos and Lemnos; (iii) exercise sea and air control in the Aegean; (iv) provide adequate air defence for the major Turkish cities and ports and for our shipping in Turkish waters.

The Prime Minister, however, preferred a draft of his own. This draft, after discussion with Sir A. Cadogan[1] and the Chiefs of Staff, was sent as a message to Mr. Eden on October 23. The Prime (c) Minister's view was that, if we forced Turkey to enter the war, she would

> 'insist on air support, etc., which could not be provided without detriment to main operations in Italy. If, however, Turkey enters on her own initiative, perhaps moving through a phase of non-belligerency, we should not have the same obligation and yet great advantages might be reaped. Obviously timing is vital and dependent upon what is the aggressive strength of the enemy in Bulgaria and Thrace. The prize would be to get into the Black Sea with supplies for Russia, warships and other forces. This is what I call giving Russia the right hand.'

Mr. Churchill said that he would like to see Turkey come in on her own and did not think that she would be overrun. 'The first step is to find out what we and the Russians want and what will help both of us most.' On October 25 Mr. Churchill sent a further telegram (d) saying that we should not discourage the Russian desire that Turkey should of her own volition enter the war. He thought that the

---

[1] Sir A. Cadogan thought the Prime Minister's draft fitted in with the views of the Foreign Office.

(a) R10557/55/44. (b) COS(43)1206; N6221/3666/38. (c) T1700/3, tel. 106 Extra to Moscow (Churchill Papers/446; R10557/55/44). (d) T1721/3, tel. 132 Extra to Moscow (Churchill Papers/446; R10557/55/44).

Russians should not be put in the position of 'arguing for this and we of simply making difficulties'. We ought to 'agree in principle and let the difficulties manifest themselves. . . . They may well be overcome or put in their proper place and proportion. Anyhow we ought not to begin by crabbing everything.'[1]

(a)   Meanwhile Mr. Eden had asked Stalin why he thought the present a good moment to get Turkey into the war. Mr. Eden pointed out that we were weak in the eastern Mediterranean, that Istanbul was vulnerable and that we could not fulfil our engagements to Turkey to send the air supplies promised in the event of attack. Stalin said that Turkey's entry would not be necessary next year and that the arms which we and the United States were supplying would have been wasted. If Turkey wanted to be at the conference table to stake her claims, she must earn her place. She could draw off now some ten German divisions, and what could Germany do against her? Germany could act only on the defensive, and the Allies would have enough air strength to cover Turkey. Mr. Eden denied this. Stalin added that, as soon as Turkey moved, the Balkan situation would become difficult for Hitler.

(b)   Mr. Eden used Mr. Churchill's telegram of October 23 as the basis for a paper setting out the British point of view on Turkey, which he circulated to the Conference on October 25. He said that there was no question that the immediate entry of Turkey into the war would help the Allies. Every new enemy hastened the destruction of Hitler. We should be able to get into the Black Sea with supplies for the Soviet Union, warships and perhaps other forces. The Germans would be obliged to keep some divisions watching the Turkish frontier, but would not be strong enough to overrun Turkey. The use of airfields in south-west Anatolia would be of great, perhaps decisive, advantage in any operations against the Aegean islands. Further, the Germans would be deprived of valuable supplies of chrome.

Mr. Eden asked what inducements could be offered to Turkey to enter the war on her own initiative. If she did so, what action did we want her to take? If, despite our offers, Turkey would not come in, Mr. Eden considered means to force her to do so. Turkey would then certainly demand immediate support for the defence of Istanbul against attack from German air forces in the Balkans. In view of Allied commitments in the Mediterranean area, especially in Italy, we could not provide even a fraction of the twenty-five squadrons which we were committed to sending Turkey as a first instalment.

---

[1] The Prime Minister also had in mind the Russian suggestion that we should try to bring Sweden into the war. See Vol. II, Chapter XXXIV, pp. 585–6.

(a) Moscow tel. 54 Space (Churchill Papers/446; R10584/55/44).   (b) N6921/3666/38.

Mr. Eden suggested that, if we could neither induce Turkey to enter the war on her own initiative nor put sufficient pressure on her to compel her to do so, there was a third possible course of action. The capture of Rhodes might lead to the opening of the Dardanelles and the passage of Allied shipping into the Black Sea. The use of Turkish airfields in south-west Anatolia was essential to the success of our operation against Rhodes. If we could induce the Turks to grant us the use of these airfields, we should not only have secured a valuable tactical advantage but have moved Turkey from an attitude of neutrality to one of non-belligerency. The step from non-belligerency to active participation in the war might then be engineered.

Mr. Hull also laid a memorandum before the Conference to the effect that the United States Government did not consider it advisable at that time to induce Turkey to enter the war. The memorandum referred to the strain on Allied resources in building up for an invasion of northern France, and the absorption of other resources in the Mediterranean in support of the Italian offensive. In view of these and other commitments the United States Government thought it unwise to undertake the additional drain on our resources which would be caused by a Turkish entry into the war owing to pressure from us. They proposed instead enquiries to the Turkish Government for the lease from Turkey as a neutral of air bases and transport facilities.

On October 28 the Conference discussed the Soviet proposal that (a) Turkey should be brought into the war immediately. Mr. Eden restated the arguments set out in his memorandum.[1] Mr. Hull also said that his Government did not think it advisable for the present to induce Turkey to come into the war. On being questioned by M. Molotov, he said that he agreed with the British and Russian view of the desirability of Turkish belligerency, but objected only to paying a price for it in view of other Allied commitments. He suggested that an early request be made to the Turks for the lease of air bases and transport facilities on the basis of Turkey remaining neutral.

M. Molotov asked why we were supplying Turkey with arms if we did not want her in the war. He thought that Turkish help was needed at once. A joint approach by the three Powers coupled with

---

[1] Mr. Eden also suggested (following a proposal by Mr. Churchill) the passage of a (b) British submarine flotilla through the Straits to destroy German transports evacuating troops from the Crimea. Mr. Molotov proposed that the naval experts should discuss this plan.

(a) Moscow tel. 121 Space, R10956/55/44. (b) Tels. 171 and 174 Extra to Moscow, Churchill Papers/446.

a threat to withhold arms might induce Turkey to come in. Mr. Eden and Mr. Hull agreed to inform their Governments of the Russian view and to ask that the Russian proposal be considered further.

(a)   Mr. Eden told M. Molotov on October 31 that he was ready to sign an undertaking that we would do our best to get Turkey into the war in 1943. M. Molotov suggested a protocol saying that the three Foreign Secretaries thought it necessary for Turkey to come into the war in 1943 in her own interests and the interests of all peace-loving nations. M. Molotov wanted to approach Turkey with this proposal and ask at once for the use of air bases. After considerable argument, Mr. Eden's view prevailed that we should first secure bases and that the entry of Turkey into the war should come later. The protocol agreed between Mr. Eden and M. Molotov stated that it was most desirable for Turkey to enter the war before the end of 1943; that Great Britain and Russia should make a suggestion to this effect to the Turkish Government as soon as possible, and should ask them immediately to give all possible aid to the United Nations by providing air bases and other facilities.

Mr. Eden reported to the Prime Minister that he had gone beyond his instructions because the Soviet Government would not have agreed to a request for air bases only unless we had undertaken to press the Turks to come in before the end of the year. Mr. Eden was convinced that it was in our interest to take this line by which we might obtain the bases at once, get Turkey into the war within the next two months and at the same time meet the wishes of the Soviet Government on a question to which they attached the utmost importance. The air bases would be only for use by British aircraft.

(b)   On November 2 the War Cabinet endorsed Mr. Eden's action. Mr. Hull agreed with the policy but could not subscribe to the
(c)   protocol without authority from Washington. The United States Government subsequently decided to join the British and Russian Governments in making immediate demands on Turkey for the use of air bases, and later in pressing Turkey to enter the war before the end of the year. This agreement was subject to the condition that no United States or British resources would be committed to the eastern Mediterranean area which the Combined Chiefs of Staff thought necessary for operations in Italy or for the cross-Channel invasion. President Roosevelt authorised Mr. Harriman to allow the letter containing the United States agreement to be attached as an annex to the protocol signed by M. Molotov and Mr. Eden.

(a) Moscow tels. 153–4 Space, R11053/55/44. (b) WM(43)149.2, C.A. (c) R13502/55/44.

(iii)

Mr. Eden's conversations with the Turkish Foreign Minister at Cairo: Turkish refusal of the request for air bases (October 27–November 20, 1943).

In the first week in October Sir H. Knatchbull-Hugessen had (a) suggested a visit to Ankara by Mr. Eden after the Conference. He mentioned the suspicion of the Turkish Government after Mr. Eden's visit to Moscow in 1941. He told Mr. Eden later that M. Numan was anxious to meet him in Cairo. Mr. Eden replied that such a (b) meeting might be inappropriate and inconvenient to him. Sir A. Cadogan thought that a little aloofness would do the Turks good, since there was no fear of their coming in on the wrong side. On October 27 therefore the Foreign Office instructed Sir H. Knatchbull-Hugessen that they could not back his arguments to Mr. Eden.

Before this telegram was sent, however, the Southern Department (c) of the Foreign Office began to think that it might be unwise to ignore this latest Turkish move. There was a political reason for bringing Turkey into the war, but hitherto there appeared to have been no military reason for doing so. Turkish belligerency might be the best if not the only way of preventing the Russians from getting control of the Balkans. The drift of the Balkan countries towards Russia was due mainly to the small prospects of Allied intervention in the Balkans in the near future, and to the inability of the Greek and Yugoslav Governments to act as rallying points of resistance in their own countries.

The Russians seemed to be refusing as a matter of policy to discuss the Balkan situation, because they knew that by keeping quiet they had nothing to lose, and that the Balkans were likely to fall under exclusive Soviet influence. If the Turks maintained neutrality, British forces would probably be unable to get into the Balkans before the Germans withdrew or before the Russians had firmly established themselves there. Furthermore we should be unable to continue our support of Turkey, whose existence in her present form was a long-term British interest, without danger of serious Anglo-Soviet friction.

The Foreign Office considered that the future of British interests in the Balkans was thus bound up with the entry of Turkey into the war. If the Soviet Government really wanted Turkey in the war, they might persuade them to come in by an offer of an agreement over south-east Europe. The terms of this offer might be that Turkey should undertake to participate in the war, and that the

---

(a) R10557, 12223/55/44. (b) Moscow tel. 87 Space, R12223/55/44. (c) R10832/55/44; R10733/111/37.

United States, Great Britain and Russia should issue a tripartite declaration or charter regarding south-east Europe. Turkey might even be a fourth signatory as the leading and only intact Power in the area. If Turkey, as the strongest of the south-east European Powers, were assured, with Russian consent, of a leading place in the new south-east European order, there might be a chance of securing independence for the Balkan States generally and of preventing a complete Russian domination of the Peninsula.

The Foreign Office thought also that with Turkey in the war we should have a better chance of capturing the Dodecanese within a reasonable time and thereby opening the Aegean and the Straits. The fact that Turkey was an ally of Russia would convince the Roumanians that unconditional surrender to Russia as well as ourselves was inevitable. The Bulgarian régime might collapse and the Bulgarians withdraw their divisions from Yugoslavia and Greece, with catastrophic consequences to Germany. Although the proposed arrangement would probably have no direct effect on the Communist bands in Yugoslavia and Greece, it might do something to strengthen the moderate influences which, owing to the feebleness of the exiled Governments, were ineffective.

The Foreign Office therefore came to the conclusion that M. Numan's offer to meet Mr. Eden would be a useful opportunity for exploring the matter with the Turks, that is to say, for telling the Turks what we wanted them to do, and also for compelling them to (a) give us an answer. The Foreign Office therefore sent a telegram to Mr. Eden on October 28. They suggested that he should say that he would be glad to see M. Numan if he had anything to tell him about (b) Turkish policy regarding the war. Sir A. Cadogan set out in a second telegram the Foreign Office views on the position of Turkey. If Mr. Eden approved of them and found M. Numan inclined to accept them, the Foreign Office would work along these proposed lines after Mr. Eden's return. On October 30 Mr. Churchill strongly (c) supported the proposal that Mr. Eden should visit Cairo.

In the light of these arguments Mr. Eden decided to go to Cairo (d) to meet M. Numan. He suggested that M. Molotov might like to send a Russian representative with him to meet M. Numan, but (e) M. Molotov left the matter in Mr. Eden's hands. On November 2 Mr. Churchill instructed Mr. Eden to ask for air bases in the name (f) of both Powers when he saw M. Numan.[1] M. Molotov gave Mr.

---

[1] This demand had, in fact, become urgent. Since the fall of Cos, on October 4, five British destroyers and two submarines had been lost and four cruisers and two destroyers

(*continued on page 149*)

(a) R10766/55/44. (b) R10766/55/44. (c) Extra 174, 194. (d) Moscow tel. 156 Space (Churchill Papers/446; R12164/55/44). (e) Tel. 210 Extra to Moscow, R11165/55/44. (f) Moscow tel. 161 Space, R11165/55/44.

Eden a free hand whether to ask for air bases in the name of both Powers or of ourselves alone. Mr. Eden preferred the latter plan since we could make our request on the basis of the treaty, and the Turks were suspicious of the Russians. M. Molotov also left it to (a) Mr. Eden to propose the date of a joint *démarche* to Turkey about entry into the war. He hoped that we would think it right to make this *démarche* soon.

On November 3 the Prime Minister sent a message to Cairo for (b) Mr. Eden. He said that the time had come to 'put the hard screw' on Turkey. The situation had changed; Turkey ought to be made to take whatever practical steps Great Britain and Russia required of her to help the Allies. Mr. Churchill did not think that the action for which we were asking would lead to an attack on Turkey, but it might be her last chance to come in with the victorious nations. The Russian request offered her 'a wonderful prospect', especially since the immediate practical action was so modest and passive. If Turkey were drawn thereby into the war, she would gain the greatest possible guarantee for the integrity of her interests and possessions.

Mr. Churchill told Mr. Eden that he need not conceal from M. Numan that Russia and Great Britain expected Turkey to declare war on Germany before the end of the year and that the request for air bases was only our first demand. Turkey would be expected to grant facilities and allow a situation to arise which might be equivalent to war. Mr. Eden could say that, if Turkey failed to act with us now, the British import of arms might be stopped at once and we should not support Turkey's case with Russia. The question of the Straits would be open, and we should regard the alliance as a fraud. (c) Mr. Eden read selected passages from Mr. Churchill's telegram in putting the British argument in favour of the grant of air bases.

M. Numan left for Cairo on November 2. The official announce- (d) ment of his departure was well received by the general body of deputies and given prominence in the Turkish press. Mr. Eden had (e) four meetings—between November 5 and 8—with M. Numan. At

---

(*continued*)
damaged by enemy air attack while supplying or patrolling the islands. On October 29 the Chiefs of Staff told the Prime Minister that unless Leros were supplied entirely by submarine the use of air bases in South-West Anatolia was essential. On October 31 Mr. Eden spoke to M. Molotov of the urgency of the need for airfields 'not only to prevent disaster in Leros and Samos but to make possible the capture of Rhodes'. General Ismay later explained the matter in detail to M. Molotov. Next day Mr. Eden again asked M. Molotov to agree to pressure on the Turks to allow the use of air bases. Mr. Eden said that Mr. Churchill had let him know that without the prompt permission to use the bases it would be impossible to hold Leros. (*F.R.U.S.*, 1943. Cairo and Teheran Conferences, pp. 144–6.) Leros fell on November 16 and Samos was evacuated three days later.

(a) Moscow tel. 163 Space, R11166/55/44. (b) R11167/55/44; Churchill Papers/446. (c) R11300/55/44. (d) R11183/55/44. (e) R12407/55/44.

the first meeting Mr. Eden put two requests to the Turkish Government. He asked, on behalf of Great Britain, for the use of air bases in south-west Anatolia for operations against Rhodes. General Ismay, who accompanied Mr. Eden at the meetings, pointed out that, if we captured Rhodes, the Germans would have to leave Crete and southern Greece, and that we should have full use of the Aegean.

Mr. Eden's second request, which he put forward on behalf of the three Allied Governments, was that Turkey should enter the war before the end of the year. The Allies asked for Turkish belligerency, though not for active military operations, in order to shorten the war (i) by compelling the Bulgarians to concentrate their forces on the Turkish-Bulgarian frontier and thus making it necessary for the Germans to replace—to the extent of some ten divisions—the Bulgarian divisions in Greece and Yugoslavia, (ii) by enabling the Allies to bomb the decisive target of Ploesti (which could be reached more easily from Turkey than from Italy, (iii) by depriving Germany of Turkish supplies of chrome. Turkish entry into the war would also have an important effect in hastening the process of disintegration in Germany and her satellites.

(a)   After this meeting Mr. Eden telegraphed to the Prime Minister: 'We have had a long, tough day with the Turks.'[1] M. Numan refused to accept a distinction between the grant of bases and the entry of Turkey into the war in 1943. He maintained that, if the Turks let us use the bases, the Germans would conclude that Turkey had decided to join the Allies; they (the Germans) would not dare not to react. M. Numan did not refuse to discuss the question of an early entry into the war, but he showed deep suspicion of possible Russian plans for penetration into the Balkans. Mr. Eden said that in our view Russia had no intentions hostile to the independence of the Balkan States, but that, even if the Turkish fears were justified, Turkey would be in a stronger position after the war if she had taken part in the defeat of Germany and thereby secured Russian goodwill. M. Numan replied that Turkish belligerency would be of no benefit to Great Britain if Turkey were left militarily exhausted. A discussion followed about the effect on Germany of Turkey's entry into the war. M. Numan argued that Bulgaria would not be compelled thereby to make any important redistribution of her forces.

---

[1] Mr. Eden has written later (*Memoirs*, III, 419) that he found the Turkish Ministers suspicious of some deal between us and the Russians, as a result of which the Russians had abandoned their demand for a second front and we had agreed to put pressure on Turkey which would end in her being involved in war with Germany. M. Numan said that he must have 'more reassurances that it would be in Turkey's ultimate interest to enter the war before he could consider such a step'.

(a) T1866/3 (Churchill Papers/446; R11300/55/44).

M. Numan asked Mr. Eden for an assurance that we would continue our supplies. He accepted Mr. Eden's answer that he could give no assurances until he knew the outcome of the conversations. Mr. Eden reported that it would be difficult to persuade the Turkish Government to separate the question of bases from the question of Turkish entry into the war. He proposed telling the Turks the next day that we could not accept their attitude as the conduct of an ally, and that if they persisted in it the whole character of our relations must be affected and we could not continue our supplies.

At the meeting on November 6 Mr. Eden restated our need for (a) air bases. He repeated that this need was urgent and that we were sure that the Germans would not declare war on the Turks if they gave us the bases. Mr. Eden threatened the stoppage of supplies if the Turks refused. M. Numan replied that the Turks could not accept our view that by giving us bases they would not be drawn into war. He said that Turkey was unable to grant us the facilities for which we asked.

M. Numan then raised the broad issue of Turkey's entry into the war. He asked whether we were really convinced that we had given the Turks enough supplies to enable them to wage war on modern lines. Further, the Turks had always thought that if they entered the war they would do so in active collaboration with the Allies. Had we decided on operations in the Balkans so that the Turks could support us there? Mr. Eden refused to discuss Allied strategy until the Turks were willing to contemplate entry into the war. He said that the best contribution the Turks could then make to the common cause was a passive role, and that they were capable of discharging this role. M. Numan said that Turkish public opinion would never agree merely to a passive part. He could only report to his Government on the question of entering the war.

Mr. Eden warned M. Numan of the consequences which refusal to meet us in either respect would have on Anglo-Turkish relations and on Turkish relations with the Allies as a whole. He pointed out that the refusal would have a bad effect on the Russian attitude to Turkey. M. Numan said that he must know more about Russia's intentions before allowing Turkey to become involved in war. Mr. Eden finally agreed that M. Numan should return to Ankara[1] and put to the Turkish Government that their reply might be that they were prepared to discuss their entry into the war and that in the discussion they would raise certain political and military questions. M. Numan would then let us know the decision of his Government;

---

[1] On November 7, however, M. Numan asked for another meeting with Mr. Eden and delayed his return accordingly.

(a) R11317/55/44.

F*BFP

M. Numan obviously did not think that they would give the answer for which Mr. Eden hoped. Meanwhile we should consult the United States and Soviet Governments about the role we would expect Turkey to play if she came into the war. Mr. Eden suggested to the Prime Minister that the Chiefs of Staff should prepare a paper for immediate communication to the United States and Russia. After the three Governments had agreed on the demands to be made, they could jointly repeat them to the Turkish Government.

(a)   On November 7 Mr. Eden asked Sir A. Clark Kerr to give M. Molotov an outline of the conversations, and to tell him that he proposed a joint invitation to the Turks to enter the war. He told Sir A. Clark Kerr for his own information that, if the Russians felt disposed to give the Turks some reassurance about the Balkans, it would help in putting pressure on the Turks. He also asked Sir A.

(b) Clark Kerr for his views on the suggestion that if the Russians wanted Turkey in the war, they should pay part of the price by offering to come to terms with her over south-eastern Europe.

(c)   On November 7 Sir H. Knatchbull-Hugessen (who had also come to Cairo) saw M. Numan. M. Numan said that he felt that Mr. Eden had been speaking on behalf of the Soviet Government. Mr. Eden had asked Turkey to come into the war immediately but had given him no information about the conditions in which Turkey would take part. Sir H. Knatchbull-Hugessen said that we were allies of Turkey and Russia, and that our main purpose was to finish the war as soon as possible. The entry of Turkey would do much to achieve this purpose. He reminded M. Numan that the latter had asked how the Turkish Government could put themselves right with Russia. M. Numan now had that advice, i.e. that Turkey should come into the war before the end of the year. Turkey could protect herself against any aggressive Russian intentions more securely by doing as we suggested than by keeping out of the war. M. Numan refused to accept this argument; he said that whatever happened Turkey would stand alone against Russia.

Sir H. Knatchbull-Hugessen thought it clear that M. Numan's own opinion was against entry into the war on the basis of the present proposals and at least until certain points could be cleared up, e.g. he could not commit his country to war without knowing the degree of co-operation we could supply; he must also be able to give assurances that Turkey would not be in danger from subsequent Russian penetration into the Balkans. If M. Numan could not give such assurances to the Turkish National Assembly, the whole régime might be swept away.

(a) R11319/55/44. (b) R11300/55/44; R11332/650/44. (c) R11412/55/44.

On November 7 Mr. Churchill telegraphed to Mr. Eden that the (a)
two main points to put to the Turks were that the Russian request
to them to join in the war was an opportunity for them to establish
a relationship with Russia which would be a protection for many
years; and that they were not asked to 'exhaust themselves' and
would get much stronger through Allied equipment if the war were
prolonged. On November 8 Mr. Eden put these arguments to M. (b)
Numan. M. Numan said that he approved of our policy towards
Russia and welcomed the Moscow decisions. His anxieties concerned
the Balkans in general and Bulgaria in particular. He said that in
the twentieth century the fate of the Balkans had come to interest
Turkey as directly as the fate of the Straits in the last century. If
Turkey were to enter the war and Russia were to establish herself
in Roumania and Bulgaria for, say, twenty-five years, Turkey would
be in a difficult position, especially if she had contributed in any
way to this result.

M. Numan complained of a change in Mr. Eden's attitude towards
Turkey, and the use of a threat when Mr. Eden had said that we
could not continue to send supplies if she refused our request. Mr.
Eden referred to the effect on British public opinion if Turkey could
not help us as early as possible regarding bases or by a favourable
answer to the joint Allied request. There was no question of our
supplying Turkey with arms if our requests were refused. Mr. Eden
appealed to M. Numan to urge his Government to return a favourable reply. M. Numan said that if his Government's response was
favourable they would attach more importance to political than to
military talks. Mr. Eden reported to Mr. Churchill that he now had
more hope that the Turkish reply might not be wholly negative.

The Northern Department of the Foreign Office noted that if the
Turks tried to extract Russian undertakings about the Balkans and
were then dissatisfied with them, we and the Americans might find
ourselves obliged to express views about the Balkans in circumstances which would be most embarrassing and might lead to
differences of view between us and the United States. For this reason
there was much to be said for following up at once the Russian
suggestion of a joint guarantee of independence and offering this to
Turkey in return for coming in, with a definite indication that she
could not expect anything else. We should thereby prevent a
situation arising in which the Turks (even though it seemed unlikely)
gave a favourable reply and then asked for a conference on political
matters.

The Russian suggestion of a guarantee had been made to Sir A. (c)

(a) T1889/3 (Churchill Papers/446; R11337/55/44). (b) R11413/55/44. (c) R11395/
55/44.

Clark Kerr on the morning of November 8. Sir A. Clark Kerr had given M. Molotov an outline of the talks with M. Numan and had explained Mr. Eden's immediate intentions. M. Molotov thought that Turkish suspicions were merely a pretext to gain time. If Turkey did in fact feel anxious, the Soviet Government would be ready to meet her half-way provided she entered the war. He thought that the Soviet Government would be willing to join in a three-Power guarantee of Turkish independence and integrity and of a place at the Peace Conference. He said that Turkey 'should be trodden on hard'. Sir A. Clark Kerr asked what he meant by this phrase. M. Molotov replied that Turkey should be invited by the three Allies to come into the war in 1943.

Sir A. Clark Kerr reminded M. Molotov that Turkey's anxieties were mainly concerned with possible Soviet penetration in the Balkans; he suggested that the Soviet Government might consider giving Turkey some kind of reassurances about the Balkans. M. Molotov asked what Turkey was afraid of and what was meant by 'penetration'. He agreed that before the invitation was made to Turkey the three Allies should consult together on what they expected her to do.[1]

(a)   On November 15 M. Numan told Sir H. Knatchbull-Hugessen that there had been a number of meetings of the Turkish Cabinet. He then read their provisional reply to Mr. Eden's requests. The Turkish Government refused the grant of air bases since such a grant would lead to war. The reply about entry into the war reaffirmed Turkish loyalty to the Allied cause, and spoke of services which Turkey 'often, at great risk to herself' had rendered to the Allied Powers. It referred to the inadequacy of Turkish defence preparations and said that, in spite of the goodwill of the British Government, the war potentiality of the Turkish forces was not appreciably increased. Chaos would follow an air attack; Turkey would in effect be put out of the war and become a liability for the United Nations. The repercussions of a war, especially in winter, made the Turkish Government draw back. Their reply spoke of the 'certain disasters' which would follow a 'precipitate entry into the struggle', as compared with the return Turkey could give after the

---

(b)   [1] On November 8 General Ismay reported to the War Cabinet that the Turks did not take our view that Germany no longer had any strength in reserve. In commenting later on this Turkish view the Prime Minister has written: 'Considering what had been happening under their eyes in the Aegean, the Turks can hardly be blamed for their caution.' Churchill, *Second World War*, Vol. V, p. 296.

Mr. Hull told President Roosevelt on November 22 that the American Ambassador at Ankara had reported from reliable Turkish sources that von Papen had recently informed the Turkish Government that the cession of even one air base would lead to an immediate declaration of war by Germany and Bulgaria with disastrous consequences for Turkey. *F.R.U.S.* 1943. Cairo and Teheran Conferences, p. 375.

(a) R11776, 11777/55/44.   (b) WM(43)151.3, C.A.

completion of precautions which Mr. Churchill had 'authoritatively defined at Adana'.

The reply of the Turkish Government referred to 'pernicious propaganda certainly fostered by the enemy' that Turkey was arming herself eventually against the Soviet Union, and said that the object of this allegation was to cause trouble between Turkey and her ally and friends. The reply stated that all Turkey's defence preparations were directed towards the west. Turkey's relations with Russia—the 'natural ally' of Turkey—sprang from their common struggle for liberty and independence.

The reply emphasised that the degree of Germany's strength had never been considered *a priori* as a determining factor in Turkey's attitude. Turkey agreed that Germany was undermined by the prospect of a defeat which seemed inevitable, but she still had means of attack against a country which had no means of counter-attack. No effective help could reach Turkey rapidly from her allies. The passive role assigned to her in the first and most dangerous stage could result in destroying every possibility of her future co-operation. In existing circumstances the Turkish Government considered the sacrifice asked of Turkey as far beyond her material capacity and incompatible with the elementary duty of the Government towards the people.

Sir H. Knatchbull-Hugessen reported to the Foreign Office that (a) he thought the Turkish Government had in principle accepted the policy of co-belligerency. M. Numan had said that this was so, and that the military arguments had been put forward as serious practical considerations. Sir H. Knatchbull-Hugessen suggested that these declarations of acceptance in principle be taken at their face value and that conversations should be begun as soon as possible. He thought that we should take Turkish anxieties about German reprisals sympathetically and give maximum satisfaction about defence against air attack. We should also provide military co-operation in the Balkans; the destruction of airfields and communications in Bulgaria would affect the Turkish estimate of German striking power.

On November 17 M. Numan gave Sir H. Knatchbull-Hugessen (b) the text of the definitive Turkish reply, which conformed exactly to the provisional reply. M. Numan said that after a twelve-hour sitting the Government group and opposition group in the Chamber had approved the Government policy. The session was stormy and the feeling in the Chamber for long one of disapproval. Party groups attached the utmost importance to adequate defence for Turkey and to co-operation with Great Britain in any action which might be taken.

(a) R11779/55/44. (b) R11860, 11906, 12309/55/44.

(a)   Sir H. Knatchbull-Hugessen thought that it would be a mistake not to see a danger signal in the fact that the first criticism of the Government's foreign policy had been heard when M. Numan reported to the party on the Cairo talks and sought approval for the Government's reply. He thought that in this reply the Government were in advance of public opinion, i.e. the small body of deputies and others who, in spite of the power of the President, the Marshal, the Prime Minister and Minister for Foreign Affairs, had influence with the people and must be reckoned with in foreign policy.

(b)   On November 18 the Soviet Ambassador received a copy of the Turkish answer. He agreed with Sir H. Knatchbull-Hugessen that it was a decision in principle to enter the war and that the points raised regarding the German reaction needed serious consideration and reasonable satisfaction. He did not suggest that these points were a pretext for avoiding entry into the war; he agreed that a triple invitation to Turkey to come in was now undesirable.

(c)   M. Numan had earlier said that if he received a triple invitation to come in, he would refuse it. Sir H. Knatchbull-Hugessen was against such an invitation at that stage, since it would defeat its object. The Turkish Government had taken an important decision in the face of a critical assembly; they would not go further until the military implications had been cleared up. He said that M. Numan was determined to act only with Great Britain as his ally. On

(d) November 20 M. Numan told the British Counsellor that the British action at Moscow and again recently had been too hasty after Adana. He said that the Moscow decision to get Turkey into the war in 1943 was 'quite absurd'. Turkey must be given the means to fight, and when she had them she would fight.

(e)   The Foreign Office agreed that the Turks had in principle accepted co-belligerency and had said so in writing for the first time. On the other hand, the Turkish Government would try to avoid entry into the war by the end of 1943 and would hope to postpone it by military arguments which in the state of British resources were hard to refute. British military experts were considering these arguments urgently to see whether we could provide sufficient support to overcome Turkish reluctance. Until this review was complete, we should not open conversations either in Ankara or Moscow.[1] Sir A. Clark Kerr was told for his own information that the Turks clearly wanted to know whether we were intending a

---

(f)   [1] M. Numan was contemplating talks with Moscow, and said that he was thinking of a Turco-Soviet treaty with a British annex on the same lines as the British treaty with its Russian annex.

(a) WP(43)592; R13218/55/44.   (b) R12038, 12588/55/44.   (c) R11861/55/44. (d) R12136/55/44.   (e) R11779, 11849/55/44.   (f) R11778/55/44.

campaign in the Balkans, and that it was much harder for us to give Turkey the necessary protection against air attack, to re-equip her armies and assure her that British and American forces would be operating in the Balkans, than it was for the Russians to give an assurance about Turkey's post-war position in the Balkans.

On November 19 the Foreign Office pointed out to Sir H. (a) Knatchbull-Hugessen that the protocol signed in Moscow committed us to bring Turkey into the war by the end of the year and to make a tripartite approach in this sense if necessary. If this approach were to be postponed, Mr. Eden must be able to reassure M. Molotov that we had a reasonable chance of bringing Turkey into the war in the very near future. Mr. Eden said that he was clearly not in a position to give this assurance. He noted on November 20 that the Turks were looking for pretexts to keep out, and that an approach (b) by the three Powers was necessary.

The Southern Department prepared a draft minute from Mr. Eden to the Prime Minister explaining that what the Turks wanted was some statement from us about our future Balkan strategy, and the part they could play in it. The draft said that although the Chiefs of Staff might be able to offer Turkey sufficient air squadrons and ground defences for her to play a defensive role, Mr. Eden doubted whether we could give the Turks much comfort on this score. He thought our chances of leading the Turks from a vague acceptance of the principle of co-belligerency to a definite commitment of entry into the war were not good, and that the prospects of conversations between the Turks and us alone were poor. Nevertheless we were entitled to begin such conversations without fear of Russian criticism that we were evading our commitment under the protocol to a tripartite demand to the Turks to come into the war. The Turkish reply to our request was a 'conditional acceptance'; any conversations in Ankara would be a continuation of Mr. Eden's talks in Cairo which M. Molotov had agreed should be the first step. It was doubtful whether, if we alone could not get what we wanted from the Turks, a tripartite approach would have more success. M. Numan appeared to have been in earnest when he said that he would refuse a tripartite invitation and that any action he took would be with His Majesty's Government as an ally. The draft minute proposed that if the conclusions of the Chiefs of Staff provided reasonable material for overcoming Turkish resistance, we should go ahead at Ankara after preliminary consultations with the Russians and Americans. We might suggest to the Russians that they could help us by giving the Turks an assurance about Bulgaria and about Turkey's own position in south-east Europe. If, however, the

---

(a) R11861/55/44. (b) R11849, 12590/55/44.

prospects of moving the Turks seemed hopeless, Mr. Eden suggested joint consultation with the Americans and Russians.

Mr. Eden approved this draft minute on November 22, although he noted that he did not take quite such a favourable view of the Turkish attitude. He attached little importance to the 'conditional acceptance' of the Turks. However, he took the minute with him to show to the Prime Minister on arrival in Cairo.[1]

(iv)

The Turkish question at the Teheran Conference: the Prime Minister's insistence upon the value of Turkish belligerency: meetings at Cairo between the Prime Minister, President Roosevelt and the Turkish President: proposals to the Turkish Government (December 4–7, 1943).

It was clear from the American attitude at the Moscow Conference that the question of Turkish entry into the war was now closely involved in the large strategical plans for 1944. The United States military authorities and the State Department thought that the Prime Minister's advocacy of plans for operations in the eastern Mediterranean might result in a serious drain on the resources which should be concentrated on the cross-Channel invasion. In any case Turkish belligerency was of less immediate importance since the Allies had not resources available to provide the arms and protection which the Turks regarded as essential to them. Furthermore the Turks themselves had shown how unwilling they were to come into the war.

At the Moscow Conference the proposal to put pressure on Turkey to enter the war and not merely to allow us the use of bases had been made by the Russians. Within a short time the Russians were less interested in Turkish entry in the war and indeed unwilling to urge it on the Turkish Government if it meant a diversion of Allied forces and, possibly, a postponement for six or eight weeks of the cross-Channel invasion. The Prime Minister, on the other hand, was more hopeful of persuading the Turks and more anxious to get them into the war. His main reason was that he regarded the full exploitation of the British and Allied forces in the Mediterranean as an essential means of reducing German strength elsewhere; he expected the entry of Turkey to be followed by a collapse of resistance in Roumania and Bulgaria.

---

[1] The Prime Minister had left Plymouth in the battleship *Renown* on November 12 for the Cairo and Teheran conferences. Mr. Eden had gone back to London from Cairo on November 10. On November 23 he flew from England to join the Prime Minister in Cairo.

The differences between the British view—or at all events the (a)
Prime Minister's view—and that of the Americans were shown at
the conference in Cairo between the Prime Minister and the
President and their respective military advisers before the meetings
at Teheran. The Prime Minister and the British Chiefs of Staff put
the familiar arguments in favour of capturing Rhodes and the
Aegean islands and securing Turkey as a belligerent. The President
doubted whether we could retain the cross-Channel invasion 'in all
its integrity and at the same time keep the Mediterranean ablaze'.
The Prime Minister thought that the cross-Channel invasion 'should
not be such a tyrant as to rule out every other activity in the
Mediterranean'. The matter was thus left open for discussion at
Teheran.

At the first plenary meeting of the Teheran Conference on
November 28 Mr. Churchill spoke of the advantages of bringing
Turkey into the war. We should have the use of air bases and with
the capture of the Aegean islands gain access to Black Sea ports.
We could then run convoys continuously to Russian ports instead of
limiting ourselves—owing to the diversion of escort vessels for the
cross-Channel preparations—to four convoys by the northern routes.
If Turkey came in, there might be 'a political landslide among the
satellite States which would enable the Greeks to revolt and hustle
the Germans out of Greece'. The Prime Minister asked whether
Stalin would be in favour of carrying out our proposed plans in the
eastern Mediterranean even if they meant a postponement of the
cross-Channel invasion for one or two months. He explained that
our plans required only two or three divisions and therefore meant
no appreciable diversion of effort from the Italian front or from the
cross-Channel preparations. Stalin said that it would be worth while
to capture the Aegean islands if the operation needed only three or
four divisions, but that we ought not to disperse Allied forces by
sending part to Turkey and elsewhere, part to southern France.
The best course would be to make the cross-Channel invasion the
basic operation for 1944, and after the capture of Rome to send all
available forces in Italy to invade southern France. He would even
suggest postponing the capture of Rome for the present if we could
send ten divisions to southern France. Stalin did not expect Turkey
to agree to enter the war, although he was in favour of trying again:
'We ought to take them by the scruff of the neck if necessary.'
President Roosevelt said that any operation undertaken in the eastern
Mediterranean would probably put off the cross-Channel invasion
until June or July, and that he was opposed to delay. The President
suggested that the military experts at the Conference should consider

---

(a) COS(43)791(O), Part II.

a time-table. The Prime Minister agreed, but said that he could not sacrifice the activities of the armies in the Mediterranean—which included twenty British and British-controlled divisions—merely to keep the date of May 1 for the cross-Channel invasion. The Prime Minister said that the question of Turkey was probably as much political as military. We had to decide (i) what we wanted the Turks to do, (ii) what offer we could make them, (iii) what would be the consequences of our offer. Stalin said that Turkey was the ally of Great Britain and on terms of friendship with the United States, and that the British and Americans should undertake the task of persuading her to come into the war. The Prime Minister thought that Turkey would be 'mad' if she refused a Russian invitation to come in on the winning side, and at the same time lost the sympathies of Great Britain. Stalin said that a number of people preferred to be mad, and that all the neutrals regarded those who were waging war as fools to fight when they might be doing nothing.

At the second plenary meeting of the Conference on November 29 General Brooke reported on his discussions with General Marshall and Marshal Voroshilov. They considered that unless some operations were carried out in the Mediterranean from the present time to the cross-Channel invasion the Germans would be able to move troops from Italy to northern France or the Russian front. On the other hand these operations must not be on a scale which would interfere with the main invasion plan. They agreed with the Prime Minister's view about the advantages to be gained from Turkish entry into the war. In the discussion at the plenary meeting the Prime Minister argued that we should keep sufficient landing craft in the Mediterranean to transport two divisions. These landing craft could be used for outflanking movements in Italy, and also for the capture of Rhodes and for opening the Aegean on the entry of Turkey into the war. The retention of the landing craft would mean a postponement of the cross-Channel invasion perhaps for six or eight weeks or the recall of assault craft and shipping already sent to the Far East. The Prime Minister said that, as the ally of Turkey, we had already accepted the task of trying to persuade or induce her to come into the war before the end of the year. If the President cared to take the lead in the matter, we should be glad to leave it to him. The Prime Minister would tell the Turks that if they refused a tripartite invitation the British Government would lose interest in Turkish territorial rights, particularly with regard to the Dardanelles and Bosphorus. In answer to a question by the Prime Minister, Stalin said that the Soviet Government would consider themselves at war with Bulgaria if as a result of Turkey's entry into the war Bulgaria were to threaten Turkey. He agreed that the Turks should be so informed. Stalin repeated his view, however, that the cross-Channel invasion was of over-riding importance; the entry of Turkey into the war, the support of Yugoslavia and the capture of Rome were relatively unimportant.

President Roosevelt put the American argument that expeditions in the eastern Mediterranean might involve increasing commitments and delay. Stalin was unwilling to agree to any delay in the invasion of northern France beyond May. The Prime Minister replied that he would do everything in his power to begin the invasion at the earliest date possible, but that the great opportunities in the Mediterranean should not be cast aside on the issue of a month or so for launching the cross-Channel operation. After further discussion the Conference agreed to ask the Chiefs of Staff to consider —on the assumption that the cross-Channel invasion would be the main plan for 1944—what subsidiary operations could be undertaken.

The Prime Minister had suggested on November 29 that the two Foreign Secretaries, and a representative of the President, should meet to discuss the best way of getting Turkey into the war. Mr. Eden, M. Molotov and Mr. Hopkins met for this purpose on (a) November 30. M. Molotov said that, in view of the results of Mr. Eden's conversations with M. Numan in Cairo, Stalin was not very hopeful that we should get Turkey into the war but that nevertheless we should make the attempt. Mr. Eden proposed that the President and the Prime Minister should invite President Inönü to Cairo to confer with them there. M. Molotov approved of the suggestion and said that he would consult Stalin.

At the plenary session on November 30 General Brooke reported that the Chiefs of Staff had considered subsidiary operations in the Mediterranean. Their view was that, of the three possible areas of operation, Yugoslavia and the Aegean were most open to doubt. They recommended that the capture of Rhodes should not be attempted unless Turkey came into the war. The question how to bring Turkey into the war still remained for discussion. The three Heads of Governments—with the Foreign Secretaries and Mr. (b) Hopkins—talked over the problem at luncheon on December 1. The Prime Minister said that we could offer the Turkish Government only limited air protection and anti-aircraft guns, but that winter was approaching and the Germans would not invade Turkey. The Turks had the Russian offer to declare war on Bulgaria if the latter attacked Turkey. We had no army to offer, but could continue to supply arms. We should give Turkey the 'priceless opportunity' of accepting the Soviet invitation to take part in the Peace Conference and of association with the victorious Powers.

Stalin said that it was possible that Turkey would not have to

---

(a) WP(44)8; Frozen 553, R12549/55/44. (b) WP(44)8.

fight, but that they would simply provide air bases. Mr. Churchill said that he would be satisfied with 'strained neutrality'. M. Molotov asked what Mr. Churchill meant when he said on November 29 that if Turkey did not enter the war her rights to the Dardanelles and Bosphorus could not remain unaffected. Mr. Churchill said that he could not commit the War Cabinet, but that in his own opinion the régime of the Straits should be reviewed.[1] He asked later whether he would have to speak on behalf of the three Powers if he met the Turkish President, or whether there would be a Soviet representative if talks took place at Cairo. M. Molotov said that the Soviet Government would be represented at Cairo by the Soviet Ambassador to Ankara, and by M. Vyshinsky who would come specially from Algiers.

This informal agreement was put on record later on December 1 in the following terms:

> 'The Conference agreed that . . . from the military point of view, it was most desirable that Turkey should come into the war on the side of the Allies before the end of the year.' They 'took note of Marshal Stalin's statement that if Turkey found herself at war with Germany, and as a result Bulgaria declared war on Turkey or attacked her, the Soviet would immediately be at war with Bulgaria. The Conference further took note that this fact could be explicitly stated in the forthcoming negotiations to bring Turkey into the war.'

(a)   On December 3 Sir H. Knatchbull-Hugessen telegraphed to Mr. Churchill and Mr. Eden that Turkey's internal and economic position were not adapted for war. The Government were not secure and were blamed for failures in the economic sphere. Public opinion, including that of the deputies, was still strongly against any war preparations. An influential body of deputies and editors might oppose the President and the Government on the issue of entry into the war under foreign pressure in the country's state of unpreparedness. Sir H. Knatchbull-Hugessen thought it essential to do nothing to impair the position of the President. The material assistance which we could give before December 31 could not solve his difficulties. Sir H. Knatchbull-Hugessen thought that the President

---

(b)   [1] On November 30 at luncheon with the Prime Minister and the President, Stalin raised the question of warm water ports; Mr. Churchill said that on the British side there were 'no obstacles'. Stalin said that, if there were no obstacles on the part of Great Britain, the question of the Straits would have to be considered. Mr. Churchill said that he wanted to get Turkey into the war, and the moment was therefore an awkward one for raising the question of the Straits. Stalin replied that the time would come later. President Roosevelt thought that the Dardanelles ought to be free to the commerce of the world. Stalin asked whether this freedom would apply to Russian commerce; the President and Prime Minister agreed that it would so apply.

(a) R12707, 13218/55/44; WP(43)592. (b) WP(44)8.

would probably be obliged to refuse entry by December 31, although much could be done in two or three months. In any case his acceptance under pressure would entail serious internal risks.

Meanwhile Mr. Churchill had invited President Inönü to a (a) meeting with President Roosevelt and himself in Cairo at which a Soviet representative would be present. The American and Soviet Ambassadors were instructed to convey similar messages. President Inönü replied that if the object of the visit were discussions on the (b) basis of a decision already taken in conversations with Stalin in Teheran, he would not come. If, however, the object were to afford an opportunity of 'free, equal and unprejudiced discussion' as to the best method by which Turkey could serve the common cause, he and M. Numan would come. On December 2 Sir H. Knatchbull- (c) Hugessen was instructed to say that the invitation was on the second basis. President Inönü then accepted the invitation. The Turkish party[1] arrived in Cairo on December 4. On the previous day the British Chiefs of Staff had suggested that the date of the Turkish (d) entry into the war should be postponed until mid-February.[2] President Roosevelt supported this view, and proposed a date between February 15 and April 1. Mr. Eden said that he thought that Russia would probably agree to postponing the date for Turkey's entry into the war from December 31, 1943, to about February 15, 1944. The proposed operations in the Aegean were thus already losing their importance.

At 5 p.m. on December 4 President Inönü met the American and (e) British delegations. Mr. Churchill said that the moment had now come when Turkey should seriously consider associating herself with the Allies. The dangers present at the time of Adana had largely passed away. He said that if Turkey entered the war on the side of the Allies, we would consider how best to help her preparations, especially against air attack. He mentioned Stalin's assurance that Russia would at once declare war on Bulgaria if the latter should join Germany in an attack on Turkey. Mr. Churchill also spoke of the 'great international changes' which would follow Turkey's entry into the war. He said that Roumania was begging for peace, that Hungary wished to get out of the war and that Bulgaria was greatly divided. He thought that the entry of Turkey into the war would cause a series of landslides in these countries.

President Inönü said that Turkey had done her best in extremely

---

[1] Sir H. Knatchbull-Hugessen came to Cairo with the Turkish Ministers. The Russian Ambassador at Ankara was not instructed to go to Cairo, and did not do so.

[2] This suggestion was made for military reasons connected primarily with the question of planning the invasion of southern France.

(a) R12548/55/44. (b) R12561/55/44. (c) R12593/55/44. (d) COS(43)791(O), Parts I–II. (e) WP(44)8; Frozen 359, R12825/55/44.

difficult circumstances to stand by her friend and ally. He was afraid of German action, especially air attack, if Turkey entered the war. Turkey wanted to collaborate with the Allies but was not prepared. She had been given help but it was not enough. If, however, the Allies were ready to meet her minimum essential requirements and if, after these requirements had been met, Turkey could be useful, she would come in. President Inönü spoke of two stages: preparation, involving supplies to Turkey, and collaboration. He could not accept a demand to come into the war blindly with a statement that when Turkey had done so she would be told what her part was to be. The Prime Minister and the President disclaimed any such demand, and said that discussions could start immediately on the two stages. The Prime Minister proposed a period of about six weeks during which material, especially for anti-aircraft defence, would be sent into Turkey, and would be followed immediately afterwards by the despatch of British and American squadrons to prepared airfields.

(a)   At 11 a.m. on December 5 Mr. Churchill and President Roosevelt met again. Mr. Churchill outlined the following programme: At the end of January the Turkish aerodromes should be fitted out with radar and anti-aircraft defences. At the beginning of February United States and British squadrons should be ready to move in to Turkey and medium bombers should start a 'softening' process from airfields in Cyrenaica. By February 15 bombing attacks on the islands should be intensified. By this time the Turks might expect some reaction from Germany, but as they grew stronger they would have to face up to greater risks. The Conference agreed that the British Chiefs of Staff should prepare a statement for presentation to the Turks showing what assistance the latter would receive if they entered the war.

(b)   At 3 p.m. on the same day the Prime Minister and President Roosevelt held another meeting with President Inönü. The latter said that Turkey had taken a decision in principle to enter the war, but that she could not do so within a matter of weeks and that the experts must first agree on a plan of preparation. Mr. Churchill proposed the despatch of supplies and technicians to prepare for the arrival of protecting air squadrons. The danger period for the Turks would be before the arrival of these squadrons. M. Numan said that the Turks could not agree to the infiltration of personnel—which he thought would provoke war—but could and did agree to the infiltration of specialists. The number suggested by the British delegation was 2,000. Mr. Churchill repeated that he wanted the preparations to begin at once with the utmost secrecy. As soon as the

---

(a) COS(43)791(O), Part II.   (b) WP(44)8; Frozen 374, R12860/55/44.

airfields were ready we should want the planes to go in. He pointed out a paradox in the discussion; we did not think that any preparation could be effective without the infiltration of personnel, while the Turks refused this plan owing to the danger of provoking Germany. No preparation could be made therefore against the risks of provoking Germany.

The Prime Minister and the President referred further discussions (a) with M. Numan to a small committee including Mr. Eden and Mr. Hopkins. M. Numan told the committee that he would accept only the required number of technicians for the supply of material. He proposed that one British and one American general should work out at Ankara with the Turkish General Staff a list of requirements and a plan of complete collaboration. At Mr. Eden's request, M. Numan confirmed that the position was as follows: (i) Our proposals for infiltration were accepted in principle, with a reservation about numbers pending consideration by the Turkish General Staff. (ii) If the infiltration programme were accepted, Turkey would not take action which she considered might lead her into war until material supplies for her use were given; the amount of these supplies had not yet been determined. (iii) Turkey had political questions to raise, including the Russian undertaking about Bulgaria. Discussions on (iii) could take place during the period of preparation and would not delay either preparation or collaboration. The infiltration programme could go ahead while the provision of supplies was being discussed.

On December 5 Sir H. Knatchbull-Hugessen told M. Numan (b) that the Turkish attitude was open to the interpretation that they were intentionally stalling, but M. Numan denied this. Sir H. Knatchbull-Hugessen pointed out that the talks about assistance to be given to the Turks and M. Numan's political conversations with the Russians might drag on indefinitely. M. Numan replied that the installation of anti-aircraft guns and radar and the sending of specialists could go ahead at once. Conversations about war material to be given to the Turks for their own use could be limited to three or four days; the political conversations could proceed simultaneously.

Another tripartite meeting was held in the early evening of December 6. President Inönü repeated his fears of German and Bulgarian attack and again spoke of the unprepared state of Turkish armaments. Mr. Churchill and President Roosevelt again tried to reassure him. President Roosevelt agreed that Mr. Churchill and (c) Mr. Eden should continue conversations with the Turks on

---

(a) WP(44)8.   (b) R13289/55/44.   (c) WP(44)8; Frozen 402, R12987/55/44.

December 7.[1] It was agreed that British experts should go to Ankara and that Turkish service representatives should come to Cairo. Other British officers would go to Ankara later to continue the conversations. Mr. Churchill suggested to President Inönü that air preparations and the discussions concerning other supplies should be continued until February 15. They should then discuss war plans, programmes for the import of munitions and political questions. President Inönü agreed to consult the National Assembly on his return and give his answer in four or five days.

Mr. Churchill proposed that on February 15 the Allies would request permission from the Turks to send in air squadrons. He made it clear that, if the Turks then refused, the Allies would direct their resources to another theatre and would give up hope of wartime co-operation with Turkey. If, however, the Turks agreed, munitions for the army and air force would continue to be sent in as quickly as possible. The sea route to Turkey would be opened; reinforcements would be provided by British anti-tank and armoured units and an agreed plan would be carried out with the full force of the Allies and Turkey.

(a)   On December 8 Mr. Eden informed M. Vyshinsky fully about the discussions with the Turks. M. Vyshinsky seemed to think the discussions satisfactory in that the Turks would be forced into a decision by February 15, but that we were not carrying out the Moscow-Teheran decision to get them into the war by the end of the year. Mr. Eden replied that the new time-table was better in our own military interest.

(b)   On December 22 the Chief of the Imperial General Staff reported to the War Cabinet that Stalin had shown little interest in the Balkan situation or in the opening of the Straits. He said that the Russians did not seem to grasp the military advantages to be gained in that part of the world, though their apparent lack of interest might have sprung from other motives.

(c)   [1] Mr. Roosevelt left Cairo on December 7. American representatives were not present at this meeting. Mr. Eden instructed the Foreign Office to inform the United States Embassy of the conclusions reached at the meeting. Admiral Leahy, who was present throughout the visit of the Turkish Ministers, noted that 'the Americans did not urge the Turks as vehemently as did the British' to enter the war. At an early stage during the visit the President told Mr. Churchill that 'if he, Roosevelt, were a Turk, he would require more assurance of aid than Britain had promised before abandoning neutrality and leading his country into war' (Leahy, *op. cit.*, p. 214). On the other hand, in a discussion with M. Numan, Mr. Hopkins strongly supported the British argument that entry into the war was in the Turkish interest. *F.R.U.S.*, 1943, Cairo and Teheran Conferences, p. 732.

(a) Frozen 422, R12986/55/44. (b) WM(43)174, C.A. (c) Frozen 412, R12985/55/44.

(v)

Large Turkish demands for defence needs: the British military mission to Ankara: breakdown of the Cairo plans; decision to recall the military mission and to stop military supplies: departure of the British Ambassador on leave from Turkey (December 11, 1943–February 28, 1944).

On December 11 M. Numan told Sir H. Knatchbull-Hugessen (a) that the Turkish Government accepted the Cairo proposals in principle, but that the crucial question was that of aid to meet their defence requirements. These requirements included 216 Spitfires, 500 Sherman tanks and 66,800 tons of petrol.[1] The Turks made it clear that their agreement to our proposals depended on our meeting these demands. They said that our offer to fly in seventeen squadrons was inadequate and that we should provide the air contingent of forty-nine squadrons agreed in April 1943.[2]

Sir H. Knatchbull-Hugessen told M. Numan that these extrav- (b) agant demands would make a very bad impression. M. Numan complained bitterly to the British and American Ambassadors that Turkey was being sacrificed to a bargain with Russia. Sir H. Knatchbull-Hugessen pointed out that the Turks were free to take their own decision on February 15, and the Prime Minister had told President Inönü that he would not call on Turkey to take a decision which she would regret. Sir H. Knatchbull-Hugessen suggested, in (c) reply to a personal enquiry from Mr. Churchill, that we could break off negotiations at once or try again to secure agreement on the basis of a Turkish decision on February 15, or discuss the Turkish proposals on the understanding that the time limit might be extended beyond February 15. In a telegram to the Foreign Office Sir H. (d) Knatchbull-Hugessen said that it was difficult to judge whether the Turkish Government were stalling, or whether they were anxious to play their part but felt unable to do so in the state of their defences. M. Numan had told him that the Turkish Government had taken into account the risk of a breakdown in the negotiations with the consequence that Turkey would be isolated. The fact that the

---

[1] The full list of equipment included 500 Sherman tanks, 7,000 lorries, 2,000 tractors (e) for guns already delivered, 550 pieces of artillery, 1,000 anti-tank guns, 470 Bofors guns, 216 Spitfires IX, 36 Mosquitos, 48 Mosquitos or Mitchells. M. Numan informed the United States and Soviet Ambassadors verbally of the Turkish demands.

[2] The offer to supply 49 squadrons of aircraft was not made by Britain alone, but by Mr. Churchill on behalf of the Allies at the Adana Conference in January 1942, when he suggested flying in 25 R.A.F. squadrons and 24 U.S. squadrons. A more precise agreement was concluded on April 13, 1943, with the Turkish General Staff, when the offer was in fact a total of 49 R.A.F. squadrons. This offer was tailored to the circumstances then existing and conditional on the political situation. (See ref. the plan 'Hardihood' in *Grand Strategy*, Vol. V (H.M.S.O., London, 1956), pp. 90–91).)

(a) R13067, 13143, 13144, 13151, 13323, 13437/55/44. (b) R13068, 13069/55/44. (c) R13140, 13141/55/44. (d) R13147/55/44. (e) 13455/55/44.

Turkish Government were willing to face this risk suggested that they must be impressed by their military and economic deficiencies and the unpreparedness of Turkish public opinion for war.

Sir H. Knatchbull-Hugessen pointed out that a breakdown at the present stage would allow the Turkish Government to claim that we had refused them the means of self-protection and had gone back on our earlier promise. German propaganda would exploit the situation both in Turkey and in other Balkan countries. We ought therefore to make a final effort to settle the matter on the basis of the Cairo programme by direct discussions between the Commanders-in-Chief and Turkish military leaders.

(a)   On December 13 the Prime Minister telegraphed to Mr. Eden in strong terms that the Ambassador should 'put the screw on hard' at Ankara.[1] He said that the Turks must be made to see that failure to comply with our request on February 15 would be 'the virtual end of the alliance, and that making impossible demands is only another way of saying no'. Meanwhile the Foreign Office should insist on the infiltration of expert personnel according to our plan. Mr. Churchill thought that the idea of a German invasion of Turkey was 'absolute rubbish'.

(b)   On December 14 the Joint Planning Staff considered the Turkish demands. They thought that we should neither accept them nor agree to negotiate about them since, in view of our other commitments, we could supply only a small fraction of the amount required. On the other hand, we should gain nothing by threats such as the Prime Minister had suggested. We might need Turkey later on and a break with her now would reveal our future plans to the enemy. The Joint Planning Staff concluded that conversations should continue and supplies go on at the rate at which they were reaching Turkey during the summer. On December 15 the Chiefs of Staff,

(c)   with the agreement of Sir A. Cadogan and Sir O. Sargent, decided for military reasons that there should be no break with the Turks. They thought that the three Commanders-in-Chief, Middle East, should go at once to Ankara for discussions. If the Turks agreed to the full programme of infiltration and preparation, we should offer them the tanks, Bofors guns, anti-tank guns and field artillery for which they asked, but not the lorries or tractors. We could offer 108 Spitfires of different types and 84 Baltimores. The limiting factor in providing the supplies would be the carrying capacity of the Turkish railways; the transport of the supplies would conflict with

---

[1] The Prime Minister was at this time ill with pneumonia in North Africa.

(a) Frozen 468 (Churchill Papers/447; R13159/55/44). (b) R13159/55/44. (c) Grand 595, Churchill Papers/447.

our own requirements under the infiltration programme. The Prime (a)
Minister agreed with these proposals.

The Foreign Office instructed Sir H. Knatchbull-Hugessen to (b)
make it clear that this latest offer was final[1] and that in the event of
a refusal or deliberate procrastination we should have to consider
stoppage of supplies and should not be able in future to take an
interest in the fate of Turkey. Sir H. Knatchbull-Hugessen was asked
to point out the position in which an isolated Turkey would find
herself with regard to Russia at the end of the war and to speak of
the end of the alliance. He was to explain that owing to the development of air warfare the status of the Dardanelles had ceased to be
a vital British interest. Turkey should not think that she could
always reckon on British support to resist Russian demands in the
matter. If the Turks argued about the danger of attack from
Bulgaria, Sir H. Knatchbull-Hugessen should refer again to Stalin's
declaration that if Turkey were involved in hostilities with Germany
and Bulgaria attacked her, the Soviet Government would declare
war on Bulgaria. The Prime Minister subsequently approved this (c)
message.

On December 16 the British Chiefs of Staff with Foreign Office (d)
concurrence reported to General Eisenhower that they still thought
a German or Bulgarian attack on Thrace unlikely and the Turkish
demands unjustified. The demand for forty-nine squadrons ignored
the diminished threat of German air attack and the disappearance
of the threat of an attack on land. The Chiefs of Staff thought that
nevertheless we should make some concession to the demands in
order to persuade the Turks to agree to our proposals for infiltration
and preparation. They proposed that the three Commanders-in-
Chief, Middle East, should go to Ankara at once. On December 18
General Eisenhower gave instructions accordingly. The Foreign (e)
Office therefore told Sir H. Knatchbull-Hugessen to inform the
Turkish Government that, while we considered their demands
excessive, we accepted their reply as a basis for further discussions
and had asked the three Commanders-in-Chief, Middle East, to go
to Ankara.

The Turkish Government, however, considered that the visit of (f)
the three Commanders-in-Chief would be a final provocation to
Germany and refused to receive them. M. Numan said that his
Government felt that we were trying to trick them into war. They
also thought that we had reached a political engagement with

---

[1] The Soviet Government was also told that our latest offer was final.   (g)

(a) Frozen 485 (Churchill Papers/447; R13265/55/44). (b) R13459/55/44. (c) Frozen
840 (Churchill Papers/447; R13459/55/44). (d) OZ4112, R13455/55/44. (e) R13459/
55/44. (f) R13407, 13408/55/44. (g) R13794/55/44.

Russia to bring them in at a specified date regardless of the consequences and without informing or consulting them. Furthermore, we had still not produced any plan for Turkish co-operation. Sir H. Knatchbull-Hugessen told the Foreign Office that we had aroused Turkish suspicions by mentioning a definite date. We had not yet produced a joint plan and the object of the visit of the Commanders-in-Chief—'proposals for infiltration and preparations'—scarcely seemed adequate. M. Numan had agreed that we could send as many technicians as the Turkish General Staff certified to be

(a) required up to 2,000. Sir H. Knatchbull-Hugessen pointed out that we should not have made our own preparations by February 15,

(b) and that this fact might provide a solution of the difficulty. The Commander-in-Chief, Levant, thought that we ought to give the Turkish Government more time rather than risk alienating them

(c) altogether. On December 22 M. Numan told Sir H. Knatchbull-Hugessen that this Government were convinced of the danger of precipitate attack from Germany and possibly Bulgaria, and that they must not take an avoidable risk of provoking German retaliation. Hence they could not agree to the visit of an Allied Commander-in-Chief to Turkey or to a visit by their own representatives outside

(d) the country. They asked that military experts of less high rank should be sent. The Chiefs of Staff and Foreign Office agreed to this suggestion, especially because we did not want an abrupt cessation of activity which would show the Germans that we had given Turkey up and that they need no longer fear a threat from that direction. In any case we wished to maintain a threat to the Germans from the eastern Mediterranean until the cross-Channel invasion.

(e)   On December 24 the Foreign Office informed Lord Halifax that M. Numan thought that we alone were putting pressure on Turkey to come into the war. The Foreign Office considered it most important for the success of the forthcoming conversations that there should be no misunderstanding on this point. Lord Halifax was instructed to ask the State Department whether they would support us in saying that our latest offer was final.

(f)   On January 11 the Foreign Office sent to Washington information from most secret sources which confirmed that Turkish official circles were counting on the Americans to support their policy towards

(g) Great Britain and Russia. On the same day, however, the State Department, with the President's approval, instructed the United States Ambassador at Ankara to point out in general terms that the United States Government hoped for an early entry of Turkey into the war. The United States Ambassador spoke in this sense to M.

(a) R13448/55/44. (b) R13526/55/44. (c) R13551/55/44. (d) R13456, 13501, 13527, 13551/55/44. (e) R13457/55/44. (f) R445/7/44. (g) R567, 780, 782/7/44.

Numan on January 14. M. Numan said that he had never doubted that the United States were as closely interested as ourselves.[1]

On January 4 Sir H. Knatchbull-Hugessen spoke to M. Orbay[2] (a) and the Deputy Secretary-General. Among other familiar arguments they said that the Turkish Government did not yet know our general plan, i.e. whether we intended attacks on Germany in other theatres. They feared that if they took action now they might be letting themselves in alone for an operation unrelated in time or capacity to attacks elsewhere. Two days later M. Numan assured Sir H. (b) Knatchbull-Hugessen that the Turkish Government would be prepared to come into the war as soon as it was clear that operations in the west had started successfully, e.g. a fortnight after their inception.[3] Mr. Eden noted that this assurance was useless to us. Since it was impossible to give detailed information about future operations to the Turks, Sir H. Knatchbull-Hugessen was instructed to say, if (c) M. Numan again reverted to the question, that they could not expect information about our general plans until they were in the war or irrevocably committed to belligerency at a definite date. He could, however, assure M. Numan that Turkey's entry into the war was part of a concerted operational plan including action in more than one theatre designed to bring about the defeat of Germany within a year.

In January 1944, Air Marshal Sir John Linnell headed a military mission to Ankara to carry on the conversations agreed to in Cairo. (d) He reported that the atmosphere was cordial but non-committal. General Orbay[4] was clearly not going to advise his Government (e) that the Turkish forces were fit to enter the war unless he had received most of the equipment in the December lists. This fact ruled out the early entry of Turkey into the war and probably also a favourable reply to the request to fly in unless the Turkish Government could be persuaded by political expediency or pressure regardless of the state of their military equipment. Sir J. Linnell

---

[1] Sir H. Knatchbull-Hugessen reported that Mr. Steinhardt had kept in close touch with him and done all he could to support him.

[2] M. Orbay had gone back from London to Ankara at the end of December.

[3] A part of the telegram from Ankara to the Foreign Office containing this information (f) appears in von Papen's *Memoirs* (London, 1952), pp. 512–13. The Foreign Office, in January 1944, had information that von Papen had secured possession from the British Embassy of documents concerned with the Cairo Conference in November, and the meetings with the Turkish Ministers at Cairo in December 1943. No subsequent leakages are known to have taken place. On January 6 M. Numan told Sir H. Knatchbull-Hugessen that the German Ambassador 'knew considerably more about what is going on than was good for him'.

[4] General Kiazim Orbay, previously Deputy Chief of the Turkish General Staff, succeeded Marshal Caknak as Chief of Staff on the latter's retirement in mid-January 1944.

(a) R295/7/44. (b) R403/7/44. (c) R448/7/44. (d) CC374, R609/7/44. (e) CC370, A466, R588/7/44. (f) R448, 1036, 1037, 1038, 1366, 1565/7/44.

thought that there were two possible courses: (a) to seek a means to maintain a threat to the Germans from the eastern Mediterranean; (b) to force an issue with the Turks at the risk of a breakdown. An attempt to bargain would lead merely to a deadlock. Such a position would be difficult to retrieve and might adversely affect the strategic

(a) plan. Sir H. Knatchbull-Hugessen thought that, when faced with the clear issue, the Turkish Government might not take the responsibility of a break with us, but there was undoubtedly a risk.

The Foreign Office obviously had to leave the Chiefs of Staff to weigh up the military arguments for and against compelling the Turks to come to a decision. The Foreign Office thought there was evidence that the Germans were seriously perturbed by our preparations and that, if our infiltration continued, they might suddenly attack the Turks. Sir A. Cadogan noted that the main object in continuing talks with the Turkish Government was to keep the Germans afraid of our designs in the eastern Mediterranean.

(b)   The Chiefs of Staff considered that we ought not to break with the Turks. We should insist on our programme of infiltration and not commit ourselves to meeting unreasonable demands for equipment. The purpose of maintaining a threat from the eastern Mediterranean would be achieved by hard bargaining even if it lead to a deadlock. If we were to raise the conversations to a governmental level in an attempt to force the issue, a breakdown would allow the Germans to conclude that they had nothing to fear from Turkey.

(c)   With the approval of the Prime Minister and Mr. Eden,[1] the
(d) Chiefs of Staff instructed the military mission on January 12 to bargain with the Turks about supplies while insisting that infiltration should have first priority as the best means of meeting any German threat. The Chiefs of Staff kept in mind the possibility of sudden developments; the situation on the Russian front was changing rapidly and might bring Turkey into the war fairly soon.

(e)   The Foreign Office instructed Lord Halifax and Sir A. Clark Kerr on January 14 to tell the United States and Soviet Governments of the reasons for the action proposed. Our Ambassadors were to explain that we realised that, if we could not succeed in securing Turkey's immediate entry into the war, we should not be carrying out the decisions taken at Moscow and Teheran, but at least we should be maintaining a threat to the Germans.

(f)   Sir H. Knatchbull-Hugessen reported on January 17 that the

---

[1] Mr. Eden and Sir A. Cadogan agreed with the instructions on the assumption that Turkey's only value now was as 'cover' to deceive the Germans.

military talks were overshadowed by political considerations and especially by the 'Turkish complex about ourselves and Russia'. We had to combat the view that we had made an 'unholy compact' with Russia about spheres of influence whereby we gave her a free hand in central and south-eastern Europe. Our attitude towards Marshal Tito and the fact that we did not appear to contemplate a joint Balkan campaign were taken as evidence of this 'compact'. In a (a) conversation on January 15 M. Numan had refused to consider further infiltration until we had met the Turkish demands for equipment. Sir H. Knatchbull-Hugessen told him that this refusal was a complete *volte face* and that he was making insuperable difficulties for political ends. M. Numan replied in a letter of January 16 insinuating that we were trying to trick Turkey into war and concentrating only on our own preparations regardless of Turkish interests. Sir H. Knatchbull-Hugessen reported that the members of the British military mission in Ankara did not expect a satisfactory solution and that there was an atmosphere of complete distrust on both sides.

On January 19 the Prime Minister sent to Mr. Eden a draft note (b) on the Turkish question. He proposed, subject to President Roosevelt's concurrence, to tell President Inönü that if by February 15 we were permitted to bring in 2,000 technicians and stores, we should be in a position to fly in twenty squadrons and offer Turkey reasonable protection against German air attacks, which were the only serious danger. If the Turkish Government obstructed the entry of these experts and forbade the flying-in of twenty squadrons, the Alliance would be at an end. We would send no more munitions and show complete disinterest in Turkey's future.

The Foreign Office had doubts about the expediency of this pro- (c) posed note. A break at this stage would determine our relations with Turkey for at least a generation. Without a friendly independent Turkey, there were small chances of British influence being felt in south-eastern Europe. An unfriendly or Russian-dominated Turkey might have effects on our position in the Near East. Before we went to extremes, we should be certain that our immediate military needs justified action contrary to our long-term political (and military) interests.

Meanwhile, on January 19 Air Marshal Linnell had a three-hour (d) conversation with General Orbay. General Orbay repeated that we must meet the December lines of requirements in full before he could tell the Turkish Government that the country was ready for war. The supply of equipment must have priority over infiltration.

(a) R873, 874, 1036, 1037, 1038, 1612, 1844/7/44. (b) M4/4, R1327/7/44. (c) R874/7/44. (d) A576, R1128/7/44.

The British military delegation were now convinced that they could make no progress and that further insistence on their part would lead to bitterness which would adversely affect future relations.

Air Marshal Linnell thought that on purely military grounds we had to decide between closing the military talks because we could not accept the terms dictated by General Orbay, and agreeing to supply the complete lists and conceding that equipment could come before infiltration. He asked whether, in view of the certainty of a leakage of information, we were in effect maintaining a threat to Germany from the eastern Mediterranean, and, if so, whether it

(a) was worth the effort in manpower and material. Sir H. Knatchbull-Hugessen also thought that the conversations in no sense constituted a threat and were more likely to be a matter of satisfaction to the Germans. The Foreign Office recognised that owing to leakages the Ankara talks were not much use as 'cover', but as long as they continued the Germans must always feel that they might lead to something tangible, whereas an open break between the British and Turkish Governments would relieve them of anxiety, and allow them to discount Turkey for the rest of the war.

(b)   On January 22 Sir H. Knatchbull-Hugessen reported that any hope of flying in on February 15 or for some time afterwards had gone; we were unable to maintain a threat which would deceive Germany or have an effect on her military dispositions. If we agreed to supply their complete lists, the Turks had other pretexts open to them for subsequent delay, such as information on general war strategy and political conversations. Sir H. Knatchbull-Hugessen recommended that we should close the military conversations. Air Marshal Linnell noted that the political background in Turkey had deteriorated in the past week, and Sir H. Knatchbull-Hugessen himself remarked on a considerable hardening of opinion against entry into the war.[1]

(c)   The Chiefs of Staff discussed the Prime Minister's minute of January 19 with Sir A. Cadogan. In a report of January 22 they mentioned once again the advantages of bringing Turkey into the war. The Chiefs of Staff said that they would recommend an ultimatum to the Turkish President if they had good grounds for hoping that it would have the desired effect. They agreed, however, with Sir A. Cadogan's opinion that we could do nothing to compel Turkey to come into the war against her will. The Turks had apparently decided on balance that they had more to gain than lose by remaining neutral; they seemed to be confident that it was not in our interest to give the Russians a free hand with them after the war.

(d)   [1] On January 27 he reported that anti-war feeling was definitely increasing.

(a) R1111/7/44. (b) R1143/7/44. (c) COS(44)57(o).; R1328/7/44. (d) R1511/7/44.

A rejection of our ultimatum could not be kept secret and would have considerable political disadvantages. The Balkan countries would turn more and more to Russia and our position in the Near and Middle East would be adversely affected. Conversely, the Germans would improve their situation in south-eastern Europe politically and militarily.

The Chiefs of Staff pointed out that the entry of Turkey into the war would not carry the immediate strategical advantages hoped for during the Cairo Conference since we had been compelled to postpone the operations contemplated against Rhodes and in the Aegean.[1] This latter fact was not known to the Germans who were showing nervousness at the possibility of such operations. We wanted to continue to play on their fears as far as possible in order to pin down German forces during the coming critical months. The Chiefs of Staff thought that the military delegation should return to Cairo. Our next step would depend on Turkey's reaction to this move, but the Chiefs of Staff favoured a compromise, i.e. we should agree to supply the complete lists and concede that equipment could come before infiltration in the hope that further negotiations under promise of the equipment would lead to a modified scale of infiltration.

The Prime Minister accepted the arguments of the Chiefs of Staff (a) and agreed to take a less drastic course than he had proposed. He suggested that we should withdraw the military mission and, without an explanation, cease sending further military supplies to Turkey. There would be no formal break with the Turks and no official publicity; it would be for the Turks to ask the meaning of our silence. Sir H. Knatchbull-Hugessen should either be recalled for consultation or confine himself to the Embassy. Mr. Churchill concluded that it remained our purpose to get Turkey into the war, and that only the method had changed.

The Foreign Office noted that the action proposed was not abandonment of Turkey but application of pressure. Mr. Eden (b) agreed generally with the Prime Minister's proposed course of action. He thought that we should cut off at first all munitions and military stores. The suspension of other supplies needed further consideration because it might affect our purchases in Turkey of commodities needed for our own use, e.g. chrome, emery, timber and dried fruit, besides enabling the Germans to recover much of the Turkish market (c)

---

[1] This postponement, or rather cancellation, was due to the unexpected slowness of the advance in Italy which caused a delay in the Anzio landings from December 20 to January 22. It was clear before January 1 that—apart from the increasing Turkish hesitation—the attack on Rhodes and other operations in the Aegean would have to be abandoned. (See *Grand Strategy*, Vol. V, pp. 207–221.)

(a) M22/4, R1345/7/44. (b) PM/44/20, R1345/7/44. (c) R1366/7/44.

which they had lost. The Chiefs of Staff also agreed generally with the Prime Minister's proposals. They assumed that infiltration of our personnel into Turkey would cease at the same time as the suspension of supplies.

(a) The Prime Minister gave instructions on January 29 that Air Marshal Linnell should be withdrawn at once without explanation; that the Ambassador should 'put up his shutters and lie low' and that all military materials then loading should be stopped. The

(b) Foreign Office instructed Sir H. Knatchbull-Hugessen accordingly on January 30.[1]

The Foreign Office informed the United States and Soviet Governments what we were doing and asked that the American and Russian Ambassadors should adopt a similar attitude to that of the

(c) British Ambassador. On February 2 Sir A. Clark Kerr told Stalin about the change in tactics. Stalin said that we were right and that the Turkish Government were afraid of being stampeded into a war against Germany. He thought that as no explanation was to be given to Turkey it would be better to recall the Ambassadors on leave of absence for a month or two. M. Molotov said that the screw should have been put on the Turks long ago and suggested that the stoppage of supplies would not make much difference. Stalin disagreed, and said that it would show that we were in earnest. On February 6 the Foreign Office telegraphed to Sir A. Clark Kerr that if the British Ambassador in Ankara were recalled, it might be difficult for him to return at the moment when his presence was needed, i.e. in the event of a decision to force the issue of Turkish belligerency. Moreover the recall of the Ambassador would dispel German anxieties about Turkey. The Foreign Office had decided

(d) on balance that Sir H. Knatchbull-Hugessen should remain at his post. On February 28 Sir A. Clark Kerr telegraphed that the Soviet Government had given similar instructions to their Ambassador at Ankara.

(e) Meanwhile on February 2 Lord Halifax had telegraphed that Mr. Wallace Murray (Department of State) agreed with our action and was taking the matter up with Mr. Hull at once so that the American Ambassador at Ankara could be instructed to conform with the attitude of the British Ambassador. The President approved

(f) of the instructions.

(g) The military delegation left Ankara on February 3. Two days later the Prime Minister directed that everything should slow down

---

[1] In view of past leakages of information, elaborate security precautions were taken in the transmission of this message to the Ambassador.

(a) M47/4, R1345/7/44. (b) R1366/7/44. (c) R1818/17/44. (d) R3246/7/44. (e) R1743, 1908/7/44. (f) R2111/7/44. (g) R1684, 2035, 2036, 2043, 2751/7/44.

and that there should be 'a general fading out'. Supplies of war material, radar and anti-aircraft equipment and infiltration of personnel ceased, some specialists were withdrawn and only construction projects already in hand were continued. The preparation of airfields ceased; the Chiefs of Staff instructed the Allied Commander-in-Chief, Mediterranean, to release for other purposes the air and anti-aircraft forces and personnel originally destined for Turkey. Turkish pilots and crews in Egypt awaiting delivery of aircraft were to be sent back to Turkey. These moves, although intended as a form of pressure on the Turks to accept our demands, had the effect of postponing the date by which Turkey would physically be able to come into the war.

The Chiefs of Staff were inclined to go slow with withdrawals of (a) equipment and personnel, since they still wanted to maintain a threat to Germany and regarded the British move as a tactical one and not as a fundamental change in policy. They thought that we should be ready to resume military supplies later if the Turkish attitude were more favourable. Mr. Eden agreed with the Chiefs of Staff and told the Prime Minister on February 8 that we did not (b) want to do anything which would hamper speedy action later on, and which did not serve the immediate purpose of showing our displeasure. On February 10 the Prime Minister let Mr. Eden know that he accepted this view, but that no one else should be sent to (c) Turkey; otherwise we should weaken 'the already rather slender rebuke' which our policy implied. The Prime Minister wanted 'just silence and fade away for the present'. With his approval Sir H. Knatchbull-Hugessen was instructed on February 10 that key (d) specialists urgently required elsewhere should be withdrawn as unobtrusively as possible, and that further withdrawals of personnel and equipment would depend on the extent of Turkish obstruction. The Chiefs of Staff kept in mind the risk of giving a chance to Germany to offer Turkey instructors.

The Foreign Office noted on February 22 that our sanctions (e) against the Turks had not been spectacular. We had not included suspension of work on projects already in hand; we had not withdrawn our instructors from Turkey or training facilities for Turkish cadets in British establishments. Supplies of oil had not been cut off (except for aviation spirit) and civilian supplies were not affected. On February 28 Sir H. Knatchbull-Hugessen left for Cairo on leave, (f) and early in March M. Orbay (who was still in Ankara) resigned from the post of Turkish Ambassador in London, ostensibly on grounds of health.

(a) OZ694, R2162/7/44. (b) PM/44/51, R2036/7/44. (c) M93/4, R2036/7/44. (d) R2036/7/44. (e) ASE(44)9, R2751/7/44. (f) R3976, 4025, 4196/7/44.

Note to section (v)

(a)   On February 6, 1944, Mr. Sterndale-Bennett wrote an analysis of the military conversations at Ankara. He pointed out that: (i) our handling of the supply problem had not been such as to give Turkey great confidence; (ii) Turkish information about Axis strength and intentions came mainly from military attachés or agents in Axis territories whose opportunities of independent assessment were limited, and the Turkish General Staff were therefore vulnerable to German attempts to plant information on them; (iii) the suddenness of some of our actions, i.e. the proposal for the Adana Conference, the request for infiltration of 7,000 men before we had answered the Turkish note of November 17 and the invitation to Cairo which followed this request, had increased the natural caution of the Turks.

We had not been able to deliver all the material which we had promised in May to deliver in 1943. We had sent much valuable material[1] but in no sort of pattern to equip an army. Consignments had been diverted to serve our own requirements in the Middle East. The Turks had not benefited as they should have done by the quantities sent out; their wish to see balanced equipment in their hands before they committed themselves was reasonable. There seemed no doubt that the Turkish General Staff genuinely feared attack by air and land if they entered the war. On the assumption that their fears were justified, the equipment asked for in their note of December 12 constituted a reasonable precaution. On a similar assumption, their fears about provocation were understandable. What had been unreasonable in their attitude was their reluctance to take into account the change in the strategical situation since the Adana meeting which affected the equipment of Turkish forces. They would allow nothing to shake their claim for equipment. Mr. Sterndale-Bennett thought that M. Numan was largely responsible for this attitude.[2]

Sir H. Knatchbull-Hugessen commented that there was enough genuine apprehension in the Turkish military point of view to exclude Turkey's entry into the war until her real needs had been met. Politics, however, had the upper hand. Mr. Eden noted on February 27 that the Anglo-Turkish Treaty was dying fast. He thought that the Prime Minister might have to warn President Inönü of the consequences of a continuation of the Turkish attitude. Some statement would soon have to be made to Parliament. Mr. Eden noted: 'I have no idea what we should say.'

(b)   [1] During 1943 His Majesty's Government gave Turkey approximately £30,000,000 worth of war material in addition to earlier deliveries under the pre-Adana commitments.

(c)   [2] The Foreign Office informed the British Embassy in Ankara on March 2 that they believed that M. Numan had divulged to von Papen details of the operational plan which Mr. Churchill had given President Inönü in Cairo. They believed that the 'technique of destruction' adopted by the Turks at the military talks was worked out with the prior knowledge of von Papen and that M. Numan discussed with him possible future Allied operations in the Balkans.

(a) R2501/7/44.   (b) R3769/7/44.   (c) R3462/7/44.

CHAPTER LII

British relations with Turkey from April 1944 to the Potsdam Conference

(i)

Anglo-Turkish relations, April–June 1944: British request to the Turkish Government to break off diplomatic relations with Germany.

THE evasions of the Turkish Government and their unwillingness to fulfil their obligations—including those of the Anglo-Turkish treaty—made it necessary for the British Government to consider the future of their relations with Turkey. Mr. Eden drew up for the War Cabinet on April 4 a short memorandum on the (a) subject. He thought that our immediate policy of withdrawing our military mission from Turkey and cutting off supplies without notification or explanation had not seriously worried the Turks; in some respects indeed our action had been a relief to them because it had also meant the cessation of political pressure. There were, however, signs of disquiet and doubt in some Turkish quarters about the rightness of Turkish official policy.

What were we to do next? Our present policy did not appear to have the full support of the Russians or Americans. The United States Ambassador at Ankara seemed to wish the deadlock to end and the Russians were said to be telling everyone that they had never wished to press Turkey to enter the war. The Turks were therefore blaming us for what had happened. We could now try to resume pressure on them to enter the war, and our pressure might take the form of threatening to denounce the Anglo-Turkish Alliance. We should be justified in a threat of this kind. We had not ourselves been able to observe all the provisions of the treaty but in the circumstances we had done everything in our power, whereas Turkey had done nothing positively to assist us. The treaty had been drawn up, in particular, to meet German and Italian aggression and with the defeat of the Axis Powers would change its character. Turkey was not likely to be called upon under the treaty to assist us against a major Power, while our obligation to assist her against the Soviet Union would remain. On the other hand, we wanted close Anglo-Turkish friendship after the war as an important factor in

---

(a) WP(44)186; R4936/101/44.

our Balkan policy and as a stabilising influence throughout the Middle East. We also wished to ensure that Turkish control of the Dardanelles was not used to our disadvantage.

We should therefore not wish to go as far as a denunciation of the Anglo-Turkish treaty. We might take the alternative course of trying to restore our former cordial political relations by means of a parliamentary statement about the alliance and by giving assurances to the Turkish Government and, probably, resuming our supplies to them. The Turks, however, would regard this course as a sign of weakness or surrender on our part. We should get nothing from it, and should only have reaffirmed our treaty obligation for the post-war period.

Our best plan therefore would be to combine our present policy of aloofness with active economic pressure. Turkey was giving Germany considerable economic assistance, and should be compelled to stop doing so. We had at our disposal the usual blockade measures which hitherto we had not applied to Turkey, but which would greatly reduce, if not disrupt, Turco-German economic relations.[1] The application of the blockade might also have the advantage of leading the Germans to think that we were now trying to coerce Turkey into war.

The War Cabinet did not discuss this memorandum until April 19. Meanwhile important steps had already been taken to warn the Turkish Government. There had been rumours in March 1944 that Dr. Clodius was coming to Ankara for commercial negotiations. In any case the existing German-Turkish agreement would be renewed unless it was denounced by April 30. Turkish commercial nego-tiations with Roumania and Hungary were also impending. On (a) March 26 the Foreign Office had instructed Lord Halifax to propose a joint Anglo-American approach to the Turkish Government. The matter was delayed for a short time because the President had earlier (b) (March 16) sent to the Prime Minister the draft of a letter to the Turkish President on the question of chrome. The letter was in cordial terms and merely asked the Turks to find a way of preventing supplies of chrome from being moved from Turkey to Germany. The Prime Minister at first—without consulting Mr. Eden—replied that he agreed that the President should approach General Inönü. Mr. Eden, however, explained to the Prime Minister why he thought that the delivery of the President's message would be a mistake. (c) Mr. Churchill telegraphed to the President on March 19 that, in

---

[1] The British Government had already put an embargo on the supply of cotton, raw wool and copper to Turkey as long as these commodities were being exported to Germany.

(a) R4300/919/41. (b) T599/4, unnumbered (Churchill Papers/447; R4925/18/44).
(c) T603/4, No. 627 (Churchill Papers/447; R4926/18/44).

Mr. Eden's view, the Turks were now in a very selfish and obstinate mood and that an appeal to their better feelings might have an opposite effect to our intention. The Turks might regard a friendly message as a sign of weakening on our part.

Mr. Winant, however, considered the Foreign Office arguments (a) 'trivial and unconvincing', and asked for the withdrawal of a telegram instructing Lord Halifax to speak to Mr. Hull on the subject.[1] Mr. Eden sent a somewhat sharp letter to Mr. Winant pointing out that, since he (Mr. Eden) disagreed with the President, it was right and proper for him to explain the position to Lord Halifax in whatever way he might think best. The United States Ambassador at (b) Ankara agreed with the British view and, after Lord Halifax had (c) spoken to Mr. Hull, the President decided on April 11 not to send his letter. Meanwhile the State Department had accepted the British proposal for a joint approach to the Turkish Government. On April (d) 14 Sir H. Knatchbull-Hugessen and the United States Ambassador (e) gave the Turkish Foreign Minister identical notes that the British and United States Governments were seriously disturbed at the economic assistance which Turkey in her trade relations with Europe had been giving to the enemy. Hitherto the two Governments had acquiesced in this trade on the understanding that Turkey was exporting only enough to buy essential goods which the United Nations could not supply. The rapidly approaching crisis of the war now compelled the two Governments to revise their attitude, though this change might cause Turkey some temporary inconvenience. They therefore warned the Turkish Government that they viewed with serious disfavour trade agreements between Turkey and Germany or her satellites under which Turkey supplied commodities essential to the conduct of the war. The renewal of such agreements or the conclusion of new agreements would entail the application to Turkey of the blockade measures applied to neutral countries.

The Turkish Government replied in a note of April 17 giving general assurances of co-operation. M. Numan told Sir H. Knatchbull-Hugessen that there would be a slowing-down of trade with Germany. The existing trade agreement would be prolonged on the same terms. Deliveries in 1943 had been only about 40 per cent of the amount promised. M. Numan would arrange that the new agreement would be even less fully executed. The negotiations with Roumania and Hungary were unimportant.

The Turkish note of April 17 did not mention the export of

---

[1] The telegram included an account of a conversation with a member of the American Embassy, and was therefore sent to Mr. Winant in draft.

(a) R4928/18/44. (b) R5151/18/44. (c) R5822/18/44. (d) R5185/101/44. (e) 5538, 5544, 5670; R6358/18/44; R3934, 4300/919/44; R6025, 6026, 6079, 6219, 6220, 6221/101/44; R6224/294/37; 6464/18/44.

chrome. This matter had been the subject of separate negotiations. On April 4 Mr. Sterndale-Bennett had said to the deputy Secretary-General at the Turkish Foreign Office that there would be trouble over the question of chrome unless the Turks stopped, or cut down radically, their deliveries to Germany. M. Numan told Sir H. Knatchbull-Hugessen four days later that the Turkish Government had decided to reduce deliveries of chrome as from April 10 to 4,200 tons a month, i.e. a reduction of about 40 per cent on recent average deliveries.

(a)   The War Cabinet had these developments in mind when they considered Mr. Eden's memorandum on April 19. The War Cabinet had to decide whether we should agree to a policy of economic collaboration with Turkey which would require us to buy Turkish products otherwise destined for Germany, and to send Turkey essential supplies. The Prime Minister thought that close collaboration would be inconsistent with our policy to Turkey since the end of January. He also pointed out that, owing to the time taken for chrome exported from Turkey to reach Germany and, to affect the flow of finished munitions to enemy forces, there was no direct connection between exports of chrome to Germany and impending military events. He suggested, therefore, that a decision should be postponed.

(b)   On May 6 Mr. Eden circulated to the War Cabinet another memorandum on British policy towards Turkey. He thought that we should take account of new and unexpected developments, including the sudden readiness of the Turkish Government to co-operate with us even at the expense of their relations with Germany. The most remarkable instance was their embargo—at our representations—on all exports of chrome to Germany, even though this action was in violation of an agreement with the Germans.[1] There were other examples of a change of policy. Hitherto the Turkish Government had refused our own and Russian requests to take steps to prevent the Roumanians or Germans from using as troop carriers in the Black Sea two Roumanian liners which had been in dock at Istanbul since 1940. The Turks argued that the ships were merchant vessels and that they had no legal right to detain them. When, however, the Russians were nearing Sebastopol, the Germans ordered the captains of the two ships to take them at once to the Black Sea for evacuation purposes. The Turkish Government intervened, took away essential machinery from the ships and put armed guards on them.

---

[1] On April 20 M. Numan announced in the Turkish National Assembly that henceforward the export of chrome to Germany and her allies would be prohibited.

(a) WM(44)52; R6480/101/44.   (b) WP(44)242 and 244.

We had also received a number of hints that the Turkish Government wanted to resume military conversations. The reason was probably that they were now becoming alarmed at their isolation, and that our policy of aloofness and indifference in political and military matters, together with our blockade measures and the increasing German difficulties in the Balkans, had convinced the Turkish Government that they were less clever in their negotiations with us during the winter than they had supposed themselves to be.

Mr. Eden did not think that we should reverse our policy. Turkey was still exporting commodities of value to Germany; we still had no firm assurance that these exports would be reduced by more than about 50 per cent. It was also not certain that the Turkish hints about resuming military conversations meant that the Turkish Government was now willing to come into the war. The Combined Chiefs of Staff were considering whether Turkish help would be of value at this stage; in any case we might find it desirable to resume the military conversations in order to deceive the Germans into thinking that we were planning to use Turkey as a base from which to invade Europe. Mr. Eden therefore suggested that we should continue our blockade and other economic warfare measures,[1] but modify slightly our attitude of aloofness. We should not start sending arms again, or give a definite answer to the hints about military conversations unless our own military advisers recommended us to do so.

The War Cabinet considered this memorandum on May 18. The (a) Prime Minister thought that, while a slight modification of our attitude would be justified, we should make it clear to the Turks that we were still far from satisfied with them and that their change of policy shown with regard to the export of chrome did not go as far as we wished. We should bring it home that the Turks had missed their chance. If, however, they showed signs of wishing to join us as allies, we should find advantage in accepting them. The War Cabinet agreed with this view.

The Chiefs of Staff were not at this time in favour of renewing the military conversations. They agreed with the Foreign Office view that the threat to Germany could be maintained equally well by economic action; the Germans believed that our recent economic pressure on the Turks was intended to force them into the war. We could increase this pressure and, after D-day, ask the Turks to break off political and economic relations with Germany. We could then decide, in the light of the progress made by our invasion, whether

---

[1] The Ministry of Economic Warfare were proposing at this time to ask the Turks to ban the export to Germany of cotton, copper, mohair and skins.

(a) WM(44)65.

and in what form we wanted Turkish military assistance before the end of the war in Europe.

The Prime Minister and the Chiefs of Staff agreed to the despatch of telegrams in this sense to Ankara and Washington on May 26.

(a)   Meanwhile in the last week of May a meeting of representatives of the Foreign Office and the Ministry of Economic Warfare discussed the problem of combining the three different policies of the British Government towards Turkey. The general aim was: (i) to deprive Germany of essential war materials from Turkey; (ii) to deceive the Germans into believing that their position in south-east Europe might be threatened by the entry of Turkey into the war or the grant of facilities after the launching of the offensive in the west; (iii) to leave ourselves free to renew negotiations later with the Turks for their entry into the war, and to create a basis for an Anglo-Greco-Turkish understanding with the object of checking Russian penetration into south-east Europe. The Ministry of Economic Warfare considered that our economic interests would be best served by signing an economic agreement—which was under discussion—as soon as possible. The Foreign Office were satisfied that this was the right action, and thought that it ought to be taken at once in view of the impending conclusion of a new German-Turkish agreement.

(b)   On June 1, therefore, the Foreign Office instructed the British Embassy in Washington that, as we had now decided to sign an economic agreement with Turkey as soon as possible, our request to the Turks for complete severance of economic and diplomatic relations with the enemy would take the form not of a demand but of a friendly proposal justified on the ground that the launching of the offensive in the west would change the situation in Europe. The Foreign Office thought that this request should be made to the Minister for Foreign Affairs jointly by the British and United States Ambassadors within ten days of the landing in Europe.

(c)   At this stage, however, the Foreign Office learnt that the Turkish Government were allowing German ships to pass through the Straits, with serious consequences to the Allied naval position in the Aegean.[1] Mr. Eden instructed Sir H. Knatchbull-Hugessen to warn the Turkish President that this action had once more compelled the British Government to question the feasibility of Anglo-Turkish co-operation. He was to make it clear to the Turkish Government that we should judge their capacity to resist German pressure and

---

[1] The vessels in question were unarmed German barges. Similar barges had previously been sent, and on arrival in the Aegean had been armed and used for military purposes. *F.R.U.S.* 1944, V, p. 859, and *F.R.U.S.* 1943, IV, pp. 1086–87.

(a) R8413/7/44.   (b) R8413/7/44.   (c) R8777/7/44.

their willingness to respect legitimate British interests by the manner in which they dealt with any more German attempts to pass ships —other than merchant vessels—through the Straits.

On June 8 Sir H. Knatchbull-Hugessen told the Turkish Prime (a) Minister that it was impossible to make progress on other points until this matter was settled. He said that he was concerned with the uncertainty of Anglo-Turkish relations; one day Turkey seemed to favour us and the next the Germans. We wanted to be sure of complete co-operation. Sir H. Knatchbull-Hugessen suggested that the Turkish Prime Minister should give us an assurance to this effect without reference to military action. The President agreed subject to an assurance on our part that relations would return to the previous basis of the alliance.

A week later the Turkish Prime Minister informed Sir H. Knatch- (b) bull-Hugessen that M. Numan had resigned as Minister for Foreign Affairs and that he was himself taking over the Ministry. M. Sara-coglu said that orders had been given to refuse German vessels passage through the Straits, with the exception of merchant vessels which would be allowed to pass after a strict search. Sir H. Knatch-bull-Hugessen asked for an assurance that Turkey would do nothing further to help Germany and that we could rely on complete co-operation. M. Saracoglu gave a categorical assurance in this sense. Sir H. Knatchbull-Hugessen reported to the Foreign Office that search of a German war transport vessel detained in the Bosphorus had revealed a concealed hold containing guns, mines and other munitions. The discovery of these arms, together with the dissatisfaction of the Cabinet in other matters, had brought about the resignation of M. Numan. On June 16 the Secretary-General (c) repeated the news of M. Numan's resignation and of M. Saracoglu's desire for co-operation.

In the first week of June Mr. Eden submitted a memorandum to (d) the War Cabinet of Russian policy in the Balkans.[1] Mr Eden considered possible ways of preventing the spread of Russian influence. He thought that the only feasible plan was to consolidate our position in Greece and Turkey, and to bring about and use Turco-Greek friendship as a fundamental factor in south-east Europe and the eastern Mediterranean.

Mr. Eden thought that this plan involved a reorientation of British policy in the direction of an Anglo-Greco-Turkish association. We should have to give up our policy of trying to force Turkey into the war under the implied threat that if she did not come in, we should

---

[1] See also Vol. III, Chapter XXXVIII, pp. 119–20.

(a) R9129/7/44. (b) R9447, R9448/789/44. (c) R9497/7/44. (d) WP(44)304; R9092/349/67.

leave her to herself after the war. Instead we should have to acquiesce in her remaining neutral during the war as long as she wished if this meant that after the German withdrawal she would be better able to collaborate with Greece as a counter-weight to Russian influence and penetration.

Sir H. Knatchbull-Hugessen had suggested that we should follow up M. Saracoglu's assurances of co-operation by asking what the Turks proposed to do. Mr. Eden thought that we should ourselves say what we wanted; otherwise we should lose the initiative and also be taking a less definite line than the Russians, who had told the

(a) Turkish Government that they should enter the war.[1] Mr. Eden suggested on June 20 to the Prime Minister that we should ask Turkey to break off relations with Germany. With the agreement of the Prime Minister and the Chiefs of Staff Mr. Eden instructed the British Embassy in Washington to raise the matter with the State Department. If the United States Government agreed, Mr. Eden would ask for their support in Ankara. The Soviet Government were also asked for general support. In a telegram to Sir A. Clark Kerr on June 24, Mr. Eden explained that pressure on the Turkish Government to enter the war at once might lead them to reopen the question of supplies of arms to meet a German attack, but that

(b) a request for breaking off diplomatic relations with Germany need not involve this question. By June 28 the State Department had sent instructions to their representative to support the British *démarche*.

(c) Two days later Sir H. Knatchbull-Hugessen was instructed to ask the Turkish Government to break off economic and diplomatic relations with Germany.

(d) Mr. Eden had spoken to the new Turkish Ambassador, M. Unaydin, of the proposed request on June 29. He said that the situation was altered by the landing of Allied armies in France. The Turkish Ambassador pointed out that his Government had not yet received arms and equipment to meet a German attack. Mr. Eden said that we were offering Turkey a last chance to take part in shortening the war. If Turkey now broke off relations with Germany, Germany could do nothing, but if Turkey failed to take this step the British and Allied peoples would not believe that she wanted an Allied victory.

(e) Sir H. Knatchbull-Hugessen carried out his instructions on June 30. M. Saracoglu was disinclined to agree to the severance of

---

(f) [1] M. Vinogradov, Soviet Ambassador at Ankara, informed Sir H. Knatchbull-Hugessen on June 13 that the Soviet Government had made this suggestion to M. Numan in response to an approach from the latter. M. Numan did not mention the Soviet proposal to Sir H. Knatchbull-Hugessen. See also below, pp. 189–90.

(a) COS(44)204(0); R9497/7/44. (b) R10983/7/44. (c) R10166/7/44. (d) R10228/7/44. (e) R10300, 10985/7/44. (f) R9411, 9412/349/67.

diplomatic relations. He said that it would be easier to approach the Chamber on the grounds of entry into the war with an active role. He suggested a declaration of war on Bulgaria in conjunction with Russia. M. Saracoglu asked Sir H. Knatchbull-Hugessen a little (a) later whether he could say to his Government that our requests were made on the basis of the alliance. Sir H. Knatchbull-Hugessen replied that they were not so made; they were the test of the survival value of the alliance. If the Turkish Government complied with our request we should be willing to deal with them on the basis of the (b) alliance. On July 4 M. Saracoglu told Sir H. Knatchbull-Hugessen that the Turkish Government had decided to accept our proposals and that he was informing the Soviet and American representatives accordingly. He told the United States Chargé d'Affaires[1] that the Turkish Government wanted to do what we asked without making conditions. They wished particularly to avoid the suspicion that they were making impossible demands in order to avoid doing anything to help us. Sir H. Knatchbull-Hugessen reported later that he was (c) now fairly certain from further remarks by M. Saracoglu that Turkey was prepared and would even have preferred to offer to enter the war outright. He thought that the Turks were anxious to reinstate themselves on our side.

M. Saracoglu's remark that the Turks were prepared to act as we wished without making conditions was something of a polite fiction. He gave Sir H. Knatchbull-Hugessen the drafts of an exchange of notes with the British Government. The draft British note gave a promise that, having taken the decision to break off relations with Germany, Turkey would find her right sanctioned to share as an equal partner in the settlement of all international questions at the end of the war and in the building of peace. Furthermore, in order to meet any eventuality which might follow the Turkish severance of relations with Germany, the British Government would resume Lend-Lease arrangements with Turkey and furnish her with war material, especially aircraft and aviation material,[2] necessary to deal with an 'initial surprise'. The British Government would also buy Turkish products left without an outlet and, as far as possible, supply civilian requirements hitherto met by Germany, furnish Turkey, in the event of an attack on her, with all possible aid and provide her with financial help to meet the exigencies of war and its consequences.

The War Cabinet discussed the Turkish reply on July 7. Mr. Eden (d)

---

[1] The Ambassador had left Turkey on leave for the United States.
[2] M. Saracoglu added lorries verbally.

(a) R10301/7/44. (b) R10450, 10451, 10453, 10461, 10484, 10985, 11305/7/44.
(c) R10453, 10485/7/44. (d) WM(44)88.3, C.A.

explained that there was some reason for thinking that the Turks might have been willing to enter the war outright. It was, however, more to our advantage that they should not go beyond breaking off diplomatic relations with Germany. They could take this action at once, whereas if we asked them to go to war with Germany we should have long discussions, e.g. over the supply of war material. The moral effect upon Germany of a breach of diplomatic relations would be almost as great as that of a declaration of war, while it would not involve us in military commitments.

The Turks, however, might find themselves involved in war as a result of their diplomatic breach with Germany. They had therefore asked for certain assurances to be given them in an exchange of letters. Mr. Eden thought that they were asking too much. He suggested that we should tell them, if possible only verbally, that, within the limits of our available resources, we would do our best to mitigate the economic disturbance which would follow the severance of diplomatic relations with Germany; that, if Turkey were involved in war as the result of her diplomatic action, we would lend her all possible economic and military assistance, and that the nature of such assistance would be the subject of conversations as and when necessary; we would also use our good offices with our allies to obtain for the Turks assistance similar to that which we ourselves undertook to afford.

Mr. Eden said that the Turks wanted to claim that their diplomatic action was sufficient to re-establish the Anglo-Turkish treaty of 1939 in full force. It was not to our advantage to accept this claim, since Turkey had hitherto failed to discharge her full obligations under the treaty. We proposed therefore to take the line that the breaking off of relations with Germany would come within the framework of the alliance. Mr. Eden thought that the Russians were not likely to regard the proposed diplomatic action as adequate, and might prefer a declaration of war or nothing. We should communicate with the Soviet and United States Governments on the subject, and the Foreign Office were also consulting the Chiefs of Staff. The Prime Minister thought that the news of the Turkish decision might have a very great effect in Germany. We could also take the line with the Russians that there was no harm in 'having two bites at the cherry'.

(ii)

Soviet dissatisfaction with the British decision not to require immediate Turkish entry into the war: Turkish announcement of the breaking off of diplomatic relations with Germany: withdrawal of British personnel from Turkey: British views on the need of close Anglo-Turkish relations after the war (June 28–October 14, 1944).

The Soviet Government were not satisfied with the British (a) *démarche* to the Turks. M. Molotov complained to the United States Ambassador on June 28 that British policy was not in accordance with the decisions of the Moscow Conference. We had expected the Turks to enter the war in 1943, and were illogical now in lowering our demands after our military successes. In a letter of June 29 to Sir A. Clark Kerr, M. Molotov said that the Turkish Government were unlikely to agree to our request, and that anyhow a breach of diplomatic relations was only a half-hearted measure which would have no serious effect on shortening the war. On July 5 the Foreign Office explained to Sir A. Clark Kerr that we had made it clear to the Turks that we did not regard compliance with our present demand as a discharge of all their treaty obligations. Our principal motive in not asking anything further at that stage was that we did not want the Turkish Government to reopen the question of supplies.

On July 10 the Soviet Ambassador complained to Mr. Eden that, (b) since the Soviet Government had told the Turks that they expected them to come into the war, we ought also to have done so. Mr. Eden said that Sir A. Clark Kerr had already explained to M. Molotov that we could get our present demand at once without the long haggling about supplies and military co-operation which would certainly ensue if we asked Turkey to go to war. Mr. Eden warned M. Gusev that if Turkey were asked to come into the war we should be unable, in view of our commitments in Italy, to send them much help; it was therefore doubtful whether the Turks would or could safely undertake a campaign on their own. He said that the situation was different last autumn when we had agreed to try to get Turkey into the war. At that time British forces in the Mediterranean were not fully committed to a successful Italian campaign. Mr. Eden explained that acceptance of Turkey's offer to break off relations with Germany did not preclude us later on from pressing her to enter the war. M. Gusev said that he understood the position.

M. Gusev also gave Mr. Eden an *aide-mémoire* containing more details of the Turco-Soviet negotiations. On May 27 the Turkish Government had proposed to Russia the establishment of closer

---

(a) R10285, 10286, 11508/7/44. (b) R10851/7/44.

political relations in the form of an agreement referring particularly to the Balkans. On June 5 the Soviet Government had replied that they were ready to consider Turkish proposals for collaboration. They pointed out, however, that the Balkans were in the hands of Germany who was at war with Russia, and that Turkey was not fighting Germany but had a friendly treaty with her and was giving her economic help. In these circumstances the political co-operation regarding the Balkans proposed by Turkey lost sense unless it meant a radical change in Turco-German relations. The only way to an agreement with Russia was the entry of Turkey into the war against Germany.

On June 27 the Turkish Government repeated that they desired more friendly relations with Russia and that their entry into the war was under consideration. On July 3 the Soviet Government replied that in their statement of June 5 they had in mind an immediate decision by Turkey to enter the war. The proposal to confirm the friendly character of Soviet-Turkish relations did not correspond with the aim of shortening the war, and general declarations could not replace actions directed against Germany.

The Soviet *aide-mémoire* stated that the Soviet position in these negotiations corresponded with the agreement about Turkey reached at the Moscow Conference of 1943 and confirmed at the Teheran Conference, and which the Soviet Government had consistently carried out. The Soviet Government complained that they had informed the British Government about the negotiations and their own position regarding them, and that the British Government had raised no objection.[1] Nevertheless at the end of June the British Government had made a new proposal to Turkey without preliminary Soviet concurrence in which they receded from the former tripartite agreement and did not insist on the immediate entry of Turkey into the war. This was in spite of the fact that the Soviet Government had replied on June 29 to the British note of June 25.[2]

(a)   On July 10 Mr. Eden told the War Cabinet the results of his discussions with the Soviet Ambassador and with the Chiefs of Staff. The latter were uneasy at the possible reactions on other operations if we had to go to the help of the Turks. M. Gusev had urged strongly that we should ask them to declare war, but he was not at

---

(b)   [1] On July 5 Mr. Eden pointed out to Sir A. Clark Kerr that he had kept the Soviet Government informed in advance of British dealings with the Turks. This was in contrast to the action of the Soviet Government regarding the Turkish proposal for a Turco-Soviet pact covering the Balkans; the Soviet Government had not informed us about the Turkish communication at the time or of their reply until after it had been delivered. In neither case had they consulted us.
[2] The Soviet reply was not received until July 1, i.e. after Sir H. Knatchbull-Hugessen had carried out his instructions.

(a) WM(44)89.3, C.A.   (b) R10407/7/44.

all sure about the assistance which they might receive in this event from the U.S.S.R. or about the Soviet requirements on specific points, e.g. what the Russians would want Turkey to do against Bulgaria. The Chief of Air Staff explained to the War Cabinet that the Germans might make small-scale air attacks with obsolete aircraft on important Turkish towns such as Istanbul. The effect of sudden air attacks, most probably by night, would be serious, since the Turks had no effective protection against them. They would ask urgently for our fighters, but we could not easily spare them from the Mediterranean area. Mr. Eden, with the support of the Prime Minister—who said that we wanted to have Turkey at the peace settlement—thought that we should continue our proposed line of policy, and might assume that the Turks themselves must have considered the possibility that Istanbul might be bombed. The War Cabinet accepted this view.

On July 12 Mr. Churchill sent a message to Stalin. He said that (a) Turkey was willing to break off relations immediately with the Axis Powers. She ought to declare war, but he feared that if the Allies told her to do that she would ask for aircraft, which we could not spare, to protect her towns, and for joint military operations in Bulgaria and the Aegean for which we had not the means. She would also ask for munitions which we could not provide because the stocks ready for her earlier had been drawn off elsewhere. Mr. Churchill thought that a Turkish breach of relations with Germany should be accepted as a first instalment. The Allies could then help her against a 'vengeance' attack from the air.

Sir A. Clark Kerr sent a letter of explanation to M. Molotov on (b) July 13. He said that the British Government proposed to regard as satisfactory the Turkish agreement to break off relations with Germany and to ask them to take this action at once. At the same time we should assure the Turkish Government: (i) that by their action they had clarified their policy and placed themselves in a better position to fill the international position at the peace making to which they aspired; (ii) that we would do our best to mitigate any economic disturbances resulting from the rupture of relations; (iii) that in the event of hostilities with Germany, we would give Turkey all possible economic and military assistance; (iv) that we would use our good offices with our allies to obtain similar help from them for Turkey. Sir A. Clark Kerr told M. Molotov that the British Government were ready to discuss with the United States and Soviet Governments the question of a declaration of war by Turkey.

Stalin answered Mr. Churchill's message on July 15. He said that (c)

(a) T1429/4 (Churchill Papers/447; R10982/17/6). (b) R11509/7/44. (c) T1453/4 (Churchill Papers/447; R11200/7/44).

the Allied Governments had asked Turkey in November and December 1943 to enter the war against Germany, and that on the initiative of the Turkish Government in May and June 1944, the Soviet Government had begun negotiations with Turkey and twice proposed that they should enter the war. Nothing had come of these proposals. In view of Turkey's evasive and vague attitude, Stalin thought that it was better to leave her in peace. This would mean the lapse of the claims of Turkey, who had evaded war with Germany, to special rights in post-war matters.

(a)   On July 17 the Prime Minister read Stalin's message to the War Cabinet. Mr. Eden agreed with the Prime Minister that the Turks had shown great unwisdom, and had risked 'missing their market'. The question was how to deal with this situation. It was clear that the Soviet Government would not co-operate on our proposed lines. The Russians might indeed be aware that Turkey was ready to enter the war, and might feel that she would have done so if we had refused any intermediate solution. There seemed no alternative now but to tell Turkey that her only chance was to declare war on Germany. In this case, however, the risk that the Germans would bomb Istanbul would be greater than if the Turks had merely taken diplomatic action. The Chief of the Air Staff said that we should find it difficult to provide the necessary fighter protection and that it was more than doubtful whether we could prevent the Germans from making at least one heavy air attack on Istanbul. The Prime Minister thought the importance of bringing Turkey into the war so great that we might have to face the disadvantage of diverting forces to her assistance. He and Mr. Eden agreed, however, that the Defence Committee should study the matter further.

(b)   On July 19 Mr. Eden wrote to the Prime Minister that Stalin's purpose in demanding that Turkey enter the war might be to make things as difficult as possible for Turkey and possibly to reopen Anglo-Turkish disagreements with effects on the alliance. Mr. Eden thought that if we could not provide fighter protection, we should revert to our programme—which we had a full right to do in view of our treaty position—of urging Turkey to break off relations at once. Although Stalin had not approved this course, he had not asked the British Government to desist from it. Mr. Eden thought that we should at least get some result from our programme 'which the world could observe and which would help our battles'.

(c)   On July 20 the United States Government informed the British Government that they agreed with our view, provided that it was made clear to the Turks that the severance of relations with Germany

---

(a) WM(44)91.5, C.A.   (b) PM/44/541, R11353/7/44.   (c) R11333, 11335, 11348, 11351/7/44.

was only the first step towards active belligerency. The United States Chargé d'Affaires at Ankara was therefore instructed to support British representations, and the Soviet Embassy in Washington was informed of these views.

On July 21 the Foreign Office instructed Sir H. Knatchbull- (a) Hugessen to tell the Turkish Government at once that we expected them to break off relations with Germany after four days, and that we regarded this action as the first step towards belligerency.[1] We considered that if she did this, Turkey would have clarified her policy, which had become obscure and confused by recent events, and would have placed herself in a better position than hitherto to fill that international position at the peace-making to which she aspired. We should remove our ban on the export to Turkey of certain commodities, and resume the provision of military supplies as soon as relations were broken off. We would also assist the Turks in measures against a possible German attack, though we regarded such an attack as unlikely. We were asking the United States Government also to resume military supplies. Sir H. Knatchbull-Hugessen was to inform his United States and Soviet colleagues of the action he was taking.[2]

On the same day (July 21) Sir A. Cadogan sent a personal tele- (b) gram to Sir H. Knatchbull-Hugessen explaining the difficulty of the situation. The Allied Governments would like to see Turkey in the war; Turkey was apparently ready to come in, but it would be most dangerous to ask her to do so because we believed that the Turks, as the result of our measures to deceive the Germans, thought that we had larger forces in the Middle East than was the case. If we asked the Turks to enter the war, they would ask what help we could give. The answer would be practically nothing, since the Chiefs of Staff would agree to provide only the minimum forces needed to meet a German air attack. This disclosure would almost certainly frighten the Turks from the idea of severing relations with Germany. It would also come to the knowledge of the Germans and give them a valuable indication as to future operations in the Mediterranean. The Russians had their own reasons for asking Turkey to come into the war. They were probably hoping either that she would suffer reverses or that, if she refused to come in, the Anglo-Turkish connexion would be broken.

Sir A. Cadogan said that we had decided merely to ask Turkey to break off relations with Germany, although this course of action

---

[1] The Turkish Government had said that they needed four days' notice.
[2] On July 21 the Foreign Office asked the British Embassies in Washington and Moscow to inform the United States and Soviet Governments respectively of these instructions.

(a) R11351, 12062, 12064/7/44. (b) R11257/7/44.

would not be easy to explain to the Russians. Since we wanted to be able later on to press the Turks to come into the war, we were reluctant to meet Turkey fully regarding the alliance and her position in the peace settlement if she only broke off relations. Turkish eagerness for satisfaction on these two points gave us a powerful weapon which we did not wish to give away until we had attained our final objective.

Sir A. Cadogan pointed out that close Anglo-Turkish friendship and even alliance were part of British policy in the eastern Mediterranean. Our existing treaty, however, was inconsistent with the Anglo-Soviet treaty. It committed us to armed support of Turkey in the event of Russian aggression, although we had obtained no military support from Turkey during the war with Italy against whom the treaty was primarily directed. We wished, therefore, to maintain the alliance, but to allow the treaty to lapse. It was not in our power alone to give Turkey the assurances she wanted about her international position. The Soviet Government had not approved our proposal that Turkey should merely break off relations with Germany; we had to be careful about the reward which we promised the Turks for the proposed action. In any case the Turks were now so far committed to breaking off relations that they could not draw back.

(a)   Sir H. Knatchbull-Hugessen told M. Saracoglu on July 22 that Turkey's refusal to agree to our proposals in January had brought about a new situation which made it necessary to proceed step by step. We thought that the severance of relations with Germany would not justify the grant to Turkey of all the advantages for which she asked. In answer to a question by M. Saracoglu, who evidently wanted an assurance that the alliance was fully restored, Sir H. Knatchbull-Hugessen said that our request was made within the framework of the alliance. He said that the Prime Minister must draw a distinction between the alliance and the treaty. The British Government attached importance to Turkish friendship and felt that a start in the right direction would be made with the severance of relations. The Ambassador was certain that in a short time the alliance would be fully revived on a basis of complete co-operation by Turkey, but M. Saracoglu was asking for a *quid pro quo* not provided for in the treaty, i.e. a voice in the peace settlement. This was not in our sole gift. Sir H. Knatchbull-Hugessen said that the terms of the treaty were not yet fulfilled, and that we should have to postpone a final answer to his question.

(b)   On July 24 M. Saracoglu informed Sir H. Knatchbull-Hugessen that relations with Germany would be broken off at midnight on

---

(a) R11474/7/44. (b) R11542, 11543, 11545, 11546, 11558/7/44.

August 2. He said that he was sure of the approval of the National Assembly. He indicated that the Turkish Government were distressed by descriptions of Turkish policy as 'obscure' and 'confused'. Sir H Knatchbull-Hugessen recommended that M. Saracoglu should be informed that his action in breaking off relations with Germany afforded proof of an alliance, and that Turkey had recovered her position as an ally. The Foreign Office accordingly instructed Sir H. Knatchbull-Hugessen that he could give a written assurance in the form of a personal letter to which M. Saracoglu might refer at the meeting of the National Assembly, although Sir A. Cadogan preferred that the actual text should not be read out. On July 27 Sir H. Knatchbull-Hugessen addressed a personal and most secret (a) letter to M. Saracoglu expressing the 'lively satisfaction' of His Majesty's Government at the decision, and stating that Turkey had thereby recovered her position as the ally of Great Britain.

Sir H. Knatchbull-Hugessen informed the Soviet Ambassador of (b) the decision of the Turkish Government. M. Vinogradov showed little enthusiasm and repeated Stalin's comment that half-measures were no use. The United States Government made a reservation (c) that, if Turkey should enter the war, they were not committed to air, military or naval support of a campaign in the Balkans. In a letter dated July 27 Sir A. Clark Kerr informed M. Molotov of the (d) latest developments. M. Molotov replied that the Soviet Government considered the Turkish position unsatisfactory. The proposals which Turkey put forward were no longer important to the common cause, and it was best to put no pressure on her. Mr. Harriman agreed with Sir A. Clark Kerr that the stubborn attitude of the Russians was due to their military successes; they had written off Turkey as a means of drawing divisions away from their front.[1]

On July 28 von Papen came back to Ankara by air and insisted (e) on an immediate interview with M. Saracoglu on the ground that he had been instructed to make an important communication to him. M. Saracoglu asked the Secretary-General to see him. At this interview, which took place on July 29, von Papen was nervous and depressed. He said he knew exactly what was planned, and recited the arrangements for the Assembly meeting. He was asked whether he could suggest anything which might prevent Turkey from making

---

[1] On August 21 Sir O. Sargent informed Sir A. Clark Kerr that the Soviet Government (f) were not interested in Turkish belligerency, but, since the Moscow Conference of 1943, were using the whole Turkish question as a stalking horse for the pursuit of their long-term objectives in the Balkans. They were treating the question of Turkey's entry into the war as a means of putting Turkey in the wrong so that at the end of the war she would be isolated and discredited as a disloyal ally and hardened neutral, and so be unable to stand in the way of Russian interests in south-east Europe.

(a) R11729/7/44. (b) R11639/7/44. (c) R11943/7/44. (d) R11873/7/44. (e) R11825, 11830/7/44. (f) R11506/7/ 4.

this move; he offered to withdraw German nationals, including consuls, to whom the Turkish Government took exception. He also proposed a German withdrawal from the Greek islands and Greece. The Secretary-General said that he knew nothing about the decision.

(a)   In response to a personal appeal M. Saracoglu received von Papen on July 29. He also reported that the Ambassador was in a state of complete despair, highly nervous and largely incoherent. He was pessimistic about the military situation. He made no threat and merely repeated that Turkey was following the road to war. On August 1 he was received by the President of the Republic and still made no threat. He read from notes an appeal to the President not to break off relations, and pointed out that by doing so Turkey would 'become like Poland'.

(b)   A secret meeting of the People's Party on the night of August 1–2 approved the severance of relations with Germany with only one dissentient vote. The meeting was stormy and one of the chief criticisms was apparently that the Government were taking action without guarantees from Russia. Sir H. Knatchbull-Hugessen heard that his letter to M. Saracoglu was an important factor in the discussion. Later on August 2 the Assembly approved the Government's motion with a unanimous vote.

(c)   Early in September Sir H. Knatchbull-Hugessen left Ankara to take up the post of Ambassador in Brussels. At a farewell lunch given to him by the President of the Republic, the Turks showed that they were anxious about their status with Great Britain and Russia. President Inönü said that if he knew more clearly the standing of Turkey with Great Britain he would know how to deal with Russia. Sir H. Knatchbull-Hugessen answered that at the time of the rupture of relations with Germany he had stated in writing to M. Saracoglu that the vitality of the alliance was restored. He said that the terms of the existing treaty would in course of time become out of date and the alliance would have to be expressed in terms corresponding with the European settlement and the British alliance with Russia. Mr. Eden noted on the telegram reporting this conversation: 'We want to keep close to Turkey.'

(d)   On September 4 the Foreign Office asked the Chiefs of Staff Committee about the possibility of slowing down the despatch of military supplies and personnel to Turkey. The Foreign Office thought it extremely unlikely that Turkey would come into the war either as the result of enemy attack or Allied pressure. If we continued to supply military material, Russia would probably point out that, as it could not be intended for use against Germany and

---

(a) R11871, 11977/7/44. (b) R12017, 14380/7/44. (c) R14197/7/44. (d) R13505, 14199, 14229/7/44; COS(44)813(0).

her satellites, it must be intended for eventual use against her.

The Chiefs of Staff Committee replied on September 8 to the Foreign Office that they did not object to giving the Turks supplies which could be spared and for which shipping was being found without difficulty. They said that a friendly Turkey was in our interest, not only because we might require facilities in connexion with the Dodecanese, but also from the point of view of the military situation in the Middle East after the war. If, however, the Foreign Office considered that the decision would not antagonise the Turks, the Chiefs of Staff were prepared to agree to the slowing down of supplies.

Four days later, however, General Wilson urgently requested (a) approval for the cancellation of the whole commitment to Turkey and withdrawal of the forces[1] in Turkey as early as practicable in view of the favourable strategic developments in the Balkans. He said that his proposal would not affect the flow of supplies for the Turks (under the Adana agreement) which was resumed when they broke off relations with Germany.

The Foreign Office commented on September 14 that, although the amount of supplies which we were prepared to give could not have much effect in strengthening Turkey against a Russian threat, the Russian advance through the Balkans made it more important for us to keep in well with the Turks. It would therefore be a very bad moment even to cut down our supplies drastically. The Foreign Office thought that nothing already sent into Turkey should be withdrawn, and that we should continue to send anything we could without prejudice to other needs. We should go on slowly until we saw Russian intentions in the Balkans more clearly.

Meanwhile on September 14 at the Quebec Conference the Chiefs (b) of Staff Committee decided to submit a minute to the Prime Minister endorsing General Wilson's recommendation. At Mr. Eden's request, however, the instructions to General Wilson were redrafted to allow (c) the gradual withdrawal of personnel. On September 16 Mr. Eden (d) telegraphed to Sir O. Sargent asking him to explain the position to the Turkish Government. Sir H. Knatchbull-Hugessen, who was in London, did not consider that the withdrawal of personnel need have a bad effect on Anglo-Turkish relations. On September 19, therefore, the Chargé d'Affaires at Ankara was instructed to remind the Turkish Government that the forces were sent into Turkey in accordance with our pledge to defend her against German attack.

---

[1] These forces amounted only to 1300–1500 R.A.F. (signals, radar, etc.), and about 40 Army anti-aircraft personnel.

(a) Medcos 188, R14229/7/44. (b) COS(44)875(o); R14229, 14734/7/44. (c) Gunfire 182, R14734/7/44. (d) Gunfire 183, R14734/7/44.

With the defeat of Roumania and Bulgaria this danger had almost vanished and would shortly disappear. Our men therefore were serving no useful purpose and were urgently needed elsewhere. Nevertheless we would withdraw them slowly so that we might avoid danger and the Turks might continue to profit by their technical knowledge. The withdrawal did not imply weakening of our feelings of friendship for Turkey or of our determination to maintain the alliance. The Turkish Government acquiesced in the withdrawal.

(a)   In a summary of the relations between the British and Turkish Governments prepared for Sir M. Peterson before he left London as Ambassador to Turkey, the Foreign Office said that we now no longer wanted Turkey to take an active part in the war. British long-term interest in Turkey was unaffected by Turkish behaviour in the past, while the recent spread of Soviet influence in the Balkans had increased the desirability of maintaining our influence. How could this be done without damage to our relations with Russia? It was difficult to say what we wanted within these limits. Turkish statesmen also seemed uncertain of the present and future services which they could render us. We were doing our best to fulfil the promise that, if Turkey broke off relations with Germany, we should make good the resultant damage to her economy. We were sending military supplies in quantities which had satisfied the Turks for the moment. We and the United States were sending civilian supplies and planning support purchases.

The Foreign Office thought that the one constructive point in recent Turkish suggestions was their insistence on the need to strengthen our relations bilaterally and without troubling too much about the United States and U.S.S.R. At first sight, therefore, revision of the treaty seemed a useful means of strengthening relations. There were, however, two overwhelming objections. The Russians would suspect the conclusion of a new treaty, and the British public would ask why we were concluding a treaty with a Government which had failed to fulfil its obligations under its previous treaty and which still remained a non-belligerent. Secondly, until the Foreign Office knew what the organisation of post-war security would be, they could not decide upon the terms of a new treaty with Turkey. Since we could not proceed with a new treaty for the moment, we must foster the alliance and develop the thesis that it was one of the main factors in our policy in the eastern Mediterranean, where the maintenance of a mutual understanding between Turkey, Greece and Great Britain would be essential to our permanent strategic interests after the war.

The Foreign Office thought that much of the value of the Anglo-

---

(a) R15838/7/44.

Turkish alliance would be lost if similar relations did not exist between Greece and Turkey. The time had not come for a new Turco-Greek treaty, but closer relations between the two Governments could be established in all spheres where they had joint interests or where their separate interests needed to be reconciled, e.g. Turkey might reach an agreement with Greece about the Dodecanese, whereby she recognised Greek sovereignty in return for the safeguarding of special Turkish interests in the archipelago. Turkey might also help Greece in her struggle for liberation and then with rehabilitation; this action in turn would assist collaboration between Great Britain, Turkey and Greece.

When on October 19 M. Hasan Saka, the Turkish Foreign (a) Minister,[1] asked Sir M. Peterson about a treaty, Sir M. Peterson said that the British Government thought that for the moment we ought to emphasise the alliance, and that the question of a new treaty ought to stand over until we could see how the new world order was shaping. M. Saracoglu also seemed greatly pleased by what Sir M. Peterson had said, but was anxious that we should not give up our position in favour of Russia. Sir M. Peterson said that there was no point in refusing to recognise the inevitable growth of Soviet influence in the Balkans. Such influence was bound to be predominant in Roumania; most Bulgarians were pro-Russian in sentiment, but in Bulgaria we ought to be able to maintain and even increase our influence. Sir M. Peterson said to M. Saracoglu that we were determined also to increase our influence in Yugoslavia, for whose entry into the war we were responsible and in which a very delicate constitutional position existed. Our influence was predominant in Greece and we intended that it should remain so. Sir M. Peterson pointed out once more to M. Saracoglu that French, German and Italian influence in the Balkans had disappeared, whether temporarily or permanently, and there was necessarily a void. It was too much to expect that this should not be partly filled by increased Soviet influence. There was no reason why British and Turkish influence should not also increase.

Sir M. Peterson reported to the Foreign Office that there was no need to say very much about the importance we attached to good Turco-Greek relations, because the Turks themselves said that that was one of their first objectives. The Greek Ambassador had told Sir M. Peterson that the Turks had formally renounced any claims to the Dodecanese. Sir M. Peterson particularly remarked that both the Prime Minister and Foreign Minister asked him anxiously for news of the Polish negotiations. They regarded the Polish question

---

[1] M. Hasan Saka was appointed Foreign Minister in mid-September 1944.

(a) R17685/7/44.

as a test whether the Russians intended to be reasonable or whether we were going to be strong enough to make them so.

(a)   Before his visit to Moscow in October 1944, Mr. Churchill suggested that President Inönü might be invited to meet him and Turkey asked to declare war. Sir O. Sargent accordingly approved a minute to Mr. Churchill saying that we wanted nothing active from Turkey. With the defection of Bulgaria and the gradual withdrawal of the Germans from Greece, Turkey's last opportunity of becoming an effective belligerent had disappeared. The Foreign Office considered the use of Turkish help in expelling the Germans from the Aegean, but this possibility was ruled out by the political repercussions which it would have caused in Greece as well as by the fact that there were no forces in the Middle East at our disposal to undertake the operation. The Foreign Office thought Turkey could not now take any political action which would help to shorten the war. The Soviet declaration of war on Bulgaria and subsequent occupation of the country had now made it unnecessary for Turkey to break off relations with Bulgaria.

The Foreign Office minute repeated the long-term arguments in favour of close Anglo-Turkish relations. Our aim was to keep Turkey after the war within the British orbit and protect her from Russian demands which might endanger her vital interests, sovereignty or territorial integrity and consequently our own position. Turkey, by her failure to come into the war when she could have been of use to the United Nations, had put herself in a very weak position with regard to Russia; her only hope was to remain in the background. A spectacular effort to rehabilitate herself would merely provoke the Russians. The closer her relations with the Greeks, the less her chances would be of finding herself completely isolated after the war in a south-eastern Europe where Soviet influence would be very powerful. The Foreign Office concluded, however, that action by the Turks on these lines would not be of decisive importance in determining the fate of Anglo-Turkish relations.[1]

(iii)

Russian demands at the Moscow and Yalta Conferences for the revision of the Montreux Convention: British attitude to the Russian demands: Turkish declaration of war on Germany and Japan (October 1944–February 1945).

The instructions to Sir M. Peterson did not refer to British policy with regard to a revision of the Montreux Convention of 1936. The

---

[1] The Prime Minister decided not to see President Inönü.

(a) R20344/7/44.

Foreign Office realised, however, that the Convention would have to be revised, and that revision would be a matter of controversy owing to the Russian demands. In view of the forthcoming visit of Mr. Eden to Moscow, Sir O. Sargent drew up on October 6, 1944, (a) a memorandum on the question for his use. He pointed out that there were technical reasons why the Convention would have to be changed. It had been drafted to fit in with the organisation of the League of Nations and with various treaties—now obsolete—dealing with the limitation of naval armaments. The provisions regarding ships of war were out of date owing to recent naval developments, such as E-boats. The Convention also needed revision on legal grounds since Japan was one of the signatories, and the Russians could reasonably object to limitations imposed on their military freedom by a State against whom they were soon to declare war.

From the British point of view, however, there were obvious difficulties in the way of revision. The Straits might now be less important to Great Britain, but the Chiefs of Staff still thought that, for our strategical security in the eastern Mediterranean and Middle East, Russia should not have physical control of them or unrestricted rights of passage. The revision of the Convention had to be considered in relation to Russian claims or threats elsewhere, particularly through the Caucasus towards Iran. The Russians probably wanted rights of egress from the Black Sea in time of war, limitations on the discretionary powers of Turkey to open or close the Straits on a threat of war, or participation in the administration of the Straits régime. The satisfaction of any of these demands would endanger Turkish neutrality in time of war and her integrity and sovereignty in general.

The British position in south-east Europe in relation to Russia was very weak; we should therefore make the most of the Anglo-Turkish alliance and of our age-long British opposition to Russian ambitions regarding the Straits; identity of interest between Great Britain and Turkey regarding the Straits was one of the basic factors of the alliance. If we gave way on the Straits, we should to some extent be throwing away the alliance. Furthermore, Mr. Eden had assured[1] the Turks that he would never discuss matters affecting Turkey with a third Power without prior consultation.

The Russians, in fact, raised the matter of the Moscow Con- (b) ference. On October 9 Stalin pointed out that if Turkey were threatened she could close the Straits, and that she was free to decide what constituted a 'threat'. Stalin said that if Great Britain

---

[1] See above, p. 82.

(a) R16013/3830/44. (b) R18327/17223/44; Print, 'Anglo-Soviet Political Conversations in Moscow, October 9–17, 1944'.

was interested in the Mediterranean, Russia was equally interested in the Black Sea. He pointed out that Mr. Churchill had expressed sympathy when he (Stalin) had raised the question in Teheran. The Convention was unsuitable and a spearhead against Russia, and should be dropped. He spoke of the danger that Turkey would 'grip Russian trade by the throat'. Mr. Churchill agreed in principle that changes were necessary. He suggested that the Russians should let us know what they wanted. Mr. Churchill added that, if they were sitting at the armistice table and Stalin asked him for free passage through the Straits for merchant ships and warships, he would say that Great Britain had no objection. Great Britain had no ties with Turkey except the Convention, which was now inadmissible and obsolete.[1] Stalin said that he did not want to hurry Mr. Churchill, but he was anxious for an admission that the Russian claim was justified. Mr. Churchill replied that Stalin should take the initiative and tell the United States what was in his mind. He thought that Russia had a right and a moral claim.

(a)   On the following day Mr. Eden wrote a minute for Mr. Churchill based on Sir O. Sargent's memorandum. He said that Stalin had made it clear that he disliked the limitations on the Russian right to send warships through the Straits in time of war, and Turkey's discretionary powers to open or close the Straits when she felt a menace of war. Mr. Eden put the arguments used by Sir O. Sargent and pointed out that under the existing régime, Russian merchant ships passed freely through the Straits both in war and peace. Except in time of war the Russian battle fleet had practically free rights of egress from the Black Sea. We had now agreed that the Soviet Government would let us know what they wanted. Mr. Eden suggested that Mr. Churchill should avoid further mention of the matter.

(b)   Mr. Churchill accepted this advice, but pointed out in a reply to Mr. Eden[2] of October 12 that there was no need to fear the movement of a Russian fleet through the Straits. Even if such a fleet were to join General de Gaulle, a British fleet and aircraft from bases in the Mediterranean would be capable of dealing with either or both. 'All Russian ships who are on the sea, warships or merchant, are hostages to the stronger naval power.' On the other hand Mr. Churchill thought that it was 'like breeding pestilence to try to keep a

---

(c)   [1] A Foreign Office note of November 9 said: 'I am not clear what exactly the Prime Minister meant by saying: "Britain had no ties with Turkey except the Montreux Convention." We have after all a Treaty of Alliance.' Mr. Eden subsequently noted: 'The Prime Minister said much, but he would have said a great deal more but for my appeals and injunctions.'

[2] This minute was not initialled by the Prime Minister. Mr. Eden initialled it on October 14.

(a) PM(M)/44/1, R16013/17223/44.   (b) M(Tol.)6/4.   (c) R18327/17223/44.

nation like Russia from free access to the broadwaters'. He thought that the assurance to Turkey of January 15, 1942, was 'more than voided' by their refusal to give any help in January 1944.

Stalin raised the question of the Montreux Convention again on (a) October 17. He said that he wanted Mr. Churchill to keep the question in mind. Mr. Churchill said that in principle his view was that the Convention ought not to remain in force. He asked Stalin to state secretly what improvement he suggested. Stalin said that he would send in his requirements and that they would not be extravagant. He repeated that it was intolerable that Turkey if threatened was entitled to close the Straits.

On November 23 Mr. Eden gave the Turkish Ambassador an (b) account of the discussions at Moscow concerning the Balkans. He said that the position of Turkey and the régime of the Straits had been discussed in very general terms. The Soviet Government were not pressing for revision of the Convention, but had pointed out that Japan was a party to the Convention, and that the régime of the Straits was bound up with the machinery of the League. Mr. Eden said that the Russians had made no proposals; if they did we would consult with the Turkish Government as we were bound to do. M. Unaydin showed uneasiness as well as the greatest interest when Mr. Eden mentioned the Straits, and Mr. Eden said that he hoped the Turkish Government would not give undue emphasis to what he had said. The fact that the Russians had first raised the matter with us showed that they realised the need for Allied co-operation in this as in all else.

On January 24, 1945, Sir A. Cadogan noted that we were still (c) awaiting Russian proposals for amendment of the Convention. The question was whether the Foreign Office endorsed Russian claims for complete freedom of the Straits in peace or war. Sir A. Cadogan added, 'We may have to', but hoped that the Foreign Office would not come to a hasty decision without asking Russia for some concession in return. He knew that Great Britain would not be able to get any concession, but thought that, if the Foreign Office could not resist a Russian demand, they should refrain from saying that it was well-founded and justified. Mr. Eden agreed with Sir A. Cadogan, and sent a minute to the Prime Minister in this sense on January 27. He said that the Russians might raise the question of the Straits at the Yalta Conference, but that it would be better for the British delegation to note what they said without giving them too much encouragement of British support. In an annex to his minute, Mr. Eden pointed out that the Turks were sensitive about Russian interest

---

(a) R18327/17223/44; Print, 'Anglo-Soviet Political Conversations in Moscow, October 9–17, 1944'. (b) R19657/17223/44. (c) R1885/44/44.

in the Straits; he thought that it would be undesirable to enter into a commitment or be led into a discussion without first consulting them.

(a)   The revision of the Convention was in fact discussed at the Yalta Conference. Mr. Eden had a preliminary discussion with Mr. Stettinius at Malta on February 1 on their way to the Conference. Mr. Stettinius said that the President had in mind the question of Russian interests in a warm water port. He asked whether the British Government knew what the Russians wanted. Mr. Eden said that the Russians wanted to revise the Convention, and that we had asked them for written proposals. He thought that they might ask for a régime for the Straits similar to that of the Suez Canal, which would allow their warships to pass from the Black Sea into the Mediterranean in time of war.

(b)   At the sixth plenary meeting of the Yalta Conference on February 10, Stalin gave notice of his intention to raise the question of revision of the Convention. He said that it was intolerable for Russia to have to beg the Turks to let her ships go through the Straits. The régime of the Straits should be similar to that of the Suez Canal. The Prime Minister said that he would support the Russian request for revision.

At a later plenary meeting on the same day, Stalin repeated his reasons for considering the Convention was out of date. He said that at the time the Convention was concluded Russian relations with Great Britain were not friendly, but he was now sure that Great Britain would not wish to strangle Russia with the help of Japan. It was impossible to put up with a situation in which 'a small state like Turkey could keep a hand on the throat of a large country like Russia'. Stalin proposed that the three Foreign Secretaries should consider the matter at their next meeting.

The Prime Minister said that he had asked Stalin in Moscow to make proposals for revision, but that he had not yet done so. He agreed that the position of Russia was unsatisfactory in regard to her Black Sea interests and her dependence upon the narrow entrance through the Straits. He accepted the suggestion that the Foreign Secretaries should examine the question. He also said that we must inform the Turkish Government before the matter was discussed, in view of our undertaking to let them know when any matter affecting their interests was about to be raised. Mr. Churchill thought that when it was proposed to alter the Convention some undertaking should be given to Turkey that her independence and integrity were not affected. Stalin said that it should be possible to give such an assurance. The Conference agreed that the Foreign

---

(a) WP(45)157.   (b) WP(45)157; Jason 336, R3043/44/44.

Secretaries at their next meeting in London[1] should consider Soviet proposals for revising the Convention, and that the Turkish Government would be informed at an appropriate moment.

Sir M. Peterson telegraphed to the Foreign Office on February 20 (a) that the Turks were enquiring whether the Balkan problems had been discussed at Yalta. The Foreign Office saw some advantage in telling the Turks at once that the question of the Straits had been raised but not discussed, and that it would be considered at the next meeting of the Foreign Secretaries. Mr. Eden said to the Turkish Ambassador on February 22 that revision of the Convention had (b) come up in much the same form as at Moscow in October. The Soviet Government had again stated their reasons for revision, and as at Moscow it had been agreed that they should put forward proposals. They said that these proposals would not prejudice the territorial integrity of Turkey.

On the day before Sir M. Peterson sent this telegram the Foreign Office had instructed him to tell the Turkish Government that they now had a chance of declaring war on Germany in circumstances which would give Turkey a place at the Peace Conference. There is a certain anticlimax in the fact that—after so many months of hesitation and evasion on the Turkish side, and so much advice and warning from the side of Great Britain—the British Government should have invited Turkey to enter the war when her services were no longer needed, and that the Turks should have accepted the invitation.

The situation was indeed unexpected. The Prime Minister had refused a suggestion from the Foreign Office that he should see the (c) Turkish Ambassador before leaving for the Yalta Conference. The Prime Minister said that he had spent much time in the past two years in trying 'to influence Turkey in the right direction'. He had met with no response, and therefore was under very little obligation to the Turks. He did not feel called upon to help Turkey to 'jump on to the bus she has missed'. At the fourth plenary meeting of the Conference on February 9, however, President Roosevelt raised the (d) question whether invitations to attend the discussions on a future World Organisation should go not only to nations which had fought against Germany but also to nations which had broken off diplomatic relations without actually taking part in the war. In the debate on the question Mr. Churchill mentioned Turkey. He said that the Turks had made an alliance with us at a dangerous time and had

---

[1] i.e. after the San Francisco Conference. The Russians had suggested a discussion while the Foreign Secretaries were in the United States for the San Francisco Conference. Mr. Churchill thought that, since British interests in the Mediterranean were closely involved, the discussion should take place in London.

(a) R3531/1723/44. (b) R4053/44/44. (c) R2265/1723/44. (d) WP(45)157.

found later that their army lacked modern equipment. They had remained friendly and helpful in many ways, although they had not taken the chance of entry into the war offered them in 1944. Mr. Churchill suggested that, if they were now ready to declare war, they should be invited to the Conference on World Organisation. It was finally agreed that invitations would be sent to States which had declared war on Germany by March 1, 1945.

President Roosevelt told the Conference that the United States Government had given a hint to certain Latin American States that a declaration of war would entitle them to an invitation to the
(a) Conference on World Organisation. Mr. Eden telegraphed to the Foreign Office suggesting that they should give a similar hint to Iceland, Egypt and Turkey. This telegram crossed a suggestion from the Foreign Office on those lines. On February 19, therefore, Sir M. Peterson was instructed to inform the Turkish Government that if they wished to be invited to the World Organisation Conference they should take steps to qualify before March 1. We were not urging the Turks to declare war, but merely calling their attention to the benefits if they did so before March 1. If Turkey did enter the war, this would not mean that we could give her any further military supplies or assistance.

(b)   The Turkish Government submitted to the National Assembly on February 23 a resolution in favour of declaring war on Germany and Japan and notifying their desire to adhere to the United Nations Declaration. Sir O. Sargent commented: 'I should have thought that the Turks would have been too proud to have done this.'

(iv)

Russian demands on Turkey for the cession of Kars and Ardahan: British proposal for a joint Anglo-American démarche to the Soviet Government: discussions on Turkey and the question of the Straits at the Potsdam Conference.

Since there was no meeting of the Council of Foreign Ministers in London before the Potsdam Conference the Russians were unable
(c) to submit to it proposals for a revision of the Montreux Convention. On March 19, 1945, however, they denounced the Russo-Turkish treaty of 1925. They informed the Turkish Ambassador at Moscow of their intention in a friendly way, but the Turkish Government believed that they were trying to put pressure on them and that they wanted to reach a direct Russo-Turkish understanding about the

---

(a) U1201/12/70. (b) U1294/12/70. (c) R5500/4476/44.

revision of the Montreux Convention before the question came up for international discussion. On March 26, the Soviet Ambassador (a) in Ankara told Sir M. Peterson that the question of the Straits was linked with the idea of a new Russo-Turkish treaty and that the Soviet Government expected to raise it at the next tripartite meeting after the San Francisco Conference.

The Turkish Foreign Minister on March 22 asked Sir M. Peterson for British advice on the reply to the Russians. He said that the Turkish Government wanted to improve their relations with Russia and hoped to do so if the Russians did not make the mistake of 'regarding Turkey as on the same footing with Bulgaria, Roumania, or Yugoslavia'. In reporting this conversation to the Foreign Office Sir M. Peterson commented that the Anglo-Turkish alliance was (b) probably the real cause of Russian irritation with Turkey.

The Foreign Office also thought that the denunciation of the (c) treaty, and recent Soviet press attacks on Turkey, were part of a process of 'softening up' with a view to demands for the revision of the Convention. Mr. Eden suggested on March 28 to the Turkish (d) Ambassador and Secretary-General (who was in London) that the Turkish reply should take note of the Russian denunciation and express a hope that conditions would soon be favourable for the negotiation of a new treaty. Mr. Eden thought that after the San Francisco Conference it might be possible to fit such a treaty into the framework of the new world security system. He suggested that, if the Russians tried to introduce the question of the Straits, the Turkish answer should be that the matter affected several countries and would have to be discussed multilaterally.

The Ambassador and Secretary-General agreed with these suggestions. The Turkish Government replied to the Soviet Government (e) on April 4 that they were ready to examine Russian proposals for a new treaty. When, however, on June 7, 1945, the Turkish Ambassa- (f) dor in Moscow made a formal approach to M. Molotov about a treaty, he was told that before proceeding with a treaty the Soviet Government wished to solve questions outstanding between the two countries. M. Molotov described these questions as follows: (i) the cessions of the provinces of Kars and Ardahan by Russia to Turkey under the Russo-Turkish Treaty of 1921, which was made under duress and required revision; (ii) the cessions of bases by Turkey to Russia in the Straits; (iii) an agreement between Turkey and Russia for revision of the Montreux Convention.

The Turkish Ambassador replied that this Government considered the treaty of 1921 to have been freely negotiated; they were not

---

(a) R5725/4476/44.   (b) R5579/4476/44.   (c) R5640/4476/44.   (d) R6103/4476/44. (e) R7128/4476/44.   (f) R10123/44/44.

prepared to revise it and they could not grant Russia bases in the Straits, and the Montreux Convention was not a matter which the two Governments alone could discuss. The Turkish Government approved the attitude of their Ambassador, and asked the British
(a) Government for advice and endorsement of their reply. Later reports suggested that the Turkish Ambassador had somewhat exaggerated the force of M. Molotov's demands and that he had been manoeuvred into asking what the Russian *desiderata* for a new treaty would be. He saw M. Molotov again on June 18 in order to confirm his earlier reply. M. Molotov then made it clear that the Russians would want bases in the Straits only in war time. The Soviet Ambassador at Ankara described the territorial demands on the eastern frontier as due to the Russian wish to 'do something for the Armenian people'.

Meanwhile the Foreign Office described the Russian demands as a 'rude shock' to the Turks, and proposed to ask the United States Government to agree to a joint *démarche* about them to Russia. They thought that they could refer to Stalin's willingness at Yalta to reassure Turkey about the maintenance of her independence and
(b) integrity. In a minute to the Prime Minister[1] on June 16 the Foreign Office pointed out that there was no reason to believe that the Turco-Soviet Treaty of 1921 had been entered into under duress on the Soviet side, and that the demands for the provinces of Kars and Ardahan and for bases in the Straits were counter to the principles of the World Organisation and to Stalin's undertakings at Yalta.

With the approval of the Prime Minister, the Foreign Office sent
(c) telegrams to Istanbul and Washington on June 17. They thought that the Turkish Government should present the Soviet Government with proposals for a new treaty. They asked whether the Turkish Government would agree to an Anglo-American approach to Russia on the points which 'had a multilateral bearing'. The Turkish
(d) Government replied on June 20 that they would welcome intervention by the British Government in Moscow with or without the support of the United States.

The telegram to Washington proposed a joint *démarche* to Russia in firm language before the meeting of Heads of Governments. If the United States Government would not agree, the British position would be weaker, but we should nevertheless have to make our position clear and to base ourselves on our alliance with Turkey and our special interests in the eastern Mediterranean. We hoped that

---

[1] Mr. Eden was ill. During his absence the Prime Minister was in charge of the Foreign Office.

(a) R10692/4476/44.   (b) PM/45/271, R10123/44/44.   (c) R10224/4476/44.
(d) R10601/4476/44.

the United States Government would at least indicate to Russia their agreement with our stand and their disapproval of the Soviet proposals to Turkey.

The United States Government, however, were unwilling to make (a) such a *démarche* before the meeting of Heads of States. The Foreign Office decided to act alone, and instructed Sir A. Clark Kerr on (b) July 5 to ask that consideration of the question be postponed until the Potsdam Conference. The Foreign Office also told the Turkish Government that we would raise the question at the Conference even if Russia did not do so. They asked the United States Government to concert action with us.

The Foreign Office consulted the Chiefs of Staff before making (c) recommendations on the policy to be adopted at the Potsdam Conference. The Chiefs of Staff had little to add to their previous recommendations. They considered the Russian demand for right of passage through the Dardanelles in time of war to be reasonable; the Russians already had a right of passage in time of war through the entrances to the Baltic. On the other hand there was no justification for Russian bases on Turkish territory to secure the right of passage. From the British point of view the best solution would be the maintenance of the *status quo* in the case of all bases covering seaways; we did not want a change in our position at Gibraltar or in relation to the Suez Canal. We should therefore try to limit the range of discussions, but if the Russians persisted in their demands for bases in the Dardanelles we should try to get the question referred to the World Organisation and not leave it to be settled bilaterally between Russia and Turkey.

The discussions on the future of the Straits at the Potsdam Con- (d) ference were inconclusive because the Russians put forward a demand for a fortified base on the Straits, and also claimed a frontier rectification including Kars and Ardahan. Mr. Churchill refused to accept these demands. President Truman thought that the territorial questions ought to be settled between Russia and Turkey, and that the Straits should be internationalised as part of a general plan for an international control of inland waterways. After the Conference the President broadcast this latter plan (under which the United States would share in the control of the Straits).

The Foreign Office instructed Sir M. Peterson to tell the Turks about the discussions at the Conference and to advise them, in reply to Russian approaches, to say that the question of the Straits must be settled on an international basis. The Foreign Office hoped that the Turkish Government would realise the importance of President

---

(a) R11554/44/44; R11021/4476/44. (b) R11430/4476/44. (c) R11554, 11695, 11962 44/44; COS(45)44(C); COS(45)449(O); JP(45)170(Final). (d) R12516/44/44.

Truman's proposal for American participation in a guarantee of the freedom of the Straits. On the other hand the President's view that territorial questions should be settled directly between Russia and Turkey weakened the British case for having a part in the matter. The Foreign Office thought that among the unavowed Russian objectives was a desire to punish the Turks for their attitude in the war, and, if possible, alter the character of the régime of Turkey in the same direction as they were shaping the régimes of other neighbouring States.

(a)   Sir M. Peterson saw the Turkish Prime Minister on July 26. M. Saracoglu hoped that the Allies were not going to give way to Russia on everything; otherwise they might make permanent Russian influence over countries in which it was still precarious. He considered that the British and United States Governments might have warned Turkey that they were going to raise the question of internationalisation. He said that it would probably mean for Turkey demilitarisation and acceptance of an International Commission in Istanbul.

Sir M. Peterson spoke of the importance for Turkey of obtaining the association of the United States in internationalisation of the Straits. The Prime Minister agreed that there was nothing to do except to await the American proposals. He said that Turkey was not interested in a treaty of alliance with Russia.[1] The Foreign Office noted on July 30 that they had not been informed of President Truman's idea in advance, and that they knew little of the details of his plan.

(b)   On August 11 M. Saracoglu told Sir M. Peterson that the Turkish
(c) Government were inclined in principle to accept internationalisation provided that Turkish sovereignty was unimpaired, and that there would be a change in the Russian attitude towards Turkey as a result. Sir M. Peterson suggested that this latter objective could best be obtained by a Turkish stipulation that normal friendly relations must exist or be re-established between Turkey and all other Powers which might join her in control of the Straits.

The Foreign Office thought that it should be possible to find some formula satisfying the Russian demand and also the Turkish claim to unimpaired sovereignty. They decided to ask the Russians once again at the Foreign Secretaries' meeting to agree to internationalisation and drop their demand for bases. Only in this way could 'normal friendly relations' between Russia and Turkey come about. A stipulation on the part of Turkey alone would not serve any purpose; the situation required general agreement among the Allies.

(d)   [1] On September 17 the Turkish Ambassador in London told Sir A. Cadogan that the Turkish Government had not sought an alliance with Russia.

(a) R12667/44/44.   (b) R13515/44/44.   (c) R13646/4476/44.   (d) R16845/44/44.

CHAPTER LIII

Syria and the Lebanon from September 1941 to December 1942

(i)

British recognition of the independence of the Syrian and Lebanese Republics: appointment of Sir E. Spears as British Minister to the Republics: Syrian and Lebanese disappointment at the French failure to fulfil promises of independence (September 1941–March 1942).

THE affairs of Syria and the Lebanon, after the extrusion of the Vichy authorities from the Levant, took up a disproportionately large amount of attention in the Foreign Office, and were among the main causes of friction between General de Gaulle and the British Government. In view of the strategic importance of the Levant States, British operational control was essential for military reasons. This control necessarily extended to political and economic matters. The problem of supplies—and especially supplies of wheat —had to be considered in relation to the Middle East as a whole; the maintenance of public order depended on a satisfactory relationship between the French and the local Governments. The implementation of the French promise of independence had more than a local importance. Arab opinion generally regarded it as a test of British as well as French sincerity.

General de Gaulle, and the majority of French officials, military or civilian, failed to understand either the policy of the British Government or the increasing emotional force of Arab and Levantine nationalism. They believed that the British Government aimed at using a situation favourable to themselves in order to supplant French by British influence in the Levant. General de Gaulle distrusted British assurances that this was not the case; he argued— and at times with some justification—that in spite of the statements of intention put forward by the Prime Minister and Mr. Eden, their representatives in the Levant States were not carrying out British policy as officially announced, but were undermining French authority and encouraging local opposition. Moreover, Frenchmen who, like General Catroux,[1] were less certain of British insincerity,

---

[1] General Catroux was appointed by de Gaulle in June 1941 'Delegate General and plenipotentiary on all Middle Eastern Affairs and Commander-in-Chief in the Middle East'.

agreed with their predecessors (including those of the Vichy administration) in rejecting as unnecessary the concessions to local
nationalism which the British Government regarded as essential.
The Free French could not give away French claims which Vichy
had upheld. General de Gaulle indeed showed in a curious way
something of the pedantic clinging to legal forms of which he accused
the supporters of Vichy elsewhere in the French Empire. Whatever
their reasons, the stubborn refusal of the French to meet nationalist
demands increased the tension between them and the local populations. This increase in tension brought more British pressure on
General de Gaulle and the French Committee to fulfil their promises
and, in turn, added to French anger at British interference. The
history of Anglo-French relations in the Levant States from the
summer of 1941 to the late autumn of 1942 and indeed later, was
thus one of continual local bickering in day-to-day affairs and, on
the highest levels of policy, a series of crises. The gravest of these
crises before 1945 came during and after a visit by General de Gaulle
himself to the Levant. This visit took place at a critical period of the
war, after the German victories in Libya and before the British
victory at El Alamein. General de Gaulle went to the Levant in a
mood of irritation over British policy in Madagascar. He angered
both the local governments and the British representatives by his
intransigence and, on his return to London at the urgent request of
the British Government, nearly broke with Mr. Churchill. After
further negotiation, however, a working agreement was reached
over the Levant States, but the deep differences and suspicions
remained.

With the approval of the British Government, General Catroux
had announced on June 8, 1941, that he was going into Syria to
end the mandatory régime.[1] In accordance with this undertaking,
he declared the independence of the Syrian Republic on September
27 and of the Lebanese Republic on November 26, 1941.[2] The
British Government also recognised the independence of the two
Republics.

---

[1] See above, Vol. I, p. 567.

[2] See Vol. I, Chapter XVII, section (ii). General Catroux issued the declaration of
Lebanese independence after discussions with the British authorities about its exact form.
Owing to General de Gaulle's insistence, the proclamation contained a phrase suggesting
some continuation of French control. The Franco-Syrian and Franco-Lebanese treaties
of December 1936 had followed a promise given by the French Government, after serious
disorders in Syria in March 1936, that Syria and the Lebanon should enjoy rights equal
to those granted to Iraq by Great Britain. Owing to the fall of M. Blum's government in
France, the treaties were not ratified. Hence the local nationalist opposition to the French
increased. In July 1939 the French High Commissioner suspended the Syrian Constitution. The situation was easier in the Lebanon (where there was a Christian majority),
but here also the French found it necessary to suspend the Constitution shortly after the
outbreak of war.

(a) E473/207/89 (1942).

Mr. Churchill had already said in the House of Commons on September 9, 1941, that the British were in Syria only to win the war and that they did not propose that full Syrian and Lebanese independence should wait until the end of the war. They wanted the Syrians and Lebanese to take an increasing part in the administration. They realised that France could not maintain her pre-war position in the two countries but recognised that French influence would predominate over that of other European countries.

On February 6, 1942, the Foreign Office appointed Major-General (a) Sir E. L. Spears[1] as the first British Minister to the Syrian and Lebanese Republics, and head of the Mission[2] to the Free French in these territories. The two Governments concerned and the local press welcomed this appointment as a further British step to complete the independence of the two Republics. Sir E. Spears's instructions were drawn up with a view to reconciling the guarantees of independence, the continuance of Free French influence and responsibility, and the need to maintain civil order in an area which British forces might have to use for military operations. As head of the Mission to the Free French, Sir E. Spears was to continue to advise the British military authorities on administrative and political questions affecting Syria and the Lebanon. He was to communicate directly with the Minister of State on all matters involving questions of principle or policy if they related solely or mainly to problems with which the Minister had powers to deal.

Sir E. Spears's instructions further stated that, while General Catroux had authority to settle all current questions concerning Syria and the Lebanon, matters of major policy such as the conclusion of treaties and questions affecting the Free French Movement as a whole must be referred to General de Gaulle. Meanwhile, British policy remained as declared by the Prime Minister on September 9. Military needs had to be the overriding consideration. The position of the Syrian, Lebanese and Free French authorities would be maintained mainly by British efforts; we therefore expected that these authorities would not hold up measures considered essential by the Commander-in-Chief, Middle East, and approved by the Minister of State. Sir E. Spears should conform to the wishes of the latter in any urgent matter vitally affecting the military position which the Minister of State did not think fit to refer to London.

---

[1] Major-General Sir E. L. Spears had been appointed by Mr. Churchill in May 1940 as his personal representative with the French Prime Minister and Minister of Defence. He became head of the British Mission to General de Gaulle in July 1940. In July 1941 he was sent as head of the British Mission to Syria and the Lebanon. Sir E. Spears had returned to England in December 1941 for discussions and was in England at the time of his appointment as Minister.

[2] The Mission was subject to the supervision of the Minister of State in the Middle East.

(a) E280/279/89; E904/207/89.

General de Gaulle had already recognised in Article 1 of the Supplementary Agreement, which he and Mr. Lyttelton had signed on July 25, 1941,

> 'that the British High Command in the Levant is empowered to take all measures of defence it judges necessary to take against the common enemy. If it should happen that any of these measures should appear to be contrary to the interests of France in the Levant, the question would be submitted to the British Government and General de Gaulle.'[1]

Sir E. Spears was instructed to bear in mind that the Free French should be encouraged to grant the Republics increasing responsibility for their own administration. We believed that, within the framework of war needs, it should be possible, without impairing efficiency, to hand over much of the administration to the local Governments. About 1,000 French officials had remained in the two countries since the Syrian armistice, although they had not rallied to the Free French cause. For reasons of military security and political policy this anomaly should be ended as soon as possible, and French officials who had not made a declaration of loyalty to the Free French Movement, and who were not carrying out this declaration, should be dismissed.[2] The policy of the British Government remained, however, that, in so far as any European country had influence in Syria and the Lebanon, the influence of France as represented by the Free French Movement would be pre-eminent. Sir E. Spears should not give any pretext to critics to assert that Great Britain intended to substitute British for French authority.

Sir E. Spears did not go back to Beirut until the latter part of March 1942. At this time the Foreign Office regarded the situation (a) in Syria as far from satisfactory. The people of the larger towns were becoming restless. The Allied setback in Libya and Japanese successes had affected opinion and Axis propaganda was making the most of the situation. The rise in the cost of living, and the feeling that military operations might take place in Syria in the spring, produced political tension. The Syrian Nationalists regarded the advent to power of the Wafdist party in Egypt as a portent. The British authorities had helped this party to power in Cairo;[3] the

---

[1] See Vol. I, p. 591.

[2] The Free French had continued to employ these officials of the Vichy régime because they had no substitutes for them. Many of the officials were strongly anti-British and were distrusted by the Syrians.

[3] On February 4, after the resignation of Sirry Pasha, partly as the result of palace intrigues, Sir Miles Lampson, British Ambassador in Cairo, had told King Farouk that the British Government insisted upon the appointment of Nahas Pasha as Prime Minister. Nahas Pasha was leader of the Wafdist party which had previously been in opposition. Nahas Pasha accepted office on the understanding that the British Government intended to collaborate with Egypt as an independent and Allied country in the execution of the Anglo-Egyptian treaty of 1936.

(a) E904, 1312/207/89.

Syrians thought that they might give help on similar lines in Syria.

The Syrian President and the Minister for the Interior put their views to British officials.[1] The President said that the failure of the Government to obtain recognition from the United States[2] and Iraq was harming its position. The Minister for the Interior complained (a) of the French attitude towards independence. The French had refused to make concessions to Syrian wishes and were insisting that all French personnel employed by the Syrian Government should be replaced by other Frenchmen when vacancies occurred. The Minister for the Interior described the population as frightened of invasion and of not being able to obtain food,[3] and the Government as unable to win support by showing concessions from the French.

Towards the end of February 1942, Sir Walter Monckton,[4] after (b) discussing the situation with Mr. J. A. Hamilton, agreed to ask General Catroux to transfer to the local Governments a number of powers which the French could cede without interfering with the conduct of the war. The Foreign Office endorsed Sir W. Monckton's instructions to Mr. Hamilton. He was told to impress upon General

---

[1] On January 15, 1942, the Syrian Minister for Foreign Affairs told Mr. J. A. Hamilton, (c) a member of the staff of the Minister of State who was acting as Sir E. Spears' deputy, that the Syrian Government were prepared to collaborate with the Free French and British during the war, but would not bind themselves to the French (Free or otherwise) in any way for the future. They would not discuss a treaty now or later with the Free French. They had had 20 years' experience of French administration and were determined that, whatever ally they sought (they realised that they could not stand alone without an ally) they would not want the French. They had also seen how Germany treated occupied countries and would rather be under British mandate than receive 'independence' at German hands.

[2] The United States Government had refused to recognise the independence of Syria and the Lebanon for several reasons. They were still in diplomatic relations with the Vichy Government, and did not want to recognise the Free French control in an area from which the Vichy Government had been extruded. They were unwilling to recognise special French privileges in the Levant in accordance with the French claims qualifying the grant of independence. They also wanted to ensure the maintenance of the rights of United States subjects in the Levant as guaranteed under a treaty of 1924.

[3] During the winter of 1941–42 there was a very serious shortage of wheat in Syria, largely due to hoarding of wheat and to smuggling across the Turkish-Iraqi borders. Some temporary relief at least from famine conditions was brought by the import (arranged by the British authorities) of about 100,000 tons. In order to check hoarding General Spears suggested to General Catroux that the British military authorities should take over responsibility for the collection and distribution of grain. General Catroux refused this proposal. After considerable negotiation an agreement was reached with the French in May 1942 for the establishment of a joint Office des Céréales Panifiables in which the two Levant States collaborated with the British and French. This Office was able to maintain adequate supplies—though at very high prices—for the rest of the war. The staff of the Office, inevitably, had to work in all areas of the country. The French authorities tended to regard the British members of the organisation as agents spreading pro-British and anti-French propaganda. In any case the French disliked, though for practical reasons they could not refuse to permit, the introduction of British officials into the Levant States.

[4] On February 26, 1942, the Minister of State, Mr. Lyttelton, had left Cairo. On March 19 Mr. Churchill announced in the House of Commons that Mr. R. G. Casey, Australian Minister in Washington, had been appointed as Mr. Lyttelton's successor. Sir Walter Monckton, Deputy Minister of State, was Acting Minister until Mr. Casey's arrival.

(a) E904/207/89. (b) E1359/207/89. (c) E1788/206/89.

H*BFP

Catroux that he had the full support of His Majesty's Government, that British good faith was involved and that, if the local population were alienated by French failure to carry out their promises of independence, Allied communications would be in danger.

(a)   Early in March the Syrian Prime Minister, Hassan el Hakim, resigned but agreed later to withdraw his resignation. One of the reasons for his action was the failure of the Free French to take steps to fulfil the promise of independence. General Catroux immediately visited Damascus, and discussed the question of concessions for the first time. He agreed in principle to hand over the police including, subject to safeguards, the *Sûreté*, but no settlement was reached over the question of the Funds of Common Interest,[1] control of customs, Bedouin control and the issue of decrees by the *Délégation Générale*.

(b) On March 6 the *Délégation Générale* informed the Lebanese Government that they would transfer to them certain services, including the issue of passports, the Diplomatic Bureau, Antiquities, the *Gardes mobiles* and the Posts and Telegraphs. The Lebanese Government regarded these concessions as inadequate.

(c)   On March 7 General Spears met Sir W. Monckton and three members of the staff of the Minister of State for a conference in Cairo. They all agreed that, if Syrian national aspirations remained unsatisfied, and the Government did not get popular support, most of the population would turn against us in a moment of danger. It was doubtful whether the danger could be offset by giving work and food. Most Syrians wanted to get rid of the French; the question for them was whether they could do so by British or by German help. Even if the time did not seem right for a change of régime, General Catroux should be compelled to make Syrian independence a reality. The question was not one of piecemeal concessions, but of a fundamental change in French policy, which could be secured only by a frank discussion with General de Gaulle.

The Foreign Office doubted whether there would be much improvement from the Allied point of view if the Governments of the Levant States had unrestricted control of affairs. Nevertheless, with the agreement of Sir E. Spears, they told the Minister of State on March 10 of their agreement that the French must do more to implement their promise of Syrian independence and to establish a Government with a measure of real popular backing. We had repeatedly promised support for the only action to this end so far recommended, i.e. the removal of unreliable French officials. The Foreign Office did not recommend taking matters up with General

---

[1] Proceeds of taxes common to both States and administered by the French. The financial basis of Free French administration depended on these revenues.

(a) E1733, 1847/207/89. (b) E1733/207/89. (c) E1559/207/89.

de Gaulle on the principle of the grant of independence. General de Gaulle was already committed to this principle; the problem was how to carry it into effect. We should put pressure on General Catroux to transfer to the Syrians everything possible without endangering the military position. If the British military authorities and representatives in Syria agreed on a line of action, the Foreign Office would do their best to see that General de Gaulle did not thwart it.

The War Office thought, however, that General Catroux would continue to avoid making concessions by referring matters to General de Gaulle and that we should have to raise the issue with him. The Foreign Office pointed out on March 12 to the War Office that they were having a dispute with General de Gaulle about Admiral Muselier;[1] until this dispute had been settled, it would not be wise to open a general conversation about Syria. There was bound to be difficulty over any Syrian question on which the Free French disagreed with us. We should inform the Free French headquarters of our views and, wherever necessary, urge General de Gaulle very strongly to authorise General Catroux to meet them, but in most cases the proper place for the threat of sanctions was not in London but in the Middle East, where the British General Officer Commanding had troops at his disposal, and the British authorities had financial control. The Foreign Office hoped that there would not be a crisis, but if one should arise, the General Officer Commanding was in a favourable position for getting his way.

(ii)

Return of Sir E. Spears as Minister: differences between Sir E. Spears and General Catroux: the question of elections (March–July 1942).

Sir E. Spears presented his letters of credence to the Lebanese (a) President on March 27, and to the Syrian President four days later. The public and press showed much enthusiasm, but almost at once a new misunderstanding showed the touchiness of the Free French with regard to their relations with the British. General Catroux took offence at Sir E. Spears's failure to call upon him soon after arrival. He sent an angry telegram to M. Dejean in London on March 29, (b) in which he complained that Sir E. Spears should have visited him as the representative of the mandatory Power and of French

---

[1] See Vol. II, Chapter XXIX, section (i).

(a) E2121, 2276/207/89. (b) E2124/279/89.

interests when he presented his letters to the two Heads of States. He said that he would ignore Sir E. Spears until he had made some reparation, and that even then he would not use him as an intermediary with the Commander-in-Chief or the Minister of State. He thought that Sir E. Spears ought not to fulfil the dual function of representing British interests and acting as liaison officer between the British authorities and the representative of the mandate.

General de Gaulle wrote a letter on the subject to Mr. Eden on April 2. He ended it by remarking that owing to the danger with which the Levant States were threatened, the Syrian and Lebanese people should have, more than ever, the impression of 'une étroite
(a) solidarité' between Free France and Great Britain. Sir E. Spears later telegraphed to London an explanation of the incident showing that he had intended no discourtesy: this explanation was passed to General de Gaulle.

(b)   Sir E. Spears had his first formal meeting with General Catroux on April 4 and discussed with him the 'most unsatisfactory position'. He trusted that General Catroux would not invoke the mandate again, since it was a legal fiction now that the States had been granted independence. He said the British Government wanted to build up the independence which they had guaranteed. General Catroux answered that he was considering the establishment of a Chamber but, as he had in mind only a nominated Chamber, Sir E. Spears thought that it would be of little value. He said that, if General Catroux would agree to collaboration with us, he would be in a position to assume the lead with British support in the background. Such collaboration was the best if not the only way of maintaining French prestige.

(c)   General Catroux's report to General de Gaulle of this conversation had a very different emphasis. According to this report, Sir E. Spears had said that Mr. Churchill was bitterly hostile to General de Gaulle and that neither he nor the French National Committee had any contacts with the British Government. In London the Free French Movement was thought to have declined in prestige, and to be of little use to the Allied cause. Sir E. Spears had asked whether General de Gaulle did not realise the deterioration which had taken place. Surely he must by now be tired of it all and have 'le dessin de liquider l'affaire'. General Catroux had answered that General de Gaulle summed up the spirit of resistance in France. He was a great leader and his followers, including General Catroux, would continue to support him. M. Dejean reported General Catroux's account of the conversation to the Foreign Office. The Foreign

(a) E2130/279/89. (b) E2158/207/89. (c) Z3024/90/17; E2268/207/89.

Office regarded the conversation as 'most deplorable'.[1] Sir E. Spears was not correct in stating that General de Gaulle was 'isolated'. Sir E. Spears did not seem to know that Mr. Eden saw him often, and had never refused to see him.

Sir E. Spears's first impression was that the situation in the Levant (a) states had become worse during his absence. The population realised that little had been done to carry out the declarations of independence. The two Governments appointed by General Catroux had proved unsatisfactory; their Presidents, in Sir E. Spears's view, were puppets in the hands of the French. The French realised their weakness and were attempting to maintain an illusion of prestige at the expense of Allied co-operation. British control had been strengthened only in financial matters. The French themselves admitted a deterioration in French military morale and dissension amongst officers and civil officials.

Sir E. Spears's conclusions were: (i) that we should do what we could to encourage and help the two Governments to gain more independence; (ii) that the test of the capacity of the Governments to achieve independence would be their handling of the Funds of Common Interest; (iii) that elections should be promised by a fixed date; (iv) that it was necessary to make General Catroux realise that the Free French could maintain their position or prestige in the Levant only by working with us.

The Foreign Office were concerned at Sir E. Spears's report. The opposition seemed to have more popular support than the Governments in power; we should not let this situation continue unless we were satisfied that security considerations were against any change. The Foreign Office realised the difficulties, particularly if changes of Government would entail a promise of elections by a fixed date. No one could foresee how the military situation would develop; it would do more harm than good to make a promise, e.g. to hold elections before the end of the year, which we were not able to fulfil. General Catroux, however, should devise some formula promising elections as soon as the military situation allowed. He appeared a month earlier to have undertaken to make a promise of this kind.

The Foreign Office asked the Acting Minister of State and Sir E. Spears[2] whether changes in the Governments were desirable at once, whether they could be made without elections or the promise of elections by any fixed date, and how far General Catroux would go in resisting our advice. We had agreed that internal political

---

[1] Mr. Eden had commented on a telegram of March 11: 'Department will bear in (b) mind that General Spears is not the most balanced of men. Mr. Lyttelton tells me that he found it always wise to discount his reports by a wide percentage.'
[2] They were instructed also to consult the British military commanders.

(a) E2224/207/89.   (b) E1688/207/89.

developments were the special province of the Free French; we should not therefore wish to intervene except in cases affecting military security. Free French support of unpopular Governments was clearly such a case; we could not agree to the continuance of this support if our civil and military authorities required a change, since they and not the Free French were responsible for defence.

(a)   Sir E. Spears sent his views on the situation on April 14. He agreed that changes should be made at once in the Governments; he proposed the nomination in each country of an 'interim Government of Affairs'[1] as a prelude to elections, but thought that these changes would not help unless elections were promised by a definite date. The populations wanted 'something positive to pocket'. He said that General Catroux could not be prevented from referring to General de Gaulle in London but that, if he did so and if General de Gaulle negotiated with His Majesty's Government, an impasse would be reached. Meanwhile the Free French—and General Catroux more than most—knew that they had much to lose by a crisis.

(b)   The Middle East War Council, at a meeting on April 20, endorsed Sir E. Spears's views. The Commander-in-Chief, Middle East, agreed with the need for firmness with General Catroux, but also wanted to avoid trouble for the time being in view of the military value of the Free French contingent in the Western Desert. The War Council thought that an announcement should be made as soon as possible that elections would be held in both States before the end of 1942, and that steps were being taken to improve the economic situation. The Council recognised that the elections might have to be cancelled in the event of major military developments. It suggested a number of administrative changes,[2] which would transform the Free French administration from an executive to an advisory role. It pointed out that the Syrian Prime Minister had asked for most of these changes a month before in a letter to General Catroux.

The Foreign Office accepted the policy agreed by the Middle East War Council. In view of the far-reaching nature of the proposals the Foreign Office considered that they should be put to General Catroux by the Commander-in-Chief, Middle East, and Sir W. Monckton, since they would be able to judge whether insistence on them would result in difficulties affecting the military value of the Free French contingent in the Western Desert. They also preferred

---

[1] i.e. government composed of officials.
[2] The Foreign Office commented: 'The administrative changes proposed will no doubt lead to a monumental row with General de Gaulle.'

(a) E2360/207/89. (b) E2503/207/89.

the Commander-in-Chief and Sir W. Monckton to make the first approach to General Catroux in order that he might realise that the British Government and the Minister of State endorsed the policy advocated by Sir E. Spears.

At this stage Mr. Welles showed Lord Halifax a telegram from (a) Mr. Engert, United States Consul-General at Beirut, to the effect that relations between Sir E. Spears and General Catroux were strained almost to breaking point and that the fault lay mainly with Sir E. Spears. The Foreign Office reply was to suggest that Mr. Engert should speak frankly to Sir E. Spears, with whom he had always co-operated closely. They thought that Sir E. Spears had a most difficult task and that the principal fault was not on his side since he was carrying out a policy accepted by the Middle East War Council and approved by the British Government, and with which Mr. Engert was understood to agree. Mr. Eden asked the State Department for support.

At the end of April Mr. Engert sent Sir E. Spears a long personal (b) letter, on instructions from the State Department, expressing the willingness of his Government to assist in bringing about a better understanding between the British and Free French and the Governments of Syria and the Lebanon. Sir E. Spears told the Foreign Office that he hoped they would not encourage the United States Government to act as arbiters between the British and Free French. He thought that Mr. Engert regarded the 'serious differences of principle' with the Free French as merely a question of personalities.

The Foreign Office already knew that General Catroux had said that 'he would be obliged to raise the greatest possible objection' to his (Sir E. Spears's) appointment as Minister.[1] The Foreign Office considered that Sir E. Spears had had to advocate a policy which the Free French inevitably disliked. The latter were anxious that Frenchmen after the war should not accuse them of having given up French interests in the Levant. They held dangerously, therefore, to all their old prerogatives, and the internal situation in Syria and the Lebanon had deteriorated to the point where it was causing anxiety for the security of British forces there. Sir E. Spears had to press the Free French to make concessions; the trouble, or so it seemed to the Foreign Office, lay in the way in which he went about his task. He thought too much about the importance of maintaining

---

[1] Sir M. Lampson had reported to the Foreign Office from Cairo on December 5, (c) 1941: 'You know that I can work with General Spears, and that I place very high his services to us in Syria. But there is no doubt that he is generally much disliked by the Free French. As a result, the Free French do not co-operate as frankly with us as they otherwise might.'

(a) E2694/207/89. (b) E2698/207/89. (c) E2694/207/89.

British prestige and his reports were coloured by his own anti-French bias and personal animosities.

(a)　　On May 1 General Catroux invited the Syrian and Lebanese Finance Ministers to give their formal approval to the 1942 budget of the Funds of Common Interest. This invitation was something new and a concession to the independent status of the countries, but it failed in its purpose; the two Ministers by previous arrangement refused to approve the budget. They presented a joint note to General Catroux asking that, pending the transfer of the Funds to the States, the budget should be left in suspense and monthly credits opened for the sums necessary for the working of the services concerned. General Catroux rejected the proposal. The Ministers therefore withdrew, and agreed provisionally between themselves that a detailed scheme for the transfer should be prepared. Lebanon would take 37 per cent of the revenues and Syria 53 per cent; the remaining 10 per cent would be put into a suspense account to be settled later.

(b)　　By the middle of May there was a deadlock between the Syrian Government and the French. The President of the Lebanese Republic and some members of the Government paid an official visit to Damascus on May 3, and Syrian Government functionaries visited the Lebanon from May 15 to 18. The purpose of these visits was to demonstrate to the French the solidarity of the two countries,

(c)　especially over the Funds of Common Interest. The Syrians brought their proposals for transfer of the Funds to be considered by the Lebanese Government and, if approved, presented jointly to General Catroux.[1]

(d)　　The problems of the two Republics were simultaneously under discussion in Cairo. In the second week of May, Mr. Casey held a series of meetings with General Catroux, General Auchinleck, General Wilson and Sir E. Spears, at which elections formed the chief subject. Mr. Casey thought that they should be held before the end of the year and that an announcement to this effect should be made as soon as possible. Subject to reference to General de Gaulle, General Catroux had agreed to an announcement by the heads of the two States that elections would be held at the end of the year.

The Foreign Office regarded these meetings as unfortunate. The British Government had approved a three-point plan for changes of government, elections and transfer of executive authority to the

---

(e)　　[1] Sir E. Spears said that the Syrian executive, even if they had the energy or ability to make a settlement, lacked the force and prestige to carry it out. They tended, therefore, to leave all troublesome matters to the Free French; at the same time they complained that the latter would never carry out the declaration of Syrian independence.

(a) E2922/207/89.　(b) E3062/207/89.　(c) E3231/207/89.　(d) E3107, 3310/207/89.　(e) E3062/207/89.

States Governments. The meetings had wrecked this plan; one point had been taken out of it, and the other two discarded. On security grounds there seemed to be serious risks if the unpopular Governments in power were to be kept in office during the whole of the pre-election period, which might last until the end of the year. The Foreign Office thought that they should tell General Catroux that an interval of six months between the announcement and the holding of elections was too long unless the Governments were changed.

Sir E. Spears—apparently in contradiction with his advice of (a) April 14—took the view that the most important issue was the wheat plan which the existing Governments had accepted after difficult negotiations.[1] We should have to rely on them to carry it out; it would be undesirable to have to negotiate the issue again with new Governments, particularly in Syria. Sir E. Spears doubted whether General Catroux's six months' period could be reduced.

On June 7, General Catroux arrived in Cairo on his way to visit (b) Free French troops at the front. He raised the question of elections with Mr. Casey the next day. After consulting the National Committee General de Gaulle had telegraphed his agreement to the holding of elections on condition that the announcement should be made as late as possible, that the elections should take place in October or, if possible, September, and that the interval between the announcement and the elections should be reduced to the legal minimum. General de Gaulle further stipulated that the announcement should be made in the name of France alone.

Mr. Casey asked General Catroux to agree to an earlier date for the announcement than that proposed by General de Gaulle. General Catroux undertook to do his best to get General de Gaulle's consent, but asked that Mr. Eden should also approach General de Gaulle. He explained that the General 'reacted unfavourably' if he suspected that the Foreign Office were trying to reach an agreement with General Catroux without telling him (General de Gaulle) in advance. Mr. Eden decided not to say anything to General de Gaulle, since the question concerning Allied military security in the Middle East should be left to Mr. Casey and General Auchinleck. The Foreign Office, however, let M. Dejean know that they regarded an early announcement of elections as important, and hoped that the French National Committee would agree to an announcement towards the end of June. The date for the holding of elections depended on the military situation and the preparation of electoral rolls. The Foreign Office hoped also that General Catroux would be given the same discretion to reach a settlement as they had given

---

[1] See above, p. 215, note 3.

(a) E3271/207/89.　(b) E3569, 3764/207/89.

to Mr. Casey. They informed Mr. Casey that the announcement should be made on the date which he had agreed with General Catroux.

(a) On June 23 Mr. Casey had a long talk with General Catroux about elections. He said that, in spite of General de Gaulle's objections, an announcement ought to be made as soon as possible that elections would take place before the end of the year. General Catroux said that, once the announcement was made, the country would enter an election period, and the position of the Government would become more difficult. The announcement should be delayed until the military situation had become clear. Mr. Casey accepted a programme that if the military situation were satisfactory, an announcement would be made at the beginning of August about the holding of elections before the end of the year. The actual date would be announced about the middle of September. The reconstruction of the Governments would then take place. The reconstructed Governments would be charged with the holding of elections. Mr. Casey pointed out that Mr. Eden had not so far taken up the question with General de Gaulle. General Catroux said that General de Gaulle had been very firm in his instructions to him; he would have to refer the matter again to him, but would recommend the plan upon which he and Mr. Casey were agreed.

Mr. Eden welcomed the programme and promised to tell General de Gaulle so if the latter raised the matter with him. Up to the beginning of July, however, the General had not shown any interest in it. Meanwhile, there had been weeks of strain in Syria caused by the British defeats in Libya. The halting of the German advance brought a slight recovery in British prestige. The immediate problem, however, in Syria and the Lebanon was still that of wheat.

(b) There were demonstrations against the shortage and high price of bread in Damascus, Beirut and other towns. The protests in Beirut rapidly developed into a political agitation against the incompetence of the Government. The Lebanese Government fell on July 23.

(c) General Catroux complained to Mr. Casey of the indiscreet language and intemperate actions of Sir E. Spears in connexion with the formation of the new Government; at the same time the President of the Lebanese Republic wrote to Mr. Eden protesting against General Spears's activities. Mr. Casey did his best to compose the differences between General Spears and General Catroux by meeting each of them.[1] On July 31 General Catroux wrote a letter to Sir

---

[1] Mr. Eden considered it necessary to send Sir E. Spears a warning about the personal difficulties with General Catroux. He said that good relations with the Fighting French were all the more necessary as General de Gaulle was coming out to Syria, and was in a helpful and co-operative mood.

(a) E3874/207/89.   (b) E4378/207/89.   (c) E4428, 4486, 4596, 4676/207/89.

E. Spears expressing the hope that their future relations would be frank and cordial.

(iii)

General de Gaulle's visit to Syria and the Lebanon: his protests about British interference in the Levant: British rejection of these protests: the Prime Minister's request to General de Gaulle to return to London (July 28– August 31, 1942).

General de Gaulle had wanted early in April to visit the territories under the administration of the French Committee. He had been persuaded to delay his visit,[1] and to agree to a second postponement in June. At the end of July he said that he could not wait any longer.[2] He wished to go to Syria and West Africa, and to be away for three weeks. Mr. Eden thought that since the beginning of June relations (a) with General de Gaulle had been easier and that we could not ask him to postpone his visit for a third time. Mr. Churchill agreed that he should go.

On July 28 General de Gaulle and Mr. Eden discussed Syrian (b) affairs. They agreed that things were not going badly. General de Gaulle, however, said that Sir E. Spears exceeded his powers and intrigued a great deal. The General said that the French regarded the British proposal for elections as inopportune. General Catroux had agreed with Mr. Casey's proposals, the French National Committee had not disapproved of them, but the situation had changed as a result of the German offensive in Libya. The French thought that at that moment elections would be most inconvenient, since one did not arrange a ballot in the middle of a battle. General de Gaulle agreed to discuss the subject with Mr. Casey. He also raised the question of the wheat supply. He referred to the establishment of the Wheat Office and complained that Sir E. Spears had introduced himself into this plan without any reason and that it would be better if he remained outside it.

On the following day, before leaving for Africa, General de Gaulle (c) saw Mr. Churchill. He said that he was not sorry to be going to the Levant; Sir E. Spears was too officious and was causing the French difficulties there. Mr. Churchill replied that Sir E. Spears had many

---

[1] See above, Vol. II, p. 332.
[2] General Legentilhomme, who had returned from the Middle East towards the end (d) of July, spoke to General de Gaulle in strong terms of the conduct of Sir E. Spears, who was 'poisoning the relations' between General Catroux and General Wilson.

(a) Z6008/608/17. (b) Z6442/90/17; Z6133/608/17. (c) Z6442/90/17. (d) E4428/ 207/89.

enemies, but he had one friend, namely, the Prime Minister. He would telegraph to Sir E. Spears and recommend him to listen to General de Gaulle. Mr. Churchill added that he had heard that the independence of the Levant States was not a reality, and that the populations were not content. General de Gaulle replied that they were as satisfied in Syria and the Lebanon as in Iraq, Palestine or Egypt. In the Levant the French were dealing with Governments which had never yet governed. It would be dangerous to leave them to themselves without a guide. Mr. Churchill told General de Gaulle that in future they must work together. General de Gaulle should make his journey and return without loss of time. If he had any difficulty, he should address himself directly to Mr. Churchill.

The Foreign Office were well aware of the difficulties of the situation, and of the problems created by the personality of Sir E.
(a) Spears. Sir E. Spears had reported at length his own views. He believed that British prestige was high in the Levant, although we had had to follow a policy which was in many ways unpopular, and public opinion had been disturbed by the lack of military success, and although there were few British forces in the area. He thought that the French had a false idea of their position, and that the difficulty was to prevent the population turning against them and appealing to the British to supplant them. He said that he had done all he could to prevent a move of this kind, and with some success. In order to induce the States to accept the existing position, we must show that we meant to keep our promises, and must insist that the French should do likewise.

Sir E. Spears pointed out that the Syrians and Lebanese had no one in London to present their case to the British Government. He therefore had to emphasise to the Foreign Office their point of view, which was often opposed to that of the French. In this way he gave an impression of personal differences with the French. He believed that the French, through whom the British must act, had neither the physical strength nor the moral hold to be of use in a crisis, though they might have created it themselves. He complained also of their 'frequently arrogant and sometimes brutal' methods.

The Foreign Office recognised that the post of Minister in Syria and the Lebanon was not an easy one, and did not want to belittle Sir E. Spears's difficulties. At the same time they continued to doubt whether he had thought out the objectives to be pursued or the methods by which we should pursue them. We were in Syria to win the war. It was to our interest, both locally and from a wider point of view, to make the best use of the Fighting French. This did not mean that we should fail to press the French to carry out their

---

(a) E4725/207/89.

promises of independence, but it did mean that we should remain on good terms with them. Sir E. Spears had been warned about his relations with General Catroux,[1] and the Minister of State had arranged for regular meetings between them. The Foreign Office thought that nothing more could be done for the moment, but that Sir E. Spears was unsuited for his post. They feared that American dissatisfaction was reflected in the reports of a projected American Special Mission to Beirut.[2]

General de Gaulle gave most of his time in Syria and the Lebanon (a) to political and propaganda activities intended to increase French influence. Sir E. Spears reported that his speeches did not mention the Allied war effort. At his first reception of French officials, he (b) reaffirmed the existence of the mandate and thanked his hearers for their successful efforts at maintaining the position of France in the Levant. The Lebanese Government objected to this remark, and published a declaration of policy with numerous references to independence. General de Gaulle then told the Lebanese Prime Minister that full liberty had already been granted and that legal formalities alone stood in the way of freedom.

On August 30 the Lebanese Prime Minister made a number of (c) demands to General de Gaulle for an extension of the powers of his Government. The demands included the transfer of almost the whole of the Funds of Common Interest and a reduction in the number of French advisers. General de Gaulle gave no reply other than a promise to study the matter. On September 11 the Lebanese Prime (d) Minister wrote to General Catroux asking for immediate transfer to the Lebanese Government of most of the services comprised in the Funds of Common Interest. He also mentioned a previous joint Lebano-Syrian request for a mixed commission to manage the customs administration. On August 30 the Syrian Prime Minister (e) wrote to General Catroux associating his Government with the Lebanese *démarche*. General Catroux replied to the Lebanese President that he was not yet prepared to hand over the Funds of Common Interest. He said that not all nations had recognised Lebanon as an independent State and that the Franco-Lebanese Treaty of 1936 had envisaged a three-year period for the gradual transfer of the various services. In the case of the Lebanon, this period should be considered as running from the proclamation of Lebanese independence on November 26, 1941.

---

[1] See above, p. 224, note 1.
[2] The Foreign Office had had the comment from an American source that Sir E. Spears's (f) real objective was, by means of his 'over-elaborate' Mission, to duplicate the French administrative system and squeeze them out, as Clive squeezed the French out of India.

(a) E5098/207/89. (b) E4899/207/89. (c) E5215/207/89; E5411/207/89. (d) E5513/207/89. (e) E5257/207/89; E5922/207/89. (f) E4725/207/89.

General de Gaulle's visit did not improve French relations with the Levant States. The most serious consequences of the visit, however, were that the General's attacks on British policy in the Middle East, and upon the British representatives responsible for carrying out this policy, led almost to a complete break with the British Government. General de Gaulle began these attacks on his arrival in Cairo and before he had even seen Syria and the Lebanon. On (a) August 14 Mr. Casey sent the Foreign Office a résumé of conversations which he had had on August 8 and 9 with General de Gaulle and General Catroux. At their first meeting General de Gaulle had taken an offensive and intransigent attitude regarding British intervention, and especially that of Mr. Casey himself, in the affairs of Syria and the Lebanon.[1] Mr. Casey had found it necessary, after consulting the Prime Minister,[2] to send for General Catroux and tell him that General de Gaulle seemed to be seeking a quarrel with His Majesty's Government. Mr. Casey had stated that we could not accept General de Gaulle's declaration that we had no part in the affairs of the Levant States: he asked General Catroux to resume discussions about elections. General Catroux assured Mr. Casey that General de Gaulle had no intention of bringing about a quarrel. Mr. Casey asked General Catroux to leave General de Gaulle in no doubt about the British attitude, and warned him that if necessary the Prime Minister would intervene. As a result, he received a verbal apology from General de Gaulle through indirect channels, and a second interview took place on friendly lines. General de Gaulle did not withdraw his declaration, but did in fact discuss Syrian and Lebanese affairs with Mr. Casey.

Early repercussions of General de Gaulle's arrival in the Levant (b) States reached the Foreign Office from American sources. On August 14 Sir R. I. Campbell saw Mr. Welles in Washington. Mr. Welles thought that he ought to know the situation in Syria as reported by Mr. Gwynn,[3] United States representative at Beirut.

---

[1] Mr. Hopkinson, who was present at the first meeting, thought that the General's intransigence was deliberate, and that he intended at once to establish the principle that the British Government had no right to interfere in Syrian and Lebanese affairs.

[2] The Prime Minister (with Sir A. Cadogan) was in Cairo from August 4 to August 10. He then went to Moscow and returned to Cairo on August 17. He flew back to England on August 24.

(c) [3] Mr. Gwynn was acting United States Consul-General. On August 25 Sir E. Spears questioned Mr. Gwynn about General de Gaulle's attack on the British. Mr. Gwynn merely said that General de Gaulle had complained that the British treated him as a small boy rather than as an ally. He admitted that he (Mr. Gwynn) had sent the State Department a gloomy telegram that Syria and the Lebanon had not one but three masters the British, the French and the local governments. Sir E. Spears inferred that he had advocated leaving control in French hands. The Foreign Office agreed with the view of Sir E. Spears that it was unfortunate—at a time when American forces were arriving in the Levant—that there was not a more friendly United States representative.

(a) E5070/207/89.   (b) E4900/207/89.   (c) E5084/207/89.

According to these reports, the situation was getting worse. General de Gaulle was refusing to agree to the holding of the immediate elections on which the British were insisting, and there were difficulties between Generals de Gaulle, Catroux and Sir E. Spears. Mr. Welles said that the United States Government could not accept the declarations which General de Gaulle was apparently making about the post-war status of Syria, since they did not recognise him as entitled to do so. Sir R. I. Campbell reported that Mr. Welles was much concerned; he had said that there would have to be a 'showdown' about Syria and General de Gaulle's attitude, but that obviously in view of the military situation the moment was not suitable.

The most important of the reports from Beirut mentioned by Mr. Welles was a telegram dated August 12 describing a conversation between Mr. Gwynn and General de Gaulle.[1] General de Gaulle had said that a decision about the future of the Levant States and the French position regarding them must be left to a future Government of France, but that in the meantime all concerned should understand that he intended to maintain the position, perhaps not quite as a mandate, but with very few minor changes. The British would have to take second place. General de Gaulle also said that unless General Spears were recalled, there would be an end of all collaboration between the Fighting French and the British. Mr. Gwynn reminded General de Gaulle that British intentions regarding the Levant States were covered by the declaration which they had made officially to the United States Government. General de Gaulle dismissed this declaration as of no value. He referred to the arguments that the British had certain rights in the Levant arising out of their military spheres in the area, and that events in Syria and the Lebanon must react on neighbouring Arab countries where the British were in charge; General de Gaulle did not regard these facts as justifying British interference in the internal administration. He said that he was determined to settle the Anglo-French controversy in the Levant States at once and regardless of cost.

On August 18 Mr. Welles again spoke to Sir R. I. Campbell (a) about the situation. General de Gaulle had again told Mr. Gwynn that unless matters changed there would be an end of all collaboration between him and the British. At one point he seemed to hint that he would welcome United States mediation.[2] The Foreign Office were aware that the State Department regarded Sir E. Spears as responsible for the position. Mr. Eden commented that it was not

---

[1] For Mr. Gwynn's report of this conversation, see *F.R.U.S.* 1942, IV, 610–12.
[2] For Mr. Gwynn's record of this conversation, see *F.R.U.S.* 1942, IV, 613–16.

(a) E4907, 5172/207/89.

easy to get a just appreciation of events and doubted whether they were so tragic, although Sir E. Spears was not proving a diplomatic Minister.

(a)   On August 17 M. Dejean left at the Foreign Office a copy of a telegram of August 14 from General de Gaulle to the Prime Minister. M. Dejean had been instructed by the General to speak to Mr. Eden on the lines of the telegram, but was reluctant to do so since he thought that the telegram was ill-advised. In any case Mr. Eden was away from the Foreign Office, so that M. Dejean would have been unable to carry out his instructions. General de Gaulle complained that the British representatives in Syria and the Lebanon were not observing the Franco-British agreement about the two States. He argued that the basis of these agreements had been a British undertaking not to pursue political aims in the Levant States, and not to attempt to encroach upon the position of France; British recognition of the continuation of the French mandate was equally a basis of these arrangements, since the mandate could be modified or terminated only by the League of Nations. General de Gaulle complained that the British representatives in Syria and the Lebanon interfered in the administration and between the local Government and the French. He regarded these interventions as incompatible with British disinterestedness and with respect for the position of France and the mandatory régime. General de Gaulle warned Mr. Churchill that British 'interventions' were leading the Arab world in the Middle East to believe that the good understanding between the British Government and Fighting France was compromised by serious divergencies. He claimed that all Frenchmen and the Syrian and Lebanese people deeply resented 'these encroachments' on the rights of the Levant States and France. He asked Mr. Churchill to re-establish in the Levant States the application of the 1941 arrangements in order to ensure the military co-operation of Great Britain and France and to demonstrate their unity to the Middle East.

The Foreign Office comments on this telegram of complaint were that General de Gaulle recognised in the Supplementary Agreement of July 25, 1941, that the British High Command was empowered to take all measures of defence which it judged necessary against the common enemy. The so-called interference of the Minister of State and Sir E. Spears was due not to a desire to supplant France in the Levant, but to the need to safeguard the British military position and to hold the French to the common pledge about the independence of the two States. On the other hand, we had not said that the mandate was bound to continue until ended by the League of Nations, since the League might never be revived. We had

_____

(a) E5071/207/89; Churchill Papers/422.

recognised that some legal formality would be necessary to define the independence of the States, and had agreed that the mandate must be regarded as in force until that time.

The French memorandum of November 5, 1941, had stated that (a) 'le Général Catroux exerce, compte tenu de la nouvelle situation de fait les pouvoirs du Haut-Commissaire de France en Syrie'.[1] The Foreign Office thought it evident from the words underlined[2] that General de Gaulle had recognised that the former powers of the High Commissioner had been modified by the declarations of the independence of the two Republics. For these reasons the Foreign Office thought they could not allow General de Gaulle's interpretation of the French and British position to pass unchallenged.

On the night of August 18–19 Mr. Casey sent to the Foreign (b) Office and to Sir E. Spears the draft of the proposed reply from the Prime Minister to General de Gaulle for any observations which the Foreign Office or Sir E. Spears might make. Sir A. Cadogan had already seen the draft, and had regarded it as satisfactory. The draft gave Mr. Churchill's assurance that we were not pursuing any political aims in the Levant States, and had not sought to undermine the French position. We recognised that the political initiative must rest with the French. Our principal political concern was to ensure that no policy was adopted which might jeopardise military security; we therefore expected to be consulted beforehand on major political developments. We were also interested as guarantors of General Catroux's declaration of June 8, 1941, announcing the intention of Free France to give the States their independence. This question was closely bound up with British relations with the rest of the Arab world.

Apart from our guarantee, the only affairs in the Levant States in which we concerned ourselves were those directly affecting our immediate military needs, and local British commercial or other interests. None of these activities constituted a violation of the letter or the spirit of the Lyttelton-de Gaulle agreements, or, as far as Mr. Churchill was aware, of the letters exchanged between the Foreign Office and the French National Committee. We understood that the mandate could be legally terminated only by international action after the war. Nevertheless, in his speech in the House of Commons on September 9, 1941, Mr. Churchill had made it clear that the position of the Fighting French in Syria could not be that

---

[1] This memorandum had been addressed only to the British Government. The same phrase occurred, however, in the letter from General de Gaulle to the Secretary-General of the League of Nations on November 28, 1941 (see below, p. 232).
[2] These words were underlined in Mr. Casey's draft reply to General de Gaulle (see below), not in the French memorandum.

(a) E7515, 7957/62/89 (1941). (b) E5072/207/89.

previously enjoyed by Vichy. General de Gaulle in his letter to the League of Nations of November 28, 1941, announcing his assumption of the responsibilities of the mandate, had stated that the independence and sovereignty of Syria and the Lebanon would not be circumscribed by any other limitations than those which were necessitated by war conditions. Mr. Casey's draft of the proposed reply by Mr. Churchill concluded by saying that our only object was to defeat the enemy, and that General de Gaulle could be assured that any British action in Syria and the Lebanon was directed towards that end alone.

(a)   On August 19 Sir E. Spears sent his comments on the draft to Mr. Casey. He thought the tone of the suggested reply 'dangerously weak' in view of the fact that General de Gaulle wanted to extract from us yet another document which he might quote against us. Sir E. Spears considered that we should not merely give assurances but that we should reject the General's position and remonstrate with him over his attitude. As far as his own official position was concerned, Sir E. Spears thought that consultation with the French was secondary to contacts with the local Governments to which he was accredited. We should therefore make it clear that these contacts, so far from being a derogation from normal procedure and dictated solely by war-time needs, were the essence of Sir E. Spears's official position.

Sir E. Spears thought that we had at least one major political aim in the Levant States, i.e. the implementation of their guarantee of independence. As this was the crux of the matter, we should not disclaim, even with subsequent reservation, a political interest in the States. In Sir E. Spears's opinion the proposed phrase '*immediate military needs*' might be used against us later on. He believed that the primary cause of General de Gaulle's outburst was his resentment at British participation in the wheat plan. Sir E. Spears claimed that 'the better sort of Frenchmen here' admitted our intervention to have been necessary to ensure Syrian co-operation. The intervention was a military act in the sense that a famine would endanger the British military position, but it was arguable that it could not be classed as an '*immediate*' military need. Sir E. Spears also suggested an alteration in the last sentence of the draft, which read: '*Our only object* is to defeat the enemy, and you can rest assured that any action by our representatives in Syria and the Lebanon is directed towards that end and that end alone.' He proposed that 'our only object' should read 'our over-riding object', and the end of the sentence should read: 'is constantly directed towards that end'.

(b)   The Foreign Office noted that for once they were in agreement with him, although they thought that his contacts with the Fighting

---

French were at least as important as—or even more important than
—his contacts with the local Governments. They also agreed that
the draft reply to General de Gaulle should be firmer on the main
point, i.e. we could not agree that we had no duties or interests in
the Levant States where, under the various agreements, our position
was based on our guarantee of the French guarantee of independence
and on the needs of military security. Mr. Eden was, however, ready
to leave to Mr. Casey, in consultation with Sir A. Cadogan, the final
drafting of the letter.

Meanwhile, in view of Mr. Casey's report of his conversations
with General de Gaulle and General Catroux on August 8 and 9,
Sir M. Peterson[1] had been instructed to point out to M. Dejean
that we could not accept communications apparently based on the
assumption that we had no interest in the course of events in the
Levant. We wanted the Fighting French to take the lead in the
Levant States, but they could not object to our satisfying ourselves
from time to time that they were pursuing the right course.

M. Dejean replied that he was sure that General de Gaulle did
not intend to suggest that we had no interest in the events in the
Levant; he was reminded that this was the tone of the General's
telegram. M. Dejean said that the Fighting French believed that the
military situation would not allow of the announcement, still less of
the holding, of elections. Sir M. Peterson replied that the Foreign
Office were waiting for Mr. Casey's view on the subject, but that it
was unfortunate that General de Gaulle had already announced the
indefinite postponement of elections. A telegram received on
August 18 from Sir E. Spears had said that General de Gaulle had
been stating in public that, after his conversations with His Majesty's
Government, elections in the near future were improbable.

On August 22 Mr. Casey sent to Beirut Mr. Churchill's reply to (a)
General de Gaulle's telegram of August 14. The original draft had
been stiffened in tone and Sir E. Spears's suggestions embodied in it.

On the evening of August 23 Mr. Hull sent Mr. Winant a message (b)
reporting a communication apparently from Mr. Gwynn. Mr.
Winant telephoned to Mr. Eden on August 25 to tell him that
General de Gaulle was not satisfied with the Prime Minister's reply
to his telegram. He had said that if he did not obtain satisfaction
about the activities of British agents in the Levant, he would have
to ask the British to leave his territory; if they refused to leave, he
would force them out.

General de Gaulle replied to the Prime Minister's telegram on (c)

---

[1] Deputy Under-Secretary of State.

(a) E5073/207/89; Churchill Papers/422.   (b) E5172/207/89.   (c) E5167/207/89.
Churchill Papers/422.

August 24.[1] He regretted that he was unable to accept Mr. Churchill's point of view that the political 'interventions' of British representatives in Syria and the Lebanon were compatible with British engagements about respect for the position of France and the continuation of her mandate. In General de Gaulle's opinion these interventions were in contradiction to the régime of independence which Fighting France had granted to Syria and the Lebanon within the framework of the mandate and the Franco-American Treaty of 1924.

The presence of British troops could not justify such intervention. Conditions of military co-operation in the Middle East and those of British troops in the Levant had been laid down by the Lyttelton-de Gaulle agreement. Relations between purely military British and French authorities in the battle of Libya and Egypt and in the defence of Syria and the Levant were very good. For this reason General de Gaulle said that he had agreed to maintain troops belonging to the French Command under the orders of the British Command in Syria and the Lebanon, in spite of the fact that the former were at that time superior in number to the British. According to the Lyttelton-de Gaulle agreement, this numerical superiority should result in the transfer of direction of Allied military affairs locally to the French Command. General de Gaulle maintained that the conditions of rivalry which interference and friction between British and French representatives had created in the Middle East were harmful in their effects on the Arab world and on public opinion in the French nation. He concluded his reply by saying that he was ready to discuss the matter with Mr. Casey at Beirut.[2]

(a)　　　Mr. Eden telegraphed to Mr. Casey on August 26 that he was not aware that there had been any 'interventions' beyond those justified by security needs and our military responsibility, or by our obligation to fulfil our guarantee of the French declaration of independence. Mr. Eden suggested that Mr. Casey should meet General de Gaulle and try to clear up the situation. If Mr. Casey went to Beirut and found the General intransigent, he would then have to tell him that Mr. Eden urged that he should return to London for consultation. Mr. Eden did not think that it would be possible to bridge a wide difference of opinion by correspondence. Mr. Casey disagreed with

(b) Mr. Eden's suggestion that he should go to see General de Gaulle at Beirut. He did not want to leave Egypt at this time;[3] he also

---

[1] The telegram containing General de Gaulle's reply was received in London on August 25.

[2] The original of General de Gaulle's reply did not reach the Prime Minister until September 1. Mr. Churchill endorsed it: 'I shall send no answer. If he wishes for discussion, let him come home.'

[3] A renewal of the German-Italian offensive was expected; the attack opened on the night of August 30–1.

(a) E5167/207/89.　(b) E5075/207/89.

thought that the atmosphere in Beirut was unfavourable to discussion. He therefore proposed to send a strongly worded telegram saying that an impasse had been reached and that General de Gaulle should come to Cairo in an attempt to find a solution; otherwise the Prime Minister had no alternative but to ask General de Gaulle to return to London immediately.

With the agreement of the Prime Minister, Mr. Eden telegraphed to Mr. Casey on August 28 that he would not press him to go to Beirut. He thought that it was useless for Mr. Casey to invite the General to Cairo; he was not likely to come or at Mr. Casey's request to leave the territory in which he regarded himself as a sovereign. The Prime Minister and Mr. Eden therefore proposed that Mr. Casey should send a message to General de Gaulle from the Prime Minister. This message would agree that the situation was serious and ask General de Gaulle to return at once to London. Sir A. Cadogan thought that General de Gaulle might later be told that we had thought of establishing him in Madagascar, but that, as long as he continued to behave as he was doing, we could not run the risk of similar embarrassment elsewhere.[1]

The telegram containing the text of a message to General de (a) Gaulle crossed a telegram from Mr. Casey that he intended to say to General de Gaulle that we could not dissociate ourselves from the administration of Syria and the Lebanon. Our military security must remain the paramount consideration. The economic and financial life of the Levant States was dependent on us, and we had important political commitments to the States. General de Gaulle should recognise that his agreement with Mr. Lyttelton and other declarations must be interpreted in such a way that we could act as partners with the French in the Levant until the end of the war. In return, Mr. Casey would be willing to give categorical assurances about British intentions to preserve the pre-eminent position of France in the Levant after the war.

On August 29 M. Dejean told Mr. Strang that he hoped that (b) General de Gaulle could be induced to return as soon as possible. The local atmosphere of intrigue and ferocious personal animosities did not favour a balanced view of the situation. There were other things more important for Fighting France than Syria, and these might be compromised unless a solution could be found. M. Dejean regretted that the United States Government had been drawn into the dispute. M. Dejean showed Mr. Strang a telegram from General de Gaulle to M. Pleven and himself. This telegram appeared to be the text of

---

[1] Sir A. Cadogan's suggestion was not included in the message to General de Gaulle.

(a) E5125/207/89. (b) E5133/207/89.

instructions from Mr. Hull to Mr. Winant to approach the British Government about the position.[1]

(a)   On August 30 Mr. Casey telegraphed that he had decided to make a last attempt to have the matter out with General de Gaulle in Cairo, and had sent him the message proposed in his telegram from Cairo to the Foreign Office on August 28.[2] If this approach failed, he would give the General the Prime Minister's message. The Foreign Office thought that nothing much could come from

(b) Mr. Casey's action. Sir E. Spears sent Mr. Casey the text of General de Gaulle's reply on August 30. The General said that Franco-British relations had been seriously compromised by British inter-ference in relations between the Fighting French and the Levant States under French mandate, and also in the internal affairs in the two countries; this interference had resulted in a diminution of the position of France which the French National Committee were bound to oppose. General de Gaulle said that he was ready to

(c) discuss military co-operation with Mr. Casey at Beirut. Mr. Casey replied that the situation in the Western Desert prevented him from leaving Cairo. He now forwarded the Prime Minister's message asking General de Gaulle to return to London.

(iv)

Further difficulties with General de Gaulle: views of Mr. Casey and Sir E. Spears: General de Gaulle's letter and memorandum of September 7 to Mr. Casey: General de Gaulle's return to London and conversation with the Prime Minister and Mr. Eden on September 30 (September 1–30, 1942).

(d)   General de Gaulle replied to Mr. Churchill's message that he would return to London as soon as possible, but that the situation did not permit him to leave Beirut for the present ('actuellement').

(e)   [1] On August 25 the Foreign Office received a telegram from Lord Halifax in Washing-ton stating that Mr. Winant had been instructed to discuss the Levant situation with Mr. Eden as soon as possible. The United States Government did not want to interfere, but they could not remain unaffected by the dispute. They thought that General de Gaulle's expressed intentions about the future of Syria and the Lebanon were at variance with the Fighting French and British declarations on the subject at the time of their entry into Syria. They thought also that Sir E. Spears had intervened in internal affairs to an unjustified extent.

(f)   [2] Mr. Casey's telegram was despatched to Beirut on the night of August 29–30. The wording of the telegram was as follows: 'My impression is that relations between your-selves and ourselves in Syria and Lebanon have reached an acute stage. Whatever the reasons for the deterioration, I believe that it is essential in [the] principal interest of us both (*sic*), namely the prosecution of the war that more satisfactory relations should be created as quickly as possible.' Mr. Casey then said that he was unable to leave Cairo; he invited General de Gaulle to meet him there. 'Failing such a meeting, I shall be obliged to submit the present position as it appears to me to the Prime Minister.' Mr. Casey asked for an 'urgent reply'.

(a) E5136/207/89.   (b) E5142/207/89.   (c) E5177/207/89.   (d) E5184/207/89; Churchill Papers/422. (e) E5074/207/89. (f) E5128/207/89.

He was still prepared to discuss matters with Mr. Casey at Beirut. He said that the maintenance of the independent position of France in Syria and the Lebanon was, for himself and for the French National Committee, an absolute duty and one of the greatest urgency. Mr. Churchill agreed with the Foreign Office that Mr. Casey should not go to Beirut. When Mr. Casey renewed the (a) suggestion that he should go, Mr. Churchill told him not to do so.

At this stage the Foreign Office considered the possibility of cutting (b) off General de Gaulle's supplies. On the ninth of every month the British Government paid £300,000 to the Fighting French towards the expenses of their administration and troops in the Levant States, and later in the month another £200,000 to £300,000. Without this subsidy General de Gaulle could supply the money for his officials and troops only for two to three weeks at most, even if he diverted to the Levant States all his private funds in London and any other funds available in Equatorial Africa and elsewhere. The Treasury opposed forcing the General to make such misuse of Fighting French funds. The Foreign Office agreed that financial sanctions need not be imposed for the moment, but Mr. Eden insisted that a French claim to assume command of the British Ninth Army must be rejected.

On September 2 Mr. Strang saw M. Dejean. Mr. Eden had asked (c) him to say that by his behaviour the General was alienating his friends and encouraging his enemies. Mr. Eden agreed with M. Dejean that, although Syria was important for Fighting France, much more important matters might be compromised unless a solution were found. Mr. Eden thought that, in the interest of the future of Fighting France and of its relations with the British Government, the sooner the General returned to London the better.

On the same day, General de Gaulle telegraphed to MM. Pleven (d) and Dejean that he was profoundly anxious about Anglo-French relations, and that British policy in the Levant consisted in establishing a *condominium*, to be replaced later by British domination. The British Government had at their disposal money, food, force and means of propaganda. They carried out their policy by insistence that Syrian and Lebanese independence was due to British initiative, by promises to the Arabs that the British would act as intermediaries between them and the local Governments, and by constant use of the pretext of military security and food supplies to encroach on French spheres of responsibility and interfere with the local authorities. General de Gaulle complained of Sir E. Spears, 'who did everything he could to throw oil on the fire' by misinterpreting his Government's instructions and the actions of the Free French. General de Gaulle instructed MM. Pleven and Dejean to explain

---

(a) E5316, 5321, 5331/207/89. (b) E5190/207/89. (c) Z6864/608/17. (d) E5217/207/89.

to Mr. Eden the urgent need to solve these problems, if Great Britain and Fighting France were to continue to co-operate. General de Gaulle said that he was staying in Syria until matters were cleared up and that he was keeping in touch with the American Consul-General and proposed to see Mr. Wilkie.[1]

M. Dejean asked Sir M. Peterson on September 2 how far we intended to press the election issue in the face of the military situation in Egypt. Sir M. Peterson said that the Foreign Office were waiting for the views of Mr. Casey and of our military authorities. The decision had been delayed not only by the military situation, but also by the unfortunate events attending General de Gaulle's visit to the Middle East. Even if immediate elections were undesirable, a statement could well be made that elections would be held when the military situation allowed. Our main cause of complaint against the Fighting French was that they had done nothing in nine or ten months since the declaration of Syrian and Lebanese independence. They must therefore find some way of making progress.

M. Dejean also asked what, if any, basis there was for General de Gaulle's suspicion that Great Britain desired a *condominium* in the Levant States, if not the complete extrusion of France. Sir M. Peterson stated that we had no intention of seeking to establish a *condominium* in the Levant, much less to exclude French influence. M. Dejean said that, on the strength of these assurances, he would telegraph to General de Gaulle urging his return.[2] He added that it was Sir E. Spears's conduct which had given rise to French suspi-

(a) cions. Mr. Eden later approved of Sir M. Peterson's answers. On September 4 he told Mr. Winant that General de Gaulle was trying to play the United States Government against the British Government. Mr. Winant agreed to suggest that the State Department should send instructions to the American Consul-General at Beirut not to encourage General de Gaulle.

Meanwhile, General de Gaulle challenged the British Government on the issue of the command of Allied military forces in Syria

(b) and the Lebanon. On September 5, Baron Benoist gave a message to Mr. Casey from General de Gaulle stating that, as the military forces in Syria and the Lebanon under French command out-numbered those under British command, the French should assume command of the Allied military forces in the area; he proposed that

---

[1] See below, p. 242, note 1.

[2] M. Dejean telegraphed to General de Gaulle that Sir M. Peterson had given him every guarantee concerning British policy, which was based on military security. There might be serious consequences for Fighting France if the United States should later undertake a military operation in North Africa and meanwhile become further prejudiced against the Fighting French Movement.

(a) E5298/207/89. (b) E5259/207/89.

the change-over should take place on September 10. M. Dejean had already handed Mr. Rooker, acting British representative with the French National Committee,[1] a copy of a similar message from General Catroux to Mr. Casey and General Alexander.[2]

The Foreign Office opposed this French proposal on legal grounds; (a) Mr. Casey, General Wilson and the Chief of the General Staff, Middle East, agreed with their view, and General de Gaulle was therefore informed that the facts did not justify his request.[3] The Foreign Office thought that he had not put forward his argument as a soldier on military grounds, but as a politician in order to challenge the British position in the Levant. He had thus raised questions which could be dealt with only in London.

On September 3 General de Gaulle sent General Alexander a (b) letter in which he repeated his demand for French command in the Levant, and further asked for the cessation of the military liaison work of the Spears Mission, the immediate employment of the Fighting French 1st Brigade in the battle of the Western Desert, and the subsequent transfer of the Brigade to the United Kingdom.

On September 7 Mr. Eden saw MM. Pleven and Dejean. Before (c) the meeting, he had received information that M. Pleven had been sending telegrams to General de Gaulle advising him to stay in Syria since, if he returned to England, he would not be allowed out again. M. Pleven had also encouraged him to continue his policy of playing off the Americans against the British. Mr. Eden now told MM. Pleven and Dejean that he had been, as they knew, a firm friend of Fighting France. General de Gaulle had promised him

---

[1] Mr. Peake appears at this time to have been ill.

[2] On September 2 Mr. Matthews, of the United States Embassy, told Mr. Strang of a (d) message from Mr. Gwynn that General de Gaulle was proposing to assume the military direction of the Allied forces in Syria on September 10. According to Mr. Gwynn, General de Gaulle had telegraphed to this effect to Mr. Casey and had proposed that they should discuss details concerned with the transfer. The Foreign Office at once instructed Mr. Casey to reject this proposal—if it were made—as contrary to the terms of the Anglo-French agreement.

[3] The British land forces in Syria and the Lebanon numbered 41,650. The total (e) number of French forces, including Troupes Spéciales and coast watchers, was about 27,000–28,000. Under agreements concluded in 1941 between General Wilson and General Catroux, the only French forces under the command of the Ninth Army consisted of one brigade in the Beirut locality.

The Troupes Spéciales were locally recruited forces financed by Great Britain. The increase in their numbers was progressively sanctioned by General Wilson. They were only bound to serve in the Levant States. Theoretically they belonged to the States and were placed at the disposal of the French. Sir E. Spears thought that they were the nucleus of a defence force for the two Republics. He did not think that they could be reckoned to be Free French troops in the same way as were the Senegalese, who were recruited in French territory.

The Foreign Office considered that the question whether the Levant States formed a zone of operations was also relevant. Mr. Casey's reply to General de Gaulle, however, dealt only with the question of numbers.

(a) E5260, 5319, 5601/207/89.   (b) E5367/207/89.   (c) E5260/207/89.   (d) E5190/207/89.   (e) E5260, 5268/207/89.

IBFP

before leaving England that he would cause no trouble in the Middle East, but that if there were difficulties, he would return for discussion. The situation had, however, become serious, and our collaboration with Fighting France was endangered. The General had become influenced by the supercharged atmosphere in the Levant;[1] hence his ridiculous suspicions that we wished to eradicate French influence and his own threats of taking over the military command by a fixed date. It was also absurd to consider playing off the Americans against us. The Prime Minister had asked General de Gaulle to return, and the latter had temporised. There was nothing more we could do; we were not prepared to offer the

(a) General assurances which might seem to be a bribe for his return. Eventually MM. Pleven and Dejean agreed to tell General de Gaulle of Mr. Eden's statement and urge his return.[2]

(b) Two days later MM. Pleven and Dejean came again to see Mr. Eden at his request.[3] Mr. Eden told them that we were about to undertake further operations in Madagascar, and had intended to invite the French National Committee to take over the administration of the territory occupied as a result of these operations. In view of General de Gaulle's attitude about the Levant States, and his unjustified suspicions of our good faith, we could not carry out this plan. If, however, the General would leave immediately for London to talk over the questions of the Levant States, we would still be ready to discuss with him the possibility of carrying out our intention about Madagascar.

M. Pleven protested that the Madagascar question should be judged on its merits, and not linked up with that of Syria; we were offering to let the French into Madagascar at the price of turning them out of Syria. Mr. Eden replied that neither General de Gaulle nor M. Pleven could really think that we were trying to displace the French in Syria. Finally, after more discussion in which M. Dejean supported Mr. Eden's suggestion, M. Pleven accepted the proposal for General de Gaulle's return at least as better than no solution.

(c) On September 10 M. Helleu,[4] former Vichy Ambassador at

(d)   [1] In a letter of September 16 to Mr. Casey Sir E. Spears pointed out that General de Gaulle's first interview with Mr. Casey, which was his worst exhibition, took place on his way to Syria and before he had had time to study the situation.
[2] M. Dejean telegraphed to General de Gaulle urging him to come back to London. The French Committee telegraphed a recommendation that he should return to Cairo.
[3] See also above, Vol. II, pp. 345–47.
[4] M. Helleu had joined the Fighting French in August 1942. Mr. Casey thought that M. Helleu hoped that General de Gaulle would make him his diplomatic adviser. Mr. Eden agreed with the view of Mr. Strang that M. Helleu, as an Ambassador of France and a man of weight, might lead the General to better behaviour in international matters.

(a) E5290/207/89. (b) Z6976/23/17. (c) E5389, 5420, 5559/207/89; Z6985/90/17. (d) E5602/207/89.

Ankara, called on Mr. Casey on his way from Syria to London. He delivered a letter from General de Gaulle to Mr. Casey dated September 7 and enclosing a forty-page memorandum. The letter claimed that Franco-British relations in Syria had not conformed with the agreements and the alliance. French concessions had 'simply encouraged British encroachments' on the rights of France and of the Levant States. British action continuously invoked two arguments: independence of the Levant States and military necessity. The first was used to prevent the Delegate-General from using powers which belonged to him until the termination of the mandate. The second was used to justify intervention in affairs reserved to France, notably the exploitation of local resources. General de Gaulle maintained that the British Government had no claim to invoke either of these arguments. Independence had been instituted by France; her word was not to be guaranteed, nor the execution of her promises controlled. The Fighting French would accept advice but not interference. They desired close Franco-British co-operation for war purposes, but British policy substituted pressure for collaboration. This policy gave the appearance of rivalry to the local population, and compromised the Franco-British alliance. General de Gaulle said that he was grateful to Mr. Churchill for the assurances of principle which he had recently renewed, but that he found in the Levant States a practice and facts which did not accord with those assurances. The memorandum accompanying the letter was a strongly worded indictment of the attitude of Sir E. Spears, the wheat plan, British intervention in financial, agricultural and industrial affairs, the activities of subordinate British officers and other matters.

In his comments to the Foreign Office on this memorandum Mr. (a) Casey refuted General de Gaulle's allegations in detail; he added that experience had shown that in almost every field, owing to lack of adequate personnel and outside resources, the French were not capable of administering the countries and supplying their needs without our aid. In some cases, e.g. the wheat plan, they had asked for this plan. In other cases it had become clear that without our help the machinery of government would have broken down, with resulting disorders which would have threatened the military situation.

Mr. Casey also thought that Syria and the Lebanon had to be regarded as part of the Middle East area as a whole and that plans for supplying them, for the control of inflation and for making the best use, in the interests of war, of their resources had had to be co-ordinated with similar activities in the rest of the Middle East.

(a) E5414/207/89.

British co-operation in these activities had proved to be necessary in all other countries of the Middle East, whenever possible under the authority of local Governments. The French seemed to think, however, that our association with them in these activities was part of a plan to obtain political and economic advantages. If they had accepted British assistance in material and personnel, whenever it was needed, they could have had it without impairing their authority. Mr. Casey proposed to reply to the memorandum that the matters in it must be dealt with in London. The Foreign Office agreed with Mr. Casey's suggestion.

(a)   The view of Sir E. Spears was that there had been a fundamental conflict of policy over the Levant States between the Fighting French and ourselves ever since the armistice. The British had looked on the area as part of the Middle East theatre of war, and its day-to-day problems from the aspect of the war effort. British officials had also tried to honour British promises of independence. The Fighting French, on the other hand, considered that their actions must not diminish and as far as possible must increase the power and prestige of France, regardless of their undertakings. This policy had led them to forget that victory was essential to the re-establishment of the French Empire, and that in their endeavour to build up their prestige they had endangered the British security position by increasing the disaffection of the local populations. Sir E. Spears thought that this conflict between British and French policy was the cause of British difficulties, but that it had taken General de Gaulle's visit to bring about a collision between the two theses.[1]

(b)   Sir E. Spears told the Foreign Office that General de Gaulle's visit had done great harm to British prestige and security and that the situation would get worse unless public confidence in British strength and promises was restored. Elections were essential, but a

(c)   promise to hold them at a distant date was not enough. The election issue had become the test of British sincerity. Mr. Casey also thought that any agreement with General de Gaulle should provide for

(d)   elections, but that it might be better to allow some latitude in their timing rather than to insist that they be held before the end of the year. Mr. Eden accepted this view.

(e)   [1] Mr. Wendell Wilkie spent September 10 in Beirut. At lunch with Sir E. Spears he discussed British troubles with the Fighting French. Reports of General de Gaulle's interview with Mr. Wilkie showed that the General had displayed profound distrust of British motives, and seemed convinced that British policy was annexation of the Levant States. Sir E. Spears pointed out to Mr. Wilkie that the best possible answer to accusations of British imperialist designs would be recognition by the United States of the Levant Republics, in accordance with our repeated suggestion. Such recognition would also encourage the Republics themselves. Before Mr. Wilkie left, he promised that he would do what he could to make General de Gaulle see reason.

(a) E5602/207/89.   (b) E5534/207/89.   (c) E5416/207/89.   (d) E5596/207/89. (e) E5511/207/89.

The Prime Minister thought that the situation in the Western (a)
Desert had been the only argument against elections. After the
recent battle[1] this argument no longer held. He considered that the
British Government should insist upon a declaration that elections
would be held before the end of the year. Meanwhile arrangements
had been made with the Treasury that they should not pay the (b)
subsidy on which the French in Syria lived until we knew that
General de Gaulle had agreed to return to London. The subsidy
was then paid.

On September 13 M. Dejean sent the Foreign Office a message (c)
from General de Gaulle to Mr. Eden. General de Gaulle referred
to the conversations between Mr. Eden and MM. Pleven and
Dejean on September 7 and 9. He inferred that we and the French
National Committee wanted to see Franco-British relations in the
Middle East established on a satisfactory basis in accordance with
the agreements, and with the position in Syria and the Lebanon.
He noted that we, in view of the new situation in Madagascar, con-
templated giving effect to the undertaking in the communiqué of
May 13 about Madagascar.[2] He appreciated the desire of Mr.
Churchill and Mr. Eden that he should return to London to discuss
this question, and hoped that the conversations would result in
closer co-operation in the war. He intended to visit Free French
Africa and be back in Cairo about September 23 ready to start for
London.

On the afternoon of September 30 the Prime Minister and Mr.
Eden met General de Gaulle. Before the meeting the Foreign Office (d)
had drawn up a memorandum for the use of the Prime Minister[3] on
the Syrian question. They considered that General de Gaulle must
give up his suspicions of British policy and recognise that we had an
interest in the Levant, as long as the war lasted, arising from our
guarantee of the French promise of independence to Syria and the
Lebanon—a promise which would have meant nothing without
British military intervention. We were entitled to insist that the
Fighting French carried out their promise. The most convincing
step would be an announcement that elections would be held within
a specified time. If this were not possible, something else must be
done, e.g. the transfer to the two States of the Funds of Common
Interest. It was also desirable to reaffirm the understanding in the

---

[1] i.e. the defeat of the German-Italian attack at the end of August.

[2] It was pointed out to M. Dejean that Mr. Eden's words to him and M. Pleven had
been that, if General de Gaulle would return to London to discuss the Levant States,
we should 'still be ready to discuss with him the possibility of proceeding with our original
intention as regards Madagascar'.

[3] For the general proposals in this memorandum, and for the record of the conversation
with General de Gaulle of June 20 on matters other than Syria, see Vol. II, pp. 358-9.

(a) M386/2, E5534/207/89.   (b) WM(42)121.   (c) Z7099/608/17.   (d) E5692/207/89.

Lyttelton-de Gaulle agreements which were intended to govern our relations with the Fighting French in the Levant.

The Foreign Office also considered the question of a change in British representation, either independently or in combination with the replacement of General Catroux. They thought that the prospects of collaboration with the Fighting French were poor as long as Sir E. Spears remained as British Minister, since, in the Foreign Office view, he was carrying out a policy of his own, namely to replace French by British influence, which was contrary to the policy of His Majesty's Government.[1]

(a)   At the meeting with General de Gaulle Mr. Churchill began by saying that he was much obliged to the General for coming back to discuss Syrian problems. Matters had gone from bad to worse while they were being discussed locally. General de Gaulle said that he had expected to find difficulties in Syria over Franco-British relations, but these difficulties had been greater than he had anticipated. The facts of the situation had worried him less than the atmosphere of unhappy rivalry. Mr. Churchill said that there was no question of rivalry. We had no aspirations in Syria, no special interest apart from winning the war and maintaining our pre-war commercial interests, which were very small. On the other hand, we had given pledges to the Syrians with General Catroux's assent, and were determined to fulfil these pledges. We could not allow our military position to be endangered by a failure to fulfil them. General de Gaulle replied that the Fighting French had special responsibilities towards the Syrians and Lebanese. They could concert, but not share, these responsibilities with the British. When General Catroux took measures in agreement with the Syrian or Lebanese Governments, he alone was responsible. There was no reason to doubt that the French would carry out their pledges. General de Gaulle thought that General Catroux went too far in meeting British wishes. Unfortunately the attitude of British representatives had compromised the independence of the Levant States.

Mr. Churchill suggested that there was one step which could be taken towards making the independence of Syria and the Lebanon more of a reality. This step was to hold elections. The local people wanted them in order to express their wishes freely, and Mr. Churchill had made a public statement to this effect in the House of Commons. We must be freed from anxiety arising out of the

---

(b)   [1] On September 28 General Holmes, commanding the Ninth Army, pointed out that General de Gaulle was not the first to realise that the British liaison services needed revision. General Holmes himself had suggested certain measures. He did not believe that General de Gaulle had dealt British prestige a severe blow. On the contrary, over 60 per cent of Frenchmen in the Levant would welcome a new deal.

(a) Z7530/90/17.   (b) E5771/207/89.

possibility of insurrections, which would endanger military security.

General de Gaulle agreed that elections should be held, but they must be genuine elections. These were impossible with the country under the occupation of two outside Powers, with a complete censorship and with the danger of a local German fifth column, especially in a country where elections always gave rise to intrigue. While the Germans were advancing in the Caucasus and at the same time threatening Alexandria, the moment was unsuitable for elections. The local populations, with whom he had been in close contact, were not asking for them; they should be postponed until the military situation improved. Mr. Eden pointed out that elections had recently been held in Egypt. Mr. Churchill said that he could not understand why there should be difficulties over the elections if the local populations were as favourable to the Fighting French as had been suggested. General de Gaulle maintained that the difficulties would arise between the different sections of the population, and not between them and the Fighting French.

On the question of local military command General de Gaulle said that he had written to General Alexander and sent instructions to General Catroux urging that they should reach agreement. He insisted, however, that the French troops in Syria should be commanded by the French. Mr. Churchill said that General de Gaulle did not realise the proportion of forces in the area; we could not agree to transfer the command to the French. On the contrary, we should take steps to maintain it, and to avoid any troubles arising out of local difficulties with the Syrians.

Mr. Eden then said that we were continually receiving complaints from the Fighting French of interference in internal affairs. We were, however, bound to play our part in such affairs, since we were the central authority for co-ordinating all questions in the Middle East concerning supply, finance and manpower. We had to relate action in one country, e.g. Syria, with action elsewhere. We had met with much French obstruction which had in many cases brought business to a standstill. Mr. Eden considered that an exchange of letters with General de Gaulle was necessary in order to provide for collaboration, which would be of an administrative rather than a political character.

General de Gaulle said that he could not admit the position under which the British raised financial questions in the form of ultimata to General Catroux or to the Syrian or Lebanese Governments. Whenever we wanted to consult the Fighting French, they were ready for consultation; they could not agree to British demands for a preponderant position. Mr. Churchill said that General de Gaulle seemed to have no idea of the real state of things. Our burdens were being made much more difficult. The local populations were being

irritated against the French. General de Gaulle was making a continual attempt to assert his local position in a way which had no
connexion with the war effort. General de Gaulle replied that the
difficulty in his view was the behaviour of the local British representatives and that it would be better to improve local contacts
rather than to discuss formulae. Mr. Churchill said that they
evidently did not agree about the Syrian position. The General
would understand that, with this extremely unhappy situation
which had grown so much worse during his visit, we were not eager
to risk similar difficulties in other theatres of war, e.g. Madagascar.
General de Gaulle refused to give way over Syria, but insisted that
the British Government should hand over the administration of
Madagascar to the Fighting French. The Prime Minister told
General de Gaulle plainly that the great difficulty lay in working
with him. Wherever he went there was trouble. He had not shown
the least will to assist us, and had himself been the greatest obstacle
to effective collaboration between the Americans and ourselves.
General de Gaulle answered that he would accept the consequences
of his action. The meeting thus ended in something very near to a
complete breach.

(v)

*Negotiations between the Foreign Office and the French National Committee
for an 'interpretative' agreement with regard to Syria: the Allied landings in
North Africa and the agreement over Madagascar: discussions with General
Catroux in London and Beirut: French agreement to an early announcement
with regard to elections (October–December 1942).*

In spite of the strong language used on both sides neither the
Prime Minister nor General de Gaulle wanted a severance of relations
between the British Government and the Fighting French. The
Foreign Office and the French National Committee were thus able
to try to bring about a settlement. The Foreign Office took the
(a) initiative almost at once. On October 2 Sir O. Sargent asked M.
Dejean to come and see him. He told him that the General's hostile
behaviour had made such an adverse impression that there could be
no further discussion between the General and the Prime Minister.
The General's prejudices and suspicions and his ideas about his
mission to defend French interests against Great Britain seemed to
make progress impossible. With goodwill and mutual confidence,
political and administrative questions in Syria could have been
settled, but the General had refused any discussion. As regards

(a) Z7531/608/17.

Madagascar, we were ready to see the Fighting French participating in the administration, if the Syrian imbroglio could be cleared up. This was an essential preliminary, since we could not risk a repetition in Madagascar of the situation in Syria.

Sir O. Sargent said that a deadlock had been reached, and that any suggestions for breaking it must come from the French. M. Dejean replied that he had already discussed possible action with General de Gaulle. After moods of great indignation and deep depression the General was in a reasonable frame of mind and had given M. Dejean authority to make certain proposals. He was ready before the end of the year to announce elections for the spring. He would drop his claims to military command in Syria if the small bodies of French troops in Syria now under British command were brought together under the command of French officers. He would also agree to the establishment of a Mixed Commission in London to deal with administrative questions. M. Dejean said that the French National Committee had passed a resolution supporting General de Gaulle, and had suggested that they should send a deputation to Mr. Eden to inform him that they considered the General the only possible leader of the Movement. Sir O. Sargent strongly deprecated such intervention by the Committee.

The Prime Minister agreed that the negotiations should be con- (a) tinued; hence on October 5 M. Dejean sent the Foreign Office an (b) *aide-mémoire* setting out formally the three proposals as a basis of negotiation: (i) the Fighting French would agree to a declaration before the end of the year that elections would be held in Syria and the Lebanon by the spring. A committee consisting of General Catroux and the General Officers commanding the 9th and 10th Armies would be asked to confirm in due course that the military situation was such that an electoral campaign could take place without risk to the security of the Levant States and the Allied forces. (ii) The Fighting French would give up their claim to command Allied troops in the Levant. Any point which they might raise later under this head would refer to their wish to group the local French forces under a unified local command. (iii) A Franco-British com-mittee[1] should be set up in London to consider difficulties for which no solution could be found locally.[2]

The Foreign Office accepted these proposals in a letter of October 8.

---

[1] The Foreign Office and Mr. Eden thought that it should be made clear that this (c) Committee would examine only problems which could not be settled locally. Sir M. Peterson pointed out that if Sir E. Spears were withdrawn, a committee in London would not be necessary.

[2] M. Dejean suggested that, in all suitable cases, Syrian and Lebanese representatives should participate in the discussions of the Committee. These representatives would be officials without diplomatic status. This suggestion was not pursued further.

(a) E5934, 5954/207/89. (b) E5948/207/89. (c) E5935, 5954/207/89.

In a subsequent letter of October 17 they suggested that the committee to pronounce on the feasibility of elections should consist of the Commander-in-Chief, Middle East, or a general nominated by him, the General Officer Commanding the 9th Army and the Commander-in-Chief of French troops in the Levant.[1] In order to complete the negotiations there should be an agreed exchange of documents defining the basis for Anglo-French collaboration in the Levant States. This formula was to be interpretative of existing agreements, and would provide the terms of reference of the Franco-British committee in London. Sir M. Peterson and M. Dejean agreed upon the draft of such an interpretative document, subject to the approval of the British Government and the French National Committee.

(a)   On October 14 Mr. Churchill had considered the question of British representation, and had decided that it would not be wise to move either Sir E. Spears or General Catroux. General Catroux was on good terms with the British representatives in Cairo and the soldiers; Sir E. Spears had defended British rights in Syria with great energy and ability. They ought to be told that they must get on with each other, and that if either had to go, both would have to go. It would have to be made clear to General Catroux that he would then have no chance of transfer to Madagascar.

The Foreign Office had meanwhile asked Mr. Casey whether he
(b) agreed with the French proposals. Mr. Casey thought them acceptable as a basis for negotiation, although he believed that the great need was for an exchange of documents defining the basis of future collaboration. He would not oppose the creation of a committee in London, provided that it was an ultimate court of appeal, and did not develop into a regular instrument of government. On October 11
(c) he sent his objections to the British draft of the interpretative document. He thought that the French should admit the British Government as a partner in the affairs of the Levant States, particularly in military security, economic, supply and financial matters. On the other hand, the draft gave Fighting France a new and unjustified right to a voice in Middle East affairs as a whole. The admission of this right might lead to embarrassing intervention by the French in British affairs in adjacent countries, and might even justify their claims to a seat on the Middle East War Council. The document should be an agreement relating to the Levant States only, and not to the whole of the Middle East.

---

[1] i.e. the French member, like the British members, should be designated by title and not by name.

(a) M442/2, Z7777/23/17. (b) E5935/207/89. (c) E5939/207/89.

Mr. Casey and Sir E. Spears thought that the new document (a) should supersede all previous agreements.[1] The Foreign Office, however, had decided that his plan would not serve the immediate purpose of restoring relations sufficiently to enable current business to be done. As a result of the improved atmosphere in London progress had been made on the questions of elections, military command and other matters which had been outstanding for months and had reached an impasse. As the first interview with General de Gaulle had ended in deadlock, the British objective had to be to secure sufficient agreement to enable practical questions to be dealt with quickly. Hence an interpretative agreement was needed rather than a comprehensive new agreement, which would have taken months to complete, since much of it would have had to be negotiated in Cairo. Moreover the interpretative agreement did not rule out the possibility of a comprehensive new agreement later.

The satisfactory progress of the Syrian conversations made it possible to raise once more the question of Madagascar. On October 8 Mr. Eden reminded Mr. Churchill that they had told General de (b) Gaulle that owing to the trouble about Syria they had found it impossible to hand over the administration of Madagascar. Mr. Eden had since learned, however, that both General de Gaulle and the French National Committee were doubtful of our good faith about Madagascar, and thought that we were using Syria as a pretext. Mr. Eden therefore proposed, as soon as General de Gaulle accepted the suggested basis for the Syrian negotiations, to offer to discuss with M. Dejean the principles for handing over the civil administration of Madagascar when the Syrian settlement was signed. This offer would help the Syrian negotiations and would also strengthen M. Dejean's position with the General. Mr. Churchill agreed that the Foreign Office should start discussions with M. Dejean on these terms.

On October 12, therefore, the question of the future administra- (c) tion of Madagascar was mentioned to M. Dejean in a preliminary way and without commitment. He was told that if the Fighting French were to take over the administration, they would do so on the basis of an agreement negotiated in London between the British Government and the French National Committee, since detailed arrangements must be made in order to avoid misunderstandings in the future. The Foreign Office were considering the clauses of such an agreement.[2]

---

[1] Middle East Command also took this view. (d)
[2] According to a report which had reached the Foreign Office, General de Gaulle was (e) prepared to accept almost any terms in order to get into Madagascar quickly.

(a) E5946, 5966, 5989/207/89. (b) Z7466/23/17. (c) Z7677/23/17. (d) E6050/207/89. (e) Z7777/23/17.

This preliminary discussion had taken place after an assurance
from M. Dejean that the terms of the Syrian agreement would be
(a) accepted. The text was in fact agreed with M. Dejean on October 15.
General de Gaulle, however, now replaced M. Dejean by M. Pleven
as Commissioner for Foreign Affairs. M. Dejean subsequently told
the Foreign Office that General Catroux had sent a telegram
criticising in strong terms the proposed agreement on Syria. General
Catroux complained that the agreement conceded every British
demand and failed to protect French interests.

(b)   M. Pleven later explained to Mr. Strang that the change in the
Commissariat for Foreign Affairs did not mean a change in policy
but was due to General de Gaulle's doubts whether he was getting
an accurate account of our attitude from M. Dejean, who had given
too optimistic a picture. M. Pleven said that he believed in the
Anglo-French alliance; he knew that the General held the same
views. They were devoted to the defence of French interests, but
were convinced that British and French interests were the same.
M. Pleven said that unfortunately the last two months had seen the
growth of a deep misunderstanding. He had been chosen for the
post of Commissioner for Foreign Affairs in order that he might try
to improve relations.

    M. Pleven thought that the cause of difficulties was not personali-
ties, but ambiguity in the sphere of action of the National Committee.
He admitted that, so far as French Equatorial Africa and the
Cameroons were concerned, there had been no difficulties, but there
was continual friction amounting to a fundamental misunderstanding
in the sphere of secret action in France.[1] There were also difficulties
about the future of territories liberated from Vichy. M. Pleven said
that the General was preoccupied with the liaison between the Syrian
and Madagascar questions. His idea was that the two agreements
should be concluded together. Mr. Strang said that the Syrian agreement was nearly ready, and could be concluded almost at once.
M. Pleven said that, if we did not wish to conclude the Madagascar
agreement unless agreement on Syria had also been reached, Mr.
Strang would understand why General de Gaulle wanted to link
the two agreements. Sir A. Cadogan commented that the Foreign
Office also wanted to link the agreements to the extent that they
must be sure of a satisfactory Syrian agreement before admitting the
French into Madagascar.

(c)   The Syrian interpretative agreement was communicated officially
to the French with the request that they should confirm their
acceptance. On October 22, however, two French officials brought to

---

[1] I have not dealt with this question.

(a) Z7846/253/17.   (b) Z8023/23/17.   (c) E6099/207/89.

the Foreign Office a new version of the text, containing amendments (a) proposed by the Committee. All the amendments reverted to points originally introduced by General de Gaulle and later omitted in return for British concessions. Mr. Eden therefore decided that we could not go on with the Madagascar negotiations. We had ready a draft agreement for that purpose, and had intended to send it to the French. Until, however, the Committee indicated that they would honour the Syrian agreement negotiated by M. Dejean, Mr. Strang could not give them the draft Madagascar agreement.

M. Pleven told Mr. Strang on October 23 that this decision was (b) very serious; he now felt bound to report to the Foreign Office that, when M. Dejean had informed them that the text of the Syrian agreement could be taken as settled, he had spoken without authority. The French side had assumed that no text would be final until the Committee had received and considered General Catroux's observations on it. M. Dejean's action was the cause of M. Pleven's appointment. M. Dejean, however, had always made it plain that there could be no question of the General actually signing the Syrian agreement before reaching an agreement about Madagascar. M. Pleven then said that the Committee were so anxious to get on with Syria that they had thought of instructing General Catroux to return to London in order that they might persuade him to withdraw his objections.

From this time, however, there was a change for the better. General de Gaulle realised that the British Government meant what they said about Syria, i.e. that they would not give up their overriding interests during the war, and that they were not attempting to supplant the French in the Levant. The French Committee also worked for an agreement, and, above all, they and General de Gaulle were afraid of losing the opportunity to secure the administration of Madagascar. On the British side the Prime Minister sent (c) a friendly personal message to General de Gaulle. The Prime Minister and Mr. Eden also wanted, in view of the approach of the North African operation, to give the French a public promise of their future position in Madagascar. Mr. Eden therefore informed (d) General de Gaulle on November 6, the day after the surrender of the Vichy Governor-General, that we were willing to continue negotiations about Madagascar, and, if General de Gaulle wished, to issue immediately a public statement saying that discussions were taking place, and that General Legentilhomme had been chosen by the French as High Commissioner for Madagascar and would shortly go there. General de Gaulle replied that he would rather defer a public statement until negotiations were complete. He agreed to an

---

(a) E6230/207/89. (b) Z8025/23/17. (c) Z8061, 8578/23/17. (d) Z8539/23/17.

earlier announcement when the Prime Minister and Mr. Eden on
November 8 told him of the African landings and explained why it
had been necessary to accept the view of the United States Government that the expedition should be regarded primarily as an
American affair, and that the Fighting French should not take part
in it.[1]

(a)   Meanwhile the French were considering the draft of the interpretative formula for Syria. After some discussion M. Helleu, as
head of the French delegation to the proposed London Committee,
put forward a counter-draft on November 5. A week later he was
informed that we could not accept the new document.[2] The Foreign
Office preferred to abandon the attempt to negotiate an interpretative agreement, and fall back on the letters exchanged between
(b)   the Foreign Office and M. Dejean on October 5 and 8. In a letter
(c)   of November 26, the French National Committee agreed to this
suggestion.

(d)   On November 27 M. Helleu brought to the Foreign Office a
letter agreeing in principle to the holding of elections. He explained
that the Fighting French would like to have them as soon as possible
after the announcement, i.e. even before the spring. He urged that
the decision in principle to hold elections should not be made public
until after General Catroux's return.[3] He added that, in view of the
change in the military situation, it was no longer necessary to take
the advice of the proposed military committee.

(e)   Sir M. Peterson had two long conversations with General Catroux
on December 1 and 3. General Catroux thought that the elections
would need strict control in order 'that pro-Axis elements might not
be returned to power'. He said that the effect on the Levantine
politicians of the announcement of elections was that of a basket of
crabs, all turning and twisting over one another in order to reach

---

[1] See above, Vol. II, pp. 389–90.

(f)   [2] There were five main changes:

(1). Words had been added to the effect that the French National Committee
continued to assume mandatory obligations in the name of France.

(2). The omission of the statement that the British Government had a legitimate
interest in the evolution of the independence of the Levant States.

(3). There was no recognition that the Middle East should be treated as a whole in
military, economic and other affairs.

(4). The French committed themselves only to paying the greatest attention to requests
submitted 'in correlation with the necessary help brought by us to the Levant
States in the interests of the war'. The Foreign Office were afraid that this wording
might exclude us, for example, from taking an interest in the extension of irrigation
works in the Levant States.

(5). The reference to the possibility of mixed commissions in the Middle East had
been omitted.

[3] General Catroux had come to London and was at this time intending to go to the
United States with General de Gaulle. See also Vol. II, Chapter XXX, section (v).

(a) E6471/207/89. (b) E5935, 5955/207/89. (c) E7044/207/89. (d) E7044/207/89.
(e) E7114/207/89. (f) E6471/207/89.

for a place of profit. General Catroux seemed pleased when he heard that the Foreign Office were considering the simplification of British representation in the Levant States.[1] He said that he would be very glad to be able to deal directly about military matters with our military representatives. He wanted to be able to send for a British military representative, but this was difficult when the representative was also the Minister.

On December 21 Sir E. Spears had a long conversation with (a) General Catroux in Beirut. General Catroux said that before leaving for the United States he proposed to issue a proclamation abrogating the decrees of 1939 whereby the Syrian and Lebanese constitutions had been suspended.[2] On the same day the two Presidents would announce that elections would shortly be held. The statutory periods for election campaigns would be observed, although they would not follow immediately upon these proclamations. Sir E. Spears and General Catroux agreed on a date for elections during the first fortnight of March. General Catroux did not object to the appointment of interim Governments, each composed of three Ministers assisted by officials.

On December 24 Sir E. Spears was informed that M. Helleu[3] (b) was leaving London immediately in order to meet General Catroux in Beirut. M. Helleu had stated that the General would make an announcement about elections before his departure. If he failed to do so, M. Helleu undertook to make the announcement in accordance with the arrangement with the British Government. The French thought that the elections should be held as soon as possible after the announcement.

On December 25 General Catroux went to the United States. (c) Sir E. Spears reported that the General's stay in Damascus, during which he was to have arranged for an interim Syrian Government, had produced no result beyond the resignation of the Syrian Prime Minister. The question of Government changes in the Lebanon had not even been discussed tentatively. General Catroux had spoken of returning in about three weeks; he did not suggest that M. Helleu during his absence should deal with the question of elections. He said that a slight delay was unimportant now that the Germans seemed no longer to be in a position to complicate matters later in

---

[1] Sir M. Peterson subsequently expressed the hope that no action would be taken to (d) reorganise the Spears Mission until the French had made good their promise to announce elections.

[2] See above, p. 212, note 2.

[3] M. Helleu was acting as Délégué-Général in General Catroux's absence. In June 1943 M. Helleu succeeded General Catroux as Délégué-Général.

(a) E7507/207/89. (b) E7527/207/89; E7508/207/89. (c) E7528/207/89. (d) E7550/207/89.

the spring. Sir E. Spears hoped that the French National Committee would instruct M. Helleu to announce elections.

On December 29 Sir M. Peterson asked the French delegation on the London Committee if they had any news of M. Helleu's arrival. They replied that M. Helleu had arrived and intended to make an announcement about elections. No announcement, however, was made about elections during General Catroux's absence in the
(a) United States. At the end of the year the French had still not taken steps to carry out their promises.

(a) E7517/207/89.

CHAPTER LIV

Syria and the Lebanon in 1943

(i)

The question of elections in Syria and the Lebanon: Sir E. Spears's complaints: the Mokaddam case (January–June 1943).

OR the greater part of 1943, and until French action provoked a serious crisis with the Lebanese, the course of events in the Levant was less troublesome than in the previous year. The Allied occupation of North Africa, the final defeat of the German-Italian attack in Egypt and the Russian victories on the south-eastern front had a calming effect on the population—and the politicians—of Syria and the Lebanon. A German invasion of the Levant was now hardly possible, and, except as a link in Allied communications, the area had lost most of its military importance. On the Allied side, General de Gaulle was occupied for the first half of the year with the relations between himself and General Giraud and the reconstruction of the French National Committee on a wider basis.[1]

Nevertheless during this time of comparative calm the Foreign Office were concerned with the question of elections and also with the relationship between the local French and British authorities in Syria and the Levant generally. This latter question, in the Foreign Office view, continued to be unnecessarily difficult owing to the attitude of Sir E. Spears. The Foreign Office realised that Sir E. Spears had a thankless and often exasperating task; they thought, however, that, although the responsibility was not wholly on his side, he had set the French authorities against him, and—a more serious consideration—had caused them to suspect British motives, and to disbelieve the sincerity of the repeated statements by the British Government that they had no intention of supplanting French influence in the Levant. There is indeed little doubt that, if the Prime Minister had not been so firm a supporter of Sir E. Spears, the Foreign Office would have secured a change in the direction of the British Mission.

At the beginning of 1943 the French had not yet announced a date for the elections. They had promised the British Government twice in writing and many times verbally that this announcement

---

[1] See above, Vol. II, Chapter XXI.

would be made before the end of 1942. In January 1943 the attitude of M. Pleven and the French National Committee was that they intended to make the announcement, but wanted to see General Catroux again before they did so. The Foreign Office were critical of this attitude, since General Catroux had only to announce the repeal of the measures of 1939 suspending the constitution and the Syrian and Lebanese Governments would then announce forthcoming elections. M. Helleu had undertaken to make an announcement if General Catroux failed to do so before leaving.[1] Sir E. Spears had reported that General Catroux took the view that elections were now less urgent because the Axis menace had receded. The Fighting French, however, had argued earlier that elections could not be held because the Axis menace was so near.

(a)   Sir M. Peterson complained to General Catroux in London on January 12 of his failure to announce elections before the end of 1942. General Catroux said that the short period which he had spent in the Levant between his two visits to London had been interrupted by Moslem holidays. He had also found it necessary to allow time to calm people down, since Sir E. Spears, contrary to the instructions which General Catroux knew he had received, had told Syrian politicians of the arrangements made between the Fighting French and the British Government. The politicians had then rushed to General Catroux in alarm for their positions. General Catroux promised that elections would be announced within a few days of his return to Syria. He hoped to form a provisional government of officials in order to hold elections in mid-March.

(b)   The Minister of State saw General Catroux[2] in Cairo on February 17, and asked his views on procedure regarding elections. Mr. Casey recommended that the Syrian and Lebanese Governments should themselves make the announcement about them. General Catroux said that he wished to consult the local notables before forming a final opinion. His provisional view was that, in order to avoid the subsequent accusation that the elections were 'rigged' by the Allies, interim governments should be nominated not by the French, but

---

(c)   [1] On January 24, 1943, the French National Committee issued a communiqué in general terms that the development of the military situation permitted a return to a constitutional régime in Syria and the Lebanon, and that they had given instructions to the Délégué-Général to put into effect the necessary arrangements after consultation with the local authorities and 'principal local political personalities'. Sir E. Spears pointed out to M. Helleu that, if General Catroux did not come back soon, and implement this general communiqué with a definite announcement of dates, the effect would be lost. M. Helleu agreed and said that he was asking for instructions to issue the announcement himself if General Catroux's return were delayed.
    [2] General Catroux was on his way back to Syria.

    (a) E273/27/89. (b) E1048/27/89. (c) E406, 511/67/89.

by the existing Syrian and Lebanese authorities as their last act before dissolution.[1]

Meanwhile Sir E. Spears complained to the Prime Minister and (a) to Mr. Eden about the difficulties of his position and, in particular, the fact that the French National Committee were able to bring up in London any proposal which the French in the Levant wanted to support or oppose. Hence the National Committee could make personal representations, while he could only telegraph, and the local Governments who were often vitally concerned were not heard at all.

Sir E. Spears also put his case to Sir A. Cadogan[2] in Cairo at the end of January. Sir A. Cadogan said that the trouble arose because Sir E. Spears was accredited to two Governments who were under a sort of mandatory control by authorities with headquarters in London. Nothing could stop the Fighting French authorities in Beirut from communicating with their headquarters in London; the Foreign Office could not refuse to receive any communications from the latter about the Levant States. Sir A. Cadogan saw no remedy for this, and Sir E. Spears could not suggest one. Sir A. Cadogan said that he would warn the authorities in London to be on their guard against the misuse of these channels.

Sir A. Cadogan reported to Mr. Eden the view of Sir E. Spears (and of Mr. Casey) that it would be difficult for them to settle questions regarding the Levant if the French appealed to the Committee in London. Sir A. Cadogan said, however, that there had been practically no appeals, and that the Committee would not receive frivolous appeals or take up cases unless they were satisfied that an attempt had been made to settle them locally and that a settlement had proved impossible. On February 19 Mr. Eden wrote to Sir E. Spears to this effect.[3]

On March 6 Mr. Casey forwarded a memorandum sent to him (b) by Sir E. Spears with the request that he should send it on to Mr. Eden with his own comments. Mr. Casey described it as a 'forthright hard-hitting memorandum written under the cumulative stress of eighteen months of frustration'. He thought that Sir E. Spears had left out of account the difficulties in London with the Fighting French as well as such questions as the Madagascar and North

---

[1] The announcements restoring the constitutional régimes, and appointing provisional Governments, were made by General Catroux in the case of the Lebanon on March 18 and in the case of Syria on March 25. The election dates for Syria were announced on June 22 and for the Lebanon on June 26. The Syrian elections were held on July 26 and those in the Lebanon on August 29.

[2] Sir A. Cadogan went with the Prime Minister to the meeting with the President of the Turkish Republic and members of the Turkish Government at Adana on January 30. See above, Chapter L, section (v).

[3] It is clear from the Office minutes that the Foreign Office regarded Sir E. Spears as causing unnecessary trouble.

(a) E928/27/89. (b) E2488/27/89.

African operations. On the whole, however, he regarded the memorandum as a 'not unfair statement of the position as seen by the British representative on the spot'.

Sir E. Spears stated in his memorandum that the French deliberately exploited the Levant States, where their one thought was to maintain and increase their hold. They had thwarted the British authorities at every turn and impeded the task of the military authorities, while attempting to make them appear ineffective in the eyes of the local populations. Sir E. Spears referred to the 'mysterious support' which General Catroux obtained in London, and claimed that owing to this support the French would always have their way. He said that they were playing 'a question of prestige against the war effort', and that they did so successfully because they were backed in London where legal arguments were invoked in favour of their theory and in opposition to the over-riding requirements of the war effort.

The Foreign Office did not acknowledge this memorandum. They felt that much indulgence had been extended to Sir E. Spears and that his representations had received more attention than those of professional diplomats holding posts of at least equal difficulty. Sir A. Cadogan drafted a letter to Mr. Casey from Mr. Eden. This draft stated that Sir E. Spears tended to brood over grievances which were not always very real, and was not very receptive to explanations intended to dispel them. Mr. Eden, however, decided
(a) not to send the letter, since he had received on April 2 another protest from Sir E. Spears about the unhelpful attitude of the Foreign Office to the problems with which he had to deal. Mr. Eden replied: 'You on your side must realise that the prevailing wind, so far as all French are concerned, blows from North Africa and that the handling of Syrian questions here, or even sometimes the leaving of them in abeyance, is dictated by considerations which are quite outside the scope of the Eastern Department.'
(b) On May 11 M. Massigli[1] called at the Foreign Office to complain about the activities of the Spears Mission. He said that Sir E. Spears and his officers were showing great and unnecessary excitement in
(c) view of the approaching elections. In particular, a notable of Tripoli named Rashid Mokaddam had recently been arrested by British military police, apparently on suspicion of possessing hashish, but in reality on suspicion of activities in connexion with an electoral list in his possession. M. Massigli also complained that officers of the Spears Mission were advising people against collaborating with the

---

[1] M. Massigli had joined General de Gaulle in the latter part of 1942, and had succeeded M. Pleven as Commissioner for Foreign Affairs in February 1943.

(a) E2346/27/89.   (b) E2759/27/89.   (c) E2484/27/89; E3632/1639/89.

provisional Governments pending the elections. He added his own opinion that the elections would serve no useful purpose.

The Mokaddam affair developed into a serious dispute during (a) June, and was finally brought before the War Cabinet. Mokaddam, who was regarded by the British authorities as a 'very undesirable character', was accused among other charges of having attempted to suborn British officers in Syria to engage in the drug traffic.[1] The French authorities wanted to secure his release from prison since they believed that he would influence the elections in their favour. The British military commander had reluctantly agreed that Mokaddam should be allowed to leave prison and return to his country house where he would be confined under strict but unostentatious surveillance. The British Chargé d'Affaires on June 26 described the French view—to which this concession had been made—as subordinating Allied co-operation in the war effort to a disreputable electioneering policy. The alternative to concession would have been to try to prolong the local impasse while the matter was fought out between the British Government and the French National Committee. The Chargé d'Affaires reported his view that settlement at that level would have taken some time; meanwhile the French might have challenged the stationing of British military police outside the prison where Mokaddam was detained. This would have meant a choice between physical clashes or unconditional acceptance of a public defeat.

The War Cabinet discussed the question on June 28. There was (b) general support for Mr. Eden's suggestion that he should take the matter up with the Committee of National Liberation at Algiers. We had entered into certain obligations after the Vichy régime in Syria had capitulated, and could not allow these obligations to be disregarded. The War Cabinet asked Mr. Eden to raise the matter with M. Massigli when the facts of the Mokaddam case were known.[2]

On July 7 the Prime Minister saw M. Massigli together with Sir (c) E. Spears and Mr. Casey.[3] The Prime Minister does not seem to

---

[1] The Foreign Office regarded the evidence against Mokaddam on these charges as 'damning', and considered that the French military authorities ought not to have acquitted him on the charge of trafficking in drugs.

[2] The War Cabinet were in a difficult position since they were at this time considering the formal recognition of the reorganised French National Committee. See above, Vol. II, Chapter XXXI, section (vii). They instructed Mr. Eden to discuss the matter in conversation with M. Massigli in such a way as to suggest that questions affecting our relations with French territories would be taken up with the Committee, but that we were not at present giving it formal recognition.

[3] Mr. Casey suggested on May 20 that he should come to England for consultation. The Prime Minister agreed on June 13 with this suggestion. On June 15 Mr. Casey proposed that Sir E. Spears should come with him. They arrived in London on June 24 and left about July 20.

(a) E3800/1639/89. (b) WM(43)89. (c) E4070, 4403/27/89.

have a record of this interview; the only account which the Foreign Office received was a verbal outline on July 8 and a subsequent letter from Sir E. Spears dated July 13.[1] According to Sir E. Spears's record the Prime Minister had said that we wanted nothing out of the war and certainly did not want Syria, and recognized French seniority in the Levant. He repeated several times that the French must allow the same freedom to the Levant as we had allowed to Iraq. The Prime Minister spoke severely to M. Massigli about the Mokaddam case; he said that we had given way locally in order not to create an incident, but he had instructed the British authorities not to give way in future in such cases until he had been consulted. The Prime Minister said that Mr. Casey and Sir E. Spears should prepare a list of their difficulties in the Levant, and send this list as soon as possible to M. Massigli. He repeated many times that the French must stop raising difficulties for His Majesty's Government in the Levant.

(ii)

Sir E. Spears's memorandum of July 5: views of the Prime Minister and the Foreign Office: Mr. Eden's meeting with M. Massigli, July 14, 1943.

(a)   Meanwhile, on July 5, Sir E. Spears had submitted a long memorandum on Anglo-French relations in Syria and the Lebanon.[2] He began by saying that, although we did not intend to substitute ourselves for the French in Syria and the Lebanon,[3] we had, and would continue to have, great interests there. British interests at present were mainly military, but a political interest arose from the guarantee of the Fighting French promise of independence to the States. Furthermore, the Middle East was a great oil-producing area and one of the great air stages of the world. Sir E. Spears claimed that on military and political counts the French had given many serious grounds of complaint. He complained of consistent obstruction by the French. He argued that the French were safe only because they

(b)   [1] A Foreign Office minute dated July 14 reads: 'This is the only record we have of what passed. I think No. 10 should keep us better informed. We are entitled to know when representations of this force are made. So far as I am aware, we were not even told when this interview would take place or what was to be raised (though we did know that the Prime Minister would speak some time to M. Massigli and prepared a note on that).' A subsequent minute says: 'I have always understood that the Prime Minister dislikes making records of this kind of conversation, his attitude being, "I know what passed and that is all that matters".' Sir M. Peterson referred to the fact that the Prime Minister had held this meeting as a 'remarkable state of affairs'.
[2] This memorandum appears to have been drawn up by Sir E. Spears for the Foreign Office. He sent a copy to the Prime Minister. The Prime Minister saw it about July 10, i.e. after his conversation with M. Massigli. Mr. Eden saw the memorandum on July 11.
[3] Mr. Eden underlined this statement.

(a) E3893/27/89.   (b) E4070, 4403/27/89.

were standing in the shadow of British power: 'All know that should they step out of it short shrift would be given them.'[1] Since we were in military occupation of the Levant, we were held responsible by local opinion for French behaviour which was daily more dictatorial. 'The Syrians cannot understand why, having the power to do so, we should not insist that the French keep their promises.'

After more detailed complaints against the French administration Sir E. Spears concluded that the French were in the Levant because British forces had conquered the country and established them there;[2] they derived the wide powers which they exercised from the state of war. The 'privileged and predominant position' conceded by us to the French did not give them the right to negative their promises of independence to the States. The French were exercising rights of censorship, powers of requisitioning, control of the gendarmerie and so on, under a delegation of military power from us; we could withdraw all these prerogatives without violating the Prime Minister's pledge that the French should have a 'privileged and predominant position' in the Levant.[3]

Sir E. Spears submitted that we should forthwith declare: that British good faith was engaged by the Fighting French proclamations of independence, and that a start be made to carry them out; the French should accept British co-operation in the treatment of such matters as supply, financial policy and the exploitation of local resources; they must undertake to meet the wishes of British military authorities in all matters covered by 'territorial command', including the use of the manpower of the States.

Sir E. Spears proposed that if these requests were not met, the powers exercised by the French should be reassumed by the supreme Allied military authority.

The Prime Minister's comments on this memorandum were that (a) he thought it 'a very powerful and able paper' and that he had no idea that the French were behaving so tyranically. He asked Mr. Eden on July 12 to circulate the memorandum to the War Cabinet, and said that the Syrian position should be discussed during the same week and that neither Mr. Casey nor Sir E. Spears should leave the country before the discussion. He also asked for the views of the Foreign Office, and concluded: 'I should think we are probably all in agreement in principle about Syria, though no doubt there will be differences of emphasis.'

The Foreign Office made Sir E. Spears's paper the occasion for a

---

[1] Mr. Eden marked this statement and queried it.
[2] Mr. Eden noted: 'They were there before.'
[3] Mr. Eden noted: 'I should not have said so.'

(a) M466/3, E3893/27/89.

general review of British policy to Syria and the Lebanon. They thought that Sir E. Spears had given a depressing but accurate account of French maladministration and misgovernment in the Levant. French colonial methods were different from British methods, and French administration in the Levant had been open to criticism by British standards since the Great War. The only new features were that the British Government had a certain responsibility, since they had financed the Fighting French and enabled them to return to the Levant. We had guaranteed the French undertaking to give Syria and the Lebanon independence and had to see that that undertaking was carried out. We also could not allow a state of affairs in which the population was made dangerously discontented in an area of military importance.

The Foreign Office had little doubt that the French intended to remain in the Levant, and that the numerous French officials hoped to be able to keep their posts. British insistence on the French granting effective independence to the States was the basis of much French antagonism. Unfortunately, matters went further than this. Although we had promised General de Gaulle that France should have a predominant place among European Powers in the Levant, British subjects in the Middle East had never accepted the idea. Most British officers and many British officials in the Middle East hoped to see the French turned out of Syria. Many hoped that this would facilitate a settlement of the Jewish question, and that an Arab federation could be formed which, as in the case of Egypt, would eventually enter into friendly relations with the British Commonwealth.[1] The French thus thought that the British were playing a double game.

The Foreign Office therefore had to take account of the conviction of the French in Syria and also of General de Gaulle that we intended to get them out of Syria. This fear of 'extrusion' influenced the French attitude to every attempt of the Spears Mission (i) to induce them to give better treatment or better administration to the Syrians and Lebanese, (ii) to prevent undesirable interference on their own part in local affairs or (iii) to insist on British participation in economic schemes they (the French) could not run themselves.

The Foreign Office disagreed with Sir E. Spears's suggestion that, if the French did not meet us on a number of points, we should threaten to withdraw some of their powers. They did not consider that French powers in the Levant were derived from the state of war by delegation of military authority from us, and that we could

---

[1] The Foreign Office pointed out that the resolutions passed on May 10–13 by the Middle East War Council were an authoritative interpretation of this view. See also p. 383.

therefore withdraw them. The use of this argument would produce a major dispute with all Frenchmen of all parties. Any advantages even from a successful issue of such a dispute would not counter-balance the harm done by it in North Africa. The French would feel that we intended to replace them in the Levant. The dispute would cancel the Lyttelton-de Gaulle agreements, and the French would argue that many of the British powers in Syria derived from those agreements and that the residual power was theirs and not ours.

The Foreign Office suggested that Mr. Eden should try to get Syrian questions placed on a new footing. Mr. Eden agreed that the attempt must be made. He thought that a note to the Prime Minister which the Foreign Office had drafted, and which he approved, should contain some reference to the views of British subjects in the Middle East on the French position in Syria.

On July 13 Mr. Eden submitted to the Prime Minister his com- (a) ments on Sir E. Spears's paper. He said that the Foreign Office agreed with the more obvious complaints against the French régime in the Levant States, but that the defective background of the paper invalidated its suggestions on policy. Mr. Eden contested Sir E. Spears's thesis that French powers in the Levant were derived by delegation from us during the continuance of a state of war. We could not treat the French in the Levant as if they were in the position of the Polish divisions in Iraq, i.e. that of refugee Allied troops who happened to occupy a particular section of the Allied front. Most of the validity of Sir E. Spears's arguments disappeared with the recognition that the French held a position in the eastern Mediterranean which we could not ignore unless we intended to limit the post-war role of France, and create a vacuum in the Middle East which might not be easy to fill. Many of Sir E. Spears's diffi-culties arose from this thesis, which had often been contradicted from London, but apparently without effect.

Mr. Eden pointed out that a second major defect in background was the claim that Great Britain had 'great' interests in the Levant. Sir E. Spears had subsequently defined our present interests more correctly as 'in the main military'. Mr. Eden said that British post-war interests were 'confined to the fulfilment of the guarantee of independence, a fulfilment which must inevitably be gradual, and the kind of general solicitude with which the predominant power in the Arab world must necessarily follow developments in any part of that world'.

Mr. Eden went on to point out as a third failure in background the exaggerated weight which the paper laid on the character and national consciousness of the Syrians and Lebanese. He referred to

---

(a) PM/43/226, E3893/27/89.

Sir E. Spears's statement that if the French emerged from the 'shadow of our power', their 'shrift' would be short. Mr. Eden asked who would make it so? Even Vichy had carried on in the Levant without undue difficulty for a year after the fall of France and without the presence of Axis forces.

Mr. Eden agreed on the need to enforce our claims based on military security in a region subject to the British High Command. He agreed in condemning French abuses and excesses, and in requiring French co-operation in matters of supply, finance and exploitation of local resources in the war interest. There was, however, a right and a wrong way of pursuing this policy. The right way was to demand French co-operation with us rather than to seek to impose our own 'partnership' upon the French. 'We do not seek equal status with the French nor partnership in Syria. To pretend we do is to fortify French suspicions of our intentions.' Mr. Eden said that these suspicions were increased by the fact, of which the French must be aware, that many British officers and officials in the Middle East wished to see the French leave the Levant States altogether, although this wish was contrary to our policy. We were entitled to claim that the forthcoming elections constituted a certain fulfilment of the guarantee of independence; the complete fulfilment of that guarantee before the end of the war was not practicable.

Finally, Mr. Eden said that lack of progress over many of the issues of which Sir E. Spears complained had been due not solely to French recalcitrance but to other causes, including the continued absences and journeyings of prominent Frenchmen, the difficulties of adjusting British relations in the Levant to the rapid changes of policy towards the Fighting French movement as a whole, and the insistence of our local authorities in the Middle East that difficult issues should be left for local settlement, and that the French should not be encouraged to raise such questions in London.

Mr. Eden suggested that he should discuss the whole matter of British policy with Mr. Casey and Sir E. Spears and later with M. Massigli rather than bring it before the War Cabinet. Mr. Churchill, (a) in a minute of July 15, agreed with this suggestion. He added: 'I am quite clear that we are being knocked about unduly and unfairly by the French and that a stiffer line should be taken against them in Syria. I should like to feel that our officers there will be supported against insolent ill-usage by the French, and that our Commander-in-Chief will not have to make ignominious compromises when he has overwhelming force at his disposal.' Mr. Churchill thought that the French position in Syria must henceforward be on the same footing as the British position in Iraq, and that British pledges to the Syrians and Lebanese must be made good.

Meanwhile arrangements were made for a meeting with M. (a) Massigli at the Foreign Office. The Foreign Office suggested a number of questions for discussion. The first main question was the supreme responsibility of the British High Command in matters of security. The Foreign Office asked that French authorities in the Levant should be told to obey the Army Commander when the safety of his forces and public security were affected. The second question was that of Mokaddam. We took the view that a man who had done things affecting military discipline and security should be punished. If he were allowed to stand for election to the Lebanese Chamber, the moral would be drawn that such crimes could be committed with impunity. The Foreign Office proposed that Mokaddam should be handed over to the military authorities for deportation.

The third main question was that of the freedom of the elections. Persons undesirable on security grounds should not be allowed to stand for election, but with this proviso the Syrians and Lebanese should be free to elect whom they chose. Strict instructions should be sent to all French officials to end intimidation and political arrests. The election of representative Chambers in Syria and the Lebanon was essential to carry out the Franco-British guarantee of independence. In the Lebanon Dr. Tabut[1] had altered the system of election by allotting many more seats to the Christian community, and had thereby exasperated the Moslems. The latter were talking of boycotting the elections and of territorial alterations. We hoped that M. Massigli would take action in the interests of tranquillity in the Arab world and the survival of the Lebanon as a state.

The meeting with M. Massigli was held on July 14.[2] Mr. Eden (b) began by referring to 'obvious stresses and strains' between the British and French in the Levant. The position was getting worse, and we should once again make British policy clear. We had no territorial ambitions as a result of the war, and no desire to undermine or challenge the French position, or to succeed to their position of predominance in the Levant. At Mr. Eden's request, Sir M. Peterson explained our more immediate objectives, i.e. the preservation of military security and the avoidance of any implication that the guarantee of independence to the Levant States would not be carried out.

---

[1] Dr. Tabut had been appointed President of the Lebanese Republic by General Catroux in March 1943.

[2] Mr. Casey, Sir E. Spears, Sir A. Cadogan and M. Viénot were also present. The minutes of this meeting were agreed with M. Massigli.

(a) E4403/27/89. (b) E4423/27/89.

M. Massigli accepted the British assurances and gave the most positive assurance on the French side that independence would be given to Syria and the Lebanon. He agreed that the situation must be improved. The elections were to be held shortly and consideration would then have to be given to the further implementation of the promise of independence, possibly on the lines followed in Iraq, or by a return to something like the 1936 treaties.[1] The problem was complicated by the fact that Syrian and Lebanese officials had little experience of government, especially in economic questions. M. Massigli referred to the list of questions forwarded to him for discussion.[2] He said that some of the matters were new to him. He had as yet no reply from Beirut to his enquiries regarding the Mokaddam case. The view (possibly incorrect) in Beirut that it was a political matter had envenomed the question.

Mr. Eden then asked Mr. Casey to state our causes for serious complaint. Mr. Casey said that we had repeatedly explained that we had no intention of establishing British predominance in the Levant, but we could not avoid the impression that the French had never believed our statements. The result of this atmosphere of distrust and lack of frank and friendly co-operation was that he had to spend almost more time over relations with the French than over all other problems. He had had to discourage the Commander-in-Chief from moving divisions into Syria because, owing to the lack of appreciation of the serious economic position and of the necessary measures to meet inflation, he had feared that their presence would unbalance the local economy. French officials did not seem to understand the needs of military security. After discussing at some length the economic and financial situation in the Levant, the meeting went on to consider security. M. Massigli asked for criticisms of French policy. Sir E. Spears said that the wishes of the Army regarding security should come first. M. Massigli said that the French were responsible for general security, of which frontier security was a part. He asked whether the British authorities were not putting forward under the heading of military security requests which the French could not accept under this heading. Military authorities, whether French or British, had a tendency to enlarge the scope of 'military necessity'; military authorities always aimed at ideal security, often without taking account of political conditions. M. Massigli said that he could not accept the principle that everything the Army wished would be granted, but he agreed that careful account should be taken of

---

[1] See above, p. 212, note 2.
[2] The list included questions referring to the behaviour of the *Gardes Mobiles* (troops under the command of French officers, but paid by the British Government).

Army needs. He asked for a short note of the cases in which Army requests on important questions had been refused.

The meeting, after dealing with other questions, discussed the Mokaddam case. Mr. Eden said that Mokaddam should not go unpunished after he had suborned British troops. Sir E. Spears suggested that Mokaddam should be deported, and claimed that he had become a protégé of the *délégué adjoint* at Tripoli for the purpose of the elections, in spite of statements to the contrary by General Catroux and M. Helleu. M. Helleu had even said that, if Mokaddam were arrested, he might have to arrest also his electoral opponent. M. Massigli promised to try and arrange a satisfactory solution.

Mr. Eden then left the meeting and Mr. Casey took the chair. He explained the problem of the *Intérêts Communs*. He said that control of its own revenues was an elementary form of independence for a State. Sir E. Spears referred to General Catroux's statement[1] to Mr. Casey that he was proposing to keep the *Intérêts Communs* as a bargaining counter in subsequent negotiations. He hoped that this argument would be dropped. M. Massigli doubted the capacity of the Syrian and Lebanese Governments to administer the funds properly. Sir E. Spears pointed out that these Governments now disposed of the major portion of their funds and had the advantage of French advisers in doing so. The meeting agreed with the view of M. Viénot that the question should be settled with the new Governments after the elections.

Mr. Casey said that General Catroux had promised over a year ago to inform Sir E. Spears in advance of important decrees which he proposed to issue. In fact the British authorities were practically never informed in advance. M. Massigli said that this was an example of a divergence of view about the exact implication of the phrase 'military security'. He felt that the question could be settled by closer personal relations and promised to discuss it with M. Helleu.

On July 19 M. Massigli came to see Mr. Eden before his return (a) to Algiers. He said that he had sent a recommendation to the Committee of National Liberation regarding Mokaddam.[2] Mr. Eden and M. Massigli agreed that an effort should be made to settle all outstanding financial problems while Mr. Casey and Sir E. Spears were in Algiers. Mr. Eden spoke about the need for a 'new deal' in the French attitude to the British in Syria. There were too many

---

[1] General Catroux had made this statement in his interview with Mr. Casey on February 17. See above, p. 256.

[2] The French agreed on August 9 to hand Mokaddam over to the British military authorities. They did so on September 16 (after the elections). The British authorities then deported him to Cyprus.

(a) E4241/27/89; Z8092/6504/69.

people causing unnecessary difficulties for the British authorities; M. Massigli hinted that there were faults on both sides. He intended, however, to do all he could to see that Anglo-French relations in Syria as elsewhere should work smoothly.

(iii)

The constitutional crisis in the Lebanon: arrest of the President of the Lebanese Republic and other Ministers, and dissolution of the Chamber on November 11: British demands of November 13: meeting between General Catroux and Mr. Casey on November 15: instructions to Mr. Casey of November 17 (November 11–18, 1943).

In spite of the friendly discussions with M. Massigli there was little improvement in the local relations between the British and French authorities in Syria and the Lebanon. On September 13 (a) M. Viénot complained to the Foreign Office of Sir E. Spears's interference in the elections. Sir M. Peterson, however, answered that the Foreign Office had felt uneasy at the extent of French interference.[1] There had been many reports that the French in the Levant States were trying to suppress public references to Arab unity. In our view the French should not regard their own retention of a modified status in the Levant as a barrier to the inclusion of the States in an Arab federation. We regarded the creation of a federation as a matter for the Arabs themselves, but did not want them to think that the French were bound to oppose it. M. Viénot professed to agree with this view.

The elections in Syria had given an overwhelming victory to the nationalists; their leader, Shukri Quwatli, was elected President of the Republic by the Chamber and a nationalist administration was formed with Saadullah Jabri as Prime Minister. In the Lebanon, where the French had expected a majority in their favour, the nationalists also won a victory. M. Khoury was elected President; Riadh es Solh, a Moslem, became Prime Minister and M. Chamoun, a Christian, Minister of the Interior.

General Catroux's proclamation in 1941 had laid down that the sovereign and independent status of Syria and the Lebanon would

---

[1] The Foreign Office asked Sir E. Spears for material to rebut M. Viénot's charges. On November 6 Sir M. Peterson gave M. Viénot an *aide-mémoire* in which these charges were answered in detail. The *aide-mémoire* pointed out that Sir E. Spears had warned M. Helleu, in view of the number of cases of serious interference by French officials (contrary to M. Helleu's orders) that the British Government were not committed to the recognition of a Chamber and Government brought into being as a result of the elections.

(a) E5525/27/89.

be guaranteed by treaties which would also define their relations with France. It was clear at the time that the French would surrender as few as possible of their previous rights and privileges, while the Syrians and Lebanese would wish to secure complete independence. After the nationalist victory in the elections, the French began to consider the terms of the treaties envisaged in the declaration; the two States, on the other hand, decided to ensure by unilateral action the constitutional changes necessary to complete their sovereignty. The French were unwilling to make further concessions before they had secured their treaties; the Levant States were unwilling to agree to treaties until they had secured all the attributes of sovereign States. They intended to secure these attributes at once, since their negotiating position would be much weaker after the re-emergence of France as a great Power. The position was complicated by the fact that the French National Committee was not a Government, and that neither the British nor the United States Governments would recognise it as competent to conclude treaties in the name of France.[1]

The two Levant Governments, after mutual consultation, decided to put their demands to the French. The Lebanese Prime Minister took the initiative in unilateral action by declaring, at the opening of the newly elected Lebanese Chamber early in October, that his Government intended to remove from the constitution the right of non-Lebanese authorities to take part in the administration. They proposed to review other conventions and regulations limiting Lebanese sovereignty and to recognise Arabic as the official language of the country.

The Foreign Office disapproved of this Lebanese announcement (a) on the ground that it ignored the French position in the Levant and that it was a mistake of the Prime Minister to commit his Government publicly to the abolition of the rights and privileges of France without even holding preliminary discussions with the French. The Foreign Office pointed out that the use of French as well as Arabic as an official language was laid down in the mandate, and that the

---

[1] Mr. Lascelles, on behalf of General Spears, mentioned these facts (which were indeed (b) common knowledge) to the Syrian President on August 23. The French National Committee took the view that this statement contributed to the refusal of the Lebanese Government to consider a treaty, and to their decision to make immediate constitutional changes. The French Committee held that, if they were competent to grant independence to the two States, they must also be competent to conclude a treaty making the grant of independence a reality. The Foreign Office proposed to the State Department early in (c) September 1943, that the French should make provisional arrangements with the two States, and defer their ratification until after the war. The State Department, as before, was unable to agree that the French should continue to hold a 'pre-eminent and privileged position', but they accepted the British proposal for provisional treaties, on condition that the rights and interests of the local populations and of the United States were safeguarded.

(a) E6451/27/89.   (b) E5070/27/89.   (c) E4520, 5088, 5196, 5329/27/89; E6791, 6875/12/89.

Lebanese would have been wiser to have asked for the employment of Lebanese assistants to the higher French officials, for example, in the administration of the *Intérêts Communs*.[1]

(a)   On October 22 M. Helleu informed the Lebanese President that the mandate was still in existence since no competent body had ended it. The French National Committee could not accept the proposed constitutional amendments, since they would prejudice the mandatory position of France, but they would examine with the Lebanese Government in a friendly manner arrangements ('aménagements') for an advance to independence. In spite of this

(b) warning, the Lebanese Prime Minister informed M. Helleu that he would continue with the revision of the constitution. On November 5

(c) M. Helleu issued a communiqué to the Lebanese press on the lines of his letter of October 22. This was contradicted by a Lebanese

(d) communiqué. M. Helleu, who had gone to Algiers and was on his way back, sent a message to say that he had certain favourable

(e) proposals to make, and asked the Lebanese to await his return. The Foreign Office learnt later that he was prepared to negotiate on the

(f) basis of the 1936 treaty. The Lebanese Parliament would not wait, and on November 9 passed a bill making the constitutional changes. The French authorities suppressed the report of the debate and the result of the voting.

(g)   Meanwhile, on November 3, Mr. Casey had met the Syrian Prime Minister and the Minister for Foreign Affairs. He advised them not to act in haste, since the French had been surprised and disappointed by the results of the elections. The Syrian Prime Minister did not want to delay, but the Minister for Foreign Affairs agreed to postpone action for two or three months. The two Ministers repeated that they would not conclude a treaty with the French authorities then in office, and asked for British support. They said that the French insisted that they would concede none of the Syrian demands until the Syrians had signed a treaty.

The Ministers asked what was the British attitude to the Middle East. Mr. Casey said that we had no territorial or political ambitions but had great interests there, including oil and communications. Hence we wanted an Arab world economically and politically contented; Syria was a part of this Arab world. The Prime Minister and Minister for Foreign Affairs said that there could be no Syrian objection to Mr. Casey's statements, and that they would gladly concede anything needed for our war effort and the security of our

(h)   [1] These views were put in a telegram to Sir E. Spears. He answered by rejecting the Foreign Office arguments. The Foreign Office therefore doubted whether he had been very active in bringing their views to the notice of the Lebanese politicians.

(a) E6459/27/89. (b) E6512, 6653/27/89. (c) E6710/27/89. (d) E6733, 6766/27/89. (e) E6902/27/89. (f) E6811/27/89. (g) E7271/27/89. (h) E6948/27/89.

troops. Mr. Casey reported that their attitude was most reasonable towards the British but unyielding towards the French. He thought it clear that the Syrians wanted to be associated with Great Britain and not France.[1]

The mood of the Lebanese Government and reports of increasing (a) tension led the Foreign Office to consider whether British intervention would be necessary to prevent disturbances. The Middle East Defence Committee, at a meeting on November 7 attended by Mr. (b) Eden,[2] agreed that British troops should not be used to keep order. The Foreign Office, however, told Mr. Casey that we could not (c) refrain from interference if it were necessary to preserve order. We had said constantly that our main objectives in the Levant were the maintenance of order, for reasons of military security, and the implementation of the promises of independence made to the two States. We should inform the French, and the Lebanese and Syrian Governments, that, if British forces had to intervene and if the French Committee and the Lebanese Government did not arrange a *modus vivendi* for the duration of the war, we should summon an immediate conference to which the French, Lebanese, Syrians and Americans would be invited. This conference would draw up the terms of a provisional arrangement to be concluded between the Levant States and the French after the war. These terms would be respected by both sides as long as the war lasted, and would permit the restoration of the parliamentary régime, if the French had interrupted it.

On the night of November 10–11 M. Helleu dined with Sir E. (d) Spears and gave his word that nothing would be done which would be liable to disturb public order. Nonetheless on the morning of November 11 at 4 a.m. the President of the Lebanese Republic and all the members of the Cabinet, except three who could not be found, were arrested by the *Sûreté* agents using French marines, including Senegalese. Sir E. Spears reported that the President was arrested in the presence of his sick wife. The house of the Prime Minister was invaded, and he was dragged out of bed. In accordance with a decree broadcast at 8 a.m. M. Helleu dissolved the Chamber and appointed M. Emile Edde[3] as Head of the State and Head of the Government. French forces surrounded the Chamber, where there were 400 deputies. Three demonstrators were wounded and one death was reported.

---

[1] A Foreign Office minute on this conversation read: 'The same Syrian Ministers tell other people that they quite definitely don't want to get the French replaced by us in any way.'

[2] Mr. Eden was on his way home from the Foreign Ministers' conference in Moscow.

[3] A former President, and regarded generally as subservient to the French.

(a) E6777/27/89. (b) E6841/27/89. (c) E6848/27/89. (d) E6848/27/89.

(a)   On November 11 the Maronite Archbishop of Beirut, speaking by authorisation of all the Christian communities, called on Sir E. Spears and demanded British military intervention in the name of Lebanese independence, which the Allies had guaranteed. The Archbishop had already protested to M. Helleu, who had refused to listen. The reaction of the other Arab States was also very strong. The Egyptian, Iraqi and Transjordan Governments protested to the British Government and the French Committee. King Ibn Saud sent telegrams of protest to the Prime Minister, President Roosevelt and General de Gaulle. There were demonstrations of protest in Cairo and Alexandria, but Nuri Pasha and King Ibn Saud advised moderation both in Iraq and in Syria and the Lebanon. Nuri Pasha, however, and King Farouk warned Sir K. Cornwallis and Mr. Shone that British prestige in the Middle East would be seriously damaged if we did not take measures to restore the Lebanese Government. Sir K. Cornwallis and Mr. Casey agreed with this warning, and pointed out that we were regarded as ultimately responsible for what happened in the Levant States. Sir E. Spears telegraphed on November 11 that, on Mr. Casey's instructions, he was making a formal protest to M. Helleu at 'action taken without consultation with us which is calculated to impede the war effort'.

The Foreign Office asked Mr. Macmillan to request[1] the immediate withdrawal of M. Helleu. On November 12, after hearing that the situation was growing worse, they sent a stronger telegram to the effect that the French must replace M. Helleu at once and release the arrested President and Ministers; otherwise we should have to dissociate ourselves from the French action.[2]

(b)   On November 12 the War Cabinet considered the situation. Mr. Eden told them of his instructions to Mr. Macmillan, and said that the French had acted without consulting us. Such information as they had given us before the event had been deliberately false. The War Cabinet considered whether we should add to our demands a request for the reinstatement of the Lebanese President and Government in order to restore the position existing before the French had acted by force. They thought, however, that we should weaken our position if we added a further demand—i.e. for reinstatement—before we had received an answer to the requests which we had already made.

(c)

[1] Mr. Eden altered this word in the draft from 'requesting' to 'urging'.
[2] Mr. Macmillan at this time was in Italy. Mr. Makins carried out the instructions on November 12. Mr. Eden directed that the Russians should be kept informed of the crisis. Instructions were sent in this sense to Moscow on November 12; the Foreign Office did not, however, want to encourage Soviet intervention. In fact the Soviet Government did not express any views on the matter.

(a) E6848/27/89.   (b) WM(43)153. E6946/27/89.   (c) E6915/27/89.

If the French refused our demands, we could threaten to withdraw our recognition of the French National Committee, and use British troops to restore order and secure communications and vital military interests in the Lebanon. The War Cabinet took the view that we should first make it clear that we would no longer recognise the French Committee unless they met our demands. We should try to avoid using British troops, but we might have to intervene. The War Cabinet agreed to a draft telegram from the Prime Minister to President Roosevelt informing him of the situation and of our proposed policy.

The War Cabinet also thought that Mr. Macmillan might warn the French more strongly about the consequences of failure to comply with our demands; he should also find out how far members of the French Committee had supported M. Helleu's action, and try to get those who had not agreed with it to support the acceptance of our demands. If the Committee refused to comply, we should repeat the demands and include a further request for the reinstatement of the Lebanese Government and the ejection of M. Edde.

We should tell Mr. Casey that for the present British troops should not be used.

The Prime Minister's message (of November 13) to President (a) Roosevelt about the crisis spoke of the 'lamentable outrages' committed by the French. He added: 'There is no doubt in my mind that this is a foretaste of what de Gaulle's leadership of France means.' The situation would be grave throughout the Middle East and the Arab world, and everywhere people would say: 'What kind of a France is this which, while itself subjugated by the enemy, seeks to subjugate others?'

Mr. Churchill thought that the British and United States Governments should together take the matter up in the strongest way. The character of the French Committee which they had recognised at the Quebec Conference had already been altered by General de Gaulle's assumption of power. The outrages in the Levant justified the two Governments, with the support of world public opinion, in bringing the issue with General de Gaulle to a head. Mr. Churchill proposed that the two Governments should insist on the liberation and reinstatement of the 'kidnapped Lebanese President and Ministers' and on a meeting of the Assembly as soon as order was restored. If General de Gaulle did not comply at once, we should withdraw recognition from the French National Committee and stop arming French troops in North Africa. The British Embassy in Washington had meanwhile kept the State Department informed (b) of the situation. The State Department had instructed Mr. Murphy

---

(a) T1952/3, No. 504 (Churchill Papers/421; E7116/27/89). (b) E7000/27/89.

to request the restoration of constitutional government in the Lebanon, and to add that unless this were done soon, the United States Government would issue a statement expressing disapproval of the French action.

(a)　　　General de Gaulle and M. Massigli saw Mr. Makins on November 12. General de Gaulle said that the position of the French Committee was based on the mandate, which could not be legally terminated during the war. They had promised independence to the States; in Syria their undertaking had been honoured and in the Lebanon elections had been held. A Government had been elected[1] which had provoked the French National Committee just as they had decided to negotiate on the basis of the 1936 treaty. In the face of this provocation the Committee could only exercise their rights under the mandate.

Mr. Makins said that, whatever the strict legal position, the British Government had continually pointed out to the French Committee that the Levant States must advance to independence as far as possible within the limits imposed by war. British recognition of the position of France in the Levant was based on the assumption that the States would attain independence. Mr. Makins then spoke as instructed by the Foreign Office. General de Gaulle said that he knew the weakness of the French position. If we forced the issue, he would give orders to withdraw all French officials and personnel from the Levant and wait upon events; he would also publish the French case to the world. He asked for the accusation against M. Helleu; Mr. Makins replied that it was one of failure to co-operate. General de Gaulle then complained of the attitude of Sir E. Spears. Finally he said that General Catroux was leaving for the Levant.

General de Gaulle told Mr. Makins on the same day that General Catroux had 'appropriate instructions', and would call on Mr. Casey on his way to Beirut. On November 13 Mr. Makins delivered
(b) a note repeating the British demands—the immediate recall of M. Helleu and the release of the Ministers—and said that British troops might have to intervene. If this intervention took place, and if the French Committee did not promise to concert at once a *modus vivendi* for the duration of the war, the British Government would summon a conference of the French, Lebanese, Syrian and American representatives to draw up a provisional arrangement between the Levant States and the French. Mr. Macmillan[2] saw M. Massigli on

---

[1] It is possible that the report of General de Gaulle's words should read: 'In Syria their undertaking had been honoured. In the Lebanon elections had been held and a Government had been elected,' etc.

[2] Mr. Macmillan returned from Italy on November 13.

(a) E6915/27/89.　(b) E6925/27/89.

the evening of November 13 and asked for a reply to the British note. M. Massigli told him that General Catroux was leaving for the Levant States. General Catroux had plenary powers to deal with the situation, and M. Helleu was thereby, in fact, suspended.

On hearing that General Catroux would call on Mr. Casey on November 14 on his way to Beirut, the Foreign Office instructed (a) Mr. Casey to make clear their expectation that the General would release the politicians immediately. The telegram to Mr. Casey continued: 'We regard what happened as nothing less than a wanton challenge to the interests, security and principles of the United Nations in an area which is still of vital importance in the prosecution of the war.'

On November 13 M. Viénot called on Sir A. Cadogan to say that (b) he did not understand what had happened during the day or two preceding the arrests. He had seen the instructions of the French Committee to M. Helleu; M. Helleu was to explain to the Government that the Committee could not accept their demand for the immediate abolition of the mandate. He was also authorised to inform the Government that the French were ready to ratify the draft treaty of 1936. He complained of the publicity given to it in the British press.

Sir A. Cadogan replied that one aspect of the incident had caused the worst possible impression in the Foreign Office. Sir E. Spears and M. Helleu were together only a few hours before the arrests, but M. Helleu had said nothing about the action which was to follow so soon. On the contrary, he had assured Sir E. Spears that nothing would be done to disturb the peace. Sir A. Cadogan spoke of 'lack of co-operation between two Allies'. He mentioned the British endorsement of the French guarantee of independence, the presence of British troops in a country now exposed to disorder, and our vital concern in other Arab countries to which disorder might spread. He hoped that General Catroux's arrival at Beirut might improve matters. On a memorandum discussing the situation Sir A. Cadogan subsequently wrote: 'Nothing can, of course, justify the *manner* of (c) the French reaction, which could not have been more stupid or deplorable.'

On November 15 the War Cabinet again considered the position (d) in the Lebanon. Sir A. Cadogan, who was present at the meeting, said that there was no further information about General Catroux's instructions since Mr. Makins's report that General Catroux was leaving for the Levant with 'appropriate instructions'. Although the French were trying to discount the gravity of the situation, there had been considerable disorder and loss of life. Mr. Casey had

---

(a) E6915/27/89. (b) E6954/27/89. (c) E7183/27/89. (d) WM(43)154; E6946/27/89.

reported from Beirut on November 14 that the French would play for time; we could not afford to let them do so, since tension was
(a) increasing. He recommended that, unless the French authority complied with our demands by the morning of Wednesday, November 17, we should insist on their agreeing to our troops patrolling the larger towns.

The Foreign Office had prepared a draft reply to Mr. Casey's telegram. They suggested that if we had to take action, we could not confine it to patrolling the larger towns. If the French rejected our demands, we should have to dissociate ourselves publicly from them and impose British martial law. The War Cabinet agreed with this view. Sir A. Cadogan said that the programme which the Foreign Office had in mind was to wait another twenty-four hours, and then if no reply were received, ask for compliance with our demands within a further twenty-four or forty-eight hours. The War Cabinet considered that they should retain for themselves authority to take a decision. A telegram was therefore sent to Mr. Casey on the lines of the Foreign Office draft.

(b)   Meanwhile, at 9.30 a.m. on November 15, Mr. Casey had met General Catroux. Mr. Casey said that the future of Anglo-French relations was involved, and that the interests of military security made it impossible to allow any disorder. Mr. Casey spoke of his week-end visit to Beirut, and pointed out that there was a grave risk of general disorder in the Lebanon unless urgent steps were taken. The British Government expected the recall of M. Helleu and the release of the Lebanese President and Ministers.

General Catroux asked that the controversy should be treated as one between France and the Lebanon, and not as one between France and Great Britain. He said that a grave factor in the situation was the general belief that Great Britain intended to undermine French authority in the Levant. The belief was largely attributable to the number of British officers engaged on political duties and in the wheat collection scheme. Mr. Casey did not admit the validity of these French complaints; even if there were any justification for them, they would not excuse M. Helleu's action.

General Catroux said that political initiative in the Levant must rest with the French and especially with himself. Any appearance of British political intervention was to be avoided. Unless France was left to handle the situation, she would prefer to withdraw her officials and troops, and place her case before the world for an impartial judgment. He repeated the arguments about the continued existence of the mandate and French rights. Mr. Casey said that public opinion in the world and particularly in the Lebanon would

(a) E6963/27/89. (b) E6915, 7010. 7387/27/89.

be unimpressed with legal niceties. The Lebanese would remember only that, whereas independence had been promised to them, freely elected members of their Government had been imprisoned.

General Catroux argued that British recognition of independence for the Levant States had been accorded within the terms of his own declaration, which linked up the grant of independence with the conclusion of treaties between the Levant States and France.[1] He said that M. Helleu had acted on his own initiative in making the arrests. M. Helleu had had instructions to inform the Lebanese Government that they had no right to reform the constitution; nonetheless they had passed constitutional amendments. Thereupon M. Helleu made the arrests, and the French National Committee knew of them only later. The Committee had then decided to send General Catroux to the Lebanon with full powers; General Catroux declared that he intended to effect a settlement which would take account of the declaration of independence and of France's responsibilities as an ally and her obligations and duties. He considered that the British demand for the recall of M. Helleu and the release of the arrested politicians was not an ultimatum but a suggestion; he must also take into account the prestige of France and the mutual relations which ought to exist between allies. He felt that, in view of his past record, he was entitled to expect us to leave him to settle the matter in his own way and time. Although he gave no undertaking about the recall of M. Helleu, the supersession of the latter by himself constituted a disavowal.

Mr. Casey agreed with General Catroux that our demands need not be regarded as an ultimatum, but repeated that Anglo-French relations were closely involved and that in the interests of the war effort we could not allow disorder. In view of military operations based on facilities in the Lebanon, urgent action was required. Mr. Casey spoke of 'the grave and immediate menace to public security'. General Catroux said that Mr. Casey seemed to have some specific operation in view, of which he (General Catroux) had no information.[2]

On November 15 Lord Halifax telegraphed to the Foreign Office (a) that from the point of view of Anglo-American relations, the Lebanon question was an awkward one with the analogy of India prominent in the American mind. The State Department took a serious view of the French action, but so far press and radio comments had been confused. Some comments were critical of the

---

[1] A Foreign Office marginal comment noted: 'That is true.'
[2] A Foreign Office minute dated November 28 on a detailed record of this conversation (b) read: 'No sign here Casey asked for reinstatement as we were told he did.' See below, p. 281.

(a) E7032/27/89. (b) E7387/27/89.

French, but the papers such as the *New York Herald Tribune* and *Washington Post*, which supported General de Gaulle, justified their action. If the British Government were obliged to use force, we might expect considerable criticism and suspicion of supposed British imperialistic designs in the Levant.

Lord Halifax warned the Foreign Office that British indignation at the arrest of the Lebanese leaders would get little sympathy in the United States press, which, however unjustifiably, would draw an analogy with the imprisonment of Mr. Gandhi and Mr. Nehru. The Americans might also argue that if we asked for their intervention in the Lebanon, we could hardly refuse it in India. Lord Halifax said that although American opinion might be divided as between France and the Lebanon, it would probably be a good deal more united in suspecting British motives. There would be little support for a change of policy towards the French National Committee based on their action in the Lebanon. Lord Halifax thought that from the point of view of American opinion, British intervention in the dispute should be minimised as much as possible. We should avoid giving a pretext for suspicion that we were trying to exploit the incident for our own ends, or that we used one set of arguments where India was concerned—that public security required the arrest of political leaders—and the opposite arguments about Syria.[1]

(a)   On November 16 the War Cabinet again reviewed the position. Mr. Eden said that there was no news of further developments, but that General Catroux was likely to play for time. The British Government might have to make clear what they would do if the Lebanese Ministers were not released within a stated time.

(b)   On the same day General de Gaulle made a statement at a specially summoned meeting of the French Consultative Assembly. He spoke of the passage of the Lebanese reform bill in spite of M. Helleu's message that he was returning with very liberal instructions. He said that the situation could not be accepted either by the Delegate-General or the French Committee because it modified unilaterally an international statute which the Lebanese Government alone were not entitled to modify, and because it was likely to disturb political and strategic conditions in a theatre of military operations. He said that the manner of the action suggested provocation of France. He then distinguished four elements of the position of France in the Lebanon: the mandate; General Catroux's proclamation of 1941; the necessity for establishing a committee of

(c)   [1]A Foreign Office comment on this telegram read: 'This is a very timely warning as regards the American attitude. On the whole we have no wish to do other than play down British intervention in the dispute, and if General Catroux can settle it on the basis of our requirements we shall, no doubt, be willing to give him the full credit.'

(a) WM(43)155; E6946/27/89.   (b) E7097/27/89.   (c) E7032/27/89.

independence[1] in relations with the Lebanon in accordance with the traditional position of France in this area; the obligation not to allow a situation in the Lebanon which could disturb strategical plans. General de Gaulle then said that the serious incident at Beirut was now being settled. M. Edde had taken office to secure the authority of the Lebanese State while the crisis lasted. General Catroux had gone to Beirut to study the best means of settlement in agreement with the Lebanon. The incident made no difference to French policy in the Lebanon. The French Committee still intended to establish a normal constitutional situation in order that they might negotiate with the Lebanese about their common concerns in complete independence.

On the morning of November 17 Mr. Macmillan saw M. Massigli (a) in Algiers. M. Massigli said that General Catroux was going to work for the release of the Lebanese Ministers. Mr. Macmillan asked for a written reply satisfactory to the British Government. He said that he had received messages from the Prime Minister and from Mr. Eden which made it clear that grave consequences would follow if an early solution were not found. M. Massigli said that he wanted to see the matter settled, and that General de Gaulle's speech had dealt moderately with the problem. General Catroux had discretion to act as he liked or to seek approval from the French Committee for the proposed measures. Mr. Macmillan left an *aide-mémoire* with M. Massigli pointing out that he had had no satisfactory reply to (b) any of the oral or written British statements. He had been instructed to issue a most serious warning to the French Committee. He asked for a reply to the communications, and more specifically to the requests for the release of the Lebanese and the recall of M. Helleu.

The War Cabinet met in the afternoon of November 17 to con- (c) sider the situation. Mr. Eden said that General Catroux had arrived in Beirut, but there had been no report of an interview between him and Sir E. Spears. Mr. Eden thought that we should now impose a time-limit. He proposed that unless General Catroux had indicated by the evening of November 18 that the French were on the point of complying with our two demands, Mr. Casey should fly to Beirut on the following day (November 19). He should there inform General Catroux that, failing compliance with these demands by 10 a.m. on November 21, British martial law would be declared and the Ministers released. If General Catroux was ready to release the

---

[1] These words appeared in the telegraphed report to the Foreign Office of General de Gaulle's statement. The French text, published in *L'Echo d'Alger* read: '. . . la nécessité d'établir l'indépendance en ce qui concerne les affaires communes au Liban et à la France. . . .'

(a) E7100/27/89. (b) E7135/27/89. (c) WM(43)156; E7146/27/89.

K*BFP

President and Ministers he should be asked to attend a conference with the released Ministers under our general good offices to negotiate a *modus vivendi*. Mr. Eden did not propose to say that if our demands were not met, we should withdraw recognition from the French National Committee. He added that the United States attitude towards us had not been too favourable, although there was much support for Great Britain in certain quarters. It was important that the United States Government should be informed of our proposed action and that, if possible, we should obtain their concurrence.

The War Cabinet considered that the quarrel was between the French and the Lebanese, and while we should do what we could to reconcile them and facilitate a settlement, we should not go so far as to undertake that in certain circumstances we would represent Lebanese interests. The War Cabinet agreed to send instructions on the lines of the discussion, and asked that the United States Government should be informed of the action proposed. Mr. Casey was (a) therefore asked to say that the declaration of martial law would be made on the grounds of military necessity, and that it would have no political implications and did not show a desire or intention on the part of the British Government to substitute their influence for that of France in the Lebanon. The telegram containing these instructions was repeated to Mr. Macmillan, who was asked to tell the French Committee that they must act without delay. Lord Halifax was instructed to inform the United States Government and to ask for their approval and support.[1]

(b)   On the following day Mr. Casey reported that he had discussed the situation with the Middle East Defence Committee. The Committee were convinced that the release of the members of the Government, without their immediate reinstatement, would not keep the peace in the Lebanon, where tension was very high and the situation was likely to deteriorate with serious effects on our base facilities and communications.[2] The Commander-in-Chief, Levant, was sending a cruiser or two destroyers to Haifa and, if necessary, to Beirut.

---

[1] The Foreign Office also informed the Soviet Government in general terms of Mr. Casey's instructions.
[2] The Secretary of State for India had also informed the Foreign Office that feeling was very strong in India against the French action.

(a) E7102/27/89. (b) E7142/27/89.

(iv)

The constitutional crisis in the Lebanon: the problem of the reinstatement of the Government: Mr. Casey's aide-mémoire of November 19: the French communiqué of November 21: release of the imprisoned President and Ministers: General Catroux's declaration of December 23 (November 18– December 24, 1943).

On November 16 the Foreign Office had received information that M. Viénot was trying to secure conciliatory action by the French. They suggested that Mr. Eden should see him in order to impress on him the strength of British feeling. Mr. Eden had no (a) time to do so, but on November 18 Sir A. Cadogan spoke to M. Viénot on his behalf. He said that Mr. Eden wanted M. Viénot to make the French Committee realise the gravity of the position. The people of the Lebanon appeared to be waiting to see the result of General Catroux's visit; if there were none, we had to be ready for trouble. Sir A. Cadogan said that he had attended the War Cabinet meetings on this question, and that the decision had been unanimous. He told M. Viénot that if our demands were not met by that afternoon, Mr. Casey was to fly to Beirut. M. Viénot promised that he would telegraph immediately to Algiers. He said that it would be extremely difficult for the French to agree to reinstate the Ministers. Sir A. Cadogan said that we had not asked yet for their reinstatement, but the question would have to be discussed later. M. Viénot did not think that the Committee could agree to the proposed conference, which he called an 'internationalisation of the question'. Sir A. Cadogan answered that 'the question' was really the present dispute, and 'internationalisation' might offer the French a way out of the difficulty. It did not necessarily mean, as M. Viénot had hinted, that we aimed at a 'co-mandatory system' in the Levant.

On November 18 the War Cabinet again considered the position. (b) Mr. Casey had telegraphed on November 17: 'In my discussions with Catroux here I have assumed that release of Lebanese Ministers meant their release as Ministers, i.e. that reinstatement of Ministers was a corollary of their release, and I consistently spoke to him in this sense.' Mr. Eden said that our demands to the French Committee had been limited to the recall of M. Helleu and the release of the Ministers, and had not included a demand for their immediate reinstatement. Our plan had been that, after the release of the Ministers, Mr. Casey should bring the French authorities and the Ministers together to reach a settlement of constitutional issues. There were two objections to insisting on immediate reinstatement:

(a) E7159/27/89. (b) WM(43)157; E6946/27/89.

(i) we would be making it almost impossible for the French to meet our demands; (ii) if the Ministers immediately resumed their functions, the deadlock between them and the French would probably continue. Mr. Eden read out to the War Cabinet a draft telegram to Mr. Casey in this sense.

In the ensuing discussion, the following points were made: (i) as Mr. Casey had already told General Catroux that the release of the Ministers implied their reinstatement, we could not recede from this position; (ii) the imprisoned Ministers were still in our view the *de jure* Government of the Lebanon; on release they would revert to their former status, and in this capacity should enter into discussions with the French; (iii) the object of negotiations by Mr. Casey and Sir E. Spears should be to bring the two sides together and arrange a settlement.

The War Cabinet considered that the Lebanese Government were not without blame, and that, if the French had not taken such precipitate and unjustified action, we might have supported them against the Lebanese. The War Cabinet agreed that they could not recognise M. Edde. They agreed also to a proposal by Mr. Eden for an extension of the time-limit by twenty-four hours. They decided that a telegram should be sent to Mr. Casey making it clear that the War Cabinet assumed that the Ministers when released would revert to their former status. The time-limit would now expire on November 22. These instructions were telegraphed to Mr. Casey on the evening of November 18.

(a) On the same evening Mr. Macmillan saw M. Massigli at the latter's request. M. Massigli said that he had made further enquiries about the disorders and the behaviour of French troops in the Lebanon, but he had not yet had full reports. In his opinion, the incidents had been neither so grave as Mr. Macmillan's information had represented nor so insignificant as he had been led to believe from his own sources. He had had two telegrams from General Catroux emphasising the difficulty that would follow the release and reinstatement of the Ministers. M. Massigli said that the French Committee had discussed the position. General de Gaulle held to the view that if we pressed the French, they could not in their position of weakness make any effective resistance. Their only course would be to withdraw altogether from the Levant. General de Gaulle now said that he could not lend himself to such a derogation from French honour and would resign from his position as President of the Committee.

M. Massigli spoke at length about the lack of comprehension in our policy. In the past, although there had been a constant struggle

(a) E7155/27/89.

in the Levant between British and French interests, the Foreign Office and the Quai d'Orsay had prevented the disputes from becoming a matter of general policy. Did we now mean to drive the French from the Lebanon? The Committee, and particularly General de Gaulle, could not resist this interpretation.

Mr. Macmillan replied that our policy was clear. For military reasons we were determined to see that there was order in the Levant States. We should deeply regret French withdrawal. Mr. Macmillan stated most strongly, and quoted phrases from different telegrams to support his statement, that we had no intention of expelling the French and still less of taking their place. Our policy was that the pledges of 1941 should be carried out. The Arab States should be made self-governing, and the French should have a position in Syria similar to our own position, e.g. in Iraq or Egypt. Meanwhile an immediate decision on the two requests was necessary. In answer to a question from M. Massigli about reinstatement, Mr. Macmillan said that we wished to get back to the position before the crisis. We wished to facilitate honourable negotiation and reconciliation, always on the basis that the French upheld their declared policy. He then gave M. Massigli a note that, unless the French complied with our requests, Mr. Casey would fly to Beirut and inform General Catroux of the attitude we now had to adopt.[1]

Mr. Macmillan also reported M. Massigli's view that Sir E. Spears's policy, which had made things difficult for a long time past, was bound to lead to rupture. Mr. Macmillan had told M. Massigli that he could not accept this view; Sir E. Spears was a Minister taking his instructions from His Majesty's Government. The account which Mr. Macmillan had given of British policy was accurate in every respect and represented the general view of the nation. No Government could stand for a moment in the state of opinion in England if it were not loyal to these idealistic concepts.

On the day following this conversation Mr. Macmillan lunched (a) with M. Massigli after a meeting of the French Committee which had lasted from 10 a.m. until 1.30 p.m. General de Gaulle at first had proposed sending an intransigent telegram to General Catroux, but had given way after long discussions. The Committee had then agreed to allow General Catroux to make a settlement on the lines which he had proposed, i.e. the President and Ministers were to be set free at once; the President was to be asked to form a government under a new Prime Minister and negotiations were to take place immediately with this government with a view to a settlement. M. Helleu would be dismissed.

---

[1] Mr. Eden telegraphed to Mr. Macmillan his approval of this statement.

(a) E7165/27/89.

M. Massigli said that the discussion showed a great improvement in the character of the Committee since its enlargement. He told Mr. Macmillan that he had made use of the conversation which he had had with him the night before, especially the solemn assurances about the principles of British policy towards the Lebanon. Mr. Macmillan told the Foreign Office that he hoped the question of automatic reinstatement of the Ministers would not prove insurmountable.

(a)　　At 5.30 p.m. on November 19 Mr. Casey and Sir E. Spears saw General Catroux at the latter's house in Beirut. Mr. Casey repeated the British demands to which no reply had been received, and said that the Ministers must revert to their former status. If the French Committee accepted this plan, we would propose an immediate conference between representatives of the Lebanese Government and General Catroux under British auspices at some point in neighbouring British territory outside the Levant in order to reach agreement on a *modus vivendi* for the period of the war. If the French Committee had not accepted the British demands by 10 a.m. on November 22, Mr. Casey would arrange for an immediate declaration of British martial law on grounds of military necessity and for the release of the prisoners. He explained that a declaration of British martial law would have no political implications, and would not denote any desire or intention to substitute British for French influence in the Levant.

Mr. Casey then handed General Catroux an *aide-mémoire* stating the British position. General Catroux said that, as the *aide-mémoire* represented an ultimatum ('mise en demeure'), he would have to refer to Algiers. When he pointed out that the time-limit was very short in view of the delay in communications between Beirut and Algiers, Mr. Casey said that we would telegraph the text of the *aide-mémoire* to Mr. Macmillan with the greatest urgency so that he could give a copy to M. Massigli. In any event the two British demands were unchanged and had been in M. Massigli's hands for a week. Mr. Macmillan in Algiers, Mr. Casey in Cairo and Sir E. Spears in Beirut had done everything possible to impress the French with a sense of the urgency of the situation. Mr. Casey reported that the tone of the discussion was calm and friendly. Each paragraph of the *aide-mémoire* was discussed to ensure that the meaning was clear beyond doubt. As he left, General Catroux said, 'This looks

(b)　like another Fashoda'. Mr. Eden approved the *aide-mémoire*, and the Foreign Office instructed Mr. Macmillan so to inform M. Massigli.

(c)　　On the evening of November 20 M. Massigli told Mr. Macmillan that the Committee had agreed to the despatch of an urgent telegram

---

(a) E7160/27/89.　(b) E7165/27/89.　(c) E7204/27/89.

to General Catroux recalling M. Helleu immediately to Algiers and agreeing to the release of the President and other Ministers. M. Massigli spoke of the delay in communications and asked that the time-limit should be postponed to allow further discussion of the other issues; Mr. Macmillan supported his appeal for more time. He reminded the Foreign Office that they took the view that the Lebanese Prime Minister had acted precipitately in passing reforms; it was therefore reasonable to negotiate about the composition of the new Ministry. Moreover, if the French made these two major concessions, they would have granted our original demand as presented in Algiers on November 13.

After he had sent this telegram, Mr. Macmillan heard from the (a) Foreign Office that they could not accept the French contention that after the liberation of the President and Ministers a new Government would have to be formed. When the existing Government had resumed office, we should try to bring about a *modus vivendi* as set out in Mr. Casey's *aide-mémoire*. Mr. Macmillan now reported that he would inform M. Massigli as instructed, but would postpone (b) his journey to Cairo. He hoped that Mr. Eden would agree to postpone the time-limit. Mr. Macmillan went on to say: 'Historians will not fail to observe that the solution now proposed is an acceptance of the only formal demand made on the French Committee.' The new demand for automatic reinstatement of the Ministers as a Government—Sir A. Cadogan had informed M. Viénot on November 18 that this demand had not yet been put forward—was made to General Catroux only on November 19, and communications were so bad that the Committee had not yet received his report. Mr. Macmillan thought that the Anglo-French relationship was being endangered and many months' work undone for a difference which was now much reduced. The vote at the French Committee that morning—only three had opposed the proposals of M. Massigli —showed a development of independence and judgment which needed fostering. Mr. Macmillan asked that his telegram should be passed to the Prime Minister.

At 9 a.m. on November 21 Mr. Macmillan told M. Massigli of (c) the insistence of the British Government on their demands as contained in Mr. Casey's *aide-mémoire* (Mr. Macmillan gave M. Massigli a copy of the memorandum). The Ministers must be reinstated. Any change in the Lebanese Government involving alteration of the *status quo* before November 8 would be discussed at the conference to be called to reach a *modus vivendi*. The time-table must stand as arranged. He urged M. Massigli most strongly to persuade the Committee to accept the demands. M. Massigli was very downcast

---

(a) E7165/27/89. (b) E7204/27/89. (c) E7218, 7534/27/89.

and talked of resignation. He said that his policy of collaboration and friendship with the English had failed. The proposal for a conference was an insult; it was a further insult to suggest a meeting under British auspices on British soil.

(a)   The Foreign Office had, however, decided on the morning of November 21 to extend the time-limit to 10 a.m. on November 24. The outstanding question was now that of reinstatement. General Catroux had been in charge of negotiations since November 13; the Foreign Office understood that Mr. Casey had informed him of the need for reinstatement on November 15, and that he had been in Beirut since November 16. It was therefore his fault if this demand was new to the French Committee. The Foreign Office thought that matters might be amicably arranged if extra time were given for settlement of the issue, although it was essential not to relax pressure on the French. They had in mind the close interest of the Arab world in the dispute.

(b)   On November 21 the War Cabinet again discussed the position. They had an account of Mr. Casey's interview with General Catroux on November 19, and a report from Sir E. Spears of an interview with the General on the following day. General Catroux had said that he had received a telegram from Algiers giving him authority to release and reinstate the President. The other Ministers were to be released but deprived of office permanently. Sir E. Spears had made clear the difficulties which would arise unless the Ministers were reinstated. General Catroux had hinted that he did not dissent from this view, but was bound by instructions from Algiers.

The War Cabinet also had before them Mr. Macmillan's report of his discussions with M. Massigli, and of the decisions of the French Committee and their request for more time to discuss other issues. The War Cabinet also knew that Mr. Macmillan strongly advised an extension of time and that he had pointed out that our original demands had not included reinstatement. Mr. Eden said that as time was short he had telegraphed to Mr. Casey that morning agreeing to an extension of the time-limit.

Mr. Eden said that we should not solve the difficulty by refraining from asking for immediate reinstatement. The negotiations for a *modus vivendi* could be conducted only with the legitimate Lebanese Government. The War Cabinet agreed with this view, and thought that General Catroux did not have plenipotentiary powers, and that we should have to negotiate with the French Committee at Algiers. Mr. Macmillan should stay at Algiers until these negotiations were concluded. We should also state that we could not go beyond an extension of forty-eight hours. At the outset Mr. Casey had told

---

(a) E7204/27/89. (b) WM(43)159; E7146/27/89; E7191/27/89.

General Catroux, whom we had then regarded as a plenipotentiary, that we demanded reinstatement.[1] Once released, the Ministers should be free to resume negotiations for a *modus vivendi* with their status unimpaired. Otherwise the negotiations might degenerate into a discussion of the personalities to be included in a new Government. The War Cabinet asked Mr. Eden to send a telegram to Mr. Casey in this sense. The Foreign Office therefore informed Mr. Casey of the extension to the time-limit and told him that there (a) could be no question of British negotiations with the French to set up a new and unconstitutional Government as Mr. Macmillan had suggested. Mr. Macmillan was asked to inform M. Massigli of this extension.

Before these instructions reached Mr. Macmillan on November 21 he had seen M. Massigli again. M. Massigli said that the French (b) National Committee had decided to release a public statement at 5 p.m. Algiers time. Later in the evening he would send Mr. Macmillan an official letter from the Committee. The original demands as stated by Mr. Macmillan on November 13 were granted; the President was restored to office, but there was an intentional ambiguity about the position of the other Ministers.[2] Mr. Macmillan hoped that Mr. Eden would now be prepared to postpone the declaration of martial law.

The text of the communiqué which was to be issued in Algiers (c) was as follows:

'Le Comité a pris connaissance des plus récents rapports et propositions du Général Catroux concernant le règlement de l'incident du Liban et constatant que l'ordre regne dans le pays.

Le Comité a décidé de donner suite à la proposition du Général Catroux tendant au rétablissement dans ses fonctions de M. Bechara Khoury, Président de la République, avec lequel le Commissaire d'Etat en mission est invité à négocier les mésures nécessaires au rétablissement rapide de la vie constitutionnelle au Liban. M. Helleu, Délégué Général et Plénipotentiaire de France, est prié de se rendre à Alger.

Le Comité a décidé, d'autre part, la mise en liberté des Ministres libanais en fonction le 8 novembre dernier.

Le Comité a confirmé sa decision d'ouvrir avec le Gouvernement de la République Syrienne les négociations nécessaires à la mise en harmonie du mandât de la France et du régime de l'indépendance promise aux Etats du Levant dans les proclamations de 1941. Dès

---

[1] The detailed record of Mr. Casey's interview with General Catroux at 9.30 a.m. on November 15 leaves this point in some doubt. See above, p. 277, note 2, and also p. 281.

[2] Mr. Macmillan reported to the Foreign Office: 'Massigli told me he had a considerable struggle in the Committee where the same divisions repeated themselves. Finally, only the Old Guard, by which he described de Gaulle, Pleven and Diethelm, stood out.'

(a) E7204/27/89.   (b) E7219/27/89.   (c) E7534/27/89.

le rétablissement de la vie constitutionnelle au Liban, des négociations analogues seront entamées avec le Gouvernement de Beyrouth.'

(a) Mr. Macmillan later told M. Massigli of the extension to the time-
limit. He also stated, verbally and in writing, the British view of the
position of the Ministers. He repeated this statement more fully in
conversation and in a note on November 22. He said that we held
to our view that the status of the released Ministers was that of the
constitutional Government of the Lebanon. The arbitrary imprisonment of members of a Government could not have the effect of
altering their status; this could only be done by normal constitutional
process. Mr. Macmillan assumed that negotiations for a *modus vivendi*
must proceed on this basis and that, in view of the strained situation
which prevailed in the Levant, they should start at once.

(b) In Beirut on the morning of November 22 General Catroux had
sent Sir E. Spears an urgent letter containing the substance of a
communication which he said had been made on the previous day
by M. Massigli in reply to Mr. Casey's *aide-mémoire*. This letter stated
that the Committee still thought that it would not be suitable for
the Lebanese Prime Minister and members of his Government to
be brought back to power at present ('actuellement'); that if a
conference seemed necessary, it should be Franco-Lebanese; that
the Lyttelton-de Gaulle agreements of 1941 did not confer the right
to proclaim martial law on the British Command; that if the British
Government were to carry out the threats contained in Mr. Casey's
aide-mémoire, they would bear the responsibility for the result, and
for the consequences on Franco-British relations.

(c) On the same day, November 22, the War Cabinet again discussed
the situation. The French National Committee had now recalled
M. Helleu; they had released and reinstated the President and had
released the Lebanese Ministers but without reinstating them. Mr.
Eden read out two telegrams from Mr. Macmillan, stating that he
had informed M. Massigli that the British Government regarded
the released Ministers as the constitutional Government and that
this fact should be the basis of negotiations for a *modus vivendi*. Mr.
Macmillan thought that public opinion generally would take the
view that France had given way to us. He also thought that the
French might try to make an arrangement with the Lebanese
President involving some change of Ministers; he asked whether we
should then insist on imposing martial law at 10 a.m. on the 24th.

Mr. Eden told the War Cabinet that he still feared that a failure
to reinstate the Ministers would mean a deadlock. The matter,

---

(a) E7221, 7248, 7534/27/89.   (b) E7247/27/89.   (c) WM(43)160; E7146/27/89;
E7248/27/89.

however, could be better handled in the Middle East than in London. There was general agreement with this view, and also with a suggestion that we should withdraw the threat to impose martial law on November 24 if our full demands had not been met then, but retain the right to do so in case of need. The War Cabinet noted statements in Mr. Macmillan's telegrams which made it clear that the majority of the French Committee had overruled General de Gaulle.

Meanwhile, before hearing these views of the War Cabinet, Mr. (a) Macmillan had written to M. Massigli that the situation in the Lebanon was so much strained that the final step in the solution of the problem (reinstatement) would have to be taken without delay. He repeated the threat of martial law by the morning of November 24. He asked for a reply to his note as soon as possible. General Catroux, however, had already telegraphed to the Committee that he had decided on his own authority to reinstate the Ministers. M. Massigli was therefore able to secure the agreement of the Committee to this decision without having recourse to Mr. Macmillan's note. Shortly after the incident was settled M. Massigli proposed that he should return the note, and Mr. Macmillan agreed.

Mr. Law[1] told the House of Commons on November 23 that the Lebanese politicians had been released, the President reinstated and M. Helleu recalled. We welcomed these developments and hoped that they would lead to the re-establishment of constitutional government.[2]

On December 1 Mr. Macmillan saw General Catroux, who had (b) returned from the Lebanon on the previous day. General Catroux seemed tired and depressed, and said that he felt humiliated as a Frenchman by receiving an ultimatum from Great Britain. Nevertheless he recognised the 'extraordinary folly' of M. Helleu's conduct, and was sure that he had acted without precise instructions; he had probably misinterpreted a general expression of support from General de Gaulle. General Catroux had seen General de Gaulle that morning, and thought that he had been impressed by the opposition of the Assembly to a dispute with Great Britain. General Catroux would attend the meeting of the Committee on the next day and

---

[1] Mr. R. Law had been appointed in September Minister of State 'to assist the Secretary of State for Foreign Affairs'. After this appointment Mr. Casey was known officially as Minister of State Resident in the Middle East.

[2] In answer to a question Mr. Law repeated that we had no desire to get political advantage for ourselves and that our policy was based solely on a desire to see the implementation of pledges which we had endorsed and to safeguard the military situation. The United States Government issued a statement on November 26 approving the action of the French National Committee in reinstating the Lebanese Government.

(a) E7310, 7319, 7346, 7724/27/89.   (b) E7582/27/89.

ask for a free hand to deal with Syria and the Lebanon. Unless he obtained it he would not continue in office.[1]

General Catroux went on to say that he would try to start direct negotiations with the Syrian and Lebanese Governments. They might be unwilling to negotiate if they thought that they would get British support for a refusal. Mr. Macmillan replied that he knew that our policy was to promote direct negotiations between France and the two Levant Governments; we wanted to see an arrangement between them similar to that which we had with Iraq. General Catroux said that Syria and the Lebanon seemed unwilling to accept a treaty. Mr. Macmillan suggested that if a treaty were impossible on legal grounds, a text could be agreed on all points at issue; this text could be initialled and regarded as a working arrangement pending final ratification. General Catroux said that he had in mind a series of individual arrangements on each separate question; the arrangements thus made could be brought together under a preamble as a single document, which would be a provisional treaty. He recognised that the Governments would wish to negotiate as independent governments; he would agree to this plan. He thought that the new committee in Algiers and the arrival of delegates to the Assembly would make possible a more progressive policy than had been possible under the old committee.[2]

The Foreign Office considered that the Syrian and Lebanese Governments would probably agree to General Catroux's idea of a series of separate agreements, which corresponded with the British

(a) idea of a *modus vivendi*. At a meeting of the French Committee on December 2 General Catroux was given full authority to deal with the situation.

(b) On December 1 the Syrian Prime Minister made a declaration of policy in the Chamber. He began by affirming the Syrian determination not to recognise the mandate. He then described the policy of his Government as: (i) recognition by the United Nations of Syrian independence and of the desire of the Syrian Government to contribute to the war effort by putting their communications and territory at Allied disposal; (ii) need for law and security in order not to hinder Allied troops; (iii) rights of independence, which he divided into two categories: those which the Syrians exercised themselves; those which they shared with the Lebanese, including certain rights hitherto reserved by the French which the Syrians were beginning to exercise. He agreed that, as long as Allied troops were in the

---

[1] General Catroux spoke highly of the correctness and delicacy of General Holmes' behaviour throughout the crisis.
[2] See above, Vol. III, p. 1.

(a) E7647/27/89. (b) E7633, 8103/27/89.

Levant, the security of the frontiers must remain in the hands of the military authorities. He said that the two States had arranged to take over the *Intérêts Communs* and the control of the customs, and that General Catroux had agreed that nothing remained to be done beyond the actual transfer of powers. The Syrians would not conclude a treaty in exchange for the transfer of rights, since treaties were only compatible with independence, and the rights which the Syrians wished to exercise completely could not be used by the 'other party' as a bargaining counter.

While the Prime Minister and Mr. Eden were in Cairo on their (a) way to and from the Teheran Conference they discussed the crisis in the Lebanon with Mr. Macmillan, Sir E. Spears and Mr. Casey. On December 10 Mr. Eden and Sir A. Cadogan saw M. Massigli (b) and General Catroux in Algiers. Mr. Eden said that we were now prepared to put pressure on the Syrian and Lebanese Governments to make reasonable agreements with the French. M. Massigli suggested that Anglo-French conversations might be held—possibly in London—about the situation.

On December 14 Mr. Eden spoke in the House of Commons of the talks in Cairo and Algiers. He said that Great Britain had deep sympathy with the national aspirations of the Arab world, and was the only country which had concluded a treaty with and withdrawn from an independent Arab State. At the same time the preservation of order and tranquillity in the Lebanon was an Allied interest, since it affected the war effort in the Middle East. Mr. Eden said that General Catroux was going back to Beirut on behalf of the French Committee, and was to conduct negotiations to try and bring about a *modus vivendi*. Mr. Eden hoped that these negotiations would be conducted in a conciliatory spirit on both sides and would lead to early agreement.

On December 18 General Catroux had a friendly talk with Sir (c) E. Spears. Sir E. Spears reported to the Foreign Office that General Catroux seemed much more optimistic about the French Committee than on his last visit, and had said that the Committee had given him full support. The Foreign Office considered General Catroux's attitude to be most satisfactory and hoped that Sir E. Spears would be able to encourage all parties to conduct negotiations for a *modus vivendi* in a conciliatory atmosphere.

On December 23, after negotiations lasting over six hours, the (d) Syrians and Lebanese agreed with General Catroux on the text of a declaration regarding the transfer to these Governments of powers exercised in their name by the French authorities. In accordance

---

(a) E7949/27/89. (b) E7772/27/89. (c) E7959/27/89. (d) E8054/27/89.

with the agreement, the *Intérêts Communs*, together with their personnel, would be transferred to the Syrian and Lebanese States with the right of enacting laws and regulations as from January 1, 1944.

The Lebanese Chamber accepted the declaration by a unanimous vote. The Syrian Parliament also met on the afternoon of December 23 and approved the declaration.

CHAPTER LV

British policy in Syria and the Lebanon from January 1944 to July 1945

(i)

Anglo-French differences of view with regard to the transfer of powers to the Levant States: French objection to the arming of the Syrian and Lebanese gendarmeries: recall of Sir E. Spears for consultation: Anglo-French discussions in London (January–September 1944).

THE essential features of British policy in the Levant were unchanged after the Lebanese crisis of November 1943. The British Government were concerned directly, and for military reasons, with the maintenance of order in the Levant. They were also pledged to the fulfilment of the promise of independence to Syria and the Lebanon; this promise did not exclude a recognition of the special position of France in relation to the two States. The Foreign Office indeed regarded it as desirable in British as well as in French interests that France should retain at least some part of her old position.

The issues between the French and the two Republics, however, were now sharper. The French had already made important financial concessions. They wanted to keep as much as possible of the other powers which they had exercised under their mandate; the Republics wanted the transfer of full powers to themselves. This conflict was aggravated, as in 1943, by a number of factors. The Syrians argued that the mandate was obsolete; the French claimed that it was legally still in existence, and as such entitled them to reject British interference. Syrian nationalism was not more reasonable or more realist than the nationalism of other small single-interest States, but the matter was of more than local concern. Arab and Moslem opinion in general watched British policy, and trouble in Syria could easily spread throughout the Middle East. The policy of the United States and of the Soviet Union did not make a Franco-Syrian settlement easier. French claims to a privileged position seemed to American opinion a form of 'colonialism' which the United States Government could not support. For different reasons the Russians also backed the Syrian demands for full independence.

In these circumstances the conduct of Anglo-French as well as Franco-Syrian relations needed the greatest tact and forbearance.

General de Gaulle on the French side did not possess either of these qualities, and would not be persuaded that the British aim was not merely to turn the French out of the Levant but to take their place. Until his recall in December 1944, Sir E. Spears added to French suspicions. The French continued to accuse him of working against them; the Foreign Office took a similar view, and considered that, after full allowance had been made for the difficulties of his position, there would be no chance of satisfactory Anglo-French co-operation unless he and his special Mission were withdrawn.

(a) On March 10 the Prime Minister, on his own initiative, sent a telegram to Sir E. Spears that his anti-French attitude was obvious to all and that he must not go too far ('surtout, pas trop de zèle').

(b) In commenting on Sir E. Spears's reply (which was a general defence of his actions) Mr. Eden said that he was known throughout the Middle East to be bitterly anti-French and that he prevented us from adequate direct contacts with the French since they would not take him into their confidence.[1] Mr. Eden also said that he could not accept Sir E. Spears's judgments on the French without careful scrutiny. The French authorities since the Lebanese crisis of November 1943 had been trying to improve matters and had removed many of their undesirable characters. Could we not make a change? The

(c) Prime Minister, however, replied on April 2 that he did not want to withdraw Sir E. Spears.

A dispute between the French and the Syrians in which the British authorities could not avoid becoming involved took place during the first half of 1944, mainly over the control of the Troupes Spéciales[2] and the transfer of the security services to the Syrian and Lebanese Governments. In each of these matters the Foreign Office thought that Sir E. Spears's intervention was contrary to the intentions of

(d) British policy. Mr. Eden complained to the Prime Minister at the end of June that 'the unfortunate and continuous tension which prevailed in the Levant' was due to the conviction held by the French 'sincerely and not without justification' that Sir E. Spears's objective was to get them out of Syria. Mr. Eden thought that Sir E. Spears's most recent actions would cause another storm. He had offered, without authority from the Foreign Office (though he

---

[1] Mr. Eden realised that Anglo-French suspicion and distrust existed in the Levant before 1939, and that the multiplicity of Allied authorities dealing with Syria and the Lebanon was bound to cause complications, delays and often contradiction in policy. These authorities included, in 1943, the Foreign Office, the War Office, the Minister of State in Cairo, the British military command in the Middle East and the British commander in Syria, the British Mission at Beirut, the French National Committee at Algiers and the British representative with this Committee, the French military and civil authorities in the Levant, and a number of economic and propaganda organisations.

[2] See above, p. 239, note 3.

(a) T527/4, Churchill Papers/423. (b) PM/44/171, Churchill Papers/423. (c) M349/4, Churchill Papers/423. (d) PM/44/476, E4066/217/89.

claimed the support of the Commander-in-Chief), to supply arms for the Syrian gendarmerie.[1] He might justify this action on technical grounds, since control of the gendarmerie had passed to the Syrian Government, but there could be no defence from the diplomatic point of view for his method of procedure, i.e. telling the French only after he had told the Syrians that he would supply the arms.

Sir E. Spears made an even more serious mistake. He had put himself in the position of an intermediary in negotiating the conditions under which the control of the Troupes Spéciales was to pass to the Syrians and Lebanese. He appeared to have inserted in these conditions a clause preventing the French from maintaining more troops in the States than were already there. Mr. Eden told the Prime Minister that, owing to French commitments elsewhere, they had only three battalions—two of them Senegalese—in the Levant.[2] Mr. Eden considered a limitation of the kind proposed by Sir E. Spears unwise in British interests, since the British Government maintained troops in Iraq and Egypt. Mr. Eden proposed therefore that Sir E. Spears should be asked to come home for consultation 'in the hope that you and I may once more be able to make our policy clear to him, which is not to undermine the French in the Levant'.[3]

The Foreign Office had meanwhile suggested—through M. Viénot (a) in London and Mr. Duff Cooper in Algiers—that the question of arming the gendarmeries of the two States should be dealt with by a special Anglo-French Committee. The French agreed with this plan, but on July 3 Sir E. Spears telegraphed to the Foreign Office (b) that he felt unable to carry out his instructions with regard to summoning the Committee. He said that the Commander-in-Chief supported his refusal. The Foreign Office could not accept this reversal of an important decision on policy. They asked the War Office to inform the Commander-in-Chief that under the Lyttelton- (c) de Gaulle agreement responsibility for the gendarmerie and general security rested with the French and that they must therefore be consulted in the matter. The Foreign Office hoped that for diplomatic

---

[1] A Foreign Office minute of July 4 noted that the Syrian and Lebanese Governments (d) had applied first to the French for arms and had secured an offer of 400 pre-1914 rifles. They had then come to the British in the hope of getting a better offer.

[2] On July 29 General Holmes, General Officer Commanding 9th Army, reported that French military strength in the Levant had not greatly decreased in the past two years. He estimated the ration strength of French and French colonial troops at about 6,000 as compared with approximately 6,300 at the beginning of 1943. The Troupes Spéciales had risen from 21,000 to 24,000.

[3] Mr. Eden added the words 'which . . . in the Levant' to the draft of the minute to the Prime Minister.

(a) E3677, 3834, 3740, 3792, 3880, 3893, 3827, 3903, 4004, 4012, 4124, 4174/217/89. (b) E3893/217/89. (c) E4004/217/89. (d) E4004/217/89.

reasons the Commander-in-Chief would accept the proposed committee.

On July 6 the Foreign Office informed Sir E. Spears of the message to the Commander-in-Chief and insisted that he should carry out his (Sir E. Spears's) instructions. In spite of these explanations,

(a) however, General Holmes on July 11 gave the French commanding general, General Humblot, a note containing decisions which the British Command had taken about the gendarmerie without consulting the French. The British authorities then handed over a considerable quantity of arms to the gendarmerie. On July 17 M. Paris complained to the Foreign Office about this action; M. Massigli also protested to Mr. Duff Cooper at Algiers. Mr. Duff

(b) Cooper telegraphed to the Foreign Office that he could not reply to the protest. 'I cannot admit to Massigli that His Majesty's Minister at Beirut has failed to carry out the policy of His Majesty's Government. . . . Your policy as I have understood it and have attempted to interpret it was that this matter should be settled by friendly Anglo-French consultation and co-operation conducted through a special Committee set up for the purpose. No such Committee has been set up nor so far as I am aware has been even suggested to the French authorities in Beirut who have been presented with a series of *faits accomplis* and whose protests have been completely ignored. The result is that a matter of minor importance is assuming alarming dimensions.' Foreign Office minutes on Mr. Duff Cooper's telegram admitted: 'I am afraid this is all true.' 'We shall never make sense of the Levant while Sir E. Spears is there.'[1]

(c) On July 19 Mr. Eden recalled Sir E. Spears immediately to London for consultation. He said that the Prime Minister and himself were concerned at the new difficulties with the French over Syria and the Lebanon just as relations with the French National Committee over larger issues were improving. Sir E. Spears at first resisted his recall in view of the tenseness of the local situation. 'It is probably more due to my influence than to any other factor that really ugly trouble has not eventuated on several occasions lately.' He finally left for London on July 24.[2] The question of arming the

---

(d)   [1] Lord Moyne also reported that he was 'not satisfied that the Legation at Beirut has advised the 9th Army Commander in accordance with the spirit or even with the letter of the Foreign Office instructions'. Lord Moyne later wrote that the trouble over the gendarmerie had been due largely 'to lack of liaison by Spears since the earliest stages, and his consistently uncompromising attitude', but he added that the French had been 'very difficult'.

(e)   [2] In this atmosphere of mistrust and dissension M. Massigli made a personal appeal to Mr. Eden. He told Mr. Duff Cooper towards the end of July that he doubted whether

(*continued on page 297*)

(a) E4174, 4259/217/89. (b) E4309/217/89. (c) E4368/217/89. (d) E4308, 4366/217/89. (e) E4424, 4500/217/89.

gendarmerie of the two States was settled for a time, after correspondence with M. Massigli, by an understanding that 2,000 rifles
should be issued to them. These weapons would be handed over to (a)
them by the French and British military commands jointly and as a
common decision.

At the beginning of July M. Massigli had suggested to Mr. Duff (b)
Cooper that Anglo-French conversations might be held in Algiers
or London to reach an agreed policy on the Levant. M. Massigli
said that the Arabs still sought—as they had done in the past—to
profit from disagreements between European nations; the French
and British were encouraging this tendency by seeming to follow
different policies, or giving the impression that the British were
taking advantage of the weakness of France to sweep her out of the
Levant. M. Massigli did not believe that this was British policy, but
found it hard to persuade his colleagues to accept his view. On
August 1 the Foreign Office told Mr. Duff Cooper that they had
considered his suggestion for a comprehensive settlement with the
French. They had arranged to hold conversations in London with
M. Massigli, but these conversations were not likely to lead to a
final settlement of differences. We could not disregard our endorsement in 1941 of the French pledge to grant independence, and the
Arab world held us jointly responsible with the French for carrying
it out. Our good name as well as that of the French National Committee was at stake. If the French were left to continue the process
of handing over powers to the States Governments, they would soon
reach a deadlock.

The telegram to Mr. Duff Cooper recognised the 'commendable
progress' of the French in the past six months in transferring powers
of self-government, but the rate of advance since 1941 had been
disappointingly slow. We had often had to restrain the Governments
of the States and to ask the French to make concessions to satisfy
the 'legitimate demands of local opinion'. This pressure on the

---

(*continued*)
British policy was being carried out. He later sent Mr. Duff Cooper for Mr. Eden a
strongly worded letter which included the passage: 'Nous nous trouvons en effet devant
l'alternative suivante: ou bien la politique suivie au Levant par les autorités britanniques
civiles et militaires reçoit l'approbation du Gouvernement de Sa Majesté, ou bien cette
politique garde un caractère personnel.' Mr. Duff Cooper concluded his own letter to
Mr. Eden: 'I think you are as convinced as I am that things can only go from bad to
worse in the Levant so long as Spears remains there, and that it would be a waste of your
time and mine to expatiate on that theme.' Mr. Eden subsequently told M. Massigli
that he did not like his letter and that he refused to take cognisance of it. After seeing
M. Massigli, however, Mr. Eden wrote to Mr. Duff Cooper: 'I have known M. Massigli
fairly intimately for 15 years, and I have confidence in his integrity. I have no doubt
that he is sincerely convinced, however mistakenly, that our local authorities are out to
destroy what remains of the French position in Syria and never miss an opportunity of
doing so.'

(a) E5207/217/89.   (b) E4122/217/89.

French would have to be continued. The French were most unpopular with the Arabs, and in the tense atmosphere of Beirut and Damascus a critical situation might arise at any moment. The telegram continued:

'It is the British task to prevent or to smooth away these continually threatened crises in Franco-Syrian and Franco-Lebanese relations, involving the risk of anti-French riots and disturbances such as might interfere with the war effort. The role of mediator which we are thus forced by circumstances to adopt is not always welcome on either side. But in this matter we are concerned not so much to please the French or the Levant Governments as to keep the peace and improve the relations between them.'

Our policy was to bring about a *modus vivendi* between the French and the States which would secure for the latter charge of all their affairs except those reserved for Allied control or advice owing to the war; a more definite settlement would eventually be necessary. Mr. Duff Cooper believed that the French would prefer to postpone a settlement until they were stronger. The Foreign Office pointed out that the Levant States were equally or even more resolved for the time not to make a lasting settlement with the French National Committee. This settlement, which would be made only after the war, might be reached under the auspices of the United Nations while Allied troops were still in the Middle East or it might be left for direct negotiation between France and the States after the evacuation of all but French troops. We would then have to use our influence to prevent the French from trying to impose a settlement by force. It seemed impossible meanwhile to reach a private understanding with the French which might limit future British freedom of action.

The Foreign Office also told Mr. Duff Cooper that they could not agree with M. Massigli's suggestion that conversations with the French National Committee should cover the whole of the Middle East. Even if the Committee were sufficiently representative of the future Government of France, French post-war interests in the Middle East might not be extensive enough to warrant such conversations. It would also be difficult to discuss Middle East affairs with the French so long as the Palestine question was not settled.

(a) The Anglo-French discussions took place in the Foreign Office on August 23 and 24.[1] At the meeting on August 23 Mr. Eden began by saying once again that the British Government did not want to replace the French in the Levant States, and that if, as was alleged, our local activities were at variance with this policy, he would be

---

[1] Mr. Eden and M. Massigli were present on August 23 only.

(a) E5185/23/89; E5207/217/89.

glad to be given evidence of them. M. Massigli replied that French policy since the occupation of Syria in 1941 had also been based on the assumption of the independence of the States. The French had assumed that the final grant of independence would be confirmed by treaties; the British Government had agreed with this view. In March 1943 General Catroux had suggested the conclusion of treaties, but the British Government had said that they should be postponed until the end of the war. After the November crisis General Catroux had transferred the *Intérêts Communs* to the States, and in doing so had told both Presidents that this arrangement was only a *modus vivendi* and that a formal treaty would be concluded later. Sir M. Peterson pointed out that in March 1943 the French Committee—as the Levant States knew—was not in the position of a government able to conclude treaties. If such a French Government came into existence, there would be no objection to treaties on the British side, but the Levant States now seemed unwilling to conclude them.

After M. Massigli had explained the French objections to the continuance of the Spears Mission, Mr. Eden and M. Massigli agreed that Sir M. Peterson, M. Ostrorog[1] and Sir E. Spears (who was now in London) should meet to examine the whole question of the functions of the Mission. A special meeting was also held to consider the arming of the gendarmerie. Sir M. Peterson reported to Mr. Eden (a) the results of these meetings. He considered that no progress would be made with the French unless there were an immediate change of British representation and the Spears Mission were withdrawn. In any case he was afraid that soon after the establishment of a French Government in Paris we should be involved in a serious dispute with them over the Levant.

Mr. Eden had suggested at the meeting on August 23 that M. Massigli should draw up a note on the question of Anglo-French policy. M. Massigli sent this note to the Foreign Office on August 25. He reaffirmed that French policy since 1941 had been based on the (b) assumption of Syrian and Lebanese independence and that this independence would be completed by treaties legally ending the mandate. He said that the British Government had advised awaiting the end of the war before the conclusion of the treaties. He then complained of British interference which he described as incompatible with the Anglo-French agreements, and seriously harmful to the French position in the Levant. He asked that this interference should cease, and that there should be a return to the exact application of the Lyttelton-de Gaulle agreement. He concluded by saying

---

[1] A member of the staff of the Délégation Générale.

(a) E5343/23/89. (b) E5144/23/89.

that the affirmation of a common Anglo-French view on the need to end the mandate by the conclusion of treaties would have a decisive influence on the attitude of the Syrian and Lebanese Governments.[1]

The Foreign Office could not accept the case put forward in M. Massigli's note. They replied to the note on August 26. M. Massigli in turn regarded the reply as unsatisfactory and said that he would have to consider his mission to London as a failure. The Foreign Office agreed to revise the draft in order to meet some of the French points; a new note, which was approved by Sir E. Spears and General Holmes, was given to M. Ostrorog on August 28 and accepted by M. Massigli. The note stated that French and British interests in the Levant were not conflicting. While making all reservations about the assertion that British authorities had interfered wrongly in local administration, the British Government confirmed that they were anxious for the closest possible local co-operation. British policy was not to supplant French influence in Syria and the Lebanon or to use British influence against French interests. The note went on to reject the French suggestion that they were misrepresenting the degree of independence achieved by the States in order to profit by French misfortunes. They had welcomed the agreement of December 22, 1943, and the progress towards a *modus vivendi* to place relations between France and the States on a basis of confidence and to enable the position to be regularised by treaties. They reserved the right to conduct direct relations with the States, especially on economic questions of importance to the war effort, but would do so wherever possible in closest association with the French and within the framework of the advisory boards and other economic organisations with French and British representation.

The note continued that the British Government had no intention of trying to regulate the internal political affairs of the two States, although the existence of diplomatic relations and the state of war prevented them from giving up the right to direct contact. They did not challenge French interest in the territorial command as defined in the Lyttelton-de Gaulle agreement. They confirmed the military provisions of this agreement, but during the war the Commander-in-Chief, Middle East, had to take a close interest in military matters, especially those affecting security. The British Government would welcome an agreement between France and the States to conclude the treaties foreseen in the declarations of independence 'as a convenient method of determining their future relations'. They

---

[1] Sir E. Spears commented on this proposal: 'I have frequently told the local Governments we would welcome a Treaty between themselves and the French, but I have never met a Syrian or Lebanese who would consider the idea.'

undertook to consider a declaration in this sense as defining their policy in the Levant. They would also consider what they could do during the war to reduce British organisations in the States.

(ii)

British advice to the Syrian and Lebanese Governments to conclude treaties with France: refusal of the two Governments to conclude such treaties: attitude of the United States Government: the Prime Minister's refusal to agree to the immediate withdrawal of Sir E. Spears.

The British Government might well declare that they were in favour of an agreement between France and the Levant States. They had indeed been making statements of this kind for the last three years and had tried to persuade the French to offer concessions which, at least for a time, might have satisfied Syrian nationalism. The difficulty, however, now came from the other side. The liberation of France and the prospect of a French Government established once more in full exercise of sovereignty increased the determination of the Syrians and Lebanese not to accept anything short of complete independence. They disregarded the legal argument that some formal arrangement was necessary to end the French mandate, and claimed that the French could not offer them anything which they were unable to provide for themselves.

In these circumstances the British Government were in a difficult position. They had put pressure on the French to make concessions to Levantine sentiment. How far were they to go in their pressure on the Levant States to come to an agreement with the French? They could, and did, begin with friendly advice, but it was clear that this advice would not be taken. Moreover, as before, the Foreign Office had the uneasy feeling that advice given through Sir E. Spears was unlikely to be presented in a way which would carry persuasion, still less conviction, with the Syrians and Lebanese.

In a letter to Mr. Eden at the end of August, Sir E. Spears said (a) that he was impressed with the 'extraordinary depth of feeling' against a treaty. The Syrian President had told him that he would cut off his right hand rather than sign a treaty with the French, and the Lebanese President that he would rather return for life to Rachaya, where he had been imprisoned in November 1943. Sir E. Spears warned the Foreign Office that if the French publicly demanded a treaty, and if it were stated that they had British support, the suggestion would be publicly repudiated by the Syrian and Lebanese Governments, the press and the Chambers, and public

---

(a) E5278/23/89.

opinion would be aroused. He expected reactions of sympathy in neighbouring Arab countries, particularly Iraq and Egypt, and thought that Russia would oppose a treaty, while the United States would not support any instrument giving the French a 'predominant and privileged position'.

(a)   Mr. Eden later told Sir E. Spears that, while we had promised freedom to the States, the position between them and the French must be regularised by a treaty, and that Sir E. Spears must work to this end.[1] Sir E. Spears suggested a British treaty with the two States on parallel lines with the French treaty, but Mr. Eden said that we had nothing to make a treaty about and that the British position in Syria was not comparable with that of the French. He also spoke about a reduction in the size of the Spears Mission, and especially in the number of political officers. Sir E. Spears said that if we removed a British officer from any district, the Syrians would immediately ask that the French officer should also go. Mr. Eden considered that a demand of this kind would be unjustified.

Meanwhile Mr. Eden had twice repeated his suggestion to the Prime Minister that Sir E. Spears should be relieved of his post. On

(b) July 30 he told the Prime Minister that Sir E. Spears had recently involved us in difficulties of his own making (over the questions of the gendarmerie and the Troupes Spéciales) and that these difficulties were only the most recent in a long series. Mr. Eden was thus driven to the conclusion that Sir E. Spears could not be trusted to carry out the spirit of his instructions or to work in pursuance of our agreed policy in the Levant. He therefore asked for authority to tell him that he would be replaced. The Prime Minister did not see this minute until August 8. On August 10—just before leaving for Italy —he asked that no decision should be taken in his absence.

(c)   On August 29, when the Prime Minister had returned to London, Mr. Eden repeated his view. He said that, apart from Sir E. Spears's unsuitability for negotiating a settlement with the French, the need of a change was now urgent on the general ground that we had to look forward to the post-war period, and that we should send out now a representative who would remain in the Levant after the war.[2]

(d)   [1] On August 25 Mr. Eden had written to Sir E. Spears: 'To my mind the resounding defeat the French sustained *vis-à-vis* the local governments at that time [November 1943] has tilted the balance somewhat unduly against them. While we must continue to urge the French to make gradual progress, it is perhaps even more necessary to exercise some restraint on the two States lest they should be tempted to think . . . there is no need for them to make some constructive and permanent effort to regularise their future relations with the French.'

(e)   [2] Lord Moyne had reported in July that Sir E. Spears himself had said that he might soon ask to be relieved. Lord Moyne thought it important that he should leave at a time when his withdrawal could not be represented as the result of French pressure.

(a) E5415/5178/89. (b) PM/44/562, Churchill Papers/423. (c) PM/44/593, Churchill Papers/423. (d) E5237/23/89. (e) T1496/4, MR/2/25243, Churchill Papers/423.

The Prime Minister drafted a reply that he could not agree to the immediate removal of 'a champion of British interests and of treaty engagements at a time like this'. Mr. Churchill, however, discussed the matter with Mr. Eden. They agreed that Sir E. Spears (who was still in England) should go back for a time, but that he should be given a strict directive and warned that he would be recalled at once if he disobeyed it. In any case the position would be reconsidered if the war came to an end suddenly, or as soon as a reorganised French Government, which we could recognise, had come into existence.

Mr. Eden therefore told Sir E. Spears on September 1 that he might go back for two months or so.[1] He gave him the proposed directive for the conduct of the Legation and the Spears Mission. The directive spoke of the 'somewhat complex relationship' between (a) the Spears Mission and the Legation. Mr. Eden wanted the Legation to be brought to the foreground; the Spears Mission was to be reduced either by suppression or by absorption into the Legation and the military command.

On September 11 Sir E. Spears spoke to the Syrian President, in (b) accordance with Mr. Eden's instructions, about a treaty with the French. He emphasised the advantages: relations between France and the Syrians would be defined, and the French would not be able to over-step these bounds; the position would be regularised, particularly with regard to the sending of French troops after the war; and economic and financial support would be facilitated. He concluded his arguments by saying that it was not British policy to take the place of France in any sphere. He then suggested that the Syrians should find out what the French had in mind; if the French put forward unfair terms, we would doubtless make representations. The Syrian President said that he would never sign a treaty with France without similar treaties with other Powers. This refusal applied even to economic and financial treaties; such treaties with France 'meant granting a licence to plunder'. He said that he would consult his Government.

On the evening of September 13 Sir E. Spears met the Syrian (c)

---

[1] Sir E. Spears wrote to the Prime Minister that he would want to leave at the end of (d) the war in Europe, but that he would like to stay until then. The Prime Minister replied to him on September 5 that he had had 'great difficulty' in securing his return: 'You did not take my advice to try to keep your francophobia within reasonable bounds, and there is no doubt that great irritation is felt by the French.' On the other hand the Prime Minister did not propose to make a change until after the French elections and the emergence of a more representative French Government. Unless the war in Europe ended sooner, Sir E. Spears would therefore be recalled in two or three months, though he would be 'given the opportunity of asking to be relieved instead of being abruptly superseded. This is the best I can do, and it certainly is in no way derogatory to you or to the services you have rendered.'

(a) E5237/23/89. (b) E5575/23/89. (c) E5681/23/89. (d) Churchill Papers/423.

Prime Minister and Minister for Foreign Affairs[1] in the presence of the Syrian President and repeated the arguments in favour of a treaty. He reported that it was a 'difficult and depressing interview'. In addition to the President's previous arguments against a treaty the Syrian Ministers said that the United States were on the point of recognising the independence of Syria without any pre-eminent position for the French. The Russian position was the same.[2] The Ministers pointed out that Great Britain had been the first Power to recognise the independence of the two States. They insisted that they would not sign a treaty with France. The Minister for Foreign Affairs said that France was not in a position to protect anyone when she had to be reinstated by Great Britain and the United States. The Syrian Ministers also referred to past experience as precluding a treaty with France. They intended to seek technical help where they thought fit, probably from Great Britain and the United States. They were determined that the Peace Conference should find them free, but they agreed upon the need of a *modus vivendi* with the French which would carry them to the end of the war. The Syrian Prime Minister said that in 1939 the Arabs were anti-British; the British Government were held to have betrayed Syria and the Lebanon after the last war. After the British occupation of Syria the position had improved, and the Arabs were beginning to trust us. We were now throwing away their confidence for the sake of France who had betrayed British interests and invited the Germans into the Levant. Sir E. Spears reported: 'I had not thought it possible that these men who were my personal friends would have expressed their views with such brutal frankness.'

The Foreign Office thought that Sir E. Spears had been wrong in asking for these formal interviews. He had been instructed to take

---

[1] Saadullah Bey Jabri, and Jamil Mardam Bey, Syrian Prime Minister and Foreign Minister respectively from December 1943.

(a)   [2] On September 7, Mr. Wadsworth, the United States Diplomatic Agent at Beirut, informed the Syrian and Lebanese Governments that his Government would recognise their independence unconditionally on receiving assurances that the rights of the United States and its nationals would be protected. These assurances were given next day. On September 19 the State Department announced that 'effective powers have been transferred to the Governments of both countries subject to the exigencies of war'. A week later the Senate confirmed the nomination of Mr. Wadsworth as Minister; in the third week of November he presented his letters of credence to the Syrian and Lebanese Presidents.

(b)   The Soviet Government had recognised Syrian independence 'in principle' on July 19, and had said that they would recognise Lebanese independence if asked to do so. On August 9 the Soviet Minister in Cairo* said to the British Chargé d'Affaires at Beirut that his Government would not recognise a privileged position for France in the Levant States. Lord Moyne informed the Foreign Office on August 10 of a reliable report that the Soviet Government had required an undertaking from the Syrian Government that they would not make a treaty limiting their independence or showing special favour to any one power.

   * The Minister was at Beirut supervising the details of Soviet recognition.

   (a) E5623, 5769, 5770, 6099, 6178, 7089/5623/89.   (b) E4848/23/89.

every chance of letting the Syrians and Lebanese know our views, but the Foreign Office had assumed that he would do so with tact and in informal conversations. He had in fact carried out his instructions in a manner which might well cause serious trouble in view of the meeting of the Arab Conference at the end of September.[1] The Foreign Office instructed him on September 20 (without much hope that he would change his methods) that, as feeling was so high, they would prefer him not to press the matter for the moment. Meanwhile Sir E. Spears had told the United States Minister of his conversations on similar lines with the Lebanese Ministers. Mr. Wads- (a) worth said that none of his own conversations in Damascus since December 1942 had given him reason to believe that Sir E. Spears would have had any other reply. He had consistently reported to his Government that Syria would not sign a treaty of alliance of special privilege with France.

Meanwhile the President of the Syrian Republic had sent a letter (b) to Mr. Churchill. He described the treaty proposal as 'a proposition that will not greatly foster the cause of peace in the Middle East'. There was no reason why Syria should enter into negotiations with the French Government. '. . . We do not wish to grant France any advantage from either the cultural, material, political or military viewpoint. We desire to treat all nations, especially the Great Powers, on a footing of complete equality.' The Syrian Government also wanted a common policy with all the Arab States to safeguard peace in the Middle East. The letter insisted that the army should . be handed over.[2] Similar letters were sent in even stronger terms to President Roosevelt and Stalin.

The Syrian Minister for Foreign Affairs telegraphed to Mr. Eden (c) on September 22 that his Government were unwilling to give France or any other State a privileged position, and refused to consider a treaty. They considered that the mandate was ended both *de jure* and *de facto*, since the setting up of liberal democratic and independent institutions, and the recognition of Syrian independence by Great Britain, Russia, the United States and other countries, including all those of the Arab world.

The Syrian attitude of angry and stubborn resistance did not change. The Syrian President and Prime Minister, after seeing General Beynet, the French Delegate General in Syria and the (d) Lebanon, and M. Ostrorog, gave an account of their interview to the United States Minister. They said that General Beynet had

---

[1] See Chapter LVI, note to section (i).
[2] On November 1 Mr. Churchill, who had been out of England in October, replied to the letter in non-committal terms.

(a) E5897/23/89. (b) E5853, 6107/23/89. (c) E5854, 6106/23/89. (d) E5810/23/89. (e) E6107/23/89.

attempted to discuss a treaty settlement which would safeguard the traditional position of France in the Levant. To this they had answered: 'This can only mean that you want to protect the Christians. The protection of our own nationals is our own affair.' They also said that at the request of the United States Government they had agreed to take over the obligations towards the United States which France had previously undertaken on behalf of the Levant States. The Syrians informed the French that the only form of treaty which they would consider would be ante-dated to November 16, 1943, and would be parallel to treaties with the majority of the United Nations Powers. During the conversation General Beynet asked: 'What can you do to maintain security?' The Syrians answered that they could maintain security if they were given the Troupes Spéciales. They threatened to get arms for the gendarmerie from some other Power if they were prevented from getting them from the British Government.

(a)   On September 26 Sir E. Spears reported that the French were pressing the Syrians hard, and saying that they were doing so in agreement with the Foreign Office. They even seemed to be going further in alleging Mr. Eden's support than the discussions with M. Massigli justified. Sir E. Spears continued: 'Seen from here we seem to be getting the worst of both worlds. Our intervention has not supported the French, and on the other hand we have done our own position in the Arab world much harm already and our attitude is being compared to our detriment with that of the United States.'

(b)   On September 22 the Minister of Labour, Mr. Bevin, wrote with some concern to Mr. Eden about the position: 'Having made use of these people during the war we are now deserting them and forcing them to accept the French.' Mr. Bevin asked whether a treaty could be arranged either between Great Britain and France or with the United Nations. 'It appears to me that we are trying to put the clock back to 1919.' Mr. Eden minuted on this letter: 'We are certainly getting into deep waters, in part because of the way Sir E. Spears is carrying out his instructions and in part because having given the French an inch they have taken an ell.' The Eastern Department reported to Mr. Eden on September 25 that they viewed the continued presence of Sir E. Spears in Beirut with the greatest misgiving. 'Sir E. Spears has consistently maintained that the French should be thrown out of Syria. He seems to have carried out his instructions about the necessity for a Syrian-French treaty in such a way that it has been the biggest possible shock to the Syrians. It seems very probable that the Syrians have never known what our real view was. . . .' The Department feared that Sir E. Spears did

---

(a) E5887/23/89. (b) E6103/23/89.

not want the crisis to pass off smoothly; they recommended that he be brought home for consultation. 'If we leave Sir E. Spears there, I think we can take it as almost certain that there never will be any understanding between the French and the Levant States. An understanding will not be easy to engineer under any circumstances.'

Mr. Eden told Mr. Bevin that he too was anxious over the situation. We did not want to force the Levant States to accept the French. In view of our undertakings, however, we could not evict the French, although we could and would ensure that they gave the States independence. Unless the States made an agreement with the French, it was difficult to confirm formally their complete independence. Mr. Eden went on to say that Sir E. Spears had carried out his instructions so brusquely and suddenly that the proposal for a treaty had not appeared—as it should have done—to the States to be the result of the continuous development of British policy. Instead Sir E. Spears had given the false impression that the proposal arose out of a private Anglo-French agreement to the detriment of the States. Mr. Eden also told the Prime Minister on September 30 (a) that he was afraid that Sir E. Spears might have acted deliberately in handling as he had done a policy which he disliked, and that he might encourage the Syrian Chamber on their reassembly to make a truculent declaration of their independence. Mr. Eden asked whether Sir E. Spears could not be brought home at once. The Prime Minister replied on October 6 that the two or three months promised to Sir E. Spears had not nearly expired, and that he did not want to take a premature decision.[1]

Meanwhile on September 27 Mr. Churchill wrote a minute to (b) Mr. Eden that, according to his recollection, we had never promised to secure the French a privileged position in Syria and the Lebanon.

> 'What we did promise was that we would in no wise seek to supplant them, as we sought nothing for ourselves. We said that if special privileges were given to any European power we should be content that the French should have them to the same extent that we had privileges in Iraq. This in no way committed us to strive for them.'

Mr. Churchill said that the situation was now 'profoundly affected' by the fact that Russia and the United States had recognised the independence of the two countries and ignored any question of

---

[1] The Prime Minister also suggested a meeting with Sir E. Spears in Cairo on his (the Prime Minister's) and Mr. Eden's return from Moscow. This meeting did not take place, but the Prime Minister and Mr. Eden discussed with Lord Moyne the question of Sir E. Spear's withdrawal. Lord Moyne told Sir E. Spears that an agreement had been reached that he was soon to go. Sir E. Spears wrote to the Prime Minister on October 24 asking that he might stay longer. The Prime Minister sent the letter to Mr. Eden saying that (c) he wanted to discuss it some time, but that there was no hurry. See also below, pp. 315–16.

(a) PM/44/628, Churchill Papers/423.   (b) M978/4, E5855/23/89.   (c) Churchill Papers/423.

French privilege. He thought it evident that British attempts to make a special treaty for France had failed. He continued:

> 'Pray have any statements made on this subject by me or in the Lyttelton Agreement looked up. I am sure we are under no obligation to struggle for an exceptional position for the French. This would lead us into the greatest difficulties with the Arab world and also into serious Syrian trouble. The French will have to make their case at the Armistice or peace table.'

(a)   On September 26 Lord Moyne had also reported that the Levant States evidently considered that a treaty giving a privileged position to France would be derogatory to their independence, although they were willing to make commercial and cultural arrangements with the French and all other nations. In view of the 'present surge of Arab nationalism', the British reputation would be damaged if the Syrian Prime Minister could show that we were trying to impose a treaty for the benefit of the French. Lord Moyne suggested that we should make it clear to both sides that, although we did not want special privileges and would welcome a treaty between the States and the French, they should settle the matter among themselves.

The Syrian Prime Minister and Minister for Foreign Affairs were (b) in Cairo at the end of September for the Arab Conference; on September 27 they asked if they could see Lord Moyne. The Foreign Office did not want the discussions transferred to Cairo. They also wished to delay them until after the Arab Conference and the departure of Sir E. Spears. They asked Lord Moyne to say that a reply to the message to Mr. Eden from the Syrian Minister for Foreign Affairs would be sent shortly through Sir E. Spears. Lord (c) Moyne told the Syrian Ministers that there had been no change in the British position and that we were not trying to impose a treaty. We had throughout supported some arrangement between the States and the French to regularise the position and prevent the raising of future claims against their independence. There were no grounds for references to secret agreements as suggested in the Syrian message to the United States; from the beginning we had made it clear that we had no intention of taking the place of France in the Levant.

Lord Moyne reported that this was his first meeting with the Syrians; he was impressed by their 'hard and unyielding attitude' They denied the need for a treaty, since Article 22 of the Covenant of the League laid down that independence was automatic after a certain degree of progress had been made.[1] They said that even under

---

[1] The Foreign Office commented that Article 22(4) of the Covenant of the League made no mention of automatic independence and did not affect the argument. They
(*continued on page 309*)

(a) E5898/23/89.   (b) E5917/23/89.   (c) E5999/23/89.

the mandate France had failed to protect Syria against aggression; they compared the French cession of Alexandretta and the Sanjak to Turkey with the British stand against Turkey over the Mosul frontier. The French had already asked for a privileged position for which they claimed British support, and had been unreasonable in the discussions.

Two days after this conversation Lord Moyne reported that tension (a) was increasing. Lord Moyne believed that the French were not trying to observe the arrangements that the details concerning the equipment of the gendarmerie should be discussed on their merits at Beirut. The Syrian Prime Minister had asked him about the British attitude if the Syrians decided to ask the United States or Russia for this equipment. They had already suggested an American gendarmerie mission on the lines of the Iranian example. General Paget and Lord Moyne thought that either of these methods of circumventing French obstruction would be derogatory to British interests and would involve serious complications. Mr. Eden shared this view. He thought that the French should be asked to agree to the issue of some arms to the gendarmerie.[1]

On October 1 Mr. Eden replied to the message from the Syrian (b) Minister for Foreign Affairs. He said that a treaty seemed necessary to end the mandate and to define the future relations between the mandatory and former mandated State. Owing to the war there had not been a French Government able to make such a treaty. The situation was altering with the liberation of France, and we would be glad to see the formal realisation of Syrian and Lebanese independence. The question was, however, more than a matter of pure form. By virtue of the mandate the French still possessed various rights and functions, some of which were also shared by British and Syrian authorities. Many other functions of government formerly exercised by the French had been transferred to the Syrians either under the agreement of December 22, 1943, or other arrangements. A number of questions which still needed adjustment could be settled only in a treaty or other agreement with the French. Mr. Eden's reply continued:

'It is not in Syria's true interest to leave them unsettled, and as disinterested friends His Majesty's Government felt entitled to tell the Syrian Government that this was their view. I would ask that the

---

(*continued*)

thought that the Syrians would have done better to stress the last sentence of the subsection, since under it the wishes of the Syrians would be taken as the primary consideration.

[1] The Foreign Office noted on October 13 that Mr. Eden was not aware that 7,000 (c) modern rifles, 600 revolvers and large quantities of motor transport and equipment had been issued to the gendarmerie, or were being issued.

(a) E6057/217/89. (b) E5855/23/89. (c) E6057/217/89.

Minister for Foreign Affairs and the President should judge the matter freely according to what they think is their country's real interest.'

Mr. Eden said once again that the British Government did not seek to replace or supplant France or substitute British for French interests in any part of Syria or the Lebanon. There were no secret agreements as hinted in the letter from the Syrian President to Mr. Churchill; British policy had been publicly defined many times and was as Mr. Eden now stated it.

(a)   Mr. Churchill sent his comments on this reply to Mr. Eden on October 2. He thought that the reply did not make clear an essential point, viz. 'that we are not responsible for procuring a position of French privilege or predominance in Syria'. Mr. Churchill thought that we could 'freely admit' a predominant position for France, but that the French must procure it for themselves by negotiation with the Syrians. If the Syrians refused and the United States and Russia recognised their refusal, we had nothing more to say. 'We are no obstacle, but we are not obliged to pull their barrow up the hill for them.' The French had no right to claim British support for their privileged position, but could say that we acquiesced in it and sought nothing for themselves nor wished to supplant them. 'This is a different thing to active and positive support.' Mr. Eden replied

(b) that he agreed. 'The position is exactly as you stated, and I agree that we are not under any obligation to procure for the French by our own active intervention a privileged position in Syria.'

(c)   Mr. Eden instructed Sir E. Spears, when he delivered Mr. Eden's reply to the Syrian Minister for Foreign Affairs, to emphasise that we were not seeking to impose any procedure or conditions on the Syrian Government, but that it would be a pity if the latter missed the opportunity to settle their relations with France. In present circumstances British influence could be used most easily to help them; such circumstances would not continue indefinitely, although we should not fail to support their independence.

Lord Halifax was instructed to inform the State Department of these exchanges and to ask the United States Government to adopt the same general attitude. The Foreign Office had consulted them in 1943 about a provisional treaty if the Syrian and Lebanese Governments wanted one with the French; the State Department

(d) had concurred. Sir A. Clark Kerr was instructed to inform the Soviet Government and Mr. Duff Cooper to inform the French Ministry of Foreign Affairs of the communications from the Syrian President and Minister for Foreign Affairs, and Mr. Eden's reply.

(a) M998/4, E5855/23/89.   (b) PM/44/648, E5855/23/89.   (c) E5855, 6825/23/89.
(d) E6106, 6240/23/89.

Lord Halifax reported that the Syrian Government had told Mr. (a) Wadsworth that the British Government were trying to force them to conclude a treaty with France. The State Department had also received the draft of a cultural agreement which the French hoped to conclude with the two Governments. The State Department felt that the draft would give exclusive benefits for the teaching of French to the detriment of English. In conversation with Lord Halifax Mr. Wallace Murray said that under the mandate the mandatory Power was expressly precluded from exercising special privileges.[1] He said that while a treaty might be the normal and desirable way of regularising the position at the end of a mandate there could be no compulsion. He acknowledged that we had been just and skilful in our dealings with Iraq, as with Egypt, and that these countries had been willing to conclude treaties. Furthermore, the British Government had possessed prestige and power and had therefore had benefits to confer and effective military support to offer. Since the fall of France, the French had had none of these assets.

Mr. Wallace Murray agreed that there was much to be said for an early treaty provided that it was not weighted on the French side. He saw that in existing circumstances British influence could be used to help the Syrians and Lebanese, and, conversely, that it might be difficult to negotiate a treaty after Allied troops had left. He also thought that if the States did not make a treaty with the French, the Russians might establish themselves in an influential position. He was concerned at what in his view was dangerous Russian penetration in the Balkans. Mr. Wallace Murray considered that the United States Government might adopt an attitude similar to the British one, on condition that the matter was taken up with the French as well as the Syrians and Lebanese. He first suggested that the French would be more amenable to British than American advice, but admitted that in view of the old fears of British designs on the Levant States the Americans might be able to help.

The Syrian Foreign Minister had earlier appealed to Mr. Hull, (b) and on October 7 the State Department telegraphed a reply that the question of treaties between Syria and other countries was one which the Syrian Government should decide. The United States Government did not want to influence their decision, but would not object to agreements defining the relationship between Syria and France provided that American interests were safeguarded. On October 9 Mr. Wadsworth was instructed to speak to the Foreign Minister in

---

[1] The Legal Adviser to the Foreign Office pointed out that the special privileges which were denied to a mandatory under a mandate were commercial treaty privileges (viz. treatment of nationals, trade) and had nothing to do with governmental powers and the stationing of troops.

(a) E6132/23/89. (b) E6309/23/89. (c) E6307/23/89.

L*BFP

support of the British view that the Levant Governments could obtain more favourable terms at this time than later in negotiations with the French.

(iii)

The question of the transfer of the Troupes Spéciales: Mr. Eden's conversations in Cairo: further dissatisfaction of the Foreign Office over Sir E. Spears's attitude towards his instructions (October 1–16, 1944).

(a)   Meanwhile the question of transfer of the Troupes Spéciales had made no progress. Sir E. Spears told General Beynet that, in view of the forthcoming reassembly of the Syrian Parliament, he was particularly worried about the apparent deadlock over the Troupes Spéciales. General Beynet told Sir E. Spears that the troops were the best bargaining counter on the French side, and that he had no instructions about their transfer. The Foreign Office did not think that it was in British interests to press the French to transfer these forces except in connexion with the treaty negotiations, when they would have to make some concessions in order to obtain a satisfactory treaty. Hence Sir E. Spears was instructed on October 2 for the moment to stop urging the French to transfer the Troupes Spéciales.

(b)   On October 3 Mr. Churchill sent a personal telegram to Sir E. Spears. He said that he was disturbed to see from Sir E. Spears's telegrams that trouble was likely when the Syrian Parliament met, if the Syrian Prime Minister could not announce an agreement for the transfer of these troops. We were most unfavourably impressed by this threat of blackmail, and by several recent indications that the Syrian Government might be contemplating direct action against the French. Mr. Churchill continued: 'The war may have left the Middle East but while this desperate conflict continues we are entitled to expect Syrians and Lebanese not to precipitate trouble which would divert any part of our war effort, especially as we have done so much for them.' In his view there was no question pending in the Levant of such urgency or importance as to justify direct action; he counted on Sir E. Spears to see that the Levant States did not precipitate another crisis.

(c)   On October 4 Sir E. Spears replied to Mr. Churchill that British influence and prestige had declined since the French had told the Syrians that we had agreed to a treaty giving the French a privileged and pre-eminent position. He described the telegram of October 2 from the Foreign Office as a bewildering change of policy. 'We pressed the French to transfer the Troupes Spéciales, stating that

---

(a) E5900/23/89. (b) T1866A/4 (Churchill Papers/423; E5900/23/89). (c) E6080/23/89.

failure to do so must inevitably increase the tension and endanger security, yet we are now apparently willing to support them in using this question as a means of bringing pressure on the Syrians for a treaty.' He said that were it not for Mr. Churchill's telegram he would have felt that it would do more harm than good to intervene further with the Syrians, 'but your name is magic still and wields a power of its own'. If the Syrians suspected that we now considered the French to be justified in using the Troupes Spéciales as a means of pressure to obtain a treaty, the two Republics would disregard our advice and their recently implanted friendship would turn to hatred. The Syrians would interpret his instructions to mean that if they did not negotiate a treaty at once they might be over-ridden by the French later, and that we would not intervene. 'The effect of taking this line with people whose independence we have guaranteed would be shattering.'

Sir E. Spears protested that he had been receiving contradictory instructions, and that the references to the mandate in his most recent instructions did not correspond with previous British or American policy on the subject or with the attitude taken during the London discussions with the French. He concluded with a reference to the 'only positive contribution the French could make to a *détente* here, namely the acceleration of the handing over of Troupes Spéciales.'

On October 15 the Foreign Office instructed Sir E. Spears that (a) the question at issue was not whether we thought that the Troupes Spéciales should be transferred, but whether it was possible to induce the French to deal with this matter alone, since obviously they were not going to give away one of their best bargaining counters in advance of a treaty settlement. Meanwhile Mr. Duff Cooper was instructed to make strong representations in Paris about the need for a *modus vivendi*, of which an agreement on the transfer of the Troupes Spéciales should form part. The last Syrian proposal of which the Foreign Office knew—in the first week of August—was that half should be transferred immediately and half at the time of the armistice with Germany. Mr. Duff Cooper was to point out that the Syrians might get arms from other sources and form their own army. The best solution would be to meet the demand for an army by the immediate transfer of part of the Troupes Spéciales. Most of these troops would presumably continue to carry out their duties for the Allies under their existing officers and chain of command. If the French were intransigent, serious local disturbances might break out.[1]

---

[1] On October 6 the Council of Ministers had met under the presidency of General de (b) Gaulle and issued a communiqué: 'M. Bidault, Minister for Foreign Affairs, reported

(*continued on page 314*)

(a) E6129/217/89. (b) E6129/217/89.

(a)   On October 9 Mr. Eden sent a telegram to Lord Moyne and Sir E. Spears.[1] He said that the various declarations about independence referred to the conclusion of treaties with France either to ensure the liberty and independence of the two States (the French and British declarations of June 8, 1941) or to replace the existing régime with a final settlement based on their independence (General Catroux's declarations of September 29 and November 26, 1941). Mr. Eden thought that it should be obvious to the Syrians that this final settlement must mean putting a formal end to the mandatory régime. Our argument for a treaty was that French rights and functions sprang from the mandate.   We should let the States Governments know that while, from a practical point of view, we had not wanted to let the existence of the mandate interfere with the grant to them of all possible control over their own affairs, there was still a legal question to be settled.   Mr. Eden said that he did not follow the reference of the Syrian Minister for Foreign Affairs to Article 22 of the Covenant of The League. Article 22 foresaw the grant of independence to mandated countries when they were able to stand alone, but did not lay down any procedure, automatic or otherwise.

Lord Moyne and Sir E. Spears were instructed to leave the Syrian Minister for Foreign Affairs to consider the matters which still needed clearing up by agreement with the French. Mr. Eden did not want to discuss the contents of a treaty with the French. Mr. Eden added for the information of Lord Moyne and Sir E. Spears that the question of French troops seemed the most important one needing an agreed settlement, and that, if necessary, they might give a hint to this effect. He did not know how the Syrian Government proposed to regulate the question except by an agreement or treaty. He did not think that it was covered by the agreed declaration of December 22, 1943, or that the Syrian Government were right in arguing that that declaration applied to the transfer of all services exercised by the French in their name, and not merely those covered by the definition of 'common interests' or any others that might be included by subsequent agreements. The Syrian Government would be prudent to avoid declarations such as that of December 22; they needed a treaty in order to avoid further misunderstanding. Mr. Eden then asked the question: 'In what way are the Levant States not finally and formally independent?' He said that they were substantially independent, and there was no reason to doubt the finality of that substantial independence. They had achieved a

(*continued*)
on the situation in Syria and the Lebanon. The Government approved his proposals, notably in regard to the status of the Troupes Spéciales.'
    [1] The Prime Minister and Mr. Eden were at this time in Moscow.

    (a) E6658/23/89.

position which already made them individual members of the family of nations, but there were certain limitations on their independence deriving from the fact that France still had rights under the mandate which had not been surrendered or even closely defined. The question of a treaty had been raised as a formal solution of these limitations. Mr. Eden said that there had been many instances, e.g. Cuba, of States substantially independent and recognised as such, but whose independence had been limited by special rights possessed by another State. Liquidation of this position required either a treaty or a unilateral surrender of all such rights by the holders of them; neither process had yet been laid down in any French pronouncements about Syria and the Lebanon.

Two days later Mr. Eden reported to Sir A. Cadogan that on his (a) way through Cairo he had had talks with Lord Moyne and General Paget about Syria, and that it was clear that the situation was 'a stubborn one and full of menace, this apart from any further difficulties created by the handling of affairs by Spears'. Lord Moyne had found that hatred of the French was deeper than he had believed. In Mr. Eden's view, there were two immediate problems: (i) the arming of the gendarmerie; (ii) the Troupes Spéciales. General Paget thought that, if the British Government did not arm the gendarmerie, the Americans or Russians would do so. Mr. Eden did not think that this was likely; we could prevent action by either Power since Syria was in the British military zone. On the other hand, Mr. Eden thought that the Foreign Office had agreed with M. Massigli that the gendarmerie should receive some arms, and that the French ought to carry out the agreement.

Mr. Eden thought that we had told the Syrians that we were in favour of the transfer of the Troupes Spéciales, and had now said that we were against it for the time being on account of their attitude towards the French.[1] 'We must be watchful not to go back on earlier undertakings to customers, however slippery, without just cause.' Mr. Eden asked Sir A. Cadogan to look into the matter: 'We have here the elements of a situation which might cause real trouble throughout the Middle East.'

In advising Sir A. Cadogan about a reply to Mr. Eden, the Eastern Department took account of a minute from the Prime Minister on the day before he and Mr. Eden left for Moscow. The Prime (b) Minister said that he hesitated to let Mr. Eden tell Sir E. Spears to send in his resignation because he was a powerful personality and a crisis was impending. He doubted whether it was the moment to

---

[1] Sir E. Spears had not in fact delivered a message to this effect to the Syrian Government.

(a) E6370/217/89. (b) M1008/4, Churchill Papers/423.

make a change. Mr. Eden took this minute with him on his journey, intending to discuss it with the Prime Minister. The Eastern Department noted: 'The whole trouble is that so long as Sir E. Spears is in Beirut, there is sure to be one crisis after another.'

(a)   On October 16 Sir A. Cadogan replied to Mr. Eden that the Foreign Office shared his concern about the situation. As for the arming of the gendarmerie, they had agreed with the French in London on a satisfactory scale of issue of rifles, revolvers, motor transport and equipment; this issue was being carried out jointly by the French and British military authorities. Sir A. Cadogan thought that the issue of rifles and other equipment should suffice to keep the situation quiet. As for the Troupes Spéciales, the Foreign Office had told Sir E. Spears to stop pressing for their transfer as a whole, but at the same time we were making further representations in Paris for some part of them to be transferred at once. We had not gone back on our undertakings to the States nor had we said that we were opposed to a transfer, although the Syrians and Lebanese might have inferred, rightly, that the Foreign Office thought the matter should be settled with the French by negotiation, either as a part of the projected treaty or separately from it.

Sir A. Cadogan told Mr. Eden that unless we obtained some agreement between the French and the States about their future relations, especially over the question of the location and strength of any French forces, there would be a clash which would upset the Middle East and in which we might have to intervene. A settlement by consent, including that of the location of French forces, was of great importance to Great Britain as well as to the other parties. Our influence could best be used to produce agreement while we still had troops in the area, but a more conciliatory spirit on the part of the French and the Levant States was indispensable.

Sir A. Cadogan hoped that Mr. Eden would be able to arrange the departure of Sir E. Spears. 'He has already mismanaged the situation badly, and is obviously out of sympathy with any policy except throwing the French out. It is true enough that he has great influence, but he will not use it in the way we require. I feel we accept a real risk in keeping him there.'

(a) E6370/217/89.

(iv)

Resolutions of the Preparatory Committee for the Arab Congress: démarche *of General Beynet: Syrian and Lebanese protests: resignation of Sir E. Spears: Lord Killearn's telegram regarding British policy in the Middle East (October 7, 1944–January 5, 1945).*

At this point both the Syrians and the French aggravated the situation by provocative action. The delegations to the Preparatory Committee for the Arab Congress had met on September 25 at Alexandria under the presidency of Nahas Pasha.[1] The Committee passed a special resolution concerning the Lebanon in the (a) following terms:

'The Arab States represented on the Preparatory Committee reaffirm severally their respect for the independence and sovereignty of the Lebanon within her present frontiers. The Governments of these States have in fact already recognised this independence and sovereignty after the Government of the Lebanon had declared their adoption of a policy of independence in a ministerial statement which received the unanimous approval of the Lebanese Parliament on October 7, 1943.'

On October 13 General Beynet told the Lebanese President that (b) the resolutions of the Conference made the conclusion of a treaty with France impossible, and invalidated General Catroux's declarations of independence.[2] The President replied that the resolutions did not preclude any Arab country from concluding a treaty provided that it was not hostile to general Arab interests. He said that Lebanese independence was established and could not be abolished.

On October 15 the Lebanese Prime Minister called on Sir E. Spears. He said that he was about to get in touch with the Syrians with a view to informing the other Arab States of this development. He proposed to inform the Iraqi Minister for Foreign Affairs, who was in Beirut. On October 21 the Syrian Minister for Foreign Affairs sent a message to Sir E. Spears that the Iraqi Minister had just left for Baghdad, and intended to address notes immediately to the British Ambassador and the United States Minister about General Beynet's *démarche*, saying that the Iraqi Government would consider any attempt to weaken Lebanese independence as an unfriendly act. The Syrian Government were sending a representative to Cairo to ask the Egyptian Government to take action similar to that of the Iraqi Government. They were also inviting the support of Trans-

---

[1] See Chapter LVI, note to section (i).
[2] M. Ostrorog subsequently told the First Secretary of the British Legation that General Beynet had acted without instructions.

(a) E6477/41/65. (b) E6653/217/89.

jordan and Saudi Arabia. The Syrian Minister said that he was meeting the Lebanese Prime Minister and Minister for Foreign Affairs on October 22 to discuss common policy in the light of the French move. He was anxious to see Sir E. Spears on October 23 before he met General Beynet and M. Ostrorog on October 24 to discuss matters generally with them.

Sir E. Spears thought that the Syrian Government were being unreasonable in going further and faster than the Lebanese who were chiefly concerned. He sent a message to Jamil Bey that he was surprised at the drastic action which he had taken without consulting the Lebanese Government. Jamil Bey replied that all actions would be postponed except that to be taken by the Iraqi Minister for Foreign Affairs, who had already left. The Syrian and Lebanese Ministers met on October 23 and decided that the Lebanese Government should press the French for an early reply to their request that General Beynet should withdraw his *démarche*. They also agreed that Jamil Bey in the name of the two Governments should demand the transfer of the Army when he saw General Beynet.

(a)   On October 21 Mr. Eden had telegraphed to the Foreign Office from Cairo that the resolutions of the Arab Conference did not preclude a treaty. He was astonished at General Beynet's attitude, which we could not endorse in view of the Lyttelton-de Gaulle agreement. He asked that M. Massigli should be told of his views. The Foreign Office had already instructed Mr. Duff Cooper to inform M. Bidault of their view that Lebanese independence was not subject

(b)   to reconsideration. Sir A. Cadogan therefore thought a representation to M. Massigli unnecessary; Mr. Eden agreed.

(c)   Mr. Churchill raised the matter in the War Cabinet on October 23. He said that the British Government might have to make clear their view that General Catroux's declarations were not invalidated by the resolutions of the Arab Conference. Sir A. Cadogan said that there would be advantage in a statement addressed not only to the French but to the Syrians who were overstating their case. The Prime Minister had had in mind a reference to the matter in his speech in the House on October 27. In the event he did not refer to it.[1]

(d)   On November 7 the Syrian Minister for Foreign Affairs replied to Sir E. Spears's representations of October 16.[2] His note stated that a treaty between Syria and France was not necessary after the

---

(e)   [1] On October 26 General de Gaulle told a press conference in Paris that the Syrians and Lebanese were independent in all respects ('de tous côtés').

[2] i.e. Mr. Eden's reply to the message of October 1 from the Syrian Minister for Foreign Affairs. See above, p. 309.

(a) E6507/23/89.   (b) E6611/23/89.   (c) WM(44)140; E6653/217/89.   (d) E7238/23/89. (e) E6613/23/89.

agreement of December 22, 1943. The note referred to the 'unpleasant memory which the Syrians still retain of former attempts to place Franco-Syrian relations on a contractual basis' and stated that Syria now enjoyed 'complete independence, both internally and externally'. There had been a great change in the external and internal position of the country since the signature of the Lyttelton-de Gaulle agreement; Syria could not tie her fate to that of France or any other nation in cultural, military, economic or political matters. The note mentioned the 'indissoluble ties' which bound Syria to the other Arab States; the resolutions of the Arab Conference precluded any arrangement which was not in their interest. After receiving the British reply on October 16 the Syrian Government had resumed negotiations with the French on October 24 to settle outstanding questions, especially the army, but the negotiations had shown that the French were trying to ensure a privileged position in Syria. Since no agreement could be reached, the Syrian Government had informed the French at the last meeting on October 30 that they intended to ask the British Government, which had assumed military responsibility in Syria for war purposes, to arbitrate on the question of the army.

During their visit to Paris on November 11–12[1] the Prime Minister (a) and Mr. Eden had an informal discussion with General de Gaulle and M. Bidault. General de Gaulle referred to Syrian independence as a part of French policy; he defined independence as including a relationship similar to that of Great Britain with Iraq, and earlier with Egypt. This relationship would not mean surrender of the dominating influence of France, but the French had no desire to annex Syria or the Lebanon. General de Gaulle asked why the British Government had pressed the French to transfer the Troupes Spéciales which were necessary to keep order. Mr. Eden said that France had undertaken to help the Levant States to create their own national armed forces. M. Bidault said that this undertaking was not to become effective until the end of the war; later he agreed that there was no stipulated date. Mr. Eden said that the whole Arab question would need to be examined, perhaps at the Peace Conference. Mr. Churchill repeated once again that we did not wish to take the place of France in Syria or the Lebanon. The French position could be analogous to the British position in Iraq and in maintaining that position France would have British diplomatic support. Mr. Churchill also said that the possession of large colonial territories would be less important in future than the possession of

---

[1] For this visit, see also Vol. III, Chapter XXXVII, section (iv).

(a) E7627/217/89.

striking power, particularly in the air. Navies were losing some of their importance and colonial possessions might sometimes be more of a liability than an asset, as Great Britain's balance sheet with India now showed.

Later the same day General de Gaulle said to Sir A. Cadogan that France by long tradition had the mission for the protection of Christians in the Levant. She was bound to fulfil that mission; her prestige would suffer if she failed. The Christian community would consider that they had been betrayed and the Moslems would consider that France had been unable to meet her obligations.

On the morning of November 12 Mr. Eden, Mr. Duff Cooper and Sir A. Cadogan discussed the question of the Levant States with M. Bidault, M. Massigli and M. Chauvel. M. Bidault said that there seemed to be an idea that France was not going to carry out her promises to the Levant States. There was no ground for this view. On the other hand France was resolved not to give up any of the rights to which she was still entitled. She would expect to retain influence in the Levant States as Great Britain had done in Iraq. Mr. Eden thought that there was no essential difference between the British and French points of view and that the situation might be regulated by a treaty.

There was then some discussion about the Troupes Spéciales. M. Bidault quoted a passage in General Catroux's declaration of independence which might be held to imply that there was no obligation to transfer these troops as long as the war lasted. Mr. Eden suggested a compromise, e.g. transfer of 25 per cent of the troops at an early date, and provision for transfer of the rest at the end of the war. M. Bidault said that it was very difficult for France to decide upon any immediate transfer of troops. If this were done, an equivalent number of French troops would have to be sent to the Levant as reinforcements. France was prepared to make in a final and comprehensive agreement every concession to which she was committed, but she did not want a series of partial agreements. Any concession made now would provoke more claims. Mr. Eden pointed out that the matter had been discussed for six months and that the demands of the Levant States did not grow less as time passed. He feared that the effect of bringing in French reinforcements would be unfortunate.

On the evening of November 12 Sir A. Cadogan went at his request to see M. Chauvel. They agreed on a formula about the Troupes Spéciales which M. Chauvel promised to submit to M. Bidault. This formula was:

'The French Provisional Government will transfer to the Syrian Government now a percentage of the Troupes Spéciales on the understanding that provision will be made for the subsequent transfer of the remainder in the final treaty or in an annex to such a treaty which could be negotiated now.'

After their return from Paris Mr. Eden asked the Prime Minister (a) to tell Sir E. Spears to send in his resignation as from December 15. The promised 'two or three months' had now passed, and the French Government had been reconstituted and recognised by Great Britain. The Prime Minister agreed with Mr. Eden's proposal. On the night of December 5 a communiqué was issued announcing Sir (b) E. Spears's resignation and the appointment of Mr. T. A. Shone as Minister to the two Republics. A further statement issued in London and the Middle East made it clear that the new appointment did not mean a change in British policy.

Mr. Shone presented his letters of credence at Beirut on December (c) 22 and at Damascus on the next day. On December 27 he called on the French Delegate-General who received him in a friendly manner. Mr. Eden had told him that he disagreed in part with the (d) statement of the position in the Syrian note of November 7. The French had handed over a number of functions to the Syrian Government, so that the latter were enjoying substantial independence, but there was a residue of rights still possessed by the French, legally speaking, by virtue of the mandate. The French had never given up their right under the mandate to have troops in Syria, although they had promised in various proclamations to relinquish various other powers at the end of the war. They exercised these powers during the war not because the Syrians had agreed, but because General Catroux had reserved them in the proclamations of independence. There was nothing as yet to show that the French were requiring any treaty rights from Syria different from the British treaty rights in Egypt or Iraq—even if they went as far—and such treaty rights had not prevented those countries from being independent or joining in the Arab Council. Mr. Shone was instructed to tell the Syrian Government that we did not think it practicable to arbitrate formally about the Troupes Spéciales.[1] They had discussed the question with the French Provisional Government, who had so far not agreed to make progress with it except as part of the negotiations for ending the mandate.

At the end of the year Lord Killearn,[2] in a telegram to the Foreign (e) Office, called attention to the increasing importance of Arab nationalism and its repercussions on British policy. He suggested that we had been pursuing two conflicting policies simultaneously,

---

[1] See above, p. 319.
[2] Sir Miles Lampson was elevated to the peerage as Lord Killearn in 1943.

(a) PM/44/705; M1116/4, Churchill Papers/423.   (b) E7473/5178/89.   (c) E7905/5178/89.   (d) E7238/23/89.   (e) E7876/23/89.

i.e. encouraging the Arab Union, and promoting Zionism in Palestine and French predominance in Syria. He pointed out that the Lebanese had signed a protocol which precluded any treaty with the French which would make the Lebanon a French military bridgehead against Syria, and that they would hardly dare to incur the open hostility of the surrounding Moslem world by breaking this agreement and siding with the French.

Lord Killearn spoke of the idea 'in some British quarters' of 'running with the hare and hunting with the hounds', i.e. that, in order to please the French, we might press the Syrians and Lebanese to sign preferential treaties with France, but if they refused, say that we could do no more. Lord Killearn thought, however, that if we supported France in the matter of a treaty, the French would go ahead, and that, unless we prevented him, General de Gaulle might use force at least against the Lebanon to impose the French terms. If we allowed the French to impose a treaty on the Lebanon by force, we should become involved in a conflict with most of the Arab world and end by losing the Middle East, unless we were prepared to keep large forces there. Lord Killearn asked whether, while we were involved in repressive action in liberated territories such as Greece, we could undertake similar action in the Egypt-Arab world.

Mr. Churchill marked this telegram to Mr. Eden 'Important'. The Foreign Office thought that Lord Killearn had misunderstood the position, but that if he had done so, the Egyptians and Arabs were much more likely to misunderstand it. Hence we should tell him and the

'high level British officials with whom he consorts, that we are looking at the Middle East as a whole and have a policy for it, and that the departure of the forceful personality of Sir E. Spears does not mean that we think that we can sit back in the Levant. . . . We may require presently to restate in Paris our view that the French Government must on no account seek to impose a settlement on the Lebanon or Syria by force. This would be likely to get them into trouble not only with the Americans and Russians, but with our own military, with our public opinion and with His Majesty's Government.'

On January 5, 1945, the Foreign Office informed Lord Killearn that they realised the need to reconcile divergent elements in British policy and to regard the Middle East as a whole. British policy towards Arab unity was one of general sympathy for the desire of the Arab States to reduce the barriers between them. If indeed we were to adopt any other policy, we should arouse all the latent xenophobia of the Arabs and be condemned by the whole Arab world as responsible for the breakdown of the discussions, which might or might not have had useful results. We could not ignore the ideals and aims of the Arab unity movement; 'in view of our great strategic and other interests in the area, we must try to guide it into spheres where we can co-operate'. We also considered that both the Arabs and Jews had very strong claims to be consulted before final decisions were taken about Palestine. As for Syria and the Lebanon, Lord Killearn had misunderstood British policy. We had under-written the French promise of independence and had no intention of pressing the States to sign it away. We did want them to reach agreement with the French about their future relations. Mr. Eden concurred with Lord Killearn's view that if there were no agree-ment, General de Gaulle might be tempted to use force to secure a decision. Such a situation would be even more serious than that which had occurred in the Lebanon in November 1943. The Foreign Office intended to do their best to prevent trouble and would have to deal firmly with it if it arose. The possibility of it, however, was precisely the reason why an agreement was so necessary. We had not said that the Syrians and Lebanese must concede everything, or indeed any specific thing, which the French asked. The Syrians and Lebanese, however, were not facing the need for an agreement. The Foreign Office could not see a satisfactory alternative to their policy of facilitating an agreed settlement between the French and the States, although it would not be easy to arrange and would take time. This policy did not seem inconsistent with their attitude towards Arab nationalism generally, unless it became clear that a settlement between the States and the French would involve some derogation from their (the States') independence. The Foreign Office thought that an agreement need not prevent Syria and the Lebanon from co-operating with the other Arab States as foreseen in the Alexandria Protocol. '. . . We fully understand here that our policy towards the Egyptian-Arab world embraces many points of major importance to us and that it has to be reconciled with our obligations under the Balfour declaration and with our policy towards the new France; also that there are undoubted difficulties and even dangers to be overcome.'[1]

---

[1] See also Chapter LVI.

(v)

Syrian and Lebanese objections to a treaty with France: meeting between the Prime Minister and Mr. Eden and the Syrian President on February 17: views of the State Department on the situation in the Levant States (January– February 1945).

(a)   On December 30, 1944, Sir E. Grigg[1] reported a conversation with M. Ostrorog, who was on his way to Beirut from Paris. M. Ostrorog said that everyone in Paris was determined on Anglo-French agreement,[2] and that there was no serious question outstanding except that of the Levant States. No French Government could allow itself to be accused of sacrificing the French position in these States. France had had 'great malheurs', and needed psychologically to keep a 'position spéciale' in the Levant States such as that of Great Britain in the other Arab States. Sir E. Grigg suggested that it was essential to exercise patience and to work for a change of feeling on the part of the States. M. Ostrorog said he and his colleagues were proposing to carry out a policy of this kind.[3] Sir E. Grigg asked whether the Levant States had been discussed with the Americans or with Russia at the time of General de Gaulle's conversations with Stalin. M. Ostrorog said that the matter had not been raised with either Government.

(b)   On December 31 Mr. Shone reported that he had found the attitude of the Syrian and Lebanese Ministers towards a treaty with France 'even harder' than he had expected. They said that a treaty was unnecessary and that they could not trust France not to use it to re-establish a situation like that under the mandate, which, whatever the legal position, they regarded as dead. They were also reluctant to make 'agreements'. The Moslem Ministers had emphasised the importance of the Arab Union. Mr. Shone reported that the French underestimated the strength of the feeling about independence and the effects on the Arab world of an attempt to re-impose French predominance. The Egyptian Prime Minister had given Mr. Shone a similar impression.

Mr. Eden minuted: 'It is certainly no part of our business to force the Syrians into a treaty with France. We can advise, we cannot impose, nor should we try. It is unfortunate that the French seem to misread the situation so badly. We must go on trying to enlighten them.' He asked for the views of the Eastern Department. The

---

[1] Sir E. Grigg was appointed Minister Resident in the Middle East on November 21, 1944. Lord Moyne had been assassinated on November 5.
[2] See Vol. III, Chapter XXXVII, section (vi).
[3] An office marginal minute read: 'Good if they do, but time is running out.'

(a) E211/8/89 (1945). (b) E8/8/89.

Eastern Department did not want anything to be imposed on the Levant States, but thought that the time had come for Syria and the Lebanon to define their future relations by agreement with France. We should not try to press the question or bring it to a head for some weeks. 'We shall sooner or later have to settle these questions though, and make sure both the French and the Levant States accept the arrangement.' The Eastern Department agreed strongly with Lord Killearn's view that 'His Majesty's Government cannot effectively run two opposed policies in the Middle East'. On January 4, 1945, Mr. Eden wrote: 'Yes. But if the Syrians won't have a treaty we cannot compel them to it.' Mr. Shone continued his warnings. On January 8 he reported: 'I think we are in for a pretty sticky time (a) before long with the Syrians.' He spoke of the 'difficulties of making any headway in Damascus without a grave risk of forfeiting their confidence'. On January 26 the Foreign Office informed him that they would not support an intransigent attitude on the part of the Syrian Government to a treaty or some arrangement with the French.

On February 3 the Syrian Government agreed to ask the French (b) to state their *desiderata*. Mr. Duff Cooper was instructed to inform M. Bidault of this decision, and to express our hope that when the French explained their proposals to the Syrians they would do so with moderation and tact. The Foreign Office asked the State Department for support in Paris and Damascus. On February 14 (c) the Syrian President spoke to Lord Killearn about the difficult situation. He said that Syria must come into the Arab *bloc* and could not exist outside it as part of an uncertain French system; the French declaration of Syrian independence and the British guarantee thereof had not mentioned the need for a treaty with France to end the mandate.

Three days later the Prime Minister, while at Cairo on his way (d) home from the Yalta Conference, met the Syrian President, M. Shukri Kuwatli, at the later part of a meeting attended by Mr. Eden, Sir E. Grigg, Sir A. Cadogan, Mr. Shone and Mr. Hankey of the Foreign Office. The Syrian President said to Mr. Eden that he hoped that the situation would improve, and that the Syrian Government would have British support in overcoming present difficulties. They wanted tranquillity in their country, but they had suffered much provocation; every effort would be made to keep the peace, but the situation might get out of hand. The President said that a special agreement about the Troupes Spéciales had been on the point of signature in the summer of 1944, but the French had suddenly said

---

(a) E207/8/89. (b) E821/8/89. (c) E1589/8/89. (d) E1415/8/89.

that there would be no transfer owing to the presence of the British Army in Syria. They did not want to be replaced by the British. Mr. Eden emphasised that there was no question of the British replacing the French. The Syrian President said that the Troupes Spéciales were composed of Syrians, and the fact that they might be used against the Government was a standing provocation to them.

After discussing a recent disturbance at Latakia Mr. Eden told the President that the French had been urged to make their proposals for a settlement to the Syrian Government. The Syrian President said he was afraid that the French would not reply or reply only very slowly to the Syrian request for proposals. They would ask for a privileged position, but it would be impossible to grant them anything which could not be granted to Russia, Turkey and other Powers. Mr. Eden said that some French proposals might be unacceptable, but that the Syrians should make counter-proposals; if these were reasonable, Great Britain and America would support them. The Syrian President explained that his Government wanted to co-ordinate their policy with that of other Arab States and were not prepared to link their fate with that of France. Mr. Eden pointed out that King Ibn Saud, members of the Government of Iraq and others took part in Arab conversations. An agreement need not mean the subordination of Syrian foreign policy to French foreign policy. He was not asking for anything contrary to Syrian independence. The matter ought to be arranged before British troops left the Levant.

The Prime Minister then came into the meeting. He said that he was anxious to convince the French that we did not aim at replacing them. We wanted nothing for ourselves. The French must recognise the independence of the States; the Syrians must not 'throw the French out altogether'. The Syrian President said he was sure that it was not the British aim to replace the French. The Syrians would guarantee the French rights to establish hospitals and schools, but the grant of a privileged position would be contrary to the interests of tranquility in Syria. He was afraid that the British Government aimed at creating a zone of influence for the French in Syria.

Mr. Eden urged the President to put his proposals in writing as soon as possible. Mr. Churchill said that the French should say what they wanted and the Syrians what they were prepared to give. The Syrians must offer something reasonable to France and the French must have a position of some sort. The Syrian President said that France would receive most favoured nation treatment. He thought that the French proposals should be made soon and that meanwhile the French should not provoke the Syrians. If there were provocation, he would ask for British help. Mr. Eden agreed about hastening French proposals, but said that the President should hasten the preparation of Syrian counter-proposals and should give the French as much as possible.

The Prime Minister said repeatedly that the Syrians should handle the question tactfully and settle it without serious quarrels. They should give the French a reasonable settlement and not trample on French *amour propre*, which had been greatly shaken by the war. They should maintain their rights but be confident in their friends and in the world organisation which would be set up. The Prime Minister said that we should not oppose any arrangements which gave France a somewhat better or different position from that of the British. Such arrangements need not affect Syrian independence. He warned the Syrians that if they did not go as far as possible to meet the French there would be trouble. General de Gaulle was a dangerous man; he (the Prime Minister) could not foresee the outcome, which might be unpleasant for everyone. British troops would not stay indefinitely in Syria.

The President said that the transfer of the Troupes Spéciales must be settled before the British forces left. The Prime Minister answered that while discussions should begin as soon as possible the Syrians should not try to force the issue prematurely. Their long-term position was not a bad one. At the Peace Conference many general arrangements would have to be made. France would be a permanent member of the World Organisation and would have many things to demand, e.g. in the Rhineland and Indo-China. The Syrians should then make a reasonable arrangement. The Syrian President later told Mr. Shone that he was satisfied with the assurances that we would not impose agreements with the French on Syria and at the Prime Minister's apparent recognition that Syria could not be expected to conclude a treaty with France on the lines of the British treaty with Iraq.

Meanwhile the State Department had replied to the British request (a) for support. They agreed with the British view of the situation and had instructed the United States Minister to try to persuade the local Governments to undertake negotiations for treaties with France which would be non-discriminatory regarding third Powers and consistent with their independence, but which would give assurances about the recognition and protection of French rights and interests. The State Department had also instructed Mr. Caffery in Paris to urge the French Government to take steps regarding the transfer of the Troupes, the equipment of the gendarmeries, and the establishment of normal diplomatic representation at Damascus and Beirut. The United States Government opposed the use of military force in the form of French-controlled native levies or French troops. The

(a) E1187, 1188, 1191/420/89.

State Department had seen the draft of a Convention Universitaire which the French were trying to conclude; its terms would injure American cultural and educational interests in the Levant States and give France privileges. The State Department assumed that the French did not want to promote their interests at American expense. The instructions to Mr. Caffery concluded that 'our policy towards the independence of Syria and the Lebanon is in our view entirely distinct and independent of our policy towards France and the French Empire'.

The British Government had invited M. Bidault to London in the latter part of February.[1] He arranged to leave for London on February 25. On the evening of February 24 he handed Mr. Duff Cooper a note on the Levant in which the French Government maintained that the Levant States were still a French responsibility and that they were repeating a statement of their position only out of a desire for Anglo-French co-operation. They could not hand over the Troupes Spéciales or make any other concessions in advance of a general settlement. Mr. Duff Cooper regarded this note as extremely unsatisfactory. He therefore saw M. Bidault again on the same evening. He said that the French attitude generally, following on the refusal of General de Gaulle to meet President Roosevelt at Algiers,[2] showed that the French had no wish for co-operation. The British and Syrian Governments had been waiting for a fortnight for the French to state their terms, but the French note gave no indication of them. M. Bidault answered that the French terms were: military and air bases; fixing of a date for transfer of the Troupes Spéciales; satisfactory safeguards for university and cultural interests; a pre-eminent position for the French Ambassador. Mr. Duff Cooper asked why he had not put forward these conditions in his note. M. Bidault said that they had received no official communication from the Syrians, and that it was 'inadmissible' that the French should state their terms to the Syrians in a note to the British.

During his visit to London[3] M. Bidault discussed the Syrian situation in general terms with Mr. Eden. M. Bidault repeated that the French wanted in Syria only a position such as the British Government had in Iraq, with their base at Habbaniyah. He did not believe that British interests in the Near East would be served if France were to leave Syria. Conciliatory instructions had been sent to the French delegate to sound the Syrian Government about a treaty. M. Bidault then stated the terms which he had mentioned to

[1] See Vol. III, p. 97.
[2] See Vol. III, pp. 97–98.
[3] See Vol. III, pp. 99–100.

(a) E1340, 1386/8/89.

Mr. Duff Cooper. Mr. Eden said that we desired nothing in Syria and only wanted the French to get their treaty. He warned M. Bidault of the strength of local opposition and told him that we had urged the Syrian President to reach agreement with the French. M. Bidault said that he was ready to have a general treaty with us covering Arab policy and mutual interests in the Near East. As for the Troupes Spéciales, M. Bidault felt that it would be more possible to set a date for their transfer if the French Government knew when British troops would be leaving Syria and the Lebanon.[1]

(vi)

Reinforcement of French troops in Syria: the Prime Minister's message to General de Gaulle of May 5: General de Gaulle's reply: French bombardment of Damascus, May 29–31: British intervention (April 30–May 31, 1945).

The Foreign Office learnt at the end of April that the French (a) Government intended to send to the Levant three battalions of French African troops. Mr. Duff Cooper was instructed to make (b) representations to the Quai d'Orsay and then to General de Gaulle on the danger of sending French reinforcements. Mr. Duff Cooper consulted the United States Embassy before taking action, but they had received no instructions. He warned General de Gaulle on (c) April 30 of the possibility of trouble in Arab countries. General de Gaulle said that he recognised this possibility, but that by the Lyttelton-de Gaulle agreement order in Syria was a French responsibility. He was sending in three battalions and intended to withdraw one. We could not expect him to hand over the Troupes Spéciales to the States without increasing the number of French troops. Mr. Duff Cooper reported to the Foreign Office General de Gaulle's continued belief that it was British policy to weaken the French position in Syria and take over responsibility. General de Gaulle said that British troops had been in Syria since General Dentz's surrender and had built permanent barracks. During the trouble in

---

[1] On February 27 the Prime Minister made a statement in the House of Commons on British policy with regard to Syria and the Lebanon. After saying that we wanted to respect the independence of the States and also to preserve the special position of France in relation to them, the Prime Minister added: 'I must make it clear that it is not for us alone to defend by force either Syrian or Lebanese independence or French privilege. We seek both, and we do not believe that they are incompatible. Too much must not be placed, therefore, upon the shoulders of Great Britain alone. We have to take note of the fact that Russia and the United States have recognised and favour Syrian and Lebanese independence, but do not favour any special position for any other foreign country.' Parl. Deb. 5th Series, H. of C., Vol. 408, p. 1290.

(a) E3828/8/89.   (b) E2643, 2709/12/89.   (c) E2733/12/89.

Greece, the British Government had withdrawn troops from Italy rather than Syria. He said that everyone in the Middle East knew that Sir E. Spears's policy had been to oust the French from the Levant, and yet he had remained there as Minister for over three years. If we withdrew all our troops from Syria, he would withdraw all French troops, even though he would not consider it wise to do so, but as long as British troops remained we could not ask him to reduce the number of French troops. He would be making a reduction if he handed over the Troupes Spéciales. He implied that he was intending to hand over the latter.

At the end of the conversation, General de Gaulle spoke of the relative prestige of the two countries in Syria. Mr. Duff Cooper assured him that it never had been the policy either of Mr. Eden or Mr. Churchill to diminish French prestige in the Levant. General de Gaulle said that that might be so, but it had been the policy of other people even before Sir E. Spears. He gave no sign that he would change his mind about the despatch of French troops to Beirut.

The Foreign Office thought that General de Gaulle's reference to the 'relative prestige of our two countries in Syria' was ominous, and that he was unlikely to halt the movement of French forces. They asked for the intervention of the Prime Minister to stop the arrival of French warships and troops at Beirut. Sir O. Sargent submitted to the Prime Minister on May 1 the view of General Paget and Mr. Shone that any French reinforcement would entail a very serious risk of trouble throughout the Middle East, and would be particularly dangerous because Franco-Syrian treaty negotiations were about to begin. General Beynet had gone to Paris early in March to get instructions and draft French terms. He was to have returned within a fortnight, but was still in Paris. He now seemed likely to arrive at the same time as a cruiser with French troops. Mr. Shone had already warned the Foreign Office that there would be a strong anti-French reaction in Syria and the Lebanon if the French terms included a demand for a military base. This reaction might be violent if the French accompanied presentation of their terms by a show of force. They might start an agitation throughout the Middle East which would matter little to General de Gaulle but a great deal to the British Government. Meanwhile one French cruiser had sailed from Toulon and was due to leave Bizerta for the Levant with the first detachment of troops before May 2. Sir O. Sargent thought that another approach must be made to General de Gaulle. He asked the Prime Minister to send a personal message, and concluded: 'Apart from this, the only thing we can suggest is to allow matters to take their course and to hope that they will not turn out so badly as we fear.'

The Prime Minister did not want to intervene:

'I do not wish to correspond with General de Gaulle directly on these matters. It would only result in my receiving some insulting answer. There is nothing he likes better than to have such opportunities presented. The matter must therefore be handled through the Embassy in Paris, and there is no reason why you should not interview M. Massigli here. . . .'

The message drafted by the Foreign Office said that the Prime (a) Minister was shocked to hear that General de Gaulle regarded the matter as one concerning the prestige of Great Britain and France in the Levant. There was no question of Great Britain trying to oust France from the Levant; we had used all our influence to get the States to come to terms with France. Mr. Churchill had spoken strongly in this sense to the Syrian President in February. The French representatives in the Levant should have reported to General de Gaulle that we were working loyally to help him. How could we continue our collaboration, for which we received no thanks from the Syrians and Lebanese, if General de Gaulle sent warships and reinforcements to the Levant against strong British recommendation?

We had recognised the special position of France in Syria and the Lebanon but our commitments and duties extended throughout the Middle East. Our main task was to ensure Allied communications to the Indian and Far Eastern theatres and the security of essential oil supplies. If General de Gaulle now reinforced his troops, the States, who had been waiting for treaty proposals for some time, would decide that he was preparing a settlement to be concluded under duress. The draft ended with a suggestion that the French and British Governments should jointly examine such questions as the transfer of the Troupes Spéciales.

The Prime Minister, after consulting the War Cabinet and the (b) Chiefs of Staff, decided to offer the withdrawal of all British troops from Syria and the Lebanon as soon as a treaty between France and the two States had been concluded and was in operation. In spite of his first refusal he sent a personal telegram to General de Gaulle. The telegram repeated what had long become a regular formula, (c) that Great Britain had no designs against French interests in Syria and the Lebanon, but that, while relations between France and the Levant States were undefined, we had to be on our guard against disturbances which might affect the whole of the Middle East. After making the offer to withdraw British troops when a treaty was in operation, the Prime Minister continued:

(a) E2733/12/89.   (b) WM(45)57 and 58; COS(45) 117th meeting.   (c) T761/5 (Churchill Papers/423; E2733/12/89).

'From this point of view it would seem a great pity if the sending in of reinforcements, above those which are needed as replacements, were to cause unrest or a rise of temperature. Of course this again might be offset if the Troupes Spéciales were handed over. It would help greatly if you could make an immediate declaration on this subject. As you imagine, it is a matter of great importance to us not to have the Arab world roused up with probable sympathetic reactions in Iraq.

If you reinforce your troops at this moment the Levant States, who have been waiting for treaty proposals for some time past, may well suppose that you are preparing a settlement to be concluded under duress. This might injure both your and our relations with them and poison the atmosphere for the negotiations you are about to begin. I hope therefore that you will help me in avoiding this addition to our troubles. Good wishes.'

(a)   General de Gaulle answered Mr. Churchill on May 6. He said that France wanted only to reconcile the régime of independence with her cultural, economic and strategic interests in the region. He mentioned French interest in communications with the Far East and in the oil of Iraq.

'Ces conditions impliquent que la France conserve des bases en Syrie et au Liban. Dès que ces divers points seront réglés d'une manière satisfaisante avec Damas et Beyrouth nous somme résolus à ne nous mêler en rien de leur gouvernement, ni de leur administration et nous leur laisserons notamment la disposition des Troupes Spéciales.'

He went on to allege British support for the attitude of the States. He took note of the Prime Minister's intention to withdraw British troops if treaties could be concluded. He said that he had published a communiqué announcing the immediate return of General Beynet to the Levant States with instructions to negotiate, and asked us to refrain from intervention during this negotiation.

'A cet égard je dois vous dire que l'entrée au Liban, telle qu'elle m'est annoncée, d'une nouvelle division britannique venant de Palestine est à notre point de vue très regrettable et inopportune.'

(b)   General de Gaulle thus did not cancel the despatch of reinforcements. The first batch arrived at Beirut on May 6 and disembarked without incident. An equivalent number of troops were re-embarked. Meanwhile the French presented their *desiderata* to the Syrian Government. The latter told Mr. Shone that they regarded them as 'absolutely incompatible with Syrian sovereignty and independence'. In reply to the French they protested against the reinforcement of French troops and refused any discussion on the basis of the French

---

(a) Churchill Papers/423; E2925/12/89.   (b) E3220, 3291, 3292, 3293, 3593/8/89.

terms. The Acting Syrian Prime Minister,[1] Jamil Bey, appealed to Mr. Churchill on May 23 to secure the withdrawal of the troops.

On the evening of May 25 Mr. Shone was instructed to warn the (a) Syrian Government that they must keep the situation under control, especially at Homs and Hama. Only a few hundred French troops had arrived; there was no reason for disorder which might affect the Allied war effort. At the same time Mr. Duff Cooper was instructed to warn the French Government of the growing tension in the Middle East and to ask them to calm their local military and civil authorities. On the following day the Foreign Office issued a statement regretting the despatch of French reinforcements and the breaking off of negotiations by the two States. On this same day Jamil Bey told Mr. Shone that the Syrian Government could not hold their people much longer.

On the night of May 27 Jamil Bey reported to Mr. Shone that disturbances had broken out in Homs and Hama and that they had been started by firing on the part of the French.[2] He could no longer be responsible for internal security, and regarded as essential the immediate transfer of the Troupes Spéciales and the withdrawal of French forces from the towns.

Mr. Churchill held a meeting on May 28 to consider British (b) action if the trouble continued. Mr. Eden, the Chief of the Imperial General Staff, Sir O. Sargent and Sir R. I. Campbell were present. Mr. Churchill approved a telegram instructing the Commander-in-Chief, Middle East, to maintain an impartial and negative attitude to French and Syrians alike and to protect British soldiers and dependants. Mr. Eden warned the Prime Minister that the course of events might force us to a decision on action by British troops, possibly within twenty-four hours.

Mr. Churchill was determined that Great Britain should not get involved in any fighting; if, however, British troops stood by while the French fought the Syrians, other countries in the Middle East would be inclined to blame Great Britain for not restraining France. Mr. Churchill strongly criticised the action of General de Gaulle and said that the French and Syrians should be left alone to fight the matter out. He was not going to intervene to save the French from their folly and was not prepared to see British troops clash with French on land to protect the Syrians. He would only agree to action by British troops jointly with American troops. If, later, Britain had

---

[1] The Syrian Prime Minister was at San Francisco.

[2] The French Government in a communiqué of May 28 said that the disorders were 'provoked artificially' and that more British troops had been moved into Syria recently without consultation.

(a) E3376, 3397, 3419, 3436, 3496/8/89. (b) E3557/8/89.

to act alone, she might do so by naval action to prevent further French reinforcements landing.

(a)   At 7.15 p.m. on May 29 heavy fighting broke out between French troops and Syrians in Damascus and the French began to shell the city. Mr. Shone, who was in Damascus, asked for full powers for the Commander-in-Chief to deal with the situation. He instructed Mr. Young[1] in Beirut to see General Beynet and demand information. Mr. Young found General Beynet in a calm and cheerful mood. He said that he had no precise information. He telephoned to General Roget at Damascus in Mr. Young's presence, and repeated to Mr. Young the following account of events: French posts in several places had been simultaneously attacked at 7.15. Machine-guns had been fired on French Delegation premises from the west, wounding some people. French artillery had fired on the Citadel. General firing was in progress.

In Mr. Young's hearing, General Beynet ordered General Roget to cease artillery fire during the night and to do as little damage as possible. General Beynet maintained that the situation was not serious. Mr. Young read to General Beynet a message from Jamil Bey to Mr. Shone: 'Just at the moment when I received Mr. Churchill's telegram[2] I summoned deputies and notables of Damascus to tell them to do nothing to upset the calm and order in the country. Now we have French aggression from every side. I have given orders to the gendarmerie on no account to fire on the French.'

(b)   On May 30 Mr. Shone reported that rifle and machine-gun fire had been going on intermittently in Damascus. Since midnight artillery had been shelling the town. Mr. Shone continued: 'Whatever the Syrians may or may not have done and whatever the French rights under the mandate, surely this ruthless bombardment of an open city, above all at night, cannot be justified.' On the same day

(c) the Syrian President begged Mr. Shone to send an urgent appeal to Mr. Churchill reminding him of the promise that no coercion on Syria would be permitted to make her sign a treaty with France. He said that Damascus was being destroyed while the British

(d) Government seemed to be doing nothing to stop French aggression. Mr. Shone urged that His Majesty's Government should consider the effect on Allied interests in the Middle East of 'this treatment of an ancient and holy city of Islam', and the effect on British prestige if we stood aside while it was destroyed. On the morning of May 30

---

[1] Mr. G. P. Young was First Secretary at His Majesty's Legations, Beirut and Damascus.

(e)   [2] This telegram was in reply to Jamil Bey's message of May 23. Mr. Churchill repeated the British wish for a settlement and asked for calm on both sides.

(a) E3498/8/89. (b) E3498/8/89. (c) E3536/8/89. (d) E3533/8/89. (e) E3591/8/89.

the Syrian President appealed to the United States Chargé d'Affaires (a) for American intervention. He pointed out that the French were bombarding Damascus with Lend-Lease material.

The Cabinet discussed the situation on the evening of May 30. (b) General Paget had reported that the French authorities could not or would not control General Roget. General Paget had proposed that he should take control of all troops in the Levant States. The Prime Minister said that under the Lyttelton-de Gaulle agreement the British Commander-in-Chief, Middle East, was responsible in the last resort for maintaining order. We must, however, avoid being manoeuvred into a position in which we had to carry alone the burden of setting matters right. It was most important to obtain the public support of the United States for our action. If possible they should send a token force to assist our troops.

The Cabinet thought that there was good reason to hope for American support. The guarantees of Syrian and Lebanese independence produced a clear issue for United States opinion. The matter also concerned them because of their lines of communication with the Far East via Egypt and the Suez Canal. On the other hand, we wanted to avoid the use of force against allies. Hence we should aim at getting the French to order their troops to withdraw to barracks and conform to the directions of the British Commander-in-Chief, Middle East. Finally, we should not give the impression in the Arab world that the British Government had done nothing to assist Syria and the Lebanon against French aggression. We could be certain of the support of the local population in any action we might take.

The Prime Minister summed up the discussion by saying that the Cabinet was in favour of approaching President Truman first to ensure United States support in action to restore order. He suggested the terms of a telegram to the President inviting his support for a message to General de Gaulle that the British Commander-in-Chief, Middle East, had been ordered to intervene to prevent further bloodshed, and calling on him to order French troops to withdraw to barracks and to cease fire except in self-defence.

The Cabinet then adjourned while the Prime Minister and the Foreign Secretary interviewed M. Massigli, who had been summoned to receive the Government's views. When the discussion was resumed, the Prime Minister said that M. Massigli had told him of a telegram from General Beynet pressing for reinforcements. The matter should be removed as soon as possible from the military to the political plane, and M. Massigli hoped that the British Government would take the initiative in making proposals. The Prime Minister had informed M. Massigli that we were issuing orders to

---

(a) E3570/8/89. (b) CM(45)2; E3675/8/89 (marked *missing* at F.O. Library).

General Paget and were asking for United States support. The wise course for the French would be to instruct their troops to cease fire, withdraw to barracks and conform to the orders of General Paget. Once order had been restored we should be glad to open discussions in London. The Cabinet authorised the immediate despatch of telegrams to President Truman and General Paget.

(a)   After the Cabinet meeting the Prime Minister and Mr. Eden told M. Massigli of the instructions to General Paget. M. Massigli urged that the manner of presenting the decision to the French Government was of the greatest importance for minimising the danger to Franco-British relations. He begged that it should be made clear in the note to the French Government and in General Paget's announcement of his orders to General Beynet that the measures which we were taking were part of a wider diplomatic action—discussions between the British, French and American Governments—to solve the problem. He also urged that the grounds for British intervention should be the need for security in the Middle East on the lines of communication for the war against Japan.

(b)   In his telegram of May 30 to President Truman the Prime Minister said that continuance of the situation in Syria would cause grave trouble throughout the Middle East and on the joint line of communication with the Far East. He was prepared to order General Paget to intervene with British troops to stop the fighting, but before doing so he asked for President Truman's support. He enclosed the draft of a telegram to General de Gaulle for the President's approval.

(c) The President did not reply until May 31. Meanwhile the Prime
(d) Minister with the approval of the War Cabinet ordered General Paget to intervene to prevent further bloodshed. Mr. Eden explained the situation to the House of Commons at 3.45 p.m. on May 31 and the Prime Minister sent a copy of this statement to the President in
(e) explanation of his own action. General Paget had earlier been
(f) instructed that, when he informed General Beynet of the action which he was about to take, he should tell him of the proposal that, as soon as firing had ceased and order had been restored, discussions should be held in London between the French, British and United States Governments.[1]

(g)   [1] Late on May 30 Mr. Shone made a personal appeal to Mr. Eden:

'When I took up this post you told me that I might telegraph to you personally in time of need. I do so now as I have never been in such difficulty, and I shall speak frankly as I know you would wish me to do.

The French have instituted nothing short of a reign of terror in Damascus. Apart from indiscriminate shelling, their troops, black and white, are behaving like madmen,

(continued on page 337)

(a) E3677/8/89. (b) T1025/5, No. 59 (Churchill Papers/423; E3830/8/89). (c) T1033/5, No. 50 (Churchill Papers/423; E3830/8/89). (d) CM(45)3. (e) T1030–1/5, Nos. 61–2 (Churchill Papers/423; E3830/8/89). (f) E3552/8/89. (g) E3626/8/89.

In the afternoon of May 31 Mr. Duff Cooper was instructed to (a)
deliver the following message from the Prime Minister to General
de Gaulle:

'In view of the grave situation which has arisen between your
troops and the Levant States, and the severe fighting which has
broken out, we have with profound regret ordered the Commander-
in-Chief Middle East to intervene to prevent the further effusion of
blood in the interests of the security of the whole Middle East, which
involves communications for the war against Japan. In order to avoid
collision between British and French Forces, we request you immediately to order the French troops to cease fire and to withdraw to
their barracks.

Once firing has ceased, and order has been restored, we shall be
prepared to begin tripartite discussions in London.'

President Truman sent a telegram on May 31 approving this (b)
message to General de Gaulle. Lord Halifax told the State Depart- (c)
ment that it would be a great help to the British Government if the
President's action were to become known. There were already
accusations in the United States that the British Government wanted
to take over the Levant States. The State Department agreed with
Lord Halifax's view, and asked for authority to announce the
President's action. Meanwhile they released the text of a note of
May 28 to the French Provisional Government.[1] At a press

(*continued*)

spraying the streets with machine-gun fire from vehicles and buildings. They do not spare
vehicles flying the British flag, and one of the armoured cars placed at my disposal
was shot at by the French when evacuating two wounded British officers, one of whom
has since died, from the Orient Palace Hotel.

It is useless to appeal to the French authorities who are clearly out to win a merciless
war on the Syrians. I have often reported before on the chaotic French disorganisation
here, and even if they had control of their troops they cannot or will not exercise it.

9th Army arranged an armistice this afternoon for the evacuation of the British and
American communities. It is now almost over, and there is no doubt that the horror
will begin again. But even during the alleged armistice there has still been firing by
the French.

Every British soldier and civilian, and every American citizen, is horrified by what
the French are doing. At an interview I have just had with the Syrian President of the
Republic and the Ministers there were the first signs of something like animosity to us.
That will inevitably increase hourly if we fail to intervene, and will surely spread
throughout the whole of the Middle East.

I can only put this to you and implore His Majesty's Government to allow the
Commander-in-Chief to intervene without delay.'

Before the receipt of this telegram Mr. Eden had already telegraphed to Mr. Shone:

'I entirely approve your handling of a most delicate situation and I am satisfied
that nothing more could have been done either at your end or elsewhere to prevent
these unhappy developments. You have our full confidence and sympathy for the very
difficult position you have been placed in.'

[1] This note expressed concern at recent developments which had given the impression (d)
that the French were using the threat of force to obtain concessions from the States, and
appealed to the French Government to review their policy with the object of making it
clear that they intended to treat the States as fully sovereign and independent countries.

(a) T1031/5 (Churchill Papers/423; E3677/8/89). (b) T1033/5, No. 50 (Churchill
Papers/423; E3830/8/89). (c) E3575/8/89. (d) E3648/420/89.

(a) conference on May 31 Mr. Grew said that the United States Government had been informed of the British decision to intervene and that the President had approved the intention.

(b)   Owing to a mischance[1] the Prime Minister's message to General de Gaulle did not reach him until about three-quarters of an hour after Mr. Eden had read the text to the House of Commons. General de Gaulle refused to see Mr. Duff Cooper later in the evening of May 31, and on June 1 issued a communiqué giving the French version of the events and also stating that the French themselves had ordered a cease-fire at 11.30 p.m. on May 30. The Foreign Office did not think that this statement was accurate. In any case, the French had not notified either the British Government in London or the British authorities at the time, and the firing had in fact continued throughout May 31.[2] On June 2 at a press conference General de Gaulle put the blame for the whole trouble on the intrigues of British agents. He said, however, that he had no anger towards the British and wanted a peaceful settlement. The Prime Minister made a conciliatory statement in the House of Commons on June 5 and also appealed (on June 3) to the Syrian President to exercise moderation.

(vii)

British and French proposals regarding a conference on Syria and the Lebanon: transfer of the Troupes Spéciales: the question of Syria and the Lebanon at the Potsdam Conference (June–July 23, 1945).

(c)   As soon as order had been restored in the Levant, the Foreign Office thought that negotiations should begin at once on a tripartite basis since isolated diplomatic representations to France were unlikely to succeed. On June 6, however, M. Massigli brought to the Foreign Office a proposal from the French Government that the scope of the proposed meeting should be enlarged and that it should take the form of a five-Power conference in Paris[3] on the Near East as a whole. M. Massigli suggested privately that if, as he expected, the British Government did not like this new proposal, they should ask the Americans to take the initiative in rejecting it. The Foreign Office approached the United States Government accordingly. On

---

[1] It is uncertain whether the telegram was sent off from London later than the Foreign Office had expected or whether the Embassy took longer than had been expected in delivering it to General de Gaulle.

[2] The French troops were withdrawn from Damascus on June 3; on the same day a British detachment entered the city.

[3] Great Britain, the United States, France, the U.S.S.R. and China.

(a) E3577/8/89.   (b) E3629. 3630, 3679, 3688, 3710/8/89.   (c) E3971, 4056, 4126, 4325/8/89; E3880, 3995/420/89.

June 8 Mr. Grew gave the French Ambassador in Washington a note saying that the United States Government did not favour a five-Power conference on the Near East as a whole, but that they would be glad to discuss with the French any further suggestions which they might make internationally towards an orderly settlement of the immediate difficulties in the Levant.

Mr. Duff Cooper was instructed on June 15 to revive the suggestion for tripartite talks in London, and to say that the Levant States might take part in them or might hold parallel talks with the British and Americans. Mr. Duff Cooper was also told to hint that we had hoped in May that General de Gaulle might have come to London, but that if he was unable to come we should welcome M. Bidault. On June 16 M. Bidault said to Mr. Duff Cooper that it would be impossible to persuade General de Gaulle to agree to a meeting in London. The Foreign Office thought, nevertheless, that they should continue to press their proposal. They submitted on June 20, for the (a) approval of the Prime Minister,[1] a draft telegram to Mr. Duff Cooper. This draft said that the Foreign Office did not want a conference in Paris, where the French would probably limit it to an examination of the reasons for British intervention in Syria, whereas the object of the meeting was to settle the main questions concerning the future relations of France and the Levant States. Furthermore, if the meeting were held in Paris, representatives of the Levant States would have to attend; we could not go to Paris to discuss their future without them. If the French were unwilling to come to London, some other place might be chosen; Beirut and Cairo were unsuitable. If we had to accept Paris, we should insist on an American chairman. The draft therefore instructed Mr. Duff Cooper to ask for an early and favourable reply to the British proposal. The Prime Minister, however, refused to approve this draft. 'Leave them alone till they come right or till we have a right to take part in controversy.'[2]

By June 24 Mr. Eden had told the Eastern Department that he (b) intended to conduct the negotiations himself and that their object should be not only a settlement of the problem of Syria and the Lebanon, but a general treaty with the French.[3] London would be the best place for the discussion, but Paris was not excluded; and Mr. Eden would himself preside if possible. The fixing of a date was

---

[1] An announcement on June 3 stated that Mr. Eden had been ordered to rest owing to a duodenal ulcer. He returned to the Foreign Office on July 10. During his absence the Prime Minister was in charge of the Foreign Office.

[2] The meaning of these words was not clear to the Foreign Office. The Prime Minister was probably referring to the British general election.

[3] This treaty would have been negotiated between the British and French, i.e. without American participation.

(a) PM/45/282, E4708/8/89.   (b) E4709/8/89.

difficult owing to the British General Election, the Potsdam Conference and Mr. Eden's health. The meeting could be held either after polling day and the end of the Potsdam Conference, i.e. about July 25 or between July 7 and 12. The later date would be more convenient for the Foreign Office if the situation allowed so long a delay.

The Foreign Office thought that it would not be easy to hold the situation in the Levant until July 25 without some concessions, especially with regard to the Troupes Spéciales. They considered a suggestion by M. Paul-Boncour that a committee of three disinterested Powers should be set up to review recent incidents in the Levant and to make recommendations about a settlement. There were disadvantages in this French proposal. It would take time to arrange such a committee, although if it were quickly agreed to the announcement might have a calming effect. It might also create a precedent for the examination of British relations with Egypt and Iraq by 'disinterested countries', since the French Government's suggestion appeared to be that the executive committee of the Preparatory Commission of the World Organisation should appoint the members of the committee. Mr. Stettinius rejected this proposal on the ground that San Francisco was not the place to raise the subject and that the executive committee was the wrong body to deal with it. He said, however, that he would consider the French suggestion if it were made through the State Department and Foreign Office. Hitherto the Foreign Office had not welcomed the French suggestion for a five-Power conference, largely on the grounds that they did not want Russia and China to be involved in discussions about the Middle East. The present French proposal did not directly involve Russian participation. Russia was, however, indirectly brought in to the extent that the question came before the World Organisation.

On hearing that Mr. Eden intended to conduct the Levant negotiations and to consider them in relation to a general Anglo-(a) French treaty, Sir A. Cadogan suggested to the Prime Minister on June 24 that M. Bidault might be so informed and invited to London. The Prime Minister agreed with reluctance. On the next morning he read in the press of General de Gaulle's treatment of Lady Spears's hospital.[1] He then instructed Sir A. Cadogan not to invite M. Bidault, and said that it was now out of the question to negotiate a treaty with General de Gaulle. Sir A. Cadogan, however, felt bound to send the Prime Minister a minute on the subject and

---

[1] The French Ministry of War had ordered the disbandment of the mobile hospital unit which Lady Spears had formed in 1941 to work with the Free French forces.

(a) E4709/8/89.

to explain that it was in British interests to seek a solution of difficulties in the Levant States. He mentioned the three outstanding issues: a French proposal for an enquiry into past events;[1] the British proposal for a three-Power conference in London; and the negotiation of an Anglo-French treaty. He wrote to Mr. Eden regarding the first proposal: 'I do not know why we should object to the French proposal for an enquiry into past events: we have nothing to hide and should come out of it all right, but that will not afford the solution which we seek.' He thought that this enquiry could run concurrently with the three-Power conference. He went on to say that he was sure that the Prime Minister would oppose an Anglo-French treaty most strongly and that it should not be raised at the moment. Mr. Eden minuted: 'The two should go together . . . I agree that we must get on with this unhealthy business. I haven't read the telegrams but feel sure we shall run grave risk of Anglo-Syrian incidents apart from further injury to Anglo-French relations. Our need of the French is almost as great as their need of us and this fact is not altered by de Gaulle's behaviour.'[2] He agreed that Sir A. Cadogan should approach the Prime Minister.

On June 29, therefore, Sir A. Cadogan raised the question of a (a) conference on the Levant with the Prime Minister. He said that General de Gaulle had written a semi-apology to Lady Spears about his treatment of her hospital. He pointed out that the French had of their own accord made a proposal to Mr. Stettinius for an international commission of enquiry into recent incidents in the Levant. Their idea seemed to be that a committee of three disinterested Powers should be set up to conduct this enquiry. It was not clear what the terms of reference of the commission would be. According to M. Massigli the intention was that the commission should enquire only into the recent incidents and the effects of British intervention. Sir A. Cadogan thought that such restricted terms of reference would not help towards a solution of the problem. Mr. Stettinius had told the French that the matter could not be dealt with by any machinery of the World Organisation, though he had not rejected the idea of nomination of a commission of neutral Governments.

Sir A. Cadogan wrote to the Prime Minister that we might be involved in increasing difficulties in Syria unless relations between France and the States were put on a new basis. Sir A. Cadogan saw no reason why we should object to a neutral commission of enquiry if it received American encouragement. Such an enquiry might do something to help the situation, but would not produce a solution

---

[1] See above, p. 338.
[2] This minute is dated June 28.

(a) PM/45/299, E4709/8/89.

of the Syrian problem; hence we ought to aim at a three-Power conference which would bring in the Levant States. He asked the Prime Minister to agree with a suggestion to M. Bidault that, if he would come to London, Mr. Eden would start discussions with him and an American representative. The Foreign Office would propose to the French and Americans that the three Governments should announce their intention to meet; such an announcement was likely to have a steadying effect in the Levant States. On July 1 Mr. Churchill accepted Sir A. Cadogan's proposed course of action. On July 3, however, M. Massigli made it clear that M. Bidault was unlikely to come to London and that, if he came, he would agree only to Anglo-French conversations.

(a)   Meanwhile the Paris press had published on July 9 a communiqué issued by M. Bidault about the transfer of the Troupes Spéciales. General Beynet had issued a declaration at Beirut that these troops would be transferred in view of the end of hostilities in Europe, and that steps to effect the transfer would be defined within forty-five days.

The French did not send an official answer to the proposal for talks in London. Hence there was nothing which the Foreign Office

(b) could do to assist in bringing about a settlement in the Levant. At the Potsdam Conference, however, the Prime Minister made a statement on the British attitude. He was answering a Russian memorandum proposing a four-Power conference—Great Britain, France, United States and Russia—on the Levant subject to prior consultation with the French Government. Mr. Churchill said that Great Britain had no intention or desire to gain any advantages in the Levant except those enjoyed by other Powers. We had told General de Gaulle that British troops would be withdrawn as soon as he made a treaty with Syria and the Lebanon satisfactory to France and those countries. An earlier withdrawal would probably lead to the massacre of French civilians and troops; the consequent excitement throughout the Arab world would increase the difficulty of maintaining order in Palestine and Iraq, and possibly Egypt. Such a disturbance in the Middle East would endanger communications to the Far East.

Mr. Churchill said that the transfer of the Troupes Spéciales gave some hope of reaching a settlement which would guarantee Syrian and Lebanese independence and secure for France some recognition of her historic cultural and commercial interests. He repeated that Great Britain did not wish to remain in Syria and the Lebanon one day longer than was necessary. As, however, the matter rested

---

(a) E4942/14/89. (b) P(Terminal) 7th meeting; Target 211; U5696, 5731/3628/70; E5483/8/89.

between Great Britain, France and the Governments of Syria and the Lebanon, he did not welcome the Russian proposal for a four-Power conference.

President Truman said that British troops had intervened with his full agreement to safeguard communications for the war against Japan. The United States Government did not agree with the British view that France should have special privileges, especially after the troubles they had provoked; they thought that no country should have special privileges in the Levant States or elsewhere. Mr. Churchill said that the British Government would like to see Syria and the Lebanon concede special privileges to France. They had not, however, undertaken to make any serious exertions to procure these privileges for her. They would go no further than give the French friendly backing in negotiations. President Truman said that the United States Government would do nothing to prevent Syria and the Lebanon from conceding special privileges to the French but he did not think it likely that they would make concessions. Stalin also held this view. In view of Mr. Churchill's statement, he withdrew his proposal for a four-Power conference.

CHAPTER LVI

The co-ordination of Anglo-American policy in the Middle East, 1942–5: Palestine: The question of oil resources: Saudi Arabia[1]

(i)

British anxiety about the effect in the Middle East of American Zionist propaganda: Anglo-American exchanges in 1943 regarding a declaration on Palestine: withdrawal of the American proposal owing to Zionist pressure: appointment by the War Cabinet of a ministerial committee on the future of Palestine.

BEFORE the entry of the United States into the war, and even in the early part of 1942, American official and military opinion was not greatly concerned with the Middle East. The long-term question of the future of Palestine was for the time in suspense, and although Zionist pressure on Congress and the Administration remained strong, there could be no question of attempting to find, still less to apply, a long-term solution until the threat of invasion had been removed. The Americans inclined to think that the British Government—and particularly the Prime Minister—exaggerated, for British imperialist reasons, the strategic importance of the Middle East in the war against Germany. There was no change in the American view that the grand strategy of the Allies should be directed towards a cross-Channel invasion, but during the latter half of the war the United States Administration began to show an increasing interest in Middle Eastern affairs, and less willingness to allow them to be settled without direct American participation. The reasons for this change were obvious. Zionist pressure became greater as the war was coming to an end and it became clear that the long-postponed decisions of policy regarding the future of Palestine would soon have to be taken. The Arabs were unable to exert a corresponding pressure on Congress or on the Administration, but American opinion was becoming more conscious of the strategic as well as the commercial importance of the vast Middle Eastern oil reserves. There was also an assumption —sometimes, though not always, consciously formulated—that the

---

[1] The co-ordination of Anglo-American policy with regard to Iran is dealt with in Chapters LVII and LVIII.

United States had now become the leading Power in the world, and, from necessity as much as from choice, must exert a positive influence to get rid of the outmoded 'imperialism' of the European Powers. President Roosevelt himself was interested in the Middle East as a favourable area for the exercise of American activities which he distinguished sharply from those of British imperialism, but which, in fact, seemed to British observers to show many of the same features. Americans in general knew little about British policy towards the Arab countries, and readily accepted the view that this policy (which in fact had accomplished more than that of any other country for Arab liberation and advancement) had been one of selfish exploitation.

This new assertion of American interest was likely to cause diffi-culties and misunderstandings with Great Britain. The Foreign Office had learned to adjust British Middle Eastern interests to those of other European Powers; British officials were bound to be disconcerted at the sudden appearance of another Great Power, especially in areas such as Saudi Arabia where British interests had long been predominant and a good relationship established with Arab rulers and peoples. The situation was not made easier by the high-handedness and lack of consideration—or so it appeared from the British angle—with which the new American policy was at times conducted. Even on matters where a common agreement seemed to have been reached, an unexpected turn in American policy might occur owing, as in the Palestine question, to Zionist influence or, as in the oil question, to personal and domestic rivalries within the United States administration.

The official American attitude on the future of Palestine was the more disturbing since it was determined largely by the domestic importance of the Jewish vote, and took little account of the actual situation in the Middle East and the probable repercussions of Zionist intransigence. American liberal opinion, though it did not go the whole way with the Zionists, was particularly embarrassing in its charges of inhumanity against British policy with regard to Jewish immigration. From the British point of view these charges were unfair. The Americans—who refused to admit any very large additional number of Jewish immigrants into the United States—seemed to be attempting to ease their consciences by diverting the problem into an area where they had no responsibility for carrying their solution into effect against opposition. Moreover there was an incongruity between the American condemnation of British im-perialism as the enforcement of British rule on weaker peoples, and American support of Zionist claims to set up, by superior force, a State of Palestine against the wishes of the great majority of its inhabitants.

Anglo-American collaboration in the Middle East was therefore one of the major issues in British diplomacy during the last two years of the war. The fact that the questions in dispute did not cause more trouble is evidence of a fundamental desire on both sides to reach agreement, but it also shows the inevitable decline of British power. The British Government, in the last resort, were unable to take major decisions against American wishes. The prolonged and anxious discussions within the War Cabinet and the Departments concerned over the future of Palestine were inconclusive largely owing to the difficulty of finding a practicable solution which American opinion would accept. At the time of the Potsdam Conference Mr. Truman reasserted in somewhat blunt though polite terms that American views must be taken into account. Mr. Eden, (a) in a memorandum of April 10, 1945, dealing primarily with the Palestine question, had already summed up the position in quiet but realist terms.

'There will no doubt be many changes in the Middle East after the war, and not all of them to our advantage. During the past 25 years Great Britain has been the predominant Power in the Arab world. The British position has been almost unchallenged by the other Great Powers. Both the Americans and the Russians are now beginning to take a new interest in the area. Already in Saudi Arabia the Americans, intent mainly on the exploitation of their important oil concessions near the Persian Gulf, have insisted on sharing in our war-time subsidy to Ibn Saud, and are indeed pressing their lavish benefactions upon him to such an extent that His Majesty's Government would have great difficulty in competing, even should they desire to do so. The friendship of Ibn Saud has been most valuable to us in the past, and we have always been able to rely on him to use his great influence with the whole Arab world on our behalf. . . . The advent of a new American patron will not necessarily mean that Ibn Saud will wish to alter his friendly relations with His Majesty's Government, but it will make him less dependent upon British assistance for his necessary supplies, and he may be less willing in the future to be helpful to us over Palestine questions.'

Mr. Eden added:

'The Russians, too, will certainly take a far greater interest in future in the Arab countries. Already they have opened new diplomatic missions in Cairo, Baghdad, Damascus and Beirut. If we lose Arab goodwill, the Americans and the Russians will be at hand and will profit by our mistakes.'

At the end of August 1942 when the military position in the Western Desert was still somewhat critical, the American Joint

---

(a) WP (45) 229; E2453/15/3

Chiefs of Staff and the State Department discussed together the serious consequences for the United Nations if the Near East (the term here covered the Near and Middle East) were lost. They regarded the position of the United States in the area as unique, since the population had 'a deep-seated conviction' that American missionary, philanthropic and educational activities had 'never been tarnished by any material motives or interests. No other member of the United Nations is in such a position'. They suggested, therefore, the issue of a declaration of policy on the Near East, which would be followed by an American Mission to the area. The propaganda and other work of this Mission would avoid being a cover for the British and Free French, though it would be carried out in close co-operation with them. The declaration would, *inter alia*, assure the support of the United States for the aspirations of the peoples of the Near East to 'independence after the war, if, in line with American foreign policy and the Atlantic Charter, these peoples actively assist in winning it'.

Mr. Winant was instructed to give the draft of the proposed declaration to the British Government. This he did on September 1, leaving the draft, an *aide-mémoire* six pages long dated August 31, (a) 1942, with Mr. Eden. Mr. Eden decided to discuss with the Cabinet on September 9 what answer should be made to Mr. Winant, and in the meantime he drafted a longish message intended for Lord Halifax in Washington which he forwarded for comment to the Prime Minister. The Cabinet authorised him to send his *aide-mémoire* to Washington. He did so on September 15, also giving a copy to (b) Mr. Winant and telling him that the Prime Minister hoped that the terms of the proposed declaration would be modified. The *aide-mémoire* pointed out that while it was certainly desirable that the United States should as far as possible use the goodwill that they had with the Middle Eastern nations in promoting unity with the Allied cause and resistance to Axis influence and propaganda, the British Government saw dangers in the publication of a declaration in the form proposed by the Americans. The emphasis on the 'promotion of liberty' seemed inappropriate in view of the fact that, with the exceptions of Palestine and Transjordania, and possibly the Levant States, all the Middle Eastern countries mentioned in the declaration already enjoyed independence 'qualified only by the exigencies of the war situation and the requirements of the Allied forces operating within their boundaries'. Axis propaganda would exploit the inevitable misunderstanding of the declaration as implying that 'liberty' was being withheld and that the United States intended to hasten its achievement. The British Government also thought that the effect

---

(a) E5353, 5299, 5491/5191/65. (b) E5491/5191/65.

of the declaration and the proposed American Mission would be misunderstood both by Jews and Arabs in Palestine, and that it could add to the difficulties of the situation in Syria and the Lebanon, where the Free French were obstructing the fulfilment of the Anglo-French Declaration of Independence. The British Government like-wise thought the declaration hardly appropriate for Turkey, although they welcomed an increase in the American influence on Turkey, both in the interests of the United Nations' war effort and as a means of keeping Great Britain better informed of the action they proposed to take.

As a result of the British representations the State Department gave up the plan for a declaration, but at the President's wish a (a) mission headed by Colonel H. B. Hoskins[1] was sent to Cairo in November. The Mission does not appear to have gone to other Arab countries.[2]

During the period from the German advance into the Balkans to the battle of El Alamein and the Allied occupation of North Africa, there could be no question of a British pronouncement on the future of Palestine. As soon as the danger of invasion receded from the Middle Eastern countries, and the victory of the Allies looked certain, Jews and Arabs alike realised that such a pronouncement would have to be made at, if not before, a Peace Conference. The period of five years under which (in the terms of the White Paper of 1939) Jewish immigration was assured would come to an end on March 31, 1944. Thereafter, if the policy laid down in the White Paper were maintained, the continuance of immigration would depend on Arab acquiescence. Arab acquiescence was unlikely; the opponents of the White Paper (including Mr. Churchill) had indeed assumed in 1939 that it would be refused. Any possibility of a com-promise between Arab and Jewish claims had been destroyed by the militant Zionists. In May 1942 an American Zionist Conference at the Biltmore Hotel, New York, passed resolutions to the effect (i) that there should be formed a Jewish military force, fighting under its own flag and under the High Command of the United Nations, (ii) that Palestine should be established as a Jewish Commonwealth,[3] and (iii) that the policy of the White Paper be totally rejected and the control of immigration into Palestine be vested in the Jewish

---

[1] Col. H. B. Hoskins was an assistant to Mr. Berle, the Assistant Secretary of State.
[2] See F.R.U.S. 1942, IV, pp. 24–36.
[3] In supporting these resolutions later in the year, the Inner Zionist Council and the Jewish Agency in Palestine, on a motion of Mr. Ben-Gurion, head of the Jewish Agency, proposed that the words 'Jewish State' should be substituted for 'Jewish Commonwealth'. Mr. Ben-Gurion also seems to have made it clear that the Biltmore resolutions, though they represented the immediate aims, were not to be taken as the ultimate aims of the Zionist movement.

(a) E6598/5191/65.

Agency. The Zionists had thus come forward openly with the demand for the establishment of a Jewish State in Palestine after the war. Some at least of their leaders had spoken of their intention of using force to secure their aims. The view of the British authorities —which this public statement by the Zionists appeared to confirm— was that fighting might well break out in Palestine after the defeat of the Axis was certain but before the end of the war; the extremists would try to present the Allies with a *fait accompli* at a time when they could not spare troops to put down disorder.

The Zionists had developed in Palestine two powerful and well-armed secret military organisations: the Hagana, of which the leadership was generally associated with the Jewish Agency,[1] and a smaller para-military organisation, known as the Irgun Zvai Leumi, maintained by the Revisionist Party. The Hagana was said in the early part of 1943 to have a strength of about 80,000, and Irgun Zvai Leumi a strength of 6–8,000. The Hagana was highly organised on military lines, with a staff and divisional and lesser commands. The British authorities believed that it employed a permanent salaried staff to supervise training, accumulate arms and transport and control the village groups. It had mobile and fixed units, the former for use in any part of the country, the latter for employment at certain points. It was well armed, and was increasing its arms by organised theft from British sources.[2] Many of its members had been trained in Continental armies; some 30,000 had received training in Palestine as regulars or auxiliaries in the police or as members of the British forces. The Irgun Zvai Leumi was thought to be similarly armed, and to have an arrangement with the Hagana for joint military command.

The British authorities had long regarded the large numbers of arms illegally held by the Jews as a danger to security, but the War Cabinet had decided in 1940 not to take measures to seize them. This decision had not been changed; the main reasons for it were that action to seize the arms would have lost much Jewish support in the war, and might have caused rioting and terrorism which would have involved the detention in Palestine of British troops urgently needed elsewhere. In the spring of 1943 the British military authorities considered that forcible disarmament would be a major undertaking which would require at least two infantry divisions.

The Jewish plans and, above all, their military organisations

---

[1] The Jewish Agency was established under the original mandate as a public body to advise and co-operate with the Palestine Administration. The Executive of the Agency in Jerusalem had come by 1939 to negotiate on terms almost of *de facto* equality with the Palestine Administration.

[2] During March 1943 there was an increase in the number of these organised thefts: 600 rifles, 23 machine guns, 3 tons of high explosive and a large quantity of ammunition were stolen from British supplies.

obviously caused great anxiety among the Arabs. The Arabs had no secret and illegal forces in Palestine corresponding to the Jewish organisations, but they too held considerable quantities of arms and many Palestinian Arabs had been trained in the police or the British forces. It was impossible to say how much military assistance the Palestinian Arabs would receive, in the case of internal trouble, from the Arab States generally, but these States were already considering closer union, primarily, though not solely, in order to safeguard themselves against attempts to establish a Jewish State by force.[1] The maintenance of friendly relations between the Arab States and Great Britain therefore turned to a large extent on the attitude of the British Government towards the irreconcilable claims of Arabs and Jews.

The United States Government as well as the British Government was concerned about the dangerous consequences of the Zionist propaganda and the extreme demands of the Jewish organisations in Palestine. The State Department had considered, in June 1942, the issue of a statement supporting an agreed Jewish-Arab settlement in Palestine and the enlistment of separate Jewish and Arab military units to fight in the war. President Roosevelt, however, told Mr. Hull on July 7 that he felt 'we [the United States Government] should say nothing about the Near East or Palestine or the Arabs at this time. If we pat either group on the back, we automatically stir up trouble at a critical moment.' In early September 1942 the State Department consulted the British Embassy about the expediency of giving passports to a Jewish delegation wishing to go to England to try to get British agreement to a Jewish army. Lord Halifax, on instructions from London, wrote to the head of the proposed delegation on October 24 that the British Government could not change their view about the undesirability of their plan. He pointed out that Jews could best make their contribution to the military effort by 'serving in the armed forces of the countries to which they owed allegiance' and that stateless Jews could join the British Army as volunteers. In January 1943 Colonel Hoskins, an American officer had told the Minister of State that after his tour of the Middle East[2] he was reporting to the State Department that, unless preventive measures were taken, fighting might break out in Palestine between Zionists and Arabs before the end of the war, and possibly even in the spring of 1943, and might lead to clashes between Jews and Arabs in other parts of the Near East.

(a)   Colonel Stanley, Secretary of State for the Colonies, brought these

---

[1] *F.R.U.S.* 1942, IV, pp. 543–4.
[2] See above, p. 346.

(a) WP(43)192; E2744/87/31.

facts to the attention of the War Cabinet in a memorandum of May 4, 1943. He said that the War Cabinet would have to come to some decision on policy before the end of the year and that he was sending the Head of the Middle Eastern Department of the Colonial Office to Palestine to study the position and to discuss it with the High Commissioner and his advisers. The Prime Minister had (a) already circulated, on April 28, a note to the War Cabinet that, while he could not recommend a new declaration, he was 'an unchanging supporter of the Balfour Declaration modified as it was by the Colonial Office White Paper [drafted by Mr. Churchill himself in 1922]' and that he could not 'in any circumstances contemplate an absolute cessation of immigration into Palestine at the discretion of the Arab majority'.[1] The Prime Minister expected that at the end of the war the pressure for a new declaration would be very strong; he also believed that President Roosevelt agreed with his views. The Prime Minister suggested that the Departments concerned should examine the possibilities of making Eritrea and Tripolitania into Jewish colonies affiliated, if so desired, to the National Home. 'Such a new departure would broaden the whole issue, and perhaps make general agreement possible between the disputants, both at home and on the spot.' Cyrenaica might well become another predominantly Arab domain.

Mr. Eden circulated a memorandum on May 10, 1943, with a (b) covering note that the War Cabinet should be aware of the disquieting developments not only in Palestine but in Egypt, Iraq, Syria and Arabia as a result of the revival of Zionist and Arab activities. Mr. Eden's suggestion, 'as the the only action which appears practicable' for the time, was

> 'an approach to the United States Government with the object of inducing them to do their best to damp down pro-Zionist utterances by American public men, such as are having unfortunate repercussions on our interests in the Middle East, though in America they may appear innocuous.'

Mr. Eden pointed out that there were signs of the rapid development of a nationalist revival in the Middle East affecting the Arabs and the Zionists, and that Zionist propagandists were responsible for an increase in tension. With the removal of the threat of war from the Middle East Arabs and Jews thought they could 'play

---

[1] The Prime Minister enclosed with his note a reprint of a speech which he had made in the House of Commons on May 23, 1939, in opposition to the policy on immigration laid down in the White Paper. This speech had been reprinted, for propagandist purposes, by the Zionist Organisation of America.

In a minute of April 18 addressed jointly to Mr. Eden and Colonel Stanley, the Prime (c) Minister described the White Paper of 1939 as 'a gross breach of faith committed by the Chamberlain Government in respect of obligations to which I was personally a party'.

(a) WP(43)178; E2742/87/31. (b) WP(43)200; E2855/87/31. (c) E2340/87/31.

politics' and that they ought to formulate their claims and secure a hearing for them at the eventual Peace Conference. The Iraqi Government clearly had this end in view when they declared war on the Axis in January 1943.[1] There was nothing unexpected in this attitude on the part of the Arabs or of the Jews. We could not do much except to go on impressing upon the Arab Governments and Jewish organisations that the requirements of the war must remain the dominant consideration.

Mr. Eden said that the intensification of Zionist activities, however, in the United States was due to deliberate policy. We had evidence that in 1941 leading members of the Jewish Agency thought they should limit its activities in Great Britain to an attempt to prevent the British Government from making new promises to the Arabs, and that they should concentrate all their efforts in the United States. This policy had been carried out and was now greatly accelerated. Mr. Eden then mentioned the Biltmore resolutions. He said that, while Mr. Hull and the State Department generally had been careful to avoid committing themselves, other members of the Administration had been less cautious. Mr. Stimson, Secretary of War, and Colonel Knox, Secretary of the Navy, had signed statements in favour of the creation of a Jewish army. The American Committee for such an army was collecting the signatures of large numbers of eminent Americans, including serving United States officials, and was publishing them in huge advertisements in the press. In March 1943 Mr. Ickes, Secretary of the Interior, had said in a speech at Boston that the United Nations should declare Palestine 'a home for those Jews who wish to abide there—not a place of exile—a respected and self-respecting member of the Commonwealth of Nations'. Two hundred and forty Senators and

---

(a)   [1] In January 1942 General Nuri informed Sir K. Cornwallis that he wanted to approach King Ibn Saud with a view to identical and simultaneous action by Saudi Arabia and Iraq in declaring war on the Axis and adhering to the United Nations Pact. The Foreign Office considered that a declaration of war by the two countries—and especially by King Ibn Saud—would have an important political effect on Arab and Moslem opinion generally, but that it would be better for an approach to King Ibn Saud to be made in the first instance by the British Government. The British Minister at Jedda was instructed to consult King Ibn Saud. The latter replied that it was neither in his own nor in British interests that he should declare war on the Axis. Saudi Arabia was completely unprepared for war, and opinion in the country would be strongly opposed to a declaration. King Ibn Saud thought that Moslems everywhere would assume, if he entered the war, that he was a tool of the British, and that he was exposing the Moslem Holy Places to danger merely in British interests.

After further discussion with General Nuri the question of a declaration of war by Iraq remained in abeyance until November 1942. General Nuri then told Sir K. Cornwallis that the Iraqi Parliament had decided, on his initiative, to adhere to the United Nations Pact and to declare war on Germany and Italy. Sir K. Cornwallis thought that this action was due to a wish to stake out Arab claims. There was no question at this time of any positive action by Iraq beyond the terms of the Anglo-Iraqi treaty.

(a) E349, 829, 1291/13/25; E340, 6664/190/93.

members of the House of Representatives had submitted a declaration to Mr. Hull, on the twenty-fifth anniversary of the Balfour Declaration in November 1942, implying that many millions of Jews in Europe should be allowed to emigrate to Palestine.[1]

Mr. Eden thought it uncertain how much this propaganda meant to the Americans themselves. Some of the Jewish Agency leaders regarded the results as disappointing; there was also evidence that anti-Jewish feeling was increasing in the United States. On the other hand the campaign had an outward appearance of success and had intensified the anxiety of the Arabs in Palestine and other Arab countries. The Arabs believed that Jewish influence predominated in the United States, and that there was little point in supporting the Allies if victory was to result in Palestine being handed over to the Jews. Arab opinion had become embittered during the last twenty years over our policy in Palestine, and we were fortunate in that we had had nothing worse to deal with in the Middle East than the Iraqi rebellion of 1941.

Mr. Eden then referred to the representations from Arab leaders about Zionist propaganda in the United States. General Nuri had suggested that the United Nations should make a definite pronouncement that they would not support the creation of a Jewish State in Palestine. Nahas Pasha had sent memoranda to the State Department on Zionist propaganda and on the impossibility of admitting into Palestine those Jews who might be rescued from Europe. King Ibn Saud had consulted the British Government on the question. The Arab Conference might be held shortly and would certainly discuss the Palestine question.

In these circumstances Mr. Eden thought that it would be desirable to support the warning which Colonel Hoskins had given to the Administration. Lord Halifax had impressed on members of the Administration, with varying success, our anxiety about American support of Zionist propaganda. The time had now come for a more formal warning that this propaganda might cause a serious handicap to the war effort. Mr. Myron Taylor, American Commissioner for Refugees, had recently told Lord Halifax that he had spoken to leading Jews in New York; moderate Jewish opinion in the United States, such as that represented by the American Jewish

---

[1] During his visit to the United States in the spring of 1943, Mr. Eden had a conversation with Mr. Welles about Palestine. Mr. Welles spoke of the political difficulty which the question was causing in the United States; he thought that the only solution was to try for a 'Greater Syria' (see note at the end of this section and also section (iii)) and then to get the Jews into discussions with the Arabs with the object of bringing another 500,000 Jewish immigrants into Palestine. Mr. Eden (and Mr. Strang, who was present at the interview) pointed out the obvious difficulties in this plan, but Mr. Welles was not much moved by them. He proposed that Palestine should be placed under some kind of international trusteeship.

Committee and the American Council for Judaism, would welcome action by the United States Government. Finally, Mr. Eden suggested that we should explain to the United States Government why we did not want to make a declaration regarding the future of Palestine unless it was essential to do so in order to calm Arab opinion.

(a)   Other Ministers also submitted papers at this time on the Palestine question. Mr. Casey, in a memorandum of June 17, gave more details of the Jewish secret military organisations, and of the recognition of the leaders that their programme would lead to disorder.[1] Mr. Casey considered that, whatever the rights or wrongs of the matter, a conflict in Palestine would seriously damage our position in the Middle East, and that Arab nationalists generally would use it as a means of pressure to remove all British influence. Mr. Casey thought that it would be most unwise for us to do nothing in the hope that, when the crisis came, we could use our forces to preserve internal security. We could not repudiate the assurances to the Arabs in the White Paper without turning the whole of Arab opinion against us and, incidentally, giving the Russians an opportunity, if they so desired, to bring the Middle East into their sphere of influence. Mr. Casey thought that the only solution was a declaration by the British and United States Governments that, subject to the fulfilment of the strategic requirements necessary to preserve world peace, they were prepared to accept any solution of the Palestine problem which might be fully agreed upon between the Arabs and Jews of Palestine, but that they would not permit or surrender to forceful changes in the administration of Palestine; in particular, they would regard the forcible establishment of a Jewish State as contrary to the Atlantic Charter and the principles upon which the peace settlement must be based.

(b)   On June 10—before the War Cabinet had considered Mr. Eden's proposal for an approach to the United States Government—Mr. Winant wrote to Mr. Eden that the State Department had asked him to inform the Foreign Office of their concern over the situation in Palestine and the probability of disturbances. The message referred to the effect upon Arab opinion of Zionist political agitation in the United States, and the consequent reaction on the Zionists. The State Department suggested that the best way of dealing with this 'spiral of increasing tension' would be the issue of a statement by the United Nations. It might be, however, that reference to the United Nations would take too long, and that some members might be unwilling to sign the statement, and others uninterested in

---

[1] This memorandum had been submitted to the Middle East War Council on April 21.

(a) WP(43)246.   (b) E3424/87/31.

Palestine. The State Department would therefore be prepared to consider the issue of the statement by a smaller group of countries such as Great Britain, the U.S.S.R., China and the United States.

The proposed statement, in the American draft, was as follows:

'The United Nations, having in mind the terms of their declaration of January 1, 1942, are agreed that, while public discussions on controversial international questions are in general desirable, in order to promote an informed public opinion and clarification of the issues involved, it is undesirable that such special viewpoints should be pressed while the war is in progress to such an extent as to create undue anxiety among the United Nations and other friendly governments and peoples.

In this connexion, the United Nations have taken note of public discussions and activities of a political nature relating to Palestine and consider that it would be helpful to the war effort if these were to cease. As in the case of other territorial problems, it is not, in their view, essential that a settlement of the Palestine question be achieved prior to the conclusion of the war. Nevertheless, if the interested Arabs and Jews can reach a friendly understanding through their own efforts before the end of the war, such a development would be highly desirable. In any case no decision altering the basic situation of Palestine should be reached without full consultation with both Arabs and Jews.'

The Foreign Office thought that the issue of a statement by the (a) United Nations or jointly by the four Powers was undesirable, but that a joint Anglo-American declaration or a simultaneous declaration by the two Governments would damp down Zionist agitation in the United States, and divide the extremists from the moderate Zionists. The Foreign Office suggested certain amendments to the text involving the substitution of a new wording in paragraph 2 after the words 'relating to Palestine'. The new draft (in the event of a simultaneous statement) ran:

'. . . which they consider are prejudicial to the maintenance of tranquillity and public order in the Middle East. His Majesty's Government and the United States Government consider that these speculations should cease and that all efforts should be concentrated on the war. Continual controversy during the war period can only prejudice the chances of future agreement, although, as stated on more than one occasion in the past, any progress which the Arabs and Jews can make towards agreement regarding Palestine will be warmly welcomed. In any case, as His Majesty's Government have already stated, no decision affecting the basic situation of Palestine should be reached without full consultation with all concerned, including both Arabs and Jews, but they wish to make it clear that they have

---

(a) E3464/87/31.

no intention of permitting or acquiescing in forceful[1] changes of any kind in the status of Palestine. The United States Government are in full accord with this assurance.'

(a)   Mr. Eden circulated Mr. Winant's note and the two drafts to the
(b) War Cabinet on June 26. On July 2 the War Cabinet, in a general discussion of the Palestinian question, considered all the memoranda submitted to them. They agreed with the Prime Minister's view that our chief aim for the present should be to keep the situation as quiet as possible and to avoid bringing the Jewish-Arab problem into undue prominence. A joint Anglo-American statement would be of great value, but the statement should not go into much detail. The War Cabinet, on the whole, preferred the American draft, but Mr. Eden pointed out that the second sentence of the second paragraph in the American draft might imply that the White Paper policy no longer held the field. While many members of the War Cabinet had opposed this policy, and would like to see it modified when opportunity offered, it would be undesirable for the present to give any public indication that modifications were being considered.

The War Cabinet therefore agreed to accept the American draft (amended to take the form of a declaration by the two Governments) with the substitution, for the last two sentences of this draft, of the proposed concluding sentences in the Foreign Office draft. The War Cabinet also decided in principle that the period during which Jewish immigration would be permitted (up to the White Paper figure of 75,000) should be extended beyond March 31, 1944, without prejudice to a later decision on immigration policy when the White Paper figures had been reached.

(c)   The War Cabinet decided to make no change for the present in their policy with regard to dealing with illegal stores of arms, Jewish or Arab. They considered that no measures should be taken to disarm the Jews unless or until equal measures could be enforced against the Arabs.[2] Finally, the War Cabinet on July 12 appointed a Ministerial Committee to consider long-term policy with regard to Palestine.[3]

On July 23, after agreement had been reached with the State Department on the text of the declaration, Mr. Winant telephoned that the State Department proposed to issue the draft on July 27.

---

[1] In the draft approved later by the War Cabinet this word read 'forcible'.

[2] It was pointed out that the Jews had accumulated their arms in large caches, while the Arabs mostly had their arms in individual possession. Since a house-to-house search for arms was impracticable, action against caches of arms would affect the Jews and not the Arabs.

[3] Mr. Herbert Morrison, Home Secretary, was chairman of the Committee. The other members were Lord Cranborne (Lord Privy Seal), the Secretaries of State for India (Mr. Amery), the Colonies (Mr. Stanley), and Air (Sir A. Sinclair) and Mr. Law.

(a) WP(43)278; E3771/87/31. (b) WM(43)92.2, C.A. (c) E4319/87/31.

This date was postponed until July 28, but on the evening of July 27 Lord Halifax telegraphed that the State Department wanted post- (a) ponement for another week in order to redraft the text and to emphasise the military aspect more strongly. Lord Halifax said that the Zionists had heard of the statement and were lobbying against it. On August 9 Mr. Winant told the Foreign Office that the United (b) States Government had decided not to issue a joint declaration. He explained that the War Department had come to the conclusion that the situation in Palestine was less 'inflammable' than they had thought and that it would be better to leave matters alone.

Lord Halifax reported on August 10 that Mr. Hull had said to (c) him that he had had some doubts about the advisability of the declaration, and had consulted Mr. Stimson. Mr. Stimson had refused to support it, and the State Department felt that they could not issue it on their own responsibility. Lord Halifax had not the least doubt that the real reason for withdrawal was intense Jewish pressure, especially on the President, after the news had begun to leak out, and that the facts were a somewhat sinister indication of the power of pressure groups in the United States. Meanwhile most of the story had appeared in the press.[1]

Note to section (i): Proposals for an Arab League: the Cairo pact of March 1945.

The Zionist demands for a Jewish State and, above all, the preparations made in Palestine for militant action led to counter-measures on the Arab side towards greater unity. The movement among the Arab States towards common action had developed before the war largely as a reply to Jewish claims in Palestine. The British Government had given indirect official recognition to the fact of common Arab action by inviting delegations from Egypt, Iraq, Transjordan, Saudi Arabia and the Yemen to the Round Table Conference in London during 1939. In a speech of May 29, 1941, Mr. Eden had stated that the British Government would welcome any scheme for strengthening the cultural, economic and political ties between the Arab States which had general Arab approval. This statement, which was made partly to tranquillise Arab opinion after the revolt of Rashid Ali, was also opportune in relation to Allied action against the Vichy forces in Syria. The Arabs also welcomed British insistence upon the fulfilment of the promise of independence given by the Free French to Syria and the Lebanon. At the end of 1942 the military situation in the Middle East encouraged Arab politicians to give more attention to the post-war

---

[1] Further information from the British Embassy indicated that the Zionist pressure (d) had been exercised principally through Mr. Morgenthau, Mr. Baruch, Mr. Stimson and Mr. Welles.

(a) E4374/87/31. (b) E4718/87/31. (c) E4718/87/31. (d) E4931, 5043/87/31.

settlement, while the rising scale of Zionist claims, the vehemence with which they were urged in the United States and the growing Jewish illegal arming in Palestine made the question of a united front seem more urgent to Arab opinion. General Nuri, who took

(a) the lead in promoting plans of Arab federation, sent a long memorandum to Mr. Casey at the time of the Iraqi declaration of war against Germany, recommending that the United Nations should declare the federation of Syria, the Lebanon, Palestine[1] and Transjordan as the basis of an Arab Union to which Iraq would adhere at once and which the other Arab States would be invited to join. Mr. Eden, in the House of Commons on February 24, 1943, renewed the assurance which he had given in 1941 to the Arab States, but added that the initiative must come from the Arabs themselves, and

(b) that hitherto no scheme commanding general Arab approval had been worked out.

General Nuri paid visits in July and August 1943 to Damascus, Beirut, Jerusalem and Cairo in order to explain his plans to other Arab leaders. He also sounded King Ibn Saud, but received a very discouraging reply. King Ibn Saud was opposed to the plan for a 'Greater Syria', since he was afraid that it might fall under the domination of the Hashimite family—the Emir of Transjordan or a member of the Iraqi royal family. The attitude of the Egyptian Government was uncertain. They had no reason to object to a 'Greater Syria', but were unlikely to join an Arab federation. For the time being Nahas Pasha seemed to be limiting himself to securing the chief part in co-ordinating the views of the Arab States. At his meeting with General Nuri in Cairo it was agreed that he (Nahas) should approach the other Arab Governments. If a sufficient measure of agreement were found, a conference would be held, probably in Cairo. After further negotiations the Arab States agreed to hold a preparatory meeting at Alexandria during September 1944 and, later, a general conference.

(c) The Foreign Office considered that the British Government ought not to oppose the holding of the conference, but that, if we were consulted, we should encourage any tendency towards postponement, in view of the probability that the delegates would pass resolutions on Palestine. We should say that we did not think it likely that the preparatory committee would reach agreement on the political side, though there might be scope for financial and fiscal and cultural

(d) co-operation. General Nuri had told Sir K. Cornwallis that Arab unity and the Arab States themselves could flourish only if they continued to strengthen their ties with Great Britain, and that he

---

[1] General Nuri proposed that the Jews of Palestine (and the Christians of Lebanon) should be given semi-autonomy, under an international guarantee, subject to supervision by the 'Greater Syrian' State.

(a) E1196/506/65.   (b) P(M)(43)11; E5635/506/65.   (c) E3686/41/65 (1944). (d) E3990/87/31.

intended to propose, as part of a common Arab policy, an alliance
with Great Britain for an initial period of thirty years.

The Preparatory Committee issued a protocol on October 7, 1944,   (a)
proposing the establishment of a League of Arab States which would
be open to all independent Arab States wishing to join it. The members would co-operate in foreign policy and in economic and cultural
matters. After a meeting early in 1945 of the Foreign Ministers of
the States a general Arab Congress met in Cairo in March 1945 and
agreed to the signature of a Pact constituting the League.

(ii)

*Renewal by Mr. Hull of the proposal for an American declaration on
Palestine: withdrawal of resolutions in Congress in favour of a Jewish State:
discussions with Mr. Wallace Murray in London, April 1944.*

The Foreign Office took a very unfavourable view of the circumstances in which the State Department had withdrawn their proposal
for an Anglo-American declaration. They thought that there was
no reason for thinking that the situation in Palestine had improved.
It was also highly dangerous for the Zionist extremists to assume
that they could paralyse Anglo-American action by means of political
pressure in the United States. The Foreign Office and the Colonial
Office therefore hoped that the Prime Minister would be able to get
the President to issue some kind of statement.

Mr. Eden raised the question with Mr. Hull during the Quebec   (b)
Conference. Mr. Hull promised to consider the British view, but
nothing was done except to agree to keep the statement in reserve
on a month to month basis for issue if the situation required it. The
President was in favour—if any statement were made—of a shorter
text to the effect that, in view of military considerations, the
Palestinian question could not be taken up at the present time. The
Prime Minister wished to add that British policy would not be
influenced by sporadic acts of violence.

At the first monthly reconsideration in the beginning of October   (c)
the Americans had not changed their minds. On December 13,
however, Lord Halifax reported that Mr. Hull had spoken to him
of the increasing Jewish pressure on the Administration. He thought
that the large question of the future of Palestine could be held over
until after the war, but that there would be serious political consequences if the Zionist extremists could say that the United States
Government were disinteresting themselves entirely in the matter.
Mr. Hull felt that he ought to make some public statement in order

---

(a) E6477/41/65. (b) E5051/87/31. (c) E5988, 7820/87/31.

to quiet opinion, at least for the next few months, but he was anxious not to embarrass the British Government. He suggested saying that the two Governments were agreed in their feeling of sympathy for the cruelties to which the whole Jewish race had been subjected; one of the purposes of victory in the war was to secure justice for the Jews. Palestine was within the responsibility of the British Government, but the United States Government, having regard to the fact that there were about four million Jews in the United States,[1] could not be disinterested in the problem, and were following with constant attention all the facts and factors affecting it. 'More than this he could not for the present say.' Lord Halifax reminded Mr. Hull of the recent British statement with regard to immigration[2] and said that we also were holding the question under constant review. He promised to ask for British comments on the proposed statement 'in the next few days' in view of Mr. Hull's wish to forestall what he described as a 'Jewish blast'.

(a)   Mr. Casey had already written to Mr. Eden on November 8 enclosing a letter from General Wilson in favour of reviving the proposal for a joint Anglo-American statement. General Wilson's argument, with which Mr. Casey agreed, was the danger of an outbreak in Palestine after the end of 1943 which, apart from other consequences, would mean withdrawing or holding back British troops from active theatres of operations. The Foreign Office were in favour of a declaration—though they did not like Mr. Hull's actual wording—since it would show Anglo-American unity in a field where British policy had been and would continue to be criticised in the United States, and would avert the great damage to British prestige in the United States in the event of disturbances in Palestine. The Foreign Office pointed out that Colonel Hoskins was in favour of a statement covering a wider field than Palestine and that the Americans themselves could be left to judge the effect on

(b) Jewish pressure groups in the United States. The Palestine Committee, however, were now opposed to a public Anglo-American statement on the lines previously agreed, since they did not want to commit themselves not to take any long-term decision about Palestine before the end of the war.[3]

Mr. Hull's new proposal, however, was in a different category.

(c) The reply to Mr. Hull was delayed (Mr. Hull asked urgently for it

---

[1] The number of Jews in the U.S.A. was given as 4,641,184 in 1941 and at the next census (1948) as 4,500,000 (Jewish Year Book, 1971).

[2] On November 10, 1943, Colonel Stanley announced in the House of Commons that the closing date of March 31, 1944, laid down in the White Paper for the quota of Jewish immigration would not apply since, owing to the war, only 44,000 out of the 75,000 places had been filled.

[3] See section (iii) of this chapter.

(a) E6916/87/31.   (b) E7847, 7984/87/31.   (c) E7977/87/31.

on December 20) because the War Cabinet were considering the report of the Palestine Committee. On December 21, however, Lord Halifax was instructed to tell Mr. Hull that we agreed about the (a) value of a public statement which would quiet Jewish opinion. We could accept Mr. Hull's draft, but it seemed to us 'unduly aloof', and we should prefer a slightly different approach. As a tentative draft we suggested:

'The United States Government, having regard to the fact that there are something like four million Jews in the United States, are particularly interested in the problems raised by the present plight of the Jews, and are giving close and constant attention to all proposals that seem likely to alleviate the Jewish lot or contribute to solving their special problems. One problem is that of Palestine, and this too, though its government and its security are a British and not an American responsibility, is receiving close attention, and it is Mr. Hull's constant hope that an eventual solution will be found that would benefit all Palestine's inhabitants, Arabs and Jews alike. If the interested Jews and Arabs, within Palestine's borders and without, could reach a friendly understanding through their own efforts, this would be exceedingly welcome to the United States.'

Lord Halifax was also instructed to say to Mr. Hull—since he had consulted us—that in our view it would be advantageous if, apart from a public statement, he felt able to warn the Zionist leaders of the dangers of their present policy. It would also be useful if the President, in reporting on his journey[1] to Congress, were able to say something about recent tension in the eastern Mediterranean, and the necessity for opinion in the United States to look at the Middle East as a whole. The mistake of the extreme Zionists was to treat Palestine in isolation and not as part of the Arab world as a whole.[2]

On January 9, 1944, Lord Halifax telegraphed that Zionist (b) pressure was steadily rising, in view of the general war situation and the approach of the Presidential election. The list of politicians who had signed Zionist statements was also growing. The small number of Americans with knowledge of the Middle East had little chance of prevailing against this pressure. Lord Halifax regarded it as most desirable that we should come to a decision soon about our policy if we wished to avoid the risk of American intervention. The Prime (c) Minister's comment on this telegram was to repeat his view that the policy of the White Paper was a disastrous breach of an undertaking for which he was 'prominently responsible. Surely we are not going

---

[1] i.e. to the Cairo and Teheran Conferences.
[2] The Prime Minister telegraphed to Mr. Eden on December 24 that he saw nothing (d) wrong in Mr. Hull's proposed statement.

(a) E7820/87/31.   (b) E195/95/31.   (c) Frozen 1256, E195/95/31.   (d) Frozen 847, E7820/87/31.

to make trouble for ourselves in America and hamper the President's chances of re-election for the sake of this low-grade gasp of a defeatist hour. The Arabs have done nothing for us during the war, except for the rebellion in Iraq.' The Prime Minister thought that the War Cabinet must come to a decision on his return to London. Meanwhile we should not commit ourselves to a new defence of the White Paper. 'Some form of partition is the only solution.'

The Foreign Office did not reply to Lord Halifax until January 29, 1944. They then told him that there was no chance of a major decision on Palestine in the near future. An announcement on the subject would almost certainly lead to disturbances in the Middle East which would prejudice the war effort. Lord Halifax should therefore take the line that we could not give attention at the present time—before victory was won—to the complicated question of the future of the Jews and Arabs in Palestine. We had already announced that Jewish immigration would continue after the 'White Paper date' of March 31, 1944, so that the full number of Jewish immigrants allowed in the White Paper would be enabled to enter Palestine.

(a)   Lord Halifax replied on February 7 that it would merely infuriate the Jews to tell them to forget about Zionism and to concentrate on winning the war. They would say that they were as much entitled as anyone else to discuss war problems, and if territorial questions affecting Poland were discussed, why not Palestine? The Jews were in fact concerned over the Prime Minister's statements that the future of Palestine was being discussed; they would certainly try to get the United States Government to see that the discussion went the right way for them.

Lord Halifax suggested that we might point out: (i) that Hitler, not the British Government, was responsible for preventing the Jews from leaving Europe—we still had 30,000 unused immigration certificates, and had been trying to get the Bulgarians to agree to release 5,000 children; (ii) that under the White Paper Jewish immigration could continue indefinitely if the Arabs agreed. Were the Arabs to be coerced into agreement, and would American troops be available for this purpose? Lord Halifax had heard nothing from Mr. Hull lately about his proposed statement, and thought that the proposal had been dropped once more.

(b)   The Prime Minister minuted on Lord Halifax's telegram that he did not think much of the arguments put forward in it. The Foreign Office, in any case, considered it dangerous for us to enter into detailed arguments which might be misinterpreted by one side or the other. It was, however, possible to point out to the Americans that the trouble in Palestine was over the conflict between the native

---

(a) E910/95/31. (b) E1571/95/31.

inhabitants, whose rights and positions were specifically guaranteed under the mandate, and the immigrants or would-be immigrants. The British Government, as the mandatory authority, in seeking to control immigration and prevent the native inhabitants from being swamped by immigrants who were not unnaturally regarded by the native inhabitants as aliens, were merely following the example of the United States and every other 'receiving country' threatened with a similar invasion. The mandate provided for immigration but stipulated that the rights of the native inhabitants should not be prejudiced. It did not justify the transformation of the indigenous majority into a suppressed minority.[1]

On January 27, 1944, two resolutions were introduced into the (a) House of Representatives proposing that the United States should use their good offices and take appropriate measures to secure the free entry of Jews into Palestine, in order that the country might become a 'free and democratic Jewish Commonwealth'. Lord Halifax reported that the resolution was likely to be approved with very little opposition. Mr. Berle[2] said to Sir R. Campbell on January 28 that the State Department would be grateful for our views on the best way of handling the matter. Lord Halifax proposed to say that it was not for us to express any opinion on action by Congress, but that the State Department might care to point out that under the White Paper Jewish immigration would continue with Arab consent. Did Congress propose that it should continue against the wishes of the majority of the population, and were they prepared to use force for the purpose?

On March 2 Lord Halifax telegraphed that he had heard from (b) the State Department that General Marshall had given evidence in a secret session of the Foreign Affairs Committee against the proposed Palestine resolutions and that as a result these resolutions in their present form would almost certainly be shelved. Since Mr. Stimson also opposed them on behalf of the War Department, the resolutions were withdrawn.[3]

On March 9 Lord Halifax reported a statement by the two (c) co-Chairmen of the American Zionist Emergency Council that the President had authorised them to say that the United States

---

[1] In their instructions to Lord Halifax the Foreign Office included a sentence: 'You could point out that the Zionists are deliberately and unjustifiably using the refugee situation, which naturally appeals to public opinion in America and England, to advance their own sectarian ends regardless of the effect upon the true interests of the United Nations.' The Prime Minister regarded this sentence as entering into the kind of controversy which the Foreign Office wanted to avoid. He commented: 'I might as well come out and say that the White Paper was a fraud and a breach of faith.'

[2] Assistant Secretary of State.

[3] The United States Government received protests against the resolutions from Egypt, Iraq, Lebanon, Saudi Arabia, Syria, Transjordania and Iran.

(a) E663/95/31. (b) E1388/95/31. (c) E1590/95/31.

Government had never given its approval to the White Paper of 1939.[1]
(a) The Foreign Office regarded this statement by the President as most
unfair, since it suggested that the United States Government had
been consulted about the White Paper and had refused their
approval of it. Nevertheless they thought it undesirable that Lord
Halifax should make, as he proposed, a reference in a public speech
to the Palestine question, especially since the withdrawal of the two
resolutions before Congress. Lord Halifax replied on April 1 that he
regarded it as necessary to answer at least some of the worst slanders
with which we were being attacked in the United States. He pointed
out that his proposed references to the Palestine question were
'exceedingly innocuous', and that they were principally a denial of
the charge that the British Government were preventing the escape
(b) of European Jews. Mr. Eden therefore took up the matter with the
Prime Minister. He suggested that Lord Halifax should be allowed
to make a statement, though in a slightly different form. Before the
Prime Minister had seen the minute Colonel Stanley wrote that he
disagreed entirely with the line proposed by the Foreign Office and
thought that it would lead only to further controversy. Mr. Eden's
minute was therefore held up, and the question discussed between
the Foreign Office and the Colonial Office. The latter were unwilling
to agree to any statement. At the beginning of May they maintained
this view. The Foreign Office considered that the Colonial Office
were giving very little help to Lord Halifax, and that they seemed
to assume that they knew more than the British Embassy in Washington about publicity in the United States. On the other hand, the
Prime Minister did not think it desirable for Lord Halifax to make
any statement, and the Foreign Office themselves were not entirely
sure that a statement, however harmless its terms, might not in the
long run do more harm than good. Lord Halifax was therefore
instructed on May 14 that the Secretary of State for the Colonies
thought that no reference to Palestine should be made in his (Lord
Halifax's) speeches.

Meanwhile the Palestine question was discussed on April 11, 1944,
with Mr. Wallace Murray and Dr. Bowman during their visit to
London.[2] Sir M. Peterson explained that our principal concern was
to prevent the spread of local agitation in Palestine, but there was
no need for us to take a fundamental decision during the war. In an
answer to questions from Mr. Murray Sir M. Peterson said that

---

[1] The Prime Minister's comment on this report was: 'The Prime Minister cordially
concurs with the President and, like him, has never given his approval to the White Paper
of 1939. On the contrary he described it at the time as a fraud and a breach of faith, and
holds the same opinion still.'
[2] See below, section (v) of this chapter.

(a) E1840, 2072, 2974/95/31.   (b) E2974/95/31.

27,000 places remained to be filled for Jewish immigration under the White Paper quota, and that, while it was true that the Prime Minister was opposed to the policy of the White Paper, nothing in the Balfour Declaration or subsequent statements had committed us to the idea of a Jewish State.

Dr. Bowman said that the Jews and Arabs did not seem likely to be able to make an agreement to manage their affairs in Palestine jointly, and that there might have to be some sort of separation between the communities on a territorial basis. There might be an understanding between the British and United States Governments about policy, but the State Department were not trying to interfere in what was essentially a British concern. Sir M. Peterson said that some scheme of division might be possible, but that the Foreign Office were not directly responsible for Palestine and that in any case the question would have to be decided by the Cabinet. Mr. Wallace Murray said that the State Department also could not answer for the views of other Departments or, for that matter, of the White House.

Mr. Wallace Murray explained that the recent resolutions in Congress went further than previous Zionist resolutions in that they called for the formation of a Jewish Commonwealth. It was inevitable that in an election year Jewish agitation should find support. Only a visit from General Marshall and a letter from Mr. Stimson had enabled the resolutions to be shelved. Sir M. Peterson pointed out that the Arab reactions to the resolutions had been entirely spontaneous and were not due to British prompting. Mr. Wallace Murray thought it a new development for the Arabs to be so 'articulate'; he had been especially surprised at the protests from Egypt. The resolutions had not been shelved owing to Arab protests, but these protests had caused surprise in Washington where public opinion knew relatively little about the Arabs. Mr. Wallace Murray raised the question whether a joint Anglo-American declaration would be of use in diminishing local tension. Sir M. Peterson said that this tension was being caused largely by the agitation in the United States. If a declaration would be helpful in America, we should certainly be prepared to consider it. As far as the local situation was concerned, we were likely to be able to keep the Arabs quiet if we did not withdraw the White Paper during the war. It was more doubtful whether we could keep the Jews quiet. Dr. Bowman said that he had no fears about the effect of Zionist agitation on American opinion. The Zionists were making increasingly wide circles in America realise how extreme their demands were. Mr. Wallace Murray gave Sir M. Peterson the text of a draft statement which, if approved, might be kept for use should later developments make its issue desirable.

(iii)

Report of the Ministerial Committee on Palestine: Foreign Office opposition to the proposals of the Committee (December 1943–October 1944).

(a)   The Ministerial Committee on Palestine submitted a report, with a note of dissent from Mr. Law, on December 20, 1943. Their main conclusions were: (i) that a policy based on partition offered the best and possibly the only solution of the Palestine problem; (ii) that we should try to secure the establishment of an association of Levant States consisting of a Jewish State, a Jerusalem Territory,[1] the larger part of the Lebanon, and a Greater Syria comprising Syria, Transjordan, the southern Lebanon and the Arab areas of Palestine; (iii) that the integrity of the Levant States should be guaranteed, if possible, by Anglo-French or Anglo-Franco-American treaties providing, *inter alia*, for the safeguarding of British and French strategic interests; (iv) that an international body consisting of British, French and possibly American representatives should be established to arbitrate on matters referred to it by the Levant States, and to supervise the observance of their treaty obligations, including the protection of minority rights.

Mr. Law's note did not dissent from the view that partition was the best solution of the Palestine problem or that it should be linked with the creation of a Greater Syria. Mr. Law's objection was that the actual scheme of partition would be violently opposed by the Arabs, since it put nearly a third of the Arab population in Palestine under Jewish control, gave the Jews the best land in Palestine, most of the Arab industries as well as all their own, and also the ports of Haifa and Jaffa. Mr. Law regarded this scheme of partition as inequitable and provocative and suggested modifications.

(b)   Mr. Casey's view of the report was that any attempt to solve the Palestine problem would cause disturbances and bloodshed. A plan for partition which also included proposals for a Greater Syria would probably cause the least trouble. In any event we should not disclose our proposals until we had at least two British divisions available in

(c)   or near Palestine. The Chiefs of Staff also commented on the report in a paper submitted to the War Cabinet on January 22. They pointed out that the partition of a small country like Palestine into three separate States would complicate military control and that the scheme of partition had military disadvantages owing to the length of frontier between Jews and Arabs, and the difficulties which

---

[1] The Committee suggested that Jerusalem and its environs should be treated as a separate 'Territory' under the administration of a British High Commissioner.

(a) WP(43)563; E8139/87/31. (b) P(M)(44)1; E95/95/31. (c) E666/95/31.

would attend the rapid movement of troops from one end of Palestine to the other. They recommended therefore that the scheme of partition should be revised. They also said that if the scheme were announced or became known before the end of the war with Germany, we could not ensure the security of the Middle East without diverting forces otherwise available for operations against Germany. Even if the announcement were not made until after the defeat of Germany, we should still be unable to meet our commitment without detriment to the deployment of forces against Japan or our plans for demobilisation or our military requirements for the occupation of Germany. The Chiefs of Staff thought that we might be faced anyhow with trouble in Palestine during the first half of 1944, and that we could not meet it unless we used Indian divisions. We ought therefore to consider whether we should not attempt to lessen possible trouble by taking measures at once to break up the Jewish secret military organisations.[1]

The Prime Minister, in a minute of January 16, commented (a) favourably on the report, but said that it would be better to defer action on it until after the defeat of Germany. He felt uncertain about the effect of the proposals, if published, on Mr. Roosevelt's election prospects. The Foreign Office were much more critical of the report than the Prime Minister. They were most emphatic on the need for deferring an announcement until after the defeat of Germany; they thought that it would be much better to postpone also any decision. It was essential to have the views of Lord Killearn and of Sir K. Cornwallis, and also to follow out the recommendations of the Chiefs of Staff for a further examination of the scheme of partition. We ought to be able, in case of need, to deny that the War Cabinet had taken a decision regarding the future of Palestine, and to say in our propaganda that we were entirely occupied with the war, and had no time to deal with so complicated a question. The Foreign Office agreed that the establishment of a Greater Syria would go some way, though not far, to offset the Arab objections to partition, but there was doubt whether the plan was practicable. The French had always opposed Arab federation, and the Syrians might well refuse negotiations on the basis of a Jewish State in Palestine.

The Foreign Office pointed out that—contrary to the Prime Minister's argument that the Arabs had done nothing for us during the war—they had in fact done about as much as we had wished,

---

[1] The Foreign Office were opposed to this proposal. They considered that it might precipitate Jewish disturbances in Palestine, and that it would start a controversy in the United States at the outset of the Presidential election campaign.

(a) E665/95/31.

and at times we had had to check proposals, e.g. from General Nuri, involving more direct participation in the war. On the other hand, the Zionist war record was not without blemish, as recent revelations of widespread organised thefts of arms from the British forces and the existence of an illicit army of 50,000 men had shown. In any case our Middle East policy should be based on a wide consideration of our interests—oil and communications—in the area.

(a)   The War Cabinet considered the reports of the Ministerial Committee and the Chiefs of Staff on January 25, 1944. Mr. Eden said that he wished to reserve his final judgment on the scheme until he knew the views of Lord Killearn and Sir K. Cornwallis. With this reservation the War Cabinet approved of the Committee's report in principle, and on the understanding that details could be further examined before a final decision was reached. Meanwhile the Colonial Secretary would arrange for the working out in detail of the Committee's recommendations.

(b)   Here the matter remained for some months.[1] Mr. Eden sent letters to Sir K. Cornwallis and Lord Killearn on February 1 asking for their views on the Committee's report. Sir K. Cornwallis considered

(c) that, while the announcement of a policy of partition might not produce an immediate and violent reaction on a large scale in Palestine, the implementation of the policy would be very difficult. The Jews would be given a tiny country; if they were to make anything of it, and satisfy the insistent demand for immigration, they would have to buy out the Arabs or get rid of them in some other way. We should be bound, in fulfilment of the second half of the Balfour Declaration, to try to safeguard the rights of the Arabs. There would certainly be strong Arab opposition within the Jewish State, and the State would become an Arab *terra irredenta*.

Sir K. Cornwallis thought the abrogation or an important 'whittling down' of the White Paper—and still more, the establishment of a Jewish State—would be regarded in Iraq as a breach of faith, and would turn Iraqi friendship towards us into distrust. We should lose our influence in the country, and the maintenance of our oil and other interests would be endangered. The reactions of other countries in the Middle East would be similar; that is to say, our relations with them would be permanently impaired and our interests imperilled. Arab political federation would also be developed much more rapidly, and against us rather than—as had happened hitherto—in a way friendly to us and our interests. The offer to

---

(d)   [1]At a conference in Cairo in April 1944, summoned by Mr. Casey and attended by the Ambassadors at Cairo and Baghdad, the Minister in Syria, the High Commissioner for Palestine and members of the Middle East Defence Committee, the High Commissioner supported partition while the two Ambassadors opposed it.

(a) WM(44)11.4, C.A.   (b) E8139/87/31.   (c) E1494/95/31.   (d) E2987/95/31.

create a Greater Syria would not soften the blow for the Arabs, since they had already assumed, from our discussions with them, our acceptance of Nuri Pasha's plans in the matter. Sir K. Cornwallis thought that there was more chance of success for the proposal to establish a Trustee State.[1] He suggested that this plan should be further examined. In any case, if we proposed to abrogate the White Paper, we should try to secure the open support of our Allies, and especially of the Americans, Russians and French. Otherwise the influence of other Governments, and especially of the United States, in the Middle East would rise as our influence fell.[2]

On June 1 the Foreign Office drew up for circulation to the Prime (a) Minister, Colonel Stanley and Mr. Morrison (as Chairman of the Palestine Committee) another memorandum on the Palestine question. They pointed out that there was general agreement that it was impracticable to continue the White Paper policy after the war, and that we should not announce our terms of settlement until after the end of the war in Europe. The Foreign Office also thought that our terms must have the backing of the United Nations, and particularly of the United States. We could not be sure what American opinion would be after the elections, and, if we were committed to a policy of partition, we ran the risk of losing to the United States the pre-eminent place which we had always held, and should continue to hold in the Arab world in view of our strategic interests, especially oil. The Foreign Office thought that the Americans had thoughts of usurping our place, 'beginning with Saudi Arabia'.[3]

As an alternative to partition the Foreign Office suggested the plan—which Mr. Eden had mentioned to Sir K. Cornwallis—for a new Palestinian State; the sovereignty over this State would lie with the United Nations who would devolve it (since sovereignty could not be exercised multilaterally) on a High Commissioner or Governor-General. The High Commissioner or Governor-General would be responsible to the United Nations but would take his day-to-day instructions from us.[4] He might be assisted by an advisory committee representing the different religions. All idea of a 'provisional' settlement or temporary mandate would thus disappear. The statute of the new State would be definitive, and renewed

---

[1] See below, pp. 375-7.

[2] Lord Killearn, in his reply, also thought that the policy of partition would be opposed (b) most strongly by the Arabs and that the British Government would be accused of bad faith. His own view was that 'we should keep Palestine ourselves as a vital link in our defence system'. The Foreign Office regarded this plan as neither possible nor desirable.

[3] See below, section (vii) of this chapter.

[4] The memorandum mentioned, as an analogy, the position of the Governor-General of the Sudan in relation to the joint sovereignty of Great Britain and Egypt.

(a) E3454/95/31.   (b) E1532/95/31.

Jewish immigration into Palestine would be rendered possible. The main cause of Arab mistrust of Jewish immigration was the suspicion that it was aimed at creating a Jewish majority upon which a permanent settlement would be based. This fear would be removed. It would also help to reconcile Arab opinion if it were possible to say that Jewish immigration was being directed to other parts of the world as well as to Palestine. If no suitable location for a Jewish settlement could be found in Africa, we might be able to persuade the Americans to allow a separate quota for Jewish immigrants or at least to publish separate returns of such immigrants.

The limits upon Jewish migration would still have to be determined, and might be fixed at a figure allowing a Jewish population of 100,000 less than the Arabs. This would allow for the gradual entry of 3–400,000 new Jewish immigrants. Within the new State a large measure of local autonomy could be granted in the country districts where the Arab and Jewish 'colonies' were fairly distinct, and in some of the big towns such as Jaffa and Tel Aviv.

(a)   Mr. Eden did not circulate this paper to the Palestine Committee until September 15, 1944.[1] He then added to it a memorandum on the case against partition, and included, as an annex, Sir K. Cornwallis's letter. He said that partition would not solve, but would merely aggravate, the problem of Jewish immigration which was the whole crux of the Palestine problem. The only condition upon which it would be possible to resume Jewish immigration without causing an upheaval in the Middle East was to offer the Arabs assurances and guarantees that neither Palestine nor any part of it would become a Jewish political State. Partition would remove all restrictions on Jewish immigration. The Zionists would not be deterred by the small size of the State from filling it with immigrants beyond its capacity. They would regard the Jewish State merely as a stepping-stone towards the realisation of their wider hopes for a larger State covering the whole of Palestine and Transjordan. The Arabs would be kept in continual tension, and there would be continuous disorders and bloodshed.

If our interests in the Middle East were so important that we could not afford to alienate the Arabs, we must find a policy in which they would acquiesce, even if this policy meant a strict control of Jewish immigration into Palestine. Mr. Eden thought that the Committee on Palestine ought to make up their minds whether or not the Middle East was vital to British interests. It was necessary to take account of American views, but we could not determine what

---

[1] Mr. Eden said that he had not circulated it because his main anxiety was not to take the matter further until the war in Europe was over.

(a) P(M)(44)11; E5660/95/31.

these views were until after the Presidential election. We might find American opinion, influenced by oil and other strategical considerations, inclining rather to the Arab than to the Jewish side.

The Palestine Committee produced the draft of a revised version (a) of their report on September 26, 1944. They maintained their original plan for partition, and put their case for it against the views held by the Foreign Office.[1] They agreed that the crucial question was that of Jewish immigration. If it were possible to put a stop to mass immigration or even to control it (as it was controlled in every other country) other solutions of the Palestine question might be acceptable. It had been shown, however, that control was impracticable. The Jews would not accept it, and could 'bring every weapon in their armoury, both here and abroad, to bear against any policy which attempted to enforce it'. Even if they failed to get the policy changed, 'no laws or regulations would prevent Jews from continuing to descend on the coasts of Palestine, and once there it would be as impossible to evict them in the future as it had been in the past'.

All chances of a bi-national Palestine, whatever the system of government proposed, broke down against this obstacle. There was no hope of agreement between Jews and Arabs on a criterion of numbers of immigrants. 'The Jews will never consent to be relegated or the Arabs to be reduced to the status of a minority community, yet in any bi-national State one of these alternatives is inevitable.' The Committee therefore agreed with the Royal Commission on Palestine of 1936–37 that partition alone offered finality, and that 'while neither race can be permitted to dominate the whole of Palestine, there is no reason why each race should not rule part of it'.

The Committee took account of the warnings from Sir K. Cornwallis and Lord Killearn; they considered, however, that in any case trouble was inevitable. The immigration quotas laid down in the White Paper would soon be filled, and a new declaration of policy would be necessary. Further immigration would have to be permitted, and the effect on Arab opinion would be much the same as the effect of an announcement of partition. The latter plan would, however, remove the Arab fears of ultimate Jewish domination.

The Foreign Office circulated to the Committee in a memo- (b) randum of October 6 their comments on the revised report. They repeated their view that partition would not remove Arab fears, especially if the Jews encouraged large-scale immigration. The

---

[1] The Committee still regarded the formation of a 'Greater Syria' as desirable, but regarded this step as impracticable for the time. They suggested the establishment of a Southern Syrian State comprising Transjordania and the Arab areas of Palestine.

(a) P(M)(44)12; E6039/95/31. (b) P(M)(44)13; E6188/95/31.

Foreign Office also regarded the final scheme of partition as unfair to the Arabs. Sixty-two per cent of the area assigned to the Jewish State was land owned by Arabs, and the whole area included nearly as many Arabs as Jews (338,980 Arabs, 391,725 Jews). All the best land, and the two principal seaports—each containing a large Arab population—were to be given to the Jews and the Jewish State included most of the Arab industries. The frontiers were very long and complicated, and their control for customs and police purposes would cause serious trouble.

The Foreign Office did not agree that it would be impossible to control Jewish immigration into Palestine. Such control had been impossible for the last ten years since illegal immigrants expelled from Palestine were liable to persecution or even death on return to their countries of origin. These conditions would not continue after the defeat of Germany, and there should henceforward be no moral or material objection to getting rid of illegal immigrants into Palestine as into any other State.

If, in spite of all these objections, the War Cabinet approved of the Committee's plan, the first step would be to try to get American approval and, if possible, public support. We might find the United States Government unwilling to give this public support; they might prefer to leave it to us to incur the hostility of Jews and Arabs and not themselves to risk the security of their oil and other interests in the Middle East. We could therefore not be sure of the American attitude. In any case we ought not to consult the United States Government and other interested parties until after the Presidential election.[1] Otherwise the American Zionists in their disappointment at not getting their full demands might put pressure on an Administration urgently requiring the support of the Jewish vote. We were also committed to prior consultation both with the Arabs and the Jews.[2]

---

[1] On October 15, 1944, Mr. Roosevelt had sent a message to a convention of the Zionist Organisation of America approving of the inclusion in the Democratic electoral programme of a statement favouring the opening of Palestine to unrestricted Jewish immigration and colonisation with the aim of establishing a free and democratic Jewish Commonwealth. The President said that, if re-elected, he would help to bring about the realisation of this aim. *F.R.U.S.* 1944, IV, 615–6. The Republican programme had included a similar statement in favour of unrestricted Jewish immigration and land ownership in Palestine. The State Department, in view of strong Arab protests, found these statements embarrassing. On December 13 Mr. Stettinius sent a memorandum to the President pointing out the possible danger to American influence and interests (notably the immensely valuable American oil concessions in Saudi Arabia) from this endorsement of Zionist aims. *F.R.U.S.* 1944, V, 648–9.

[2] Lord Cranborne had said in the House of Commons on May 6, 1942, that we should not enter into commitments regarding the future of Palestine without such consultation.

(iv)

Assassination of Lord Moyne by Jewish terrorists: Sir E. Grigg's proposals for a Palestinian settlement: the question of Jewish immigration beyond the White Paper quota: Mr. Truman's note of July 24, 1945, to the Prime Minister (October 1944–July 1945).

During Mr. Eden's absence in Moscow the Foreign Office drew (a) up a draft paper for submission to the War Cabinet stating the arguments against the partition schemes. This paper was not circulated at the time because the discussion of the Committee's report in the War Cabinet was postponed after the assassination of Lord Moyne by two Jewish terrorists on November 6.[1] There was further delay owing to Colonel Stanley's absence in West Africa. Mr. Eden then went to the Yalta Conference. Early in March 1945, the Foreign Office were informed that the Cabinet were likely to consider the revised report of the Committee some time during the month. Mr. Eden, however, did not want to circulate the Foreign Office memorandum until he had considered proposals which Sir E. Grigg was putting forward as an alternative policy to partition. After these proposals had been received Mr. Eden circulated the (b) memorandum (on April 10) with a concluding note that he intended later to put forward more positive proposals based on Sir E. Grigg's recommendations.

Mr. Eden's memorandum repeated the Foreign Office view that the Palestine problem was one of a territorial conflict between two new and rapidly growing nationalisms. Our concern in it was not to back either Arabs or Jews but (i) to keep our word (as far as it was possible to fulfil undertakings which were in themselves most difficult to reconcile); (ii) to produce a workable system within which the two communities could exist and develop; and (iii) to maintain our position in the Middle East where our interests were of vital importance. After describing these interests—oil, communications and bases—the memorandum pointed out that we had secured Arab goodwill and obtained for ourselves a reputation for fair dealing and good intentions. We should have to face in future a new American and Russian interest in the Middle East as well as a movement for Arab unity.

In the light of these facts the memorandum examined the question

---

[1] An attempt had been made on August 8 by terrorists to kill Sir Harold Macmillan, the retiring British High Commissioner in Palestine. On October 18 it was stated in the House of Commons that Jewish terrorists had killed ten British, three Arab and two Jewish members of the Palestine police force since the beginning of 1944. The Jewish Agency repudiated these terrorist attacks. Dr. Weizmann sent a message to the Prime Minister deploring the attack on Lord Moyne.

(a) E435/15/31 (1945). (b) WP(45)229; E2453/15/31.

of partition from the Arab point of view. The Arabs regarded
Palestine as for centuries past a purely Arab country. In 1918 it had
an Arab population of about 600,000, and only about 55,000 Jews.
The Jewish immigrants, mostly from eastern Europe, had come in
by virtue of the mandate, but without Arab consent; they had no
previous connexion with the country. To the Arabs partition meant
the establishment of a Jewish State for the benefit of these eastern
European 'interlopers'. The establishment of a Jewish *Home* in
Palestine was our settled policy, though the Arabs strongly resented
the fact that we had set up this home in Palestine rather than in some
British territory. An attempt on our part to establish a Jewish *State*
with unrestricted immigration would appear to the Arabs 'as an
outrage', the more so because during the war years, when we most
needed Arab goodwill, we had done our best by our propaganda to
convince the Arabs that the 'policy of calling a halt to Jewish
immigration represented the firm and indeed "final" policy of His
Majesty's Government'. Mr. Eden agreed with Sir K. Cornwallis
and Lord Killearn in thinking that the reaction to any form of
partition with unrestricted immigration would be 'deep-rooted,
permanent and very severe'. After stating the special objections to
the scheme of partition put forward by the Committee, the memorandum suggested that the Committee's proposals were based on
the hypothesis that it would be as difficult to control Jewish immigration in the future as it had been in the past, and that partition
would be a 'final solution'. Mr. Eden, in putting the Foreign Office
argument that the position about immigration would change with
the end of the persecution of the Jews in Europe, mentioned that
Sir Herbert Emerson, International Commissioner for Refugees, had
said in a confidential report of 1944 that it was essential in the
interests of the Jews that the 'centrifugal movement' from Europe
should be actively discouraged. On the second point Mr. Eden
asked whether we could assume that the Jewish Agency and the
Zionists would accept the proposed frontiers as final. The Zionists,
especially after the 'prudent hand of Dr. Weizmann' was removed,
would fill up their State far beyond its capacity, and so 'prove their
need for more living space—first, no doubt, the Jerusalem State'.
With the funds available to American and British Zionism, there
should not be 'any real economic deterrent to such a policy'. In any
case it would be

> 'extremely improvident to create a new State and undertake to
> defend it by force of arms unless we are as certain as possible that
> we are also the controlling influence in that State. . . . The danger
> to ourselves . . . in the proposed Jewish State is that the highly
> organised, active, and irresponsible Zionists in America (and not in
> America only), and even American political leaders also, will be

perpetually influencing the policy of the new State in a sense that will exasperate the Arabs surrounding it, and that the responsibility for defence will rest, under our scheme, apart from the Jews themselves, entirely upon us.'

Sir E. Grigg set out his proposals in a memorandum circulated to (a) the War Cabinet on April 4. He began by putting the arguments, with which he agreed, against partition. These arguments repeated, generally, those already stated by Mr. Eden and the Foreign Office. Sir E. Grigg summed up the Arab view against partition:

'They [the Arabs] believe, with good reason, that a Jewish State would be strongly nationalist, authoritarian and aggressive, and would not be content for long to remain within the frontiers laid down for it. They also fear that the Jewish State would enjoy external support in its expansionist ambitions, which have been made amply clear in public utterances by Zionists of all shades of opinion. They have learnt, moreover, in the last five years how States with large financial resources and expansionist ambitions can now equip themselves for terrorism against poorer and more primitive peoples, and they fear that the English-speaking democracies might once again be ready to let events take their course in this region of the world . . . if intervention seemed to involve another threat of war. They would therefore regard the establishment of a Jewish State as a threat to the security not only of the Arabs of Palestine, but to that of all the surrounding countries which now form the Arab League.'

Sir E. Grigg pointed out that the Jews would also resist partition because: (i) it would defeat the primary object of political Zionism which was to obtain possession of the whole of Palestine; (ii) it would frustrate many of the Zionist plans and greatly narrow the scope of the economic and industrial development of Palestine;[1] (iii) it would cut them off from some of the places, e.g. Jerusalem, which they most desired and venerated; (iv) they thought that they could mobilise a large measure of support in the United States and elsewhere in their resistance to it.

Sir E. Grigg considered that there was no reason why we should not continue to hold a mandate for a bi-racial State if we corrected the defects in the existing mandate. The greatest defect was that we were solely responsible for deciding the amount of Jewish immigration. This responsibility should be placed upon an international body consisting of representatives of Great Britain, the United States, the U.S.S.R., France and (through the Arab League) the Arab States and two Jews (to be chosen by the United States Government on the advice of Jewish organisations).

---

[1] Sir E. Grigg mentioned large-scale irrigation schemes which could not be carried out if the country were broken up into independent States.

(a) WP(45)214; E2263/15/31.

(a)   Mr. Eden circulated to the War Cabinet on April 13 a memorandum on Sir E. Grigg's proposals. He said that he needed more time for a careful study of the proposals, but that his impression was that the proposals offered a suitable alternative to partition. He mentioned certain difficulties in the plan. A bi-national State in which neither side was able to dominate the other might lead to a deadlock and total administrative paralysis on matters where Arab and Jewish interests were opposed. The proposal for an international body to decide upon Jewish immigration might result in a situation in which a non-British body took important decisions (perhaps against British advice) on immigration, while British troops alone would suffer casualties if the decision led to disturbance and revolt.

Mr. Eden considered that the Colonial Office and other Departments concerned (including the Foreign Office) should be invited to prepare for submission to the War Cabinet a definite scheme on the basis of Sir E. Grigg's proposals. This preparation would take some time; the Committee on Palestine would therefore doubtless wish to consider proposals for approaching the Arab States to secure their consent to a temporary continuance of Jewish immigration into Palestine after the exhaustion of the White Paper quotas in September.[1]

Owing to Colonel Stanley's illness and the preoccupations of other Ministers the discussion of Sir E. Grigg's proposals was postponed.[2] No decision could be reached while Mr. Eden and Lord Cranborne were at San Francisco; it was also evident that a decision on long-term policy could not be taken until after the British General Election. Meanwhile, as Mr. Eden had pointed out, an immediate decision was necessary on what was to be done about immigration. During the latter part of May the Colonial Office and Foreign

(b)   Office jointly drew up a memorandum summarising possible courses of action, two of them long-term and three short-term. The two long-term projects were the Committee's proposals for partition and Sir E. Grigg's suggestions (not yet fully worked out) for a new trusteeship arrangement. The three short-term proposals were: (i) to adhere, if only temporarily, to the White Paper policy, and not to allow further Jewish immigration after the exhaustion of the quota without Arab consent; (ii) to continue to administer Palestine as at present, and to consult the Arabs with regard to the matter, but to insist on allowing further Jewish immigration even in the event of

---

[1] The actual date of exhaustion on the quota of the monthly figure of 1,500 immigrants was likely to be the end of November 1945.

(c)   [2] At a conference in Cairo in April 1945, the British diplomatic representatives in the Middle East, the High Commissioner for Palestine and the three Service Commanders endorsed Sir E. Grigg's criticisms of partition.

(a) P(M)(45)3; E2263/15/31. (b) E3975/15/31. (c) E2297/15/31.

an Arab refusal; (iii) to insist on further Jewish immigration without prior consultation with the Arabs.

The first of the three short-term proposals might be agreed to by the Arabs, since it would concede the point which they were most anxious to establish, namely, that the White Paper policy was still accepted by the British Government. The Arabs would ask whether this policy was final, but we could reply that the whole mandate system was now under review by a World Organisation of which they were members, and that for this reason there could be no finality in respect of any matter affecting mandated territories. There were, however, difficulties which seemed to make this first proposal impracticable: (i) the British Government might be unwilling to reassert the White Paper policy; (ii) if they reasserted this policy, the Government might have to meet serious opposition in Parliament. There would also probably be an outcry from the United States, unless the United States Government agreed with the policy and were ready to say so in a public statement. There would almost certainly be trouble from the Jews in Palestine; (iii) if we quoted the White Paper in the hope of getting Arab consent to further immigration, and if the Arabs refused their consent, we should be bound by this refusal.

There was very little chance of getting Arab consent under the second short-term proposal. The Arabs held to the White Paper policy and, if we did not reassert this policy, they were unlikely to assist us in getting out of an embarrassment. They considered that, having regard to the small size of Palestine, they had already made a greater contribution to the solution of the refugee problem than any other country and that they should not be asked to do more. They might regard the matter as a sound case on which to test the strength of the new Arab League. It was at least possible that, if we decided that Jewish immigration must continue, the repercussions would be less serious if we stated the fact plainly in the first instance rather than asked Arab consent and then overrode their refusal.

The dangers in the second and third short-term courses were thus similar, though they differed slightly in degree: (i) the Arabs would regard the abrogation of the White Paper policy as a breach of faith; (ii) abrogation would involve us in military commitments in various parts of the Middle East; (iii) the resentment thereby caused would estrange the Arab countries from Great Britain and result in their turning to Russia for support. Arab grievances would also be exploited as a Moslem grievance and would be used by anti-British elements to stir up trouble in India.

Since there were serious difficulties in the way of each one of the possible courses of action, it was essential to obtain the views of the

Chiefs of Staff, the British diplomatic representatives in the Arab States, the High Commissioner for Palestine, and the Viceroy of India and Lord Halifax. These views should be obtained within the next month or six weeks, since an announcement on policy should not be delayed longer than the end of September. If it were decided to consult the Arab States, we should approach them early in August.[1]

(a)   Lord Halifax gave his reply in a long despatch of July 1. He pointed out that five million United States citizens were Jews, and that they were thus about half of the remaining Jews in the world.[2] Many of them held prominent positions round the White House, in the administration and in the press. The Jewish vote could turn the scale in the key electoral state of New York. The Jews, however, were not as powerful as they were vocal. They had to carry non-Jewish opinion with them, and in particular win the support of leading non-Jews in the Administration and in Congress. Non-Jewish opinion was not greatly interested in the Palestine issues apart from the question of immigration, but liberal opinion held that we ought to have admitted more Jews into Palestine, and that Palestine was now the national asylum for the many Jews who wanted to leave Europe. 'The average citizen does not want them in the United States, and salves his conscience by advocating their admission to Palestine. On this issue the Jews can therefore carry with them both liberal humanitarians and many anti-Jews.' Non-Jewish opinion also suspected that we were encouraging the Arabs against the Jews for our own political interests.

Any solution, therefore, which appeared to shut out needy and victimised Jews from Palestine would be represented as an act of inhumanity dictated by selfish reasons, and any disturbances involving the use of force by British troops against Jews would cause a violent reaction in the United States against the British Government. Since there was no Arab vote in the United States, the Arabs could not exercise direct political pressure. On the other hand, President Roosevelt's reception of King Ibn Saud and King Farouk on his return from Yalta, the formation of the Arab League and events in the Levant States had aroused considerable American public interest in the Arab world.[3] This interest had been increased by the return

---

[1] This memorandum was not brought before the War Cabinet. It was sent out by the Foreign Office and Colonial Office as part of a plan to have complete information to submit to the new government when it took office.

[2] See above, p. 360, note 1.

[3] Lord Halifax pointed out that, in a letter of April 5 to King Ibn Saud, President Roosevelt, notwithstanding his earlier statements to American Zionists (see above, p. 372, note 1) had renewed a previous assurance to the King that the United States Government desired that 'no decision be taken regarding the basic situation in [Palestine] without full consultation with both Arabs and Jews'. King Ibn Saud had informed the British Minister at Jedda of the President's letter.

(a) E4849/15/31.

of numbers of American servicemen from North Africa, and by the presence at San Francisco of representatives of sovereign Arab States with a common outlook, comparable, *mutatis mutandis*, to that of the Latin American countries. A growing realisation of the importance of Middle Eastern oil had also focused attention on the Arab world. The State Department was, in fact, more favourable to the Arab than to the Jewish case, but the United States Government was in the comfortable though illogical position that their wishes could not be ignored, and yet they did not have to bear any share of the responsibility.

Lord Halifax thought that non-Jewish opinion in the United States would be favourable to partition if it were freely accepted by Jews and Arabs. Sir E. Grigg's plan for an international body to settle the question of immigration would also be well received. Lord Halifax suggested that the main difficulty in the plan might be met by giving the British Government the right to refer to the World Organisation any decision about immigration which they regarded as impracticable or likely to lead to disturbance.

The first of the short-term proposals would be acceptable only if the Arabs gave their consent to further immigration. Non-Jewish opinion had never grasped that the White Paper had laid down that immigration should be based on the principle of consent. The second short-term plan would also be acceptable, especially if it could be put into effect without reference to the White Paper. The third plan would have no advantages over the second, and would have the disadvantage that the Arabs could claim that in spite of the promises made to them they had not even been allowed to state their case.

Lord Halifax therefore thought that something on the lines of Sir E. Grigg's plan would be the best choice; otherwise he recommended the second short-term plan. He asked whether, as a variant to the latter, it might be possible to persuade the Arabs to agree to the admission, as a special humanitarian action, of some 100,000 Jews who wished to leave Europe. Lord Halifax also asked whether it was essential to our interests to continue to take the sole responsibility for the Palestine mandate.

The Foreign Office stated their own views in a memorandum of (a) July 26 after all the replies had been received to the memorandum of June 11. They pointed out that each of the two long-term projects at present recommended had been brought forward before it was known whether international arrangements would be made to replace the existing system of mandates. It was now clear that, if the charter signed at San Francisco were ratified, we should have to decide whether or not Palestine was to be placed under international

(a) E5452/15/31.

trusteeship. If it were so placed, new terms of trust would have to be negotiated. An attempt therefore on our part to predetermine the character of the trust by announcing a long-term policy might cause unfavourable criticism.

Apart from this consideration, the Foreign Office stated that our representatives in the Middle East thought that the scheme of partition proposed by the Cabinet Committee would have a disastrous effect on Anglo-Arab relations and that the Arabs would not acquiesce in it. The Jews might agree to partition in principle, but would resist the present scheme as bitterly as the Arabs. The Arab and Jewish reactions would affect the attitude of other Powers, especially of the United States. Lord Halifax thought that a decision to partition Palestine would probably be favourably received by non-Jews in the United States if it were freely accepted both by the Jews and by the Arabs; any policy involving force against either Arabs or Jews would be condemned.

Sir E. Grigg's proposal would be less likely to provoke violent Jewish or Arab resistance in Palestine and would therefore have more chance of commending itself to public opinion in the United States. It was not certain, however, whether the United States Government would want to give up its freedom from responsibility for any decisions about Palestine affairs and take part in the regulation of Jewish immigration. Moreover the Arabs would not welcome the introduction of the United States—whose policy they regarded as specially exposed to Zionist influence—into Palestinian affairs. The Arabs would also dislike the abandonment of the fixed limit of immigration laid down in the White Paper.

Since it was improbable that we could take at present a long-term decision, there remained the three possible short-term proposals. Our representatives in the Middle East regarded the first short-term course as the only plan likely to be approved by the Arab States. Lord Halifax thought that if Arab consent were given, but not otherwise, American opinion would support the policy. The Zionists would protest against the dependence of their immigration on Arab consent, but the *de facto* continuance of this immigration would take the sting out of their protest and probably deprive them of an adequate pretext for a resort to violence.

The second and third short-term proposals would also have serious consequences if the Arabs refused to accept a continuance of immigration. The Prime Minister had assured King Ibn Saud that he would keep him informed of our policy, and that he would propose nothing contrary to the 'rules of justice and equity which are the foundation of all true friendship'. Mr. Roosevelt had also told King Ibn Saud of the desire of the United States Government that no decision should be taken without full consultation with both Arabs and Jews. The King would regard failure to consult him as a personal affront; the other Arab Governments would be equally shaken in their belief in the sincerity of British policy towards them and the value of their present close attachment to us.

The best solution might therefore be consultation with the Arabs regarding the continuance of Jewish immigration on a temporary basis; if the Arabs refused their consent, we should inform them that we had decided to refer the matter to the Big Five, as the appropriate interim procedure pending the coming into force of the Charter, and that the five Powers would give the interested parties an opportunity of stating their views before reaching a final decision.

While these enquiries were taking place, the Prime Minister had (a) sent a minute (July 6) to the Colonial Secretary and the Chiefs of Staff that the question of Palestine would have to be settled at the Peace Conference, and that it might be 'touched upon' at Potsdam. The Prime Minister thought that we should not 'take the responsibility on ourselves of managing this very difficult plan while the Americans sit back and criticise'. He asked:

> 'Have you ever addressed yourselves to the idea that we should ask them [the Americans] to take it over? I believe we should be the stronger the more they are drawn into the Mediterranean. At any rate the fact that we show no desire to keep the mandate will be a great help. I am not aware of the slightest advantage which has ever accrued to Great Britain from this painful and thankless task. Somebody else should have their turn now. However, the Chiefs of Staff should examine the matter from the strategic point of view.'

The Chiefs of Staff replied to the Prime Minister on July 12 that (b) the presence of the United States in Palestine would certainly be 'an insurance to our general strategic position in the event of a breakdown of the World Security Organisation', since it would 'deter unwanted Powers from pursuing their aims in the Middle East itself', and would also 'go some way towards ensuring the early intervention of the United States in a general European war, if that occurs'.

On the other hand, there were grave disadvantages in giving up our responsibility. We should be thought to have abandoned our predominant position in the Middle East. 'This abrogation of responsibility would have evil consequences, not only in the Middle East but in India and beyond.' The safeguarding of our strategic interests in the Middle East would virtually depend upon the policy pursued by the United States in Palestine. If that policy were hostile to our interests, we should be 'faced with an increased internal security

---

(a) E4939/15/31. (b) E5141/15/31.

commitment in the Middle East and an embarrassing conflict of policy with the United States'.[1]

On balance, therefore, the Chiefs of Staff did not support the Prime Minister's suggestion, though they would 'welcome a distribution of responsibilities in Europe and the Middle East, which imposed a permanent commitment upon the United States'. The report of the Chiefs of Staff also included certain points put to them by the Foreign Office: (i) The Russians might regard the entry of the United States into the Middle East as somehow aimed at them, and might feel that they must take action to protect themselves. (ii) The United States might pursue a strongly pro-Zionist policy which would arouse Arab opposition. We might feel bound, owing to our special interests in the Middle East, to support the Arabs, and thus bring about a clash, at least of opinion, with the United States. If, on the other hand, we did not support the Arabs, the Russians might take the opportunity of doing so.

The Prime Minister's proposal was not put into effect, but the need for a decision at least on a short-term policy was even more (a) urgent owing to an approach from the American side. On July 24 at Potsdam President Truman sent a minute to the Prime Minister in the following terms:

'There is great interest in America in the Palestine problem. The drastic restrictions imposed on Jewish immigration by the British White Paper of May 1939, continue to provoke passionate protest from Americans most interested in Palestine and in the Jewish problem. They fervently urge the lifting of those restrictions which deny to Jews, who have been so cruelly uprooted by ruthless Nazi persecutions, entrance into the land which represents for so many of them their only hope of survival. Knowing your deep and sympathetic interest in Jewish settlement in Palestine, I venture to express to you the hope that the British Government may find it possible without delay to take steps to lift the restrictions of the White Paper on Jewish immigration into Palestine. While I realise the difficulties of reaching a definite and satisfactory settlement of the Palestine problem, and that we cannot expect to discuss these difficulties at any length at our present meeting, I have some doubt whether these difficulties will be lessened by prolonged delay. I hope, therefore, that you can arrange at your early convenience to let me have your ideas on the settlement of the Palestine problem, so that we can at a later but not too distant date discuss the problem in concrete terms.'

The Prime Minister gave this note to Mr. Eden, with a request

---

[1] In their report (prepared for the Chiefs of Staff by the Joint Planning Staff) this point is put somewhat more clearly: 'If troubles occurred in the Middle East as a result of American policy over which we should have little control, our internal security commitments in other countries, notably India, might well be increased.'

(a) E5474, 5539/15/31.

for his views about a reply. The Foreign Office considered that the reply would have to be worded with great care. The President had almost certainly intended his *démarche* mainly 'for the record' and would make known at least the general nature of our reply in some statement after his return to the United States. They also thought it important to correct the impression in his letter that Palestine rather than the countries of which they were nationals was the proper home of all Jews.

Owing to the change of Government in Great Britain it was impossible to give a reply at once to the President's minute. The Foreign Office and Colonial Office suggested on July 28 in a telegram to Sir A. Cadogan at Potsdam that the reply should state that the question was under urgent examination in London and would be laid before the new Government at an early date, and that the President would no doubt realise that no statement of policy could be given to him until the new Government had had time to consider the matter. Mr. Bevin sent a minute to Mr. Attlee on July 30 that he agreed with the suggested answer. He also wrote a minute for Sir A. Cadogan that 'this matter will become urgent. I shall need a summary of the position to date together with the repercussions on the whole Middle East and the U.S.A. to enable the consideration of the steps to be taken to arrive at definite conclusions'.

(v)

British proposals for a general approach to the United States Government on the co-ordination of Anglo-American policy in the Middle East, June–July 1943: Mr. Wallace Murray's visit to London, April 1944.

In addition to a proposal for common action in an attempt to stop inflammatory Zionist propaganda on Palestine the Foreign Office considered in the early summer of 1943 a more general approach to the United States Government on Middle Eastern policy. On May (a) 10–13 the Middle East War Council held a special meeting in Cairo to discuss British policy in the Middle East in the changed circumstances after the removal of any serious threat of invasion by Axis forces. At this meeting the Council recommended the establishment of a Middle East Regional Council including British and American representatives related to a possible wider international organisation. Mr. Casey suggested after the meeting that he should come to England for consultation. The discussions during his visit brought out very clearly the need for the co-ordination of British and

---

(a) WP(43)247; E3234/2551/65.

American policy in the Middle East. The Foreign Office were disquieted at what seemed to them the increasing lack of consideration shown by the Americans for British interests. They did not know the motives behind American policy or indeed what this policy was. They wanted American help in the Middle East and realised that they could not obtain it without a general agreement on policy. Hence they supported a proposal made by Mr. Casey for an approach to the United States Government. The first stage would be the communication of a memorandum explaining British policy and stating the general grounds on which it was based. We should hope, as a further stage, to arrange for a high official of the State Department to come to London for a detailed discussion.

(a)   Mr. Eden submitted a draft memorandum on this proposal to the War Cabinet on July 12, 1943.[1] In a covering note he mentioned some of the more recent difficulties with the State Department. Thus in Afghanistan, where until recently the United States had no diplomatic representation, the State Department had instructed their newly appointed Minister to Kabul to intervene against our interests in negotiations which we and the Russians were conducting with the Afghan Government over the activities of certain persons subsidised by the Axis Legations. In Iran the Americans had accused us in 1942 of dealing with the Iranians in a manner likely to make the task of the United States advisers more difficult and to prejudice the Allied position. We had had little difficulty in explaining our policy to the State Department but their general doubts about our intentions remained. The State Department had also insisted, against our wishes, upon opening an American Consulate at Bahrein, although there were only 100 American citizens in the total foreign colony of 16,000. In Saudi Arabia, where again the Americans had recently established a Legation,[2] the United States Consul at Jedda had been told to instruct the authorities to apply for arms to Washington and not to London. The Consul had promised that, if it were feasible, the supplies would be granted. This offer took no account of the unofficial Anglo-American understanding regarding zones of responsibility for the supply of arms or of the obvious importance which, in view of our responsibility for defending and maintaining order in neighbouring Arab countries, we attached to preventing excessive supplies of arms from reaching the Arabian peninsula. We had also been surprised that, without consultation with us, the President had invited King Ibn Saud or one of his sons to Washington

---

(b)   [1] The memorandum was embodied in a despatch to Lord Halifax (see below, p. 386) I have included here some additional details mentioned in the despatch.
    [2] See below, section (vii) of this chapter.

(a) WP(43)301; E4079/2551/65. (b) E4462/2551/65.

for a discussion of the Palestinian problem. Mr. Eden pointed out in his covering note that we had to overcome the prejudiced American opinion that Great Britain had exploited the Middle Eastern terri tories for her own imperialist ends and had retarded political progress in them. We had in fact done more than any other Power both to further Arab freedom and to develop the Middle Eastern countries. The proposed memorandum would attempt to correct the American misunderstanding on this matter.[1]

We did not want to have an argument conducted through an exchange of notes. Our hope was that we might get a high official of the State Department to come to London for a detailed discussion of Middle Eastern affairs. We could not expect the Americans to sacrifice their interests to ours in the Middle East, but we might persuade them to allow us to 'play the hand there from a political point of view', and to come to an agreement with us on such matters as the proposal for a Central Economic Council for the Middle East.

Mr. Casey also circulated a memorandum to the War Cabinet in (a) which he developed, in particular, proposals for Anglo-American co-operation on a Middle East Economic Council. The War Cabinet (b) considered Mr. Eden's and Mr. Casey's proposals on July 14. Mr. Eden said that he had submitted his memorandum largely at the suggestion of the Minister of State, who thought that British authori- ties in the Middle East would find it helpful if a memorandum on our general Middle Eastern policy were communicated to the United States Government. Mr. Casey explained that there seemed to be no definite American policy in the Middle East. Some American actions seemed to be based on suspicion of British policy or even on opposition to our interests. Mr. Casey thought that we should invite the Americans to recognise that the British Commonwealth and Empire had a predominant interest in the Middle East, whereas American interests were relatively minor and subsidiary. During the discussion Mr. Casey mentioned American prospecting for oil in the Middle East; he thought that British oil interests might welcome a discussion with the Americans. The question was raised whether an approach might be made to the President on the subject. The Prime Minister, however, thought it undesirable to raise at present the far-reaching issues involved in the oil question.

---

[1] Mr. Eden said that we were also faced with the unfriendly attitude of Mr. Wallace Murray, who was Political Adviser for Middle East Affairs (including India) in the State Department. We had proof of his hostility in connexion with Iran. It was desirable, therefore, to have an open discussion on our policy. The British Embassy in Washington (c) had reported to the Foreign Office on April 6, 1942, that Mr. Murray always gave one 'the strong impression of casting envious eyes on the Middle East, and of wishing to promote United States interests in that area not always to British advantage'.

(a) WP(43)302. (b) WM(43)99; E4264/2551/65. (c) E2420/773/93 (1942).

(a)   The War Cabinet accepted the proposals (with minor changes) at a meeting on July 19. They considered that the best method of approach to the United States Government would not be through a written memorandum, but that such a memorandum might be given to Lord Halifax as the basis for conversations with the President or

(b) Mr. Hull. The memorandum was sent in the form of a despatch to Lord Halifax on August 8.

(c)   Lord Halifax spoke to Mr. Stettinius on November 2 on the proposal for a full exchange of views.[1] Mr. Stettinius said that a discussion was especially necessary on the oil question. Lord Halifax

(d) left with Mr. Stettinius a formal *aide-mémoire* and received a memorandum in reply on November 29. The State Department asked what questions were to be discussed and what were the British views about them. They also thought it better to hold the meeting in Washington, since a number of British technical experts were already there, while the United States Government had not a similar staff in London.

Lord Halifax said that the Foreign Office would not like the suggestion that the talks should be held in Washington. Mr. Stettinius said that the memorandum had been drawn up by Mr. Wallace Murray who did not much want to come to London. Later Mr. Stettinius said that the President was in favour of discussions but wished to talk over the matter with Mr. Hull before giving a definite reply.

(e)   On December 1 Lord Halifax telegraphed that Mr. Stettinius had told him on November 26 that the reply of the State Department to our invitation to discuss Middle East affairs was that it would be better to await the meeting between the President and the Prime Minister. Lord Halifax also said that the Foreign Office had taken note of Mr. Stettinius's suggestion about the importance of an early discussion on oil. The British Government would be very ready to include oil in the general discussion, but the oil question covered a larger area than the Middle East. Mr. Stettinius said that the President had said that he did not want the oil question taken up until he had been able to talk about it with the Prime Minister.[2]

(f)   Lord Halifax was instructed on December 15 that we could not agree to hold the discussions on the Middle East in Washington. A number of different Departments would be concerned with the

---

[1] The reason for this long interval was that Lord Halifax was waiting first, until the appointment of a successor to Mr. Welles, and then until the conclusion of the Moscow Conference.

(g)   [2] On December 23 the Foreign Office were informed that the Prime Minister had had no discussions with the President on oil policy during their meetings.

(a) WP(43)312; WM(43)101; E4265/2551/65. (b) E4462/2551/65. (c) E6647/2551/65. (d) E7735/2551/65. (e) E7526/2551/65. (f) E7735/2551/65. (g) E7526/2551/65.

questions discussed and, as the recent Lebanese crisis had shown, our interest in the Middle East was greater and more immediate than the American interest.[1] The State Department, however, replied on January 7, 1944. They repeated their wish to hold the conversations (a) in Washington. They argued that no one on the staff of the United States Embassy in London had served in the Middle East and that it would be difficult to spare any of the limited number of officials in the State Department who were familiar with the subjects to be discussed.

The Foreign Office considered early in February a reply explain- (b) ing that their idea was not to hold formal conversations and that they did not expect to conclude specific agreements. They had in mind merely an exchange of views aiming at a certain co-ordination of policy. If the conversations showed a general agreement, so much the better; if they showed differences of opinion, it would do no harm to see whether they could be eliminated by friendly discussion before they led to any serious divergencies. There was no need to discuss complex technical matters; we had already agreed to separate oil discussions.[2] We had no intention of 'springing any surprises' on Mr. Wallace Murray.

This reply was not sent, since the proposals for Middle East conversations were necessarily held up during the somewhat controversial exchange over the oil talks. The Foreign Office also thought it better to wait to raise the question with Mr. Stettinius on the latter's visit to London.[3]

The State Department finally agreed that Mr. Wallace Murray should come to London with Mr. Stettinius. Six meetings were then (c) held between April 11 and 26, 1944. Sir M. Peterson, Mr. Baxter and Mr. Hankey took part on the British side, and Mr. Wallace Murray brought with him Dr. Isaiah Bowman,[4] Vice-Chairman of the Advisory Council in the State Department on post-war foreign policy. An agreed minute at the end of the conversations stated that there was a general community of aims and outlook between the Foreign Office and the State Department on Middle Eastern questions. British policy was necessarily influenced by commitments for the administration and defence of certain areas; American policy was affected by special economic interests, but these different preoccupations should not lead to any conflict. During discussions on

---

[1] See above, Chapter LIV, sections (iii) and (iv).
[2] See section (vi) of this chapter.
[3] Mr. Stettinius was coming to London for informal conversations of a general kind on post-war questions.
[4] President of Johns Hopkins University. See above, section (ii) for the discussion on Palestine, and below, section (vii), for that on Saudi Arabia.

(a) E488/16/65. (b) E417/16/65. (c) E2736/16/65.

the best method of dealing with complaints made on either side about Middle Eastern policy Mr. Wallace Murray said that he was seriously concerned at the political consequences of these complaints. In the United States, for example, political bodies or pressure groups with an axe to grind might use a few minor questions for creating dangerous currents of opinion which might affect issues on a higher level than those to which the complaints originally referred. Mr. Murray did not think that the use of the term 'anti-British' in relation to American policy was justified. It was agreed that arrangements should be made for dealing, if possible, locally with mutual complaints or criticisms, and that the British and United States Diplomatic and other Missions in the Middle East should be informed accordingly.

(vi)

American requests for conversations at a ministerial level on oil questions with special reference to the Middle East: British objections to the American proposals: experts' conference on oil, April–May 1944: Lord Beaverbrook's mission to the United States: American withdrawal from proposed oil agreement (July 1943–January 1945).[1]

As the exchanges of view with the United States Government on the Palestine question had overlapped and broadened into a more general discussion on Anglo-American co-operation in the Middle East, so these discussions in turn were affected by American proposals for a general consideration of oil resources in the Middle East. In 1933 the Standard Oil Company of California[2] had obtained a large exploratory concession in Saudi Arabia. Five years later they began the exploitation of oil in the Dhahran Peninsula. In 1939 they built a pipeline from the oilfield in this area to the Persian Gulf and by 1944 their production of oil was on a large scale. These facts alone—together with the past history of rivalry between British and American oil interests in the Middle East—would have led at least to local friction, and to efforts to extend American influence, but the question of oil was given wide publicity in the United States owing to reports of the rapid depletion of American oil reserves. For this reason the Administration decided in July 1943 to set up a Petroleum Reserves Corporation to secure the future of American

---

[1] I have dealt with these complicated and technical discussions only from the Foreign Office point of view, i.e. in relation to their repercussions on Anglo-American political relations. A full account of them would require the use of the archives of the Ministry of Supply.

[2] The company was renamed in 1936 the California-Arabian Standard Oil Company and in 1944 the Arabian-American Oil Company (Aramco). In 1936 the Texas Oil Company had acquired a 50 per cent interest in the operation of the company.

concessions by developing and operating oilfields in other parts of the world, especially in the Middle East. The Directors of this Corporation were: Mr. Cordell Hull, Secretary of State, Mr. Stimson, Secretary for War, Colonel Knox, Secretary for the Navy, Mr. Leo I. Crowley, Director of the Office of Economic Warfare, and Mr. Harold Ickes as Chairman. This Corporation almost at once brought forward a plan to acquire the total stock of the Californian-Arabian Standard Oil Company (including the share of the Texas Oil Company). The Company, however, refused this offer, and was equally unwilling to accept other offers which would have given the Corporation only part control of their activities.

The matter now became even more complicated owing to acute (a) differences of opinion between Mr. Hull and Mr. Ickes, the Petroleum Administrator for War and the founder and president of the Petroleum Reserves Corporation.[1] Mr. Hull wanted a discussion with Great Britain, under his own leadership, with a view to an Anglo-American agreement over oil reserves. The British representative in the United States of the Petroleum Division of the (b) Ministry of Supply regarded the Petroleum Reserves Corporation, and Mr. Ickes's activities, as likely to result in a very dangerous form of competition with British interests; he therefore recommended that the British Government should take the initiative in suggesting an exchange of views with the United States. The Foreign Office and the Ministry of Supply supported this recommendation, but while they were considering the best way of approaching the United States Government, the State Department, on December 2, 1943, (c) sent to Lord Halifax an invitation to the British Government to hold such an exchange. The State Department referred only to the oil resources of the Middle East, and suggested 'informal and preliminary discussions . . . for the purpose of formulating appropriate recommendations to the two Governments'. They regarded the matter as urgent, and asked for a reply 'at the earliest possible moment'.

The Foreign Office view was that this invitation was given in order to provide a 'safety valve' for domestic criticism; opposition to the Petroleum Reserves Corporation was gaining ground in the

---

[1] The 'acute differences of opinion' referred to are not reflected in either of the documents W2486 or 2920, but in another document in the same file, W2863/34/76, a telegram from Lord Halifax dated February 21, 1944, which states: 'Stettinius told me in fact what happened here over oil. Ickes went one day to the President who said, "I like your thought, Harold, why should you not preside over our Group?" When Hull heard this he went straight to the President, and said State Department must be in charge of all foreign negotiations. The President said, "Well, so we will make you chairman and Harold can preside when you are not there".'

(a) WP(44)119; W2486, 2920/34/76 (1944). (b) A9194, 9286/3410/45; A10103, 10104/3410/45 (1943). (c) E7686/3710/65.

United States, and from the British point of view there was less need for Anglo-American conversations. There was also no special reason on our side for haste. The State Department had often kept us waiting over similar requests and, in view of the preoccupation of Ministers with the problems of the cross-Channel invasion, the time was unsuitable for raising very large questions of post-war policy which might well lead to public controversy between the two countries. On the other hand, the Foreign Office realised that American public opinion was excited over the question of oil reserves and that too long delay would be politically dangerous. In any case it soon became clear that the Americans would not accept procrastination or an evasive answer to their invitation; there were also signs of a revival of the activities of the Petroleum Reserves Corporation. These activities included a project for the construction of a pipeline from Saudi Arabia to the eastern Mediterranean. Mr. Ickes later described the announcement of this project as in the nature of a 'blunderbuss shot' intended to accelerate the opening of international discussion.

(a)   On January 11, 1944, Mr. Stettinius sent a reminder to the Foreign Office and asked for an early reply. The British Embassy in Washington and the representative of the Ministry of Supply sent warning that there were serious risks of misunderstanding, and of

(b) damage to British interests, if the reply were not sent, but the Petroleum Division of the Ministry of Fuel and Power took a long time to give their considered views. Hence the Foreign Office were unable to send the British reply until February 2. They had already made it clear that they wanted the discussions to be world-wide in scope and not limited to a particular area. They now instructed

(c) Lord Halifax that they would prefer the talks to be held in London, since the President wanted them to begin with Middle Eastern oil, and we should therefore have to provide the necessary information. For this reason we wished to know what the Americans proposed to discuss. We should also refuse to commit ourselves to sending a Ministerial mission to Washington during the coming critical weeks. The actual note of reply did not mention London, but suggested that the discussions should begin with the Middle East and should be extended to cover the subject of oil in its general aspect. The note also invited the United States Government to suggest 'the precise level at which . . . the discussions should be held'.

(d)   These instructions crossed another message from Lord Halifax asking for a reply to the invitation of December 2. On February 10

(e) the State Department sent a note to the British Embassy with a

---

(a) W746/34/76. (b) W746/34/76. (c) W872/34/76. (d) W2196/34/76. (e) W2198/34/76.

'tentative' list of questions—including concession rights—for discussion. The note explained that five 'staff members', headed by the Petroleum Adviser of the State Department, would conduct the conversations on behalf of the United States Government. The United States Government thought that it might be desirable to extend the scope of the conversations beyond the Middle Eastern area, but did not commit themselves on the matter.

Lord Halifax thought that we should be unable to get the talks in London, partly owing to interdepartmental rivalries in the United States, and partly because Congress and American public opinion would be suspicious of the choice of any place except Washington. On February 11—that is to say, the day before the American reply reached London—the *New York Times* published a report that the British Government were sending a delegation to Washington to discuss the details of a programme for developing the oil resources of the Middle East and that a Russian mission was also expected. Mr. Stettinius proposed to issue a 'corrective' statement which would have committed the British Government to a conference on Middle Eastern oil with all the producing and consuming interests concerned 'in accordance with the principles enumerated in the Atlantic Charter'.

The Foreign Office informed the State Department that they (a) could not agree to more than a statement that the two Governments were 'undertaking preliminary and exploratory discussions on petroleum questions. These conversations will embrace first of all Middle Eastern questions. Should these preliminary discussions lead to conclusions, no decision affecting producing areas would be taken without consultation with the Governments of the countries concerned'.

The State Department replied that they would give the matter further consideration. On the night of February 15–16, however, (b) Lord Halifax telegraphed that the State Department had changed their ideas about the composition of the American delegation. They now proposed that the delegation should consist of Mr. Hull, Mr. Ickes, Mr. Patterson (Under-Secretary of War), Mr. Forrestal (Under-Secretary of the Navy), the Petroleum Adviser of the State Department and the Vice-Chairman of the War Production Board. Mr. Stettinius had told Lord Halifax that Mr. Hull and, in his absence, Mr. Ickes would preside at the meetings. Mr. Stettinius hoped that the discussions would take place in about a fortnight. He wanted to announce the composition of the American delegation on February 16.

Lord Halifax said that he had pointed out 'with bluntness' to the State Department that an announcement of names would prejudge

---

(a) W2293/34/76. (b) W2433/34/76.

the level of the conversations; that Mr. Stettinius himself had said that the latter need not be held on a Ministerial level, and that the British Government had said that they could not at this time commit themselves to the despatch of a Ministerial mission from England. The announcement would also prejudge the question of venue, since Mr. Hull and Mr. Ickes would obviously not come to London. Lord Halifax's comment was that 'these fits and starts on the American side are infuriating. Apart from being the inevitable consequence of no trained civil service and no cabinet unity, they are due in this case to a prolonged tussle between the State Department and Ickes and their manoeuvring for intervention by the White House'. On the other hand, Lord Halifax thought that 'all concerned', including the President, wanted the talks as soon as possible and that, from our point of view, their attitude was as favourable as we could expect.

The Foreign Office telegraphed on the afternoon of February 16 that the latest American proposals entirely altered the position; we could not agree to an announcement until we had reconsidered the whole matter in its new form. On the following day the Foreign Office sent to Lord Halifax a draft reply which had not been submitted to the Secretary of State but had been drawn up with the approval of other Ministers concerned. The telegram explained that Ministers were objecting strongly to the American procedure of 'asking us to agree to far-reaching proposals at the shortest notice and then introducing sudden and fundamental changes'.

The draft Foreign Office reply suggested that a conference at a Ministerial level should not take place until after the holding of preliminary discussions. These preliminary discussions should be held in London, especially in view of the intention to concentrate on Middle Eastern questions. The British Government were preparing comments on the agenda proposed by the State Department, but meanwhile they would 'welcome an assurance that the discussions will not be concerned with existing rights over oil property or products . . . but will be directed to promoting the fullest and most economical development by each country of its resources in foreign fields in the interests of the war effort and to the revival and expansion of international trade as soon as the war is over'. Lord Halifax was instructed that, in view of reports of the recommendations of the Truman Committee,[1] this assurance was essential to our consent to hold any discussions.

---

[1] This Committee, which was investigating the American defence programme under the chairmanship of Mr. Truman, issued a report on February 16. According to the British press, they proposed that the allies of the United States—and especially Great Britain—should be asked to transfer to the United States reserves of oil to compensate for the 'excessive depletion' of American reserves owing to war demands.

Lord Halifax replied on the night of February 17–18 that the (a) proposed reply would only make matters worse, and that there was no chance of getting the Americans to agree to hold the discussions in London. He regarded the American action as due to the 'civil war' between the American departments concerned and not to a deliberate or latent wish to make difficulties for us. In view of Lord Halifax's opinion the Foreign Office decided not to include in their note a demand for an assurance with regard to existing oil rights, but they instructed Lord Halifax to get this assurance, if possible in writing, and to make it clear that in any case our representatives would be debarred from discussing such rights. We could not at the present time arrange for talks at a Ministerial level, and must leave open the question whether the talks should be held in London or Washington.

On February 18–19 Lord Halifax sent three telegrams reporting (b) his interviews on February 18. The first reported a meeting in the morning with Mr. Stettinius and Mr. Rayner, who referred to the note of February 10 to the British Embassy and to the recommendations of the Truman Committee. Mr. Stettinius telephoned in Lord Halifax's presence to Mr. Ickes, who asked that Mr. Eden should be informed that he had not seen the report of the Truman Committee before publication. In his second telegram Lord Halifax (c) reported that Mr. Stettinius had telephoned him to say that the President had refused to agree to the British proposals about the conversations on oil. The President thought that we should reserve existing rights, but otherwise approach the whole question as complete partners. He wanted the discussion to be held in Washington as soon as possible. He attached great importance to the early publication of the names of the six American representatives, and insisted that some announcement should be made on February 19. Later, in the afternoon, Lord Halifax had spoken with Mr. Stettinius and four other members of the State Department. Mr. Stettinius again explained that in their note of February 10 they intended the phrase 'concession rights' to apply to future concessions. They did not want to 'jockey' us or to seek advantages at our expense. He said that he had fought and won a hard ten days' battle to secure control of the talks for the State Department, and that it was of value for us that Mr. Hull and not Mr. Ickes had been given charge of them. He much regretted the difficulties which the American demands were causing us, but political pressure in the press made it very difficult for the President to act otherwise.

Lord Halifax telegraphed that he had argued with Mr. Stettinius for nearly two hours. He told him that the Americans 'were treating

---

(a) W2625/34/76. (b) W2626/34/76. (c) W2641/34/76.

us shockingly, and that they were being as cavalier as U.J.', and that his own instructions were 'no less categoric than the President's and that we ought not to behave in this shotgun way to each other'. If the United States Government put out their unilateral statement, the result might be that there would be no talks.

Lord Halifax regarded the position as so very unsatisfactory that he had asked for an interview with the President. He reported the (a) result of this interview in his third telegram. He said that he had told Mr. Roosevelt of the difficulties felt by the British Government with regard to the American proposals. They might have to refuse to hold immediate conversations. In any case the unilateral action by the Americans was not a hopeful sign for Anglo-American co-operation. Mr. Roosevelt said that his single idea was that we should work together in a field of vital importance to both of us. He wanted frank discussion and exchange of information. He was willing to hold up any announcement for a few days, e.g. until about February 22. He expected that the conversations would soon become technical, but he proposed to take the chair at the first meeting, and hoped that we could send a Minister at the head of our delegation.

Lord Halifax thought it desirable to accept the President's proposals. The Foreign Office did not take this view. Mr. Law, with Mr. Eden's agreement, submitted a minute to the Prime Minister explaining the position. Mr. Law said that there was no doubt that the Americans had 'behaved very badly' in the matter. The President probably wanted some spectacular gesture to demonstrate that he was not in our pocket and to impress his own business community with his ability to defend American interests. The essential difference between our own and the American proposals was that under our plan the talks would be conducted by officials and technicians, with the minimum of publicity and political pressure, and neither Government would be committed by them. On the American plan, with a conference opened by the President and with Mr. Hull in charge of the proceedings, there would be a maximum of publicity and, possibly, of political pressure. We could not therefore be sure of avoiding any commitments. Mr. Law told the Prime Minister that, in Mr. Eden's view, it would be most dangerous to enter a conference of this kind without full preparation. The pressure which was driving the President to insist on his proposals would be intensified during the conference and the conference would raise expectations in the United States which could be satisfied only at our expense. There would be great anxiety in Parliament and the press, and this anxiety would be expressed in ways damaging to Anglo-American

---

(a) W2642/34/76.

relations. Mr. Eden therefore hoped that the Prime Minister would take up the matter directly with the President.

The Prime Minister telegraphed to the President on February 20. (a) He said that the oil question could surely be considered with patience

'between us before it is flung into public discussion on both sides of the Atlantic. A wrangle about oil would be a poor prelude for the tremendous joint enterprise and sacrifice to which we have bound ourselves. . . . There is apprehension in some quarters here that the United States has a desire to deprive us of our oil assets in the Middle East on which, among other things, the whole supply of our Navy depends. This sensitiveness has, of course, been greatly aggravated by the five Senators.'[1]

After stating the objections put to him by the Foreign Office the Prime Minister concluded:

'International conferences at the highest level should surely be carefully prepared beforehand, and I would beg you to consider whether it would not be more advisable to proceed as a first step for official and technical talks on the lines which had, I understand, already been agreed between the State Department and ourselves.'

President Roosevelt replied on February 22 rejecting the Prime (b) Minister's proposal. He answered the Prime Minister's reference to British anxiety about American intentions by saying that he was

'disturbed about the rumour that the British wish to horn in on Saudi Arabian oil reserves. Problems and questions which give rise to rumours and apprehensions of this sort also clearly indicate the strong need for arriving at a basic understanding between the two Governments regarding Middle Eastern oil, which understanding should lead to oil agreements of a broader scope.'

The President agreed that 'the actual working technical discussions should be at the expert staff level', but, 'in view of the great long-range importance of oil to the post-war international security and

---

[1] The reference is to five Senators (including two members of Mr. Truman's committee) (c) who went on a world inspection of American forces, installations, etc., in the summer of 1943. Their report—and a number of their comments—were printed in the Congressional Record. Some of their conclusions were directly or indirectly extremely critical of British action. The British view was that this criticism was ignorant and ill-founded. The Prime Minister telegraphed to Mr. Hopkins on October 10 that he proposed to make a statement correcting some of the errors of fact. Mr. Hopkins telegraphed back that he thought it would be unwise for the Prime Minister to mention the Senators by name. Other 'unfriendly or misinformed people' in the United States were making similar statements. Mr. Hopkins thought that the Prime Minister's proposed statement was 'very good'. The Prime Minister did not issue his statement, but said in reply to a parliamentary question on October 19 that he was having a full statement of the facts drawn up for record and, if necessary, for publication. One of the allegations made by the Senators was that too much American oil (and too little from other sources) was being used. See Parl. Deb. 5th Ser. H. of C., Vol. 392, cols. 1211–12.

(a) T348/4, No. 583 (Churchill Papers/322; W2642/34/76). (b) T378/4, unnumbered (Churchill Papers/322; W2968/34/76). (c) A9175, 9345, 9408, 9946, 9959, 9961, 10443, 10641, 11191/6274/45; A9653/6274/45.

economic arrangements', he was 'firmly convinced that these technical discussions should take place under the guidance of a group at Cabinet level'. He could not therefore change his position. He wished to preside at the first meeting of the joint group to be held in the Cabinet Room of the White House. He wanted all the discussions to be in Washington, and to set no limitations on the problems to be discussed. He assured the Prime Minister that the United States Government had in mind a 'mutually satisfactory agreement' which would strengthen Anglo-American collaboration.

(a)   With the approval of the War Cabinet the Prime Minister replied
(b) on February 24 that the War Cabinet had expressed the view that the enquiry should be on an official level in the first instance in order to ascertain the facts; they would prefer it to take place in London, and wished to state in Parliament that no proposal would be made to change the existing ownership of oil interests in the Middle East (on which the British Navy depended) or elsewhere. 'Your telegram dismisses all these points and, if you will allow me to say so, seemed to convey your decision on these matters.'

The Prime Minister said that the War Cabinet were 'very much disturbed' at the possibility of a wide difference opening between the two Governments 'on such a subject and at such a time'. He intended to bring the matter before the War Cabinet again in a few days, and hoped meanwhile that the President would make no public announcement. If the matter became public otherwise than by agreement, debates would take place in Parliament 'at which all kinds of things would be said which would darken counsel and be resented on your side of the ocean'.

(c)   On February 8 Lord Beaverbrook had sent a minute to the Prime Minister suggesting that the American request should be 'put in a pigeon hole'. Lord Beaverbrook thought that pressure would be put on us to agree to divide our oil resources with the United States. The Prime Minister asked that Lord Beaverbrook's minute should be circulated to the War Cabinet.

The Foreign Office thought that Lord Beaverbrook's suggestion
(d) was wrong. Mr. Eden therefore circulated a paper to the War Cabinet stating the Foreign Office view in reply to Lord Beaverbrook's paper. This Foreign Office paper was not finally settled until February 19, and therefore took account of the sudden change in the views of the State Department. Mr. Eden pointed out that the President himself, in his latest report on Lend-Lease, had dealt effectively with the uninformed criticism of British policy in regard to oil which disturbed Lord Beaverbrook. The Americans would

---

(a) WM(44)25.   (b) T388/4, No. 591 (Churchill Papers/322; W2968/34/76).
(c) W2486/34/76. (d) WP(44)119; W2920/34/76.

have no justification in asking us to cede oil resources to them, and Article 7 of the Mutual Aid agreement protected us from being asked to do so in return for Lend-Lease, since the consequent reduction in our earning power would 'burden our commerce' and postpone the possibility of unrestricted economic expansion. We should, however, keep in mind that we had received and were receiving far more oil from the United States than we were able to supply. We were greatly dependent on the United States for the release of equipment for production, refining and distribution, including pipelines and tanker tonnage. Without this equipment the development of our oil resources in the Middle East would soon be brought to a standstill. Hence a refusal to allow the United States Government an opportunity even to discuss oil problems would almost certainly prejudice the development of our oil industry after the war. Such a refusal would play into the hands of all the enemies of Anglo-American co-operation, including the members of a senatorial committee now investigating the activities of the Petroleum Reserves Corporation. We should also alienate many of our proved friends, including Mr. Ickes and Mr. Davies, of the War Petroleum Administration.

The President replied on March 3 to the Prime Minister's message (a) of February 24. He asked the Prime Minister to accept his assurances that the United States Government were 'not making sheeps' eyes at your oilfields in Iraq or Iran'. At the same time the President said that he could not 'hold off the conversations much longer'. Mr. Eden asked Mr. Law to prepare a draft reply for the Prime Minister. In submitting a draft Mr. Law said that Mr. Eden was extremely disquieted about the position, and that the most serious aspect of it was that Mr. Stettinius was being embarrassed by our delay in sending an answer. Mr. Law's own view, which he had also expressed to Mr. Eden, was that talks about oil were not as dangerous for us as some members of the Cabinet feared. Mr. Ickes would like to extort concessions from us, but Mr. Hull was bitterly opposed to him, and likely to have his way on an issue of this kind. Mr. Law thought that there was no reason for us to 'give anything away'. If we could not get from the President the assurances which we wanted in regard to existing concessions, the Prime Minister might say definitely in the House of Commons that no question of the cession of rights or properties would arise in connexion with the talks.

After consideration of the question in the War Cabinet the Prime (b) Minister replied on March 7[1] that the War Cabinet welcomed the (c)

---

[1] Mr. Churchill sent an *interim* reply on March 4 that we also had no intention of 'trying to horn in' on American property or interests in Saudi Arabia.

(a) T444/4, No. 485 (Churchill Papers/322; W3697/34/76).   (b) WM(44)28.3, C.A. (c) T472/4, unnumbered (Churchill Papers/322; W3697/34/76).

President's assurance that there was 'no desire on the part of the United States Government to propose the transfer of our property and interests in Iraq and Iran which we presume includes our properties elsewhere'. Hence we no longer objected to the talks being held in Washington and not in London, and would send a delegation to the United States. We still felt, however, that the delegation should be 'official and expert, and once the ground is clear and facts established, that higher authorities should then intervene'. Since the fact of our sending a delegation would be known, the Prime Minister suggested the issue of a communiqué in the following terms:

> 'The Governments of the United States and the United Kingdom are undertaking preliminary and exploratory discussions on petroleum questions. These discussions will be, in the first instance, at the official and expert level, and will take place in Washington.'

The Prime Minister concluded by saying that, since he was likely to be questioned in Parliament on the subject, he must reserve the right to make it clear that no question would arise of any transfer of existing rights or properties in oil.

The President accepted the Prime Minister's proposal. The expert talks therefore took place in Washington from April 18 to May 3. (a) The British delegation were instructed to 'explore possible bases of an Anglo-American agreement on oil policy for consideration by Ministers'. They were not to make any commitments, and to refuse to consider proposals involving existing rights or properties in oil or the transfer of oil products without payment. They were to try to reach agreement with the United States delegation on the facts of the world oil situation, and not merely on the Middle Eastern situation, and to point out that there was no 'present or immediately prospective shortage of oil in the Middle East or in the world generally'. On this basis the delegation was to explore possible machinery for the orderly development of oil resources,

> 'always provided that no machinery can be considered which would prevent the development of British-controlled resources to the fullest extent necessary to maintain first the communications and the military security of the British Empire, and secondly the maintenance not only of the industrial capacity of the United Kingdom but also the general commercial position of the United Kingdom and the foreign exchange thereby obtained.'[1]

---

[1] I have not dealt in detail with the discussions in Washington. The instructions to the British delegation were drawn up by a ministerial committee appointed by the Prime Minister on March 28, and were approved by the War Cabinet on April 5. The instructions had the approval of the Chiefs of Staff who thought that, on balance, an American interest and strategic commitment in the Middle Eastern oilfields was to our advantage. The British delegation, under the chairmanship of Sir William Brown, consisted of
(*continued on page 399*)

(a) WP(44)179; W5619/34/76.

On their return to London the British delegation reported to the Ministerial Oil Committee, and the latter in turn submitted a memo- (a) randum to the War Cabinet on May 24, 1944. The delegation had found the discussions in Washington both frank and friendly, and considered it desirable to go on to the next stage, i.e. the Ministerial discussions, before there was any 'change of atmosphere'.[1] The United States delegation had brought forward at an early stage in the discussions a 'draft memorandum of understanding' in the form of draft agreement between the two Governments. This memorandum removed one of the causes of public disquiet in the United States by accepting the view that the world resources of oil were adequate 'for the foreseeable future'. The first article declared the intention of the two Governments (i) to ensure an adequate supply of oil, on an equitable and non-discriminatory basis, to all 'peace-loving countries'; (ii) to apply the principle of equal opportunity to the 'acquisition of exploration and development rights in areas not now under concession' and (iii) to 'respect all valid concession contracts and lawfully acquired rights'. Article 2 proposed a multilateral conference of Governments of all oil producing and consuming countries. Article 3 set up a joint Anglo-American Petroleum Commission to prepare estimates of world supply and demand and to make recommendations both on general questions of oil policy and on short-term problems of common interest.

The Foreign Office also pointed out once again the difficulties which a non-Moslem adviser was likely to meet in Saudi Arabia both in obtaining information and getting his advice accepted. Hence, in view of American and British wishes for an improvement in Saudi finance it 'still seems to us more practical to give Ibn Saud the sort of adviser he wants'.

The Ministerial Oil Committee recommended that the draft agreement, with certain changes in the text, should be taken as the basis of further discussion. They suggested that, since it was difficult for British Ministers to go to Washington at the present time, or for United States Ministers to come to London, Lord Halifax should be instructed to continue the discussions in Washington with the assistance of experts sent out for the purpose and to conclude an agreement on the general lines of a revised British draft. The committee thought that we should try (i) to find a form of words acceptable

---

(continued)
representatives of the Treasury, Foreign Office, Admiralty (representing, by agreement, the three Service departments) and the Petroleum Division, and two leading oil experts, Sir William Fraser and Sir Frederick Godber.

[1] The delegation had in mind that the question might again become an electoral issue in American politics.

(a) WP(44)269; W8641/34/76.

OBFP

to the United States Government which would reserve our full rights to make any provision we thought fit in the interest of national security, and (ii) to persuade the United States Government to agree to a joint declaration of support by each Government of concessions held by the other's nationals. Even if our efforts in these two respects were unsuccessful, we should conclude the agreement. The War
(a) Cabinet appointed another Committee on May 31 to consider the draft 'memorandum of understanding' and to make suggestions with regard to the next stage of the discussions.

(b)   On the night of June 2–3 Lord Halifax telegraphed that there was serious danger in further delay. Mr. Ickes had said to Lord Halifax on May 5 that he was most anxious to conclude an agreement, and that he was afraid of political trouble unless we could settle the matter quickly. The Foreign Office agreed on the need for
(c) a rapid settlement, but the Prime Minister sent a minute on June 5 to Mr. Eden that he inclined to reply to Lord Halifax:

> 'Pray do not let yourself be overfretted by the activities of Ministers or prominent personalities who are anxious to shove themselves into prominence. There are great advantages in using the powers of delay. In principle, I am not in favour of concluding any negotiations before the Presidential Election is decided. There may be exceptions to this; but they have to be proved nevertheless.'

The Foreign Office thought that a message of this kind would be most unfortunate. The point of the tentative agreement on oil reached in Washington was not that Mr. Ickes should secure a personal success, but that the Administration should be able to show that they could co-operate advantageously and practically with us, and to forestall the misuse by their political opponents of the most formidable pressure capacities of the immense American oil industry. The principal though by no means the sole advantage of the agreement to ourselves as well as to the Administration in Washington was that by the establishment of a merely advisory body it would prevent us being rushed into unwise action. It would be wholly imprudent of us to use the 'instrument of delay' in dealing with friends like Mr. Stettinius. The President and his Administration believed that they were in agreement with us on all larger questions of post-war policy, and that they had not let us down for electoral reasons on any important point. They would be deeply resentful if they saw that we were deliberately delaying until after the Presidential election in November the negotiation of an agreement to which they attached the greatest importance.

Mr. Law regarded this latter consideration as decisive. He also

---

(a) WP(44)313; WM(44)70; W8818, 8969/34/76.   (b) W9348/34/76.   (c) M684/4, W9348/34/76.

pointed out that the Americans had already given way on the two matters upon which we had held out—a preliminary conference at official level, and an assurance that we should not be asked to give up any of our existing rights. Mr. Eden sent a minute to the Prime Minister on June 8 suggesting that he (the Prime Minister) should not send his proposed telegram to Lord Halifax.[1]

The special committee appointed on May 31 reported to the War Cabinet on June 14. They proposed certain additional changes in (a) the draft agreement, and the withdrawal of the suggestion for a mutual guarantee, since this proposal might alarm other nations and was incompatible with the multilateral arrangements towards which the agreement was a first stage.

After further delay, and another appeal from Mr. Hull and Mr. Ickes for haste, a Ministerial delegation headed by Lord Beaverbrook arrived in Washington to conclude the agreement. These talks lasted until August 8, when the text was finally signed. The War (b) Cabinet sent a telegram of congratulation to Lord Beaverbrook on the result of his negotiations. The British Embassy in Washington was not so well pleased with the result. In his despatch of August 24[2] (c) Sir R. I. Campbell pointed out that the American Administration had confidently expected such an agreement to be signed ever since the end of April, not in favour of the unpopular oil industrialists but as a matter of policy and as the first of a series of agreements by which the President was hoping to prove the possibility and utility of international agreements. Lord Beaverbrook had succeeded in resisting the inclusion of terms which seemed too hampering to the British, but at the cost of delay and the irritation of those who were most friendly to this country. Furthermore, Mr. Ickes was not regarded as a friend of the oil industry, and in any case during an election year the Administration could not risk the charge of deferring to big business, and especially the unpopular oil business.[3]

The negotiations, when at last they were begun, ran into unexpected difficulties, partly owing to the American irritation over the long and unexplained delay, partly because of the sudden emphasis of the British delegation on the need to safeguard the British exchange position, though the Americans thought that sufficient safeguards were already provided. A deadlock arose on

---

[1] As in other matters, it should be remembered that the Prime Minister was at this time anxious and fully occupied over the cross-Channel invasion. There is no direct evidence in the Foreign Office papers on the reasons why the Prime Minister had suggested his draft telegram to Lord Halifax, but indirect evidence seems to suggest that Lord Beaverbrook, as earlier, was in favour of delaying the oil negotiations.

[2] This despatch was formally addressed by Sir R. I. Campbell to Lord Halifax and transmitted by him to the Foreign Office.

[3] The Foreign Office agreed with Sir R. I. Campbell's view.

(a) WP(44)313; W9880/34/76. (b) W11910/34/76; W12368/34/76. (c) W12956/34/76.

this point—which could have been avoided by earlier explanation—
and was removed only by the informal intervention of the Embassy
which was taking no official part in the negotiations.

In fact the whole negotiation came to nothing. The American oil
interests regarded the agreement as an unnecessary interference by
the Administration in matters where industry wanted to receive
official support of a general political kind but did not want official
control. The oil interests used their influence against the acceptance
of the agreement, with the result that in January 1945, after strong
criticism in the Senate, the President withdrew the proposals. He
suggested a revision of the terms in consultation with the British
Government, but at the end of the war the Administration was still
engaged in discussions with the oil companies.

(vii)

*British and American policy towards Saudi Arabia: insistence of the State
Department upon the preponderance of American financial and economic
interests: the question of the subsidy to King Ibn Saud.*

Throughout the Anglo-American discussions on oil the Foreign
Office had been, on the technical side, no more than a channel of
communication; their intervention to hasten the Cabinet and depart-
mental decisions in London was due to their realisation of the
political importance of meeting American wishes, as far as possible,
in a matter which was arousing in the United States wide popular
feeling and a good deal of distrust of British motives. The Foreign
Office wanted, obviously, to safeguard British and, for that matter,
Western European supplies of oil, and to secure a free field for
British enterprises in competition with those of the United States,
but they were not trying to secure a monopoly at American expense.
As the Chiefs of Staff foresaw, the development of American interests
in Middle Eastern oil was on balance to British advantage since it
provided an additional and extremely powerful counterweight to
Russian designs.

These large considerations of policy on the British side were less
clearly realised in the United States and did not prevent a good deal
of local rivalry and discord in the oil areas primarily concerned, and
especially in Saudi Arabia. Here again the Foreign Office was not
unaware that the development of a great oil industry would change
the whole economy of a tribal kingdom, backward in culture and,
apart from its oil, poor in natural resources, and hitherto drawing
its revenues almost entirely from pilgrims to the Moslem Holy Places
in its dominions. The Foreign Office papers do not show any attempt
to hamper, still less to supplant, American oil interests in Saudi

Arabia. On the other hand the Foreign Office seems to have assumed that this development could take place without the substitution of American for British political influence in Saudi Arabia. The British Government had maintained a close and friendly association with King Ibn Saud. The Association, which had existed long before the emergence of an American interest in the country, was of great value as a stabilising factor in Arab and Moslem opinion generally. British strategic interest in the Middle East as a centre of communications was far wider and more direct than American interest. The British Government had taken very great risks in 1940 in holding their military position in the Middle East generally. They had fought almost the whole of the campaign against the Italians. They considered that they had a claim to take the lead in determining and executing Allied policy in the Middle East, and that their political interests in the area were and would remain greater than those of the United States. They were often exasperated by American methods and by the inexperience of Americans in dealing with Moslem peoples. They were also taken aback by the contrast between the general and ill-informed American criticism of British imperialism, and the official application of a policy which was not easily to be distinguished from imperialism in matters where American business interests were concerned.

At the outbreak of the war the Americans did not even have separate diplomatic representation in Saudi Arabia. Until 1940, when the United States established a separate Legation at Jedda, Saudi-American relations had been dealt with locally by the American (a) Minister to Egypt. The payment of a subsidy to King Ibn Saud was a British affair and had been considered by the British Government in the summer of 1938. It was then thought that if, in the event of war, overseas pilgrimages to Mecca were cut off, King Ibn Saud would be in an extremely difficult financial position, and probably unable to maintain his Government. In February 1939 the British Government took the decision that, if necessary, they would offer a subsidy which might have to be as large as that paid to Sherif Hussein during the war of 1914–18.

Towards the end of 1939 it was clear that King Ibn Saud was in serious financial difficulties, and also that he was expecting British financial help. The matter became urgent when in January 1940 the Italian Minister at Jedda informed the King that Hitler had asked Mussolini to obtain permission for Dr. Grobba[1] to go to Jedda.

---

[1] Former German Minister at Baghdad and also accredited to King Ibn Saud. Dr. Grobba was leaving Baghdad owing to the rupture of relations between Iraq and Germany.

(a) E3406/325/25 (1944).

The King refused to give permission and, before sending his refusal, told the British Minister at Jedda that he might now incur Italian as well as German hostility, and that he looked for British help, including a credit of £250,000 for the purchase of foodstuffs in India. King Ibn Saud regarded a preliminary offer of £100,000 as inadequate to his dignity and his needs. The offer was raised to £200,000, and was increased after the extension of the war to the Middle East, when the continuance of the King's benevolent neutrality was of the greatest importance. The amount provided in 1940 was thus about £400,000.

King Ibn Saud asked for a larger sum in 1941. He also approached the Californian Arabian Oil Company. The latter in turn suggested to President Roosevelt in April 1941 that the United States Government should make an advance of six million dollars annually for five years to King Ibn Saud and receive an equivalent in oil from the company. The President found, however, that he had no legal way of assisting the King, and the increase in the subsidy was made by the British Government. In 1941 the figure was £1,211,375, in 1942 just under £3,000,000 and in 1943 £3,840,855.[1] Towards the end of 1942, however, the Californian Arabian Oil Company was greatly concerned that the increasing influence of the British Government, through the subsidy, over King Ibn Saud would affect the maintenance of American interests in the country after the war. They argued that, since Great Britain was receiving large sums in Lend-Lease from the United States, the British subsidy amounted to an indirect form of Lend-Lease to Saudi-Arabia. The company therefore proposed in February 1943 that the United States should make Lend-Lease payments available directly to Saudi Arabia, and that in return they would make extremely favourable terms with the United States Government in setting aside oil reserves for them and in the sale of oil. On February 18, 1943, President Roosevelt declared Saudi Arabia eligible for Lend-Lease.

The distrust of British intentions, however, remained. On March (a) 1, 1944, Lord Halifax telegraphed that General Hurley[2] had said that he was advising the President not to allow the British to supply arms to Saudi Arabia, since he had heard 'on the best authority' that the Foreign Office had given instructions that American

---

[1] A large proportion of the subsidy was paid in kind. In July 1941 President Roosevelt sent a note to Mr. Jesse Jones, Federal Loan Administrator: 'Will you tell the British I hope they can take care of the King of Saudi Arabia. This is a little too far afield for us.' *F.R.U.S.* 1941, III, p. 643.

[2] General Patrick J. Hurley had been sent by President Roosevelt on a special mission to the Middle East in 1943 and had made wholly unfounded criticisms that British policy in Iran was unfriendly to American interests.

(a) E1496, 1839/63/25.

interests were to be 'squeezed out of Saudi Arabia'. General Mac-ready[1] had told General Hurley that this report was nonsense, but he was unconvinced. Lord Halifax was instructed on March 3 to say to General Hurley from Mr. Eden that the report was completely and utterly unfounded and to ask him not to spread stories of this kind until he had verified them. Lord Halifax also spoke to Mr. Stettinius and Mr. Hull. Mr. Stettinius made no attempt to defend General Hurley, and admitted that he had been doing a good deal of mischief.

A Foreign Office memorandum—drawn up in view of the visit of (a) Mr. Stettinius and Mr. Wallace Murray to London—considered the future of British policy towards Saudi Arabia. The memorandum pointed out that in future the main financial support of the country would be the revenue from the American oil industry. American influence was thus bound to increase, and it was of the first importance that this increase should not lead to rivalry between the Americans and ourselves, but that our respective relations with Saudi Arabia should be conducted in a spirit of co-operation. The Americans were already tending to suspect us of trying to exclude them and to oppose any increase in their influence. We should therefore make it clear to Mr. Wallace Murray that we recognised the growing commercial interest of the United States in the country and did not wish to prevent them from taking a part in Saudi Arabian affairs corresponding to the importance of this interest.

At the same time the United States Government should recognise that we had a strong economic as well as political interest in Saudi Arabia in addition to our general interest in a territory neighbouring on Palestine, Transjordan, Iraq and our vital imperial communications. Apart from the large subsidy which we had been giving King Ibn Saud during the last four years our economic interest consisted in trade with India and with other surrounding countries more or less under our influence, and in the economic features of the pilgrimage. King Ibn Saud's support was important to us politically in connexion with the pilgrimage, and the large Moslem populations with which we had to deal, and also in regard to impending Arab questions, especially that of Palestine. We had therefore to try to make the State Department understand that, while we did not want to 'queer their pitch' in any way in Saudi Arabia, and would welcome their co-operation, and while the development of the oil industry might alter the economic position in the future, Saudi

---

[1] Chief of the British Army Staff in Washington.

(a) E2678/325/25.

Arabia was still more important to us than to the United States.[1]

Since 1940 we had paid King Ibn Saud over £8 million, and had also undertaken to pay the outstanding debt of the Saudi Arabian Government to the United Kingdom Commercial Corporation for essential supplies in 1943, after deducting therefrom a portion of the pilgrimage revenues. A good deal of the subsidy was wasted owing to the lavish expenditure of the royal family and the corruption of officials. On the other hand, the pilgrimage revenues were now increasing again, and we ought to agree with the Americans about cutting down the subsidy. An agreement with the Americans was also necessary because King Ibn Saud was being encouraged in his extravagance by getting supplies of silver from the United States. King Ibn Saud had in fact asked us for an adviser to reorganise the finances of the country; since we were providing most of the financial assistance to him, obviously we and not the Americans should provide the adviser (if a suitable Moslem could be found).

(a)   Before Mr. Wallace Murray came to London, an American military mission arrived in Saudi Arabia without the agreement or even the knowledge of the British Government. Mr. Wallace Murray explained that this mission was intended solely to instruct Saudi Arabians in the use of arms provided under Lend-Lease and that it

(b)   would be withdrawn after it had fulfilled its purpose. Mr. Jordan, British Minister at Jedda,[2] however, telegraphed on April 16 that

---

(c)   [1] The memorandum stated that American methods of dealing with King Ibn Saud were much too pushful, and that the King's resentment of them would cause us much embarrassment, but that we should be unable to make the Americans understand the need for more subtlety in their approach to him. The Foreign Office regarded American attempts to change King Ibn Saud's attitude on the Zionist question as typical of this lack of understanding. In the latter part of July 1943, President Roosevelt had sent Colonel Hoskins on a special mission to present to King Ibn Saud a message (from the President) suggesting that he might receive Dr. Weizmann. The Foreign Office had no doubt that the King would refuse this proposal. He not only refused it but, in a reply of August 20 to Colonel Hoskins, described Dr. Weizmann as his 'enemy', since he had had 'the outrageous impudence' to ask him (Ibn Saud), through 'a certain European'* to abandon his support for the rights of Arabs and Moslems in Palestine in return for a payment of £20,000,000 to be guaranteed by the President. Dr. Weizmann had earlier told the State Department that the Prime Minister had suggested using King Ibn Saud to bring about a Zionist solution of the Palestine problem. The Foreign Office, on enquiring from the Prime Minister, found that he had given Dr. Weizmann no authority to speak in his name.

* This overture was made through Mr. Philby.

(d)   [2] One of the local difficulties in the way of Anglo-American co-operation was that the Americans appeared to believe that Mr. Jordan, whose relations with King Ibn Saud were excellent, was working against American interests. The Foreign Office defended Mr. Jordan against the American charges—some of which were obviously absurd—and, in the British view with better reason, complained of the aggressive and unfriendly attitude of Mr. Moose, the United States Minister. In 1944 both Ministers were withdrawn to other posts, though the Foreign Office continued to have confidence that Mr. Jordan had carried out his instructions to act in close co-operation with the Americans.

(a) E2736/16/65. (b) E2354/325/25. (c) E815, 826, 2342, 4437, 4743, 5242, 5469, 5554/87/31.   (d) E2720, 2811, 3105, 3358, 3398, 3693, 3838, 3976, 4582, 5522, 5524/128/25; E4157/325/25.

the Americans wanted to extend the scope of the instructional mission, and that, doubtless for this reason, King Ibn Saud had asked us to send a military mission composed of Moslem officers in order to neutralise criticism that he was becoming increasingly dependent on foreign Christian Powers. Mr. Jordan thought that, in view of the King's helpful attitude over Arab political affairs, we should do our best to assist him. Mr. Jordan's view was that the Americans were making 'determined but clumsy attempts to gain political and economic predominance' in Saudi Arabia, though he was not sure whether these attempts were 'prompted by Washington or carried to excess by United States military interests in the Middle East'.

Mr. Wallace Murray gave a tactful warning that there would be resentment on the American side if we accepted King Ibn Saud's request for a mission composed of Moslem officers, and that it would be better to secure a joint military mission under a British officer, not a Moslem. After the return of Mr. Stettinius and Mr. Wallace (a) Murray to the United States, the State Department telegraphed on May 1 their agreement to a joint military mission under British leadership, but claimed for themselves the leadership in any 'economic or financial mission', owing to the 'preponderant American economic interests in Saudi Arabia'.

The Foreign Office were now in some difficulty because the (b) Treasury considered that we should insist upon British leadership of an economic mission, while the War Office did not want to give up British leadership of a military mission. The Foreign Office view was that neither mission would be of much use, and that the financial mission in particular would be unpopular with the Saudi Arabians. In any case, the Americans were jealous and resentful of our influence in Saudi Arabia and unlikely to change their attitude. There was also the problem of persuading King Ibn Saud—who had asked us for the missions in order to avoid accepting Americans—to agree to the American proposals.

Sir M. Peterson, who replied for the Foreign Office to the United States Embassy on June 8 accepting the proposals for a joint military mission headed by a British officer, pointed out that King Ibn Saud might be unwilling to receive Christian officers. In this latter event, we should ask the State Department whether they would like us to supply Moslem officers only or to drop the whole plan. On the question of an economic or financial mission we assumed that the American condition did not apply to the King's request for a Sunni Moslem financial adviser to help him in reorganising the country's

---

(a) E2702/325/25.   (b) E3025/325/25.

finances.[1] There was as yet no question of an economic or financial mission. We did not know how far King Ibn Saud would approve of any such plan, but, if and when the question of sending an economic mission arose, we should 'be inclined to agree that the leadership of it should be determined according to which party has the predominant interest in Saudi Arabian economy and finance at the time'.

We had agreed with Mr. Wallace Murray that 'the larger financial and supply problems of Saudi Arabia ought to be dealt with as far as possible on a joint basis in consultation between the two Governments'. We wished to maintain this agreement and hoped that each country would give full support to the experts which either selected for those important places where we had joint interests. We had done everything possible to support Dr. Millspaugh in Iran[2] and to make the Iranians understand that he and his staff had our entire confidence. Similarly we hoped that when the Middle East Supply Centre sent a representative to Jedda (they had appointed an American officer) we could count on the support of both our Legations and that we would work in the joint interest of the two countries.

Sir M. Peterson added that the suggestion of the appointment of a Sunni Moslem to the post of financial adviser and Sunni Moslem officers on the military mission was made by King Ibn Saud himself without any prompting from British sources. King Ibn Saud had to be extremely careful not to expose himself to criticism that, as guardian of the Holy Places of Islam and as leader of one of the strictest Moslem sects, he had come under foreign influence, and had accepted Christians to administer his affairs.

(a) The reply of the State Department was received on July 7. The State Department recognised the Near East as an area of 'primary British military operational responsibility', but claimed that the

'preponderant interest in Saudi Arabian economy is unquestionably American in character and will presumably remain so for many years to come. . . . For this reason the question does not arise as to which party may have a preponderant economic and financial interest in Saudi Arabia at such time as a financial mission might be formed. Saudi Arabia's traditional commercial relations with neighbouring British countries, however, must be taken into consideration. Thus it is sincerely hoped that satisfactory arrangements may be worked

---

[1] A Sunni Moslem was necessary because the Treasury was at Mecca. A member of the United States Embassy told the Foreign Office on May 30 that, in his opinion, the reference in the reply of the State Department to an 'economic mission' did not imply the appointment of a financial adviser.
[2] See p. 417, note 1, and Chapter LVII, *passim*.

(a) E4063/325/25.

out to deal jointly with the larger Saudi Arabian financial and supply problems.'

The State Department proposed that a joint military mission should be headed by 'a British officer of Anglo-Saxon extraction' and that an American financial adviser should be appointed to function either singly or as head of a joint financial mission.[1] The State Department proposed that the British and United States Ministers to Saudi Arabia should advise King Ibn Saud accordingly, but added that, if the British Government felt unable to concur in this proposal, the State Department might instruct their Minister to visit the King.

The Foreign Office replied on July 20 to this somewhat brusque (a) letter that the American view of the economic position was based on false premises since, apart from the fact that the small export trade carried on by Saudi Arabian merchants was largely with British possessions and the sterling area generally, the American calculations took no account of the revenues from pilgrims—a large proportion of whom were British subjects, while even those of other nationalities came largely from the sterling area. The income from oil resources was likely to increase, but so also was the revenue from pilgrims when the Indian and Far Eastern pilgrimages were resumed. In any case the position could be reconsidered if Saudi Arabia in the future ceased to depend mainly on economic relations with sterling area countries. The Foreign Office also pointed out once again the difficulties which a non-Moslem adviser was likely to meet in Saudi Arabia both in obtaining information and getting his advice accepted. Hence they stated that in view of American and British wishes for an improvement in Saudi finance, it 'still seems to us more practical to give Ibn Saud the sort of adviser he wants'.

Here the matter rested for some time. The State Department did not answer the letter of July 20. At the end of October the India (b) Office, which had obtained from the Government of India the name of a suitable Moslem adviser, asked urgently that a decision should be taken. After consulting the Treasury and the War Office, the Foreign Office wrote on November 23 to the United States Embassy that the State Department seemed to have misunderstood our proposal. There was no question of a 'financial mission'. The financial adviser would be in the employment of King Ibn Saud, not of the British Government, and would merely perform, more efficiently, the functions now exercised by members of the King's own administration who were responsible for giving him advice. The appointment would not be the first step towards the establishment of a

---

[1] The State Department thought King Ibn Saud could set off the difficulty of employing a non-Moslem adviser by moving his Treasury from Mecca.

(a) E4201/325/25.   (b) E6628/325/25.

financial mission corresponding to Dr. Millspaugh's Mission in Iran.

We were ourselves in some hesitation about the proposal. We doubted whether in present Saudi-Arabian conditions, even the best and most tactful financial advice would be accepted, or put into practice. A foreign financial adviser would probably incur much unpopularity; this unpopularity would affect the Saudi-Arabian attitude towards foreigners in general. On the other hand, we thought it most desirable that Saudi Arabia should have experienced foreign advice 'during the startling developments which are now taking place during its transition from the purely tribal stage to that of a modern and prosperous oil-bearing State'. King Ibn Saud was dissatisfied with his present financial advisers and had good reason for his dissatisfaction. The King's proposal was very sensible; we were reluctant to refuse it, especially since we had found a suitable man for the post. Finally it was in the interests of the United States and the British Governments, as well as of King Ibn Saud himself, that he should get the best advantage from the subsidy, the pilgrimage (a) revenues and the oil subsidies. The reply of the State Department was sent to the Foreign Office on December 13 from the United States Embassy. The reply stated that the State Department had intended their view to apply to a proposal for a financial adviser who might be employed and paid by King Ibn Saud. The State Department had not changed this view and were therefore 'gratified that the British Government is prepared to agree not to proceed any further with the proposal'.

The Foreign Office did not think that it was worth while having dispute over the matter with the Americans at a time when they were sharing the subsidy, though they felt that the State Department ought not to be allowed to forget that we had 'disobliged Ibn Saud in order to oblige them'.

The arrangements for sharing the subsidy were made, at the suggestion of the State Department, in July 1944. This agreement was unlikely to last. Mr. Hull has stated in his memoirs[1] that the Americans were afraid the British Government might obtain oil concessions in return for their subsidy. In fact the British Government were at this time most anxious to cut down the subsidy, and to tell King Ibn Saud that he must expect a smaller sum in 1945. (b) For this reason, early in 1945 the Foreign Office thought it essential to come to an agreement with the Americans about the joint subsidy for the year. The Foreign Office view was that the 1945 subsidy

---

[1] Hull, *Memoirs*, Vol. II, p. 1515.

(a) E7674/325/25. (b) E1377/60/25.

should be on a reduced scale owing to the resumption of pilgrimages and the increase in King Ibn Saud's oil revenues. The United States Government, however, proposed that the 1944 arrangements should continue throughout the first half of 1945. The Chancellor of the Exchequer regarded this proposal as financially impossible for Great Britain, and suggested that we should aim now at terminating the subsidy altogether after the end of 1945. The Foreign Office thought that for political reasons we should keep ourselves free to continue the subsidy if the Americans were unwilling to stop it. King Ibn Saud was our most influential friend among the Arabs; we needed his support in connexion with the Levant and Palestine and indeed in his own country, where on economic questions the Americans were 'running us hard'. The greater financial strength of the Americans enabled them to continue the running.

CHAPTER LVII

British policy towards Iran from the signature of the Anglo-Russian-Iranian Treaty to the Teheran conference

(i)

Signature of the Treaty of Alliance with Iran: security questions: expulsion of the Japanese Legation: arrest of Axis supporters in Iran: food and currency problems (January 29–November 7, 1942).

THE Anglo-Russian military occupation of Iran in the autumn of 1941[1] had been necessary owing to the obstinate refusal of the Shah to get rid of the German fifth column in the country. The Allies already had enough experience in Europe of German fifth column tactics to realise that they were a serious military danger; there was also ample evidence that Rashid Ali's rebellion in Iraq had been planned in Iran. After their failure the rebel leaders had escaped to Teheran; some had gone on to Turkey, but there was a well-organised body of Germans and pro-German partisans ready to arrange a *coup d'état* in Iran at a favourable moment. After the Anglo-Russian advance to the capital and the removal of the Shah in 1941, most of the Germans in the country who had not managed to escape were rounded up by the British or the Russians, but the Iranian Government and the Majlis still hesitated over making a
(a) treaty with the Allies. Mr. Lyttelton described the Iranian Prime Minister, M. Firoughi, as widely respected, but 'hardly of stern enough stuff to face the times in which he lives'. The Foreign Office
(b) realised M. Firoughi's difficulties. He had to conclude a treaty of alliance with the two Powers who were traditionally feared and suspected by the Iranians, and who had recently invaded the country. The Government, and the public, believed that Russia was assisting a separatist movement in Azerbaijan, if not plotting to annex the province. Berlin radio accused the Prime Minister of treachery and corruption, and at the same time announced that the German armies would soon reach Iran.

The terms of the treaty finally signed on January 29, 1942, were intended to reassure public opinion. Great Britain and Russia

---

[1] See above, Vol. II, Chapter XIX, section (v).

(a) E1438/14/34. (b) E281, 312/23/34.

undertook to respect the territorial integrity, sovereignty and political independence of Iran, and to defend her from aggression. Iran undertook to co-operate with the Allies in order that they might be able to fulfil this undertaking and to give them the unrestricted right to use, maintain, guard and, in case of military necessity, control all communications, to assist in obtaining material and recruiting labour and to establish a censorship. The Allies could maintain land, sea and air forces in Iran, but their presence was not to constitute a military occupation, and would disturb as little as possible Iranian administration and economic life. Allied forces were to be with-drawn not later than six months after the end of the war. The Allies undertook jointly to do their best to 'safeguard the economic existence of the Iranian people' against wartime privations and difficulties.

M. Taqizadeh, Iranian Minister in London, asked Mr. Eden whether he could supplement his announcement in Parliament of the signature of the treaty by giving an additional reassurance to Iran about her territorial integrity and independence. Mr. Eden therefore repeated in the House of Commons on February 4 that the British and Soviet Governments had undertaken to respect the territorial integrity, sovereignty and political independence of Iran, and had no designs or ambitions which would conflict with this undertaking. He pointed out that in a speech to the Moscow Municipal Soviet on November 6, 1941, Stalin had said: 'We do not and cannot have such war aims as the conquest of foreign terri-tory and the enslaving of other nations, and this applies to territories and peoples in Europe and Asia.' Moreover, when the signature of the Atlantic Charter was first announced, Sir R. Bullard had quoted the Charter to the Iranian Prime Minister and the Minister for (a) Foreign Affairs as an additional guarantee for the execution of British and Soviet undertakings to Iran. The Iranian Government secured the insertion of a reference to the Charter in the treaty.

Both sides were disappointed with the carrying out of the treaty.[1] The Iranian Government ignored shipping and economic difficulties (b) in the rest of the world, and tried to interpret the promise of econo-mic aid as binding the Allies to supply large quantities of lorries, motor tyres, spare parts, wheat and other commodities. The Allies for their part met with little co-operation from the Iranians, who made practically no effort to solve the internal difficulties resulting from the war and demanded Allied assistance at every turn. On a number of occasions the Allies could not get even their essential

---

[1] The Foreign Office had commented on January 9 that the Soviet Government (c) probably had no intention of fulfilling the treaty in detail.

(a) E1245/122/34. (b) E2450/239/34 (1943). (c) E158/23/34.

military requirements without the strongest diplomatic pressure, and once or twice a threat of force.

The general attitude of the Iranian public remained for some time pro-German rather than pro-Ally. The Russian offensive which began in December 1941—especially the recovery of Rostov by the Russians—and the entry of the United States into the war, encouraged the supporters of the Allies, but the early Japanese successes were an influence on the other side. The Japanese Legation at Teheran maintained propaganda and intelligence services on such a scale that the Allies found it urgently necessary early in February 1942 to ask the Iranian Government to break off relations with Japan. The Iranian Government were not obliged under the terms of the treaty to take this step; they did everything possible to keep the Legation, which they probably regarded as their last re-insurance link with the Axis. According to the Prime Minister, a secret session of the Majlis was in favour of maintaining relations with Japan. At the suggestion of the British Government the United States Government made the grant of Lend-Lease facilities and the provision of expert advisers dependent on the severance of diplomatic relations with Japan. The Soviet Government agreed to inform the Iranian Government that they had no objection to such a severance. Nevertheless the Iranians held out for two months against continuous British representations. At last, on April 12, they agreed to instruct the Japanese Minister to leave Iran within one week. The Minister and his staff left Teheran on April 23.

(a)

(b)

Another cause of dissatisfaction with the Iranian Government was their failure to take measures to stop Axis propaganda or even to make it illegal. In December 1941 Sir R. Bullard had informed the Foreign Office that it was most important to round up Iranian fifth columnists and pro-Germans. The Foreign Office, however, preferred to try to collaborate with the Iranians rather than to make a number of arrests immediately after the signature of the treaty. They were willing to authorise action against a few Iranians as a deterrent to others, provided that there was evidence against them subsequent to the signature of the treaty and that action was taken with the consent of the Iranian Government. They would not agree to large-scale arrests (other than of German nationals) unless an invasion of Iran was imminent.

(c)

At the end of February 1942 the British Legation prepared a list of seven Axis supporters against whom there was sufficient evidence, and obtained Soviet co-operation in the submission of the list to the Iranian Government with a request that the suspects should be detained under Iranian police supervision in eastern Iran. After

---

(a) E2197/98/34. (b) E2197/98/34; E4078/3655/34. (c) E6157/122/34.

some delay the Iranian Government promised to take action. The
Legation soon learned, however, that three of the men were still at (a)
large. The Foreign Office therefore agreed that Sir R. Bullard should
ask for an audience with the Shah. At this audience on April 22
Sir R. Bullard demanded the immediate delivery of six of the suspects
to the British military authorities. It was apparent that the Shah
had heard of Russian and British troop movements and previous
British warnings, since he said that most of the six had been arrested
that morning. The seventh suspect, Atabai, a brother-in-law of the
Shah, was still to be detained in eastern Iran under police supervision. After considerable hesitation the Iranians handed over five
of the suspects at the end of April to the British military authorities
for internment at Kermanshah under Anglo-Iranian supervision.
The sixth suspect disappeared under the eyes of the police.

As the result of further requests the Iranian police detained some
Germans and a few more Iranians. In mid-June, when there was a (b)
recrudescence of Axis activity, the Legation asked the Prime Minister
to hand over eighteen more suspects. After much procrastination the
Prime Minister agreed on July 22 that within three days he would
produce eleven of the eighteen suspects, but he did nothing and soon
afterwards fell from power. Meanwhile the continued German
advance towards the Caucasus had increased the danger from the
fifth column in Iran, and had also discouraged the Iranians from
taking action in favour of the Allies.[1] The Foreign Office thought
that the collapse of M. Soheily's Government, partly as a result of
his failure to hand over the suspects, made matters considerably
more difficult. In the last resort we could enforce our demands in
Iran, but we had always been careful to avoid disregarding the
wishes of the Government since the collapse of their authority would
greatly increase our responsibilities. When, therefore, M. Soheily
was succeeded by M. Qawam-es-Saltaneh,[2] the Foreign Office
decided to try to establish an agreed procedure which would avoid
haggling for each suspect or group of suspects and constant complaints because men already under arrest had been moved elsewhere,
etc.

The Foreign Office instructed Sir R. Bullard that, provided we (c)

---

[1] The Iranians were not alone in regarding a total Russian collapse on the south-eastern
front as possible. Mr. Churchill did not hold this view but his military advisers—including
General Brooke—thought it not unlikely that the Germans would reach Iran, though
not in any great strength, before the end of 1942. The Iranians could not be unaware
of the inadequacy of the forces available at this time for resisting a German invasion.

[2] A wealthy landowner who had taken part in Iranian politics before the rise to power
of Riza Shah, and had been Prime Minister in the early period of Riza Shah's rule.
M. Soheily had succeeded M. Firoughi in March 1942, on the latter's resignation owing
to lack of support in the Majlis.

(a) E2501/122/34. (b) E2806, 3715, 4434, 4555/122/34. (c) E4611/122/34.

secured control of persons placed under detention, we should make every possible concession to the Iranians. The Legation drew up a new list of forty-five names, including a few named in the list of eighteen, and several Germans, and consisting entirely of persons implicated in evidence given by Germans or Iranians already in

(a) British custody. The Prime Minister obtained the arrest of nearly all the persons on the list; he handed over the Germans, but held out for the detention of the Iranian suspects at Teheran, and appealed to the Foreign Office through the Iranian Minister in London. Meanwhile the press began a violent campaign against the Allies on this question. The Prime Minister's appeal to London failed owing to the proved unreliability of the Iranian police; he then agreed to Sultanabad as a place for detention. The procedure governing the detention and interrogation of all suspects was worked out and agreed to by the Iranian Government and Sir R. Bullard.[1]

Meanwhile economic questions were causing great difficulty in the country and much Anglo-Iranian friction. In Iran, as elsewhere in the Middle East, the food situation became serious in the winter of 1941–42. The Government asked the British and Americans for large supplies of wheat but, in spite of representations from Sir R. Bullard, did little to secure a better distribution of supplies or to prevent hoarding. Although the Government possessed, from Shah

(b) Riza's time, large monopoly powers for the purchase of grain, Sir R. Bullard reported in May 1942 that the inefficiency and corruption of the Iranian officials were the chief obstacles to the efforts of the British authorities. Between September 1941 and May 1942 the Iranians were supplied with nearly 50,000 tons of wheat, 9,000 tons

(c) of flour and 30,000 tons of sugar.[2] Nonetheless the Iranian Government, through their Minister in London, sent notes in May and June expressing their disappointment at the amount of economic assistance given to them, and putting forward a list of minimum requirements. The Foreign Office regarded this list, which included

---

(d)   [1] Sir M. Peterson wrote to Sir R. Bullard on November 3 congratulating him on achieving so large a measure of success with so little support from the Americans or Russians.

   [2] In addition the British authorities gave 4,400 tons of wheat to the Russians for the use of the people in the Russian zone of occupation. They also imported another 20,000 tons of wheat before the end of July 1942. The Russians added greatly to the difficulties of supplying the civilian population owing to their own demands for grain and rice and their unwillingness (notwithstanding M. Maisky's assurances to the contrary) to allow the transport of wheat to Teheran from Azerbaijan and Khorassan. Sir R. Bullard reported to the Foreign Office more than once that British purchases—though they did not include wheat—of vegetables and other local produce tended to raise prices. Thus the military authorities exported potatoes from Iran for the British forces in Iraq without an export licence from the Iranian Government. The purchase of supplies for some 100,000 Polish refugees in Iran (see above, Vol. II, Chapter XXXV, sections (i) and (ii)) also aggravated the problem.

   (a) E4682, 4693, 4782/122/34.   (b) E2875/122/34.   (c) E3523, 3560/122/34. (d) E5158/122/34.

120,000 tons of wheat, as absurdly large in spite of another poor harvest in southern Iran. They pointed out that Iran was normally self-supporting in wheat, and that the Government should deal with hoarding and supervise the collection and distribution of supplies. Sir R. Bullard, however, continued to report that the Government were incompetent to meet these problems.

The question of the supply of wheat was also complicated by difficulties with the Iranian Government and the Majlis over the provision of currency. The British military authorities needed large quantities of rials for developing the supply route to Russia and maintaining their forces in Iran. An Anglo-Iranian Financial Agreement of May 26, 1942, had defined arrangements for the purchase of rial currency with sterling and dollars. By mid-August, however, a further increase in the Iranian note issue was needed to meet the growing demand for currency. In spite of the provisions of the Financial Agreement, the Iranian Government were reluctant to go to the Majlis with a bill to add to the note circulation.

After his appointment as Prime Minister M. Qawam-es-Saltaneh (a) set up an unofficial commission to report on a long-term policy for the note issue, with particular regard to arrangements for its cover.[1] This commission was still studying the question when the currency situation became so acute that immediate action by the Government and Majlis was necessary. The Majlis accordingly passed a bill on September 12, 1942, authorising an increase in the note issue. This measure was in the nature of a stop-gap. Sir R. Bullard thought that the additional issue should suffice for seven or eight weeks at the current rate of British spending. There was, however, hostile criticism during the debate on the bill to the effect that the increase in money supply would raise the already high cost of living. The general tone of the debate as published in the local press ascribed the responsibility for the increased cost of living to the obligation to supply local British currency needs.[2] Sir R. Bullard later protested

---

[1] Early in 1942 Sir R. Bullard had suggested the appointment of American advisers to assist the Iranian Government in financial and revenue matters and the distribution of imported supplies. Mr. Eden agreed with this suggestion and instructed Lord Halifax to let the State Department know his view. After some correspondence—during which the United States Government were unwilling to send a full military mission to Iran—and formal applications for assistance from the Iranian Government, Dr. A. G. Millspaugh went to Teheran in the autumn as financial adviser. Dr. Millspaugh (of whose appointment Sir R. Bullard and the Foreign Office fully approved) was an American citizen who had been an Adviser to the Iranian Government between 1922 and 1927. Mr. J. P. Sheridan, another American citizen, was appointed American Adviser on fuel supplies. He came to Teheran in September 1942.

[2] The cost of living in Teheran, on a rough estimate, almost doubled between June (b) 1941 and June 1942. During the next six months there was a steeper rise, and at the end of 1942 the cost of living figure was already four times that of 1939. The note issue per head of the population, however, was twice as great in Iraq and greater in Turkey.

(a) E6154/3655/34. (b) E1988/69/34.

to the Prime Minister against the publication of anti-Allied speeches made in the Majlis.

The opposition in the Majlis, however, continued, and as a result the Iranian Government in October threatened to withhold supplies of local currency for the Allied forces as from November 2 unless
(a) the Allies gave them some assurance about future supplies of wheat. On October 21 the Foreign Office received from Sir R. Bullard the text of a food agreement which the Iranian Government wanted the British and United States Governments to sign. The Iranian Government would undertake to carry out all measures recommended by Mr. Sheridan, e.g. to prevent hoarding and introduce rationing, as well as the recommendations of the Road Transport Committee.[1] In return, the British and United States Governments would undertake to make good any deficiency of grain until the following harvest. Sir R. Bullard reported that the Iranian Prime Minister had attempted to secure from him an undertaking to recommend acceptance of the food agreement for the period of the war in return for his promise to get the approval of the Majlis to an issue bill for 2,000 million rials.[2] Sir R. Bullard had refused to give an undertaking of this kind; he had pointed out that the Iranian Government already had an obligation under the financial agreement to supply us with unlimited rials, and that M. Qawam was now asking for a long-term guarantee about food while giving only a short-term guarantee about rials. In order to meet an immediate critical situation and to enable the Government to introduce an emergency bill on October 20 providing a fortnight's supply of rials, Sir R. Bullard and Mr. Dreyfus[3] had promised to forward the food agreement, limited in its duration until the next harvest, to their Governments.

(b)   Between October 21 and 27 Sir R. Bullard telegraphed about the gravity and urgency of the situation, and the daily increase in British unpopularity. In view of the opposition of the Majlis, the Government might be forced to resign and, unless we found a solution by about November 3, we should have no money and might have no Iranian Government through whom to work. Sir R. Bullard pointed out that the British Legation were carrying practically the whole burden of negotiation. The crisis was political as well as economic in character, and affected American aid to Russia.[4] The aloofness of

---

[1] This committee of Iranian, British, American and Russian representatives was established in the autumn of 1942.
[2] This bill had been rejected in Committee.
[3] United States Minister at Teheran.
(c)   [4] On October 24 Mr. Casey pointed out that aid to Russia was liable to suffer to the extent of two-thirds of a ton for every ton of imported wheat sent to Teheran.

(a) E6108/144/34.   (b) E6169, 6299/144/34.   (c) E6240/144/34.

the Russians was less justifiable in view of the fact that they were co-signatories of the treaty with Iran, that they too needed Iranian currency in increasing amounts and that without Russian help we could not settle questions of supplies and transport or deal with the opposition of the Majlis and the formation of an alternative Government to that of M. Qawam. Sir R. Bullard had asked the Foreign Office in August to try to secure the co-operation of the Soviet Legation in Teheran. Mr. Eden appealed to M. Maisky on October (a) 30 for Russian support.

On November 1 the Foreign Office instructed Sir R. Bullard that (b) we did not want to incur American and Russian disapproval by using force except in the event of a stoppage in the rial supply. There was, however, a limit to the price which we would pay to ensure anything less than a guaranteed supply for the rest of the war. Sir R. Bullard was therefore given discretion, subject to American concurrence, to conclude a food agreement even against a short-term guarantee of rials. The Foreign Office did not want the food agreement to cover the duration of the war unless the Iranians would provide a long-term guarantee. In any case Sir R. Bullard was told to make it clear that we intended to secure the necessary currency and the fulfilment of our existing financial agreement and would use force to this end if the supply were cut off.

On November 7 Sir R. Bullard informed M. Qawam that in (c) return for their concession in regard to a food agreement, and for undertaking to send to Iran as soon as possible a reserve of 20–25,000 tons of wheat, His Majesty's Government expected to receive immediate satisfaction about currency. If M. Qawam did not propose to dissolve the Majlis, the Majlis must ratify the financial agreement, and as a corollary give up its right to limit the note issue. Sir R. Bullard said that with the draft food agreement in hand, M. Qawam ought to be able to impose this policy on the Majlis and people, and put an end to a situation where the central Government had no authority, the local officials were supine, the Majlis malevolently obstructive and the press engaged in a campaign of ignorant hostility. The Iranian Prime Minister did not question Sir R. Bullard's view of the situation. He agreed that the Government could not continue its present policy. He said that he would like to dissolve the Majlis, but that he did not know how Russia would take such a proposal.

(a) E6371/144/34; E2450/239/34 (1943). (b) E6371/144/34. (c) E6542/144/34.

(ii)

Sir R. Bullard's proposals for dealing with Iranian opposition: settlement of the wheat and currency questions: the Teheran riots of December 8 and 9, 1942: American criticism of British policy: Foreign Office reply (November 7, 1942–January 6, 1943).

(a) Meanwhile Sir R. Bullard had suggested to the Foreign Office more drastic action. He thought that satisfaction from the Iranian Government on currency alone was insufficient if other important issues were left at the mercy of the Government dependent on the Majlis. Concessions on wheat in return for currency would mean that further concessions would have to be made when other issues arose. Sir R. Bullard therefore recommended that we should inform the Iranian Prime Minister that we and the United States Government (if they agreed) were prepared to support the Iranian Government only if they would co-operate with the war effort. In particular they should give us immediate satisfaction on a guaranteed supply of currency, enforcement of anti-hoarding legislation, an effective system of price-fixing, control of the press and security. In order to enable the Government to honour its engagements under these points, we should expect it to obtain emergency powers from the Majlis for the Council of Ministers for a year or six months. The Majlis might be left in being for debate, but without power to reject measures introduced by decree of the Council under its emergency powers. We might call upon the Prime Minister at any time to get rid of unco-operative elements in his Cabinet and include Ministers (military officers if necessary) recommended by us. The Prime Minister should receive concessions about food only if he accepted these conditions. Sir R. Bullard realised that this policy might lead to the fall of the Government; but he felt that the situation had deteriorated to a point where we might be faced with 'guns and political chaos'.

The Foreign Office, however, thought that the proposals went much too far, and that Sir R. Bullard should follow his previous instructions. They had realised that pressure of events might force us to exercise greater control over Iranian affairs; they did not want to adopt such a policy unless it were necessary and supported by the Soviet and United States Governments. This support was unlikely. The Russians were concerned to keep M. Qawam-es-Saltaneh in power, and thought that the Allies ought to interfere as little as possible in Iranian administration. The Americans believed that we should get better results from a friendly and sympathetic attitude.

(a) E6371/144/34; E6512/122/34.

The Foreign Office informed Sir R. Bullard that in any case they (a) did not approve his detailed proposals. We could not expect the Iranian Prime Minister to agree in advance to alter his Cabinet whenever we wished and to replace non-co-operative members by our nominees. It was unreasonable to expect that the Majlis could be induced to sign away its own powers, and its dissolution seemed preferable. We need not take an immediate decision because the Iranian Prime Minister had agreed that we should continue to draw rials during the course of the negotiations.

Mr. Dreyfus had meanwhile telegraphed Sir R. Bullard's proposals (b) to Washington for instructions. He thought that the demands were not acceptable to the Iranians, and would bring about the fall of the Cabinet. The Allies would then probably be forced to organise a puppet Government or to proceed to a military occupation of the capital, or even to take both these courses. The State Department considered that nothing should be done that would lead to the fall of the Cabinet; they therefore sent instructions to Mr. Dreyfus that an announcement about wheat might be made without any conditions. Mr. Dreyfus could suggest that the Iranian Prime Minister should seek full powers from the Majlis. He was also given discretion to urge strict fulfilment of the Anglo-Iranian financial agreement.

The State Department telegraphed to the United States Embassy in London a statement deprecating the adoption of Sir R. Bullard's proposals. On November 11 Mr. Gallman[1] told the Foreign Office that the State Department were instructing Mr. Dreyfus to propose immediate publication of the wheat agreement, and assumed that Sir R. Bullard would receive similar instructions. Mr. Gallman's letter referred to the added responsibilities of the United States in Iran through the operation by the United States Army of supply routes into Russia[2] and the furnishing of numerous American advisory missions, particularly the group of financial advisers under Dr. Millspaugh. The United States Government wanted to see a co-operative, stable Government in Iran with popular support.

---

[1] First Secretary of the United States Embassy.

[2] It was clear in the summer of 1942 that the British technical troops in Iran were insufficient to deal with the growing volume of supplies in transit to Russia. On Mr. Churchill's visit to Moscow in 1942, a decision was reached to increase the supplies sent through Iran. Since no more British personnel were available the United States agreed to take over the operation of the ports, the Trans-Iranian railway and most of the road traffic to Russia. The British authorities remained responsible for inland water transport, lighterage and security arrangements. They also continued to provide road transport for material sent through Kermanshah.

The proposal made at this time by the Prime Minister, and accepted by the President, for sending an Anglo-American air force to the southern front of the Russian armies would have added to the amount of material to be transported across Iran.

The American technical troops began to arrive in December 1942.

(a) E6558/122/34. (b) E6335, 6611/122/34.

(a)   The Foreign Office thought that, while shipments of wheat should be made as soon as possible, the food agreement should be accepted only in exchange for a long-term currency settlement. They explained to Mr. Gallman that we had not agreed with Sir R. Bullard's more extreme proposals, but that we considered a long-term financial policy essential. If the Iranians fulfilled their obligations under the financial agreement with us, our own needs would be met, but not those of the Russians or the Americans. The Russians recognised this difficulty and had recently submitted proposals for a financial agreement to the Iranians. As long as the Majlis retained the power to restrict the note issue, the Allies would be liable to be held up to ransom. Mr. Gallman agreed to telegraph to Washington in this sense.

(b)   On November 17 an official of the British Embassy in Washington explained the position to Mr. Wallace Murray and members of the Near Eastern Division of the State Department. The Americans thought it better to accept a short-term solution of the currency question than to use force to obtain a long-term solution. The British representative said that we would use force only with extreme reluctance and in a grave emergency when no other methods were available, but that we could not do without Iranian currency. As a

(c)   result of the British representations to the Soviet Government, M. Smirnov was at last instructed to co-operate with Sir R. Bullard and Mr. Dreyfus to secure without recourse to force the currency needed to supply Allied troops in Iran and transport goods to Russia. On

(d)   November 17 the Iranian Prime Minister submitted to the Majlis a Bill giving him full powers regarding currency, including freedom to increase the note issue. On November 19 the Majlis decided to transfer authority for the note issue to a Note Reserve Control Committee on which the American financial adviser (when he arrived) would serve.

(e)   Sir R. Bullard, Mr. Dreyfus and the Iranian Minister for Foreign Affairs signed the food agreement on December 4, 1942. The British and United States Governments undertook to do their best to provide cereals to make up any unavoidable deficiency before the harvest of 1943, on condition that the Iranian Government carried out all the measures recommended by Mr. Sheridan— including measures to prevent hoarding and to introduce rationing —as well as the recommendations of the Road Transport Com-

(f)   mittee. If the Iranian Government undertook responsibility for the distribution of cereals and for ensuring that a deficiency in one area was met by supplies from another, the British and United States

---

(a) E6611/122/34. (b) E6842, 6843/122/34. (c) E6811/122/34. (d) E258/82/34 (1943). (e) E6938, 7106/144/34. (f) E2450/239/34 (1943).

Governments would help with transport for distribution. In addition, Sir R. Bullard and Mr. Dreyfus informed the Minister for Foreign (a) Affairs that the British and American Governments were arranging to import jointly into Iran as soon as possible 25,000 tons of wheat.[1] The Soviet Government were invited to participate in the food (b) agreement, but refused in view of their own difficulties. They were told that the replacement from overseas cereals purchased in Iran for the Russian forces would interfere with the carriage of goods and war material to Russia.

Although the Soviet Government had now promised to assist in (c) the transport of grain from the north, their local representatives continued to hold up supplies.[2] For a long time no wheat came in from Khorassan or Azerbaijan, and the local Iranian officials did nothing to collect wheat in centres from which it could be transported to Teheran, or alternatively seized by the Russians. With the coming of winter transport in many districts was impossible. The Iranian Minister of Food went in person to Tabriz to try to improve the situation and British army lorries carried back loads of wheat south from Azerbaijan.[3]

During this difficult period the Iranian Prime Minister was continually being attacked in the press and by the Majlis on the rise in the cost of living and the shortage of food, transport and consumer goods. On December 8 and 9 there was serious rioting in Teheran; the Prime Minister's house and a number of shops and food depots were looted. In view of the inability of the Iranian Government and (d) army to maintain order, Sir R. Bullard arranged for a battalion of British troops to come to Teheran from Qum.[4] There was some evidence that the disorders were not displeasing to the Shah,[5] and that he and some of the generals planned to take charge of public affairs for a while. Sir R. Bullard thought that the Shah had come out of the affair very badly; he had taken sides openly and violently

---

[1] The British Government had intended, irrespective of a food agreement, to provide this amount to replace 5,000 tons of wheat and 15,000 tons of barley which the Iranians had undertaken to supply to the Russians.

[2] M. Molotov had admitted that there was a surplus of 50,000 tons of wheat in northern (e) Iran. The Foreign Office thought that, even after Russian military needs had been met, a considerable amount should be available for Teheran.

[3] When Mr. Sheridan wanted to send his American assistant to Azerbaijan, the Russians (f) were unwilling to give him a pass. He was allowed to go in February 1943, but by that time transport was becoming increasingly difficult.

[4] These troops did not enter the city. See below, pp. 425–6.

[5] Mr. Churchill, while on his way to Moscow in August, had met the young Shah (g) and had later told Mr. Eden: 'I was much impressed with his intelligence and goodwill, both of which were in marked contrast to his brother-in-law. He expounded the principles of the Allied cause with the greatest vigour, and explained why he was convinced that the interests of Iran lay wholly with Britain and the United States.'

(a) E7106/144/34. (b) E6470/122/34; E258, 6519/82/34 (1943). (c) E6851, 6884, 7006/122/34; E7346/144/34. (d) E7555/19/34; E7167, 7247/14/34. (e) E6558/122/34. (f) E2301/48/34 (1943). (g) E5027/122/34; WM(42)118.2, C.A.

against a Prime Minister who was supported by the British, United States and Soviet representatives.

The State Department were extremely disturbed over the riots in Teheran and the difficulties with the Iranian Government. On

(a) December 11 Mr. Welles told Lord Halifax that he was satisfied that British and American policy was identical, but that Sir R.

(b) Bullard was evidently not carrying out this policy. The Foreign Office commented that the State Department was unreasonable in complaining about our methods while benefiting by our action.

(c) Mr. Eden had already spoken to Mr. Winant in strong terms about the attitude of Mr. Dreyfus, while he praised the work of Sir R. Bullard.

(d)   On December 15 Mr. Gallman brought to the Foreign Office a memorandum to the effect that American prestige in the country made it possible for the United States to bring considerable influence to bear in United Nations interests and was an asset of such importance that it ought to be conserved and used. Further, owing to the number of American advisers in Iran, it was essential to secure conditions favourable for their work. The United States Government had made heavy commitments with regard to supplies for Russia, and were directly concerned in maintaining the supply route.[1] The memorandum then referred to American complaints in detail. On December 15 Sir M. Peterson discussed these complaints with Mr. Gallman. Mr. Gallman was somewhat apologetic about them, but in order to check 'these incipient misunderstandings', the Foreign Office drew up for the Americans a full explanation of British policy in Iran. Sir A. Cadogan commented on the draft reply that the Americans were handicapped by a belief in 'American prestige' in various countries and a fear that this might be diminished. The prestige depended on the expectation of benefits to come; the Americans would be unpopular when they began to take part in the administration. They based their right to criticise British policy on their responsibility for organising transport across Iran; they forgot that in North Africa, where we were doing all the fighting, they did not admit our right to a voice in the ordering of affairs.

(e)   The memorandum was sent to the United States Embassy on January 6, 1943, with a letter from Mr. Eden to Mr. Freeman Matthews. Mr. Eden wrote that we were in substantial agreement on the main issues. He denied the State Department's implication that Sir R. Bullard had been carrying out a policy not in accordance with the views of the Foreign Office and creating unnecessary

---

[1] See p. 422, note 2.

(a) E7259/122/34.   (b) E6795, 7020/14/34.   (c) E7263/14/34.   (d) E7330/122/34. (e) E7330/122/34.

difficulties with the Iranians. He said that Sir R. Bullard was loyally carrying out the policy of His Majesty's Government, and that he had the fullest confidence in him.[1] He suggested that Mr. Dreyfus should co-operate more actively in maintaining United Nations interests in Iran.[2]

The memorandum also stated that British and American policies in Iran were very similar. The Foreign Office agreed about the increasing importance of American interests in the country, and confirmed their desire for greater co-operation. British policy was not to occupy Teheran, but to allow the Iranian Government to administer the country with as little interference as possible. Although the policy of collaboration with the Iranians had been successful hitherto, it had been necessary in the interests of the war effort to bring strong pressure to bear and to contemplate measures which had apparently led the Iranians to complain to the United States Government. The matters in question were (i) the provision of local currency for the United Nations forces in Iran, (ii) the wheat problem, (iii) security measures against Axis agents. The memorandum defended British policy in detail, and referred to the importance of maintaining the supply route to Russia. It pointed out that between the military operations of August 1941 and the summer of 1942, 50,000 tons of wheat had been imported from British and United States sources to satisfy Iranian civil needs.

The memorandum confirmed that the signature of the Anglo-American-Iranian agreement for wheat had been delayed to ensure a satisfactory long-term currency settlement. Rials were essential for the United Nations forces in Iran. His Majesty's Government felt therefore that they must insist on some new currency arrangement, so that the Majlis would no longer create difficulties whenever they were asked to provide rials. As soon as a satisfactory solution had been reached, the signing of the food agreement had not been delayed to impose more difficult conditions on the Iranian Government. As distinct from the agreement, we had at all times—and irrespective of disputes with the Iranians—tried to hasten the despatch of wheat urgently needed, owing primarily to the Soviet demand in northern Iran. A battalion of British troops had been sent to Teheran in the rioting solely to protect Allied property and military stores. The Foreign Office denied that food for Teheran

---

[1] In mid-December—after discussing Middle Eastern problems with Mr. Casey—Mr. Eden had sent a personal telegram to Sir R. Bullard congratulating him on his handling of the recent crisis in Teheran.

[2] On a visit to Washington in January 1943, Mr. Casey had a long conversation with (a) Mr. Wallace Murray and the State Department officials concerned with Iran. Mr. Wallace Murray read out some of Mr. Dreyfus's telegrams at the time of the October–November wheat and rial crisis. The telegrams consisted only of criticism of Sir R. Bullard.

(a) E932/932/65.

was delayed for political reasons; such delay would not have been in accord with our views and intentions. Any delay had been due to transport difficulties. Sir R. Bullard had not threatened the Shah or Iranian Prime Minister with the possibility that we might withhold supplies already arranged.

(iii)

Anglo-Soviet relations in Iran from the signature of the Treaty to the summer of 1943.

(a)   Shortly after the joint occupation of Iran Sir R. Bullard had suggested the establishment of a permanent Anglo-Russian-Iranian Commission in Teheran to deal with non-military matters arising out of the invasion. The Foreign Office supported this plan, but the Soviet Government refused it, apparently because they were afraid that their representatives would always be in a minority. The refusal was typical of the Soviet attitude of aloofness except in matters which might allow the Allies to secure important strategic controls. Thus the Russians tried to secure for themselves a larger share in the general management of the Trans-Iranian railway. Sir R. Bullard pointed out to them that the British Government had sent railway experts and provided rolling stock and other material and were already directing the railway administration before the Russian experts, without any materials, had arrived in Teheran. The Russians also tried, without success, to get British agreement to the prolongation of as far as Qum of the Russian-controlled section of the railway; this extension would have given them control of the central railway administration in Teheran. Later the Russians were unfavourable to the transfer to American management of the British-controlled section of the railway. They also warned Iranian politicians against the 'principle' of accepting American technical advisers.[1]

If the Russians suspected British and American aims, the British Government were equally suspicious of Soviet policy. Owing to Russian preoccupation elsewhere this policy was not at first clearly (b) defined. The Russian occupation of the northern provinces had been carried out with unnecessary harshness, e.g. in requisitioning motor vehicles, but once in occupation the Russians behaved, politically, better than the Iranians had expected. The worst feature of their occupation was their treatment of the forces of order; they disarmed the gendarmerie and the police, and then refused to assist

---

[1] See also below p. 437, note 1.

(a) E6024/3326/34 (1941). (b) E3655/3655/34 (1942).

in the maintenance of order on the ground that such action would be an interference in the internal affairs of Iran. They asked almost at once for a large extension in their consular representation throughout Iran. The Iranians accepted their requests and put forward counter-proposals based on reciprocity. They received in reply a declaration of sympathy for the 'principle' of the extension of Iranian consular representation in the U.S.S.R. after the war.

Sir R. Bullard was well qualified by temperament and experience to deal both with the Russians and the Iranians. He had been British Consul-General in Leningrad from 1931 to 1934; he had not previously served in Iran, but most of his official career had been in the Middle East. His own views on dealing with the Russians were extremely sensible. In a report to the Foreign Office at the end of (a) April 1942 he said that he realised the long-term danger to British interests from Russian policy, but that the Russians were our Allies and at a critical stage of the war we ought to give them the fullest assistance against the enemy. We had to run the risk of endangering our future position, since our main objective was to defeat Germany. Our position in Iran after the war would depend on the general world situation; our attitude to the Russians should be firm, as over the management of the railway in Azerbaijan, but also reasonable and not based on pre-war apprehensions. We should cultivate friendly local relations and try to allay Russian suspicions. We should ensure that the Russians had no excuse for alleging that we were not helping them to the full.[1]

After the Russian victory at Stalingrad there was no danger of a German invasion beyond the Caucasus. The only reason for continuing the Allied occupation of Iran was the supply of materials to Russia. The use of Iranian territory for this purpose, however, remained a most disturbing factor in the economy of the country. Iranian transport facilities, although greatly enlarged and improved by British and American engineers, were insufficient to carry the volume of military traffic across the country and also to meet domestic needs. The presence of an occupying force, and the heavy expenditure on local labour, added to the inflationary difficulties. The Iranian Government and administration were more of a hindrance than a help to the solution of these problems. The population

---

[1] On May 4 Mr. Eden informed Sir R. Bullard that he agreed with his views. On (b) May 9 the Minister of State, Cairo, reported that both he and the Commander-in-Chief, Middle East, also agreed and that the British military authorities would do everything possible to establish friendly local relations. Sir R Bullard considered it easier to be patient with the Soviet officials 'if one knew the false view of ourselves in which they had been (c) brought up, and the terror under which they lived'. He worked on the rule that if we were to co-operate, most of the goodwill and frankness must come from us, and if we secured even a little co-operation from the Russians we had done well.

(a) E2571/122/34. (b) E2956/122/34. (c) E7537/122/34.

generally became increasingly resentful over the rising cost of living, the shortage of goods and the interference with their traditional routine and habit. The resentment took various forms, open grumbling and, more serious, opposition by hoarding or smuggling to measures of control. The Iranians put most of the blame for their troubles on the British military and civil officials.[1] for the somewhat absurd reason that they were most active in putting the necessities of war, and particularly the movements of supplies to Russia, before the convenience of the Iranian people. This policy, as Sir R. Bullard had pointed out and as the Foreign Office understood, was obviously not in the long-range interests of Great Britain. The position was the more fantastic because the Russians were well satisfied to allow the British to incur unpopularity and dislike in consequence of their loyalty in giving prior regard to Russian needs.

(a)   In a report of March 2, 1943, Sir R. Bullard referred once again to the dangerous consequences of allowing the Iranians to believe that their troubles were caused by British mismanagement. The shortage of oil, for example, was due to the cutting down of local supplies in the interest of Russian demands; the British-controlled oil companies were being blamed for it, though they had no freedom of action in the matter. Sir R. Bullard thought that we were not only making ourselves unnecessarily disliked but that our failure to provide adequately for civilian needs was in fact reducing the efficiency of Iran as a supply route. The Foreign Office, as earlier, realised the force of these arguments and the readiness of the United States and Russia to leave us to bear the unpopularity of measures applied in the interests of the Allies as a whole. We could not, however, change our policy of providing Russia with the maximum volume of supplies. Moreover, in spite of their criticism of us, many Iranians realised that the danger of post-war interference with the territorial integrity and independence of their country came from the U.S.S.R. and not from Great Britain.

On March 16 the Foreign Office suggested possible ways of
(b) meeting Iranian complaints. Mr. Casey visited Iran in April 1943. He agreed in general with Sir R. Bullard's views. He regarded Iran as our 'most formidable political problem' in the Middle East and was afraid of a breakdown of government unless the monetary inflation could be kept under control. He thought that the Russians would not be unwilling to see administrative chaos in the country since they would hope to profit later by it. The Shah told Mr. Casey

---

[1] The British military authorities were also responsible for Allied security arrangements outside the Russian area of occupation. The Americans had no combat units in Iran.

(a) E1279/82/34. (b) E2368/38/34.

that he wanted an alliance with Great Britain to block Russian penetration.

The Foreign Office considered that Mr. Casey exaggerated the 'Russian menace'. On the other hand, the economic problem caused by inflation combined with hoarding and profiteering was not peculiar to Iran but was common to the whole of the Middle East, and unavoidable in view of the vast British military expenditure (some £200,000,000 a year) and the surplus purchasing power thereby created. As far as Iran was concerned we could only give full support to Dr. Millspaugh.[1]

On May 17 Sir A. Cadogan, at Mr. Eden's request, drew up a (a) report on the situation. He pointed out that hitherto the Foreign Office had been able to suggest palliatives but no radical remedy. He was still unable to propose a remedy, although he thought that the situation was bad both for Iran and for Great Britain. He ruled out the assumption by Great Britain of the administration of Iran. We ought to see, however, that we gained some credit for what we did and that we were not blamed for everything that went wrong, whether it was due to us or not. He suggested that the clearance of the 18,000 tons of Iranian civil supplies which were blocked in Iranian ports would not seriously hamper the transport of material to Russia, and that we could assist in the distribution of these supplies by the provision of lorries, tyres and petrol. As for the British position in Iran, the main trouble was that the Iranians were more frightened of the Russians than of the British on whom they vented all their resentment. We ought to do all we could to make the Russians associate themselves with us. We were in Iran to help them and they would suffer most if we refused to act owing to their unwillingness to collaborate with us. Sir A. Cadogan also suggested intensifying British propaganda, even at the risk of giving some offence to the Russians. If we decided to improve Iranian supplies and help in other ways, we could make our aid dependent on the suppression of anti-British propaganda and on effective control of the press. Sir A. Cadogan concluded his survey of the Iranian situation: 'I am afraid these are no very heroic remedies, but I confess I see none.'

Mr. Eden thought that Sir A. Cadogan's proposals should be put into effect as soon as possible, although he expected that we should have 'to drive hard to get our way'. On May 24 he instructed Sir R. Bullard that, after serious consideration, he had come to the conclusion that there was no case for modifying policy in the hope of improving matters. We could not abandon the policy of sending

---

[1] See above, p. 417, note 1.

(a) E2368/38/34; E3054/82/34.

maximum aid to Russia, and as long as this policy continued we had to expect unfavourable reactions in Iran. Mr. Eden was also opposed to taking over more direct control of the administration, because it would be against British, Indian and Iranian interests to give the Russians a lead for a similar move in their zone. In these circumstances only limited action was open to us. Even if this were successful, we could not expect any great or sudden improvement. Mr. Eden then put Sir A. Cadogan's proposals. He said that he intended to discuss with the Americans at once the clearance of civil supplies. He thought that we should continue and intensify our efforts to associate the Russians with us whenever action had to be taken.

(a)   In a despatch of May 3, 1943, Sir R. Bullard gave his views on probable post-war developments in Iran. He thought that the Russians would withdraw their troops within six months of the end of the war. They were not likely to bring upon themselves the accusation of imperialism by failing to carry out the treaty, though later on they might encourage a separatist movement in Azerbaijan. In any case they would assert themselves more in Iran. They would have established their position as one of the three greatest Powers and would have seen that the Iranian people were a favourable ground for their activities. The command of Iran with its oil and warm-water ports would be valuable in itself, and would provide access to India, where self-government would give greater opportunities for Russian penetration; the combination in Iran of intense poverty and hardship with the offer of an attractive remedy should be strong. If Iran were left to herself after the war—without the aid, for example, of American advisers—her Government was likely to degenerate into anarchy or an authoritarian régime. The British Government would have a difficult time in dealing with the Iranians. Their resentment at the Anglo-Russian occupation would remain strong, and would probably appear in violent newspaper attacks, in the persecution of any Iranians who might be held to have helped Great Britain during the war and in revenge on the Anglo-Iranian Oil Company.

Sir R. Bullard thought that Russia would be able to count on two important factors: the waning of British public interest in Iran, and the 'existence among the British public of a pro-Russian feeling so strong and so blind that any British Government will have to take it into account'. Russia would find it easy to encourage Iranian hostility to British interests in secret while outwardly preserving a correct attitude. On the other hand, Iran could be defended against

(a) E2939/82/34.

Russian domination only through a wide system of co-operation. For the present the British Government should try to discover Iranians less venal and conservative than most of those attaining to high office, and induce them to adopt a policy of reform 'suitable to the human material to which it is to be applied'. On the other hand, Iranian inertia would be a strong passive force when Soviet troops had left the country. Criticism of Soviet actions during the war would grow when Soviet troops had gone. The British still enjoyed much respect and goodwill in southern Iran. If the independence of their country were menaced the Iranians would turn first to Great Britain for sympathy and assistance, although the remedy would have to be sought within the wider framework of world security.

The Foreign Office view was that the Russian attitude probably was in the main defensive. To the Russians, British and especially American activity, might look like an exaggerated interest in Iranian affairs. They would suppose that we were taking advantage of their military preoccupations elsewhere to entrench ourselves in Iran. The Foreign Office thought that Russian foreign policy was based on self-interest without any element of idealism or altruism, and that we often attributed to Soviet actions far greater significance than they possessed. Sir R. Bullard's report suggested that the success of the American advisers in Iran was the best hope for establishing and maintaining a régime that suited British interests. M. Oumanski had told a member of the Foreign Office of the suspicion aroused in Moscow by the discovery at French General Headquarters, after the collapse of France, of plans for a Franco-British attack on Baku.[1] The Foreign Office noted that Abadan and the Persian Gulf were a similar vital interest to us, and the oil-bearing Arabian littoral was becoming an important American interest; if we wished it, the Americans were likely to join us in trying to convince the Russians that we had no desire or intention to dominate in Iran. We had, however, our vital oil interests to the south as they had to the north, apart from the general principle in the Atlantic Charter to respect the independence and self-government of all States.[2]

---

[1] The reference is probably to the French proposals of March 25, 1940. See above, Vol. I, Chapter IV, sections (iii) and (iv). The British Government had never accepted these plans.

[2] On March 30, 1943, the Foreign Office had informed Sir R. Bullard that all the (a) exchanges of views between Great Britain and Russia about post-war territorial changes had been limited to Europe, and that the Soviet Government had never expressed any views or claims affecting Iran after the war.

(a) E1530/82/34.

(iv)

Discussions regarding Iran at the first Quebec Conference: visit of M. Hajir to London: Iranian complaints about British policy: Foreign Office reply (August–November 1943).

(a)   At the end of March 1943 German agents were dropped by parachute in Iran with the purpose of organising sabotage, especially on the railway, and if possible exploiting discontent against the Government and the occupying Powers. The German activities were discovered during the course of the summer.[1] Sir R. Bullard recommended the arrest of certain dangerous Iranians, including seventy railway employees known to be implicated in railway sabotage organisations, since the matter affected the transport of supplies to Russia. Sir R. Bullard asked the Soviet Chargé d'Affaires[2] for his co-operation. The latter replied that he had already asked his Government for authority to request the Iranian Government to arrest certain suspects. The Foreign Office asked the Soviet Government for joint action and the United States Government for general friendly support.

(b)   On August 20, at the Quebec Conference, the President raised the question of Iran with Mr. Eden. He read extracts from a State Department report representing the position as serious. Mr. Hopkins subsequently asked Mr. Eden how serious he considered it to be, and what Anglo-American action could be taken to improve it. Mr.

(c)   Eden consulted the Foreign Office. On August 22 Sir O. Sargent replied that he also took a serious view. The most urgent problem was security. The tribes near Shiraz were rebellious, and the trouble might spread. The German parachutists were trying to increase disorder and divert our troops and probably to damage the oil installations and railway. The Foreign Office and Sir R. Bullard had wished to see British troops stationed at Shiraz to keep the situation under control, but the Commander-in-Chief had not had sufficient forces. The Foreign Office had consequently to concentrate on efforts to improve the local Iranian administration and to ensure drastic security measures. In the past few days one German[3] who had organised a widespread plot with the assistance of prominent Iranians, and two German parachutists, had been captured by our

---

(d)   [1] The War Office believed that the Germans were preparing a systematic campaign of sabotage in the Middle East, and to this end had dropped parachutists in Iraq, Iran and Syria.

[2] The Soviet Ambassador was in Moscow.

[3] The reference is probably to Franz Mayr, a German agent who had escaped the earlier 'round-up'. Mayr was caught in Teheran on August 15, 1943.

(a) E4378, 4398, 4589, 4744, 5128, 5164/38/34; E5658/239/34; E5899/82/34.
(b) Welfare 245, E5061/38/34.   (c) Concrete 490, E5061/38/34.   (d) E4769/38/34.

security authorities and a mass of new evidence against Iranian suspects had come into our hands. The political situation was unsatisfactory. M. Soheily was ineffective as Prime Minister.[1] The Iranian Government commanded no confidence and had little authority. The financial situation was bad and likely to get worse. In spite of a large harvest, administrative inefficiency might again result in shortages.

Sir O. Sargent said in his telegram to Mr. Eden that we should welcome closer American co-operation, and that lack of American support was one of the greatest difficulties. At the moment the most important thing was to have this support for action on security questions. If the Americans for their part in the light of experience gained by their advisers had suggestions for improving Iranian administration, the Foreign Office would do their best to help. Mr. Eden gave instructions that the Prime Minister should see Sir O. Sargent's telegram. The Prime Minister proposed that the matter should be raised at a meeting of the conference on August 24. On August 23 Mr. Eden discussed it with Sir A. Cadogan, who suggested that the United States Government should consider an increase in the import of consumer goods to Iran to the extent of two shiploads. On the same evening Mr. Eden discussed the situation with the President and Mr. Hopkins. He took it up with Mr. Hull on August 24 and promised to let him have a note about it. On August 28 a summary of Sir O. Sargent's telegram, with the addition of the suggestion about supplies, was left in the form of a note with the (a) State Department.

On August 29 Sir R. Bullard gave the Iranian Prime Minister (b) and Minister for Foreign Affairs an Anglo-Soviet list of 162 suspects with a request that they should be arrested and sent to Sultanabad for detention and interrogation. The Prime Minister promised to give orders for the arrests to begin on August 30. Sir R. Bullard later reported that the Iranians were carrying out the arrests efficiently. On September 2 the Iranian Government, in agreement (c) with the Soviet and British Ambassadors, issued a communiqué justifying their action. Out of the 162 suspects whom the Iranian Government were asked to arrest, 138 were handed over at Sultanabad. The names of ten additional suspects were given to the Prime Minister on October 10; eight of them were arrested. The Foreign Office remarked on the 'fairly satisfactory' results of British repre- (d) sentations to the Iranian Government, and thought that they were

---

[1] M. Soheily had succeeded Qawam-es-Saltaneh as Prime Minister on February 14, (e) 1943.

(a) E5061/38/21; E5138/38/34. (b) E5164/38/34; E5899/82/34. (c) E7569/239/34. (d) E5658/239/34. (e) E2453/239/34.

due largely to improved Russian and American collaboration.

(a)   Meanwhile the Iranian Government had formally notified the British, American and Soviet representatives that they wanted to adhere to the United Nations declaration. Early in July they had asked to be informed of the obligations and advantages involved. The three Governments returned an agreed reply, and on September 9, a day after the surrender of Italy, Iran declared war on Germany. Sir R. Bullard thought that the declaration came at an opportune moment, when the arrest of German agents in the country provided the Iranian Government with justification for their action. The Majlis and the press received the declaration very well. Sir R. Bullard spoke of 'complete unanimity of opinion'. The Iranian Government signed the United Nations Declaration on September 14.

(b)   On August 12 M. Hajir, the Iranian Minister for Roads and Communications, arrived in London with instructions to present a letter to Mr. Churchill from the Shah on 'recent developments, which give rise to some anxiety'. M. Hajir saw the Parliamentary Under-Secretary of State for Foreign Affairs and Sir M. Peterson and, on September 9, Mr. Eden.[1] In a memorandum on the questions

(c)   which he wanted to discuss M. Hajir claimed that the Iranian Government had tried to carry out their obligations to the Allies, but that the Allies had not done so with regard to Iran. They had not fulfilled their promises of economic assistance; they had not taken account of Iranian needs in their use of communications or of their engagement to disturb Iranian administration as little as possible. They had introduced American forces into the country without consulting the Iranian Government; the British and Soviet Governments had undertaken to respect the territorial integrity of Iran but had been unwilling to intervene when the Iranians complained of Russian breaches of this undertaking. M. Hajir argued that the political and economic difficulties of Iran were due mainly to the failure of the Allies to fulfil their treaty obligations. Allied demands were presented haphazardly and at short notice; the Iranian Government had difficulty in carrying them out and persuading the country of their necessity. As a result the Allies had sometimes resorted to direct action. The authority of the Iranian Government had declined and this decline had resulted in further intervention. In order to re-establish their authority, the Iranian Government asked generally for a closer observation of the treaty, and particularly for reference direct to London of all problems which could not be

---

(d)   [1] The Prime Minister received M. Hajir on October 7.

(a) E338, 705, 3993, 4822, 5393, 5424, 5456, 5567/338/34; E5658/239/34. (b) E4850, 5094, 5435/82/34. (c) E5621, 6840/82/34. (d) E5659/82/34.

settled expeditiously in Teheran,[1] the avoidance of independent action by the Allies and of direct reference by the Allied authorities to the different departments of the Iranian Government; the establishment of a tripartite committee consisting of a British, Russian and Iranian representative,[2] and support for Iranian representation at the Peace Conference on the same footing as other Allied nations.

The Foreign Office asked Sir R. Bullard and Mr. Casey for their (a) views on M. Hajir's complaints. They pointed out to Mr. Casey on October 2 that the memorandum was the first Iranian protest against the Middle East Supply Centre system as such. They asked him to consider urgently whether the Iranians could be given more opportunities, either in Cairo or Teheran, to state their views on supply questions.

Sir R. Bullard was certain that a tripartite committee would be (b) unworkable, and that the Russians would never agree to discuss their affairs with Iranians in the presence of British representatives. He thought that the most important thing was to ensure that the British, Russian and American representatives received parallel instructions from their Governments to co-operate on financial and economic questions. He and Mr. Casey proposed that Iran should be represented on the Anglo-American Combined Supplies Committee at Teheran which considered Iranian import requirements and made recommendations to the Middle East Supply Centre. The Foreign Office agreed that the Iranians had a reasonable claim to more effective representation where supply matters affecting their interests were in question.

Mr. Eden sent a long and detailed reply on November 15 to M. (c) Hajir's memorandum. He explained that the degree to which Great Britain could help Iran must depend on the extent to which Iran helped herself. He mentioned his discussions during his visit to Teheran on the way to the Moscow Conference. He stated that we wished to see Iran strong, united and independent, and enjoying internal security and political and economic stability. He said that a tripartite committee would require the agreement of too many authorities to any course of action and would interfere unnecessarily with the liberty of action of the Iranian Government. He suggested closer Iranian association with existing supply arrangements. He pointed out that Great Britain and the United States had arranged to pool their resources during the war, and that the import of supplies

---

[1] The Foreign Office thought that this demand was a complaint against the Middle East Supply Centre.

[2] The Foreign Office noted: 'This proposal . . . would probably enable the Russians (d) to prevent the American Advisers getting any reforms through.' For Sir R. Bullard's earlier proposal for a joint committee, see above, p. 426.

(a) E5621/82/34. (b) E5993, 6369/82/34. (c) E6840/82/34. (d) E5435/82/34.

for Iran could be dealt with only by a joint Anglo-American organisation, and not by either of the two Governments separately. For this reason the reference of questions direct to London would not be in the interests either of the Allies or Iran.

Mr. Eden referred at some length to shipping and supply difficulties. He explained that in the eighteen months after September 1941, 100,000 tons of wheat and flour had been imported into Iran from British and American sources. The allocation of space on the railway for Iranian civil requirements including oil represented a total of 35,000 tons a month, or more than twice the entire estimated capacity of the railway in 1941. In conclusion, Mr. Eden urged the Iranian Government to support their American advisers who had full British backing, and to reform their own administration.

(v)

Discussions regarding Iran before and during the Moscow Conference: the three-Power declaration at the Teheran Conference (October–December 1943).

(a)   Before the Moscow Conference of Foreign Ministers in October 1943, the Foreign Office reviewed the general question of Allied collaboration and friction in Iran. They thought that experience there—the only country in which the three major Allies had worked together—would be a useful guide for collaboration elsewhere, e.g. in certain countries of liberated Europe.

(b)   The Foreign Office asked Sir R. Bullard for his views. He considered that the American failure to give support in 1942 had been due to the traditional hostility of the State Department to British policy in Iran as 'imperialistic', and to the unfriendly reports of the United States Minister.[1] The State Department had complained to the Foreign Office about the alleged harshness of British policy; our firm reply and the attitude of the Minister of State when in Washington had brought a change. American co-operation had greatly improved, especially in security matters. Russian co-operation had also improved; instructions from Moscow to the Soviet Embassy in Teheran had brought co-operation with Sir R. Bullard in the currency and security issues. In both issues aid to Russia had been threatened. Sir R. Bullard thought that the Soviet Embassy preferred to leave the odium of interference to us unless their interests as opposed to the general Allied interests, were in danger. Actual friction with the Russians was rare except in matters of the passage of British subjects into and through the Russian zone. Sir R. Bullard

---

[1] See above, p. 425, note 2.

(a) E5444/82/34. (b) E5626/82/34.

attributed friction in other matters to a lack of candour on the part of the Soviet Embassy.

On October 5 the Foreign Office informed the United States (a) Embassy in London of the line which the British delegation would take at the Moscow Conference. They proposed to say that the success or otherwise of Allied policy in Iran had been found to depend on the degree of co-operation between the Allied representatives in Teheran, and that the three Allied Governments should give full support to the American advisers.[1] Dr. Millspaugh's recent reports had shown that the economic and financial position of Iran was critical. The question of an American credit was under consideration, and the Anglo-Iranian Oil Company had agreed to an advance of royalties. The Soviet contribution might take the form of a revision of certain contracts which were a heavy burden on the Iranian budget.

The British delegation also proposed to suggest that the whole of Iran, including the areas where Soviet, American or British troops were stationed, should be treated as a single administrative and economic unit over which the Iranian Government should be able to exercise control, and that Allied policy should be simply defined in terms of the utmost development of Iran as a channel for supplies to Russia for the duration of the war in Europe. At the same time, everything should be done to ease the strain of this policy on Iran. After the war there should be rapid withdrawal of Allied controls. The United Nations should respect the integrity and independence of Iran, and enable her to remain stable administratively by economic aid. On October 9 the Foreign Office were informed that the State Department agreed with this policy.

Although Mr. Eden did not regard the Iranian question as one of the major issues for discussion at the Moscow Conference, he (b) submitted to it a memorandum on Iranian affairs containing a draft declaration intended to reassure opinion in the country.[2] At a discussion of the British proposal on October 24 Mr. Eden suggested the appointment of a sub-committee to consider the draft declaration, and also economic questions, transport, railway finance and co-ordination of trade policy. Mr. Hull supported this proposal. M. Molotov said that before the Conference the Iranian Ambassador had said to M. Kavtaradze[3] that, in accordance with the provisions

---

[1] On September 1 a member of the State Department asked Sir R. I. Campbell (c) whether we could bring pressure to bear on the Russians to give more support to Dr. Millspaugh. The Foreign Office elsewhere described the Russian attitude to the American advisers as one of 'non-co-operation tempered with obstruction'.

[2] This draft was on the lines of paragraph 1 and the first half of paragraph 2 of the three-Power declaration mentioned below.

[3] Assistant Commissar for Foreign Affairs.

(a) E5935/82/34. (b) N6921/3663/38. (c) E5220/38/34; E5396, 6097/82/34.

of the Treaty, the Iranian Government ought to take part in any discussions at the Conference affecting Iran. The Ambassador had been told that it was not proposed to take any decisions affecting the country. M. Molotov now asked whether the Conference approved the reply. He pointed out that the United States Government were not yet in treaty relations with Iran.[1]

Mr. Eden agreed that if the Conference were to make any new decisions of policy Iranian representatives should be present, but that there could be no objection to a general survey of the situation, especially if the result were to benefit Iran. M. Molotov then accepted the appointment of a sub-committee. The British representatives submitted two draft declarations to the sub-committee at its first meeting on October 25.[2] The first document was a draft three-Power declaration of general support, with a promise of the withdrawal or reduction to 'a normal peace-time establishment' of the 'non-military governmental organisations' now operating in Iran 'in connexion with the United Nations war effort'. The second draft was of an Anglo-Soviet declaration repeating the assurances in the Treaty with regard to the respect for Iranian territorial integrity and the withdrawal of British and Soviet forces from Iran after the war. The United States delegation proposed a parallel declaration of their own to the two-Power declaration. The American documents would state that the American military organisations in Iran were solely technical and administrative. Their only purpose was to facilitate the transport of supplies to Russia; they would be withdrawn after the war.

The British representatives accepted the American proposals.[3] The Russian representatives asked for more time to study the British and American documents. The British representatives then suggested that the sub-committee should examine food supplies, transport, local purchase policy, trade policy, railway finance and the payment of Iranian taxes, and monthly or more frequent meetings between British, American and Russian representatives at Teheran on economic and financial issues.

At their second meeting, on October 26, the sub-committee examined the draft documents. The British and American representatives maintained that the declarations would have a good effect. The American representatives said that the Iranian Government

---

[1] The United States Government were in fact discussing with the Iranian Government a treaty on the lines of the Anglo-Russian-Iranian Treaty to regularise the position of United States troops in Iran.

[2] They also submitted a draft financial agreement concerning the Iranian State Railways.

[3] The American representatives also proposed some amendments to the three-Power declaration.

would hear that Iran was being discussed and would expect something from the Conference. The Russian representatives, however, thought that Iran did not expect reaffirmation of the Treaty undertakings. Article 6 of the Treaty already provided for consultation with Iran. M. Molotov said again that he had informed the Iranian Ambassador that no decisions about Iran would be taken without consultation with his Government. The American representatives suggested that if necessary, after the declarations had been agreed, the Iranian Government should be informed of them and asked whether they would like them to be published. The British representatives agreed with this proposal.

The Russian representatives then said that any declaration might embarrass the Allies by leading Iran to expect more than was intended. The Americans thought that there would be a favourable reaction to tripartite assurances and that the effect would extend outside Iran. The Conference had been convened to consider good relations between Allies. There was no country in which there was such close contact as in Iran.

The Russian representatives asked for explanations on certain points in the documents. They did not favour a proposal that they should submit counter-drafts. They had no objection to reaffirming the treaty position, but thought that there was no need for public declarations, and that most of the points raised by the British representatives were being discussed in Teheran and were also highly technical. At the third meeting, on October 30, M. Kavtaradze said that the appropriate time for a declaration would be after the signature of the American-Iranian agreement. A joint three-Power declaration would then be possible. The American representatives replied that they had consulted Mr. Hull on the expediency of a declaration. He had said that the Russian position 'made sense' to him; the British and Russian Governments had given undertakings, he saw no reason to renew them 'every time the moon changed'. At the same time the Conference seemed an appropriate occasion for reassurance.

The Russians did not agree with the British and Americans that the Iranians were uneasy. They referred to Iran's declaration of war on Germany, and said that the Allies had kept their undertakings to interfere as little as possible with the economic life of the country. They mentioned the allotment of 25,000 tons of Soviet wheat from the north to Teheran.[1] The Iranians would attach more

---

[1] In the second week of April the Soviet Government, without previously consulting (a) the British or American Governments, announced that they would despatch 25,000 tons of wheat to Teheran at the rate of 7,500 tons a month. Earlier, on January 11, Mr. Eden
(*continued on page 440*)

(a) E258/82/34; E3868/239/34.

ᴅ°ʙꜰᴘ

importance to the adoption of measures at the Conference for
shortening the war against Hitler than to the superfluous renewal
of existing obligations.

The Americans then said that their Government would prefer
not to give reassurances unless the situation demanded it; they
thought that the signature of the American-Iranian Agreement
would be a suitable moment. The sub-committee reported to the
Conference that there was no fundamental difference in the policy
of any of the three Governments to Iran; that they were unable to
agree about a declaration and that the matter might be further
considered by the representatives of the three Governments in
Teheran.

One of the members of the American delegation in Moscow stayed
(a) in Teheran for a few days after the Conference. He told Sir R.
Bullard that, acting on Mr. Hull's instructions, he had informed the
Shah and the Minister for Foreign Affairs, to their satisfaction, that
the Russians had repeatedly declared their intention of carrying out
the treaty. Sir R. Bullard also thought that the news had brought
relief; he asked the Foreign Office whether he should make a similar
statement. The Foreign Office replied that the Russians had not
given any such explicit assurances and that it seemed best not to
supplement the American statement by a British communication.

(b)	The British representatives on the sub-committee at the Conference
reported later to the Foreign Office that from the outset the Russians
did not want to go beyond vague talks. The sub-committee on Iran
had made little headway. The Russians had been unwilling to discuss
economic and financial questions. On the other hand, the general
exchange of views might have done good. The Russians had said
that reaffirmations of treaty commitments were not necessary, since
the Iranians had faith in Allied intentions. The British representatives had taken the Russians to mean that they intended to honour
their obligations, and did not want suspicion cast on their intentions
by unnecessary reaffirmations.

(c)	On November 29, after his arrival at Teheran for the three-Power
Conference, Mr. Eden called on the Iranian Prime Minister. M.
Soheily said that Teheran was expecting the publication of a communiqué regarding Iran as a result of the Conference. He suggested
that this communiqué should state that Iran had done her best to

---

(*continued*)
had appealed to the Soviet Government for urgent aid in sending wheat to Teheran.
The Soviet Government made great propagandist use of this delivery, though in fact it
was less than the normal quantity which would have reached Teheran from the northern
provinces (where the harvests had been better than in the south) if the Russians had not
prevented the export of grain from their zone of occupation.

(a) E6770, 7040/82/34.　(b) E7424/82/34.　(c) E7833/82/34.

help the Allies, and that it should confirm the treaty assurances about the integrity and independence of Iran, and refer to economic assistance. Mr. Eden said that he did not object to the proposal, but that M. Soheily should also speak to the Russians.

On November 30 Mr. Churchill and Sir R. Bullard, and at a (a) separate meeting President Roosevelt, met the Shah in the presence of the Iranian Prime Minister and Minister for Foreign Affairs. On the following day Stalin called on the Shah. The Iranian Prime Minister stated later that these conversations showed complete understanding. The Iranian Government presented an *aide-mémoire* in identical terms to the Allied Governments. This *aide-mémoire* outlined the contents of the proclamation which the Iranian Government hoped the Conference would issue.

As a result of the talks on December 1 the three Heads of Governments at the Teheran Conference issued a joint declaration regarding (b) Iran. The declaration made no reference to the withdrawal of troops after the end of the war, but recognised the contribution which Iran had made to the war, reaffirmed their promises of economic assistance and their desire for the maintenance of Iranian independence, sovereignty and territorial integrity. The declaration seems to have satisfied Iranian opinion; the Shah sent a message of thanks to Mr. Churchill and Mr. Eden for their part in securing it.

(a) E7648/82/34. (b) E7710/82/34.

CHAPTER LVIII

British policy towards Iran from the Teheran conference to the Potsdam conference

(i)

Anglo-American exchanges on the lack of Russian co-operation in Iran: Russian demand for an exclusive oil concession in northern Iran: British and American attitude to the Russian demand (January 1–November 9, 1944).

At the time of the Teheran Conference the Foreign Office regarded the Russian attitude as satisfactory. For over two years they had been warned that the Russians were penetrating Iran and would ultimately install a Communist régime and eliminate British influence. There had been no evidence of any such long-term Soviet policy. The Russians had done nothing to assist good government, but were doing nothing to overturn it. At the worst their policy seemed to be the promotion of disorder in the country in order to maintain their hold in the north. Mr. Eden agreed with the Foreign Office view that serious Anglo-Russian disagreement over Iran was unlikely.

The optimism of the Foreign Office about Russian intentions in Iran was not lasting, and indeed could hardly have survived a careful study of Russian policy in the northern provinces, including, for example, the favour shown by the Soviet authorities to the Tudeh party.[1] The American advisers to the Iranian Government found themselves unable to extend their reforms to the areas under Russian control or even to visit them freely, while in Teheran Russian propaganda attacked the advisers and also the Iranian Government for 'subservience' to them. The State Department now became seriously disturbed at the situation. They suggested that Mr. Wallace Murray should discuss the question of Russian economic exploitation of Iran during his visit to London in April 1944.[2]

---

[1] This party had been founded after the abdication of the Shah by an opposition group, most of whom had been in prison and were released only after the fall of the dictatorial régime. The party was pro-Russian and reformist, but not by any means proletarian. It included a number of landowners dispossessed by Reza Shah. Russian support of the party—at first somewhat guarded—became more open in 1943, when the military situation enabled the Soviet authorities to take a more active part in Iranian affairs. They then applied the familiar methods of putting their protégés of the Tudeh party in local control in the area under Soviet occupation.

[2] See above, Chapter LVI, section (v).

Sir R. Bullard regarded the Russian interference in Iranian (a) administration as disastrous, and thought that the British and United States Governments might well make representations about it to the Soviet Government. The Foreign Office, on the other hand, were doubtful about the expediency of raising the question of the access of the American advisers to the territory under Russian control. They were afraid that the Russians might raise the general question of the advisability of employing American advisers. In practice, even if the Russians admitted an American adviser into northern Iran, they would not be any more forthcoming, for example, about the transport of wheat from the Russian zone. The general conclusion reached in the discussions with Mr. Stettinius and Mr. Wallace Murray was that the two Governments might approach the (b) Russians with proposals for closer co-operation on the basis of the Moscow agreement and the Teheran declaration. Neither the British nor the Americans wanted the establishment of foreign domination or zones of influence in Iran; the Americans believed that they could assist in bringing Iran back to normal conditions and in relieving tension between Great Britain and Russia. They also regarded the situation in Iran as a test of the ability of the three Powers to co-operate in applying the principles of the Atlantic Charter. The British and Americans agreed upon the desirability of setting up a tripartite committee in Teheran. They thought it expedient to mention the proposal at once to the Russian Ambassador in London. The Russians did not object to discussions in Teheran. At the end of May they instructed the Soviet Ambassador at Teheran[1] to (c) discuss economic questions with the British and American Ambassadors.[2] Some discussions took place in June, but the Soviet Government did not think it necessary to set up a Higher Supplies Committee including Iranian representatives.[3] Meanwhile, from the Iranian point of view, the position looked easier; the end of the war with Germany seemed imminent and the question of supplies was therefore likely to become less difficult.

A new and serious crisis arose, however, early in September 1944. On September 6 the Soviet Government informed the Iranian (d) Ambassador in Moscow that they were sending M. Kavtaradze on

---

[1] M. Maximov, who had replaced M. Mikhailov on May 21, 1944. Sir R. Bullard described M. Maximov, who had been Counsellor of Embassy at Teheran at the time of his appointment, as 'sensible and business-like'.

[2] In February 1944 the British Legation at Teheran was raised to the status of an Embassy. The United States Government took a similar step in regard to their Legation.

[3] This committee would have taken the place of the Anglo-American Central Supplies Committee which, in so far as it dealt with imports, was concerned only with those coming on the Gulf route. The Russians thought that talks between the diplomatic representatives at Teheran would be sufficient.

(a) E2202/94/34.   (b) E2167, 2212, 2570, 2659, 2660/94/34.   (c) E3238, 3342, 3350, 3635, 3708, 4019, 6559/94/34. (d) E6357/6058/34; E6016/94/34.

a special mission to Teheran to ask for a revival of the oil concession in the district of Khavir Kumian (south of Semnan), formerly granted to an Iranian company in which the Soviet Government had been interested.[1] M. Kavtaradze arrived in Teheran on September 13. A fortnight later he told the Shah that the Soviet Government wanted not only to discuss the Khavir Kumian concession but also to ask for a five-year exploratory concession covering all the five northern provinces of Iran, an area of some 200,000 square miles. The exploratory concession would be followed by a grant of rights over a smaller area on which oil had been found. The Russians based their request on a similar concession granted to a Russian subject in 1916.[2] They also demanded that other foreign oil companies should be excluded from the northern area to which their proposed concession applied.

(a)   Sir R. Bullard considered that Iranian acceptance of the Russian demands would have serious political consequences. If the Russians were given this concession to the exclusion of any competitors they would have gone far towards making northern Iran into an autonomous Soviet republic. Soviet troops were unlikely to stay in Iran after the war in contravention of the treaty; the Russians, however, could encourage 'spontaneous' applications for annexation, and create economic enclaves in northern Iran under the guise of oil concessions.

Sir R. Bullard thought that we were entitled to say (i) that as oil resources were a valuable but wasting asset, applications for concessions must be examined with the greatest care, and that if the Iranian Government encouraged competition in the south, why not in the north also? He thought that the Iranians would probably try to postpone the grant of any new concessions until the withdrawal of foreign troops. Since there was urgent need of a British concession, a postponement would be a victory for the Russians, but it would be better than our getting no oil while the Russians had a free hand in the north. Sir R. Bullard was afraid that if the Russians succeeded in their demand, the Iranians would conclude that the British Government was a spent force in Iran, and would rush to conciliate the Russians in every way.

---

[1] This concession had been abandoned and the exploratory rights granted under it transferred to the American Iranian Oil Company, who had in turn also surrendered it.

[2] The Iranian Government had later regarded the concession of 1916 as invalid. The Concession was, in fact, abandoned in the Soviet-Iranian Treaty of 1921. There was, however, a precedent for a grant of an exploratory concession over a very wide area. The Anglo-Iranian Oil Company, at the revision of their agreement with the Iranian Government in 1933, had obtained such a five-year grant covering an area of 100,000 square miles (the Russian claim covered an area of over 200,000 square miles). In this case also the exploratory grant was to be followed by an exploitation grant over a smaller area.

(a) E6058/6058/34.

The difficulty both for the British and United States Governments was that the Russians had not been the first to make a move during the war in asking the Iranians for oil concessions. With the consent of the United States Government (in November 1943) the Standard-Vacuum Oil Company and another American group had applied to the Iranian Government for concessions; the Shell Oil Company, with British consent, had made a similar application. The Iranian Government had delayed a decision on the applications, and had called in two American experts to advise them about the terms on which any concessions should be granted. The difference between the Anglo-American and Russian applications was that the latter was exclusive,[1] and in view of the Russian state control of all industrial enterprises entirely governmental, and that, as Sir R. Bullard had pointed out, Russian monopoly control of oil resources would certainly be followed by political control. The British and American Governments, however, could not use this argument plainly with the Russians since they would at once deny it; in any case the argument was weakened by the fact that the Americans in particular were obtaining something very like indirect political predominance in Saudi Arabia.[2]

The Prime Minister and Mr. Eden were at this time about to leave for Moscow.[3] The Foreign Office therefore drew up for Mr. Eden (a) a memorandum on the oil question. They pointed out that the Russian application had to be considered in the light of British political interests in preventing northern Iran from becoming a Russian dependency, and of the desirability of obtaining for a British company a concession in southern Iran. They explained the position with regard to the British and American requests in the south, and said that the Ministry of Fuel and Power was anxious that the Shell Company should get the concession if possible, and so provide a further much needed source of sterling oil. The Russians had let it be known that they were not concerned with the question of a concession in the south, but they assumed that they had the field to themselves in the north. We had never admitted such an exclusive Russian right. It was, however, fairly certain that no British company would apply for a concession in the north; the Foreign Office would not advise a British company to do so in view of the difficulties which the Russians would place in their way. In practice, therefore, no question of competition arose. We could not ask the Iranians to

---

[1] As early as February 1944 the Russians had stated through the Iranian press, in view of the British and American applications, that they had prior rights to the exploitation of oil in northern Iran.

[2] See Chapter LVI, section (vii).

[3] See Vol. III, Chapter XXXVIII, section (vi).

(a) E6262/6058/34.

refuse the Russian request by saying that British companies might want to apply for concessions in the north. At the same time, it would not be wise to try to persuade the Iranians to refuse a concession to the Russians, since the latter would then doubtless put strong pressure on them to be equally obstructive about granting a concession in the south. If the Russians raised the question at the Moscow Conference the Foreign Office proposed that Mr. Eden should support a fair field for all and due regard for the interests of Iran. This meant that the Iranian Government should not be hurried into granting any concession. The American and British applications had been referred to foreign advisers. The Iranians had every right, if they so wished, to treat the Russian application in a similar way.

(a)　　The Shah informed Sir R. Bullard on October 9 that the Iranian Government would refuse the Russian request and would explain the refusal by saying that no oil rights would be granted in Iran until after the war. Sir R. Bullard did not suggest that the British application should be granted regardless of other considerations, because he was sure that Iran could not have Russia exploiting oil in its territory and remain the buffer state which Great Britain wanted it to be. He thought also that the Iranian Government would not give a concession to a British or American company in the south while rejecting a Russian demand in the north. He agreed with the Shah's view that the grant of oil rights to Russia would mean the end of Iranian authority in the north. The Ministry of Fuel and Power thought that a refusal of the Russian request in the north might lead to an increase of Russian interest further south. From the point of view of British interests in oil, they suggested a solution by which the Russians would receive a concession in the north at the same time as the Shell Company received one in the south.

The Foreign Office view was that if the Iranians were advised to grant a concession either to the British or Americans in the south they could not be advised simultaneously to refuse a concession to the Russians in the north. If oil deposits were to be exploited in northern Iran, the Russians were the only people likely in practice to be able or willing to exploit them. There appeared therefore to be a conflict between British oil interests, which made the grant of a concession in southern Iran desirable, and British political interests which Sir R. Bullard considered would be prejudiced by the grant of a concession to the Russians. The decision of the Iranian Government not to grant any oil rights until after the war at least had the political advantage for Britain of keeping the Russians out. The first reaction of the Foreign Office was that they should approve the attitude of Sir R. Bullard on this question.

(a) E6186/6058/34.

There was, however, some division of opinion. One view was that, if the Ministry of Fuel and Power thought that their interests were best served by not instigating or supporting an Iranian refusal to give a concession to the Russians, it might be better to take the same line, for political as well as practical reasons. The Foreign Office were not confident that the Iranians would maintain their refusal of the Russian demand. If, as was probable, the Russians increased their pressure the Iranians would be likely to give way. We might then find that we had held up the grant of an oil concession to a British company in the south, aroused Russian resentment by obstruction which could be based only on political grounds and had nevertheless failed to achieve our object. Even if the Russians did not frighten the Iranians into giving them the concession, they could achieve complete political and strategic domination of the north Iranian provinces politically and strategically by other means.

Mr. Eden telegraphed from Moscow on October 11 that he had (a) seen the memorandum of October 5; he agreed with Sir R. Bullard's view that the grant of a concession to the Russians would endanger the position which we wanted Iran to maintain, and bring about the end of Iranian authority in the north. Mr. Eden asked the Foreign Office to consider whether it would not be better that neither we nor the Russians should compete for new oil concessions in Iran, and thereby divide the country up into British and Russian spheres of influence.

On October 16 Sir R. Bullard telegraphed his opinion that the (b Russian demand was a test case, and that we were entitled to object to it on principle. He said again that Russian exploitation of the oil area in the north would be incompatible with Iranian independence. The Iranian Prime Minister believed, rightly, in Sir R. Bullard's view, that acceptance of the Soviet demand would mean presenting the Russians first with part and then with the whole of the north. Once the north had gone the rest of Iran could hardly hold out, if only because it was economically dependent on the north.

Sir R. Bullard said that his opinion was shared by all Iranian and foreign observers whose views His Majesty's Government would regard as worth consideration. If, for reasons of policy, the Russians were allowed a free hand, the life of Iran as an independent state and buffer for our protection was not likely to be long. The oil controversy had strengthened the widespread belief in Iran that the Government would not be free until the Soviet troops had gone. Sir R. Bullard hoped that as soon as Iran had ceased to be a road for aid to Russia, British troops would be withdrawn from Teheran and kept as far south as was compatible with the protection of British

---

(a) Hearty 45, E6262/6058/34. (b) E6367/6058/34.

oil interests until the defeat of Japan and the complete evacuation of Iran. He hoped that everything would be done to persuade the Russians to reduce to a minimum the area in which they kept troops.

(a) On October 17 the Foreign Office informed the Ministry of Fuel and Power of the Iranian decision to refuse oil concessions until after the war. They said that they could not take the responsibility of advising the Iranian Government to reverse this decision. The decision would have certain political advantages if the Iranians could maintain it, but it was doubtful whether they would be able to do so. If the Russian need for oil were great, they were likely to bring further pressure to bear. In that event the Foreign Office considered that we ought not to advise the Iranians to resist. If, however, the Soviet action was a clear breach of their treaty under-taking given jointly with us to recognise Iranian independence and integrity, we might be able to take the question up with the Russians, not on the ground that they had no right to obtain a concession but on the ground that their methods of obtaining it were inadmissible. The Foreign Office asked for the concurrence of the Ministry of Fuel and Power in their instructions to Sir R. Bullard.

These instructions, which were sent on October 18, were to the effect that, if the Iranian Government asked his advice, Sir R. Bullard should say that the British Government appreciated their difficulties, and did not wish to dispute their decision provided that it was equally maintained. They were not prepared to advise the Iranian Govern-ment as to the lengths to which they should go to maintain it. If the decision were changed, the British Government would expect that an application by British nationals for a concession would be con-sidered. Sir R. Bullard was told for his own information that if Russian pressure were to take a form incompatible with Iranian independence, thus constituting a breach of the treaty, the Foreign Office might take the matter up with the Soviet Government. Sir

(b) R. Bullard was further informed on October 22 that the choice did not seem to lie between 'letting the Russians have a free hand' and inciting the Iranian Government to resist. If we had to try to restrain the Soviet Government, the best method would be a direct approach to them. The Foreign Office asked for the views of the American Ambassador and Dr. Millspaugh.

(c) On October 21 Sir R. Bullard reported that a number of news-papers were carrying out a pro-Russian campaign, and were attack-

(d) ing the Prime Minister[1] on the charge that he was opposing Russian interests. On the previous day the Prime Minister had made a

---

[1] M. Saed had become Prime Minister on March 18, 1944. He had been Iranian Ambassador in Moscow from 1938 to 1942 and Iranian Foreign Minister since 1942.

(a) E6262/6058/34. (b) E6367/6058/34. (c) E6461, 6530/6058/34. (d) E6575/6058/34.

statement in the Majlis explaining the attitude of the Government. He told Sir R. Bullard that he had most of the House with him. No vote was taken. Sir R. Bullard believed that the Iranians in general were opposed to the grant of a concession to the Russians.

The Soviet authorities continued the 'war of nerves' against the (a) Prime Minister and his Government. On October 22 lorry loads of armed Russian troops ranged about the streets of Teheran, particularly in the neighbourhood of the Majlis. On October 27 there were demonstrations by Tudeh supporters in Teheran and towns in (b) the north. They were followed by a more serious incident in Tabriz where Russian military authorities prevented Iranian police and troops from trying to keep order. At Teheran the deputies were subjected to pressure; one of them was told by the Russians that they considered relations with the Iranian Government 'severed'. The Russians used the Iranian radio to broadcast the Soviet point (c) of view in a violent form.[1] They stopped the movement of grain to Teheran on northern railways.[2]

After an attack on the Iranian Prime Minister in the Soviet press, (d) the Foreign Office suggested that he should make a restrained statement of his point of view. On October 29 he made such a statement (e) to the Iranian press; the Russian censor suppressed the statement and the attacks continued.[3] The Prime Minister was ready to resign (f) if his resignation would relieve the tension, but the Shah felt that he should stay in office as long as possible since he (the Prime Minister) had his confidence and that of the Majlis. The Iranians then asked whether the British or Americans could make representations to the (g Soviet Government.

In reporting this request Sir R. Bullard telegraphed that the Russians were exerting pressure while they had troops in Iran and control over news to other countries, and in the belief that loyalty and policy would probably compel Great Britain and the United States to keep silent. He was not sure that Russia could dominate northern Iran in any case if she wished. If Iran could stand by her decision to postpone the grant of oil concessions until after the war, she had some chance of resisting political pressure in the press. After the war there would be the weapon of publicity, which 'the Russians so much dislike and fear'. He thought also that Iran could be made much less dependent on Russia than in the past.

---

[1] The Iranian Government had undertaken to allow the Soviet and British Governments opportunities for broadcasting from the Teheran radio station.
[2] The interference with supplies caused the G.O.C. in C., Iran and Iraq Command, to protest to the War Office.
[3] See also below, p. 452. (h)

(a) E6515/6058/34; E6603, 7037/6058/34. (b) E6714, 6865/189/34. (c) E6530/6058/34. (d) E6883, 6967/6058/34. (e) E6516/6058/34; E6526/189/34. (f) E6526, 6574, 6622, 6870, 6876, 6997, 7061/189/34. (g) E6515/6058/34. (h) E7198/6058/34.

Sir A. Cadogan considered that he ought to submit Sir R. Bullard's telegram to the Prime Minister since it was a proposal for a remon-
(a) strance to Russia.[1] He sent it to the Prime Minister on October 27. He mentioned Sir R. Bullard's warning that this was a test case and that, if the Iranians were forced to give way, the chances of Iran again becoming an independent buffer state were small. However this might be, there was no doubt that Russian behaviour was not consistent with Iranian independence, which the Russians, British and Americans had undertaken to respect. The Iranian Prime Minister, backed by the Shah, had shown courage, but Russian pressure might soon increase. Sir A. Cadogan therefore thought the time had come to ask for American support in an approach to the Russians. He submitted a draft telegram asking Lord Halifax to
(b) approach the State Department. On October 25 Sir R. Bullard reported that, in answer to the Iranian request for representations to Russia, the United States Ambassador had replied that he could not make any recommendation to his Government; he would transmit the request although, owing to the war situation and the imminence of the United States elections, it was not made at a good moment.

(c)   Lord Halifax reported on October 26 that the State Department had asked for the British view of the oil question. They had received disquieting reports of the attitude of the Soviet representative at Teheran and of the tone of the Soviet press. As soon as Mr. Churchill and Mr. Eden left Moscow, the Soviet press had begun to speak of fascism in Iran and of the failure of the Iranian authorities to punish those guilty of sabotage and pilfering of supplies for Russia. The State Department were afraid that this propaganda campaign might be intended to work up a case against Iran on the familiar German model.

Lord Halifax said that the United States Government were prepared to accept the Iranian decision to refuse any applications for concessions during the war. If the Russians tried to compel Iran to grant a concession against her will, the State Department considered that their action would raise the question of the Teheran Declaration. If this declaration were to be set aside, it would be a bad omen for future agreements with the Russians. The State Department proposed representations by the British and United States Governments in Moscow.

With the approval of the Prime Minister, the Foreign Office

---

[1] Mr. Eden was visiting Athens and Rome, and had not returned to London with the Prime Minister.

(a) PM/44/660, E6515/6058/34.   (b) E6573/6058/34.   (c) E6605/6058/34; E6515/6058/34.

instructed Lord Halifax on October 28 to tell the State Department that, in view of the undertakings in the Treaty and the Teheran Declaration, the British Government were considering an approach to Russia on the lines that they did not contest the Russian right to seek an oil concession in northern Iran, but that Iran also had a right to decide the question for herself. His Majesty's Government had accepted the decision to grant no more concessions during the war. They felt that Iran should not be forced to concede the Russian demand during the war. If the Russian attitude were hostile, the Foreign Office would quote attacks on the Iranian Prime Minister in the Soviet press as evidence of unfair pressure. They asked whether the United States Government would do the same.[1]

On October 31 Lord Halifax reported that the State Department (a) agreed with the proposed *démarche* and were telegraphing instructions to their Chargé d'Affaires in Moscow to send a note to the Soviet Government. The note would state the view of the United States Government that sovereign and independent countries such as Iran had the right to withhold or grant concessions in their own territory. The United States Government were particularly concerned over the maintenance of this principle in view of the Teheran Declaration, and could not concur in any action constituting undue interference in Iranian internal affairs.

In order to avoid the appearance of 'ganging up' the Foreign Office therefore instructed Sir A. Clark Kerr on November 1 to approach the Soviet Government without reference to the American action and to say that information reaching the Foreign Office indicated that M. Saed had the support of responsible elements in Iran, and the fact that he had remained in office bore this out. M. Saed's Government—the legal Government of Iran—had fulfilled its treaty obligations, and had the right to expect that Russia and Great Britain would do likewise. The Foreign Office knew of nothing to support the assertion from Soviet-inspired sources that M. Saed's Government had obstructed the passage of supplies to Russia.

The United States Chargé d'Affaires sent a note to the Soviet (b) Government on November 1 and Sir A. Clark Kerr on November 2. On November 3 the Iranian Ambassador spoke to Sir A. Cadogan (c) about the gravity of the situation and the unexpectedness of the Russian demand. He said that his Government were standing on their decision not to grant any concessions until after the war, and even if the Government were to change the new Government would

---

[1] The instructions were telegraphed to Mr. Eden for his information. He replied that (d) he agreed with them, but thought that action should be taken very quickly.

(a) E6670/6058/34. (b) E7325/6058/34. (c) E6769/6058/34. (d) E6698/6058/34.

(a) maintain the same attitude. He asked for British support. On November 3 Sir A. Bullard reported that as from the previous day

(b) the Russians seemed to have effected a change in policy. The same day he telegraphed that there were signs that they were about to drop their demand. They were, however, insisting on the resignation of the Iranian Prime Minister, who was prepared to resign if he could secure postponement of the oil issue. The State Department also received a report of a sudden change in the Soviet attitude. They thought that the representations in Moscow had had some effect.

(c)   Sir R. Bullard considered that the failure of the campaign for an oil concession would damage Russian credit abroad, especially if their use of the 'Hitler technique' became known. The Iranians had seen a Russian diplomatic defeat, which they had thought impossible, and had learnt that it was not suicidal to stand up to the Russians. For the first time since the occupation the Iranian press, which had often criticised the British and Americans, had now criticised the Russians.

Sir R. Bullard was certain that the Russians had given up their plan owing to the British and American representations in Moscow. He thought that some credit should go to the Iranian Prime Minister, who had refused to resign even when many deputies and high officials had wavered. M. Saed's reply to the Russian delegate had received wider credence than M. Kavtaradze's accusations. Mr. Eden doubted whether Sir R. Bullard was right about the reasons for the change in the Russian attitude. The Foreign Office also

(d) thought the representations could not have been the decisive factor in a change which was already noticeable on November 2. In his telegram of November 3, Sir R. Bullard had attributed the change to the publicity given to the Iranian case outside Iran. The Foreign Office agreed that this might have had much to do with it. The Russians had organised press campaigns in Teheran and Moscow representing their demand for oil rights as backed overwhelmingly by the Iranian people. They had alleged that the Iranian Prime Minister had given promises to M. Kavtaradze which he had repudiated. At the same time the Russian censor in Teheran had stopped all press messages—even a statement by the Iranian Prime Minister—giving the Iranian version of the facts. The Foreign Office had, however, arranged for the substance of M. Saed's statement to be published in London.

The Foreign Office also thought that the Russians had failed to foresee that we and the Americans would not object to the Iranian decision to postpone the grant of oil concessions.

(a) E6767/94/34. (b) E6783, 6862/6058/34. (c) E6868, 6978/6058/34. (d) E6978/6058/34.

(ii)

Resignation of the Iranian Prime Minister: Iranian refusal of all demands for oil concessions (November 9, 1944–January 20, 1945).

Mr. Eden noted on November 9, with regard to the Iranian crisis: 'We are probably not out of the wood yet.' In fact, on this same day M. Saed resigned. He had previously heard from the Russians that (a) if he resigned the oil question would be dropped and M. Kavtaradze would leave Teheran. Before his resignation M. Saed made a statement of the history of the oil question for the Majlis and for publication.[1] He refused to allow the Tudeh party to make a demonstration on November 7.[2]

Sir R. Bullard reported that, although M. Saed was still assured (b) of the support of the Majlis, he hoped by resigning to induce the Russians to resume relations while dropping the oil question. The Shah said that he had accepted the resignation of M. Saed to gain time, and out of fear of some extreme action by the Russians, such as encouragement of a separatist movement in Azerbaijan. The Shah also said that freedom to discuss the oil question would come not with the end of the war but with the departure of foreign troops. Sir R. Bullard agreed that negotiations could not be equal while the Russians were able to cut off the food supplies of Teheran and stop Iranian Government telegrams in violation of the censorship agreement.[3] Attacks on M. Saed continued to appear in the Soviet press after he had resigned. An article in the *Red Star* on November 15 (c) claimed that the growing unity between the Allies showed that the efforts of politicians such as M. Saed to cause disagreements were doomed to failure and that the fate of M. Saed showed that no Government could remain in power in Iran which conducted a policy hostile to Russian interests.

On November 16 the Foreign Office informed Sir A. Clark Kerr (d) that M. Kavtaradze was still in Teheran. This fact did not suggest that Russia had decided to drop the oil question. Press attacks on M. Saed reported by Sir A. Clark Kerr also seemed to suggest that the Russians were preparing to renew their pressure. Mr. Eden instructed Sir A. Clark Kerr to impress on M. Molotov that we were bound to take a close interest in the matter since we were a party to the joint guarantees of Iranian integrity. Mr. Eden

---

[1] A further statement by M. Saed was given to the Foreign Office on November 23, (e) and published in the British press.
[2] A Teheran Tass message dated November 3 given by all papers in Moscow on (f) November 7 reported more anti-Saed demonstrations in Iran.
[3] The joint Anglo-Russian-Iranian censorship did not apply to official statements.

(a) E6978, 7323/6058/34. (b) E7101, 7182/6058/34. (c) E7061/189/34; E7101, 7164/6058/34. (d) E7101/6058/34. (e) E7037, 7227/6058/34. (f) E6909/189/34.

also suggested to the State Department that similar instructions should be sent to the American Ambassador in Moscow. The situation seemed likely to get worse if there was delay in making the Russians realise the strength of British and American views.

(a)   On November 18 Sir A. Clark Kerr telegraphed that he doubted the wisdom of asking M. Molotov for an explanation of Soviet pressure as long as there was hope that it might be withdrawn. Such a demand might make the Russians more obstinate. He suggested a note to M. Molotov that the British and American Governments were watching the situation. The United States Ambassador in Moscow shared this view and agreed that the best check on Soviet policy would be a hint to M. Molotov that the joint guarantee of Iranian integrity would come up at the next meeting of the Heads of Governments.

(b)   Meanwhile, on Mr. Eden's instructions, Sir A. Cadogan had spoken to an official of the Soviet Embassy in London on November 18.[1] Sir A. Cadogan explained that Mr. Eden was disturbed at the Russian action regarding northern Iran. The Iranian Government had announced their decision three weeks ago to postpone the grant of oil concessions until after the war, but M. Kavtaradze was still in Teheran. There were indications that Russia intended to renew pressure, and attacks on M. Saed in the Soviet press. Sir A. Cadogan pointed out that, although we were co-signatories of the treaty, Russia had not taken us into her confidence before adopting a hard attitude in attempting to force the issue and compel the resignation of the Iranian Government. Mr. Eden was attempting to restrain criticism in the British press, but would find it difficult to keep up this restraint unless we could say that the question would be left until the end of the war. He expected questions in Parliament in the next week. The Soviet official promised to ask his Government to

(c)   explain their intentions.[2] On the instructions of the Foreign Office Sir A. Clark Kerr wrote to M. Molotov on November 20 that uneasiness about the situation in Iran was beginning to find public expression in Great Britain. It would assist the British Government in dealing with criticism if they could say that, in common with Great Britain and America, Russia had agreed that the questions of oil concessions in Iran should be left until after the war.

(d)   The War Cabinet discussed the Iranian oil dispute on November 21. Mr. Eden said that the Russian objective was not clear, but the Foreign Office were uneasy at the pressure that was being brought

---

[1] The Soviet Ambassador was ill at the time.

[2] Mr. Eden noted: 'Excuses won't help. They must let the Iranians alone.'

(a) E7115/6058/34. (b) E7164/6058/34. (c) E7115, 7813/6058/34. (d) WM(44)152.5, C.A.; E7067, 7376/6058/34; E7153/6058/34.

to bear on Iran, and representations had been made both to M. Molotov and to the Soviet Counsellor in London. The United States Government had collaborated with us. No reply had been received to the representations made in London or Moscow. Mr. Eden felt that British public opinion would be critical if, as a result of Russian pressure, a new Iranian Government were formed which would grant the concession.

Mr. Eden said that there were four possibilities: (i) After a new Iranian Prime Minister had been appointed, Sir R. Bullard might inform him that we trusted that he would follow the policy of his predecessor about the concession. (ii) Sir R. Bullard might tell the Shah or the Minister at Court of our representations to the Soviet Government. (iii) The Iranians might be informed that we proposed to discuss these matters at the next meeting of the Heads of Governments. (iv) Mr. Churchill might suggest to the President a joint statement to Russia that we proposed to discuss these matters at the next meeting of Heads of Governments. Mr. Eden thought that public opinion would be critical of an apparent surrender to Russian demands. If we said nothing, the Russians might be able to say that they had not been warned of the strength of our view.

The Prime Minister spoke in favour of a joint message by President Roosevelt and himself that they would like to discuss the matter at their next meeting with Stalin, and that they felt confident that Russia would not take any action until they had done so. The Prime Minister told the War Cabinet that any such discussion would be confined to new concessions in the north and would not affect existing concessions in southern Iran.

The War Cabinet agreed that Mr. Eden should instruct Sir R. Bullard as he had proposed in his first three suggestions and, in accordance with his fourth suggestion, the Prime Minister and the President—if the latter was willing to do so—should send a joint message to Stalin. The instructions to Sir R. Bullard were despatched (a) the same evening. He replied that the Iranians were already hoping that the Heads of Governments might discuss the crisis, and thought that such a move would greatly encourage the Shah and his Prime Minister. Meanwhile the Foreign Office received a telegram from (b) Lord Halifax that Mr. Harriman was leaving Washington for Moscow and was to stop at Teheran on the way. The State Department would prefer to await his recommendations before making a further approach to the Russians in Moscow. They had not received any reports from the Ambassador at Teheran in the past few days that the situation was getting worse. The State Department were ready to say more in Moscow if Mr. Harriman recommended it.

(a) E7153/6058/34; E7186/6058/34.   (b) E7206/6058/34; E7376/6058/34.

Mr. Eden and Sir A. Cadogan agreed that, in view of the quieter local situation, Mr. Churchill's approach to President Roosevelt
(a) should await Mr. Harriman's report to the State Department. The Foreign Office noted that attacks continued in the Soviet press against the Iranian Government. On the other hand, there had been no recent reports of much activity in Teheran by the Russians and their tone had been more conciliatory. The Prime Minister agreed to postpone his message to the President.

(b)   On November 23 M. Bayat, the new Iranian Prime Minister, told Sir R. Bullard that he would follow the policy of M. Saed in the matter of oil concessions, since this was the policy desired by the Majlis and most of the people. Sir R. Bullard said to the Shah and the Prime Minister that the attitude of the former Government was understood in Great Britain and had won general sympathy. Mr.
(c) Eden instructed him to continue to speak in this sense. Sir R. Bullard later told the Minister at Court that His Majesty's Government had protested to Russia and had asked for information.

(d)   On November 29 Lord Halifax reported that the State Department were still inclined to await a report from Mr. Harriman from Moscow. Lord Halifax suggested to them that they should authorise either the United States Ambassador or Mr. Harriman to say some-
(e) thing encouraging to the Iranians. The State Department finally instructed the Ambassador to inform the Iranian Prime Minister of the American *démarche* in Moscow, and to say that it was made in the spirit of the Teheran Declaration.

At this point the oil question took an unexpected turn. On
(f) December 2 Dr. Mussaddiq, a leading Iranian politician and oppo-
nent of all oil concessions (including those of the Anglo-Iranian Oil Company). brought forward a bill which the Majlis rushed through under double urgency procedure. Article 1 provided that no Prime Minister, Minister or Under-Secretary, had the right to enter into conversations about oil concessions with official or legal effect or to sign any agreement about oil. Article 2 provided that the Prime Minister and the Cabinet might discuss the sale of oil or the manner in which the Iranian Government was to exploit and control the country's oil deposits, but must inform the Majlis of these discussions. Article 3 provided that offenders against the first two articles would be sentenced to solitary confinement for a period of three to eight years and permanently dismissed from the Government service. Sir R. Bullard was informed that the Tudeh deputies had opposed the bill and mustered only seven votes, whereas about eighty voted for it.

(a) E7274/189/34. (b) E7177, 7207/6058/34; E7446/189/34. (c) E7241, 7546/6058/34. (d) E7335/6058/34. (e) E7383/6058/34. (f) E7415, 7439, 7796/6058/34.

Mr. Harriman called on the Soviet Ambassador just after the (a) passing of the bill. The Soviet Ambassador and M. Kavtaradze said that they could not accept this rebuff from the Iranians. M. Maximov suggested to Mr. Harriman that the law was directed against the (b) United States and Russia, since Great Britain already had a concession.[1] Mr. Harriman replied that his Government were interested only in the application of the Teheran Declaration and the independence of small nations. M. Maximov said that the land of Iran was (b) owned by 300 families, that the Majlis represented only 5 per cent of the population and that the Government must become more (b) democratic. He subsequently demanded from the Minister of Foreign Affairs the suppression of five of the leading newspapers which had opposed the Russian demand.

On December 4 Mr. Harriman told the Shah that the United (c) States Government had expressed its concern to Russia at the crisis in Iran, but that while they (the United States) and presumably the British Government viewed the matter with concern and sympathy, it was an Iranian-Russian problem. Mr. Harriman told Sir R. Bullard that he had found the Shah firm but worried at reports that demonstrators had been collected in Russian lorries for meetings in northern towns on the question of autonomy. Mr. Harriman said that the Iranian Government could not expect sympathy unless they were able to offer the people prospects to compete with those held out by Russian sympathisers. The Shah agreed. Sir R. Bullard told Mr. Harriman that for three years he had been giving the Shah and the Iranian military authorities similar warnings. He had suggested to them long ago that, in order to forestall demands for autonomy from the northern provinces, they should apply to all provinces the provision in the constitution for the creation of provincial councils.

M. Maximov and M. Kavtaradze called on the Iranian Prime (d) Minister on December 7. M. Maximov said that the Soviet Government were dissatisfied with their relations with Iran, and that the passing of the oil concession bill had increased the difficulties. M. Kavtaradze told the Prime Minister that he was leaving for Moscow by the first aircraft. M. Maximov also said to M. Bayat that the (e) Soviet Government expected the oil concession law to be amended; he suggested as an alternative that the Shah should refuse to ratify the law. The Prime Minister pointed out the difficulties, but said

---

[1] The United States Ambassador reported that there were rumours in Teheran that the new oil measure had been brought forward at British suggestion. The Ambassador did not believe these rumours and was confirmed in his view by the fact that he was with Sir R. Bullard when the latter heard about the passing of the law. He said that Sir R. Bullard was taken completely by surprise at the news. *F.R.U.S.* 1944, V, 480–1.

(a) E7439/6058/45.　(b) E7425/6058/34.　(c) E7425/6058/34.　(d) E7546/6058/34.　(e) E7654/6058/34.

that the law permitted the Iranian Government to discuss the sale
of oil. M. Maximov said that the Iranian Government had no capital
for the exploitation of oil, and that the only practical way was that
(a) proposed by the Russians. He later informed M. Bayat of instructions from Moscow that relations with Russia could not be good
until the law had been amended.

The departure of M. Kavtaradze meant a lull in the Soviet-
(b) Iranian dispute. In view of the Soviet attitude, however, the Foreign
Office did not expect a long respite. They thought that the Russians
might renew pressure by threats of social disturbances or separatist
movements in the north, and that the Iranian Government should
consider means to improve their position with regard to Russia
before this happened. The Foreign Office suggested that they should
take immediate steps to carry out measures of social reform on the
lines advocated by Sir R. Bullard and Mr. Harriman, and also to
show that they were planning alternative methods of exploiting
Iranian oil deposits. The Foreign Office thought that if the Iranians
did nothing in these ways the Russians could represent their attitude
as purely obstructive. Sir R. Bullard was instructed, if he saw no
objection, to speak to the Shah and the Prime Minister in this sense.

Sir R. Bullard was told for his own information that the Iranians
were unlikely to be able to debar the Russians indefinitely from a
share in exploiting the oil of northern Iran. They could, however,
postpone negotiations until they could take place in conditions enabling Iran to obtain reasonable terms, i.e. after the withdrawal of
Russian troops. If the Iranians were to hold the Russians off until
then, it was important that they should lose no opportunity of
strengthening their case. Their general line of action also should be
one which would justify British support if this were needed.

(c)   Sir R. Bullard spoke strongly to the Shah and Prime Minister on
these lines. He reported that the Shah had always pressed for
reforms, including the breaking up of big estates, and that he welcomed the British recommendation on this point. The Prime Minister
foresaw excellent results from the transfer, which he hoped to effect,
of the economic powers of Dr. Millspaugh to himself or his nominees.
He claimed to have planned to distribute essential commodities to
the rural and tribal areas. He professed to be ready to break up
state lands into small holdings.

The Shah and the Prime Minister said they realised that the
development of oil in the north could not be postponed indefinitely.
They had already planned a bill for presentation to the Majlis
providing for the formation of an Iranian company to bore for oil.
Sir R. Bullard did not feel that the Prime Minister appreciated the

---

(a) E7822/6058/34.   (b) E7546/6058/34.   (c) E7822/6058/34.

difficulty of exploiting the oil deposits. He thought that it would be necessary, as the Foreign Office had pointed out, to give the Russians an interest in northern oil, but the Majlis seemed likely to be jealous about the manner and extent of Russian participation.

The British Chargé d'Affaires in Moscow reported on December (a) 21 that Mr. Harriman thought Iranian fears about Russian aggressiveness were not groundless. Mr. Harriman said that his visit to Teheran had been undertaken as a minor hint to Russia that the United States Government were keeping an eye on developments. The Foreign Office inferred that the Americans were not going to take a firm line about the dispute. They did not want American support which was so half-hearted as to show disagreement, as in the affairs of Greece and Poland. For the moment there was nothing more to be done. They hoped, however, that the question would be discussed at the next meeting of Heads of Governments.[1]

On December 29 the Soviet Government replied to the British (b) notes of November 2 and 20. They referred to the change in the attitude of M. Saed's Government 'under the influence of pressure behind the scenes'. They spoke of 'this disloyal attitude' on the part of M. Saed and the 'unfavourable attitude adopted by the British' with regard to Soviet-Iranian negotiations for an oil concession. They did not agree that the grant of a concession to Russia could effect the sovereignty of Iran; if this argument were valid, it would apply first to Great Britain. The note concluded by alleging that the 'unconstitutional Majlis resolution was adopted under the influence of the intrigues of hostile elements such as Saed'.

The Foreign Office thought that this note was 'highly unsatisfactory', and that it implied a continuance of Soviet pressure on Iran. The note misrepresented the British attitude, namely, that the Iranian Government was entitled to dispose as it saw fit of its undeveloped oil resources. The most important feature of the note was its attempt to represent the affair as an Anglo-Soviet dispute, when the British position was identical with the Americans. Russian

---

[1] A memorandum of December 19, 1944, from Mr. Wallace Murray to Mr. Stettinius is of interest as showing the attitude of the State Department (and the President) at this time towards British interests in the Middle East. Mr. Wallace Murray was discussing a suggestion by the President that Mr. Harriman should talk to Stalin about a possible international trusteeship to operate the Iranian railways and a port on the Persian Gulf. Mr. Wallace Murray thought that neither the Iranians nor the Russians would favour such a proposal, and that the British Government would be strongly against it. British policy for a century had been to prevent Russia or any other Great Power from establishing itself on the Persian Gulf. There was good reason for maintaining this policy. 'If we proceed on the assumption that the continuance of the British Empire in some reasonable strength is in the strategic interests of the United States (and I understand the strategists of the War Department proceed on this assumption) it is necessary to protect the vital communications of the British Empire between Europe and the Far East.' *F.R.U.S.* 1944, V, pp. 485–6.

(a) E7838/6058/34. (b) E39/24/34 (1945).

intervention had prevented both British and American representatives from obtaining a new concession.

The Foreign Office replied to the Soviet note on January 20, 1945. They pointed out that representatives of a British oil company and of certain American oil companies had applied for concessions in southern Iran before the Soviet Government made their application. The attitude of the Iranian Government—not to grant new concessions while Allied troops were in their country—towards all applications had been identical. The British note denied that we had had any interest in the passage of the law of December 2, and regretted that Soviet persistence in pressing their demands, after they knew the Iranian attitude, had apparently provoked the Majlis into passing it. The note said that as an independent sovereign State, Iran had a right to grant or withhold concessions. His Majesty's Government did not intend to try to persuade the Iranian Government or Majlis to adopt a less negative attitude. The British attitude to the Soviet-Iranian negotiations had been unfavourable; we had not contested the Soviet right to apply for a concession in northern Iran. If the Iranian Government were willing to negotiate, they would have no ground for objection to a concession granted by free negotiation as with the Anglo-Iranian Oil Company concession.[1]

(a) At the end of the year Sir R. Bullard sent the Foreign Office a long telegram of warning about the oil question. He doubted whether Russian participation in the exploitation of Iranian oil could ever be reasonable. He pointed out that any Soviet company or organisation was a branch of the Soviet Government and that exploitation of oil deposits by such company or organisation would involve encroachment on Iranian sovereignty. If Iran had to submit, she would do so only because she was weak and because the assurances in the treaty and the Teheran Declaration were worthless. Even Russian participation in the exploitation of oil in the north meant effective Russian control of exploitation, since other partners, Iranian or foreign, could not withstand Russian pressure. Control of the exploitation of oil involved control of the oil area, and it was then a short step to the Russian control of northern Iran and the end of Iranian independence.

Sir R. Bullard said that Russian pressure in the north was very great. At first the Russians had demanded oil, knowing that political control was likely to follow. They had now reversed the process, and were using measures approaching political control to obtain oil. Sir R. Bullard reported the only hopeful suggestion he had heard to keep the oil question quiescent until foreign troops had gone. This

---

[1] The Foreign Office sent the text of the Russian note to the State Department.

(a) E7943/6058/34.

suggestion was, that the Iranian Government should invite Russia to assist them in exploiting northern oil resources, by choosing experts from any country neutral in the question, i.e. any country other than Great Britain, the United States and the U.S.S.R. Sir R. Bullard asked whether the Foreign Office approved of this suggestion. Sir R. Bullard was certain that, unless the Russians obtained a concession in the north, they would attempt to secure cancellation of the Anglo-Iranian Oil Company's concession in the south, and might succeed. Against this risk, however, he thought there must be set the far graver risks inherent in their obtaining a northern concession. This would lead to the termination of Iranian independence and hence to the termination of the Anglo-Iranian Oil Company.

The Foreign Office did not think that the solution proposed by Sir R. Bullard was practical. Our attitude was that the Iranians were justified in refusing to grant concessions until foreign troops were withdrawn, but not that we wished to keep the Russians away from the northern oil deposits for ever. We wanted the survival of Iran as an independent State until the withdrawal of foreign troops, when Iran would be in a position to negotiate freely with the Russians, as well as with the Americans and British, about the development of her oil resources outside the Anglo-Iranian Oil Company concession.

The Foreign Office suggested that when the question of Iran was raised with Stalin at the Yalta Conference, a hint should be given of the possibility that when foreign troops had withdrawn, Russia, the United States and Great Britain, as the Great Powers chiefly responsible for world security, might discuss the future of the undeveloped Iranian oil deposits with the Iranians. This might remove any Russian suspicions that our real aim in supporting Iranian independence was to exclude them permanently from Iranian oil.

(iii)

Question of the date of withdrawal of Allied troops from Iran (January 1944–January 1945).

At the end of December 1943 Sir R. Bullard had raised with the (a) Foreign Office the question of the maintenance of foreign troops in Iran between the defeat of Germany and the defeat of Japan. The Foreign Office asked the War Office for their views. The War Office referred to the vital importance of the oil areas until Japan had been defeated. Even after the end of the war with Japan, the

---

(a) E155/155/34; E1175/260/34 (1944).

security of the oilfields would be indispensable economically to Britain. There was also the question of an air reinforcement route during the war from the Middle East to India. As for the eventual withdrawal of British troops, the War Office thought that no undertaking should be given that British troops would not be stationed in Iran until future needs could be better assessed. The War Office realised the implications of the treaty but thought that it might be replaced by another agreement.

The Foreign Office had always recognised that a Russian refusal to withdraw their troops from northern Iran might force us to leave some troops in the south. They regarded such a development as politically undesirable, and thought that we should not try to obtain facilities from Iran to maintain troops. On April 8 they instructed Sir R. Bullard that if the Russians wanted to keep troops in Iran until six months after the Japanese armistice, we should have no legal ground for objection. The Foreign Office view had been that in any post-war security scheme for the Middle East and Persian Gulf, Abadan and the Iranian oilfields would have to be defended from bases outside Iran, i.e. in Iraq or on the Arab shore of the Gulf. Our need to retain Iran as an independent buffer state could be met only if we and the Russians withdrew our troops by the due date and did not try to set up permanent garrisons. The Foreign Office added that no Iranian Government would allow such garrisons except under compulsion.

(a)   Sir R. Bullard agreed that the Russians could legally stay in Iran until six months after the end of the war with Japan. Once Germany was defeated there would be no aid to Russia through Iran, and troops would not be needed to guard lines of communication. The oil in the south would, however, still be vital to us. The question was whether we should retain troops to guard the oil area. If we did so, the Russians might keep forces in the north, to the detriment of the economy and morale of Iran. If, on the other hand, British troops left the country when the war was over, the Russians could hardly stay.

The Foreign Office did not think that the Russians would withdraw their troops before the end of the Japanese war under the moral compulsion that we had done so, or that the political advantages of freeing Iran from the presence of foreign troops outweighed the risk involved in leaving our vital strategic oil supplies unguarded. We needed the oil supplies of the Persian Gulf for the war against Japan; in any case the effects of our evacuating Iran on the internal position were so hard to foresee that we ought to stay at least in the oilfields area until we had beaten Japan. The War Office agreed

(a) E3089/94/34.

with the Foreign Office view. The Foreign Office therefore instructed (a)
Sir R. Bullard on June 27 that they shared his view of the desirability
of getting Russian troops out of the north as soon as possible, but
that unfortunately we had to consider our own needs in the war
against Japan, and to keep troops at least in the oilfields area while
this war lasted. The effect of our withdrawal on the Russians was
not certain; they might say that they would stay until the end of the
treaty period irrespective of what we did.

On June 14 the Foreign Office had asked for the advice of the (b)
Chiefs of Staff on post-war strategic requirements in the Levant and
the Middle East, including arrangements for the defence of the south
Iranian oilfields. The Foreign Office pointed out that, according to
the terms of the Soviet-Iranian Treaty of February 26, 1921, which
was still in existence, Russia had the right to send forces into Iran
if a third Power introduced forces to make the country a base for
operations against the Soviet Union. The Foreign Office thought
that we could not promote Iranian independence and internal
stability if parts of the country were occupied by troops. If there
were any need after withdrawal for intervention to defend the oilfields against internal disturbance or external aggression, we should
have to operate from bases outside Iran. After the war Russia would
take a much closer interest in the Middle East. A Soviet Legation
had been set up in Cairo and another was to be established in Iraq.
It was impossible to foresee how our relations with Russia would
develop. Our policy was to try to make the Anglo-Soviet Treaty a
reality, to draw Russia into closer collaboration in world affairs
wherever possible and desirable, and oppose any tendency on her
part to withdraw into isolation. The Foreign Office believed that
Russia would want to maintain peaceful conditions in adjacent
territories. If this belief were justified, a satisfactory arrangement
with her was possible. On the other hand we had to take into account
in assessing our strategic needs the risk that Anglo-Soviet relations
might be more difficult and strained.

The question of the withdrawal of British troops remained in
abeyance until the end of October 1944, when the War Office again (c)
raised it. The Commander-in-Chief, Iran and Iraq Command,
proposed to construct a summer camp at Kermanshah. This proposal suggested the retention of troops in Kermanshah after the end
of the war or even after aid to Russia through Iran had ceased. The
War Office, in asking for the views of the Foreign Office, said that
the presence of troops in Iran was desirable from an imperial and
military point of view, but that political factors might require their
withdrawal. The Foreign Office replied that they expected that

---

(a) E3692/351/34. (b) COS(44)524(o); U5908/748/70. (c) E6744/260/34.

QBFP

British troops would be withdrawn after the defeat of Germany to the immediate vicinity of the oil area in the south and that they would leave altogether after the end of the treaty period. It would therefore be a waste of money to build a camp at Kermanshah. Such a step would probably have adverse political effects, since the Russians would notice it and draw their own conclusions as to British intentions. Our efforts to secure the withdrawal of Russian troops from the north would be prejudiced if the Russians were able to say that we were planning to maintain troops as far north as Kermanshah.

The War Office did not authorise the construction of the camp at Kermanshah. Meanwhile news of the project had led Sir R. Bullard (a) to write a personal letter to Mr. Eden on November 19. He said that the Iranians wanted to postpone all talk of oil concessions until foreign troops had left the country. This was their wish because, as long as there were Russian troops in the north, Iranian police and troops could be brow-beaten or excluded, sympathisers with Russia encouraged to violence, food supplies for the capital held up and other forms of pressure applied. Our political interest was that foreign troops should leave Iran as soon as possible, but in our military interests we had decided to keep troops in the oil area until the defeat of Japan. As long as British troops remained in the south Russian troops were not likely to leave the north.

Sir R. Bullard pointed out that the force needed to protect the refineries and oilfields was not large but had to be spread over a large area. The Russians would then probably keep troops in a large area, e.g. all Azerbaijan. If a camp were built at Kermanshah, the Russians would retain something as an offset, e.g. Meshed and Khorassan. Even after the defeat of Germany, therefore, Great Britain and Russia would be retaining troops in a large area. Sir R. Bullard pointed out that it would be a great gain to Iran if even Teheran were evacuated, since the Iranian Government would be less exposed to direct pressure. On the other hand, as long as large quantities of aviation spirit for Russia from Abadan had to go by rail through Iran, the railway would still have to be controlled by the Allies and guarded as far as Teheran by the British. This control probably meant the retention of British and Russian troops in Teheran. Hence, if Russia joined the war against Japan, and if we had to continue the supply of aviation spirit through Iran, we should be unable to withdraw British troops to the south. Sir R. Bullard commented: 'What luck the Russians have! The more we help them, the greater their chance of strangling Iran.' He thought that as far as military interests permitted we ought to reduce to the smallest limits and as soon as possible the area occupied by troops

(a) E7549/260/34.

in the hope that Russia would follow our example. Mr. Eden agreed.[1]
He noted that: 'The military will stay for ever in Iran if they can
but we want to get them and the Russians out.'

In December Sir R. Bullard reported continuation of work on (a)
three airfields in east Iran might have aroused Soviet suspicion. He
said: 'However mistaken and even dishonest Soviet accusations in
such matters may be, we should consider seriously all possible causes
of suspicion with a view to their elimination or diminution wherever
possible.' Mr. Eden again agreed.

The Foreign Office thought that the question of closing the Iranian
route was largely a technical one involving such points as: (a) the
ability of Russian Black Sea ports to handle all cargo then being
shipped from America via the Persian Gulf. (b) The possibility of
supplying Russia with aviation fuel from some other source than
Abadan, or alternatively of supplying tankers to ship the oil from
Abadan to the Black Sea instead of sending it across Iran by
railway. (c) The possibility of diverting American cargo from
Russian ports in the Far East if Russia came into the war against
Japan. On December 11, therefore, the Foreign Office sent a note
on the subject to the Allied Supplies Executive.[2]

After making interdepartmental enquiries, the Allied Supplies
Executive agreed on January 2, 1945, that oil supplies to Russia (b)
from Abadan could not be diverted to the Black Sea route until the
end of June 1945, and that there was no hope of closing the Iranian
route before that date; that no new commitment to supply oil to
Russia from Abadan should be made without prior consideration of
the withdrawal of troops from the transport route.

The Chiefs of Staff confirmed the view that the need to protect (c)
the oil area would require British troops to remain in south and west
Iran until the end of the war with Japan. They agreed with the
Foreign Office on a policy of mutual withdrawal *pari passu* with the
Russians as soon as aid to Russia over the Iranian route had ceased.
In that event British troops should be withdrawn to the south
Iranian oilfields, but retention of the Kermanshah camp was
essential in view of the climate of the south Iranian plain.[3]

---

[1] Mr. Eden had written on an earlier telegram from Sir R. Bullard in the same sense: (d)
'For what purpose do we keep troops in Iran? Presumably only in order to protect
Russian supplies going through. If so, mightn't we suggest some mutual withdrawal?'

[2] i.e. the ministerial committee responsible for all questions of Allied supplies to Russia.

[3] Towards the end of January 1945, the Foreign Office asked the General Manager of (e)
the Anglo-Iranian Oil Company at Abadan, Mr. Pattinson, privately by Mr. Baxter for
his view on the need to keep British troops in the oilfields area until the end of the war
with Japan. Mr. Pattinson thought that the important thing was not when British troops
left but how the withdrawal was arranged. He suggested a period of six months or more

(continued on page 466)

(a) E7717/189/34. (b) ASE(45)1; E125/103/34. (c) E398/103/34. (d) E7088/189/34.
(e) E398, 856/103/34.

(a)   Meanwhile on December 19 Mr. Churchill, in view of the general
difficulties with the Russians, had written to Mr. Eden that we
ought not to withdraw the British garrison from Iran. He thought
that there were so many questions unsettled: 'It is easy to go and
hard to return.' Mr. Eden replied on January 1 that there was no

(b) immediate question of withdrawal. The problem was to get the
Russians out of Iran; we should withdraw only *pari passu* with them.
Subject to Russian reciprocation Mr. Eden had in mind a withdrawal in two stages, namely withdrawal from forward positions to
the oil area in the south as soon as the supply route closed, probably
in not less than six months' time, and a final withdrawal from Iran
when military conditions allowed but in any case not later than the
end of the treaty period. Mr. Eden referred to the danger of a permanent Russian hold on the north. He said that Sir R. Bullard
wanted the Iranian Government to reassert its authority as soon as
possible; the first condition of this was that the area occupied by
Russian troops should be reduced and that they should leave
Teheran. Mr. Eden therefore thought that we should propose to the
Soviet Government withdrawal *pari passu* from certain areas of
which Teheran would be the first.

Mr. Eden said that he saw only two alternatives for Iran. Either
we and the Russians must agree to keep out and leave the Iranians
free to run their country for themselves, or else there would be some
form of partition or division of Iran into spheres of influence as in
1907. The first alternative was the right one for us, and alone
accorded with the Anglo-Russian undertakings to respect Iranian
independence. The second alternative would involve an indefinite
military commitment, constant friction with the Iranians and
Russians, and American criticism. We should also be at a disadvantage since the Russians would always be in a better position
to exert strong pressure on Iran.

(c)   Mr. Churchill replied on January 2 that he did not object to
withdrawal *pari passu* with the Russians, but doubted if they would
agree. He thought that there was no harm in raising the point. The

(d) Foreign Office subsequently informed Sir R. Bullard that withdrawal must be carried out *pari passu* with the Russians. They did
not favour even a partial withdrawal as a gesture in the hope that
the Russians might follow our example.

(*continued*)
during which Iranian and British troops should remain in the area side by side. There
should be no sudden withdrawal of British troops, leaving no one capable of keeping
order.

(a) M1233/4, E103/103/34.   (b) PM/45/3, E103/103/34.   (c) M13/5, E103/103/34.
(d) E246/103/34.

(iv)

British proposals for the discussion of the Iranian question at the Yalta Conference: Russian attitude at the Conference (January–February 1945).

At the end of 1944 the Foreign Office had given up hope of real Russian collaboration in Iran. They expected indeed that, in view of the refusal of their demands for an oil concession, the Russians would now try to undermine the position of the Anglo-Iranian Oil Company, and also that, having failed to secure political control in the north by economic measures, they would do all they could to weaken Iranian authority and establish their own protégés (the Tudeh party) while their troops were still in Iran. Hence, as earlier, the Foreign Office were most anxious to secure the withdrawal of all foreign forces from Iran. Meanwhile they considered it desirable to get the Americans to join them in raising the question of Iran at the forthcoming conference of Heads of Governments.

On January 14 Mr. Eden suggested to the Prime Minister that he (a) should send a message to this effect to the President. Mr. Eden explained that in the last month the situation in Iran had not suddenly deteriorated, but that the Russians had asked for the amendment of the oil concession bill and the suppression of several Iranian newspapers which had criticised the Russian demands. Unless we made it clear that Iranian independence was an important British interest, we were much more likely to have trouble later with the Russians. Mr. Eden proposed a message to the President suggesting that the British and American Governments should tell the Russians now that they intended to raise the matter at the forthcoming conference. The Prime Minister sent a message on these lines to the President. (b)

On January 16 the Iranian Ambassador told Sir A. Cadogan that (c) Russian pressure in northern Iran was increasing. The Russians refused to allow any Iranian armed forces to enter their zone and terrorised the population into making demonstrations. They were also demanding the repeal of the oil concession bill. The Ambassador asked whether the British Government would put the Iranian case at the Conference, and try to secure that Russian policy should conform to the treaty and the Teheran declaration. Sir A. Cadogan said that we should probably raise the question at the Conference. The Shah also sent a message asking whether three points could be discussed: (d) (i) the independence and integrity of Iran and the behaviour of the Russians in the north; (ii) the right of Iran to postpone discussion

---

(a) PM/45/26, E438/20/34. (b) T97/5, No. 890 (Churchill Papers/237; E438/20/34). (c) E482/20/34 (d) E568/20/34.

of oil concessions until the departure of foreign troops; (iii) the evacuation of troops, especially the immediate evacuation of
(a) Teheran. Sir R. Bullard again warned the Foreign Office that, as long as British troops remained in the oil area, there was no hope of saving the Iranians from the cumulative and already disastrous effects of Russian occupation. If Russian troops remained until the end of the war with Japan, the authority of the Iranian Government would probably disintegrate completely, and we might lose the use of the oilfields permanently.

(b)   The Foreign Office prepared a brief on Iran for the British representatives at the Yalta Conference. They pointed out that the Soviet Government were maintaining pressure on the Iranians over the oil question. If the Russians succeeded in coercing the Iranians, they would have taken a long step towards establishing a zone in northern Iran which would remain indefinitely under their control. Our interest required us to prevent the establishment of such a zone, or any other permanent sphere of influence in Iran.

We would need American support if we were to move the Russians. We should therefore base our case on the joint guarantees of Iranian independence in the treaty and declaration, which safeguarded Iranian rights and British and Allied interests. We should also argue that the moral position of the Great Powers would be undermined in other questions such as those concerned with the World Organisation unless they honoured specific undertakings. Apart from certain limitations laid down in the treaty the Iranian Government should be free to take their own decisions. Otherwise competitive interference in Iranian internal politics would develop, to the embarrassment of inter-Allied relations and with a disastrous effect on Iran herself. Such interference if prolonged might lead to a return to spheres of influence, involving constant friction with the Russians, a heavy British military commitment and a breach of all the Allies' pledges to the Iranians. A self-denying ordinance by the three Powers to refrain from interference in Iranian affairs was the only alternative to a series of international complications.

The Foreign Office suggested that the Russians should agree not to bring forward the oil question until the withdrawal of troops from Iran. We might agree in return that the future exploitation of Iranian oil resources, not already covered by existing concessions, should be the subject of discussions with the Iranian Government, if they were willing to hold them, after the withdrawal of troops.

(c)   The Foreign Office thought that the Iranian question could be linked with the proposals for a veto on the Security Council. They could point out to the Americans, and later to the Russians, that the

---

(a) E744/103/34.   (b) E1101/103/34; E2497/103/34.   (c) E2497/103/34.

widespread dislike of a Great Power veto would be dangerously increased if in the first test case of Iran, one of the three Powers was seen to be breaking specific obligations in its private interest and the other two to be making no effective protest. The Foreign Office suggested that we should not meet Stalin fully over the veto until he agreed to stop putting pressure on Iran. Sir A. Cadogan, however, pointed out that this proposal would mean giving way to the Russians over the veto in exchange for evidence of Russian good intentions for the moment. He hoped that we should agree to the veto only in the last resort, and that in exchange we should at the least get the Russians to withdraw their demand for participation in the World Organisation of their sixteen republics. On January 25 Mr. Eden minuted that he agreed with Sir A. Cadogan, except that he would regard giving way to the Russian thesis over the veto as near to a calamity and would fight very hard to prevent it. Mr. Eden continued: 'If I got my way over Poland and Iran and Sir A. Cadogan's condition above, I might consider it. I pray, but I don't expect, that we shall be really firm in negotiation with Russia this time. America in particular has a strong hand, if she will play it well, for Russia has much need of her.'

At his first conversation with Mr. Stettinius on February 1, Mr. (a) Eden raised the question of Iran. He said that it was essential to maintain the independence of the country against Russian threats, mainly in connexion with the oil dispute. He suggested an Anglo-Russian withdrawal of troops *pari passu* after the supply route through Iran was no longer needed (possibly about June 1945).[1]

The United States delegation agreed that a default by the three Powers on their undertakings to Iran would have repercussions elsewhere and that the two delegations should try to get the Russians to agree to a withdrawal *pari passu* of the foreign troops in Iran, and also to admit that the Iranian Government were entitled to decline to negotiate oil concessions as long as these troops were in the country.

At the third plenary meeting of the Yalta Conference on February (b) 7 the question of Iran was referred, at Mr. Churchill's suggestion, to the Foreign Secretaries. The Foreign Secretaries considered the question next day. Mr. Eden mentioned the Teheran declaration and the treaty and pointed out that, apart from engagements under these documents, the Iranians should be free to take their own decisions; otherwise the Great Powers might become involved in

---

[1] Mr. Eden made a reservation, however, that British troops might be needed after that date for the protection of the oilfields in south Iran.

(a) WP(45)157; U1688/888/70; E1063/103/34. (b) WP(45)157; E1102/103/34.

competitive interference in Iranian affairs. Mr. Eden suggested a self-denying agreement by each of the Powers to refrain from interference in Iran.

He then said that Great Britain did not wish to prevent the Russians from getting oil from northern Iran, for which Russia was the natural market, or to raise any obstacle in the way of a Russian concession if the Iranians were willing to grant it. He suggested that the three Powers should agree to leave the question until the withdrawal of their troops. He went on to suggest that they should make a statement that they would start withdrawing earlier than the final date in the treaty and as soon as the supply route to Russia was closed.

M. Molotov then gave a summary of the Russian oil negotiations. He pointed out that the Iranians would benefit economically by granting a concession to the Russians. M. Kavtaradze had now left Iran. There were no negotiations in progress with the Iranians, but the Soviet Government might resume them later. The problem was not acute, and there was no need for a self-denying agreement. Russia had no intention of disturbing the British concession. As for the withdrawal of troops, they could act only in accordance with the treaty; if the treaty needed alteration, they would have to study the matter.

Mr. Stettinius said that the United States Government had not signed any treaty with Iran during the war. Certain American oil companies had been negotiating at the same time as the Russians, and their negotiations had been cut short. He supported Mr. Eden's statement about the withdrawal of troops, and said that the only reason for the presence of American troops was to serve Russian interests by the transport of military supplies. As for oil, he was content that negotiations should not be resumed until after the end of the war.

Mr. Eden repeated that His Majesty's Government did not oppose the negotiation by Russia of an oil concession in Iran. Mr. Stettinius said that the United States Government held a similar view. Mr. Eden said that negotiations for another British concession had been proceeding before the Russian negotiations had begun, and that they had also come to an end as a result of the decision of the Majlis. He again suggested a statement to reassure the Iranians and make negotiations for concessions easier. M. Molotov thought that the meeting should limit itself to an exchange of views, and that the matter was not urgent.

(a)   Mr. Eden later prepared a draft statement which he submitted to the other Foreign Secretaries on February 9. Mr. Stettinius said

---

(a) WP(45)157; E1290/103/34.

that the statement was acceptable to the United States Government. M. Molotov said that he had not yet had an opportunity of looking at it, but would discuss it later.

At a meeting of the Foreign Secretaries the next day, Mr. Eden asked whether M. Molotov had considered the statement for inclusion in the final communiqué of the Conference. M. Molotov thought that it was undesirable to make any reference to Iran in the communiqué. He did not support a proposal by Mr. Stettinius that the communiqué should say that Iranian problems had been discussed and the situation clarified. He also objected to a proposal by Mr. Eden that they might say that Iranian problems had been examined and the Teheran declaration reaffirmed.

Mr. Eden told the Prime Minister on February 10 that the Foreign (a) Secretaries had not agreed, although Mr. Stettinius had supported the British proposals. Mr. Eden asked the Prime Minister, when the question of Iran came up at the plenary meeting on that day, to say that we were concerned at the situation in view of Russian pressure on the Iranian Government. We wished to record the great importance of adhering to the terms of the treaty and declaration. Mr. Eden suggested that Mr. Churchill might ask that the British and American military representatives in Moscow should begin to examine with the Russians the problem of withdrawal of troops.

On February 11 the Prime Minister and Mr. Eden discussed Iran (b) with Stalin and M. Molotov. Mr. Churchill spoke in accordance with Mr. Eden's suggestions. The Russians repeated that they had no intention of putting pressure on the Iranians and that they stood by the treaty and declaration. They refused further discussion of Iran at the Conference. They also refused to agree to preliminary discussion of the withdrawal of Allied forces from Iran.

The confidential protocol of the Conference merely stated that the (c) situation in Iran had been discussed, and that it had been agreed to pursue the question through diplomatic channels. Mr. Eden thought that this meagre result was disappointing, but that at least the Russians were aware of our strong views on Iran.[1]

---

[1] Mr. Hankey of the British delegation wrote to the Foreign Office on February 11: (d)

'. . . My own feeling is that Molotov knows he stuck his foot in it badly last autumn and got a bad rebuff and is genuinely afraid of being taken further to task. Stalin, talking to the Secretary of State, was rather jocular about Molotov's sensitiveness on the subject and said that, when he spoke to him about Iran, he was sometimes almost in a "frenzy!" However, I am afraid that, in spite of the asseverations both of Stalin and Molotov, that they did not intend to make trouble in Iran, I do not feel any confidence on this topic.

It is satisfactory that Molotov should have disclaimed any intention of challenging the position of the A.I.O.C. You will, however, see that he suggested that the Iranian Government might change their opinion again about the Russian oil concession and

(*continued on page 472*)

(a) PM(A)17, E1102/103/34. (b) E1064/103/34. (c) WP(45)157. (d) E1102/103/34.

(v)

*Further Russian interference in Iranian affairs: Foreign Office disagreement
with the Chiefs of Staff on the withdrawal of British troops: discussion of
Iranian questions at the Potsdam Conference: Russian agreement to the
withdrawal of troops from Teheran (April–August 1945).*

(a)   For a short time after the Yalta Conference there was a slight
improvement in the Russian attitude towards Iran. Nevertheless
Russian aims seemed unchanged and early in April the Foreign
(b) Office had to consider what they could do to meet a renewal of
pressure on the Iranian Government. The Russians had shown in
Poland, Bulgaria and Roumania their methods of dealing with a
government which they wished to destroy. They alleged that this
Government was unable to keep order, and that the resulting disorder was a threat to Soviet security, and also that the Government
was 'fascist' and should be replaced by a 'democratic' Government
which would represent the will of the people or, in M. Vyshinsky's
words, 'give their efforts to the service of the people'. On such
pretexts the Russians might claim that their interests were threatened
by disorders in Azerbaijan or even in Teheran, and that the Iranian
Government was 'fascist'. The Foreign Office were aware that this
Government did not in fact represent public opinion; a Russian-
sponsored Government would be less representative and not more
effective in promoting the welfare of the people.

If the Russians tried shock tactics, as in Roumania, the Foreign
Office thought that we should make immediate representations, and
disprove any claim that the Russian nominees represented the
'democratic forces' of the country. We should have ready a list of
the most important cases in which the Russians had made it impossible for the Iranian Government to keep order by preventing
Iranian troop movements, restricting the numbers of police and
gendarmerie and interfering with their work. We should also secure
publicity for the Iranian case, and prevent the Russians from stopping critical messages from press correspondents. Meanwhile we

---

(continued)

that he also stated that the Majlis "decision" was not a "genuine one". I tried to get
this controverted at a high level but it did not seem to be possible as so many other
major questions were being discussed. . . .

It was unfortunate that the Iranian question hung fire till towards the end of the
conference and only really became active on the last day, but the statesmen were
naturally interested first of all in the future of Germany, reparations, the World
Organisation and other questions of absolutely major importance. However, I think
we showed a red light, which was what we principally set out to do, and the Americans
supported us most satisfactorily.'

(a) E1801/103/34.   (b) E2318/20/34.

should continue to impress upon the Shah and his Ministers that they should introduce measures of social reform.

In the Foreign Office view the only real safeguard for the Iranians would be the withdrawal of foreign troops. Hence, as earlier, the Foreign Office were most disquieted at the unwillingness of the British military authorities to agree to a rapid withdrawal of the British forces in the south. On May 19, 1945, the Iranian Government (a) sent notes to the British, Russian and United States Governments asking for the withdrawal of Allied troops from their country. Mr. Eden (b) told the Prime Minister on June 1 that he had proposed to the Russians on May 30 that Allied troops should start withdrawing *pari passu* and in stages before the final treaty date. He now wanted to make a public statement in the House of Commons on June 6 offering to withdraw British troops entirely before the final treaty date provided that all other foreign troops were withdrawn at the same time. He wished to add that the British Government were prepared, if the Soviet and United States Governments would do the same, to make an immediate start by withdrawing British troops from Teheran. There was, however, a difficulty about announcing that the British Government were prepared to withdraw their troops entirely from Iran, because the Chiefs of Staff wanted to retain troops in the oil area of south-west Iran until the end of the war with Japan. They also wanted to provide for these troops summer stations near Kermanshah.

Mr. Eden said that if British troops were retained in such a large area the Russians would insist on keeping troops in an equivalent area in the north. They could then continue their interference in Iranian internal affairs. Mr. Eden thought that it was more important to get the Russians out of northern Iran than to keep a few British troops in the south guarding the oilfields; the Iranian army could perform this latter task. Mr. Eden asked whether the Chiefs of Staff could reconsider the problem as a matter of urgency. Mr. Churchill agreed with Mr. Eden and referred the question to the Chiefs of (c) Staff. They replied on June 4 that they were aware of the political advantages of withdrawal, and would not advise keeping any British troops in Iran if they were sure that an interruption of oil supplies would not affect operations against Japan. They were urgently examining the problem and asked meanwhile that proposals for withdrawal should have no publicity.

Mr. Law brought the matter again to the attention of the Prime (d) Minister on June 5. He said that Mr. Eden and Sir R. Bullard would be greatly concerned if it were not possible to make a statement

---

(a) E3211, 3499, 3735/103/34; E3420/103/34. (b) E3499, 3735/103/34; PM/45/218, E3935/103/34. (c) E3936/103/34. (d) PM/45/237, E3935/103/34.

even about immediate withdrawal from Teheran. The Prime Minister, however, was unwilling to overrule the Chiefs of Staff.

(a)   On June 6 the Chiefs of Staff gave their view that it would be unwise to withdraw all British forces during the war against Japan unless other means were found to protect the oil installations against sabotage and damage by bandits. The Chiefs of Staff had therefore asked the War Office whether protection could be provided by a non-military police force under British officers but nominally under Iranian control. Meanwhile they asked again that any public announcement of a proposed withdrawal policy should be deferred.

On June 15 the Foreign Office took up the question with the War Office. They said that they agreed with Sir R. Bullard's view that all foreign troops should leave Teheran as soon as possible, and pointed out that on June 30 the transfer of the southern section of (b) the railway to the Iranian State Railways was due to be completed. On June 20 the Chiefs of Staff agreed to the withdrawal of British troops from Teheran.

Mr. Eden continued to think that we should make as soon as possible a public offer to withdraw all our forces before the treaty (c) date. Sir A. Cadogan therefore raised the matter again with the Prime Minister on July 5. He said that the subject of troop withdrawals from Iran was on the agenda of the Potsdam Conference. The Foreign Office wanted to take the opportunity of raising the matter with the Russians, who had not yet replied to the British proposal that Allied troops should start withdrawing *pari passu* and in stages before the final treaty date. Sir A. Cadogan said that the Chiefs of Staff were ready to withdraw the British troops from Teheran. They were, however, still unwilling to agree to evacuation of the oil areas before the end of the war with Japan, or to give up certain camps used as summer stations in areas far north of the oilfields near Kermanshah. Sir A. Cadogan explained that in order to get the Russians out of northern Iran the Foreign Office favoured complete withdrawal of all Allied forces from the country, including the oilfields area, as soon as possible. Even if British troops had to be kept in the south a little longer, we should withdraw from the rest of Iran, including the summer camps at Kermanshah. Sir A. Cadogan asked the Prime Minister to direct the Service Departments to make their plans on the assumption that, even if total withdrawal were not decided on, the policy of His Majesty's Government might make it necessary for them to withdraw their forces at short notice from all parts of Iran outside the oil area.

On July 13 Mr. Eden also sent a minute to the Prime Minister. The Chiefs of Staff had meanwhile agreed with the War Office that

---

(a) E3937/103/34. (b) E4361/103/34. (c) PM/45/316, E4438/103/34.

it was militarily undesirable that British and Indian forces should (a) be withdrawn from the oilfields at least until the end of the war with Japan. Mr. Eden repeated that the Russians hold on Iran was (b) becoming tighter, and that the remedy was to secure a complete withdrawal of Russian forces as soon as possible. We could do this only if we were prepared to offer complete withdrawal of British forces. Mr. Eden said that he wanted to settle the matter at Potsdam by an offer of complete joint withdrawal in three stages: (i) complete withdrawal from Teheran at once; (ii) British withdrawal from Iran except Abadan and the oilfields area in return for Russian withdrawal from Iran except for a zone in the north; (iii) complete withdrawal by both Powers. Mr. Eden pointed out that the Chiefs of Staff were not ready to carry out any of these proposals. They were prepared to withdraw a battalion stationed at Teheran, but wanted to keep a headquarters there to supervise the disposal of assets. They wanted to retain summer camps near Kermanshah, and were not willing to leave the protection of the oilfields to the Iranians. Mr. Eden thought that there was much more risk to the oilfields if we failed to get the Russians out of the country than in leaving their protection, as in the past, to the Iranians.

On July 19 Mr. Eden sent another minute to the Prime Minister. (c) He pointed out that the Chiefs of Staff had greatly exaggerated a possible danger to the security of the oilfields after the withdrawal of British troops. He also told the Prime Minister that he wanted to circulate to the Conference a paper on proposals for withdrawal in three stages. The Prime Minister replied on July 20: 'By all means (d) circulate your paper.'

Mr. Eden's insistence had been due to further reports (which he sent to the Prime Minister) from Sir R. Bullard in July that the (e) Russians were making a 'tremendous effort' to obtain control over Iran before the withdrawal of their troops. They were attacking the Iranian Government in the Soviet press, and over Radio Teheran; the newspapers under their control in Teheran were openly anti-British in their propaganda. A strong Russian trade union delegation had come to Teheran to support the Tudeh party in stirring up industrial unrest. Tudeh party agents were at work in the villages in the north and north-west; if they were not accompanied by Russian soldiers, these soldiers often happened to be in the neighbourhood. The opposition was too much frightened to act. In parts of northern Kurdistan, where they would not allow the Iranians to send troops, the Russians were encouraging a Kurdish independence movement.

(a) COS(45)460(o); COS1009/5, E5232/103/34. (b) PM/45/326, E5238/103/34. (c) COS(45)460(o); PM/45/4T, E5908/103/34. (d) M(Ter)8/5, E5330, 5908/103/34; COS(Term.) 6th meeting. (e) E5045/20/34.

Sir R. Bullard did not think that the Russians would try a violent *coup* against the Iranian Government; they would force their candidates on the electorate and secure the dominance, if not a majority control, of the Majlis by the Tudeh party. Sir R. Bullard repeated that the withdrawal of the foreign troops from a large part of Iran would have an excellent effect; even a withdrawal from Teheran would encourage the Iranians. If the Russians refused to leave Teheran, a British withdrawal would nonetheless be desirable, since it would be difficult for the Russians to convince public opinion of the genuineness of elections in the areas under their military control.

On July 15 the United States delegation to the Potsdam Conference gave the British delegation a copy of their brief on Iran,
(a) dated June 23. This brief stated that the Commanding General, Persian Gulf Command, had publicly announced the termination of his mission as from June 1, and that the withdrawal of American forces had begun several months earlier. The United States Government had replied to that effect to the Iranian note of May 19, and had given assurances that withdrawal would continue as rapidly as military exigencies allowed. In order to help restore Iranian administrative control and to reduce the dangers of Allied friction over Iran, the American delegation were instructed to favour the withdrawal of all forces not needed for the war against Japan. If the Russians were unwilling to agree to withdraw their forces in view of the continued presence of American and British forces, the American delegation would propose that the British and Russian Governments agree to the progressive reduction *pari passu* of their forces both as regards numbers and the areas occupied.

At the opening of the Potsdam Conference, the British Govern-
(b) ment's list of subjects for discussion included 'the mutual withdrawal of troops' from Iran. Iran was not among the subjects mentioned either by President Truman or Stalin at the first plenary meeting, but
(c) on July 21 the British delegation submitted a memorandum on their proposals for a withdrawal of Allied forces in three stages. Mr. Churchill referred to this memorandum at the seventh plenary
(d) meeting of the conference on July 23. He asked the views of his colleagues on the proposals. Stalin said that the proposals seemed to be based on the assumption that the period during which Allied forces might remain in Iran by virtue of the treaty had already expired. The Soviet view was that it had not yet expired and would not do so until after the end of the war with Japan. Nevertheless the Soviet Government accepted the proposal in the British memorandum that Allied forces should be withdrawn from Iran *pari passu*

(a) E5405/103/34; F.O. Potsdam archives 15(1). (b) P(Terminal)1. (c) P(Terminal) 16. (d) P(Terminal) 7th meeting.

and in stages before the final treaty date was reached. They agreed further that the first of three stages proposed by the British delegation —the withdrawal of British and Soviet forces from Teheran—should begin at once.

Mr. Churchill said that the British Government had been anxious to secure agreement that the two further stages should follow immediately upon the first, so that the whole operation could be completed within the treaty time-limit. They had assured the Iranian Government that British troops would be withdrawn after the end of the war with Germany. More than two months had passed since this event, and the British Government wished not only to carry out the first stage of withdrawal but also to agree on the second and third stages. The whole process might then take place in an orderly manner within the treaty time-limit. Stalin, however, refused to commit himself to anything more than immediate withdrawal from Teheran. He said that the treaty time-limit was still some way ahead, and that the proposals for further withdrawals could be considered later on. Mr. Churchill suggested that the Conference should approve immediate withdrawal from Teheran and should agree that the further stages of withdrawal should be considered at the first meeting of the Council of Foreign Ministers to be held in London in September 1945.

Stalin accepted this suggestion. Mr. Truman also agreed to the proposal. He said that the United States Government did not propose to delay the withdrawal of all their troops from Iran, since these troops were needed elsewhere for the war against Japan. The withdrawal of all American forces in Iran might be completed within sixty days. Stalin said that in case the United States Government had any anxieties on the point, he would assure the President that Russia had no intention of taking action against Iran.

On July 25 Sir R. Bullard was informed of this decision. He was (a) instructed to get in touch at once with the Soviet Ambassador and, as soon as the latter had received the necessary instructions, to arrange for simultaneous notification to the Iranian Government of the decision to withdraw from Teheran. Sir R. Bullard reported that the news that Teheran was to be evacuated was obviously (b) unwelcome to the Soviet Ambassador. The Foreign Office let the Soviet Government know that, whether or not the Soviet Ambassador received similar instructions, Sir R. Bullard would shortly inform the Iranian Government of the decision. Sir R. Bullard was instructed to do so not later than August 2.

When Sir R. Bullard made an oral communication to the Iranian (c) Minister for Foreign Affairs on August 2, the Soviet Ambassador

---

(a) E5482/103/34. (b) E5531, 5576/103/34. (c) E5693/103/34.

had still received no instructions and the United States Ambassador
(a) had not heard from his Government. The Minister for Foreign
Affairs said that he had hoped for much more than the evacuation
of Teheran. On the other hand the Shah appeared to be satisfied.
On August 8 the Foreign Office asked Sir A. Clark Kerr to inform
the Soviet Government that they had already instructed Sir R.
Bullard to discuss details of withdrawal from Teheran with his
Soviet colleague. Sir A. Clark Kerr was to ask that similar instruc-
(b) tions be sent to the Soviet Ambassador in Teheran as soon as possible.
The Soviet Ambassador finally took action on August 9.

(a) E5721, 5791/103/34.   (b) E5825/6511/34.

CHAPTER LIX

British relations with China from the spring of 1941 to the Anglo-Chinese Treaty of January 11, 1943

(i)

Relations between Great Britain and China during 1941.

THROUGHOUT the year 1941 the Chinese under the leadership of General Chiang Kai-shek maintained what might be called a passive or at best a harassing resistance to the Japanese. There was, in fact, little fighting. Two American officers attached to the United States Military Mission to China[1] reported in November 1941 that they had observed no contact between Chinese and Japanese troops at the front, and that

'the interest of the Chinese towards any aggressive action seems quite negligible, regardless of their statements that all they need are airplanes, tanks and artillery in order to drive the aggressor from their shores.'[2]

In December one of these officers reported in even more disillusioned terms that

'the general idea in the United States that China has fought Japan to a standstill, and has had many glorious victories, is a delusion. Japan has generally been able to push forward any plan she wanted to. . . . The will to fight an aggressive action does not yet exist in the Chinese army. . . . This attitude is being changed by diplomatic persuasion from without, but it will require well-directed propaganda from within to give the proper mental attitude to the soldiers who are to do the fighting.'

Even more ominously, the American observer continued:

'Many small things all pointing in the same direction have caused me to have a feeling, stronger than a suspicion, that the desire of the Chinese for more modern *matériel* was not, before December 8, for the purpose of pressing the war against Japan, but was to make the Central Government safe against insurrection after diplomatic pressure by other nations had forced Japan out of China.'[3]

---

[1] See below, p. 484, note 1.

[2] F. Romanus and R. Sunderland, *Stilwell's Mission to China* (United States Army in World War II), p. 36.

[3] *Id.*, pp. 43–4. In the early part of 1941 the staff and a large number of disabled men (a)

(*continued on page 480*)

(a) F4787/3653/10.

The administrative incompetence and corruption of the Chinese Government had indeed destroyed disinterested loyalty to it, although General Chiang Kai-shek himself retained wide personal support. American experts reporting in August 1941 on the inefficiency, waste and delays affecting traffic on the Burma Road made recommendations which the Chinese authorities largely ignored. The general situation in the areas still under the control of the Chinese Government continued to get worse. Sir O. Niemeyer of the Bank of England, who went to China in September 1941 at the request of the British Government to advise on the economic and financial situation, reported at the beginning of December that (a) there was little chance of improvement during the war. Ministers and officials were incompetent to deal with problems of administrative reform. Internal forces were out of control and foreign help such as the export credits and stabilisation loans provided at the end of 1940[1] or the grants in 1941 under Lend-Lease, were stopgaps unrelated to a general scheme accompanied by proposals for reform. In any case the Japanese had been cutting off, one by one, the routes by which supplies could be brought into the country. Lend-Lease material, for example, was accumulating at Rangoon during the autumn of 1941 to an extent likely to prove dangerous in the event of war between Great Britain and Japan.

Chinese morale, such as it was, was supported throughout the year largely by the expectation that Great Britain and the United States would become involved in war with Japan. Hence the Chinese were disappointed and discouraged by the Anglo-American policy of avoiding extreme provocation of Japan. They had also been alarmed by the Japanese-Soviet pact of April 13, 1941, since it seemed possible that the Soviet Government would cut off supplies, already meagre enough, to China. In this respect the fears of the Chinese were for the time unfounded, but, until the German attack on Russia, there was a possibility that German pressure would compel the Russians to change their policy towards China. German propaganda at the time of the Japanese-Soviet pact also spread

---

(*continued*)
of the so-called New Fourth Army, which was predominantly Communist, were reported to have been killed by Government troops while crossing the Yangtze.

In February 1942 Brigadier General J. A. Magruder, Chief of the U.S. Military Mission to China, reported in equally strong terms about the lack of offensive action by the Chinese, and the danger to American war plans if they were based on the wildly exaggerated propaganda which influenced American opinion. *F.R.U.S.* 1942, China, pp. 13–15. The State Department thought General Magruder's indictment of Chinese military weakness went too far, but the United States Ambassador in Chungking agreed about the unwisdom of the American press in accepting Chinese reports of military victories. *Id.*, 24–5.

[1] See Vol. II, p. 117.

(a) F13300/1/10.

suspicion among the Chinese that Great Britain might desert them. These suspicions increased when Mr. Roosevelt made statements to the press on April 15 and 18, 1941, about aid to China, and no similar counter-move to the Russian pact came from London. On April 14, General Chiang Kai-shek had asked for a definite answer (a) as soon as possible to the question whether Great Britain would assist in the defence of Yunnan, if the Japanese attacked this province at a time when Great Britain and Japan were not at war. The question was connected with another Chinese proposal for an international air force of 500 aircraft to be manned by British and American pilots. The British Government had been willing to agree to this proposal, if it were accepted by the United States, to the extent of releasing for the purpose aircraft ordered by them in America, but, in view of the policy of averting war with Japan, they would not allow British subjects to volunteer for the international force.[1]

There was, however, no change in the general policy of giving as much help as was practicable to China. In order to reassure Chinese opinion, a statement to this effect was made in Parliament on May 14, 1941. Sir A. Clark Kerr was also instructed on May 10 to tell (b) General Chiang Kai-shek that the rumours of a British arrangement with Japan at Chinese expense were false. On the other hand, we could not undertake new commitments, such as the defence of Yunnan, in advance of an outbreak of war between Japan and Great Britain. We had to concentrate upon the Atlantic and the Mediterranean; the survival of China as well as of Great Britain depended upon the outcome of the fighting in these areas.

The message had some effect. General Chiang Kai-shek sent a (c) friendly answer to the Prime Minister on May 20, 1941, and the Prime Minister replied on May 24. The German attack on Russia brought hope to the Chinese of a great coalition of Russia, Great Britain, the United States and the Netherlands against Germany and Japan, but these distant prospects depended on the duration of Russian resistance, and in any case could provide no immediate relief to China. There might have been a temporary respite if the Japanese had taken the chance of attacking the Russian eastern armies, though this respite would have been paid for later in the event of a Russian collapse. Japanese caution, however, in resisting German pressure was of no immediate advantage to China since, if Japan did not move against Russia, she could safely concentrate her forces against the Chinese without the risk of Russian interference.

---

[1] The United States Government did not wish to be associated publicly with the plan, (d) but allowed the Chinese Government to recruit volunteers for it in the United States. In July 1941 a number of these American volunteers were allowed the use of British airfields in Burma.

(a) F3017/60/10. (b) F3796/60/10. (c) F4276/60/10. (d) F5325/145/10.

Even the prospects of a change in Japanese policy alarmed the Chinese, since they continued to be afraid that the United States and Great Britain might compromise at their expense.

At the beginning of July 1941 the Chinese Government broke off diplomatic relations with Germany and Italy, after these two Powers had recognised the puppet régime in Nanking. Mr. Eden stated in the House of Commons that this recognition of the Nanking régime would make no difference to British policy, and that we should (a) continue to do what we could to help China to maintain her independence. The Chinese Government were also informed that after the war we should be willing to negotiate the abolition of extra-territorial rights, the rendition of concessions and the revision of treaties with China on a basis of reciprocity and equality.

The Chinese Government approved the freezing of Japanese and Chinese assets after the entry of Japanese troops into Indo-China,[1] but this Japanese move increased Chinese fears of an attack on the (b) Burma Road. The Chinese Ambassador[2] asked Mr. Eden on July 25, 1941, whether we could give military help, especially in the air, if the Road were attacked. Mr. Eden said that the despatch of the Royal Air Force to fight Japanese aircraft attacking China would be an act of war on our part, and that the Japanese were likely to (c) attack Thailand rather than the Burma Road. On August 13 Dr. Koo brought another appeal from General Chiang Kai-shek about the International Air Force. General Chiang Kai-shek said that over a hundred American pilots and mechanics had already arrived in China or were in Burma on their way to China. He asked most urgently that we should allow the formation of a British volunteer squadron on similar lines.

Mr. Eden pointed out that, unlike the Americans, we were at war and could not spare any of our trained pilots. Dr. Koo said that General Chiang Kai-shek realised our position, but hoped that we could meet his request, since the psychological effect in China would be great. He also asked whether we could give air assistance from Malaya if the Japanese attacked the Chinese from northern Indo-China. Mr. Eden had to say once more that the employment of (d) the R.A.F. against the Japanese would mean war with Japan. Dr. Koo renewed his request later in the month and again on September 19. He then said that, although General Chiang Kai-shek understood why we were unable to co-operate with the International Air Force, he wondered whether we could not strengthen our own Air

---

[1] See Vol. II, pp. 139.
[2] Dr. Wellington Koo assumed charge of the Chinese Embassy in London on July 3, 1941.

(a) F9693/5163/10. (b) F6815/26/10. (c) F7768/145/10. (d) F8279/145/10.

Force in Burma and, if the Burma Road were attacked, transfer one or two squadrons to China in order to work with the American squadrons in the International Air Force. Mr. Eden said that we could not do this unless we were prepared to face war with Japan, since the Japanese would not accept the sudden transformation of a British squadron into a squadron of the International Air Force operating from British territory.

The Ambassador seemed to accept the answer as final. No more requests for help of this kind were made until the end of October. On October 30 General Chiang Kai-shek told Sir A. Clark Kerr (a) that he feared an early Japanese attack on Yunnan in order to cut the Burma Road. If the attack succeeded, the Chinese armies would be encircled and there would be an end of Chinese resistance. The General said that he could meet the Japanese on the ground, but that he had no means, other than the small International Air Force, of resisting them in the air and that without such means his armies must be defeated. Although he was sorry that he had to repeat an appeal which had been rejected, he felt bound to tell the British and United States Governments what was likely to happen if he did not secure immediate Anglo-American help in the form of a volunteer air force. He did not think that Japan would go to war with Great Britain or the United States as a consequence of this aid to China.

General Chiang Kai-shek sent a message to Mr. Churchill explain- (b) ing the reasons for his appeal. Mr. Churchill answered on November 11 that he too thought that south China might be the next Japanese objective; he was not certain, however, that the Japanese had decided to attack Kunming. He was therefore examining the possibility of strengthening the International Air Force. General Chiang Kai-shek also appealed to President Roosevelt. The President replied that the United States Government would give all possible help, and that the American Air Force in Manila was much stronger than the Japanese knew. In spite of these assurances, the American negotiations with Japan continued to cause disquiet in China. Moreover there had been a lack of detailed co-ordination between British and American aid to China. Sir A. Clark Kerr had pointed out in (c) August that although most of General Chiang Kai-shek's requests had been met, or were about to be met, in one way or another, there was still no concerted Anglo-American plan for dealing with Chinese needs. Sir A. Clark Kerr suggested the establishment of an Anglo-American-Chinese Committee in Washington (with a Russian member for the discussion of military questions) and a sub-committee in Chungking.

(a) F11674, 11702/145/10. (b) T778/1; T799/1, Churchill Papers/90; F11714, 12144/145/10. (c) F8415, 8652/145/10.

The Foreign Office thought that better co-ordination was necessary, but that the difficulty lay on the American side. We always informed the United States Government fully of our views and intentions on Far Eastern matters. It was not easy for them to treat us similarly, since they had to take care to avoid giving the impression that their policy was tied to or dictated by British policy. Hence they had often acted in important matters affecting our own or the Dutch position without previous warning or with the minimum warning necessary for us to take parallel action. We had had no knowledge, for example, of the despatch of a special American

(a) military mission[1] to China before an announcement in the press on August 27. It was thus difficult for us, when we were uncertain about American policy, to define our own Far Eastern policy. A further source of trouble was that American policy itself was often confused, because the President inclined to deal with General Chiang Kai-shek personally, without consulting either the State Department or the United States Ambassador at Chungking.

The disastrous opening to the Far Eastern war made general strategic planning more urgent. For many months after the surprise attack on Pearl Harbour the Americans had to remain on the defensive over most of the Pacific. The Japanese followed up their advantage by the capture of the islands of Guam and Wake and by an immediate attack on the Philippines. They began landings on the main island of Luzon on December 10 and entered Manila on January 3, 1942.[2] The Japanese also attacked Hong Kong. Here the small garrison of a few battalions had to withdraw to the island, after resisting for three days an invading force which had crossed from China into the leased Kowloon territory. Since there was no chance of relief by sea, the fall of the island was only a matter of time. The safety of Malaya itself was endangered by the sinking of the *Prince of Wales* (a new battleship) and the *Repulse* by Japanese shore-based aircraft on December 10.

Within a short time, therefore the military position had become

(b) extremely critical. General Chiang Kai-shek proposed a council at Chungking to advise on every aspect of the Allied war effort in the

---

[1] The American decision to send this mission had been taken in the latter part of July. The Chinese Government were told of the decision on August 20.

[2] The American garrisons had been in process of gradual withdrawal before 1939. American forces were due to leave in 1945 when the Philippines would have obtained full independence. The President of the Philippines, Manuel Quezon, had secured the services of General MacArthur, a former Chief of the United States Army Staff, to organise a defence force. General MacArthur had tried to make the defences of Luzon strong enough to hold out against invasion until the arrival of reinforcements, but he had not received sufficient war material to complete the work. The partly-trained Philippine army of 100,000 men had as yet little military value, and there were less than 20,000 American troops in the island, with about half this number of trained Philippine scouts.

(a) F8572/145/10.   (b) F13573, 13575/13540/23.

Far East. The Foreign Office agreed with the need for co-ordination of policy, but considered that until the question had been discussed with the Americans and the Dutch the best plan would be for General Chiang Kai-shek to exchange senior military officers with General Wavell, Commander-in-Chief in India. Meanwhile, Mr. Eden sent a message to General Chiang Kai-shek in answer to his proposal for an alliance. Mr. Eden referred to a statement by the (a) Prime Minister in the House of Commons on December 11 describing China as an ally.[1] He also reaffirmed the promises made by the British Government to give China all possible help in prosecuting the war, and said that we should consider with sympathy, in the light of the views of the other Governments concerned, the General's proposal for a military alliance between the British Empire, the United States, the U.S.S.R., the Netherlands and China.

The Foreign Office at this time did not wish Great Britain alone to be committed to an agreement with China not to sign a separate peace, since they were afraid that the Chinese Government might thereby have the power to be 'embarrassingly obstructive' (for example, on the question of Manchuria) in negotiating a peace settlement. They were also opposed to pressing the Soviet Government to declare war upon Japan, and thus to divert some of their strength from the war in the west. In any case the Soviet Government were unwilling to take the initiative against Japan. Stalin told General (b) Chiang Kai-shek that he had been obliged to draw largely upon men and material in Siberia, and that for the present he could not attack Japan. Sir A. Clark Kerr and Mr. Gauss, the United States (c) Ambassador at Chungking, thought that it was most desirable to sign a pact with China at once. The Allied defeats, and especially the situation at Hong Kong, were having a bad effect on Chinese morale. If the Burma Road were cut, and the Japanese then offered terms, General Chiang Kai-shek might find it hard to resist the defeatists, who were already saying that China had chosen the wrong side.[2]

The British and Americans were actually moving more quickly than General Chiang Kai-shek realised towards the co-ordination

---

[1] On the day of the Japanese aggression at Pearl Harbour Mr. Churchill sent a message (d) to General Chiang Kai-shek: 'The British Empire and the United States have been attacked by Japan. Always we have been friends: now we face a common enemy.' General Chiang Kai-shek replied on December 10 in similar terms.

[2] In the spring of 1941 a report which reached the Foreign Office had pointed out that (e) common hostility to the Communists might be a face-saving method whereby a defeatist party in China could come to terms with the Japanese.

(a) F13469, 13493/13469/10. (b) F13922/421/23. (c) F14155/13469/40. (d) WM(41) 125; F13498, 13566/13469/10; T936, 988/1, Churchill Papers/158. (e) F4787/3653/10.

(a) of plans. Mr. Roosevelt suggested to the Soviet Government and General Chiang Kai-shek on December 14 that each should call an inter-allied military conference to agree by December 20 on preliminary recommendations to prepare the way for common action. The President asked the British Government to hold a naval and military conference at Singapore and to invite Chinese and Dutch as well as Dominion representatives. This conference would also report by December 20. The War Cabinet accepted the plan, and instructed Mr. Duff Cooper, who had been appointed Resident Minister of Cabinet rank at Singapore for Far Eastern affairs, to call a conference at once.

The date of report was chosen by the President in order to enable him to have the recommendations before him in time for discussions which he was preparing to hold with Mr. Churchill. At these discussions the President and Mr. Churchill agreed to appoint General Wavell as Supreme Commander-in-Chief in the South-West Pacific area. They sent a message to General Chiang Kai-shek explaining General Wavell's appointment, and suggesting that General Chiang Kai-shek should himself assume the supreme command over the Chinese theatre of war. This theatre would include at first such parts of Thailand and Indo-China as might become accessible to troops of the Associated Powers.[1]

The American representatives at the staff talks were much concerned at the possibility of a weakening of the Chinese war effort. They therefore thought it desirable to increase the amount of assistance to China. They regarded the isolation of China and the general scarcity of munitions as the chief obstacle to a better utilisation of Chinese resources.[2] They proposed to suggest to General Chiang Kai-shek measures for improving communications on the Burma Road, and for closer collaboration in China with the American military officers.

These arrangements were put forward at a time when the full measure of the Japanese attack was not realised. The British and American view was that the defeat of Germany should be the prior objective, but there was still hope of holding Singapore and Rangoon and the Dutch East Indies, if not the Philippines. There was also some expectation that the Russians would attack the Japanese in March or April, if the Japanese had not earlier taken the initiative against them.

---

[1] Burma was excluded from General Chiang Kai-shek's area of supreme command.
[2] Mr. Churchill considered that the President, and American opinion generally, greatly overestimated the contribution which the Chinese could make to the 'general war'.

(a) F13672/13549/23.

(ii)

Chinese reactions to the Allied losses in the Far East: General Wavell's visit to Chungking: General Chiang Kai-shek's visit to India (December 22, 1941–March 6, 1942).

As a further response to General Chiang Kai-shek's desire for closer co-operation, General Wavell had already been instructed to (a) visit Chungking. He reached there on December 22 with Major-General Brett, Chief of the Air Corps of the United States Army. General Chiang Kai-shek outlined to them proposals for discussions (b) about combined Allied strategy, the conduct of the war in the Pacific area and an inter-Allied war council. General Wavell said that, although discussions on these subjects would be of interest and value, no decisions could be reached about them at Chungking, and that it would be better to use the time available for their meeting to settle matters of immediate concern, e.g. the defence of the Burma base, the disposal of the limited air forces available for this purpose, Chinese assistance in the defence of Burma and the pooling of Lend-Lease material. General Brett supported this view.

Although General Wavell reported that General Chiang Kai-shek seemed pleased to see his visitors, and that the atmosphere was cordial, the Foreign Office had reason to believe that, in fact, General (c) Chiang Kai-shek resented the way in which his attempt to discuss the wider strategy of the war was brushed aside. Mr. T. V. Soong[1] stated in Washington that the visit of the two generals had made a very painful impression, since they were unable to hold any real discussions. A Chungking broadcast by Reuter's representative on January 16 repeated this view, and added that General Wavell had asked for everything from China and had himself nothing to offer in return. Sir A. Clark Kerr thought Mr. Soong's report very much exaggerated, but that, even so, General Chiang Kai-shek had been disappointed.[2]

The Chinese attitude improved somewhat after the signature of the Declaration of the United Nations (including China) at Washington

---

[1] Mr. T. V. Soong went to Washington on a special mission in 1940. At the end of 1941 he was appointed Chinese Foreign Minister but remained in Washington until October 1942.

[2] Mr. Churchill telegraphed to General Wavell on January 23 that General Chiang Kai-shek had complained to President Roosevelt about the British unwillingness to accept Chinese help. General Wavell replied that the facts as stated by the Chinese were wrong. He agreed that British prestige in China was low, but thought that it could hardly be otherwise until we had had some successes. The Prime Minister accepted General Wavell's answer, and said that he would take an opportunity of explaining the facts to the President. See also p. 488, note 1.

(a) F1173/74/10 (1942). (b) F14016/13549/23. (c) F84, 350/74/10 (1942).

(a) on January 1, 1942, and the announcement that, in accordance with the suggestion made at Washington, General Chiang Kai-shek had accepted the Supreme Command in the Chinese theatre. In spite of this recognition General Chiang Kai-shek continued to feel

(b) neglected and resentful. Sir A. Clark Kerr reported in the last week of January that the General complained at the failure to give him information about Malaya. He was most anxious about the position at Singapore. He had heard that some reinforcements had reached Malaya and that others were expected, but these reports were mostly hearsay. He felt that he was entitled to be taken into our confidence, and asked why we were not being frank with him.

(c)   Sir A. Clark Kerr thought that our withdrawals in Malaya were having a very bad effect on Chinese morale. The Chinese believed rumours that we were rejecting their military help in Burma,[1] and considered generally that we were not treating them as equals in the alliance. They also were dismayed at British and American statements that the defeat of Germany must be our first aim. Finally, they observed that while Mr. Roosevelt had declared that he would use all American resources to secure the deliverance and independence of the Philippines, no such declaration came from Great Britain to give Indians something for which to fight. Hence the Chinese considered that we were insincere in our talk about securing the independence of the subjugated nations of Asia.

(d)   The Foreign Office realised the importance of trying to meet Chinese grievances, but we could not do much while we were suffering heavy military reverses. In any case it was not easy to meet the Chinese criticisms. The Chinese were inclined greatly to exaggerate the part which they could play in the war; they had been making demands on us for years past which we could not fulfil. We had given them everything we could spare in our own urgent need, and the Americans had been very generous under the Lend-Lease programme. One reason why the Chinese armies were not better equipped was the incompetent and corrupt Chinese management of the Burma Road. It was also difficult for us to allow information about military plans to be sent to the Chinese, since there were many Japanese spies with contacts in Chungking, and the Japanese could probably decypher Chinese code telegrams.

(e)   [1] General Wavell, in fact, accepted on December 23, 1941, the offer of two Chinese divisions. Their arrival was delayed partly by difficulties of communication and supply, but partly also by a decision to keep the Chinese Sixth Army in Kunming until it was known whether the Japanese were intending to attack Yunnan and not Burma. The Japanese intentions were not discovered until their attack had begun. In any case, Chinese help had been conditional on the impracticable provision of a separate line of communication in Burma for the Chinese Fifth Army.

(a) F109/107/61.　(b) F838/74/10.　(c) F1030/74/10.　(d) F1173/74/10.　(e) F1330/4/23.

At the same time the Foreign Office considered that the greatest care should be taken to meet General Chiang Kai-shek's demands for treatment as an equal with the war leaders of Great Britain and the United States. It seemed clear that he had expected Generals Wavell and Brett to consult him about the general plan of campaign in the Pacific area. All that had happened was that he had been told how he could be useful to us in his own area. The discussion was limited to the defence of the Burma base and the release to us of American Lend-Lease goods for China. He was not told anything of our plans for other parts of the Pacific, including Malaya. We ought therefore to arrange that General Chiang Kai-shek should receive all the information which could safely be communicated to Chung-king, and that he should send personal representatives to take part in discussions in Washington and London. There was no need for us to exaggerate Chinese military activity—the Chinese would do it for themselves. Indeed, one difficulty was that the Chinese tended (a) to write up their own exploits—when in fact they were doing little or nothing—and then to contrast this rose-coloured picture with the British disasters on land and sea. On the other hand, without accept-ing the fantastic claims of the Chinese, we could emphasise in public statements their refusal to accept defeat, the valuable contribution which they were making to the cause of the free nations and the importance of securing full Chinese independence at the end of the war. The Chinese had a real fear that, after the defeat of Germany, we might make a compromise peace with Japan at their expense.

Meanwhile General Chiang Kai-shek had taken the initiative in (b) suggesting, on January 24, that he should pay short unofficial visits to Burma and India.[1] He wanted to discuss with the Governor and Commander-in-Chief the military situation in Burma, and in India to get in touch with the Viceroy, and also to see Mr. Gandhi and Mr. Nehru in order to impress on them the need to co-operate fully in the common cause. Sir A. Clark Kerr was strongly in favour of assenting to these suggestions. Sir R. Dorman-Smith, the Governor of Burma, also supported the proposed visit to Burma. The Foreign Office therefore replied to Sir A. Clark Kerr that, subject to the approval of the Government of India, General Chiang Kai-shek's visit would be welcomed. On the other hand, since the General was generally regarded as Head of the Chinese State, there was some difficulty about the proposal that he might intervene between the Government of India and private individuals who had hitherto refused co-operation. The Foreign Office suggested that General

---

[1] For documentation of British and Indian policy and reactions to Chiang Kai-shek's visit, see N. Mansergh, *Transfer of Power* 1942–1947, 3 vols. (HMSO, 1971.)

(a) F1356/5/10; 1448/54/10. (b) F834/74/10.

Chiang Kai-shek might discuss the matter with the Viceroy. In other respects the General's contacts with civil and military authorities would be of great value to the co-ordination of the Allied war effort in the Far East.

The War Cabinet thought that the Viceroy should invite Mr. Gandhi, Mr. Nehru and Mr. Jinnah to meet General Chiang (a) Kai-shek at Delhi, but the General did not want the Indian leaders to come to Delhi. He considered that, according to Chinese etiquette, he should make the first call since he was the younger man. On (b) February 3, the day before General Chiang Kai-shek left Chungking, the Prime Minister sent him a personal message that a visit to Mr. Gandhi and Mr. Nehru, except by arrangement with the Viceroy, would make a bad impression in Great Britain and throughout the Empire. Mr. Churchill also thought that, if General Chiang Kai-shek were to see any of the leaders of the Indian Congress Party, he should also see Mr. Jinnah and representatives of the Indian princes and of the depressed classes.

(c)   Sir A. Clark Kerr, who was accompanying General Chiang Kai-shek to India,[1] suggested changes in the wording of the message. The Prime Minister accepted these changes, but was still most anxious to avoid the possibility of anything which might appear to be an intervention on the part of General Chiang Kai-shek in matters affecting the relations between the Government of India and Mr. Gandhi and Mr. Nehru. The Viceroy of India and the Foreign Office were less inclined to fear any risks in letting the interviews be arranged as General Chiang Kai-shek insisted. Sir A. Clark Kerr felt very strongly that, as one of the purposes of the General's visit was to use his personal influence in inducing the Indian leaders to support the war effort, an attempt to deflect him by persuasion was unlikely to succeed, and that it would be a great mistake to give an impression of doubting his good faith and dis-(d) cretion. Nonetheless the Prime Minister thought it desirable to send another message to General Chiang Kai-shek strongly advising him not to go to visit Mr. Gandhi.

The Foreign Office regarded the Prime Minister's attitude as inexpedient at a moment when events in the Far East were at a critical stage.[2] General Chiang Kai-shek was the only man who could keep China in the war if the Japanese occupied Burma. It was therefore much better to accept the disadvantages of a visit to

---

[1] Sir A. Clark Kerr had been appointed Ambassador at Moscow, and was in any case leaving Chungking. Sir Horace Seymour succeeded him as Ambassador to China.

[2] The British Commander at Singapore had surrendered to the Japanese on February 15.

(a) F1070/74/10. (b) F1317/74/10. (c) F1317/54/10, F1102, 1318/74/10. (d) F1523/74/10.

Mr. Gandhi than to cause offence by refusing to allow it. General (a) Chiang Kai-shek, however, was ready to give way to the Prime Minister's wish. He saw Mr. Nehru at Delhi, but did not go to see Mr. Gandhi at Wardha. Mr. Gandhi, who had refused to come to Delhi, then decided to meet the General on the latter's way home through Calcutta.

General Chiang Kai-shek left Calcutta on his return journey on February 23, and after spending some days in Kunming reached Chungking on March 6, two days before the evacuation of Rangoon. During his visit he and General Wavell discussed further mutual (b) assistance and co-operation. He also came to an agreement with the Government of India on the forwarding of Lend-Lease stores to China, road construction and the assembly of military aircraft. General Chiang Kai-shek was much concerned about Indo-Burmese communications with China, and asked the British authorities to (c) maintain touch with the Chinese armies. The Viceroy reported the (d) discussions as of the greatest value in the closer co-ordination of plans to meet Japanese attack. In a message to Mr. Churchill on his (e) return to Chungking, General Chiang Kai-shek was grateful for his warm reception in India, and said that another step forward had been taken towards closer military collaboration and the solidarity of China and India. Sir A. Clark Kerr reported that for the first (f) time the General had been brought fully into the confidence of his allies, and had been promised the fullest support India could give China. This confidence had pleased him, and had made him feel that at last he was being treated as an equal.

During the Delhi discussions it was agreed that there should be reciprocal appointments of Chinese and Indian representatives at Delhi and Chungking with the rank of Minister. At the end of (g) February the Government of India appointed a Chinese Relations Officer at Calcutta to co-ordinate the activities of various Indian authorities in matters concerning China, e.g. the transport of supplies.

Note to section (ii): General Chiang Kai-shek's proposal for a Chinese-American guarantee of a British promise to grant Indian independence: President Roosevelt's exchanges with Mr. Churchill and General Chiang Kai-shek.

General Chiang Kai-shek's visit to India did not have the effect of correcting his misconceptions about the situation in India. He failed to see, or at any rate to take account of, the seriousness of the Hindu-Moslem problem or to realise that the satisfaction of Hindu

---

(a) F1523/24/10.   (b) F1823, 1858/74/10.   (c) F1851/74/10.   (d) F1823/74/10.
(e) F1914/74/10. (f) F2140/74/10. (g) F3751/1689/10.

demands would not bring about Indian national unity.[1] The General's misunderstanding went deeper because Chinese politicians and 'political generals' cared little for the rights of minorities in China or elsewhere. The Chinese regarded the Indian Congress Party as the natural ally of the Kuomintang and expected them to take power as the Kuomintang had done, by absorbing the State. They also were bound to notice that a 'Congress India' would be a convenient neighbour, not strong enough to interfere in Chinese affairs and perhaps sufficiently weak to allow a certain amount of Chinese expansion. Finally, the Chinese wanted the British to leave India just as they wanted China to be free of all 'servitudes' to Western Powers. They were unlikely to favour a British-Indian compromise which would certainly weaken the power of Congress and might delay a British withdrawal after the war.

General Chiang Kai-shek knew that he could not change British policy, but that the United States was in a much stronger position to do so. He knew also that American opinion was very critical of British policy in India. He therefore tried to persuade President Roosevelt to put pressure on the British Government.

General Chiang Kai-shek telegraphed on February 24 to Mr. Soong asking him to give to the President a copy of a message he was sending to Mr. Churchill. The message was to the effect that he (General Chiang Kai-shek) had been greatly shocked by the military and political situation in India, and was afraid that Mr. Churchill did not know 'the real situation'. General Chiang Kai-shek wanted to say that, if the British Government gave the Indians real power and did not allow different parties in India to cause confusion, he was sure that the Indian attitude would change.[2] Mr. Roosevelt was at this time under considerable pressure from American critics of British policy towards India. To a considerable extent the President agreed with these criticisms, though he was obviously more aware of the difficulties of interfering in what was primarily a British-Indian affair. The Foreign Relations Committee of the Senate was arguing that the United States would be justified in dictating to the British Government the grant of independent status to India. The President telegraphed to Mr. Winant on the night of February 25 that he was concerned about the Indian situation from the point of view of defence. He asked Mr. Winant or Mr. Harriman (who was in London on business dealing with Lend-Lease) to let him know the Prime Minister's view. Mr. Roosevelt said that he hesitated to send a direct message to Mr. Churchill 'because, in a strict sense, it is not our business. It is, however, of great interest to us from the point of view of the conduct of the war'.

Mr. Harriman saw Mr. Churchill and was told by him of the discussions (preparatory to the Cripps mission) going on in London

---

[1] The Chinese tended to equate Indians and Hindus since the same Chinese term covered them.

[2] *F.R.U.S.* 1942, I, pp. 604–6.

and India. Mr. Churchill had also explained to him—from the point of view of Indian defence—that about three-quarters of the Indian forces were Moslems and that only some 12 per cent of the total sympathised with the Indian Congress group. Mr. Churchill would not take any political step which would alienate the 100,000,000 Moslems.[1] On March 4 Mr. Churchill telegraphed to the President that the War Cabinet were considering 'a declaration of Dominion status after the war, carrying with it if desired the right to secede'. Mr. Churchill repeated that we could not break with the Moslems or forget our duty to the 30–40 million untouchables and to 80 million people of the states of the Indian princes. He also sent the President statements by Mr. Jinnah and Sir Firoz Khan Noon on the Moslem attitude, a note from the India Office about the Indian Army and, later, a report from the Governor of the Punjab.

Mr. Roosevelt replied on March 10 with a fairly long message about the historical development of the constitution of the United States with special reference to the formation of a temporary government under the Articles of Confederation of 1783. He thought that a similar plan might well solve the Indian difficulty.[2]

On March 11 Mr. Churchill announced the Cripps mission. Ten days before the failure of this mission was officially made public Lord Halifax said to Mr. Welles that he thought the acceptance of the British proposals unlikely because Congress knew that they themselves could not come to terms with the Moslems; hence they wanted to leave us with the responsibility for failure which would otherwise have been placed upon them. Lord Halifax did not expect serious consequences from the breakdown of the discussions.[3] American opinion was in fact most critical of the British refusal to accept the Congress demands. Mr. Churchill sent to the President a copy of Sir S. Cripps' telegram about the final discussions and the cause of failure. The President's reply was that American opinion regarded the responsibility for the breakdown as on the British side and that Americans could not see why Great Britain, if she were willing to allow 'the component parts of India to secede' from the Empire after the war, refused to allow them to enjoy what was tantamount to independence during the war. The President again mentioned his own proposal on the analogy of the American Articles of Confederation. Mr. Churchill answered that he could not take responsibility for the defence of India 'if everything has again to be thrown into the melting pot at this critical juncture'.

The Foreign Office had tried to get a statement of the facts about

---

[1] *F.R.U.S.* 1942, I, pp. 604 and 608. Mr. Churchill said that he had explained to the President the background of the Indian situation when he was in Washington (in December 1941). According to Mr. Churchill (*Second World War*, V, p. 185) he had 'reacted so strongly and violently' to the President's exposition on the 'usual American lines' that Mr. Roosevelt 'never raised (the question) verbally again'.

[2] *F.R.U.S.* 1942, I, 615–6. Mr. Churchill (*Second World War*, V, 190) has described this message as illustrating 'the difficulties of comparing situations in various centuries and scenes where almost every material fact is totally different'.

[3] *F.R.U.S.* 1942, I, 623.

India to General Chiang Kai-shek directly through Sir H. Seymour in Chungking and indirectly through Dr. Koo in London, but the General remained convinced that the responsibility for preventing a settlement lay entirely with the British Government. On July 25,[1] when the Congress Party was threatening a mass movement of non-co-operation, General Chiang Kai-shek sent another long message to President Roosevelt. Mr. Soong summed up the General's view as based on the belief that the British Government did not realise the dangers of an explosion of opinion in India and the possibility of a Japanese military move in the near future. General Chiang Kai-shek thought that Congress represented the desires of the Indian people and was comparable in importance and representative capacity with the Kuomintang in China. He believed that Congress would accept less than they were asking from the British if the United States and China were to underwrite the British promises to India and thus make possible a compromise arrangement with Congress for the period of the war. Mr. Roosevelt sent a copy of the message to Mr. Churchill (Mr. Soong had already shown it to Sir R. I. Campbell in Lord Halifax's absence). Mr. Churchill, who was in Cairo, replied on August 8[2] that he had no doubt about the ability of the Government of India to maintain order and secure India's maximum contribution to the war 'whatever Congress may say or do, provided of course that their authority is not undermined'.

(a)   The President replied on August 9 to Mr. Churchill that he had let General Chiang Kai-shek know that he did not think it 'wise or expedient for the time being to take any of the steps' suggested by him since they might undermine the authority of the Indian Government at a critical time, but he would be glad to keep in touch with General Chiang Kai-shek on this and other questions affecting the United Nations. Mr. Roosevelt told Mr. Churchill that he had made this suggestion because the General might otherwise act on his own initiative. The President sent his message to General Chiang Kai-shek on August 8. He also said in the message that the British Government believed that their offer to the Indian peoples offered an 'adjustment fair to both sides'.

On August 9 the Government of India ordered the arrest of Mr. Gandhi, Mr. Nehru and other leading members of the Congress Party in view of their threat of a mass movement to enforce their demand for a British withdrawal. Mr. Attlee, in the Prime Minister's absence in Cairo, had sent a message to the President on August 7

(b)   [1] This message is reproduced in *F.R.U.S.* 1942, I, 695, where it is dated 'Chungking July 25', but it appears again under the date July 29, when President Roosevelt quotes it verbatim in a telegram to Mr. Churchill beginning, 'I have today received an urgent message from Chiang Kai-shek . . . etc.'. It is repeated again in the same form as Annex 1
(c)   to a War Cabinet Paper.
(d)   [2] This telegram was actually transmitted on July 31, though quoted in *F.R.U.S.* under August 8, the date on which it was handed to the Chinese Foreign Minister.

(a) T1098/2, No. 176, Churchill Papers/470. (b) T1056/2, Churchill Papers/470.
(c) WP(42)334, Annex 1. (d) T1056/2, Churchill Papers/470.

explaining the need for drastic action to prevent the crippling of India's war effort. Mr. Attlee pointed out that the Viceroy's Council which was taking this action consisted of eleven Indian members and only five Europeans (one of whom was absent) including the Viceroy and Commander-in-Chief.[1] The President thought it best not to reply to Mr. Attlee's message. Mr. Hull agreed that the United States Government had nothing to add to their previous statements, though he believed that a repetition of the British offer, with full emphasis on the proposal for independence at the end of the war, and a statement of immediate adjustments, might lead to a resumption of discussions.[2]

General Chiang Kai-shek sent another message to Mr. Roosevelt on hearing of the arrest of the Congress leaders. The President replied on August 12 that he deplored the situation, but that, without becoming parties to the 'internal controversy' between the British Government and Mr. Gandhi, there was nothing more which he or General Chiang Kai-shek could do. The President thought that he and General Chiang Kai-shek should let both parties know that while they had no moral right to force themselves upon either side, they stood 'in the position of friends who would gladly help if . . . called on by both sides'. The President then put to General Chiang Kai-shek the analogy with the action of the American colonies in 1783.[2] Mr. Hopkins told Sir R. I. Campbell about General Chiang Kai-shek's proposal. He (Mr. Hopkins) had said to Mr. Soong that the plan was impracticable. Mr. Soong said that the General had also written to Mr. Nehru. Mr. Nehru had replied that he would accept Dominion status for India if it were promised under a Chinese-American guarantee. Mr. Hopkins had pointed out that the decision   (a)
lay not with Mr. Nehru but with Mr. Gandhi.

Meanwhile General Chiang Kai-shek had told Sir H. Seymour that the Indian leaders might go over to the Japanese side, if they felt that they could not count upon sympathy from the United Nations. General Chiang Kai-shek said that the British Government should   (b)
ask the United Nations to approach the United States, and that the latter should guarantee the grant of independence to India after the war. General Chiang Kai-shek said to Sir H. Seymour that he had sent personal telegrams to Mr. Gandhi, Mr. Nehru and Mr. Azad,   (c)
and that Madame Chiang Kai-shek had sent messages to Mrs. Naidu and Mrs. Nehru. General Chiang Kai-shek asked Sir H. Seymour to let the Viceroy know of these telegrams, and to request that a Chinese Commissioner should be allowed to deliver them in person and to see Mr. Nehru, if possible, alone. The General thought that such an interview might be helpful. About the same time Dr. Tsiang Ting-fu, who was to lead a Chinese educational visit to India, issued a

---

[1] *F.R.U.S.* 1942, I, 705 and 721–2.
[2] *F.R.U.S.* 1942, I, 714–7.

(a) F5705/2428/10.   (b) F5756/2428/10.   (c) F5797/2428/10.

statement that China would be glad to intervene in order to help to improve the situation in India.

The Viceroy replied on August 14 that he could not allow the messages to be conveyed. He pointed out that the attitude of General and Madame Chiang Kai-shek was already much resented in Moslem circles, and that Chinese interference in Indian domestic politics would be as intolerable as British attempts to interfere in the domestic politics of Chungking.

(a) The Foreign Office gave a reasoned answer to General Chiang Kai-shek's views on August 23. Sir H. Seymour was instructed to explain why rapid action was necessary, and to point out that Congress had no claim to speak for the whole of India, and that an agreement between the Government of India and Congress would not make a solution easier. Sir S. Cripps's proposals, which Congress had rejected, might have led to a settlement, since they would probably have been acceptable to the other communities. Congress was now asking the British Government to throw over these communities and to allow British troops to be used as mercenaries of a Hindu *raj*. The Government of India could deal with civil disobedience but not with communal civil war; they were unwilling to attempt to coerce the martial races of India in the interest of Congress rule.

In view of the stubbornness with which General and Madame Chiang Kai-shek held to their opinions on Indian affairs, the Prime Minister decided to set out in a personal message to the General the reasons why the British Government and the Government of India could not accept the General's proposal for Chinese-American (b) mediation. The Prime Minister was in Egypt, and sent his draft for consideration by the Foreign Office and the India Office.

Mr. Churchill began by pointing out that Congress was almost entirely a Hindu organisation, and could not be taken as representing India which, like Europe, was inhabited by many different races, nations and religions. There were, for example, 95,000,000 Moslems, 45,000,000 'Untouchables' and 90,000,000 subjects of the Indian principalities. Moreover, Congress had nothing in common with the fighting races of India, of whom over a million had volunteered for the army during the war. Mr. Churchill thought that if in the future, as the result of the constitutional process to which Great Britain was committed, our own troops were withdrawn from India, the Moslem warriors would soon dominate the Hindu parliamentarians. Mr. Gandhi could not set up Hindu ascendancy over all India unless he had at his disposal a Japanese army to hold down the Moslems and other non-Hindu elements and the Indian States. The Japanese would not provide an army unless they had a free passage through India to join up with the Germans.

Mr. Churchill thought it a wise rule for allies not to interfere in

---

(a) F5886/2428/10. (b) F6122/54/10.

each other's internal affairs. We were resolved in every way to respect the sovereign rights of China, and had abstained from comment even when the differences between the Kuomintang and the Communists were most acute. Mr. Churchill therefore hoped that General Chiang Kai-shek would not allow himself to be drawn into political correspondence with the India Congress, or with individuals who were trying to paralyse the war effort of the Government of India and to disturb peace and order. Otherwise General Chiang Kai-shek would estrange powerful sections of British opinion, who would feel that he had increased the British war burden against Germany, Italy and Japan.

Mr. Churchill then said definitely that no British Government of which he was head, or a member, could accept American mediation on a matter affecting sovereign rights, and that Mr. Roosevelt would be unwilling to make any proposal for mediation. Finally, Mr. Churchill described the war situation. He said that he had found Stalin confident about the future. The German attack on Russia, in spite of its gains, was less strong than in 1941. The Japanese appeared to be unwilling to attack Russia until they knew the position at the beginning of winter. This might mean a heavier task for China, and increase the importance of the defence of India, but Mr. Churchill was persevering with plans for an offensive against Japanese lines of communication along the Burma Road and other roads between Siam, Malaya and China. He had asked General Wavell to meet him in Cairo to discuss these plans, and hoped that before many months had passed we could do something to relieve the pressure upon the Chinese people under General Chiang Kai-shek's leadership.

This message was telegraphed to Chungking on August 26. General Chiang Kai-shek was not in Chungking; it was therefore impossible to deliver the message to him at once. Meanwhile, on September 1, (a) General Chiang Kai-shek sent a friendly message to Mr. Churchill on the third anniversary of the outbreak of war in Europe. Mr. Churchill replied in similar terms, and gave instructions that this second message should be given to the General twenty-four hours after the first message on India.

On September 23 General Chiang Kai-shek told Sir H. Seymour that he had received and read the Prime Minister's message on India. He was clearly determined to say no more on the subject, and Sir H. Seymour hoped that he would leave it alone, at all events for the time. The Chinese press was also giving the whole matter less prominence.

(a) F6442/54/10.

(iii)

Proposals for loans to China from Great Britain and the United States: the question of the abolition of extra-territoriality (January–April 1942).

(a)   In December 1941 General Chiang Kai-shek asked for a loan of £100,000,000 from England and $500,000,000 from the United States on the grounds that he wanted to give a psychological stimulus to his people, and restore their faith in their own currency. Sir A. Clark Kerr explained to him that the Chinese could not make full use of foreign exchange at that time. General Chiang Kai-shek said that this did not matter; he wanted 'a picture on the wall' to display to the people and the Chinese armies, and did not much care whether he could use the loan or not.

(b)   On January 5, 1942, Dr. Koo raised the question of the loan with Mr. Eden. He explained that events in the Far East had caused great anxiety for China. Moreover, China had always been helped by remittances from overseas, especially from Malaya and the

(c)   Netherlands East Indies, but these were now at an end. On January 25 the Foreign Office telegraphed to Lord Halifax that the British Government proposed to reply that they had decided to make available to China on Lend-Lease terms all the munitions and military equipment which we could supply. The limiting factors on the material help we could give were our own war needs and obligations to the other Allies, and the amount which could be transported over the Burma Road. Although our power to help in China's financial difficulties was very limited, we were ready to go forward with a loan if the United States Government would take parallel action. We recognised that very large sterling and dollar loans, though of no actual help to China at that time, would have a psychological value, but we could not grant a large loan in view of the difficulty we should have in maintaining our balance of payments after the war. We could not add to these future difficulties by placing a large amount of sterling at China's disposal after the war. The position of the United States with enormous supplies of gold was different. Mr. Eden asked Lord Halifax to find out what scheme for financial assistance to China the United States Government might have in mind.

(d)   On January 28 Sir A. Clark Kerr reported to the Foreign Office that, in view of the general despondency at Chungking, he feared the effects of explaining our views to the Chinese Government. The promises of ammunition and military equipment were too distant to affect the present problem and the store of supplies in Burma was

---

(a) F14398/1/10. (b) F196/7/10. (c) F252/7/10. (d) F998/7/10.

very small. There was nothing, therefore, in our offer which General Chiang Kai-shek could use to give his people the stimulus which he sought and they needed. Could we not protect ourselves by a condition that any sums now promised should be used only for sterling area expenditure directly connected with the war or that any proposal for detailed expenditure should be subject to specific agreement?

The Foreign Office replied that we had now decided to offer (a) financial assistance to China parallel to that proposed by the United States. On February 1 the United States Government sent word that they were asking Congress to approve a loan of $500,000,000. This loan was approved on February 2. Our offer was to lend China £50,000,000 on terms to be agreed by the British and Chinese Governments. The loan would not be available for post-war expenditure, but was limited to war purposes. Owing to the great disparity between British and American financial resources, the British offer could not exceed £50,000,000.

The announcement of the British and American loans had an (b) excellent reception in Chungking, in spite of the reservations placed upon the British loan. The loan negotiations, however, were long and difficult. In the first week in February the Foreign Office sent to the Treasury a warning from Sir O. Niemeyer that the Chinese (c) might put forward unacceptable conditions. They would probably ask for the provision of foreign currency reserve to Chinese notes which were now being issued; the United States Government might agree to this proposal, but it would involve us in a post-war drain of considerable size without doing anything for China's war needs. Sir O. Niemeyer thought that there might also be demands for industrial equipment of no importance to the war and probably, in view of the already large Lend-Lease commitments, far beyond the limited war transport possibilities.

On February 19 the Treasury replied to Sir O. Niemeyer through (d) the Foreign Office that their interpretation of 'war purposes' would not exclude guarantees for an internal war loan if the Chinese asked for them, but we could not regard more than £10,000,000 as available for this purpose. In any case, the Treasury intended to interpret 'war purposes' primarily as expenditure in the sterling area for war needs, and excluding anything covered by the Lend-Lease arrangement. Sir O. Niemeyer warned the Treasury that the Chinese were (e) difficult to handle on details; he advised the British Government not to raise minor objections, which would cause great irritation without doing any good.

(a) F1109/7/10. (b) F1261/74/10. (c) F1314/7/10. (d) F1706/7/10. (e) F1751/7/10.
R*BFP

(a)   On March 21 the United States signed an agreement with China for a $500,000,000 loan, which was specifically for post-war as well as war purposes. Lord Halifax reported that the Americans intended to leave the Chinese a very free hand in the use of the money. The Chinese press publicised the loan as proof that the Americans had attached no reservations. No mention was made of the British credit.

(b) On March 25 Dr. Y. C. Koo, Vice-Minister of Finance, complained to Mr. E. L. Hall Patch, British member of the Stabilisation Board in Chungking, that the British Government had imposed restrictions on the use of the money and were slow in negotiation. 'The Americans attached no strings, and we did.'

(c)   The Chinese Minister of Finance, Dr. Kung, told Sir H. Seymour on March 26 that, as he had concluded an arrangement with the United States, he now wanted to come to a similar arrangement with Great Britain as soon as possible. It had been more convenient to negotiate the American loan first as the Chinese Minister for Foreign Affairs, Mr. T. V. Soong, had been in Washington. Dr. Kung gave Sir H. Seymour a copy of the American agreement and an *aide-mémoire* setting out the purposes for which the Chinese Government wished to use the British credit.

(d)   On March 31 Dr. P. W. Kuo of the Chinese Embassy in London made a similar approach to the Treasury. He was told that, in view of the limited amount of our own exchange resources and the great calls on them, we felt we could best help China if the credit were made available primarily for expenditure in the sterling area. Our object was to give the maximum financial help to China during the war. We recognised the importance to China of post-war reconstruction, but this matter should be dealt with separately. After the war we should have to maintain our balance of payments without external help. This would be difficult for some years; hence we could not regard any part of the £50,000,000 loan to China as available for post-war use. Subject to this reservation the Treasury sent Mr.

(e) Hall Patch on April 3 the text of an agreement to make £50,000,000 sterling available to the Chinese Government.

The Chinese, however, continued to ask for a change in the British conditions, and as the matter dragged on it became a question of personal prestige with Dr. Kung, whose administration seemed to the British Government as disastrous as his personal influence on General Chiang Kai-shek.[1] He proposed a number of compromises,

---

(f)   [1] On February 3 Sir A. Clark Kerr described Dr. Kung (who was General Chiang Kai-shek's brother-in-law) as China's 'Old Man of the Sea': 'It is hard to reflect upon or to write of Dr. Kung with any patience. He is a cancer in the belly of China. His
(*continued on page 501*)

(a) F1752, 2072, 2473/7/10.   (b) F2540/7/10.   (c) F2568/7/10.   (d) F2540/7/10. (e) F2697/7/10.   (f) F4351/113/10.

all of which would have left the Chinese free to accumulate sterling credits for post-war purchases.

During the long-drawn-out negotiations over a loan the British Government had been considering the question of the abolition of extra-territoriality. On March 28 the Foreign Office informed (a) Sir H. Seymour that they had in mind a new treaty with China to encourage the Chinese as a preparation for post-war co-operation, and a counterpoise to a possible Chinese agreement with Russia. The most promising subject for a treaty was the abrogation of British extra-territorial rights; the British Government were already committed to negotiate on this question when peace was restored.[1] The Foreign Office asked Sir H. Seymour what effect the offer to negotiate such a treaty would have on the Chinese. Would they regard it as a generous gesture and react accordingly? Or would it appear in present circumstances as an act of weakness? There was bound to be opposition from firms trading in China, but in any case at the end of the war we could not maintain our extra-territorial privileges. We intended to consult the Dominions and the United States before we approached the Chinese Government. On the other hand, if we took action on the proposals, we should like the Chinese Government to know that the initiative came from Great Britain.

Sir H. Seymour considered that we should take the initiative now, (b) although an offer to do so would be regarded as a sign of our weakness in the Far East. He said that the Chinese would not accept any provisions other than those which were usually included in treaties between equal States. From the point of view of encouraging the Chinese during the war, and preparing for post-war collaboration, the proposals should be framed and negotiations conducted in such

---

(*continued*)
mischievous hand may be detected everywhere. His varlets are in every post. It is probably fair to say that many of the acutest of China's present financial and economic problems are due to his ignorance, his cocksureness and his preference for his own interests over those of his own country. . . . Nothing in the life of Dr. Kung would become him more than his disappearance from office. . . . Dr. Kung is an urgent danger to China and therefore to the Allied cause.'

[1] The question had been in abeyance since 1931. Negotiations had continued between 1929 and 1931 and had ended in June of that year with a draft treaty acceptable to both sides except for two crucial articles regarding certain reserved areas and the duration of the treaty. Negotiations were not resumed after the Japanese invasion of Manchuria. The British attitude was that we had gone as far as we could to meet the wishes of the Chinese and that the matter must be suspended until other Powers had made similar progress (apart from the Americans, no other Power had taken up the question) and China appeared likely to be able to implement a treaty resulting from the negotiations. Mr. Churchill had stated in Parliament on July 18, 1940: 'When peace is restored in the Far East, His Majesty's Government will be ready to negotiate with the Chinese Government the abolition of extra-territorial rights, the rendition of concessions, and the revision of treaties on a basis of reciprocity and equality.' This statement was reaffirmed by Mr. Eden on June 11, 1941, and in a note to the Chinese Government of July 4, who in reply expressed 'profound gratitude'. In June 1941 the United States Government published an exchange of letters with the Chinese Government to the same effect.

(a) F2031/74/10. (b) F2757/828/10.

a way as to make it clear throughout that the treaty was between equals and allies. Sir H. Seymour agreed on the importance of ensuring that China realised that the initiative came from Great Britain.

(a)   The Foreign Office subsequently decided that, at the present stage of the war and in view of Chinese disappointment, an approach would be regarded as evidence of weakness and would not produce the desired effect. He would therefore wait until the tide had begun to turn against Japan. Meanwhile, if the Chinese Government raised the issue the position would be different, and we would respond sympathetically. The State Department agreed with the British view.

(iv)

Anglo-Chinese relations in the summer of 1942: further negotiations for a British loan to China (April–December 1942).

During the months between the return of General Chiang Kai-shek from India and the Allied victories in the late autumn of 1942 Anglo-Chinese relations became increasingly strained. The Foreign

(b) Office thought it necessary early in May to ask Lord Halifax to call the attention of Mr. T. V. Soong to the publication of anti-British propaganda in the Chinese press. About the same time Sir H.

(c) Seymour remarked on an 'increasingly unreasonable attitude of coldness' on the part of the Chinese at Chungking. Sir O. Niemeyer also reported that 'British stock stands low at the moment in China', while the Chinese were 'much set in their new equality as a Great Power'.

After their meeting in the latter part of June 1942, Mr. Churchill and President Roosevelt issued a statement that they had discussed with their military advisers methods to be adopted against Japan

(d) and for the relief of China. On July 4 Mr. Churchill approved an encouraging message to the Chinese press:

> 'The world has watched with admiration the mighty efforts made by China not only on the field of battle, but also in the sphere of internal reconstruction. . . . The war in Europe and the Middle East is as much part of the defence of China as the war in the Far East is part of the defence of Britain. We are determined to extend to the Chinese people every material, moral and spiritual help in our power.'

(e)   Nonetheless Dr. Currie[1] in Chungking believed at the end of July

---

[1] Dr. Currie was President Roosevelt's principal adviser on Far Eastern Affairs. He arrived in Chungking on July 20.

(a) F2757, 3807/828/10.   (b) F3187, 3343/3187/10.   (c) F3187/3187/10.   (d) F4846/3187/10.   (e) F5456/54/10.

that Chinese disappointment over the progress of the Pacific war had led to anti-British sentiment so strong that it was a danger to the common war effort. The Chinese had refused twice to accept from British sources arms which the United States could not supply. Dr. Currie thought that an unfortunate position was developing in which the United States were supplying, in the highly popular form of aircraft, the only visible Allied help to China.

In spite of their disparagement of British activities the Chinese themselves at this time and indeed throughout 1942 were doing little fighting in their own country against the Japanese. The Japanese moved into considerable areas of Chekiang and Kiangsi during the (a) summer, partly to raid grain and other supplies and also in order to prevent the Allies from using landing grounds in eastern China. They began to move back in July and from September the front remained unchanged. The Chinese press represented the Japanese advance as a large-scale offensive strongly contested by the Chinese armies and finally defeated by a counter-offensive. In fact the Japanese met hardly any opposition either in their advance or in their withdrawal. The Chinese admitted that for this campaign the Japanese had been able to use 100,000 troops taken from elsewhere in China; Chinese pressure was clearly not severe. Sir H. Seymour, with the agreement of the Russian military attaché at Chungking, thought that many of the Japanese units were below strength. In some respects it was surprising that the Japanese did not try to finish off the war in China and thus free themselves for all-out offensives against Australia or Russia or India. They could have occupied Chungking, and possibly put an end to the somewhat passive resistance under General Chiang Kai-shek, but the Chinese might have gone back to Lanchow and thus compelled the Japanese to garrison an enlarged area of occupation. In any case an advance to Chungking would have required some military effort and was hardly worth while —China was no longer a serious danger and could not be used as a base for an Allied offensive.[1] The Japanese also drew a considerable amount of supplies, including antimony and tungsten, from Free China by a system of trading at which the authorities on each side connived—the Japanese because they wanted the Chinese raw materials, and the Chinese because they had no other way of getting foreign goods.

The isolation of China from her allies was at this time almost

---

[1] A high official of the Chinese Military Intelligence Service remarked in September to one of the British service attachés that the Japanese could have reached Chungking if they had wished to do so, but that China had ceased to be a menace to Japan and could be left alone, except for the rounding-up of any Chinese force which showed signs of activity, until after the victory of the Axis Powers.

(a) F7252, 7411/1689/10.

complete. Proposals had been made for the opening of routes into
China from Mandalay and Myitkyina, but these plans had to be
given up after the loss of Burma in May. Investigations were then
made into the feasibility of sending pack caravans from India along
the old tea route to China across the highlands of Tibet. The
Tibetan Government agreed with the Government of India in July
to allow the transport of non-military supplies through their territory.
The Chinese, however, regarded the good offices of the Government
of India in a matter concerning Tibet as derogatory to their position
as suzerain. They tried to deal directly with Tibet, and thus produced
a deadlock in the negotiations since the Tibetan Government looked
to India for support against Chinese encroachment.

In any case the pack route could not have carried more than a
very small amount of supplies; the only other solution was the
development of a lorry service or a railway from Baluchistan through
eastern Iran, Russian Central Asia and Chinese Turkestan. The
British Government did their best to develop this route. At the end
of 1942 they had arranged, as a beginning, for transport of 2,000 tons
a month[1] by rail and lorry from India, via Meshed in Iran to Askabad
on the Russian trans-Caspian railway. The Russians would take
over the service from Askabad to Alma Ata in eastern Turkestan by
rail and thence by lorry to Hami in eastern Sinkiang. The Chinese
would then carry on from Hami to Lanchow and beyond. The
greatest of many practical difficulties in carrying out this plan was
to provide and maintain the lorry service on the Russian and Chinese
sections of the route. During 1942 the only effective link between
China and her allies was the air service.

(a)   The situation in China appeared so grave that on August 23 Mr.
Eden submitted a memorandum on the subject to the War Cabinet.
He said that the assistance which we had been able to give had not
been sufficient to meet the requirements of China. The Chinese war
effort was being maintained largely by the leadership of General
Chiang Kai-shek, who needed our continued support. The Chinese
wanted more aircraft but there were no facilities for them in China
even if they could have been spared from India. If the United States
could not provide more assistance and if we were unable to help,
there was a serious danger that China would fall out of the war
owing to her isolation and loss of confidence, with 'moral and
material results of far-reaching gravity'.

(b)   The War Cabinet agreed on August 31 that every effort should be
made to send a British squadron from India to China, and that its

---

[1]About a tenth of the tonnage which entered China by the Burma Road in the last
months of 1941.

(a) WP(42)375; F5995/24/10, F6228/54/10.   (b) WM(42)119.

despatch would have a political value out of all proportion to the sacrifice involved. The Foreign Office asked Sir H. Seymour whether (a) effective Chinese resistance would go on in the next twelve months, and how continued isolation would affect Chinese morale. He replied that Allied defeats had weakened Chinese confidence in her allies (b) and that an increase of assistance was badly needed. There was, however, no reason to expect that Chinese resistance would collapse if the Japanese kept to the existing scale of activities, if there were no major allied disaster, especially in the Middle East or India, and if crops were sufficient to ensure food supplies. Large-scale Chinese military activity could not be expected, whatever supplies were available, unless the Chinese Government felt that they could attack without serious risk as a result of the weakening of Japan by events elsewhere. The Chinese were hoping for an attack on Burma. Sir H. Seymour considered that it was most important that the Chinese should not have a feeling of desertion in favour of activities on fronts more important to the Allies. The small and diminishing American air force should be increased as much as possible by British and American aircraft. Such support would have the greatest effect on morale and the stiffening of Chinese resistance.

Efforts to increase supplies in China by using transport aircraft, however, failed. In the first week of October the Air Ministry said (c) that no transport aircraft were available for Chinese internal air routes or for a British air service between India and China. The Royal Air Force in India was much below strength in transport aircraft for military purposes alone.[1]

In this unfavourable atmosphere it was not surprising that the loan negotiations should have dragged on unsatisfactorily during the summer and autumn months. On April 20 the Chinese Ambassador (d) said to Mr. Eden that the terms of the British loan seemed very different from the unconditional American loan. The Chinese Government had hoped that both loans might be on the same basis. In particular, they disliked the restriction on the use of the credit. They did not object to the loan being made available in the sterling area only, but would regret its restriction to the purchase of goods. They wanted to use it for the support of an internal loan. General Chiang Kai-shek was anxious that the Chinese people should not

---

[1] The War Cabinet decided in August to send a Parliamentary mission to China. The (e) proposal for a goodwill mission had been made in March 1942, and was renewed by General Chiang Kai-shek in May. The decision to send a mission was announced in Parliament on September 10. The Mission—consisting of Lord Ailwyn, R.N., Lord Teviot, Captain S. Wedderburn and Mr. J. J. Lawson, reached Chungking on November 10 and stayed a fortnight. Sir H. Seymour reported that the Mission had been an outstanding success.

(a) F6229/1689/10. (b) F6316/1689/10. (c) F7840/24/10. (d) F3043/7/10. (e) F8545/54/10.

compare the British and American attitude unfavourably, and hoped that on this occasion, as a political gesture, we would waive our conditions.

Mr. Eden replied that we understood the primary purpose of the loan to be political; we hoped that this fact was clear from the promptness with which the loan had been made. Our only general limitation was that the loan should be solely for war purposes, but obviously transport difficulties now imposed limitations on its use. We did not object to the use of a portion of the money as support for an internal Chinese loan. Mr. Eden promised Dr. Koo that we would examine the terms of the American loan to see whether we could not meet the Chinese request by suitable presentation of our own terms.

(a)   On April 23 Mr. Hall-Patch saw Dr. Kung. The latter, in agreement with General Chiang Kai-shek, had instructed the Ambassador in London that the Chinese Government could not accept less favourable terms from Great Britain than those granted by the United States. He would not agree to any reservations, e.g. that the credit agreement should terminate at the end of the war, or that only £10,000,000 could be earmarked for guaranteed loans. Dr. Kung did not accept the explanation that our draft agreement followed the American terms as closely as our circumstances permitted; he asked for the employment of identical terms, and maintained that this was the spirit of the agreement between the Prime Minister, Mr. Morgenthau and Mr. Soong.[1] Mr. Hall-Patch sent a warning that Dr. Kung had the support of General Chiang Kai-shek. If we were not prepared to give way, we should have to meet a campaign of thinly veiled abuse, and a comparison of our meanness with American generosity. The Chinese would then consider as a sign of weakness the grant under pressure of concessions which had at first been refused.

(b)   On May 13 Mr. Eden wrote to Dr. Koo that we had examined the United States agreement carefully in an effort to meet the Chinese Government's wish that our agreement should be on the same basis. We had revised the draft although certain differences still remained. Within a limit of £10,000,000, the credit could be used to guarantee an internal Chinese loan. We hoped that the Chinese Government would accept the revised draft agreement. Mr. Eden pointed out that, apart from financial aid, we were

---

(c)   [1] Dr. P. W. Kuo on April 20 had said that when Mr. Churchill was in the United States, he had agreed with the President and Mr. Morgenthau that the terms of the two loans should be identical, and had authorised them to inform the Chinese accordingly.

(a) F3188/7/10.   (b) F3468/7/10.   (c) F3043/7/10.

supplying without claim to repayment all the arms, munitions and equipment which we could spare for the Chinese forces.

On May 16 the Foreign Office informed Lord Halifax that we (a) had made it clear to the Chinese from the beginning, with Mr. Morgenthau's knowledge, that we could lend only for war purposes. We thought it most important to convince the United States Government on this point. Otherwise the Chinese would at once notice a difference of opinion between us and the United States, and the influence of both in China would suffer. We trusted the (b) United States Government would not encourage the Chinese to refuse our conditions, which were reasonable and necessary. Unless the United States supported Great Britain, most of the political value of the joint financial assistance would be lost.

On May 30 Mr. Eden discussed Anglo-Chinese relations with (c) Dr. Koo. Dr. Koo said that the Chinese Government accepted limitation of the loan to the sterling area and to use in war. They did not like the condition, however, that the concurrence of the British Government would be required for purchases which they wished to make. Mr. Eden said that we had tried to model our proposals on those of the United States, even though there were more conditions attached to the British loan, but our position was difficult, and financially Great Britain was much less strong. Mr. Eden promised, however, to consult the Chancellor of the Exchequer.

On June 6 Dr. Koo asked that the loan should be made available (d) 'for other urgent national purposes arising out of the war, particularly guaranteeing internal Chinese loans and strengthening Chinese currency reserves'. Five days later Sir A. Cadogan told Dr. Koo (e) that we had to stand by the terms already attached to the loan. Dr. Koo argued that on these terms the loan was largely meaningless, since it was impossible to obtain material to the value of £40,000,000 in the sterling area.

A letter handed to Dr. Koo on June 17 set out our position in (f) more detail. We were prepared to agree to make available £10,000,000 for a guarantee of Chinese internal loans; this maximum should cause no difficulty for the Chinese Government since, with loans already secured on United States credit, the market was unlikely to be able to absorb a greater amount now or in the near future. As regards the use of the loan for strengthening Chinese currency reserves, China's external needs would be met during the war largely by Lend-Lease supplies from Great Britain and the United States; hence any sterling sums made available for this purpose could not be used effectively during the war, and would be

---

(a) F3613/7/10. (b) F3749/7/10. (c) F4096/7/10. (d) F4252/7/10. (e) F4383/7/10. (f) F4333/7/10.

available only for post-war purposes. As we and the Chinese Government had agreed that the loan should be available only for war purposes in the sterling area during the war, we could not accept the Chinese proposal.

The letter ended with the hope that the Chinese Government would agree to early signature, and pointed out that the draft provided that there should be no restrictions on our giving the Chinese Government all the financial help in our power during the

(a) war. Dr. Koo admitted that we had now put the matter in the most favourable light possible, although the Chinese Government would be disappointed at the terms. On July 2 Mr. Eden informed Sir H. Seymour that we agreed on the importance of an early settlement, but for strong practical reasons we were unable to go further in concessions. The loan had been asked for and granted primarily as a symbol of Anglo-Chinese solidarity. Sir H. Seymour was asked to ensure that our position was understood at Chungking, and to urge early signature of the agreement.

(b) On July 6 Sir H. Seymour saw Dr. Kung. He went over the history of the negotiations with him, and said that we could not accept the Chinese plan. He thought that Dr. Kung was frightened about the Chinese economic situation and its political results, and had persuaded himself that it could be remedied by foreign loans. Dr. Kung's view was that if we could not fall in with Chinese wishes the Chinese Government would drop the proposal for a loan. Sir H. Seymour had thought ever since the discussions started that the Chinese Government would be content with nothing less than the United States terms. This was still their position.

(c) Dr. Koo called on Mr. Eden on July 9 to renew the proposal that £30,000,000 of the proposed £50,000,000 loan should be placed at the disposal of the Chinese Government in England as a reserve for the Chinese note issue. Mr. Eden said that the loan was still open but only on the terms offered. Dr. Koo replied that the Chinese currency position was most serious, and asked again for support for

(d) the note issue. In a letter of July 21, Mr. Eden told him that we had gone over the whole matter most sympathetically, but could not do what the Chinese wanted. We could not agree to post-war commitments to China which we had not undertaken even in the case of the Dominions or our Colonies. The Chinese later put forward two

(e) compromise suggestions to the Foreign Office, but no satisfactory

(f) formula had been found by the first week in September. Sir H. Seymour and the Foreign Office reached the same conclusion, i.e.

(a) F4590/7/10. (b) F4884/7/10. (c) F4940/7/10. (d) F5049, 5227/7/10. (e) F7252/1689/10. (f) F5726, 5835/7/10.

that tension over this question was largely due to the fact that Dr. Kung had led General Chiang Kai-shek to expect that he could force us to concede terms as favourable as those of the United States.

On September 28 Mr. Eden informed Sir H. Seymour that it was (a) important politically that we should not be represented as obstructing the loan plans. We wanted to please General Chiang Kai-shek as well as benefit the Chinese people, and to make the former understand that the blame for Dr. Kung's mismanagement did not lie with us. Mr. Eden suggested that Sir H. Seymour should tell General Chiang Kai-shek what we were prepared to do, and so forestall any allegation that we were holding up immediate action for China's benefit. We thought that the initiative towards breaking the deadlock should come from the Chinese side. Some approach by Sir H. Seymour might give the General an opening for instructing Dr. Kung to begin further discussions on lines we could accept, and make it more difficult for Dr. Kung to throw the blame on us.

Sir H. Seymour agreed that the only way out of the deadlock was (b) through some compromise; there was, however, no sign that the Chinese would make an approach to us. By October arrangements for concluding the loan had been delayed for more than six months. (c) The delay had undoubtedly had a 'deplorable effect' on Sino-British relations, owing to the feelings of the high Chinese personalities involved. Sir H. Seymour thought that £10,000,000 for a loan guarantee would be well spent if the deadlock could be broken. On November 20 Sir H. Seymour reported that he had spoken some (d) days before to the Minister for Foreign Affairs[1] on the credit question, and had explained our difficulties in making an agreement likely to commit us to post-war currency demands for which we should receive nothing in return. Mr. Soong said that he would discuss the matter with those dealing with it. He suggested later that he should (e) seek power to discuss the credit question with Mr. Churchill and Mr. Eden during his visit to London. Sir H. Seymour thought that this procedure would conform to our original idea that the next step should come from the Chinese side, and would enable an exchange of views to take place without loss of face either to General Chiang Kai-shek or to Dr. Kung; the Foreign Office therefore (f) accepted the proposal. Sir H. Seymour believed that the £50,000,000 (g) credit—'this thorn in the side of Sino-British relations'—remained a handicap to goodwill. The British attempt to follow the Americans in their generosity had so far produced only unfortunate results.

---

[1] Mr. T. V. Soong arrived in Chungking from Washington on October 25.

(a) F6717/7/10. (b) F7411/1689/10. (c) F7031/7/10. (d) F7860/7/10. (e) F8013/7/10. (f) F8339/7/10. (g) F8510/1689/10.

(v)

*Extra-territoriality negotiations, September 1942–January 11, 1943:
British views on post-war policy in the Far East, September 1942.*

Meanwhile the question of extra-territoriality had remained a
possible source of friction between China and her allies. Sir H.
(a) Seymour had thought in June that the abolition of extra-territorial
rights was of little practical importance to British trade with China.
(b) The policy of the Chinese Government was tacitly to assume that
extra-territoriality had already disappeared. By the first week in
September, the development of American opinion on this matter
made it desirable to take up the question at an early date. The
(c) United States Government proposed a joint *démarche* to the Chinese
Government offering to negotiate brief treaties (which would be
followed later by a more comprehensive settlement) to end extra-
territorial and related rights. The War Cabinet approved this
proposal in principle.

The Foreign Office instructed Sir H. Seymour on September 15
that the moment was not the most opportune, but they thought that
no better occasion was likely to arise in the near future, and that it
was wise to take the initiative while we still had it. In considering
the question, the Foreign Office had in mind the Coral Sea and
Midway victories and the Solomon Islands advance. General Wavell
had just said publicly that the tide had turned. The Chinese had
commented favourably on our operations in Madagascar, the news
that we had largely made up our war-time losses of naval vessels
and the statement by the Commander-in-Chief in India that we
were determined to reconquer Burma. The Allied successes in the
Middle East and south-west Pacific had also affected Chinese
opinion. The United States had now made an offer of concerted
instead of parallel action; they did not often make such an offer to
us in matters affecting their relations with China. We should get
better terms from the Chinese by a joint approach than by acting
alone; we should also avoid the danger that they would treat our
concession as a 'discard from weakness'.

The installation of a new Chinese Ambassador at Washington,[1]
(d) early in October 1942, gave urgency to the question. Mr. Winant
informed Mr. Eden that the Chinese Government might approach
the United States Government at any time to end the extra-territorial
system. The date chosen for the opening of negotiations was more

---

[1] Dr. Wei Tao-ming.

(a) F5218/1689/10. (b) F4629/1689/10. (c) WP(42)404; WM(42)121; F6361/5087/10;
F6183, 6388/828/10. (d) WP(42)448; WM(42)131 and 132; F6977/5087/10.

fortunate than the Allies knew. They made their first approach early in October. Before the treaty was signed the Russians had taken the offensive, and had isolated the German and Roumanian divisions around Stalingrad. In Libya the German and Italian armies were in retreat, and further west the Allies had established themselves in French North Africa. In Australasian waters the Japanese had lost the initiative and were slowly being driven out of New Guinea.

On October 7 the Foreign Office told Sir H. Seymour of the (a) proposal from the United States Government that they and the British Government should inform the Chinese representatives in Washington and London on October 9 that they had been considering the relinquishment of consular jurisdiction in China, and expected to present the Chinese Government shortly with draft treaties. The United States Government gave the Foreign Office a draft of their treaty. We had let Mr. Winant know that we agreed generally with their proposal, although we reserved the right to suggest amendments to the draft treaty.[1] On October 9 Mr. Eden (b) handed an *aide-mémoire* to the Chinese Chargé d'Affaires announcing the British proposals.

The 'well-timed and totally unexpected announcement' of the (c) British and American intentions was made on October 10, China's National Day and the anniversary of the military uprising at Wuchang which began the Chinese revolution in 1911. The reception by the Chinese political leaders, press and public of this gesture of goodwill was excellent. The British draft treaty was sent to Sir (d) H. Seymour on October 18. The United States Government were to present their draft to the Chinese Ambassador in Washington on October 24. Sir H. Seymour was instructed to tell the Chinese Government on that day that His Majesty's Government were still in consultation with the Dominions and India, but expected their draft treaty to follow closely the text of the United States draft and to provide also for the rendition of the British Concessions at Tientsin and Canton. The Foreign Office intended that negotiations for this treaty should be conducted by Sir H. Seymour in Chungking. The British draft was presented to the Chinese Government on October 30.[2] Mr. Eden thought that the improved atmosphere resulting from (e) Great Britain's extra-territoriality gesture would facilitate an

---

[1] All the Dominions had concurred in principle in the renunciation of extra-territorial (f) rights by His Majesty's Government, but Canada and Australia wanted to conclude separate treaties.

[2] This draft provided for abrogation of British rights of jurisdiction, the cancellation of (g) the Final (Boxer) Protocol of 1901, the rendition of the British concessions at Tientsin and Canton, and the abandonment of British rights in the International Settlements of Shanghai and Amoy.

(a) F6940/828/10.   (b) F7010/828/10.   (c) F8215/1689/10.   (d) F7220, 7319/828/10.
(e) F7458/828/10.   (f) F6940/828/10.   (g) F8510/1689/10.

approach to General Chiang Kai-shek about the deadlock over the loan negotiations.

The Chinese, however, did not merely accept the surrender of privileges offered to them. They asked for more. On November 13 (a) the Chinese Government produced a counter-draft which went far beyond the British offer. It differed from the British draft in the addition of a new article providing that Sino-British relations were based on the principle of equality and reciprocity, the addition to the article regarding rendition of concessions of a clause providing for termination of the Kowloon Lease Convention of 1898,[1] and an exchange of notes providing for inclusion in the abrogation of extra-territorial and related rights of further unequal treaty rights, including those concerned with coastal trade and inland navigation.

(b)   The Chinese Minister for Foreign Affairs said that the Chinese Government had not raised the question of Hong Kong, but that they felt the 1898 Convention ought to be included in this treaty. Sir H. Seymour thought that the Chinese Government were determined upon the abrogation of all rights resulting from unequal treaties, and that public opinion was solid on the matter. The demands now put forward by the Chinese did not affect American interests, and American public opinion continued to regard China as the blameless victim of Western imperialism. As far as Sir H. Seymour could judge, there was no reason why the United States Government should not accept such minor modifications in the new treaty as might affect them. The Chinese, therefore, were in a strong position, of which they were fully aware.

(c)   Sir H. Seymour was not surprised that the Chinese Government had raised the question of the Kowloon leased territory. They were unlikely to drop it, since they considered leased territories to be in the same category of unequal treaty rights derogatory to Chinese sovereignty as our Concessions and the Shanghai Settlement. The whole question of the treaty negotiations had aroused great interest in Chungking. The Chinese attitude was that no foreign Power should continue to occupy their territory. Sir H. Seymour thought there was much to be said for accepting their demands, which did not include a request for the use of any British territory, including Kowloon. There was some value in the tacit acceptance by China that Hong Kong, including Kowloon, was British, and did not come within the scope of the negotiations.

On December 5 Mr. Eden informed Sir H. Seymour that he was

---

[1] Great Britain had acquired the lease of the Kowloon territory adjacent to Hong Kong in 1898 for 99 years under the Convention for the Extension of Hong Kong Territory signed at Peking.

(a) F7741/828/10. (b) F7742/828/10. (c) F7822/828/10.

not prepared to consider the Kowloon lease in connexion with the present treaty, since it had nothing to do with extra-territoriality; it was an enlargement of British territory, and thus in a different category from the concessions and settlements in China in which we were relinquishing special rights. He preferred to stand on this argument. If, however, Sir H. Seymour thought that we should have to go further, the Foreign Office would inform the Chinese Government, if necessary in writing, that at the end of the war His Majesty's Government looked for a reconstruction in the Far East which would secure peace and order for all, both on land and on sea. We would be ready to consider with the Chinese Government the future status of the Kowloon territory during the currency of the lease.

On December 7 Sir H. Seymour reported that he was not sure (a) whether the introduction of the question into the negotiations by the Chinese was tentative, or whether they would make an issue of it. He thought that the latter alternative was more likely, and that the Chinese would not acquiesce in the continuance of the lease after the war. He agreed that the best course was to stand if possible on a refusal to include the Kowloon lease, but that it might prove necessary to make a statement to show that the question was not shelved indefinitely. A week later Sir H. Seymour told Dr. Soong (b) that we were not prepared to discuss the Kowloon question. Dr. Soong said that the Chinese public regarded the leased territories and the Concessions as in the same category; that the matter had been raised in the People's Political Council; that it was desirable to remove all causes of misunderstanding between Great Britain and China, and that the Chinese Government felt that a treaty which did not secure settlement of the Kowloon lease would fail to achieve this purpose.

On December 14 Mr. Han Lih-wu[1] left a personal message for (c) the Ambassador from Dr. Soong. Dr. Soong doubted whether General Chiang Kai-shek and Dr. Kung would conclude the treaty if cancellation of the lease were not included. Mr. Han Lih-wu suggested that the Chinese Government should address a communication to His Majesty's Government stating that, while they recognised that the question was not concerned with the treaty, they desired to raise it later. Sir H. Seymour recommended that the British Government should accept this compromise. On December 18 the Foreign Office informed Sir H. Seymour that the United (d)

---

[1] Secretary-General of the Sino-British Cultural Association working for improvement of Sino-British relations. Mr. Han Lih-wu was one of the few men in General Chiang Kai-shek's confidence, and in this capacity acted as a liaison between the General and the British Embassy.

(a) F8188/828/10. (b) F8287/828/10. (c) F8287/828/10. (d) F8299/828/10.

States Government had nearly concluded their negotiations and were proposing to the Chinese Government signature on January 1 (the first anniversary of the United Nations declaration). We should
(a) like to sign on the same day. On December 21 the War Cabinet gave authority for a statement that, while the Kowloon lease was outside the scope of the treaty, we would be prepared to discuss it
(b) after the war. Six days later Dr. Koo said that his Government had considered the proposal to deal with the Kowloon leased territory by an exchange of notes. They had decided that no solution would be acceptable unless it contained a statement that we intended to return the territory to China. They had no objection to dealing with the matter outside the treaty and making arrangements after the war, but unless the proposed statement of our intentions were made they would not sign the treaty.

Sir H. Seymour replied that the treaty was highly satisfactory to the Chinese Government, and that we had gone a long way to meet them in offering an exchange of notes stating our readiness to discuss the matter after the war. We would not agree to settle the matter
(c) now. Sir H. Seymour later reported to the Foreign Office that, if the Chinese Government refused to sign the treaty unless we made a statement of our intention to return the territory to China, our relations would deteriorate just when they had begun rapidly to improve.

(d)   On December 28 Dr. Soong told Sir H. Seymour that the Chinese Government had had two discussions on the proposed exchange of notes, but could not accept the British solution. He said both Government and people felt strongly against the continued existence of the leased territory, and asked that His Majesty's Government should declare their readiness to return it to China, on the understanding that details could be negotiated later. Although such a declaration could be separate from the treaty, a settlement which left out the Kowloon lease would fail to establish relations on a basis of mutual confidence. Sir H. Seymour thought that the text of the treaty and note should be agreed subject to the Kowloon question.[1]

The Foreign Office, however, considered that if the Chinese persisted in their demand we should have to do without the treaty.
(e) Mr. Eden asked Lord Halifax to try to get the help of the United States Government in persuading the Chinese to abandon an attitude

---

[1] Sir H. Seymour's meaning is not clear. It is possible that the text should read 'subject to reservations on the Kowloon question', i.e. the treaty would be initialled and notes would be exchanged regarding the readiness of the British Government to discuss the question after the war, but the question of a declaration in the sense requested by the Chinese Government would be left open.

(a) WP(42)600. WM(42)171. F8287, 8299, 8397/828/10; F8552/828/10. (b) F8482/828/10. (c) F8482/828/10. (d) F8515/828/10. (e) F8482/828/10.

which would make it impossible to sign the treaty. In a letter to the United States Chargé d'Affaires of December 29, Mr. Eden said (a) that we had wanted to co-operate with the United States as closely as our differing positions allowed, and to make the signing of the treaties an Anglo-American-Chinese act of political solidarity. We were unable to withdraw from our position about the leased territory and so lay ourselves open to further Chinese pressure on other matters. On December 30 Sir H. Seymour informed Dr. Soong that (b) we were not prepared to go beyond the proposed exchange of notes. The Chinese Government after another protest agreed not to raise the Kowloon question in connexion with the treaty, but reserved the right to raise the question later. The treaty was ready for signature on January 1, 1943. It was not signed until January 11 owing to a delay at Washington over the Chinese text of the treaty with the United States.

The Anglo-Chinese treaty of January 11, 1943, was a considered act of policy even though in important particulars the concessions made to Chinese nationalist feeling went beyond the original intention of the British Government, and involved the risk of sacrificing legitimate British interests built up over a long period of years. These concessions were greater than those required from the United States; one important reason for making them was the overriding need to keep as far as possible in line with American policy.

It was impossible at this stage of the war to frame detailed proposals for a post-war settlement. Nevertheless the Foreign Office was aware of the danger of allowing opinion, especially in the United States, to develop on lines unfair to Great Britain and unlikely to secure the stability and welfare of Asia. American opinion was inclined to dismiss too summarily the past contribution of Great Britain to the power of Asia as nothing more than selfish imperialism, and to ignore the sense of responsibility which governed British colonial and Far Eastern policy.

We had therefore to formulate at least in general terms the kind of settlement which Great Britain would desire in the Far East. An attempt to draw up the general principles of a settlement had been (c) made in a memorandum of September 1942 after joint consultation between the Foreign Office, the India Office, the Dominions Office and the Colonial Office. The memorandum was overtaken by events, but it remains of considerable interest as an indication of the British view at a time when, after three years of war, the tide had begun to turn against the Germans and their allies, and ultimate victory at last seemed certain.

The memorandum did not deal with India. Here the British

(a) F8482/828/10. (b) F8557, 8566/828/10. (c) F6441, 6720/695/61.

Government and the Government of India had made definite promises; the fulfilment of these promises was only a matter of time and the obstacles were local to India. There was no question of keeping British control. Similarly in Burma the declared policy of the British Government was the establishment of full Burmese self-government within the Commonwealth. At this time it was regarded not merely as impracticable but as unfair to the Burmese to hand the country over to them for self-government without practical assistance in recovery. We should therefore aim at retaining administrative control during a period of reconstruction. This period would have a stated time-limit and, in accordance with our previous declarations, we should consult with representative Burmese on the best means of transition to full self-government.

The general policy which we should recommend for the whole Pacific area would be based on three main principles: the general interest of all concerned in securing the defence of the area and preventing a revival of Japanese aggression; the general interest in securing free access to raw materials, markets and ocean ports, and opportunities for investment and development; the application of the principles of Article III (1) of the Atlantic Charter[1] and of Article VII of the Anglo-American Mutual Aid Agreement.[2] We had not expressly admitted the applicability of Article III of the Charter to the Far East, but the United States had done so, and we could not withhold a similar admission.

The application of these principles raised certain large questions. Were we to maintain our sovereignty over our colonial territories on the pre-war basis, or to treat these territories as the United States had treated the Philippines, or should we look for some 'half-way' between the retention of full sovereignty and the grant of complete independence? From the economic point of view, we required nothing more than the free access which was desirable for all. From

---

[1] 'They (the signatory Powers) respect the right of all peoples to choose the form of government under which they will live; and they wish to see sovereign rights and self-government restored to those who have been forcibly deprived of them.'

[2] 'In the final determination of the benefits to be provided to the United States of America by the Government of the United Kingdom in return for aid furnished under the Act of Congress of March 11, 1941, the terms and conditions thereof shall be such as not to burden commerce between the two countries, but to promote mutually advantageous economic relations between them and the betterment of world-wide economic relations. To that end they shall include provision for agreed action by the United States and the United Kingdom, open to participation by all other countries of like mind, directed to the expansion, by appropriate international and domestic measures, of production, employment and the exchange and consumption of goods, which are the material foundations of the liberty and welfare of all peoples; to the elimination of all forms of discriminatory treatment in international commerce; and to the reduction of tariffs and other trade barriers; and, in general, to the attainment of all the economic objectives set forth in the Joint Declaration made on August 12, 1941, by the President of the United States of America and the Prime Minister of the United Kingdom.'

the defence point of view, we could not again make ourselves responsible for the defence of vast territories with inadequate forces and no certainty of help. We needed therefore a system of collective defence in which we should take our share. From an administrative point of view, we could fulfil our obligations in the interest of the peoples concerned only if we had adequate internal responsibility. There was, however, nothing incompatible between this local responsibility, which admitted the principle of trusteeships and participation in some general international arrangement such as the establishment of a United Nations Council for the Pacific. We should therefore offer to accept the supervision of an international body of this kind, subject to American participation, and to similar acceptance by all other Powers concerned.

CHAPTER LX

British relations with China from January 1943 to July 1945

(i)

Chinese insistence on 'equality of treatment' as a Great Power: Madame Chiang Kai-shek's attitude towards Great Britain: revival of the loan proposals (January–December 1943).

WITH the Allied victories in 1943 the Chinese Government were assured that they were on the winning side and that the expulsion of the Japanese from China was only a matter of time. Furthermore, owing to the support of the United States, they had secured for themselves the status of a leading Great Power, and the long-postponed abolition of extra-territoriality in the treaties of January 11 was a legal recognition of their changed relationship with the West. The practical consequences of the surrender of extra-territorial privilege were small since British and other interests had already disappeared under the Japanese occupation,[1] but the psychological effect was important. In a broadcast on January 12, 1943, General Chiang Kai-shek spoke of the new status. The Chinese did not regard it as due to an act of grace by their allies but as something which they had themselves achieved in fulfilment of one of the chief aims of Sun Yat-sen's revolution. They tried to get full and almost unlimited practical recognition of their equality. General Chiang Kai-shek asked for a rapid increase of military supplies, and claimed the right to be consulted over strategic decisions and post-war plans.

These claims were put forward, for propagandist reasons, with more vehemence because they diverted attention from the domestic weakness of the Government. The hold of General Chiang Kai-shek on the country was becoming weaker. The provincial governors in the area nominally under Kuomintang control were acting with increasing disregard of the central authority, though their own rule was not less inefficient and corrupt. The central authority was itself

---

(a) [1] On January 1, 1943, the Japanese announced to the puppet Chinese Government at Nanking their own surrender of extra-territorial privileges. The Nanking Government declared war on Great Britain and the United States on January 9. The Japanese handed over to the Nanking Government more than 1,000 items of 'enemy property' confiscated since December 9, 1941, and including factories, schools and hospitals.

(a) F1208/254/10.

falling into disrepute owing to General Chiang Kai-shek's unwilling-ness to listen to criticism or even to keep in employment people who ventured to tell him the truth. He continued to refuse to dismiss his brother-in-law, Dr. Kung, from the post of Finance Minister, although he (Dr. Kung), owing to his inefficiency as well as his dishonesty, was more responsible than anyone else in China for the maladministration which had led to a galloping inflation; prices in 1943 were 200 times those of 1937.[1] The Kuomintang army, which lived largely on the country, was almost as great a burden to the peasants as the Japanese. The leaders in Chungking had no intention of expending their forces in China against the Japanese; their plan was to harbour them, such as they were, for employment against rebels, and particularly the Communists in the north, after the war.[2] Already in 1943 a large number of the better-trained troops were being employed to ward off any further advance of the Communists. The only value of Chinese resistance to the Allies was that, mainly in a passive way, it occupied a number of Japanese troops.

The Foreign Office did not believe that this resistance would (a) collapse if it were not supported by a large-scale diversion of Allied resources or that such a diversion would hasten the defeat of Japan. On the other hand, American opinion took a different view. The President had access to first-hand information which would have given him a true picture of the situation, but even if he had wished to do so, he could hardly have resisted the general popular view—which united different *blocs* of American opinion—of the importance of China in the war and the need in American interests to give full backing to General Chiang Kai-shek. The war effort of China was indeed regarded in some quarters as comparable with that of Great Britain, and also as more disinterested, and untainted with 'im-perialism'.

Chinese propaganda in the United States thus met with wide and (b) uncritical sympathy. The warnings about disaster for China unless help were given on a much larger scale strengthened the suspicion that 'Downing Street's preoccupation with Europe' was the main obstacle to increased aid to China, and that Great Britain was deliberately keeping out of the war in the Far East except in relation to her own colonial interests. In China General Chiang Kai-shek took a similar line. He thanked both Great Britain and the United States for the treaties of January 11, but said that the attitude of the United States was especially gratifying. since it was 'at one with us in our hopes and aspirations' and 'made no reservations whatsoever'.

---

[1] See above, p. 500, note 1.
[2] See p. 479.

(a) F1208/254/10. F351/351/23. (b) F1317/1317/61.

The Chinese press was enthusiastic, and at the same time regretted that the Kowloon Leased Territory had not been dealt with in the treaty. Sir H. Seymour reported that influential members of the Government were said to hold the view that the peace aims of China and the United States were identical, while those of China, the United Kingdom and Soviet Russia diverged.

At the end of the Casablanca Conference the Prime Minister and
(a) the President sent a message to General Chiang Kai-shek that 'the vital importance of aiding China has filled our minds'. The Prime
(b) Minister also sent, at the President's suggestion, a personal message assuring the General that, if Germany should collapse before Japan, Great Britain would at once bring the largest forces possible to the Far Eastern theatre and would continue the war against Japan to the end. Early in February Sir John Dill went to Chungking with General Arnold, the Chief of the United States Air Force, for military discussions with the Chinese on plans for the reconquest of Burma.
(c) General Chiang Kai-shek wrote to the Prime Minister on February 7 that he had greatly appreciated this visit, but he made large and impracticable demands for supplies by air. After the meeting
(d) General Chiang Kai-shek refused to publish the official communiqué of the conference, and was said to be much disappointed at the results. The Chinese press also noted that the Casablanca Conference seemed to have confirmed the intention of the Allies to deal with Germany before Japan. They attributed this decision mainly to British influence and complained that China was not brought into the most secret Anglo-American strategic discussions. A Chinese military mission in Washington had hoped for admission to membership of the Combined Chiefs of Staff, but left in January without obtaining it.

Madame Chiang Kai-shek's popularity in the United States, where she had come at the end of November 1942,[1] also caused some difficulties. The Foreign Office hoped that she might be
(e) encouraged to visit Great Britain. Sir H. Seymour felt that such a visit might go a long way towards disabusing her of some of the prejudices she had against us. Many of these were 'American' owing to her American education, and her stay in the United States in a very critical attitude would only increase the ill-feeling there towards Great Britain on Indian and colonial questions.
(f)   On January 2, 1943, the Chinese Embassy informed Lord Halifax that Madame Chiang Kai-shek's health prevented her from accept-

---

[1] Madame Chiang Kai-shek came to the United States for medical treatment.

(a) T75/3, Stratagem 225, Churchill Papers/420. (b) Stratagem 241, Churchill Papers/420. (c) T108A/3, Churchill Papers/158. (d) F931/25/10. (e) F8452/4072/10 (1942). (f) F73/73/10.

ing any invitations. The Foreign Office thought that her reluctance
to commit herself to a visit might be due partly to misgivings whether
her reception would be in accordance with her estimate of her
position.[1] Although her status was not that of the wife of the head
of a State, the Foreign Office were most anxious, from the point of
view of British relations with the United States and China, that her
reception should not be compared unfavourably with that accorded
to Mrs. Roosevelt. Sir A. Clark Kerr confirmed their fear that (a)
Madame Chiang Kai-shek would not come unless she was assured
beforehand that she would be invited to stay at Buckingham Palace. (b)
At the request of the Foreign Office the King and Queen agreed to
offer her hospitality at Buckingham Palace or Windsor Castle at
any time after February 1. Lord Halifax was instructed to urge her
to come, but failed to secure a definite answer; on February 23 (c)
Madame Chiang Kai-shek said that owing to her health she could
make no firm plans.[2]   (d)

Madame Chiang Kai-shek addressed Congress (where she was (e)
given an enthusiastic reception) on February 18. She spoke strongly
against the view that the defeat of Hitler was the first concern of the
United States and Great Britain. She argued that the Japanese, in
their areas of occupation, controlled greater resources than Germany
and the longer they were left the stronger they must become. Lord
Halifax thought that Congress might be swept on a wave of public
emotion into making promises to China which, in view of the
shipping situation, would be difficult to fulfil.[3]

In this atmosphere a broadcast by Mr. Churchill on March 21[4]
caused an unfortunate impression both in China and the United

---

[1] The Prime Minister noted later (May 21): 'The lady gives herself royal airs and (f)
considers herself co-ruler of China.' She apparently demanded to be present at military
discussions, and was offended with her husband for telegraphing that Mr. Soong alone
would speak for China.

[2] Lord Halifax believed the plea of ill health to be genuine and that Madame Chiang (g)
Kai-shek really wanted to visit England. She did not give a definite refusal until June 9.
She arrived back in Chungking via Canada on July 3. On the Prime Minister's visit to
Washington in May 1943, Madame Chiang Kai-shek invited him to meet her in New
York, but refused an invitation from the President to meet the Prime Minister at the
White House.

[3] In a minute dated April 15, 1943, Mr. N. Butler wrote: 'The American obsession (h)
for China has been consolidated by Madame Chiang Kai-shek to an extent that it requires
a definite mental effort on the part of persons in this country [Great Britain] to understand.'

[4] The theme of this broadcast was to warn the people of Great Britain that, in spite of
recent victories, they could not relax, and return to politics and planning for peace-
time, etc. In order to make his warning clear Mr. Churchill outlined his own idea of the
course of events, the defeat of Germany, and then the final effort against Japan, in which
it would be physically impossible to employ all the forces used against Germany. Hence
there was likely to be a partial demobilisation. Mr. Churchill then spoke in very general
terms of post-war conditions at home, and the world settlement. He said that the 'three
great victorious Powers' would discuss World Organisation.

(a) F8550/4079/10 (1942).   (b) F352/73/10.   (c) F1111/25/10.   (d) F1156/73/10.
(e) F1317/1317/61.   (f) F2704/73/10.   (g) F3070/25/10.   (h) F1878/25/10.

States. Critics noticed the omission of China from the list of victorious Great Powers, and the announcement of the partial demobilisation of British forces after the defeat of Hitler and before that of Japan. They assumed that we were not determined to fight to the end in the Far East. The misunderstanding was aggravated because the Chungking Press Attaché omitted from the report of the speech the one sentence that really concerned China, namely that physical reasons precluded us from moving to the Far East all the millions of troops who would become available on Germany's defeat. In these circum-
(a) stances, and in view also of the President's insistence at a talk with Mr. Eden on March 16 of the need to associate China with other world Powers in the solution of world problems, the Foreign Office drafted, for the approval of the Prime Minister, a telegram to be sent to Mr. Eden.[1] The draft pointed out that the Prime Minister was referring specifically to Europe, and suggested that Mr. Eden might like to make it clear again on a future occasion that in the task of world reconstruction 'we look upon China as one of the four leading Powers who have the greatest contribution to make'. Mr. Churchill thought it unnecessary to send this telegram. He regarded it as untrue to say that China was a world Power equal to Great Britain, the United States or Russia, and did not want to subscribe to a statement to this effect.

Madame Chiang Kai-shek's oratory in the United States continued, however, to cause anxiety, or at all events irritation, to the Foreign Office and also to the Government of India.[2] At the end of
(b) April Lord Halifax was instructed, at the Viceroy's request, to protest to Mr. Soong about Madame Chiang Kai-shek's public

---

(c)   [1] During conversations with Mr. Eden in Washington on March 27, the President repeated his view that China must be included among the four Great Powers. He based his arguments on population, the probability of a development in China in the next 50 years similar to that in Japan in the nineteenth century, and the view that China would have no aggressive aims or imperialistic ambitions, and would be a useful counterpoise to the Soviet Union.

(d)   [2] The Government of India regarded as extremely discourteous the fact that, in November 1942, Madame Chiang Kai-shek had flown over Indian territory without notifying the Government of India of her intention to do so. The Americans were also involved in the matter since they had arranged her flight. Mr. Soong was well aware of the British views on this piece of bad manners, though nothing had been said to Madame Chiang Kai-shek, but it had been intended to raise the question with her on her visit to Great Britain. Mr. Eden had also spoken to Mr. Winant on the subject in December 1942. On her return to Chungking in July 1943, Madame Chiang Kai-shek again flew unannounced over India. At the request of the India Office and the Viceroy Sir H. Seymour spoke to the Vice-Minister for Foreign Affairs at Chungking. The latter put the responsibility on the Americans. Protests through Mr. Winant did no more than produce an answer that the United States Air Transport Command were not in the habit of giving notification when carrying distinguished passengers. General and Madame Chiang Kai-shek crossed India by air unannounced on their way to the Cairo Conference. On this occasion Madame Chiang Kai-shek had been asked to inform the British authorities of the arrangements for herself and her husband, but failed to do so.

   (a) F1725/25/10.   (b) F2079/20/10.   (c) F1878/25/10.   (d) F8117/4072/10 (1942); F4369, 5563, 6538/73/10.

references to the Indian situation and criticism of British action with regard to the Congress leaders. Lord Halifax was asked to point out that we had taken the greatest care to avoid any public criticism of the deplorable dissensions in China between the Nationalists and Communists which militated against a united Chinese war effort. (a) Mr. Soong agreed that neither country ought to make in public any criticism of the internal problems of the other.

The relations with the Chinese Government during the summer and autumn of 1943 turned mainly on military questions.[1] Mr. Soong visited London from July 23 to August 11. It was clear from his questions that he was interested mainly in the immediate question of British strategy in the war against Japan, but that he also wanted to know our plans for the Far East after the war. Mr. Eden told Mr. Soong in general terms the proposals for a security organisation (b) based on the four Great Powers and on our wish to prevent further Japanese aggression and to see a strong China.[2]

The Foreign Office on their part were interested in the post-war plans of the Chinese Government. The general Chinese attitude towards post-war territorial changes in the Far East seemed likely to include a claim for all regions that had comprised the Manchu Empire of the nineteenth century before concessions had been granted to foreign Powers. According to this theory China would not lay direct claim to Thailand, Indo-China, Burma, Malaya or other European colonial possessions in the Southern Seas, but would certainly try to recover the leased and ceded territories and islands along the China coast, as well as Manchuria, Outer Mongolia and autonomous Tibet. The Chinese Government constantly protested to the British Embassy that atlases and maps issued by the Ministry of Information and British publishers marked the three Eastern Provinces and sometimes Outer Mongolia as being separate from the rest of China. They also objected strongly to the term 'Manchukuo'.

In his book *China's Destiny*[3] General Chiang Kai-shek advanced

---

[1] I have not dealt with these questions since they fall outside the scope of this History.

[2] On July 7, 1943, Mr. Eden spoke in similar terms about British post-war policy in the Far East at a 'Salute to China' meeting in the Albert Hall.

[3] *China's Destiny* was first published on March 10, 1943. It was at once hailed in China (c) as the 'book of the century' and the 'New Testament' of China's political bible (Dr. Sun Yat-sen's *Three Principles of the People* representing the Old Testament). An English translation was ready for simultaneous publication in May in Great Britain, America and India but was postponed owing, it was said, to fear of adverse foreign reactions. The main theme was that the unequal treaties imposed by the foreign Powers were primarily responsible for all the ills of China during the past 100 years. A revised edition, published on January 1, 1944, attempted to tone down some of the denunciations of foreign action and included an appeal to the Chinese to 'abstain from raking up past things and harbouring old hatreds'. Exaggerations and distortions, however, still remained. The
(continued on page 524)

(a) F2244, 2369/73/10. (b) F3864/182/10. (c) F1250/310/10 (1944).

the theory (asserted in the second edition as an historical fact) of the common ancestral origin of the Hans, Manchus, Mongols, Tibetans and Chinese Moslems.[1] Sir H. Seymour suggested that the purpose of this theory seemed to be to supply an historical justification for a policy of economic, cultural and political assimilation of the border peoples which might otherwise have invited the stigma of imperialism. General Chiang Kai-shek claimed that the natural geographic boundaries of historic China included an area absolutely necessary
(a) for national defence and national economy. The Foreign Office found it difficult to agree with President Roosevelt's belief (expressed to Mr. Eden on March 27) that China had no imperialist ambitions. They regarded China as determined not only to reassert political dominion over the border peoples, but also to exercise a preponderating influence in Thailand, Indo-China and possibly Burma. Herein lay the most important difference between Sino-American and Sino-British relations. The United States had no territorial interests to defend in south-east Asia. Relations between Great Britain and China on the other hand were overshadowed by the threat of a direct clash over Tibet[2] and Hong Kong and the possibility of friction over the future of China's south-western neighbours.

This threat did not materialise in 1943. The Chinese continued to refuse a formal recognition of the autonomy of Tibet even with the British condition allowing for Chinese suzerainty, but no more incidents were reported and the Chinese desire for the return of
(b) Kowloon and Hong Kong was not made a serious issue. There was a widespread and deep-seated feeling in the south-east provinces of

---

(*continued*)
first complete authorised English translation of the revised version was published in New York in January 1947. The appendix contains the earlier version of altered passages.
(c) A Foreign Office note of February 15, 1944, on the book pointed out that, in spite of his views on self-determination in Asia, General Chiang Kai-shek claimed that Tibet and Mongolia were necessary to China for her defence, and that 'no area' could 'of its own accord assume the form of independence'.
(d) [1] The Chinese Moslems originated in Arabia, Iran and Turkey; most of them have kept their own distinctive identity in the Moslem districts of western China. Under the Kuomintang Government they attained a position of considerable importance among the peoples who formed the National Republic of China.
(e) [2] The question of the status of Tibet was raised in connexion with the organisation of a supply route through the country to China. The Chinese and Tibetans mutually accused each other of threats of aggression. The Government of India were more concerned than the Foreign Office over the possibility of a Chinese attack on Tibet. The Tibetans seemed over-anxious on the matter, but the Chinese, though denying that they had hostile intentions against Tibet, claimed that the country was Chinese territory and that any movement of troops on the border was from the point of view of the Chinese Government a domestic matter. The view of the British Government—and, more directly, the Government of India—was that the Chinese Government, while maintaining suzerainty over Tibet, had recognised the *de facto* autonomy of the country since the fall of the Manchu Empire. The Chinese Government refused to accept this view and the United States Government, while disclaiming support of any other 'colonial' or imperialist Power, did not seem disposed to question the Chinese claim.

(a) F1878/25/10. (b) F4485/254/10. (c) F803/310/10 (1944). (d) F3512/113/10 (1942). (e) WP(43)267; WM(43)94.

China for their return, though the demand was not put forward officially.

The Chinese were not interested in British 'imperialism' from the point of view of Hong Kong alone. The large Chinese populations in Malaya and Burma and elsewhere aroused their concern in the future of these British-administered territories. One or two incidents during the year suggested that China might have territorial designs on northern Burma. Part of the Burma-China border was un-demarcated; the Chinese attempted to extend their influence over the disputed area by the penetration of irregulars and in a map published by the Chinese Ministry of Information on July 7 they included all northern Burma as undisputed Chinese territory.[1]

Mr. Soong, however, had told Mr. Eden during his visit to the (a) United States in March that China had no territorial ambitions in Thailand, Indo-China, Burma or Malaya. He knew that at some time there might have been doubts in our minds whether the Chinese would not wish to stay in Burma, but he reminded Mr. Eden that Chinese troops went to Burma at our invitation and would be withdrawn as soon as their military work had been done. Mr. Soong repeated this assurance during his visit to London. General Chiang Kai-shek had already, on February 26, 1943, given a solemn pledge that China had no territorial designs on Thailand and no intention of violating her independence.

During his discussions in London Mr. Soong also referred to (b) economic questions. He said that, although there would be no opening for 'concession-hunting', the Chinese Government wanted to secure foreign technical advice and capital. Mr. Soong was told that British firms in China would expect treatment comparable with that of foreign firms in Great Britain, and that they had been discouraged by the tendency of the Chinese Government to establish monopolies and by confusion over the rules affecting shareholding in joint Chinese and foreign companies.[2] Mr. Soong, however, was not very forthcoming in his answers.

---

[1] The Chinese acceptance of the status of a leading world Power was also shown in (c) their attitude towards the Four-Power declaration in Moscow. The Chinese Government received their inclusion in the declaration as a matter of right; the Chinese Ambassador in Moscow told Sir A. Clark Kerr that the declaration was of particular value as a guarantee that the Soviet Union would not claim any Chinese territory in the event of their entry into the war against Japan. In general the Chinese attitude towards the Russians was that they wanted Russian assistance but were afraid of the price which they might have to pay for it. The Chinese, however, had themselves taken advantage of Russian difficulties to resume political control of Sinkiang in 1942–3.

[2] One such disquieting move had been the monopolising of foreign exchange by the (d) Chinese Central Bank. This measure particularly affected the two British banks in Chungking. In September, however, the Chinese Government removed restrictions on the ratio of capital in these joint enterprises and no longer required Chinese directors to be in a majority on company boards.

(a) F1520/73/10. (b) F4032/182/10. (c) F5834/3801/10. (d) F3774/254/10.

(a) Towards the end of the year 1943 the Chinese revived their interest in the British loan. Dr. Kung was criticised at the People's Political Council in September for not having utilised the British credit; in conversation with a member of His Majesty's Embassy he argued that the question of the loan was a major obstacle to good Anglo-Chinese relations—a view which, according to the British Embassy, was not held by anyone else.

(b) At Cairo on November 26 Mr. Eden told Dr. Wang Chung-hui[1] that the British and United States Governments were prepared to start work on a new Commercial Treaty even before the end of the war. Dr. Wang then produced some new proposals for the £50,000,000 loan which he hoped would be more acceptable to us. Mr. Eden said that under these proposals we should still be obliged after the war to deliver to China goods ordered during the war in the sterling area on a considerable portion of the proceeds of the loan and that we were most unlikely to accept such an obligation. He explained to Dr. Wang the serious position of our post-war balance of trade, but promised that his proposals should be examined in London and a detailed reply given.[2]

(ii)

British views on the China situation in 1944: the question of British intervention in the interest of Chinese unity and American suspicions of British policy in the Far East.

From this time Anglo-Chinese diplomatic relations were not of great importance. There were indeed few diplomatic exchanges with the Chinese Government. Sir H. Seymour's telegrams and despatches were limited mainly to a political commentary and to reports on negotiations between the Chinese Government and the Communists. There was no British representative with the Communists and, as the Foreign Office noticed with a certain impatience, the accounts of Communist activities from unofficial British sym-
(c) pathisers were superficial and uncritical. Sir H. Seymour himself wrote in March 1944 that 'the lot of foreign representatives here [Chungking] is made no easier by the fact that the Minister for Foreign Affairs has for most of the last three years been either abroad or in trouble here'.

---

[1] Secretary-General of the Chinese Supreme Council of National Defence.
(d) [2] See above, Chapter LIX, sections (iii) and (iv). The loan agreement was finally signed on May 2, 1944. The terms were those upon which the British Government had insisted during the negotiations, i.e. the amount to be used for backing an internal loan was not to exceed £10 million, and the loan was to be spent during the war.

(a) 5813/39/10.   (b) F6618/25/10.   (c) F2247/34/10.   (d) F1959/4/10.

Admiral Mountbatten, as Supreme Allied Commander, South- (a)
East Asia, tried at the end of 1943 and in the early part of 1944 to
secure the appointment of a Minister of State in the Far East, but
the Prime Minister was disinclined to give the proposal much
support. The main issues at this time and later in the Far East were
strategic, and the controversies over them were now more Anglo-
American than Anglo-Chinese. Since the Americans indeed had
taken practical responsibility for the relations between China and
the Allies, there was little for the British Government to do in the
matter. American policy was itself uncertain, and affected not only
by serious differences of opinion about the part which China could
play in the war against Japan, but also by an increasing exasperation
that Chinese behaviour continued to be very different from the
idealised version of it built up in the United States. In spite of the
large claims made by General Chiang Kai-shek, Chinese resistance
to the Japanese remained almost negligible; between July and
November 1944 the Japanese moved without difficulty into Chang-
sha, Hangyang and Kweilin and destroyed the aerodromes which
were being constructed for an eventual attack on Japan. Meanwhile
the internal situation grew even worse, and as the administration of
the Kuomintang became more and more discredited the hopes and
demands of the Communists rose. During and after the late summer
of 1943 these demands had gone beyond the possibility of any compromise, even though they were still put in a polite form and at
least nominally with a view to the formation of a united Government
and a united military command. The Communists, however, were
consolidating their position in the areas under their control, and
there seemed little chance of avoiding civil war in China after the
expulsion of the Japanese. Negotiations between General Chiang
Kai-shek and the Communists continued throughout 1944. They
were discussed fully at the meeting of the Chinese People's Political
Council in September, but no agreement was reached.

The Foreign Office, as well they might, regarded these developments in China with great anxiety. A minute of October 12, 1944, (b)
on a report of the proceedings of the People's Political Council, read:

> 'China is certainly in a mess at present and I am not sure that we
> shall not have to consider very soon some positive action to get her
> out of it—or at least to try. Pressure on Chiang Kai-shek to promote
> unity by coming to terms with the Communists and attempts to find
> out where the Communists themselves stand are matters which we
> have so far left to the Americans. Chinese circles in touch with the
> Embassy have deprecated our intervention and it is quite clear that
> the Americans want to keep China as their own preserve, politically,

---

(a) F757, 759, 948, 1379. 1824/757/61; F1177/73/10. (b) F4609/159/10.

militarily and economically. But after the Presidential Election I am not sure that we shall not have to assert ourselves. A strong and united China—if such is attainable at all—is going to be a very important British interest after the war and if unity cannot be achieved during the remainder of this war, it is not likely to be achieved afterwards.'

(a)　　On October 21, 1944, Mr. Sterndale-Bennett[1] wrote a private letter to Sir H. Seymour asking whether he thought it desirable for the British Government to try to establish direct contact with the Communist authorities. Mr. Sterndale-Bennett said that hitherto the Far Eastern Department had inclined to think that in view of the weakness of the Central Government it would be dangerous to get in touch with the Communists and to put pressure on General Chiang Kai-shek to reach a settlement with them. The Department could not see what they could do to remove the deepening gloom in Chungking or promote Chinese unity. 'We do not seem well placed to make any positive contribution and our intervention would probably be disliked as much by the Americans as by the Chinese.' At the same time, we had a great interest in building up a strong, united, democratic China. Mr. Sterndale-Bennett repeated the view that if China could not achieve greater unity during the war, she was unlikely to achieve it afterwards. The proceedings at the People's Political Council suggested that there was still a chance of a settlement; slight progress seemed to have been made, partly by American pressure. Mr. Sterndale-Bennett wondered whether we could not add to this pressure, perhaps by saying that if the Central Government wanted to be treated as a Government of China and as one of the Big Four, they must come to an understanding with the Communists. We might achieve our purpose simply by showing an active interest in the Communists, as the Americans were doing. We could not let matters drift, for if the Kuomintang and Communists did not reach a settlement, the Communists might drift into the Russian orbit. Russia might enter the war against Japan. She might later demand special security arrangements in Manchuria and, owing to her relations with the Communists in north-west China, might penetrate north China to such a degree as to prevent the unification of the whole country. 'Is it not therefore in our interests to cultivate the Chinese Communists and to do what we can to bring about a reconciliation between them and the Kuomintang for the sake of Chinese independence and unity?'

Mr. Sterndale-Bennett asked Sir H. Seymour what chances there

---

[1] Mr. Sterndale-Bennett had succeeded Mr. Ashley Clarke as head of the Far Eastern Department.

(a) F4857/34/10.

were of securing national unity in China. Many arrangements were being made on the theory that China would remain one of the Big Four, but these arrangements seemed to be risky if China were likely to relapse into factions, particularly if unanimity among the Big Four were needed for the most important decisions of the new World Organisation.

Sir H. Seymour replied on November 7: 'It seems a long time (a) now since the best times of Chinese resistance, and it is sad to watch the gradual fading of the bright hopes which were then entertained for the unification of China as a reaction to Japanese pressure. Recent tendencies have all been the other way.' Provincial leaders had lost confidence in the ability of the Central Government to protect them. The Kuomintang was divided within itself, and was widely regarded as mainly an organisation for distributing lucrative posts. The use of the Chinese army seemed 'childishly incompetent', and the high potential value of the Chinese soldier was squandered. In these conditions factionalism was likely to increase. Even if the Central Government were able to re-occupy areas at present under the Japanese, it would still be a long time before a strong, united, democratic China emerged, and even then it would be on a basis of considerable provincial autonomy.

Sir H. Seymour said that the Communists knew the strength of their position, and that there was no sign that they would surrender any point which they regarded as vital to their continued existence. Hitherto they had held control of their own armies to be vital. The Communist administration could not be called a democracy, but seemed to have popular support. It was doubtful whether their system would work in more densely populated and richer parts of China. Sir H. Seymour pointed out that the Communists were well placed geographically; they were deeply suspicious of the Kuomintang; they were receiving encouragement from abroad and were likely to cling to their position. It was therefore difficult for General Chiang Kai-shek to offer a solution which would not produce a split-off of the Communist area. The most that could be hoped, and that without confidence, was for a compromise which would enable both sides to get on with the war. Sir H. Seymour did not think that we could do anything to promote an agreement. He mentioned former British statements at the time of General Chiang Kai-shek's intervention in Indian affairs that we did not interfere in his internal affairs. General Hurley[1] was trying to find a settlement, and owing to their operations in the China theatre the United States Government

---

[1] See below, p. 538.

(a) F5408/34/10.

had a better *locus standi* than the British Government. The Chinese looked to them far more than to Great Britain for post-war help. Sir H. Seymour did not think that we could intervene without an American invitation; even so, combined pressure was likely to defeat its own object. A *modus vivendi* might result from General Hurley's efforts, but the chances were not good.

Sir H. Seymour referred to the suggestion that Russia might penetrate north China. All observers in Yenan (the Communist centre) thought that there was no direct contact with Moscow; General Mao Tse-tung said that he feared Russian intervention, and wanted British and American help against it. Sir H. Seymour pointed out that hitherto British contacts with the Communists were confined to contacts with Communist representatives in Chungking. He did not see how we could open a consular post in a Communist area against the wishes of the Chinese Government.

In Sir H. Seymour's view, China was not really one of the Big Four; she would not be in a position for many years to help in suppressing a threat of aggression. At recent international conferences, however, Chinese delegates had often made a good contribution, although they had nothing behind them. Sir H. Seymour did not think that serious danger would arise from the fiction that China was a powerful State. 'The Chinese know in fact perfectly well that they are not.' He concluded: 'I only wish I could recommend an ideal cure for the present situation, but I do not think there is one.'

The Foreign Office thought that the situation was dominated by American ascendancy in China; the United States were trying to get the control of Chinese forces in China into the hands of an American general, and had undertaken intervention in the Communist problem. They seemed to aim at improving China's war production and planning her post-war industrialisation. They might establish a monopoly in China, although the Chinese would not favour such a development and the Russians would probably oppose it. American influence might cause Allied disunity; it might also handicap the rehabilitation of British commerce and other activities in China after the war. There might be combined American and Chinese pressure on imperial issues, e.g. Hong Kong. The remedy was closer Anglo-American co-operation in China. Sir A. Cadogan wrote on November 28: 'It does not appear that there is any opportunity for our intervention in any field at present.'

Note to section (ii): President Roosevelt's views on the future of Indo-China.

Anglo-American co-operation in the Far East was also complicated (a)
by President Roosevelt's views about Indo-China. On July 21, 1943,
the President said at a meeting of the Pacific Council[1] that the French
should not be allowed to retain their colonial possessions in Indo-
China on the ground that they had 'done nothing for the population,
but had misgoverned and exploited it', and that their return to
Indo-China would 'make bad feeling through the Far East'. The
President proposed a régime of trusteeship under the United Nations
as a preparation for independence on the model of the American
treatment of the Philippines.

The Foreign Office considered that the President's views on Indo-
China were not based on knowledge of the facts but arose largely
out of his prejudice against the colonial policies of the Western
Powers. A refusal to allow the return of Indo-China to France would
cause the deepest resentment among the French people. Moreover
the United States Government had in fact given explicit pledges
with regard to the integrity of the French Empire.[2] Apart from these
pledges to the French the Foreign Office regarded the proposal for
international control of Indo-China as unsatisfactory, since it would
allow Chinese, and ultimately Japanese, intrigues. Direct Chinese
control was not wanted by the inhabitants and would probably be
a threat to British interests.

After his return from the Teheran Conference President Roosevelt (b)
received the Chinese and Turkish Ambassadors, the Egyptian
Minister, the Soviet and Iranian First Secretaries (in the absence of
their chiefs) and the British Minister.[3] He told them, in confidence,
that he had been working very hard to prevent Indo-China from
being restored to France, which during the last hundred years had
done nothing for the Chinese people under their care. The latter
were as poor and as uneducated as ever they had been, and this state
of affairs could not be allowed to continue.

---

[1] Dr. Hornbeck (of the State Department) told Mr. Ashley Clarke in October 1943 (c)
that he did not know that the President had expressed his views at the Pacific Council.
Dr. Hornbeck said that the Departments of the United States Government were not
always kept very fully informed of what happened in the Pacific Council.

[2] The two chief commitments of the United States Government regarding the French (d)
Empire were: (i) A letter from Mr. Atherton to M. Pleven of October 14, 1941, stating:
'The policy of this Government as regards France is based upon the maintenance of the
integrity of France and of the French Empire, and on the eventual restoration of the
complete independence of all French territories.' (ii) Mr. Murphy's letter to General
Giraud immediately before the North African landings stating: 'I am able to assure you
that the restoration of France in its complete independence, in all its grandeur and the
extent it possessed before the war, in Europe as well as overseas, is one of the war aims of
the United Nations. It is understood that French sovereignty will be re-established, as
soon as possible, in all the territories, continental and colonial, over which the French
flag flew in 1939. The Government of the United States considers the French nation as
an ally and will treat it as such.' These letters were not published. The Foreign Office
did not think that the President had ever made a personal statement, but the letter to
General Giraud could hardly have been sent without his approval.

[3] The Ambassador was unwell.

(a) F4646, 6780/1422/61. (b) F6656/1422/61. (c) F5456/4023/61. (d) F6656/1422/61;
F223/66/61 (1944).

The President thought that the Indo-Chinese were not yet ready for elective institutions of their own, and that they should be placed under some United Nations Trusteeship which should take them towards the stage when they could govern themselves.[1] Mr. Roosevelt did not make it clear whether he was thinking of a United Nations Trusteeship for all peoples in this category or whether the administration was to be in the hands of a single country or of all or several of the United Nations. The President went on to say that 'we' should have great trouble with the French over this plan, but that 'we' must nevertheless carry it out. He also referred to Dakar as an example of an important place which, if it were in the hands of a country too weak to defend it, might become a threat to the whole western hemisphere.

(a)
The Foreign Office were much concerned over these remarks. They were sure that the remarks would be repeated, probably in a distorted form, and would have a bad effect. The British military authorities in south-east Asia were equally alarmed. They considered that the French reactions would be extremely serious, and that French co-operation would be essential in the reconquest of Indo-China from the Japanese. A small French force was already on its way to the Far East. We could not employ Frenchmen for our own ends and then refuse to give them back their territory.

(b)
The Prime Minister—whom Mr. Eden consulted by telegram— replied on December 21 that he had often heard the President express his views about Indo-China and Dakar, and that he (the Prime Minister) had never given his assent to them. He did not think that the Americans intended to take territory from France forcibly and without agreement with the French after a French Government had formed on the basis of the will of the French people. The Prime Minister considered that if we were informed officially of the statements made by the President we should state clearly and at once that we had no part in them. We should also mention the various declarations made by the President in favour of the integrity of the French Empire.

(c)
The Foreign Office instructed Lord Halifax to ask Mr. Hull confidentially whether the President had considered his proposals in relation to American pledges to France, and whether the policy which they represented had been agreed with the State Department.

(d)
Mr. Hull's answer was that he knew no more of the matter than Lord Halifax, and that he reminded the President from time to time of the pledges given to France. Mr. Hull thought that the President and he would probably discuss the matter later.

The Foreign Office inferred from this answer that the President's remarks did not represent a settled policy. The Prime Minister (to

---

[1] The President had in mind the developments in the Philippines under United States rule.

(a) F79/66/61 (1944).   (b) Frozen 769 (Churchill Papers/178; F6815/4023/61).
(c) F6656/1422/61.   (d) F66/66/61.

whom the facts were telegraphed) suggested to Mr. Eden on January   (a)
12, 1944, that the Foreign Office should 'develop a very strong movement on this issue' through the State Department and leave until a
later stage any direct communication between himself and the
President.

On the night of January 18–19 Lord Halifax reported a conver-   (b)
sation with the President himself on the matter. Mr. Roosevelt
said that his remarks on December 16 represented his considered
opinion, and that he did not mind if they were repeated to the
French. He did not think that his pledges about the French Empire
were of importance. He said that Mr. Murphy had committed
himself on the subject more definitely than he should have done.
Lord Halifax reminded the President that Mr. Welles had also made
a strong public statement which had not been withdrawn.

The Foreign Office submitted to the War Cabinet, on February 16,   (c)
1944, a memorandum on the future of Indo-China and other French
possessions. This memorandum recommended strongly that we
should try to get the support of the Dominions for the retention by
France of Indo-China and the French possessions in the Pacific. We
should propose arrangements for international consultation, joint
use of bases, etc., with regard to our own colonies and suggest that
France should accept similar arrangements for her colonies, including, if necessary, United Nations bases in Indo-China.

The War Cabinet accepted these proposals on February 24, 1944.   (d)
Once again, however, in the pressure of other and more immediate
business, the matter was postponed. The consultation with the
Dominions and with the United States Government had not taken
place when M. Massigli came to London in August 1944 for discussions. The Foreign Office therefore considered that we could not   (e)
make a statement of policy to M. Massigli but that we should suggest
to the French direct conversations with the United States Government, and that we should ask whether they would accept in respect
to Indo-China the arrangements for mutual security and consultation
which we were willing to accept for the British Empire. The War
Cabinet agreed with this suggestion, but thought that, in the circum-   (f)
stances, Mr. Eden might be more explicit about our policy.

M. Massigli told Mr. Eden that he did not expect the French   (g)
Government to object to the kind of arrangement we had in mind.
The Foreign Office hoped that the matter might be raised at the
Quebec Conference. Nothing was said about it at the Conference,
but the Prime Minister promised to discuss it later with the President.   (h)
No such discussion took place. The President kept obstinately to his
views about Indo-China, and had not given them up at the time of the
San Francisco Conference.

(a) Frozen 1255 (Churchill Papers/178; F118/66/61). (b) F360/66/61. (c) WP(44)111;
F980/66/61.   (d) WM(44)25; F1075/66/61.   (e) WP(44)444; F3789/66/61.
(f) WM(44)106. (g) F4348/66/61. (h) F1272, 1421/11/61 (1945).

(iii)

The problem of Anglo-American co-operation in the Far East: American suspicions of British policy: General Hurley's visit to London, April 1945.

The possibility of closer Anglo-American co-operation in the Far East depended on the willingness of the United States Government to agree that the two countries had a common purpose. Unfortunately American opinion, official and unofficial, did not take this
(a) view. In May 1944 Lord Halifax reported somewhat pessimistically about public criticism of British policy. The attitude of Government departments in Washington was equally distrustful. American officials assumed that British aims in the Far East were self-seeking and in conflict with more generous American principles. The State Department had recently told the British Embassy that British policy towards Thailand would 'augment' the distrust of our intentions in the Far East. The Office of War Information had said that they could not collaborate fully with us in propaganda to the Far East owing to a fundamental divergence of attitude about the future status of Asiatic peoples and their relationships with them.

The Foreign Office regarded it as difficult to meet these American suspicions until we had worked out a more definite policy of our
(b) own for the Far East. At the beginning of June 1944 they suggested that we should propose an exchange of plans with the State Department on post-war collaboration in Far Eastern affairs. Owing to the immediate concentration on Western affairs little was done during the summer and early autumn towards the first stage in this
(c) plan, the formulation of British policy. At the beginning of November the Prime Minister agreed to the revival of the inter-departmental Far Eastern Committee which had existed before the outbreak of war against Japan. This Committee held three meetings before the
(d) end of the year, but could not make much progress. Before their third meeting the Foreign Office had received a note from the United States Embassy to the effect that President Roosevelt expected the United States Government to be consulted about *any* arrangements for the future of south-east Asia. The reason for this note seemed to be that the State Department had heard reports that the British and Dutch might have come to an agreement on political, security and economic questions in the Pacific, and that the French were to be included in the talks.

The Foreign Office thought that this communication was an example of the American suspicions which were our greatest potential difficulty in the Far East. We had made no agreements with the

---

(a) F2300/993/61.   (b) F2469/993/61.   (c) F5388/757/61.   (d) F5868/168/61.

Dutch or French about the Far East; the only agreement under consideration was one with the Dutch about civil affairs in the Netherlands East Indies, of which the Americans knew. We were not in a position to start discussions with the United States about south-east Asia or the Pacific, and would not be able to do so for some time, since there were too many unknown factors, and Cabinet approval and Dominion concurrence were needed. On the other hand, the longer discussions were delayed the greater was the risk of differences growing, and of American governmental opinion hardening in directions which might create trouble later. The Foreign Office again proposed that we should have an informal exchange of views with the Americans. We should then work out our own attitude on issues arising from this exchange of views, in consultation with the Dominions. As a third stage we should hold a formal discussion with the Americans. The Foreign Office did not expect that the first stage of this programme could be carried out until after an interval of two months.

Early in January 1945 the Foreign Office consulted Sir H. (a) Seymour on the possibility of collaboration with the United States in aid to China. The Foreign Office realised that we had little to give, but thought that if we merely stood aside when China was in danger of complete collapse, our own standing and prestige would be affected. Furthermore, the position in China concerned the Allies generally; it was therefore undesirable to treat all decisions as a kind of American monopoly. In any case the Russians were unlikely to agree to this monopoly.

Sir H. Seymour replied on January 17. He was in favour of an (b) approach to the United States Government, though he did not think an immediate Chinese collapse likely to occur unless the Japanese again started serious operations in the country. He considered that British aid would be valuable, though it would become known only to a small circle and would have little propaganda effect. The South East Asia Command was to take a more important part in the war against Japan, but the Chinese and Americans would discount it on the ground that Great Britain was concerned mainly with the recovery of her colonies. Our best contribution to China would be through air operations. On the other hand, the Americans, in their task of getting order in the 'Chinese chaos', would want to keep everything under their own control, and would not want British collaboration except possibly in production and similar fields. They would think that our help would be too small to be worth the additional complications. Sir H. Seymour recommended that if we had anything substantial to give, we might offer it. We should not

(a) F136/136/10.   (b) F458/186/10.

get far merely by saying that we should like to help if the Americans could think of anything we might do. Any important operations by the British Fleet would have a great effect in China.[1]

(a)   Meanwhile the Chiefs of Staff had considered the telegram from the Foreign Office to Sir H. Seymour, and had differed from some of the views expressed in it. They pointed out that it had long been accepted that we and even the Americans could do nothing to make China a potential military asset in sufficient time to pay even a minimum dividend in the war. They believed that a breakdown of the Chungking Government would not have an 'incalculable' effect on the Far Eastern war; the effect on prestige and morale would be considerable, but militarily it was doubtful if the consequences would be so disastrous. At worst we should lose the Chinese contribution to the Burma campaign and the use of American airfields. China's main contribution, i.e. tying down large Japanese forces by guerrilla activity, would remain. With China in or out of the war, the value of the China coast for air bases remained the same; there would be little difference in the effort necessary for their recapture. The Chiefs of Staff considered that militarily China had made no progress; she had been a weak, unstable and disorganised State for too long, and assistance to her would have to be on a scale so large that the effort would not be commensurate with the results. We could not provide her with air transport; we were very short of it in Burma, and depended on American help to continue the campaign.

On January 27, therefore, the Foreign Office told Sir H. Seymour to regard their telegram as 'suspended'.[2] At the same time they warned the Chiefs of Staff of the danger of underrating the long-term political issues. Our post-war aim was the establishment of a strong and united China. The political disadvantage of the collapse of the Chungking Government would be the delay or removal of all chance of realising this aim. If unification were not delayed or did not altogether vanish, it might come about under the aegis of Russia. In any case the rise of Russian influence in China might be another result of collapse.

(b)   [1] Mr. Dening, Political Adviser to Admiral Mountbatten, agreed with Sir H. Seymour. He pointed out that the South East Asia Command was itself in great need of material, and particularly of transport aircraft and motor transport. This need would continue when the war in Europe was over. Mr. Dening added: 'Though in American eyes it may be an almost indictable offence for us to recover British territory in the process of destroying Japanese forces opposed to us, this will not prevent us from being savagely criticised if we fail to succour the population of Burma (and later of Malaya) and allow it to starve. . . . It might therefore be a long time before there would be any British surpluses to offer to China.'

[2] i.e. the telegram was not to be taken as a statement of policy. The Foreign Office sent the comments of the Chiefs of Staff to Sir H. Seymour, and said that the whole question of policy was under further review.

(a) COS(45)17; F439/186/10. (b) F587/186/10.

On March 2 the Foreign Office, in a review of developments in (a)
China, pointed out the disadvantage of a 'situation in which we
remain in a position of passivity and seeming detachment while the
Americans pursue single-handed their endeavour to promote a strong
and united China'. China was going through a critical phase in her
history, and was trying to continue fighting while at the same time
building up her strength and cohesion. The difficulties to be overcome—political, financial and economic—were 'vast and complex.
. . . If China failed to cope with them successfully the Allies might
find themselves confronted at the end of the Pacific war with a
Chinese chaos akin to the Grecian chaos but on a vast scale.'

The Foreign Office thought that Russia would not favour an
American 'monopoly' in China after the war. Either an American or
a British-American-Chinese *bloc* might produce a collision with the
Russians. The best safeguard seemed to lie in recognition of the fate
of China as a United Nations interest, and it was in this direction
that we could exert our influence.

The Foreign Office considered that the Chinese reaction to an
American monopoly might not be in British favour. It might take
an anti-foreign form as unfavourable to Great Britain as to the
United States, or it might be in favour of Germany and Japan. In
any case the Chinese struggle for self-development would probably
prove hard to reconcile with consideration for foreign interests after
the war. A broadening of the basis of foreign aid to China during
the critical period of the war seemed the best safeguard against later
hostility to foreign interests.

The Foreign Office then went on to discuss the accusations in
China and the United States of British lack of interest in China, and
the suspicion that we did not want a strong and united China to
emerge because we still had imperialist designs, or because
we feared that China might be aiming at the break-up of
the British colonial system in the Far East. It was difficult to
dispel these suspicions as long as Great Britain remained inactive.

The reduction of the 'Chinese chaos' to order depended not only
on American or, as the British Government hoped, Anglo-American
material aid, but on agreement among the Chinese themselves.
Unfortunately the gap between the Chinese Government and the
Communists remained as wide as ever. In June 1944 President
Roosevelt had sent Mr. Henry Wallace, who was then Vice-
President, to discuss with General Chiang Kai-shek the possibility
of an agreement with the Communists, and also of a Chinese-
Russian agreement which would secure the Chinese Government
from Soviet interference on the Communist side. General Chiang

---

(a) F1331/409/10.

Kai-shek was pessimistic about the chances of persuading the Communists to accept terms which would not leave them in a position, from the Government point of view, of dangerous independence. On the other hand, he was willing, for obvious reasons, to try to come to an arrangement with the Russians.

In August 1944 the President sent two more personal representatives, General Patrick Hurley and Mr. Donald Nelson, to China.[1] On his way to Chungking General Hurley travelled through Moscow. He was told by M. Molotov that the Soviet Government were not supporting the Chinese Communists, and that they approved of American efforts to bring about unity in China, but that until General Chiang Kai-shek tried by a change in policy to improve Soviet-Chinese relations, the Soviet Government 'did not intend to take any interest in Chinese affairs'.

President Roosevelt therefore hoped that, at the Yalta Conference, he might reach a satisfactory agreement with the Russians on their own demands in the Far East, and on their collaboration in bringing about Chinese unity. In fact the President found the Russians more grasping than he had expected, but he had to give way to them, not merely because he thought their help essential against Japan; he also wanted their support for the unification of China. The latter
(a) question was raised at the meeting between Mr. Eden and Mr. Stettinius at Malta.[2] It was then said that the President doubted whether the British wanted Chinese unity. Mr. Eden replied that we were most anxious that unity should be secured; Mr. Stettinius added that he had not heard the report about the President's doubts. The Foreign Secretaries agreed that the military situation in China had improved, partly through the diversion of two divisions from Burma and partly through the reopening of the Burma Road. Mr. Stettinius asked that the British, Soviet and United States Governments should make every effort to bring about agreement between General Chiang Kai-shek and the Communists.

Neither the Foreign Office nor Sir H. Seymour thought that the British Government could do anything to promote a settlement
(b) between the Kuomintang and the Communists. Sir H. Seymour considered that the Chinese Government would be most suspicious of Soviet participation, and that it would be almost impossible to put forward a plan acceptable both to the Russians and Americans.

---

[1] The President appears to have kept a close personal control of American policy towards China to the exclusion of the State Department. The immediate purpose of the Hurley-Nelson mission was to try to settle the dispute between General Chiang Kai-shek and General Stilwell. General Hurley succeeded Mr. Gauss as United States Ambassador to China in February 1945.

[2] Neither the British nor the American record of the Conference gives an indication which delegation raised the subject.

(a) WP(45)157; F310, 970/35/10; F804/186/10.   (b) F1085/186/10.

He thought that there was a danger of transferring the Kuomintang-Communist dispute into an argument between major allies; it would be difficult to refuse to give support to the United States if they wanted it, but British participation would not affect the result.

The Foreign Office agreed that an appearance even of joint or concerted pressure on General Chiang Kai-shek to come to terms with the Communists would probably harm the joint war effort. They doubted whether it was still possible to talk of a settlement; the partiality shown to the Communists by the British and American press and the B.B.C. had made them unwilling to listen to a compromise. Here, as far as British policy was concerned, the matter ended. The Chinese themselves came no nearer to unity. On American advice, General Chiang Kai-shek included a Communist in the Chinese delegation to the San Francisco Conference, but in mid-June Sir H. Seymour reported evidence of fighting between the Kuomintang and Communist forces. General Hurley, who had been recalled to Washington for consultation, returned to Chungking in April 1945, through London. He arrived in London on April 4 and left on April 7. Owing to his many American engagements he had not very much time to discuss matters with British officials, but he saw the Prime Minister once and Mr. Eden twice[1] and also attended a meeting of the Chiefs of Staff. He told the Chiefs of Staff that, after (a) conversations with M. Molotov and others in Moscow, he had established that the Chinese Communists were not really Communists, and were not supported by the Soviet Government. The latter wanted to establish good relations with the Chinese Government. General Hurley told Mr. Dening that there was a strong (b) feeling in the United States that American assistance should not be made available for the recovery of British colonial territory, since this violated the fundamental principle upon which the existence of the United States rested. He put this point to the Prime Minister in a slightly different form. He said that Lend-Lease material should (c) not be used for the recovery of colonial territories. He also mentioned to the Prime Minister the question of the return of Hong Kong to the Chinese Government. The Prime Minister, who described General Hurley as 'very friendly' and as 'rather an old-world American figure', noted that he (the Prime Minister) 'took him up with violence' about Hong Kong and said that he would never yield

---

[1] One of the minor complaints which he made was about the quantity of supplies which were being flown into China for British use in American aircraft. General Wedemeyer seemed to suspect that we were bringing in material for some nefarious purpose. It was pointed out to him that these supplies were for the British Embassy, the Canadian and Australian Legations, the British Red Cross and the representatives of the Ministry of Information as well as the Service organisations. Mr. Eden was about to leave for Washington, and did not make a record of his conversations.

(a) F2218/127/61. (b) F2144/127/61. (c) Churchill Papers/159.

an inch of the territory that was under the British flag. On the question of Lend-Lease material the Prime Minister 'offered to take all the Lend-Lease pistols and weapons away from the soldiers there and supply them again here after the defeat of the Germans'.

General Hurley went on to Moscow and left there under the impression that Stalin had given him a promise of support for American policy in China, and was willing to continue to recognise the National Government under the leadership of General Chiang Kai-shek.

(a) Mr. Kennan, at this time United States Chargé d'Affaires in Moscow, however, took a different view of Stalin's statements. Mr. Kennan thought that Stalin had kept himself free to argue that unity was possible in China only if far-reaching concessions were made to the Communists, including strong representation in the Central Government.

The Foreign Office agreed with Mr. Kennan's view that the Soviet Government wanted to secure, through the Communist representatives, influence at Chungking equal to that of the Western Powers, and that otherwise they would work for a disunited China. Later events were to show only too clearly the accuracy of the forecast.

(a) F2844/186/10.

INDEX

c.1

D
750
W62
v.4

c.1

D
Woodward, E. L.   750
British foreign policy in W62
the Second World War.   v.4

DATE	ISSUED TO

CARLOW COLLEGE
Grace Library
Pittsburgh, Pa. 15213